Message Filter (237) How can a component avoid receiving uninteresting messages?

Message History (551) How can we effectively analyze and debug the flow of messages in a loosely coupled system?

Message Router (78) How can you decouple individual processing steps so that messages can be passed to different filters depending on a set of conditions?

Message Sequence (170) How can messaging transmit an arbitrarily large amount of data?

Message Store (555) How can we report against message information without disturbing the loosely coupled and transient nature of a messaging system?

Message Translator (85) How can systems using different data formats communicate with each other using messaging?

Message (66) How can two applications connected by a message channel exchange a piece of information?

Messaging Bridge (133) How can multiple messaging systems be connected so that messages available on one are also available on the others?

Messaging Gateway (468) How do you encapsulate access to the messaging system from the rest of the application?

Messaging Mapper (477) How do you move data between domain objects and the messaging infrastructure while keeping the two independent of each other?

Messaging (53) How can I integrate multiple applications so that they work together and can exchange information?

Normalizer (352) How do you process messages that are semantically equivalent but arrive in a different format?

Pipes and Filters (70) How can we perform complex processing on a message while maintaining independence and flexibility?

Point-to-Point Channel (103) How can the caller be sure that exactly one receiver will receive the document or perform the call?

Polling Consumer (494) How can an application consume a message when the application is ready?

Process Manager (312) How do we route a message through multiple processing steps when the required steps may not be known at design time and may not be sequential?

Publish-Subscribe Channel (106) How can the sender broadcast an event to all interested receivers?

Recipient List (249) How do we route a message to a dynamic list of recipients?

Remote Procedure Invocation (50) How can I integrate multiple applications so that they work together and can exchange information?

Request-Reply (154) When an application sends a message, how can it get a response from the receiver?

Resequencer (283) How can we get a stream of related but out-of-sequence messages back into the correct order?

Return Address (159) How does a replier know where to send the reply?

Routing Slip (301) How do we route a message consecutively through a series of processing steps when the sequence of steps is not known at design time and may vary for each message?

Scatter-Gather (297) How do you maintain the overall message flow when a message must be sent to multiple recipients, each of which may send a reply?

Selective Consumer (515) How can a message consumer select which messages it wishes to receive?

Service Activator (532) How can an application design a service to be invoked both via various messaging technologies and via non-messaging techniques?

Shared Database (47) How can I integrate multiple applications so that they work together and can exchange information?

Smart Proxy (558) How can you track messages on a service that publishes reply messages to the Return Address specified by the requestor?

Splitter (259) How can we process a message if it contains multiple elements, each of which may have to be processed in a different way?

Test Message (569) What happens if a component is actively processing messages but garbles outgoing messages due to an internal fault?

Transactional Client (484) How can a client control its transactions with the messaging system?

Wire Tap (547) How do you inspect messages that travel on a Point-to-Point Channel?

Praise for *Enterprise Integration Patterns*

Enterprise Integration Patterns details an emerging trend that will affect all software and business process architects in financial services, and supports our efforts to be innovative and competitive while still leveraging our customers' legacy system investments. This topic is timely, and the Messaging and Workflow patterns are described in a concise and execution-driven fashion—highly relevant and immediately applicable in today's event-driven and information-intensive environments.

—Glenn Cameron, Director of Middleware Solutions Architecture, Thomson Financial

In addition to covering basics like pub-sub and guaranteed delivery, *Enterprise Integration Patterns* provides an architect's sourcebook of higher-level patterns that describe how messaging is actually *used.* This book is as much about describing and building messaging-based applications as it is about integration. The patterns—such as Routing Slip, Aggregator, or Resequencer—will serve developers well in both integration and in ground-up application development projects.

—Paul Brown, CEO, FiveSight Technologies, Inc.

Enterprise Integration Patterns is a landmark achievement. The integration world has been plagued by a veritable lack of consistency in even the language used to talk about integration, never mind the software or protocol standards. This book finally provides the opportunity to change all of that so that everyone—vendors, consultants, developers, and end-users—can start communicating via a common lexicon. If there is any one development that will move integration best practices out of the middle ages and launch a renaissance movement towards creating a formal discipline for integration worldwide, this is it! A must-have for the bookshelf of every IT architect, developer and integrator.

—John Schmidt, Board Member, EAI Industry Consortium

Enterprise Integration Patterns provides a timeless foundation to understanding the present and future of integration. The authors use patterns to effectively capture and share their tremendous wisdom and experience. I learned a great deal in reviewing and reading this book, and I look forward to relying on its advice in the years to come.

—Luke Hohmann, author of *Beyond Software Architecture*

This book not only provides valuable recipes for approaching integration problems with messaging, it also shows tremendous insight into why each approach is useful. The authors have captured and articulated the most common uses of messaging in integration and shown clear ways of approaching complex problems using messaging channels.

—Dave Chappell, Vice President and Chief Technology Evangelist, Sonic Software, author of *Enterprise Service Bus, Java Web Services,* and *Java Message Service*

If you are involved with the operation or development of an enterprise application, there will doubtless come a time when you will need to integrate your application with another using the emerging preferred approach of messaging. When that time comes, this book will be your most valuable reference. Bobby and Gregor have done a masterful job of collecting the hard-won wisdom of the software development profession on the topic of application integration using messaging, and neatly organizing it into a set of patterns, the preferred form for communication of design knowledge between software professionals. The result is a vocabulary and set of proven solutions that software professionals can use to design and discuss enterprise application integrations.

—Randy Stafford, Chief Architect, IQNavigator, Inc.

Enterprise Integration Patterns

Designing, Building,
and Deploying Messaging Solutions

Gregor Hohpe
Bobby Woolf

With Contributions by
Kyle Brown
Conrad F. D'Cruz
Martin Fowler
Sean Neville
Michael J. Rettig
Jonathan Simon

✦Addison-Wesley

Boston • San Francisco • **New York** • **Toronto** • **Montreal**
London • Munich • Paris • **Madrid**
Capetown • Sydney • Tokyo • **Singapore** • **Mexico City**

Many of the designations used by manufacturers and sellers to distinguish their products are claimed as trademarks. Where those designations appear in this book, and Addison-Wesley was aware of a trademark claim, the designations have been printed with initial capital letters or in all capitals.

The authors and publisher have taken care in the preparation of this book, but make no expressed or implied warranty of any kind and assume no responsibility for errors or omissions. No liability is assumed for incidental or consequential damages in connection with or arising out of the use of the information or programs contained herein.

The publisher offers discounts on this book when ordered in quantity for bulk purchases and special sales. For more information, please contact:

U.S. Corporate and Government Sales
(800) 382-3419
corpsales@pearsontechgroup.com

For sales outside of the U.S., please contact:

International Sales
(317) 581-3793
international@pearsontechgroup.com

Visit Addison-Wesley on the Web: www.awprofessional.com

Library of Congress Cataloging-in-Publication Data

Hohpe, Gregor.
    Enterprise integration patterns : designing, building, and deploying messaging solutions / Gregor Hohpe, Bobby Woolf.
        p.   cm.
    Includes bibliographical references and index.
    ISBN 0-321-20068-3
    1. Telecommunication—Message processing.   2. Management information systems.   I. Woolf, Bobby.   II. Title.

TK5102.5.H5882 2003
005.7'136—dc22

2003017989

ISBN 0-321-20068-3

Text printed in the United States on recycled paper at Courier in Westford, Massachusetts.

Fifteenth Printing   May 2011

*To my family and all my friends who still remember me
after I emerged from book "crunch mode"*

—Gregor

To Sharon, my new wife

—Bobby

Contents

Foreword

by John Crupi

What do you do when a new technology arrives? You learn the technology. This is exactly what I did. I studied J2EE (being from Sun Microsystems, it seemed to be the logical choice). Specifically, I focused on the EJB technology by reading the specifications (since there were no books yet). Learning the technology, however, is just the first step—the real goal is to learn how to effectively apply the technology. The nice thing about platform technologies is that they constrain you to performing certain tasks. But, as far as the technology is concerned, you can do whatever you want and quite often get into trouble if you don't do things appropriately.

One thing I've seen in the past 15 years is that there seem to be two areas that software developers obsess over: programming and designing—or more specifically, programming and designing effectively. There are great books out there that tell you the most efficient way to program certain things in Java and C#, but far fewer tell you how to design effectively. That's where this book comes in. When Deepak Alur, Dan Malks, and I wrote *Core J2EE Patterns*, we wanted to help J2EE developers "design" better code. The best decision we made was to use patterns as the artifact of choice. As James Baty, a Sun Distinguished Engineer, puts it, "Patterns seem to be the sweet spot of design." I couldn't agree more, and luckily for us, Gregor and Bobby feel the same way.

This book focuses on a hot and growing topic: integration using messaging. Not only is messaging key to integration, but it will most likely be the predominant focus in Web services for years to come. There is so much noise today in the Web services world, it's a delicate and complex endeavor just to identify the specifications and technologies to focus on. The goal remains the same, however—software helps you solve a problem. Just as in the early days of J2EE and .NET, there is not a lot of design help out there yet for Web services. Many people say

Web services is just a new and open way to solve our existing integration problems—and I agree. But, that doesn't mean we know how to design Web services. And that brings us to the gem of this book. I believe this book has many of the patterns we need to design Web services and other integration systems. Because the Web service specifications are still battling it out, it wouldn't have made sense for Bobby and Gregor to provide examples of many of the Web service specifications. But, that's okay. The real payoff will result when the specifications become standards and we use the patterns in this book to design for those solutions that are realized by these standards. Then maybe we can realize our next integration goal of designing for service-oriented architectures.

Read this book and keep it by your side. It will enhance your software career to no end.

John Crupi
Bethesda, MD
August 2003

Foreword

by Martin Fowler

While I was working on my book *Patterns of Enterprise Application Architecture*, I was lucky to get some in-depth review from Kyle Brown and Rachel Reinitz at some informal workshops at Kyle's office in Raleigh-Durham. During these sessions, we realized that a big gap in my work was asynchronous messaging systems.

There are many gaps in my book, and I never intended it to be a complete collection of patterns for enterprise development. But the gap on asynchronous messaging is particularly important because we believe that asynchronous messaging will play an increasingly important role in enterprise software development, particularly in integration. Integration is important because applications cannot live isolated from each other. We need techniques that allow us to take applications that were never designed to interoperate and break down the stovepipes so we can gain a greater benefit than the individual applications can offer us.

Various technologies have been around that promise to solve the integration puzzle. We all concluded that messaging is the technology that carries the greatest promise. The challenge we faced was to convey how to do messaging effectively. The biggest challenge in this is that messages are by their nature asynchronous, and there are significant differences in the design approaches that you use in an asynchronous world.

I didn't have space, energy, or frankly the knowledge to cover this topic properly in *Patterns of Enterprise Application Architecture*. But we came up with a better solution to this gap: find someone else who could. We hunted down Gregor and Bobby, and they took up the challenge. The result is the book you're about to read.

I'm delighted with the job that they have done. If you've already worked with messaging systems, this book will systematize much of the knowledge that you and others have already learned the hard way. If you are about to work with messaging systems, this book will provide a foundation that will be invaluable no matter which messaging technology you have to work with.

Martin Fowler
Melrose, MA
August 2003

Preface

This is a book about enterprise integration using messaging. It does not document any particular technology or product. Rather, it is designed for developers and integrators using a variety of messaging products and technologies, such as

- Message-oriented middleware (MOM) and EAI suites offered by vendors such as IBM (WebSphere MQ Family), Microsoft (BizTalk), TIBCO, WebMethods, SeeBeyond, Vitria, and others.

- Java Message Service (JMS) implementations incorporated into commercial and open source J2EE application servers as well as standalone products.

- Microsoft's Message Queuing (MSMQ), accessible through several APIs, including the System.Messaging libraries in Microsoft .NET.

- Emerging Web services standards that support asynchronous Web services (for example, WS-ReliableMessaging) and the associated APIs such as Sun Microsystems' Java API for XML Messaging (JAXM) or Microsoft's Web Services Extensions (WSE).

Enterprise integration goes beyond creating a single application with a distributed n-tier architecture, which enables a single application to be distributed across several computers. Whereas one tier in a distributed application cannot run by itself, integrated applications are independent programs that can each run by themselves, yet that function by coordinating with each other in a loosely coupled way. Messaging enables multiple applications to exchange data or commands across the network using a "send and forget" approach. This allows the caller to send the information and immediately go on to other work while the information is transmitted by the messaging system. Optionally, the caller can later be notified of the result through a callback. Asynchronous calls and callbacks can make a design more complex than a synchronous approach, but an asynchronous call can be retried until it succeeds, which makes the communication much more reliable. Asynchronous messaging also enables several other advantages, such as throttling of requests and load balancing.

Who Should Read This Book

This book is designed to help application developers and system integrators connect applications using message-oriented integration tools:

- **Application architects and developers** who design and build complex enterprise applications that need to integrate with other applications. We assume that you're developing your applications using a modern enterprise application platform such as the Java 2 Platform, Enterprise Edition (J2EE), or the Microsoft .NET framework. This book will help you connect the application to a messaging layer and exchange information with other applications. This book focuses on the integration of applications, not on building applications; for that, we refer you to *Patterns of Enterprise Application Architecture* by Martin Fowler.

- **Integration architects and developers** who design and build integration solutions connecting packaged or custom applications. Most readers in this group will have experience with one of the many commercial integration tools like IBM WebSphere MQ, TIBCO, WebMethods, SeeBeyond, or Vitria, which incorporate many of the patterns presented in this book. This book helps you understand the underlying concepts and make confident design decisions using a vendor-independent vocabulary.

- **Enterprise architects** who have to maintain the "big picture" view of the software and hardware assets in an enterprise. This book presents a consistent vocabulary and graphical notation to describe large-scale integration solutions that may span many technologies or point solutions. This language is also a key enabler for efficient communication between the enterprise architect and the integration and application architects and developers.

What You Will Learn

This book does not attempt to make a business case for enterprise application integration; the focus is on how to make it work. You will learn how to integrate enterprise applications by understanding the following:

- The advantages and limitations of asynchronous messaging as compared to other integration techniques.

- How to determine the message channels your applications will need, how to control whether multiple consumers can receive the same message, and how to handle invalid messages.

- When to send a message, what it should contain, and how to use special message properties.

- How to route a message to its ultimate destination even when the sender does not know where that is.

- How to convert messages when the sender and receiver do not agree on a common format.

- How to design the code that connects an application to the messaging system.

- How to manage and monitor a messaging system once it's in use as part of the enterprise.

What This Book Does Not Cover

We believe that any book sporting the word "enterprise" in the title is likely to fall into one of three categories. First, the book might attempt to cover the whole breadth of the subject matter but is forced to stop short of detailed guidance on how to implement actual solutions. Second, the book might provide specific hands-on guidance on the development of actual solutions but is forced to constrain the scope of the subject area it addresses. Third, the book might attempt to do both but is likely never to be finished or else to be published so late as to be irrelevant. We opted for the second choice and hopefully created a book that helps people create better integration solutions even though we had to limit the scope of the book. Topics that we would have loved to discuss but had to exclude in order not to fall into the category-three trap include security, complex data mapping, workflow, rule engines, scalability and robustness, and distributed transaction processing (XA, Tuxedo, and the like). We chose asynchronous messaging as the emphasis for this book because it is full of interesting design issues and trade-offs, and provides a clean abstraction from the many implementations provided by various integration vendors.

This book is also not a tutorial on a specific messaging or middleware technology. To highlight the wide applicability of the concepts presented in this book, we included examples based on a number of different technologies, such as JMS, MSMQ, TIBCO, BizTalk, and XSL. However, we focus on the design decisions and trade-offs as opposed to the specifics of the tool. If you are interested in learning more about any of these specific technologies, please refer to one of the books referenced in the bibliography or to one of the many online resources.

How This Book Is Organized

As the title suggests, the majority of this book consists of a collection of *patterns*. Patterns are a proven way to capture experts' knowledge in fields where there are no simple "one size fits all" answers, such as application architecture, object-oriented design, or integration solutions based on asynchronous messaging architectures.

Each pattern poses a specific design problem, discusses the considerations surrounding the problem, and presents an elegant solution that balances the various *forces* or drivers. In most cases, the solution is not the first approach that comes to mind, but one that has evolved through actual use over time. As a result, each pattern incorporates the experience base that senior integration developers and architects have gained by repeatedly building solutions and learning from their mistakes. This implies that we did not "invent" the patterns in this book; patterns are not invented, but rather discovered and observed from actual practice in the field.

Because patterns are harvested from practitioners' actual use, chances are that if you have been working with enterprise integration tools and asynchronous messaging architectures for some time, many of the patterns in this book will seem familiar to you. Yet, even if you already recognize most of these patterns, there is still value in reviewing this book. This book should validate your hard-earned understanding of how to use messaging while documenting details of the solutions and relationships between them of which you might not have been aware. It also gives you a consolidated reference to help you pass your knowledge effectively to less-experienced colleagues. Finally, the pattern names give you a common vocabulary to efficiently discuss integration design alternatives with your peers.

The patterns in this book apply to a variety of programming languages and platforms. This means that a pattern is not a cut-and-paste snippet of code, but you have to *realize* a pattern to your specific environment. To make this translation easier, we added a variety of examples that show different ways of implementing patterns using popular technologies such as JMS, MSMQ, TIBCO, BizTalk, XSL, and others. We also included a few larger examples to demonstrate how multiple patterns play together to form a cohesive solution.

Integrating multiple applications using an asynchronous messaging architecture is a challenging and interesting field. We hope you enjoy reading this book as much as we did writing it.

About the Cover Picture

The common theme for books in the *Martin Fowler Signature Series* is a picture of a bridge. In some sense we lucked out, because what theme would make a better match for a book on integration? For thousands of years, bridges have helped connect people from different shores, mountains, and sides of the road.

We selected a picture of the Taiko-bashi Bridge at the Sumiyoshi-taisha Shrine in Osaka, Japan, for its simple elegance and beauty. As a Shinto shrine dedicated to the guardian deity for sailors, it was originally erected next to the water. Interestingly, land reclamation has pushed the water away so that the shrine today stands almost three miles inland. Some three million people visit this shrine at the beginning of a new year.

Gregor Hohpe
San Francisco, California

Bobby Woolf
Raleigh, North Carolina

September 2003
www.enterpriseintegrationpatterns.com

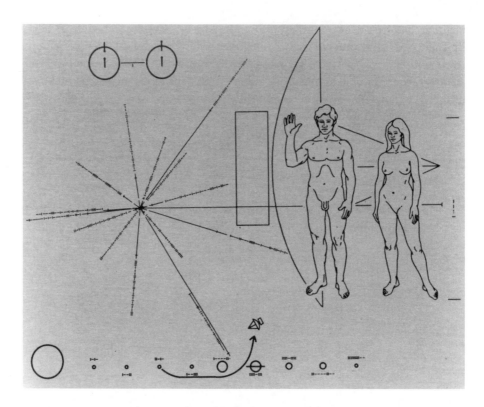

The Pioneer Plaque by Dr. Carl Sagan
A message to extraterrestrial life forms.

Acknowledgments

Like most books, *Enterprise Integration Patterns* has been a long time in the making. The idea of writing about message-based integration patterns dates back to the summer of 2001 when Martin Fowler was working on *Patterns of Enterprise Application Architecture (P of EAA)*. At that time, it struck Kyle Brown that while *P of EAA* talked a lot about how to create applications, it touches only briefly on how to integrate them. This idea was the starting point for a series of meetings between Martin and Kyle that also included Rachel Reinitz, John Crupi, and Mark Weitzel. Bobby joined these discussions in the fall of 2001, followed by Gregor in early 2002. The following summer the group submitted two papers for review at the Pattern Languages of Programs (PLoP) conference, one authored jointly by Bobby and Kyle and the other by Gregor. After the conference, Kyle and Martin refocused on their own book projects while Gregor and Bobby merged their papers to form the basis for the book. At the same time, the *www.enterpriseintegrationpatterns.com* site went live to allow integration architects and developers around the world to participate in the rapid evolution of the content. As they worked on the book, Gregor and Bobby invited contributors to participate in the creation of the book. About two years after Kyle's original idea, the final manuscript arrived at the publisher.

This book is the result of a community effort involving a great number of people. Many colleagues and friends (many of whom we met through the book effort) provided ideas for examples, ensured the correctness of the technical content, and gave us much needed feedback and criticism. Their input has greatly influenced the final form and content of the book. It is a pleasure for us to acknowledge their contributions and express our appreciation for their efforts.

Kyle Brown and Martin Fowler deserve special mention for laying the foundation for this book. This book might have never been written were it not for Martin's writing *P of EAA* and Kyle's forming a group to discuss messaging patterns to complement Martin's book.

We were fortunate to have several contributors who authored significant portions of the book: Conrad F. D'Cruz, Sean Neville, Michael J. Rettig, and Jonathan Simon. Their chapters round out the book with additional perspectives on how the patterns work in practice.

Our writers' workshop participants at the PLoP 2002 conference were the first people to provide substantial feedback on the material, helping to get us going in the right direction: Ali Arsanjani, Kyle Brown, John Crupi, Eric Evans, Martin Fowler, Brian Marick, Toby Sarver, Jonathan Simon, Bill Trudell, and Marek Vokac.

We would like to thank our team of reviewers who took the time to read through the draft material and provided us with invaluable feedback and suggestions:

Richard Helm

Luke Hohmann

Dragos Manolescu

David Rice

Russ Rufer and the Silicon Valley Patterns Group

Matthew Short

Special thanks go to Russ for workshopping the book draft in the Silicon Valley Patterns Group. We would like to thank the following members for their efforts: Robert Benson, Tracy Bialik, Jeffrey Blake, Azad Bolour, John Brewer, Bob Evans, Andy Farlie, Jeff Glaza, Phil Goodwin, Alan Harriman, Ken Hejmanowski, Deborah Kaddah, Rituraj Kirti, Jan Looney, Chris Lopez, Jerry Louis, Tao-hung Ma, Jeff Miller, Stilian Pandev, John Parello, Hema Pillay, Russ Rufer, Rich Smith, Carol Thistlethwaite, Debbie Utley, Walter Vannini, David Vydra, and Ted Young.

Our public e-mail discussion list allowed people who discovered the material on *www.enterpriseintegrationpatterns.com* to chime in and share their thoughts and ideas. Special honors go to Bill Trudell as the most active contributor to the mailing list. Other active posters included Venkateshwar Bommineni, Duncan Cragg, John Crupi, Fokko Degenaar, Shailesh Gosavi, Christian Hall, Ralph Johnson, Paul Julius, Orjan Lundberg, Dragos Manolescu, Rob Mee, Srikanth Narasimhan, Sean Neville, Rob Patton, Kirk Pepperdine, Matthew Pryor, Somik Raha, Michael Rettig, Frank Sauer, Jonathan Simon, Federico Spinazzi, Randy Stafford, Marek Vokac, Joe Walnes, and Mark Weitzel.

We thank Martin Fowler for hosting us in his signature series. Martin's endorsement gave us confidence and the energy required to complete this work.

We thank John Crupi for writing the foreword for our book. He has observed the book's formation from the beginning and has been a patient guide all along without ever losing his sense of humor.

Finally, we owe a great deal to the editing and production team at Addison-Wesley, led by our chief editor, Mike Hendrickson, and including our production coordinator, Amy Fleischer; our project manager, Kim Arney Mulcahy; our copy-editor, Carol J. Lallier; our proofreader, Rebecca Rider; our indexer, Sharon Hilgenberg; as well as Jacquelyn Doucette, John Fuller, and Bernard Gaffney.

We've likely missed some names and not given everyone the credit they deserve, and we apologize. But to everyone listed and not listed who helped make this book better, thank you for all your help. We hope you can be as proud of this book as we are.

Introduction

Interesting applications rarely live in isolation. Whether your sales application must interface with your inventory application, your procurement application must connect to an auction site, or your PDA's calendar must synchronize with the corporate calendar server, it seems that any application can be made better by integrating it with other applications.

All integration solutions have to deal with a few fundamental challenges:

- *Networks are unreliable.* Integration solutions have to transport data from one computer to another across networks. Compared to a process running on a single computer, distributed computing has to be prepared to deal with a much larger set of possible problems. Often, two systems to be integrated are separated by continents, and data between them has to travel through phone lines, LAN segments, routers, switches, public networks, and satellite links. Each step can cause delays or interruptions.

- *Networks are slow.* Sending data across a network is multiple orders of magnitude slower than making a local method call. Designing a widely distributed solution the same way you would approach a single application could have disastrous performance implications.

- *Any two applications are different.* Integration solutions need to transmit information between systems that use different programming languages, operating platforms, and data formats. An integration solution must be able to interface with all these different technologies.

- *Change is inevitable.* Applications change over time. An integration solution has to keep pace with changes in the applications it connects. Integration solutions can easily get caught in an avalanche effect of changes—if one system changes, all other systems may be affected. An integration solution needs to minimize the dependencies from one system to another by using *loose coupling* between applications.

Over time, developers have overcome these challenges with four main approaches:

1. *File Transfer* (43)—One application writes a file that another later reads. The applications need to agree on the filename and location, the format of the file, the timing of when it will be written and read, and who will delete the file.

2. *Shared Database* (47)—Multiple applications share the same database schema, located in a single physical database. Because there is no duplicate data storage, no data has to be transferred from one application to the other.

3. *Remote Procedure Invocation* (50)—One application exposes some of its functionality so that it can be accessed remotely by other applications as a remote procedure. The communication occurs in real time and synchronously.

4. *Messaging* (53)—One application publishes a message to a common message channel. Other applications can read the message from the channel at a later time. The applications must agree on a channel as well as on the format of the message. The communication is asynchronous.

While all four approaches solve essentially the same problem, each style has its distinct advantages and disadvantages. In fact, applications may integrate using multiple styles such that each point of integration takes advantage of the style that suits it best.

What Is Messaging?

This book is about how to use messaging to integrate applications. A simple way to understand what messaging does is to consider the telephone system. A telephone call is a synchronous form of communication. I can communicate with the other party only if the other party is available at the time I place the call. Voice mail, on the other hand, allows asynchronous communication. With voice mail, when the receiver does not answer, the caller can leave him a message; later, the receiver (at his convenience) can listen to the messages queued in his mailbox. Voice mail enables the caller to leave a message now so that the receiver can listen to it later, which is much easier than trying to get the caller and the receiver on the phone at the same time. Voice mail bundles (at least part of) a phone call into a message and queues it for later consumption; this is essentially how messaging works.

Messaging is a technology that enables high-speed, asynchronous, program-to-program communication with reliable delivery. Programs communicate by sending packets of data called *message*s to each other. *Channel*s, also known as queues, are logical pathways that connect the programs and convey messages. A channel behaves like a collection or array of messages, but one that is magically shared across multiple computers and can be used concurrently by multiple applications. A *sender* or *producer* is a program that sends a message by writing the message to a channel. A *receiver* or *consumer* is a program that receives a message by reading (and deleting) it from a channel.

The message itself is simply some sort of data structure—such as a string, a byte array, a record, or an object. It can be interpreted simply as data, as the description of a command to be invoked on the receiver, or as the description of an event that occurred in the sender. A message actually contains two parts, a header and a body. The *header* contains meta-information about the message—who sent it, where it's going, and so on; this information is used by the messaging system and is mostly ignored by the applications using the messages. The *body* contains the application data being transmitted and is usually ignored by the messaging system. In conversation, when an application developer who is using messaging talks about a message, she's usually referring to the data in the body of the message.

Asynchronous messaging architectures are powerful but require us to rethink our development approach. As compared to the other three integration approaches, relatively few developers have had exposure to messaging and message systems. As a result, application developers in general are not as familiar with the idioms and peculiarities of this communications platform.

What Is a Messaging System?

Messaging capabilities are typically provided by a separate software system called a *messaging system* or *message-oriented middleware* (MOM). A messaging system manages messaging the way a database system manages data persistence. Just as an administrator must populate the database with the schema for an application's data, an administrator must configure the messaging system with the channels that define the paths of communication between the applications. The messaging system then coordinates and manages the sending and receiving of messages. The primary purpose of a database system is to make sure each data record is safely persisted, and likewise the main task of a messaging system is to move messages from the sender's computer to the receiver's computer in a reliable fashion.

A messaging system is needed to move messages from one computer to another because computers and the networks that connect them are inherently unreliable. Just because one application is ready to send data does not mean that the other application is ready to receive it. Even if both applications are ready, the network may not be working or may fail to transmit the data properly. A messaging system overcomes these limitations by repeatedly trying to transmit the message until it succeeds. Under ideal circumstances, the message is transmitted successfully on the first try, but circumstances are often not ideal.

In essence, a message is transmitted in five steps:

1. *Create*—The sender creates the message and populates it with data.

2. *Send*—The sender adds the message to a channel.

3. *Deliver*—The messaging system moves the message from the sender's computer to the receiver's computer, making it available to the receiver.

4. *Receive*—The receiver reads the message from the channel.

5. *Process*—The receiver extracts the data from the message.

The following figure illustrates these five transmission steps, which computer performs each, and which steps involve the messaging system:

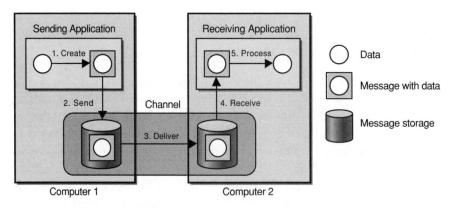

Message Transmission Step-by-Step

This figure also illustrates two important messaging concepts:

1. *Send and forget*—In step 2, the sending application sends the message to the message channel. Once that send is complete, the sender can go on to other work while the messaging system transmits the message in the background. The sender can be confident that the receiver will eventually receive the message and does not have to wait until that happens.

2. *Store and forward*—In step 2, when the sending application sends the message to the message channel, the messaging system stores the message on the sender's computer, either in memory or on disk. In step 3, the messaging system delivers the message by forwarding it from the sender's computer to the receiver's computer, and then stores the message once again on the receiver's computer. This store-and-forward process may be repeated many times as the message is moved from one computer to another until it reaches the receiver's computer.

The create, send, receive, and process steps may seem like unnecessary overhead. Why not simply deliver the data to the receiver? By wrapping the data as a message and storing it in the messaging system, the applications delegate to the messaging system the responsibility of delivering the data. Because the data is wrapped as an atomic message, delivery can be retried until it succeeds, and the receiver can be assured of reliably receiving exactly one copy of the data.

Why Use Messaging?

Now that we know what messaging is, we should ask, Why use messaging? As with any sophisticated solution, there is no one simple answer. The quick answer is that messaging is more immediate than *File Transfer* (43), better encapsulated than *Shared Database* (47), and more reliable than *Remote Procedure Invocation* (50). However, that's just the beginning of the advantages that can be gained using messaging.

Specific benefits of messaging include:

- *Remote Communication.* Messaging enables separate applications to communicate and transfer data. Two objects that reside in the same process can simply share the same data in memory. Sending data to another computer is a lot more complicated and requires data to be copied from one computer to another. This means that objects have to be "serializable"—that is, they can be converted into a simple byte stream that can be sent across the network. Messaging takes care of this conversion so that the applications do not have to worry about it.

- *Platform/Language Integration.* When connecting multiple computer systems via remote communication, these systems likely use different languages, technologies, and platforms, perhaps because they were developed over time by independent teams. Integrating such divergent applications can require a neutral zone of middleware to negotiate between the applications, often using the lowest common denominator—such as flat data files with obscure formats. In these circumstances, a messaging system can be a universal translator between the applications that works with each one's language and platform on its own terms yet allows them to all to communicate through a common messaging paradigm. This universal connectivity is the heart of the *Message Bus* (137) pattern.

- *Asynchronous Communication.* Messaging enables a *send-and-forget* approach to communication. The sender does not have to wait for the receiver to receive and process the message; it does not even have to wait for the messaging system to deliver the message. The sender only needs to wait for the message to be sent, that is, for the message to be successfully stored in the channel by the messaging system. Once the message is stored, the sender is free to perform other work while the message is transmitted in the background.

- *Variable Timing.* With synchronous communication, the caller must wait for the receiver to finish processing the call before the caller can receive the result and continue. In this way, the caller can make calls only as fast as the receiver can perform them. Asynchronous communication allows the sender to submit requests to the receiver at its own pace and the receiver to consume the requests at its own different pace. This allows both applications to run at maximum throughput and not waste time waiting on each other (at least until the receiver runs out of messages to process).

- *Throttling.* A problem with remote procedure calls (RPCs) is that too many of them on a single receiver at the same time can overload the receiver. This can cause performance degradation and even cause the receiver to crash. Because the messaging system queues up requests until the receiver is ready to process them, the receiver can control the rate at which it consumes requests so as not to become overloaded by too many simultaneous requests. The callers are unaffected by this throttling because the communication is asynchronous, so the callers are not blocked waiting on the receiver.

- *Reliable Communication.* Messaging provides reliable delivery that an RPC cannot. The reason messaging is more reliable than RPC is that messaging uses a *store-and-forward* approach to transmitting messages. The data is packaged as messages, which are atomic, independent units. When the sender sends a message, the messaging system stores the message. It then delivers the message by forwarding it to the receiver's computer, where it is stored again. Storing the message on the sender's computer and the receiver's computer is assumed to be reliable. (To make it even more reliable, the messages can be stored to disk instead of memory; see *Guaranteed Delivery* [122].) What is unreliable is forwarding (moving) the message from the sender's computer to the receiver's computer, because the receiver or the network may not be running properly. The messaging system overcomes this by resending the message until it succeeds. This automatic retry enables the messaging system to overcome problems with the network so that the sender and receiver don't have to worry about these details.

- *Disconnected Operation.* Some applications are specifically designed to run disconnected from the network, yet to synchronize with servers when a network connection is available. Such applications are deployed on platforms like laptop computers and PDAs. Messaging is ideal for enabling these applications to synchronize—data to be synchronized can be queued as it is created, waiting until the application reconnects to the network.

- *Mediation.* The messaging system acts as a mediator—as in the *Mediator* pattern [GoF]—between all of the programs that can send and receive messages. An application can use it as a directory of other applications or services available to integrate with. If an application becomes disconnected from the others, it need only reconnect to the messaging system, not to all of the other messaging applications. The messaging system can employ redundant resources to provide high availability, balance load, reroute around failed network connections, and tune performance and quality of service.

- *Thread Management.* Asynchronous communication means that one application does not have to block while waiting for another application to perform a task, unless it wants to. Rather than blocking to wait for a reply, the caller can use a callback that will alert the caller when the reply arrives. (See the *Request-Reply* [154] pattern.) A large number of blocked threads or threads blocked for a long time can leave the application with too few available threads to perform real work. Also, if an application with a dynamic number of blocked threads crashes, reestablishing those threads will be difficult when the application restarts and recovers its former state. With callbacks, the only threads that block are a small, known number of listeners waiting for replies. This leaves most threads available for other work and defines a known number of listener threads that can easily be reestablished after a crash.

So, there are a number of different reasons an application or enterprise may benefit from messaging. Some of these are technical details that application developers relate most readily to, whereas others are strategic decisions that resonate best with enterprise architects. Which of these reasons is most important depends on the current requirements of your particular applications. They're all good reasons to use messaging, so take advantage of whichever reasons provide the most benefit to you.

Challenges of Asynchronous Messaging

Asynchronous messaging is not the panacea of integration. It resolves many of the challenges of integrating disparate systems in an elegant way, but it also introduces new challenges. Some of these challenges are inherent in the asynchronous model, while other challenges vary with the specific implementation of a messaging system.

- *Complex programming model.* Asynchronous messaging requires developers to work with an event-driven programming model. Application logic can no longer be coded in a single method that invokes other methods, but instead the logic is now split up into a number of event handlers that respond to incoming messages. Such a system is more complex and harder to develop and debug. For example, the equivalent of a simple method call can require a request message and a request channel, a reply message and a reply channel, a correlation identifier and an invalid message queue (as described in *Request-Reply* [154]).

- *Sequence issues.* Message channels guarantee message delivery, but they do not guarantee when the message will be delivered. This can cause messages that are sent in sequence to get out of sequence. In situations where messages depend on each other, special care has to be taken to reestablish the message sequence (see *Resequencer* [283]).

- *Synchronous scenarios.* Not all applications can operate in a send-and-forget mode. If a user is looking for airline tickets, he or she is going to want to see the ticket price right away, not after some undetermined time.

Therefore, many messaging systems need to bridge the gap between synchronous and asynchronous solutions.

- *Performance.* Messaging systems do add some overhead to communication. It takes effort to package application data into a message and send it, and to receive a message and process it. If you have to transport a huge chunk of data, dividing it into a gazillion small pieces may not be a smart idea. For example, if an integration solution needs to synchronize information between two existing systems, the first step is usually to replicate all relevant information from one system to the other. For such a bulk data replication step, ETL (extract, transform, and load) tools are much more efficient than messaging. Messaging is best suited to keeping the systems in sync after the initial data replication.

- *Limited platform support.* Many proprietary messaging systems are not available on all platforms. Often, transferring a file via FTP is the only integration option because the target platform may not support a messaging system.

- *Vendor lock-in.* Many messaging system implementations rely on proprietary protocols. Even common messaging specifications such as JMS do not control the physical implementation of the solution. As a result, different messaging systems usually do not connect to one another. This can leave you with a whole new integration challenge: integrating multiple integration solutions! (See the *Messaging Bridge* [133] pattern.)

In summary, asynchronous messaging does not solve all problems, and it can even create new ones. Keep these consequences in mind when deciding which problems to solve using messaging.

Thinking Asynchronously

Messaging is an asynchronous technology, which enables delivery to be retried until it succeeds. In contrast, most applications use synchronous function calls—for example, a procedure calling a subprocedure, one method calling another method, or one procedure invoking another remotely through an RPC (such as CORBA and DCOM). Synchronous calls imply that the calling process is halted while the subprocess is executing a function. Even in an RPC scenario, where the called subprocedure executes in a different process, the caller blocks until the subprocedure returns control (and the results) to the caller. In contrast, when using asynchronous messaging, the caller uses a send-and-forget approach that allows it to continue to execute after it sends the message. As a result, the calling procedure continues to run while the subprocedure is being invoked (see figure).

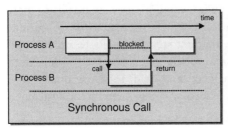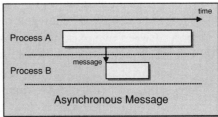

Synchronous and Asynchronous Call Semantics

Asynchronous communication has a number of implications. First, we no longer have a single thread of execution. Multiple threads enable subprocedures to run concurrently, which can greatly improve performance and help ensure that some subprocesses are making progress even while other subprocesses may be waiting for external results. However, concurrent threads also make debugging much more difficult. Second, results (if any) arrive via a callback mechanism. This enables the caller to perform other tasks and be notified when the result is available, which can improve performance. However, this means that the caller has to be able to process the result even while it is in the middle of other tasks, and it has to be able to remember the context in which the call was made. Third, asynchronous subprocesses can execute in any order. Again, this enables one subprocedure to make progress even while another cannot. But it also means that the sub-processes must be able to run independently in any order, and the caller must be able to determine which result came from which subprocess and combine the results together. As a result, asynchronous communication has several advantages but requires rethinking how a procedure uses its subprocedures.

Distributed Applications versus Integration

This book is about enterprise integration—how to integrate independent applications so that they can work together. An enterprise application often incorporates an *n*-tier architecture (a more sophisticated version of a client/server architecture), enabling it to be distributed across several computers. Even though this results in processes on different machines communicating with each other, this is application distribution, not application integration.

Why is an *n*-tier architecture considered application distribution and not application integration? First, the communicating parts are tightly coupled—they dependent directly on each other, so one tier cannot function without the others. Second, communication between tiers tends to be synchronous. Third, an application (*n*-tier or atomic) tends to have human users who will only accept rapid system response times.

In contrast, integrated applications are independent applications that can each run by themselves but that coordinate with each other in a loosely coupled way. This enables each application to focus on one comprehensive set of functionality and yet delegate to other applications for related functionality. Integrated applications communicating asynchronously don't have to wait for a response; they can proceed without a response or perform other tasks concurrently until the response is available. Integrated applications tend to have a broad time constraint, such that they can work on other tasks until a result becomes available, and therefore are more patient than most human users waiting real-time for a result.

Commercial Messaging Systems

The apparent benefits of integrating systems using an asynchronous messaging solution have opened up a significant market for software vendors creating messaging middleware and associated tools. We can roughly group the messaging vendors' products into the following four categories:

1. *Operating systems.* Messaging has become such a common need that vendors have started to integrate the necessary software infrastructure into the operating system or database platform. For example, the Microsoft Windows 2000 and Windows XP operating systems include the Microsoft Message Queuing (MSMQ) service software. This service is accessible through a number of APIs, including COM components and the System.Messaging namespace, part of the Microsoft .NET platform. Similarly, Oracle offers Oracle AQ as part of its database platform.

2. *Application servers.* Sun Microsystems first incorporated the Java Messaging Service (JMS) into version 1.2 of the J2EE specification. Since then, virtually all J2EE application servers (such as IBM WebSphere and BEA WebLogic)

provide an implementation for this specification. Also, Sun delivers a JMS reference implementation with the J2EE JDK.

3. *EAI suites.* Products from these vendors offer proprietary—but functionally rich—suites that encompass messaging, business process automation, workflow, portals, and other functions. Key players in this marketplace are IBM WebSphere MQ, Microsoft BizTalk, TIBCO, WebMethods, SeeBeyond, Vitria, CrossWorlds, and others. Many of these products include JMS as one of the many client APIs they support, while other vendors—such as SonicSoftware and Fiorano—focus primarily on implementing JMS-compliant messaging infrastructures.

4. *Web services toolkits.* Web services have garnered a lot of interest in the enterprise integration communities. Standards bodies and consortia are actively working on standardizing reliable message delivery over Web services (i.e., WS-Reliability, WS-ReliableMessaging, and ebMS). A growing number of vendors offer tools that implement routing, transformation, and management of Web services-based solutions.

The patterns in this book are vendor-independent and apply to most messaging solutions. Unfortunately, each vendor tends to define its own terminology when describing messaging solutions. In this book, we strove to choose pattern names that are technology- and product-neutral yet descriptive and easy to use conversationally.

Many messaging vendors have incorporated some of this book's patterns as features of their products, which simplifies applying the patterns and accelerates solution development. Readers who are familiar with a particular vendor's terminology will most likely recognize many of the concepts in this book. To help these readers map the pattern language to the vendor-specific terminology, the following tables map the most common pattern names to their corresponding product feature names in some of the most widely used messaging products.

Enterprise Integration Patterns	Java Message Service (JMS)	Microsoft MSMQ	WebSphere MQ
Message Channel	Destination	MessageQueue	Queue
Point-to-Point Channel	Queue	MessageQueue	Queue
Publish-Subscribe Channel	Topic	—	—
Message	Message	Message	Message
Message Endpoint	MessageProducer, MessageConsumer		

Enterprise Integration Patterns	TIBCO	WebMethods	SeeBeyond	Vitria
Message Channel	Subject	Queue	Intelligent Queue	Channel
Point-to-Point Channel	Distributed Queue	Deliver Action	Intelligent Queue	Channel
Publish-Subscribe Channel	Subject	Publish-Subscribe Action	Intelligent Queue	Publish-Subscribe Channel
Message	Message	Document	Event	Event
Message Endpoint	Publisher, Subscriber	Publisher, Subscriber	Publisher, Subscriber	Publisher, Subscriber

Pattern Form

This book contains a set of patterns organized into a pattern language. Books such as *Design Patterns*, *Pattern Oriented Software Architecture*, *Core J2EE Patterns*, and *Patterns of Enterprise Application Architecture* have popularized the concept of using patterns to document computer-programming techniques. Christopher Alexander pioneered the concept of patterns and pattern languages in his books *A Pattern Language* and *A Timeless Way of Building*. Each pattern represents a decision that must be made and the considerations that go into that decision. A pattern language is a web of related patterns where each pattern leads to others, guiding you through the decision-making process. This approach is a powerful technique for documenting an expert's knowledge so that it can be readily understood and applied by others.

A pattern language teaches you how to solve a limitless variety of problems within a bounded problem space. Because the overall problem that is being solved is different every time, the path through the patterns and how they're applied is also unique. This book is written for anyone using any messaging tools for any application, and it can be applied specifically for you and the unique application of messaging that you face.

Using the pattern form by itself does not guarantee that a book contains a wealth of knowledge. It is not enough to simply say, "When you face this problem, apply this solution." For you to truly learn from a pattern, the pattern has to document why the problem is difficult to solve, consider possible solutions that in fact don't work well, and explain why the solution offered is the best available. Likewise, the patterns need to connect to each other so as to walk you from one problem to the next. In this way, the pattern form can be used to teach not just what solutions to apply but also how to solve problems the authors could not have predicted. These are goals we strive to accomplish in this book.

Patterns should be prescriptive, meaning that they should tell you what to do. They don't just describe a problem, and they don't just describe how to solve it—they tell you what to do to solve it. Each pattern represents a decision you must make: "Should I use *Messaging*?" "Would a *Command Message* help me here?" The point of the patterns and the pattern language is to help you make decisions that lead to a good solution for your specific problem, even if the authors didn't have that specific problem in mind and even if you don't have the knowledge and experience to develop that solution on your own.

There is no one universal pattern form; different books use various structures. We used a style that is fairly close to the Alexandrian form, which was first popularized for computer programming in *Smalltalk Best Practice Patterns* by Kent Beck. We like the Alexandrian form because it results in patterns that are more prose-like. As a result, even though each pattern follows an identical, well-defined structure, the format avoids headings for individual subsections, which would disrupt the flow of the discussion. To improve navigability, the format uses style elements such as underscoring, indentation, and illustrations to help you identify important information at a quick glance.

Each pattern follows this structure:

- *Name*—This is an identifier for the pattern that indicates what the pattern does. We chose names that can easily be used in a sentence so that it is easy to reference the pattern's concept in a conversation between designers.

- *Icon*—Most patterns are associated with an icon in addition to the pattern name. Because many architects are used to communicating visually through diagrams, we provide a visual language in addition to the verbal language. This visual language underlines the composability of the patterns, as multiple pattern icons can be combined to describe the solution of a larger, more complex pattern.

- *Context*—This section explains what type of work might make you run into the problem that this pattern solves. The context sets the stage for the problem and often refers to other patterns you may have already applied.

- *Problem*—This explains the difficulty you are facing, expressed as a question. You should be able to read the problem statement and quickly determine if this pattern is relevant to your work. We've formatted the problem to be one sentence delimited by horizontal rules.

- *Forces*—The forces explore the constraints that make the problem difficult to solve. They often consider alternative solutions that seem promising but don't pan out, which helps show the value of the real solution.

- *Solution*—This part explains what you should do to solve the problem. It is not limited to your particular situation, but describes what to do in the variety of circumstances represented by the problem. If you understand a pattern's problem and solution, you understand the pattern. We've formatted the solution in the same style as the problem so that you can easily spot problem and solution statements when perusing the book.

- *Sketch*—One of the most appealing properties of the Alexandrian form is that each pattern contains a sketch that illustrates the solution. In many cases, just by looking at the pattern name and the sketch, you can understand the essence of the pattern. We tried to maintain this style by illustrating the solution with a figure immediately following the solution statement of each pattern.

- *Results*—This part expands upon the solution to explain the details of how to apply the solution and how it resolves the forces. It also addresses new challenges that may arise as a result of applying this pattern.

- *Next*—This section lists other patterns to be considered after applying the current one. Patterns don't live in isolation; the application of one pattern usually leads you to new problems that are solved by other patterns. The relationships between patterns are what constitutes a pattern language as opposed to just a pattern catalog.

- *Sidebars*—These sections discuss more detailed technical issues or variations of the pattern. We set these sections visually apart from the remainder of the text so you can easily skip them if they are not relevant to your particular application of the pattern.

- *Examples*—A pattern usually includes one or more examples of the pattern being applied or having been applied. An example may be as simple as naming a known use or as detailed as a large segment of sample code. Given the large number of available messaging technologies, we do not expect you to be familiar with each technology used to implement an example. Therefore, we designed the patterns so that you can safely skip the example without losing any critical content of the pattern.

The beauty in describing solutions as patterns is that it teaches you not only how to solve the specific problems discussed, but also how to create designs that solve problems the authors were not even aware of. As a result, these patterns for messaging not only describe messaging systems that exist today, but may also apply to new ones created well after this book is published.

Diagram Notation

Integration solutions consist of many different pieces—applications, databases, endpoints, channels, messages, routers, and so on. If we want to describe an integration solution, we need to define a notation that accommodates all these different components. To our knowledge, there is no widely used, comprehensive notation that is geared toward the description of all aspects of an integration solution. The Unified Modeling Language (UML) does a fine job of describing object-oriented systems with class and interaction diagrams, but it does not contain semantics to describe messaging solutions. The UML Profile for EAI [UMLEAI] enriches the semantics of collaboration diagrams to describe message flows between components. This notation is very useful as a precise visual specification that can serve as the basis for code generation as part of a model-driven architecture (MDA). We decided not to adopt this notation for two reasons. First, the UML Profile does not capture all the patterns described in our pattern language. Second, we were not looking to create a precise visual specification, but images that have a certain "sketch" quality to them. We wanted pictures that are able to convey the essence of a pattern at a quick glance—very much like Alexander's *sketch*. That's why we decided to create our own "notation." Luckily, unlike the more formal notation, ours does not require you to read a large manual. A simple picture should suffice:

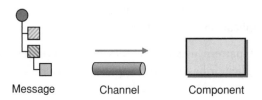

Message   Channel   Component

Visual Notation for Messaging Solutions

This simple picture shows a message being sent to a component over a channel. We use the word *component* very loosely here—it can indicate an application that is being integrated, an intermediary that transforms or routes the message between applications, or a specific part of an application. Sometimes, we also depict a channel as a three-dimensional pipe if we want to highlight the channel itself. Often, we are more interested in the components and draw the channels as simple lines with arrow heads. The two notations are equivalent. We depict the message as a small tree with a round root and nested, square elements because many messaging systems allow messages to contain tree-like data structures—for example, XML documents. The tree elements can be shaded or colored to highlight their usage in a particular pattern. Depicting messages in this way allows us to provide a quick visual description of transformation patterns—it is easy to show a pattern that adds, rearranges, or removes fields from the message.

When we describe application designs—for example, messaging endpoints or examples written in C# or Java—we do use standard UML class and sequence diagrams to depict the class hierarchy and the interaction between objects because the UML notation is widely accepted as the standard way of describing these types of solutions (if you need a refresher on UML, have a look at [UML]).

Examples and Interludes

We have tried to underline the broad applicability of the patterns by including implementation examples using a variety of integration technologies. The potential downside of this approach is that you may not be familiar with each technology that is being used in an example. That's why we made sure that reading the examples is strictly optional—all relevant points are discussed in the pattern description. Therefore, you can safely skip the examples without risk of losing out on important detail. Also, where possible, we provided more than one implementation example using different technologies.

When presenting example code, we focused on *readability* over *runnability*. A code segment can help remove any potential ambiguity left by the solution description, and many application developers and architects prefer looking at 30 lines of code to reading many paragraphs of text. To support this intent, we often show only the most relevant methods or classes of a potentially larger solution. We also omitted most forms of error checking to highlight the core function implemented by the code. Most code snippets do not contain in-line comments, as the code is explained in the paragraphs before and after the code segment.

Providing a meaningful example for a single integration pattern is challenging. Enterprise integration solutions typically consist of a number of heterogeneous components spread across multiple systems. Likewise, most integration patterns do not operate in isolation but rely on other patterns to form a meaningful solution. To highlight the collaboration between multiple patterns, we included more comprehensive examples as interludes (see Chapters 6, 9, and 12). These solutions illustrate many of the trade-offs involved in designing a more comprehensive messaging solution.

All code samples should be treated as illustrative tools only and not as a starting point for development of a production-quality integration solution. For example, almost all examples lack any form of error checking or concern for robustness, security, or scalability.

We tried as much as possible to base the examples on software platforms that are available free of charge or as a trial version. In some cases, we used commercial platforms (such as TIBCO ActiveEnterprise and Microsoft BizTalk) to illustrate the difference between developing a solution from scratch and using a commercial tool. We presented those examples in such a way that they are educational even if you do not have access to the required runtime platform. For many examples, we use relatively barebones messaging frameworks such as JMS or MSMQ. This allows us to be more explicit in the example and focus on the problem at hand instead of distracting from it with all the features a more complex middleware toolset may provide.

The Java examples in this book are based on the JMS 1.1 specification, which is part of the J2EE 1.4 specification. By the time this book is published, most messaging and application server vendors will support JMS 1.1. You can download Sun Microsystems' reference implementation of the JMS specification from Sun's Web site: *http://java.sun.com/j2ee*.

The Microsoft .NET examples are based on Version 1.1 of the .NET framework and are written in C#. You can download the .NET Framework SDK from Microsoft's Web site: *http://msdn.microsoft.com/net*.

Organization of This Book

The pattern language in this book, as with any pattern language, is a web of patterns referring to each other. At the same time, some patterns are more fundamental than others, forming a hierarchy of big-concept patterns that lead to more finely detailed patterns. The big-concept patterns form the load-bearing members of the pattern language. They are the main ones, the *root patterns* that provide the foundation of the language and support the other patterns.

This book groups patterns into chapters by level of abstraction and by topic area. The following diagram shows the root patterns and their relationship to the chapters of the book.

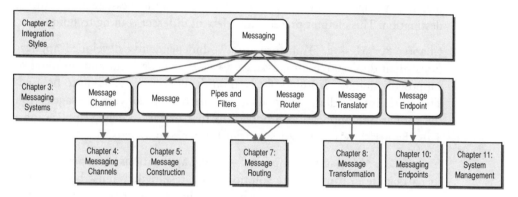

Relationship of Root Patterns and Chapters

The most fundamental pattern is *Messaging* (53); that's what this book is about. It leads to the six root patterns described in Chapter 3, "Messaging Systems," namely, *Message Channel* (60), *Message* (66), *Pipes and Filters* (70), *Message Router* (78), *Message Translator* (85), and *Message Endpoint* (95). In turn, each root pattern leads to its own chapter in the book (except *Pipes and Filters* [70], which is not specific to messaging but is a widely used architectural style that forms the basis of the routing and transformation patterns).

The pattern language is divided into eight chapters, which follow the hierarchy just described:

Chapter 2, "Integration Styles"—This chapter reviews the different approaches available for integrating applications, including *Messaging* (53).

Chapter 3, "Messaging Systems"—This chapter reviews the six root messaging patterns, giving an overview of the entire pattern language.

Chapter 4, "Messaging Channels"—Applications communicate via channels. Channels define the logical pathways a message can follow. This chapter shows how to determine what channels your applications need.

Chapter 5, "Message Construction"—Once you have message channels, you need messages to send on them. This chapter explains the different ways messages can be used and how to take advantage of their special properties.

Chapter 7, "Message Routing"—Messaging solutions aim to decouple the sender and the receiver of information. Message routers provide location independence between sender and receiver so that senders don't have to know about who processes their messages. Rather, they send the messages to intermediate message routing components that forward the message to the correct destination. This chapter presents a variety of different routing techniques.

Chapter 8, "Message Transformation"—Independently developed applications often don't agree on messages' formats, on the form and meaning of supposedly unique identifiers, or even on the character encoding to be used. Therefore, intermediate components are needed to convert messages from the format one application produces to that of the receiving applications. This chapter shows how to design transformer components.

Chapter 10, "Messaging Endpoints"—Many applications were not designed to participate in a messaging solution. As a result, they must be explicitly connected to the messaging system. This chapter describes a layer in the application that is responsible for sending and receiving the messages, making your application an endpoint for messages.

Chapter 11, "System Management"—Once a messaging system is in place to integrate applications, how do we make sure that it's running correctly and doing what we want? This chapter explores how to test and monitor a running messaging system.

These eight chapters together teach you what you need to know about connecting applications using messaging.

Getting Started

With any book that has a lot to teach, it's hard to know where to start, both for the authors and the readers. Reading all of the pages straight through assures covering the entire subject area but isn't the quickest way to get to the issues that are of the most help. Starting with a pattern in the middle of the language can be like starting to watch a movie that's half over—you see what's happening but don't understand what it means.

Luckily, the pattern language is formed around the root patterns described earlier. These root patterns collectively provide an overview of the pattern language, and individually provide starting points for delving deep into the details of messaging. To get an overall survey of the language without reviewing all of the patterns, start with reviewing the root patterns in Chapter 3.

Chapter 2, "Integration Styles," provides an overview of the four main application integration techniques and settles on *Messaging* (53) as being the best overall approach for many integration opportunities. Read this chapter if you are unfamiliar with issues involved in application integration and the pros and cons of the various approaches that are available. If you're already convinced that messaging is the way to go and want to get started with how to use messaging, you can skip this chapter completely.

Chapter 3, "Messaging Systems," contains all of this pattern language's root patterns (except *Messaging* [53], which is in Chapter 2). For an overview of the pattern language, read (or at least skim) all of the patterns in this chapter. To dive deeply on a particular topic, read its root pattern, then go to the patterns mentioned at the end of the pattern section; those next patterns will all be in a chapter named after the root pattern.

After Chapters 2 and 3, different types of messaging developers may be most interested in different chapters based on the specifics of how each group uses messaging to perform integration:

- *System administrators* may be most interested in Chapter 4, "Messaging Channels," the guidelines for what channels to create, and Chapter 11, "System Management," guidance on how to maintain a running messaging system.

- *Application developers* should look at Chapter 10, "Messaging Endpoints," to learn how to integrate an application with a messaging system and at Chapter 5, "Message Construction," to learn what messages to send when.

- *System integrators* will gain the most from Chapter 7, "Message Routing"—how to direct messages to the proper receivers—and Chapter 8, "Message Transformation"—how to convert messages from the sender's format to the receiver's.

Keep in mind that when reading a pattern, if you're in a hurry, start by just reading the problem and solution. This will give you enough information to determine if the pattern is of interest to you right now and if you already know the pattern. If you do not know the pattern and it sounds interesting, go ahead and read the other parts.

Also remember that this is a pattern language, so the patterns are not necessarily meant to be read in the order they're presented in the book. The book's order teaches you about messaging by considering all of the relevant topics in turn and discussing related issues together. To use the patterns to solve a particular problem, start with an appropriate root pattern. Its context explains what patterns need to be applied before this one, even if they're not the ones immediately preceding this one in the book. Likewise, the next section (the last paragraph of the pattern) describes what patterns to consider applying after this one, even if they're not the ones immediately following this one in the book. Use the web of interconnected patterns, not the linear list of book pages, to guide you through the material.

Supporting Web Site

Please look for companion information to this book plus related information on enterprise integration at our Web site: *www.enterpriseintegrationpatterns.com*. You can also e-mail your comments, suggestions, and feedback to us at *authors@ enterpriseintegrationpatterns.com*.

Summary

You should now have a good understanding of the following concepts, which are fundamental to the material in this book:

- What messaging is.

- What a messaging system is.

- Why to use messaging.

- How asynchronous programming is different from synchronous programming.

- How application integration is different from application distribution.

- What types of commercial products contain messaging systems.

You should also have a feel for how this book is going to teach you to use messaging:

- The role patterns have in structuring the material.

- The meaning of the custom notation used in the diagrams.

- The purpose and scope of the examples.

- The organization of the material.

- How to get started learning the material.

Now that you understand the basic concepts and how the material will be presented, we invite you to start learning about enterprise integration using messaging.

Chapter 1

_____

Solving Integration Problems Using Patterns

This chapter illustrates how the patterns in this book can be used to solve a variety of integration problems. In order to do so, we examine common integration scenarios and present a comprehensive integration example. As we design the solution to this example, we express the solution using the patterns contained in this book. At the end of this chapter you will be familiar with about two dozen integration patterns.

The Need for Integration

Enterprises are typically comprised of hundreds, if not thousands, of applications that are custom built, acquired from a third party, part of a legacy system, or a combination thereof, operating in multiple tiers of different operating system platforms. It is not uncommon to find an enterprise that has 30 different Web sites, three instances of SAP, and countless departmental solutions.

We may be tempted to ask: How do businesses allow themselves to get into such a mess? Shouldn't any CIO who is responsible for such an enterprise spaghetti architecture be fired? Well, as in most cases, things happen for a reason.

First, writing business applications is hard. Creating a single, big application to run a complete business is next to impossible. The Enterprise Resource Planning (ERP) vendors have had some success at creating larger-than-ever business applications. The reality, though, is that even the heavyweights like SAP, Oracle, Peoplesoft, and the like perform only a fraction of the business functions required in a typical enterprise. We can see this easily by the fact that ERP systems are one of the most popular integration points in today's enterprises.

1

Second, spreading business functions across multiple applications provides the business with the flexibility to select the "best" accounting package, the "best" customer relationship management software, as well as the "best" order-processing system for its needs. Usually, IT organizations are not interested in a single enterprise application that does it all, nor is such an application possible given the number of individual business requirements.

Vendors have learned to cater to this preference and offer focused applications around a specific core function. However, the ever-present urge to add new functionality to existing software packages has caused some functionality spillover among packaged business applications. For example, many billing systems started to incorporate customer care and accounting functionality. Likewise, the customer care software maker takes a stab at implementing simple billing functions, such as disputes or adjustments. Defining a clear, functional separation between systems is difficult: Is a customer dispute over a bill considered a customer care or a billing function?

Users such as customers, business partners, and internal users generally do not think about system boundaries when they interact with a business. They execute business functions regardless of how many internal systems the business function cuts across. For example, a customer may call to change his or her address and see whether the last payment was received. In many enterprises, this simple request can span across both the customer care and billing systems. Likewise, a customer placing a new order may require the coordination of many systems. The business needs to validate the customer ID, verify the customer's good standing, check inventory, fulfill the order, get a shipping quote, compute sales tax, send a bill, and so on. This process can easily span five or six different systems. From the customer's perspective, it is a single business transaction.

In order to support common business processes and data sharing across applications, these applications need to be integrated. Application integration needs to provide efficient, reliable, and secure data exchange between multiple enterprise applications.

Integration Challenges

Unfortunately, enterprise integration is no easy task. By definition, enterprise integration has to deal with multiple applications running on multiple platforms in different locations, making the term *simple integration* pretty much an oxymoron. Software vendors offer Enterprise Application Integration (EAI) suites that provide cross-platform, cross-language integration as well as the ability to interface with many popular packaged business applications. However, this technical infrastructure addresses only a small portion of the integration complexities. The true challenges of integration span far across business and technical issues.

- Enterprise integration requires a significant shift in corporate politics. Business applications generally focus on a specific functional area, such as customer relationship management (CRM), billing, and finance. This seems to be an extension of Conway's famous law: "Organizations which design systems are constrained to produce designs which are copies of the communication structures of these organizations." Many IT groups are organized in alignment with these same functional areas. Successful enterprise integration needs to establish communication not only between multiple computer systems but also between business units and IT departments—in an integrated enterprise application, groups no longer control a specific application because each application is now part of an overall flow of integrated applications and services.

- Because of their wide scope, integration efforts typically have far-reaching implications on the business. Once the processing of the most critical business functions is incorporated into an integration solution, the proper functioning of that solution becomes vital to the business. A failing or misbehaving integration solution can cost a business millions of dollars in lost orders, misrouted payments, and disgruntled customers.

- One important constraint of developing integration solutions is the limited amount of control the integration developers typically have over the participating applications. In most cases, the applications are legacy systems or packaged applications that cannot be changed just to be connected to an integration solution. This often leaves the integration developers in a situation where they have to make up for deficiencies or idiosyncrasies inside the applications or differences between the applications. Often it would be easier to implement part of the solution inside the application endpoints, but for political or technical reasons, that option may not be available.

- Despite the widespread need for integration solutions, only a few standards have established themselves in this domain. The advent of XML, XSL, and Web services certainly marks the most significant advance of standards-based features in an integration solution. However, the hype around Web services has also given grounds to new fragmentation of the marketplace, resulting in a flurry of new "extensions" and "interpretations" of the standards. This should remind us that the lack of interoperability between "standards-compliant" products was one of the major stumbling blocks for CORBA, which offered a sophisticated technical solution for systems integration.

- Existing XML Web services standards address only a fraction of the integration challenges. For example, the frequent claim that XML is the lingua franca of system integration is somewhat misleading. Standardizing all data exchange to XML can be likened to writing all documents using a common alphabet, such as the Roman alphabet. Even though the alphabet is common, it is still being used to represent many languages and dialects, which cannot be readily understood by all readers. The same is true in enterprise integration. The existence of a common presentation (e.g., XML) does not imply common semantics. The notion of "account" can have many different semantics, connotations, constraints, and assumptions in each participating system. Resolving semantic differences between systems proves to be a particularly difficult and time-consuming task because it involves significant business and technical decisions.

- While developing an EAI solution is challenging in itself, operating and maintaining such a solution can be even more daunting. The mix of technologies and the distributed nature of EAI solutions make deployment, monitoring, and troubleshooting complex tasks that require a combination of skill sets. In most cases, these skill sets are spread across many different individuals or do not even exist within IT operations.

Anyone who has been through an EAI deployment can attest that EAI solutions are a critical component of today's enterprise strategies—but they make IT life harder, not easier. It's a long way between the high-level vision of the integrated enterprise (defined by terms such as straight-through-processing, T+1, agile enterprise) and the nuts-and-bolts implementations (What parameters did System.Messaging.XmlMessageFormatter take again?).

How Integration Patterns Can Help

There are no simple answers for enterprise integration. In our opinion, anyone who claims that integration is easy must be incredibly smart (or at least a good bit smarter than the rest of us), incredibly ignorant (okay, let's say optimistic), or have a financial interest in making you believe that integration is easy.

Even though integration is a broad and difficult topic, we can always observe some people who are much better at it than others. What do these people know that others don't? Since there is no such thing as "Teach Yourself Integration in 21 Days" (this book sure ain't!), it is unlikely that these people know all the answers to integration. However, they have usually solved enough integration problems that they can compare new problems to prior problems they have solved. They know the "patterns" of problems and associated solutions. They learned these patterns over time by trial-and-error or from other experienced integration architects.

The patterns are not copy-paste code samples or shrink-wrapped components, but rather nuggets of advice that describe solutions to frequently recurring problems. Used properly, the integration patterns can help fill the wide gap between the high-level vision of integration and the actual system implementation.

The Wide World of Integration

We intentionally left the definition of *integration* very broad. To us it means connecting computer systems, companies, or people. While this broad definition gives us the convenience of sticking whatever we find interesting into this book, it is helpful to have a closer look at some of the most common integration scenarios. Over the course of many integration projects, we repeatedly came across the following six types of integration:

- Information portals
- Data replication
- Shared business functions
- Service-oriented architectures
- Distributed business processes
- Business-to-business integration

This list is by no means a complete taxonomy of all things integration, but it does illustrate the kind of solutions that integration architects build. Many integration projects consist of a combination of multiple types of integration. For example, reference data replication is often required in order to tie applications into a single, distributed business process.

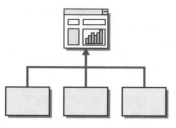

Information Portal

Many business users have to access more than one system to answer a spe-cific question or to perform a single business function. For example, to verify the status of an order, a customer service representative may have to access the order management system on the mainframe plus log on to the system that manages orders placed over the Web. Information portals aggregate informa-tion from multiple sources into a single display to avoid having the user access multiple systems for information. Simple information portals divide the screen into multiple zones, each of which displays information from a different system. More sophisticated systems provide limited interaction between zones; for example, when a user selects an item from a list in zone A, zone B refreshes with detailed information about the selected item. Other portals provide even more sophisticated user interaction and blur the line between a portal and an integrated application.

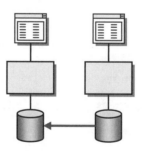

Data Replication

Many business systems require access to the same data. For example, a cus-tomer's address may be used in the customer care system (when the customer calls to change it), the accounting system (to compute sales tax), the shipping system (to label the shipment), and the billing system (to send an invoice). Many of these systems have their own data stores to store customer-related information. When a customer calls to change his or her address, all these systems need to change their copy of the customer's address. This can be accomplished by implementing an integration strategy based on data replication.

There are many different ways to implement data replication. For example, some database vendors build replication functions into the database; alternatively, we can export data into files and re-import them to the other system, or we can use message-oriented middleware to transport data records inside messages.

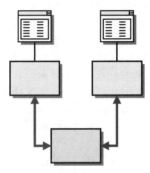

Shared Business Function

In the same way that many business applications store redundant data, they also tend to implement redundant functionality. Multiple systems may need to check whether a social-security number is valid, whether the address matches the specified postal code, or whether a particular item is in stock. It makes sense to expose these functions as a shared business function that is implemented once and available as a service to other systems.

A shared business function can address some of the same needs as data replication. For example, we could implement a business function called Get Customer Address that could allow other systems to request the customer's address when it is needed rather than permanently store a redundant copy. The decision between these two approaches is driven by a number of criteria, such as the amount of control we have over the systems (calling a shared function is usually more intrusive than loading data into the database) or the rate of change (an address may be needed frequently but change very infrequently).

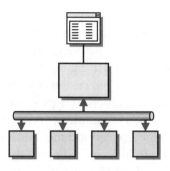

Service-Oriented Architecture

Shared business functions are often referred to as services. A service is a well-defined function that is universally available and responds to requests from "service consumers." Once an enterprise assembles a collection of useful services, managing the services becomes a critical function. First, applications need some form of service directory, a centralized list of all available services. Second, each service needs to describe its interface in such a way that an application can "negotiate" a communications contract with the service. These two functions, service discovery and negotiation, are the key elements that make up a service-oriented architecture (SOA).

SOAs blur the line between integration and distributed applications. A new application can be developed using existing remote services that may be provided by other applications. Therefore, calling a service can be considered integration between the two applications. However, most SOAs provide tools that make calling an external service almost as simple as calling a local method (performance considerations aside), so that the process of developing an application on top of an SOA resembles building a distributed application.

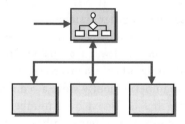

Distributed Business Process

One of the key drivers of integration is that a single business transaction is often spread across many different systems. A previous example showed us that a simple business function such as placing an order can easily touch half a dozen systems. In most cases, all relevant functions are incorporated inside existing applications. What is missing is the coordination between these applications. Therefore, we can add a business process management component that manages the execution of a business function across multiple existing systems.

The boundaries between an SOA and a distributed business can be fuzzy. For example, you could expose all relevant business functions as services and then encode the business process inside an application that accesses all services via an SOA.

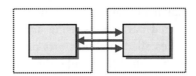

Business-to-Business Integration

So far, we have mainly considered the interaction between applications and business functions inside a single enterprise. In many cases, business functions may be available from outside suppliers or business partners. For example, the shipping company may provide a service for customers to compute shipping cost or track shipments. Or a business may use an outside provider to compute sales tax rates. Likewise, integration frequently occurs between business partners. A customer may contact a retailer to inquire on the price and availability of an item. In response, the retailer may ask the supplier for the status of an expected shipment that contains the out-of-stock item.

Many of the above considerations apply equally to business-to-business integration. However, communicating across the Internet or some other network usually raises new issues related to transport protocols and security. Also, since many business partners may collaborate in an electronic "conversation," standardized data formats are critically important.

Loose Coupling

One of the biggest buzzwords in enterprise architecture and integration is *loose coupling*. It is in fact such a popular term that Doug Kaye wrote a whole book titled after this ubiquitous concept [Kaye]. The benefits of loose coupling have been known for quite some time now, but they have taken center stage more recently due to the surging popularity of Web services architectures.

Loose Coupling

The core principle behind loose coupling is to reduce the assumptions two parties (components, applications, services, programs, users) make about each other when they exchange information. The more assumptions two parties make about each other and the common protocol, the more efficient the communication can be, but the less tolerant the solution is of interruptions or changes because the parties are tightly coupled to each other.

A great example of tight coupling is a local method invocation. Invoking a local method inside an application is based on a lot of assumptions between the called and the calling routine. Both methods have to run in the same process (e.g., a virtual machine) and be written in the same language (or at least use a common intermediate language or byte code). The calling method has to pass the exact number of expected parameters using agreed-upon data types. The call is immediate; that is, the called method starts processing immediately after the calling method makes the call. Meanwhile, the calling method will resume processing only when the called method completes (meaning the invocation is synchronous). Processing will automatically resume in the calling method with the statement immediately following the method call. The communication between the methods is immediate and instantaneous, so neither the caller nor the called method has to worry about security breaches in the form of eavesdropping third parties. All these assumptions make it very easy to write well-structured applications that divide functionality into individual methods to be called by other methods. The resulting large number of small methods allows for flexibility and reuse.

Many integration approaches have aimed to make remote communications simple by packaging a remote data exchange into the same semantics as a local method call. This strategy resulted in the notion of a Remote Procedure Call (RPC) or Remote Method Invocation (RMI), supported by many popular frameworks and platforms: CORBA (see [Zahavi]), Microsoft DCOM, .NET Remoting, Java RMI, and most recently, RPC-style Web services. The intended upside of this approach is twofold. First, synchronous method-call semantics are very familiar to application developers, so why not build on what we already know? Second, using the same syntax and semantics for both local method calls and remote invocations would allow us to defer until deployment time the decision about which components should run locally and which should run remotely, leaving the application developer with one less thing to worry about.

The challenge that all these approaches face lies in the fact that remote communication invalidates many of the assumptions that a local method call is based on. As a result, abstracting the remote communication into the simple semantics of a method call can be confusing and misleading. Waldo and colleagues reminded us back in 1994 that "objects that interact in a distributed system need to be dealt with in ways that are intrinsically different from objects that interact in a single address space" [Waldo]. For example, if we call a remote service to perform a function for us, do we really want to restrict ourselves to only those services that were built using the same programming language we use? A call across the network also tends to be multiple orders of magnitude slower than a local call. Should the calling method really wait until the called method completes? What if the network is interrupted and the called method is temporarily unreachable? How long should we wait? How can we be sure we communicate with the intended party and not a third-party "spoofer"? How can we protect against eavesdropping? What if the method signature (the list of expected parameters) of the called method changes? If the remote method is maintained by a third party or a business partner, we no longer have control over such changes. Should we have our method invocation fail, or should we attempt to find the best possible mapping between the parameters and still make the call? It quickly becomes apparent that remote integration brings up a lot of issues that a local method call never had to deal with.

In summary, trying to portray remote communication as a variant of a local method invocation is asking for trouble. Such tightly coupled architectures typically result in brittle, hard-to-maintain, and poorly scalable solutions. Many Web services pioneers recently (re-)discovered this fact the hard way.

One-Minute EAI

To show the effects of tightly coupled dependencies and how to resolve them, let's look at a very simple way of connecting two systems. Let's assume we are building an online banking system that allows customers to deposit money into their account from another bank. To perform this function, the front-end Web application has to be integrated with the back-end financial system that manages fund transfers.

The easiest way to connect the two systems is through the TCP/IP protocol. Every self-respecting operating system or programming library created in the last 15 years is certain to include a TCP/IP stack. TCP/IP is the ubiquitous communications protocol that transports data between the millions of computers connected to the Internet and local networks. Why not use the most ubiquitous of all network protocols to communicate between two applications?

To keep things simple, let's assume that the remote function that deposits money into a person's account takes only the person's name and the dollar amount as arguments. The following few lines of code suffice to call such a function over TCP/IP (we chose C#, but this code would look virtually identical in C or Java).

```
String hostName = "finance.bank.com";
int port = 80;

IPHostEntry hostInfo = Dns.GetHostByName(hostName);
IPAddress address = hostInfo.AddressList[0];

IPEndPoint endpoint = new IPEndPoint(address, port);

Socket socket = new Socket(address.AddressFamily, SocketType.Stream, ProtocolType.Tcp);
socket.Connect(endpoint);

byte[] amount = BitConverter.GetBytes(1000);
byte[] name   = Encoding.ASCII.GetBytes("Joe");

int bytesSent = socket.Send(amount);
bytesSent    += socket.Send(name);

socket.Close();
```

This code opens a socket connection to the address finance.bank.com and sends two data items (the amount and the customer's name) across the network. No expensive middleware is required: no EAI tools, RPC toolkits—just 10 lines of code. When we run this code, it tells us "7 bytes sent." Voila! How can integration be difficult?

There are a couple of major problems with this integration attempt. One of the strengths of the TCP/IP protocol is its wide support so that we can connect to pretty much any computer connected to the network regardless of the operating system or programming language it uses. However, the platform-independence works only for very simple messages: byte streams. In order to convert our data into a byte stream, we used the BitConverter class. This class converts any data type into a byte array, using the internal memory representation of the data type. The catch is that the internal representation of an integer number varies with computer systems. For example, .NET uses a 32-bit integer, while other systems may use a 64-bit representation. Our example transfers 4 bytes across the network to represent a 32-bit integer number. A system using 64 bits would be inclined to read 8 bytes off the network and would end up interpreting the whole message (including the customer name) as a single number.

Also, some computer systems store their numbers in big-endian format, while others store them in little-endian format. A big-endian format stores numbers starting with the highest byte first, while little-endian systems store the lowest byte first. PCs operate on a little-endian scheme so that the code passes the following 4 bytes across the network:

232 3 0 0

$232 + 3 * 2^8$ equals 1,000. A system that uses big-endian numbers would consider this message to mean $232 * 2^{24} + 3 * 2^{16} = 3,892,510,720$. Joe will be a very rich man! So this approach works only under the assumption that all connected computers represent numbers in the same internal format.

The second problem with this simple approach is that we specify the location of the remote machine (in our case, finance.bank.com). The Dynamic Naming Service (DNS) gives us one level of indirection between the domain name and the IP address, but what if we want to move the function to a different computer on a different domain? What if the machine fails and we have to set up another machine? What if we want to send the information to more than one machine? For each scenario, we would have to change the code. If we use a lot of remote functions, this could become very tedious. So, we should find a way to make our communication independent from a specific machine on the network.

Our simple TCP/IP example also establishes temporal dependencies between the two machines. TCP/IP is a *connection-oriented* protocol. Before any data can be transferred, a connection has to be established first. Establishing a TCP connection involves IP packets traveling back and forth between sender and receiver. This requires that both machines and the network are all available at the same time. If any of the three pieces is malfunctioning or not available due to high load, the data cannot be sent.

Finally, the simple communication also relies on a very strict data format. We are sending 4 bytes of amount data and then a sequence of characters that define the customer's account. If we want to insert a third parameter, such as the name of the currency, we would have to modify both sender and receiver to use the new data format.

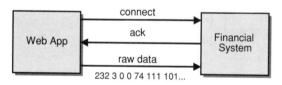

Tightly Coupled Interaction

Our minimalist integration solution is fast and cheap, but it results in a very brittle solution because the two participating parties make the following assumptions about each other:

- Platform technology—internal representations of numbers and objects
- Location—hardcoded machine addresses

- Time—all components have to be available at the same time

- Data format—the list of parameters and their types must match

As we stated earlier, coupling is a measure of how many assumptions parties make about each other when they communicate. Our simple solution requires the parties to make a lot of assumptions. Therefore, this solution is tightly coupled.

In order to make the solution more loosely coupled, we can try to remove these dependencies one by one. We should use a standard data format that is self-describing and platform-independent, such as XML. Instead of sending information directly to a specific machine, we should send it to an addressable *channel*. A channel is a logical address that both sender and receiver can agree on without being aware of each other's identity. Using channels resolves the location dependency but still requires all components to be available at the same time if the channel is implemented using a connection-oriented protocol. In order to remove this temporal dependency, we can enhance the channel to queue up sent requests until the network and the receiving system are ready. The sender can now send requests into the channel and continue processing without having to worry about the delivery of the data. Queuing requests inside the channel requires data to be chunked into self-contained *messages* so that the channel knows how much data to buffer and deliver at any one time. The two systems still depend on a common data format, but we can remove this dependency by allowing for data format transformations inside the channel. If the format of one system changes, we only have to change the transformer and not the other participating systems. This is particularly useful if many applications send data to the same channel.

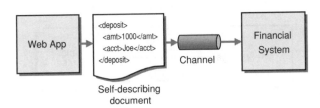

Loosely Coupled Interaction

Mechanisms such as a common data format, asynchronous communication across queuing channels, and transformers help turn a tightly coupled solution into a loosely coupled one. The sender no longer has to depend on the receiver's internal data format nor on its location. It does not even have to pay attention to whether or not the other computer is ready to accept requests. Removing these dependencies between the systems makes the overall solution more tolerant to change, the key benefit of loose coupling. The main drawback of the loosely coupled approach is the additional complexity. This is no longer a 10-lines-of-code solution! Therefore, we use a *message-oriented middleware* infrastructure that provides these services for us. This infrastructure makes exchanging data in a loosely coupled way almost as easy as the example we started with. The next section describes the components that make up such a middleware solution.

Is loose coupling the panacea? Like everything else in enterprise architecture, there is no single best answer. Loose coupling provides important benefits such as flexibility and scalability, but it introduces a more complex programming model and can make designing, building, and debugging solutions more difficult.

A Loosely Coupled Integration Solution

In order to connect two systems via an integration solution, a number of issues have to be resolved. These functions make up what we call middleware—the glue that sits between applications.

Invariably, some data has to be transported from one application to the next. This data could be an address record that needs to be replicated, a call to a remote service, or a snippet of HTML headed for a portal display. Regardless of the payload, this piece of data needs to be understood by both ends and needs to be transported across a network. Two elements provide this basic function. We need a communications *channel* that can move information from one application to the other. This channel could consist of a series of TCP/IP connections, a shared file, a shared database, or a floppy disk being carried from one computer to the next (the infamous "sneakernet"). Inside this channel, we place a *message*—a snippet of data that has an agreed-upon meaning to both applications that are to be integrated. This piece of data can be very small, such as the phone number of a single customer that has changed, or it can be very large, such as the complete list of all customers and their associated addresses.

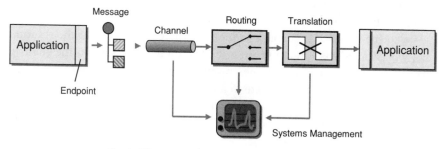

Basic Elements of Message-Based Integration

Now that we can send messages across channels, we can establish a very basic form of integration. However, we promised that simple integration is an oxymoron, so let's see what is missing. We mentioned that integration solutions often have limited control over the applications they are integrating, such as the internal data formats used by the applications. For example, one data format may store the customer name in two fields, called FIRST_NAME and LAST_NAME, while the other system may use a single field called Customer_Name. Likewise, one system may support multiple customer addresses, while the other system supports only a single address. Because the internal data format of an application can often not be changed, the middleware needs to provide some mechanism to convert one application's data format in the other's format. We call this step *translation*.

So far, we can send data from one system to another and accommodate differences in data formats. What happens if we integrate more than two systems? Where does the data have to be moved? We could expect each application to specify the target system(s) for the data it is sending over the channel. For example, if the customer address changes in the customer care system, we could make that system responsible for sending the data to all other systems that store copies of the customer address. As the number of systems increases, this becomes very tedious and requires the sending system to have knowledge about all other systems. Every time a new system is added, the customer care system would have to be adjusted to the new environment. Things would be a lot easier if the middleware could take care of sending messages to the correct places. This is the role of a *routing* component, such as a message broker.

Integration solutions can quickly become complex because they deal with multiple applications, data formats, channels, routing, and transformation. All these elements may be spread across multiple operating platforms and geographic locations. In order to have any idea what is going on inside the system, we need a *systems management* function. This subsystem monitors the flow of data, makes sure that all applications and components are up and running, and reports error conditions to a central location.

Our integration solution is now almost complete. We can move data from one system from another, accommodate differences in the data format, route the data to the required systems, and monitor the performance of the solution. So far, we assumed that an application sends data as a message to the channel. However, most packaged and legacy applications and many custom applications are not prepared to participate in an integration solution. We need a *message endpoint* to connect the system explicitly to the integration solution. The endpoint can be a special piece of code or a *Channel Adapter* (127) provided by an integration software vendor.

Widgets & Gadgets 'R Us: An Example

The best way to understand message-based integration solutions is by walking through a concrete example. Let's consider Widgets & Gadgets 'R Us (WGRUS), an online retailer that buys widgets and gadgets from manufacturers and resells them to customers.

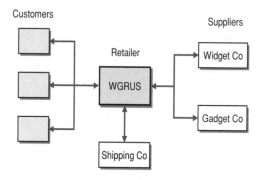

WGRUS Ecosystem

For this example, we assume that the solution needs to support the following requirements. Naturally, we simplified the requirements a bit for sake of brevity, but nevertheless these types of requirements occur frequently in real businesses.

- **Take Orders:** Customers can place orders via Web, phone, or fax.

- **Process Orders:** Processing an order involves multiple steps, including verifying inventory, shipping the goods, and invoicing the customer.

- **Check Status:** Customers can check the order status.

- **Change Address:** Customers can use a Web front-end to change their billing and shipping address.

- **New Catalog:** The suppliers update their catalog periodically. WGRUS needs to update its pricing and availability based on the new catalogs.

- **Announcements:** Customers can subscribe to selective announcements from WGRUS.

- **Testing and Monitoring:** The operations staff needs to be able to monitor all individual components and the message flow between them.

We tackle each of these requirements separately and describe the solution alternatives and trade-offs using the pattern language introduced in this book. We will start with a simple message flow architecture and introduce more complex concepts, such as a *Process Manager* (312), as we address increasingly complex requirements.

Internal Systems

As in most integration scenarios, WGRUS is not a so-called "green field" implementation, but rather the integration of an existing IT infrastructure comprised of a variety of packaged and custom applications. The fact that we have to work with existing applications often makes integration work challenging. In our example, WGRUS runs the following systems (see figure).

Web Interface	WGRUS	Billing/ Accounting
Call Center		Shipping
Inbound Fax		Widget Inventory
Outbound E-mail		Widget Catalog
		Gadget Inventory
		Gadget Catalog

WGRUS IT Infrastructure

WGRUS has four different channels to interact with customers. Customers can visit the company Web site, call the customer service representative at the call center, or submit orders via fax. Customers can also receive notifications via e-mail.

WGRUS's internal systems are comprised of the accounting system, which also includes billing functions, and the shipping system that computes shipping charges and interacts with the shipping companies. For historic reasons, WGRUS has two inventory and catalog systems. WGRUS used to sell only widgets but acquired another retailer that sells gadgets.

Taking Orders

The first function we want to implement is taking orders. Taking orders is a good thing because orders bring revenue. However, placing orders is currently a tedious manual process, so the cost incurred with each order is high.

The first step to streamlining order processing is to unify taking orders. A customer can place orders over one of three channels: Web site, call center, or fax. Unfortunately, each system is based on a different technology and stores incoming orders in a different data format. The call center system is a packaged application, while the Web site is a custom J2EE application. The inbound fax system requires manual data entry into a small Microsoft Access application. We want to treat all orders equally, regardless of their source. For example, a customer should be able to place an order via the call center and check the order status on the Web site.

Because placing an order is an asynchronous process that connects many systems, we decide to implement a message-oriented middleware solution to streamline the order entry process. The packaged call center application was not developed with integration in mind so that we have to connect it to the messaging system using a *Channel Adapter* (127). A *Channel Adapter* (127) is a component that can attach to an application and publish messages to a *Message Channel* (60) whenever an event occurs inside the application. With some *Channel Adapters* (127), the application may not even be aware of the presence of the adapter. For example, a database adapter may add triggers to specific tables so that every time the application inserts a row of data, a message is sent to the *Message Channel* (60). *Channel Adapters* (127) can also work in the opposite direction, consuming messages off a *Message Channel* (60) and triggering an action inside the application in response.

We use the same approach for the inbound fax application, connecting the *Channel Adapter* (127) to the application database. Because the Web application is custom built, we implement the *Message Endpoint* (95) code inside the application. We use a *Messaging Gateway* (468) to isolate the application code from the messaging-specific code.

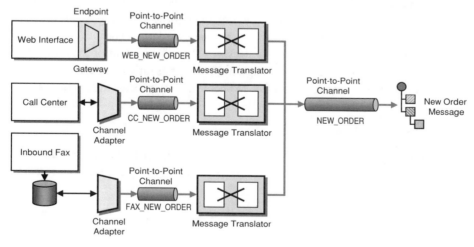

Taking Orders from Three Different Channels

Because each system uses a different data format for the incoming orders, we use three *Message Translator*s (85) to convert the different data formats into a common New Order message that follows a *Canonical Data Model* (355). A *Canonical Data Model* (355) defines message formats that are independent from any specific application so that all applications can communicate with each other in this common format. If the internal format of an application changes, only the *Message Translator* (85) between the affected application and the common *Message Channel* (60) has to change, while all other applications and *Message Translator*s (85) remain unaffected. Using a *Canonical Data Model* (355) means that we deal with two types of messages: canonical (public) messages and application-specific (private) messages. Application-specific messages should not be consumed by any component other than that application and the associated *Message Translator* (85). To reinforce this policy, we name application-specific *Message Channel*s (60) starting with the name of the application: for example, WEB_NEW_ORDER. In contrast, channels carrying canonical messages are named after the intent of the message without any prefix: for example, NEW_ORDER.

We connect each *Channel Adapter* (127) to the *Message Translator* (85) via a *Point-to-Point Channel* (103) because we want to be sure that each order message is consumed only once. We could get away without using a *Message Translator* (85) for the Web interface if we programmed the transformation logic into the *Messaging Gateway* (468). However, hand-coding transformation functions can be tedious and error-prone, and we prefer to use a consistent approach. The additional *Message Translator* (85) also allows us to shield the New Order flow from minor changes in the Web interface data format. All *Message Translator*s (85) publish to the same NEW_ORDER *Point-to-Point Channel* (103) so that orders can be processed off this channel without regard to the order's origin.

The NEW_ORDER *Message Channel* (60) is a so-called *Datatype Channel* (111) because it carries messages of only one type: new orders. This makes it easy for message consumers to know what type of message to expect. The New Order message itself is designed as a *Document Message* (147). The intent of the message is not to instruct the receiver to take a specific action, but rather to pass a document to any interested recipient, who is free to decide how to process the document.

Processing Orders

Now that we have a consistent order message that is independent from the message source, we are ready to process orders. To fulfill an order, we need to complete the following steps:

- Verify the customer's credit standing. If the customer has outstanding bills, we want to reject the new order.

- Verify inventory. We can't fulfill orders for items that are not in stock.

- If the customer is in good standing and we have inventory, we want to ship the goods and bill the customer.

We can express this sequence of events using a Unified Modeling Language (UML) activity diagram. Activity diagrams have relatively simple semantics and are a good tool to depict processes that include parallel activities. The notation is very simple; sequential activities are connected by simple arrows. Parallel activities are connected by a thick black bar representing fork and join actions. A fork action causes all connected activities to start simultaneously, while the join action continues only after all incoming activities have been completed.

Our activity diagram (see figure) is designed to execute the Check Inventory task and the Validate Customer Standing task in parallel. The join bar waits until both activities are completed before it allows the next activity to start. The next activity verifies the results of both steps: Do we have inventory, and is the customer in good standing? If both conditions are fulfilled, the process goes on to fulfill the order. Otherwise, we transition to an exception-handling activity. For example, we may call to remind the customer to pay the last invoice or send an e-mail letting him or her know that the order will be delayed. Because this book focuses on the design aspects of message-oriented integration rather than on workflow modeling, we leave the details of the exception-handling process aside for now. For a very good discussions of workflow architecture and workflow modeling, refer to [Leyman] and [Sharp].

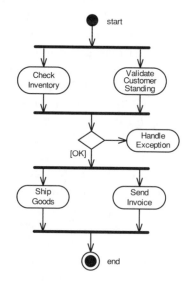

Activity Diagram for Order Processing

It turns out that the activities in the activity diagram map relatively nicely to the systems in WGRUS's IT department. The accounting system verifies the customer's credit standing, the inventory systems check the inventory, and the shipping system initiates the physical shipping of goods. The accounting system also acts as the billing system and sends invoices. We can see that the processing of orders is a typical implementation of a distributed business process.

To convert the logical activity diagram into an integration design, we can use a *Publish-Subscribe Channel* (106) to implement the fork action and an *Aggregator* (268) to implement the join action. A *Publish-Subscribe Channel* (106) sends a message to all active consumers; an *Aggregator* (268) receives multiple incoming messages and combines them into a single, outgoing message (see figure).

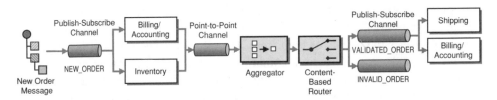

Order Processing Implementation Using Asynchronous Messaging

In our example, the *Publish-Subscribe Channel* (106) sends the New Order message to both the accounting system and the inventory system. The *Aggregator* (268) combines the result messages from both systems and passes the combined message to a *Content-Based Router* (230). A *Content-Based Router* (230) is a component that consumes a message and publishes it, unmodified, to a choice of other channels based on rules coded inside the router. The *Content-Based Router* (230) is equivalent to the branch in a UML activity diagram. In this case, if both the inventory check and the credit check have been affirmative, the *Content-Based Router* (230) forwards the message to the VALIDATED_ORDER channel. This channel is a *Publish-Subscribe Channel* (106), so the validated order reaches both the shipping and the billing systems. If the customer is not in good standing or we have no inventory on hand, *Content-Based Router* (230) forwards the message to the INVALID_ORDER channel. An exception-handling process (not shown in the figure) listens to messages on this channel and notifies the customer of the rejected order.

Now that we have established the overall message flow, we need to have a closer look at the inventory function. As we learned in the requirements section, WGRUS has two inventory systems: one for widgets and one for gadgets. As a result, we have to route the request for inventory to the correct system. Because we want to hide the peculiarities of the inventory systems from the other systems, we insert another *Content-Based Router* (230) that routes the message to the correct inventory system based on the type of item ordered (see figure). For example, all incoming messages with an item number starting with W are routed to the widget inventory system, and all orders with an item number starting with G are routed to the gadget inventory system.

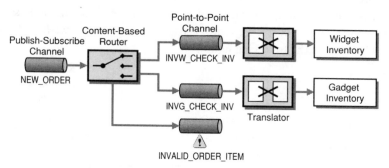

Routing the Inventory Request

Note that the intent of messages on the *Point-to-Point Channels* (103) between the *Content-Based Router* (230) and the inventory systems is different from the previous channel. These channels contain *Command Messages* (145), messages that instruct the system to execute the specified command, in this case verifying the inventory of an item.

Because the widget inventory system and the gadget inventory system use different internal data formats, we again insert *Message Translators* (85) to convert from the canonical New Order message format to a system-specific format.

What happens if the order item starts neither with W nor G? The *Content-Based Router* (230) routes the message to the INVALID_ORDER channel so that the invalid order can be processed accordingly, by notifying the customer, for example. This channel is a typical example of an *Invalid Message Channel* (115). It highlights the fact that the meaning of a message changes depending on what channel it is on. Both the NEW_ORDER channel and the INVALID_ORDER channel transport the same type of message, but in one case a new order is being processed, while in the other case the order is deemed invalid.

So far, we have assumed that each order contains only a single item. This would be pretty inconvenient for our customers because they would have to place a new order for each item. Also, we would end up shipping multiple orders to the same customer and incur unnecessary shipping costs. However, if we allow multiple items inside an order, which inventory system should verify the inventory for this order? We could use a *Publish-Subscribe Channel* (106) to send the order to each inventory system to pick out the items that it can process.

But what would then happen to invalid items? How would we notice that neither inventory system processed the item? We want to maintain the central control the *Content-Based Router* (230) gives us, but we need to be able to route each order item individually.

Therefore, we insert a *Splitter* (259), a component that breaks a single message into multiple individual messages. In our case, the *Splitter* (259) splits a single Order message into multiple Order Item messages. Each Order Item message can then be routed to the correct inventory system using a *Content-Based Router* (230) as before; see the following figure.

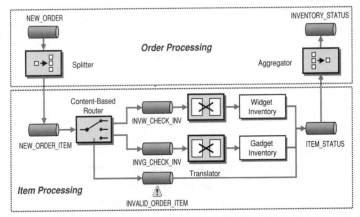

Processing Order Items Individually

Naturally, when the inventory for all items has been verified, we need to recombine the messages into a single message. We already learned that the component that can combine multiple messages into a single message is the *Aggregator* (268). Using both a *Splitter* (259) and an *Aggregator* (268), we can logically separate the message flow for individual order items from the flow for a complete order.

When designing an *Aggregator* (268), we have to make three key decisions:

- Which messages belong together (correlation)?
- How do we determine that all messages are received (the completeness condition)?
- How do we combine the individual messages into one result message (the aggregation algorithm)?

Let's tackle these issues one by one. We can't correlate order items by the customer ID, because a customer may place multiple orders in short succession. Therefore, we need a unique order ID for each order. We accomplish this by inserting a *Content Enricher* (336) into the part of the solution that takes orders (see figure). A *Content Enricher* (336) is a component that adds missing data items to an incoming message. In our case, the *Content Enricher* (336) adds a unique order ID to the message.

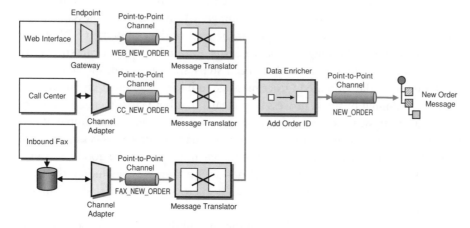

Taking Orders with Enricher

Now that we have an order ID to correlate Order Item messages, we need to define the completeness condition and the aggregation algorithm for the Order Item *Aggregator* (268). Because we route all messages, including invalid items, to the *Aggregator* (268), the *Aggregator* (268) can simply use the number of items in the order (one of the fields in the Order message) to count until all order items arrive. The aggregation algorithm is similarly simple. The *Aggregator* (268) concatenates all Order Item messages back into a single Order message and publishes it to the VALIDATED_ORDER channel.

The combination of a *Splitter* (259), a *Message Router* (78), and an *Aggregator* (268) is fairly common. We refer to it as a *Composed Message Processor* (294). To simplify the figure, we insert the symbol for a *Composed Message Processor* (294) into the original message flow diagram:

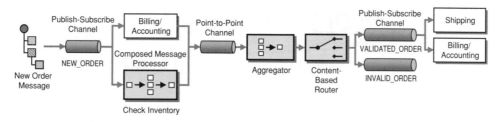

Revised Order Process Implementation

Checking Status

Despite connecting the systems via *Message Channels* (60), fulfilling an order can take some amount of time. For example, we may be out of a certain item and the inventory system may be holding the Inventory Check message until new items arrive. This is one of the advantages of asynchronous messaging: the communication is designed to happen at the pace of the components. While the inventory system is holding the message, the accounting system can still verify the customer's credit standing. Once both steps are completed, the *Aggregator* (268) publishes the Validated Order message to initiate shipment and invoicing.

A long-running business process also means that both customers and managers are likely to want to know the status of a specific order. For example, if certain items are out of inventory, the customer may decide to process just those items that are in stock. Or, if the customer has not received the goods, it is useful if we can tell him or her that the goods are on their way (including the shipping company's tracking number) or that there is an internal delay in the warehouse.

Tracking the status of an order with the current design is not so easy. Related messages flow through multiple systems. To ascertain the status of the order in the sequence of steps, we would have to know the "last" message related to this order. One of the advantages of a *Publish-Subscribe Channel* (106) is that we can add additional subscribers without disturbing the flow of messages. We can use this property to listen in to new and validated orders and store them in a *Message Store* (555). We could then query the *Message Store* (555) database for the status of an order (see figure):

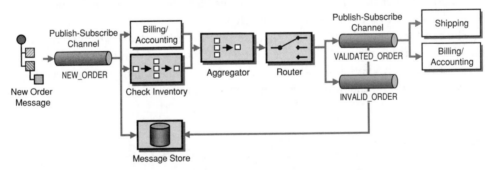

Adding a Message Store to Track Order Status

In situations where we use a *Point-Point Channel* (103), we cannot simply add a subscriber to the channel, because a *Point-to-Point Channel* (103) ensures that each message is only consumed by a single subscriber. However, we can insert a *Wire Tap* (547), a simple component that consumes a message off one channel and publishes it to two channels. We can then use the second channel to send messages to the *Message Store* (555); see figure.

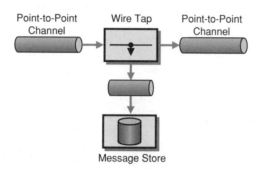

Tracking Messages with a Wire Tap

Storing message data in a central database has another significant advantage. In the original design, each message had to carry extraneous data in order to continue processing the message down the line. For example, the Validate Customer Standing message may have had to transport all sorts of customer data even though it required only the customer ID. This additional data is necessary so that the resulting message still contains all data from the original order message. Storing the New Order message in a *Message Store* (555) at the beginning of the message flow has the advantage that all subsequent components can refer to the *Message Store* (555) for important message data without all intermediate steps having to carry the data along. We refer to such a function as *Claim Check* (346)—messages can "check in" data for later retrieval. The downside of this approach is that accessing a central data store is not as reliable as sending messages across asynchronous *Message Channels* (60).

Now, the *Message Store* (555) is responsible for maintaining data related to the new message as well as the progress of the message within the process. This data gives us enough information to use the *Message Store* (555) to determine the next required steps in the process rather than connecting components with fixed *Message Channels* (60). For example, if the database contains reply messages from both the inventory systems and the billing system, we can conclude that the order has been validated and can send a message to the shipping and billing systems. Instead of making this decision in a separate *Aggregator* (268) component, we can do it right in the *Message Store* (555). Effectively, we are turning the *Message Store* (555) into a *Process Manager* (312).

A *Process Manager* (312) is a central component that manages the flow of messages through the system. The *Process Manager* (312) provides two main functions:

- Storing data between messages (inside a "process instance")

- Keeping track of progress and determining the next step (by using a "process template")

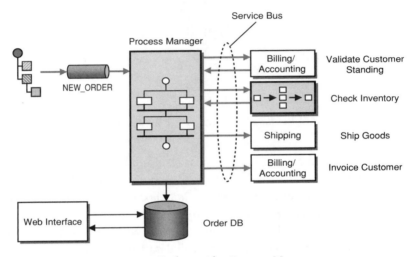

Processing Orders with a Process Manager

This architecture turns the individual systems (e.g., the inventory systems) into shared business functions that can be accessed by other components as services, thus increasing reuse and simplifying maintenance. The services can be wired together via a message flow (for example, using a *Composed Message Processor* (294) to check inventory status for each order item) or orchestrated via a *Process Manager* (312). Using a *Process Manager* (312) makes changing the flow of messages much easier than our previous approach.

The new architecture exposes all services to a common services bus so that they can be invoked from any other component. We could turn the WGRUS IT infrastructure into an SOA by adding facilities to look up ("discover") a service from a central service registry. In order to participate in this SOA, each service would have to provide additional functions. For example, each service would have to expose an interface contract that describes the functions provided by the service. Each request-reply service also needs to support the concept of a *Return*

Address (159). A *Return Address* (159) allows the caller (the service consumer) to specify the channel where the service should send the reply message. This is important to allow the service to be reused in different contexts, each of which may require its own channel for reply messages.

The *Process Manager* (312) itself uses a persistent store (typically files or a relational database) to store data associated with each process instance. To allow the Web interface to query the status of an order, we could send a message to the *Process Manager* (312) or the order database. However, checking status is a synchronous process—the customer expects the response right away. Because the Web interface is a custom application, we decide to access the order database directly to query the order status. This form of *Shared Database* (47) is the simplest and most efficient approach, and we are always ensured that the Web interface displays the most current status. The potential downside of this approach is that the Web interface is tightly coupled to the database, a trade-off that we are willing to take.

One difficulty in exposing systems as services results from the fact that many legacy systems were not built with features such as *Return Address* (159) in mind. Therefore, we "wrap" access to the legacy system with a *Smart Proxy* (558). This *Smart Proxy* (558) enhances the basic system service with additional capability so that it can participate in an SOA. To do this, the *Smart Proxy* (558) intercepts both request and reply messages to and from the basic service (see figure).

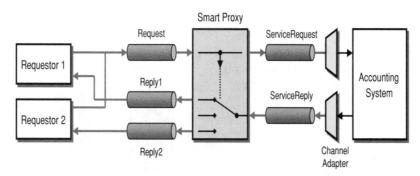

Inserting a Smart Proxy to Turn a Legacy System into a Shared Service

The *Smart Proxy* (558) can store information from the request message (e.g., the *Return Address* [159] specified by the requestor) and use this information to process the reply message, (e.g., route it to the correct reply channel). A *Smart Proxy* (558) is also very useful to track quality of service (e.g., response times) of an external service.

Change Address

WGRUS needs to deal with a number of addresses. For example, the invoice has to be sent to the customer's billing address, while the goods are shipped to the shipping address. We want to allow the customer to maintain all these addresses through the Web interface to eliminate unnecessary manual steps.

We can choose between two basic approaches to get the correct billing and shipping addresses to the billing and shipping systems:

- Include address data with every New Order message

- Store address data in each system and replicate changes

The first option has the advantage that we can use an existing integration channel to transport the additional information. A potential downside is the additional data flowing across the middleware infrastructure; we pass the address data along with every order even though the address may change much less frequently.

When implementing the first option, we need to consider that the billing and shipping systems are packaged applications and were likely not designed with integration in mind. As such, they are unlikely to be able to accept addresses with a new order but rather use the address that is stored in their local database. To enable the systems to update the address with the New Order message, we need to execute two functions in the billing system (and the shipping system): First, we must update the address, and then we must send the bill (or ship the goods). Because the order of the two messages matters, we insert a simple *Process Manager* (312) component that receives a New Order message (which includes the current shipping and billing addresses and publishes two separate messages to the billing (or shipping) system (see figure).

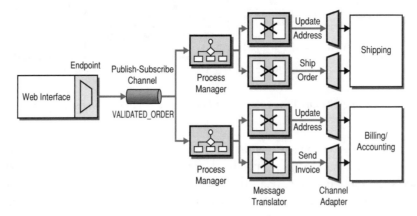

Including Address Data in the New Order Message

We need to keep in mind that the *Channel Adapter*s (127) require messages to be formatted in the proprietary formats used by the applications (using so-called private messages). Because the New Order message arrives in the canonical message format, we need to perform a translation between the two formats. We could build the transformation into the *Process Manager* (312), but we actually prefer external *Message Translator*s (85) so that the logic inside the *Process Manager* (312) is not affected by the possibly complicated data format required by the applications.

The second option uses data replication to propagate address changes to all affected systems independently of the New Order process. Whenever the address information changes in the Web interface, we propagate the changes to all interested systems using a *Publish-Subscribe Channel* (106). The systems store the updated address internally and use it when an Order message arrives. This approach reduces message traffic (assuming customers change addresses less frequently than they place orders). It can also reduce coupling between systems. Any system that uses an address can subscribe to the ADDRESS_CHANGE channel without affecting any other systems.

Because we are dealing with multiple types of addresses (shipping and billing addresses), we need to make sure that only the right type of address is stored in each system. We need to avoid sending an address change message to the shipping system if the address is a billing address. We accomplish this by using *Message Filters* (237) that pass only messages matching certain criteria (see figure).

We also use *Message Translator*s (85) to translate the generic Address Change message into the specific message format used by the applications. In this case, we do not have to use a *Message Translator* (85) for the Web interface because we define the *Canonical Data Model* (355) as equal to the format of the Web interface application. This could limit our flexibility if we want to introduce other ways of changing addresses in the future, but for now it is sufficient.

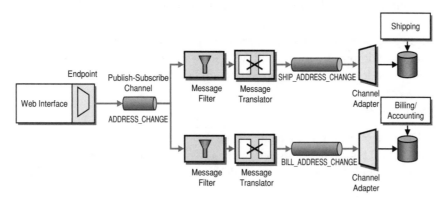

Propagating Address Changes via a Separate Publish-Subscribe Channel

Both the shipping and the billing systems store addresses in a relational database, so we use a database *Channel Adapter* (127) to update the data in each system.

How do we decide between the two options? In our situation, the message traffic is not much of a concern because we process only a few hundred orders a day, so either solution would be reasonably efficient. The main decision driver is going to be the internal structure of the applications. We may not be able to insert the addresses directly into the database, but rather through the applications' business layer. In this case, the applications may perform additional validation steps and record the address change activity. The system may even be programmed to e-mail a confirmation message to the customer every time the address changes. This would get very annoying if the update occurred with every order. Such a condition would favor propagating address changes using dedicated messages that are sent only when the customer actually changes the address.

In general, we prefer well-defined, self-contained business actions such as "Change Address" and "Place Order" because they give us more flexibility in orchestrating the businesses processes. It all comes down to a question of granularity and the associated trade-offs. Fine-grained interfaces can lead to sluggish systems due to an excessive number of remote calls being made or messages being sent. For example, imagine an interface that exposes a separate method to change each address field. This approach would be efficient if the communication happens inside a single application—you update only those fields that changed. In an integration scenario, sending six or seven messages to update an address would be a significant overhead, plus we would have to deal with synchronizing the individual messages. Fine-grained interfaces also lead to tight coupling. If we change the address format by adding a new field, we have to define new message formats and change all other applications to send an additional message.

Coarse-grained interfaces solve these issues, but at a cost. We send fewer messages and are therefore more efficient and less tightly coupled. However, interfaces that are too coarse can limit our flexibility. If Send Invoice and Change Address are combined into one external function, we will never be able to change an address without sending a bill. So, as always, the best answer is the happy medium and depends on the specific trade-offs at work in the real-life scenario.

New Catalog

To place orders, customers need to see the currently offered items and their prices online. WGRUS's catalog is driven by the offerings from the respective suppliers. However, one of the services that WGRUS provides to its customers is allowing them to view widgets and gadgets on the same site and to order both types of items in a single order. This function is an example of an Information Portal scenario—we combine information from multiple sources into a single view.

It turns out that both suppliers update their product catalog once every three months. Therefore, it makes relatively little sense to create a real-time messaging infrastructure to propagate catalog changes from the suppliers to WGRUS. Instead, we use *File Transfer* (43) integration to move catalog data from suppliers to WGRUS. The other advantage of using files is that they are easily and efficiently transported across public networks using FTP or similar protocols. In comparison, most asynchronous messaging infrastructures do not work well over the public Internet.

We still can use translators and adapters to transform the data to our internal catalog format. However, these translators process a whole catalog at once instead of one item at a time. This approach is much more efficient if we are dealing with large amounts of data in the same format.

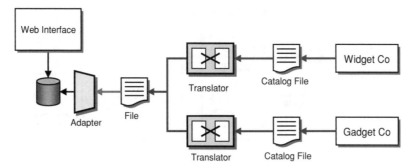

Updating Catalog Data via File Transfer

Announcements

In order to improve business, we want to announce specials to our customers every once in a while. To avoid annoying the customers, we allow each customer to specify which messages interest them. We also want to target specific messages to a specific subset of customers. For example, we may announce special deals only to preferred customers. When we need to send information to multiple recipients, a *Publish-Subscribe Channel* (106) immediately comes to mind. However, a *Publish-Subscribe Channel* (106) has some disadvantages. First, it allows any subscriber to listen to the published messages without the publisher's knowledge. For example, we would not want smaller customers to receive special offers intended for high-volume customers. The second downside of *Publish-Subscribe Channels* (106) is that they work efficiently only on local networks. If we send data across wide-area networks via a *Publish-Subscribe Channel* (106), we have to send a separate copy of the message to each recipient. If a recipient is not interested in the message, we would have incurred unnecessary network traffic.

Widgets & Gadgets 'R Us: An Example

Therefore, we should look for a solution that allows subscribers to issue their subscription preferences and then send individual messages only to interested (and authorized) customers. To perform this function, we use a *Dynamic Recipient List* (249). A dynamic *Recipient List* (249) is the combination of two *Message Routing* (78) patterns. A *Recipient List* (249) is a router that propagates a single message to a set of recipients. The main difference between the *Recipient List* (249) and a *Publish-Subscribe Channel* (106) is that the *Recipient List* (249) addresses each recipient specifically and therefore has tight control over who receives messages. A *Dynamic Router* (243) is a router whose routing algorithm can change based on control messages. These control messages can take the form of subscription preferences issued by the subscribers. A dynamic *Recipient List* (249) is the result of combining these two patterns.

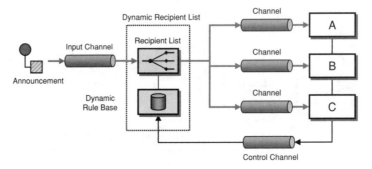

Sending Announcements with a Dynamic Recipient List

If customers receive announcements via e-mail, the implementation of these patterns can use the mailing list's features typically supplied by e-mail systems. Each recipient channel is then identified by an e-mail address. Likewise, if customers prefer to receive announcements via a Web services interface, each recipient channel is implemented by a SOAP request, and the channel address is the URI of the Web service. This example illustrates that the patterns we use to describe the solution design are independent of a specific transport technology.

Testing and Monitoring

Monitoring the correct execution of messages is a critical operations and support function. The *Message Store* (555) can provide us with some important business metrics, such as the average time to fulfill an order. However, we may need more detailed information for the successful operation of an integration solution. Let's assume we enhance our solution to access an external credit agency to better assess our customer's credit standing. Even if we show no outstanding payments, we may want to decline a customer's order if the customer's credit ranking is particularly poor. This is especially useful for new customers who do not have a payment history with us. Because the service is provided by an outside provider, we are charged for its use. To verify the provider's invoice, we want to track our actual usage and reconcile the two reports. We cannot simply go by the number of orders, because the business logic may not request an external credit check for long-standing customers. Also, we may have a quality of service (QoS) agreement with the external provider. For example, if the response time exceeds a specified time, we may not have to pay for the request.

To make sure we are being billed correctly, we want to track the number of requests we make and the time it takes for the associated response to arrive. We have to be able to deal with two specific situations. First, the external service can process more than one request at a time, so we need to be able to match up request and reply messages. Second, since we treat the external service as a shared service inside our enterprise, we want to allow the service consumer to specify a *Return Address* (159), the channel where the service should send the reply message. Not knowing to which channel the reply is being sent can make it difficult to match request and reply messages.

Once again, the *Smart Proxy* (558) is the answer. We insert the *Smart Proxy* (558) between any service consumer and the external service. The *Smart Proxy* (558) intercepts each request to the service and replaces the *Return Address* (159) specified by the service consumer with a fixed reply channel. This causes the service to send all reply messages to the channel specified by the *Smart Proxy* (558). The proxy stores the original *Return Address* (159) so that it can forward the reply message to the channel originally specified by the consumer. The *Smart Proxy* (558) also measures the time elapsed between request and reply messages from the external service. The *Smart Proxy* (558) publishes this data to the *Control Bus* (540). The *Control Bus* (540) connects to a management console that collects metrics from many different components.

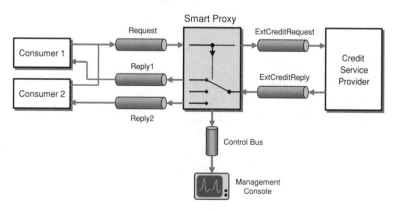

Inserting a Smart Proxy to Track Response Times

Besides tracking our usage of the external credit service, we also want to make sure that the service is working correctly. The *Smart Proxy* (558) can report to the management console cases where no reply message is received within a specified time-out period. Much harder to detect are cases where the external service returns a reply message but the results in the message are incorrect. For example, if the external service malfunctions and returns a credit score of zero for every customer, we would end up denying every order. There are two mechanisms that can help us protect against such a scenario. First, we can periodically inject a *Test Message* (66) into the request stream. This *Test Message* (66) requests the score for a specific person so that the result is known. We can then use a *test data verifier* to check not only that a reply was received but also the accuracy of the message content. Because the *Smart Proxy* (558) supports *Return Addresses* (159), the *test data generator* can specify a special reply channel to separate test replies from regular replies (see figure).

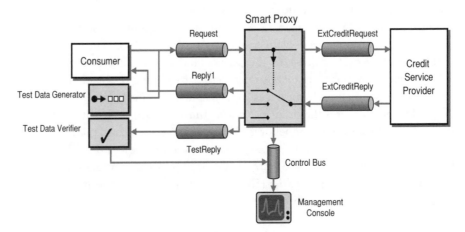

Inserting Test Messages to Verify Accurate Results

Another effective strategy to detect malfunctioning services is to take a statistical sample. For example, we may expect to decline an average of less than one in 10 orders due to customers' poor standing. If we decline more than five orders in a row, this may be an indication that an external service or some business logic is malfunctioning. The management console could e-mail the five orders to an administrator, who can then take a quick look at the data to verify whether the rejections were justified.

Summary

We have walked through a fairly extensive integration scenario using different integration strategies such as *File Transfer* (43), *Shared Database* (47), and asynchronous *Messaging* (53). We routed, split, and aggregated messages. We introduced a *Process Manager* (312) to allow for more flexibility. We also added functions to monitor the correct operation of the solution. While the requirements for this example were admittedly simplified, the issues and design trade-offs we had to consider are very real. The solution diagrams and descriptions highlight how we can describe each solution in a vendor-neutral and technology-neutral language that is much more accurate than a high-level sequence diagram.

The integration scenario in this chapter focuses primarily on how to connect existing applications. For a detailed description of how to publish and consume messages from inside a custom application, see the examples in Chapter 6, "Interlude: Simple Messaging," and Chapter 9, "Interlude: Composed Messaging."

The remainder of the book contains detailed descriptions and code examples for each of the patterns that we used in our solution design, as well as many related patterns. The patterns are categorized by their primary intent between base patterns, channel patterns, message patterns, routing patterns, transformation patterns, endpoint patterns, and system management patterns. This arrangement makes it easy to read all patterns in sequence or to look up individual patterns as a reference.

Chapter 2

Integration Styles

Introduction

Enterprise integration is the task of making disparate applications work together to produce a unified set of functionality. These applications can be custom developed in house or purchased from third-party vendors. They likely run on multiple computers, which may represent multiple platforms, and may be geographically dispersed. Some of the applications may be run outside of the enterprise by business partners or customers. Other applications might not have been designed with integration in mind and are difficult to change. These issues and others like them make application integration complicated. This chapter explores multiple integration approaches that can help overcome these challenges.

Application Integration Criteria

What makes good application integration? If integration needs were always the same, there would be only one integration style. Yet, like any complex technological effort, application integration involves a range of considerations and consequences that should be taken into account for any integration opportunity.

The fundamental criterion is whether to use **application integration** at all. If you can develop a single, standalone application that doesn't need to collaborate with any other applications, you can avoid the whole integration issue entirely. Realistically, though, even a simple enterprise has multiple applications that need to work together to provide a unified experience for the enterprise's employees, partners, and customers.

The following are some other main decision criteria.

Application coupling—Integrated applications should minimize their dependencies on each other so that each can evolve without causing problems to the others. As explained in Chapter 1, "Solving Integration Problems Using Patterns," tightly coupled applications make numerous assumptions about

Introduction

how the other applications work; when the applications change and break those assumptions, the integration between them breaks. Therefore, the interfaces for integrating applications should be specific enough to implement useful functionality but general enough to allow the implementation to change as needed.

Intrusiveness—When integrating an application into an enterprise, developers should strive to minimize both changes to the application and the amount of integration code needed. Yet, changes and new code are often necessary to provide good integration functionality, and the approaches with the least impact on the application may not provide the best integration into the enterprise.

Technology selection—Different integration techniques require varying amounts of specialized software and hardware. Such tools can be expensive, can lead to vendor lock-in, and can increase the learning curve for developers. On the other hand, creating an integration solution from scratch usually results in more effort than originally intended and can mean reinventing the wheel.

Data format—Integrated applications must agree on the format of the data they exchange. Changing existing applications to use a unified data format may be difficult or impossible. Alternatively, an intermediate translator can unify applications that insist on different data formats. A related issue is **data format evolution and extensibility**—how the format can change over time and how that change will affect the applications.

Data timeliness—Integration should minimize the length of time between when one application decides to share some data and other applications have that data. This can be accomplished by exchanging data frequently and in small chunks. However, chunking a large set of data into small pieces may introduce inefficiencies. Latency in data sharing must be factored into the integration design. Ideally, receiver applications should be informed as soon as shared data is ready for consumption. The longer sharing takes, the greater the opportunity for applications to get out of sync and the more complex integration can become.

Data or functionality—Many integration solutions allow applications to share not only data but functionality as well, because sharing of functionality can provider better abstraction between the applications. Even though invoking functionality in a remote application may seem the same as invoking local functionality, it works quite differently, with significant consequences for how well the integration works.

Remote Communication—Computer processing is typically synchronous—that is, a procedure waits while its subprocedure executes. However, calling a remote subprocedure is much slower than a local one so that a procedure may not want to wait for the subprocedure to complete; instead, it may want to invoke the subprocedure asynchronously, that is, starting the subprocedure but continuing with its own processing simultaneously. Asynchronicity can make for a much more efficient solution, but such a solution is also more complex to design, develop, and debug.

Reliability—Remote connections are not only slow, but they are much less reliable than a local function call. When a procedure calls a subprocedure inside a single application, it's a given that the subprocedure is available. This is not necessarily true when communicating remotely; the remote application may not even be running or the network may be temporarily unavailable. Reliable, asynchronous communication enables the source application to go on to other work, confident that the remote application will act sometime later.

So, as you can see, there are several different criteria that must be considered when choosing and designing an integration approach. The question then becomes, Which integration approach best addresses which of these criteria?

Application Integration Options

There is no one integration approach that addresses all criteria equally well. Therefore, multiple approaches for integrating applications have evolved over time. The various approaches can be summed up in four main integration styles.

File Transfer (43)—Have each application produce files of shared data for others to consume and consume files that others have produced.

Shared Database (47)—Have the applications store the data they wish to share in a common database.

Remote Procedure Invocation (50)—Have each application expose some of its procedures so that they can be invoked remotely, and have applications invoke those to initiate behavior and exchange data.

Messaging (53)—Have each application connect to a common messaging system, and exchange data and invoke behavior using messages.

This chapter presents each style as a pattern. The four patterns share the same problem statement—the need to integrate applications—and very similar contexts. What differentiates them are the forces searching for a more elegant solution. Each pattern builds on the last, looking for a more sophisticated approach to address the shortcomings of its predecessors. Thus, the pattern order reflects an increasing order of sophistication, but also increasing complexity.

Introduction

The trick is not to choose one style to use every time but to choose the *best* style for a particular integration opportunity. Each style has its advantages and disadvantages. Applications may integrate using multiple styles so that each point of integration takes advantage of the style that suits it best. Likewise, an application may use different styles to integrate with different applications, choosing the style that works best for the other application. As a result, many integration approaches can best be viewed as a hybrid of multiple integration styles. To support this type of integration, many integration and EAI middleware products employ a combination of styles, all of which are effectively hidden in the product's implementation.

The patterns in the remainder of this book expand on the *Messaging* (53) integration style. We focus on messaging because we believe that it provides a good balance between the integration criteria but is also the most difficult style to work with. As a result, messaging is still the least well understood of the integration styles and a technology ripe with patterns that quickly explain how to use it best. Finally, messaging is the basis for many commercial EAI products, so explaining how to use messaging well also goes a long way in teaching you how to use those products. The focus of this section is to highlight the issues involved with application integration and how messaging fits into the mix.

File Transfer

by Martin Fowler

An enterprise has multiple applications that are being built independently, with different languages and platforms.

> How can I integrate multiple applications so that they work together and can exchange information?

In an ideal world, you might imagine an organization operating from a single, cohesive piece of software, designed from the beginning to work in a unified and coherent way. Of course, even the smallest operations don't work like that. Multiple pieces of software handle different aspects of the enterprise. This is due to a host of reasons.

- People buy packages that are developed by outside organizations.

- Different systems are built at different times, leading to different technology choices.

- Different systems are built by different people whose experience and preferences lead them to different approaches to building applications.

- Getting an application out and delivering value is more important than ensuring that integration is addressed, especially when that integration doesn't add any value to the application under development.

As a result, any organization has to worry about sharing information between very divergent applications. These can be written in different languages, based on different platforms, and have different assumptions about how the business operates.

Tying together such applications requires a thorough understanding of how to link together applications on both the business and technical levels. This is a lot easier if you minimize what you need to know about how each application works.

What is needed is a common data transfer mechanism that can be used by a variety of languages and platforms but that feels natural to each. It should require a minimal amount of specialized hardware and software, making use of what the enterprise already has available.

Files are a universal storage mechanism, built into any enterprise operating system and available from any enterprise language. The simplest approach would be to somehow integrate the applications using files.

Have each application produce files that contain the information the other applications must consume. Integrators take the responsibility of transforming files into different formats. Produce the files at regular intervals according to the nature of the business.

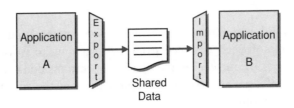

An important decision with files is what format to use. Very rarely will the output of one application be exactly what's needed for another, so you'll have to do a fair bit of processing of files along the way. This means not only that all the applications that use a file have to read it, but that you also have to be able to use processing tools on it. As a result, standard file formats have grown up over time. Mainframe systems commonly use data feeds based on the file system formats of COBOL. UNIX systems use text-based files. The current method is to use XML. An industry of readers, writers, and transformation tools has built up around each of these formats.

Another issue with files is when to produce them and consume them. Since there's a certain amount of effort required to produce and process a file, you usually don't want to work with them too frequently. Typically, you have some regular business cycle that drives the decision: nightly, weekly, quarterly, and so on. Applications get used to when a new file is available and processes it at its time.

The great advantage of files is that integrators need no knowledge of the internals of an application. The application team itself usually provides the file. The file's contents and format are negotiated with integrators, although if a package is used, the choices are often limited. The integrators then deal with the transformations required for other applications, or they leave it up to the consuming applications to decide how they want to manipulate and read the file. As a result, the different applications are quite nicely decoupled from each other. Each application can make internal changes freely without affecting other applications, providing they still produce the same data in the files in the same format. The files effectively become the public interface of each application.

Part of what makes *File Transfer* simple is that no extra tools or integration packages are needed, but that also means that developers have to do a lot of the work themselves. The applications must agree on file-naming conventions and the directories in which they appear. The writer of a file must implement a strategy to keep the file names unique. The applications must agree on which one will delete old files, and the application with that responsibility will have to know when a file is old and no longer needed. The applications will need to implement a locking mechanism or follow a timing convention to ensure that one application is not trying to read the file while another is still writing it. If all of the applications do not have access to the same disk, then some application must take responsibility for transferring the file from one disk to another.

One of the most obvious issues with *File Transfer* is that updates tend to occur infrequently, and as a result systems can get out of synchronization. A customer management system can process a change of address and produce an extract file each night, but the billing system may send the bill to an old address on the same day. Sometimes lack of synchronization isn't a big deal. People often expect a certain lag in getting information around, even with computers. At other times the result of using stale information is a disaster. When deciding on when to produce files, you have to take the freshness needs of consumers into account.

In fact, the biggest problem with staleness is often on the software development staff themselves, who frequently must deal with data that isn't quite right. This can lead to inconsistencies that are difficult to resolve. If a customer changes his address on the same day with two different systems, but one of them makes an error and gets the wrong street name, you'll have two different addresses for a customer. You'll need some way to figure out how to resolve this. The longer the period between file transfers, the more likely and more painful this problem can become.

Of course, there's no reason that you can't produce files more frequently. Indeed, you can think of *Messaging* (53) as *File Transfer* where you produce a file with every change in an application. The problem then is managing all the files that get produced, ensuring that they are all read and that none get lost. This goes beyond what file system–based approaches can do, particularly since there are expensive resource costs associated with processing a file, which can get prohibitive if you want to produce lots of files quickly. As a result, once you get to very fine-grained files, it's easier to think of them as *Messaging* (53).

To make data available more quickly and enforce an agreed-upon set of data formats, use a *Shared Database* (47). To integrate applications' functionality rather than their data, use *Remote Procedure Invocation* (50). To enable frequent exchanges of small amounts of data, perhaps used to invoke remote functionality, use *Messaging* (53).

Shared Database

by Martin Fowler

An enterprise has multiple applications that are being built independently, with different languages and platforms. The enterprise needs information to be shared rapidly and consistently.

▼

How can I integrate multiple applications so that they work together and can exchange information?

▲

File Transfer (43) enables applications to share data, but it can lack timeliness—yet timeliness of integration is often critical. If changes do not quickly work their way through a family of applications, you are likely to make mistakes due to the staleness of the data. For modern businesses, it is imperative that everyone have the latest data. This not only reduces errors, but also increases people's trust in the data itself.

Rapid updates also allow inconsistencies to be handled better. The more frequently you synchronize, the less likely you are to get inconsistencies and the less effort they are to deal with. But however rapid the changes, there are still going to be problems. If an address is updated inconsistently in rapid succession, how do you decide which one is the true address? You could take each piece of data and say that one application is the master source for that data, but then you'd have to remember which application is the master for which data.

File Transfer (43) also may not enforce data format sufficiently. Many of the problems in integration come from incompatible ways of looking at the data. Often these represent subtle business issues that can have a huge effect. A geological database may define an oil well as a single drilled hole that may or may not produce oil. A production database may define a well as multiple holes covered by a single piece of equipment. These cases of *semantic dissonance* are much harder to deal with than inconsistent data formats. (For a much deeper discussion of these issues, it's really worth reading *Data and Reality* [Kent].) What is needed is a central, agreed-upon datastore that all of the applications share so each has access to any of the shared data whenever it needs it.

Shared Database

Integrate applications by having them store their data in a single *Shared Database,* and define the schema of the database to handle all the needs of the different applications.

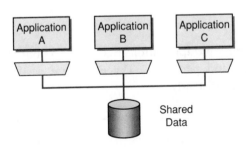

If a family of integrated applications all rely on the same database, then you can be pretty sure that they are always consistent all of the time. If you do get simultaneous updates to a single piece of data from different sources, then you have transaction management systems that handle that about as gracefully as it ever can be managed. Since the time between updates is so small, any errors are much easier to find and fix.

Shared Database is made much easier by the widespread use of SQL-based relational databases. Pretty much all application development platforms can work with SQL, often with quite sophisticated tools. So you don't have to worry about multiple file formats. Since any application pretty much has to use SQL anyway, this avoids adding yet another technology for everyone to master.

Since every application is using the same database, this forces out problems in semantic dissonance. Rather than leaving these problems to fester until they are difficult to solve with transforms, you are forced to confront them and deal with them before the software goes live and you collect large amounts of incompatible data.

One of the biggest difficulties with *Shared Database* is coming up with a suitable design for the shared database. Coming up with a unified schema that can meet the needs of multiple applications is a very difficult exercise, often resulting in a schema that application programmers find difficult to work with. And if the technical difficulties of designing a unified schema aren't enough, there are also severe political difficulties. If a critical application is likely to suffer delays in order to work with a unified schema, then often there is irresistible pressure to separate. Human conflicts between departments often exacerbate this problem.

Another, harder limit to *Shared Database* is external packages. Most packaged applications won't work with a schema other than their own. Even if there is some room for adaptation, it's likely to be much more limited than integrators would like. Adding to the problem, software vendors usually reserve the right to change the schema with every new release of the software.

This problem also extends to integration after development. Even if you can organize all your applications, you still have an integration problem should a merger of companies occur.

Multiple applications using a *Shared Database* to frequently read and modify the same data can turn the database into a performance bottleneck and can cause deadlocks as each application locks others out of the data. When applications are distributed across multiple locations, accessing a single, shared database across a wide-area network is typically too slow to be practical. Distributing the database as well allows each application to access the database via a local network connection, but confuses the issue of which computer the data should be stored on. A distributed database with locking conflicts can easily become a performance nightmare.

To integrate applications' functionality rather than their data, use *Remote Procedure Invocation* (50). To enable frequent exchanges of small amounts of data using a format per datatype rather than one universal schema, use *Messaging* (53).

**Shared
Database**

Remote Procedure Invocation

by Martin Fowler

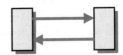

An enterprise has multiple applications that are being built independently, with different languages and platforms. The enterprise needs to share data and processes in a responsive way.

How can I integrate multiple applications so that they work together and can exchange information?

File Transfer (43) and *Shared Database* (47) enable applications to share their data, which is an important part of application integration, but just sharing data is often not enough. Changes in data often require actions to be taken across different applications. For example, changing an address may be a simple change in data, or it may trigger registration and legal processes to take into account different rules in different legal jurisdictions. Having one application invoke such processes directly in others would require applications to know far too much about the internals of other applications.

This problem mirrors a classic dilemma in application design. One of the most powerful structuring mechanisms in application design is encapsulation, where modules hide their data through a function call interface. In this way, they can intercept changes in data to carry out the various actions they need to perform when the data is changed. *Shared Database* (47) provides a large, unencapsulated data structure, which makes it much harder to do this. *File Transfer* (43) allows an application to react to changes as it processes the file, but the process is delayed.

The fact that *Shared Database* (47) has unencapsulated data also makes it more difficult to maintain a family of integrated applications. Many changes in any application can trigger a change in the database, and database changes have a considerable ripple effect through every application. As a result, organizations that use *Shared Database* (47) are often very reluctant to change the database, which means that the application development work is much less responsive to the changing needs of the business.

What is needed is a mechanism for one application to invoke a function in another application, passing the data that needs to be shared and invoking the function that tells the receiver application how to process the data.

▼

Develop each application as a large-scale object or component with encapsulated data. Provide an interface to allow other applications to interact with the running application.

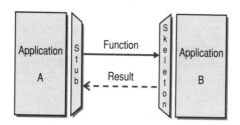

Remote Procedure Invocation applies the principle of encapsulation to integrating applications. If an application needs some information that is owned by another application, it asks that application directly. If one application needs to modify the data of another, it does so by making a call to the other application. This allows each application to maintain the integrity of the data it owns. Furthermore, each application can alter the format of its internal data without affecting every other application.

A number of technologies, such as CORBA, COM, .NET Remoting, and Java RMI, implement *Remote Procedure Invocation* (also referred to as Remote Procedure Call, or RPC). These approaches vary as to how many systems support them and their ease of use. Often these environments add additional capabilities, such as transactions. For sheer ubiquity, the current favorite is Web services, using standards such as SOAP and XML. A particularly valuable feature of Web services is that they work easily with HTTP, which is easy to get through firewalls.

The fact that there are methods that wrap the data makes it easier to deal with semantic dissonance. Applications can provide multiple interfaces to the same data, allowing some clients to see one style and others a different style. Even updates can use multiple interfaces. This provides a lot more ability to support multiple points of view than can be achieved by relational views. However, it is awkward for integrators to add transformation components, so each application has to negotiate its interface with its neighbors.

Since software developers are used to procedure calls, *Remote Procedure Invocation* fits in nicely with what they are already used to. Actually, this is more of a disadvantage than an advantage. There are big differences in performance and reliability between remote and local procedure calls. If people don't understand these, then *Remote Procedure Invocation* can lead to slow and unreliable systems (see [Waldo], [EAA]).

Remote Procedure Invocation

Although encapsulation helps reduce the coupling of the applications by eliminating a large shared data structure, the applications are still fairly tightly coupled together. The remote calls that each system supports tend to tie the different systems into a growing knot. In particular, sequencing—doing certain things in a particular order—can make it difficult to change systems independently. These types of problems often arise because issues that aren't significant within a single application become so when integrating applications. People often design the integration the way they would design a single application, unaware that the rules of the engagement change dramatically.

To integrate applications in a more loosely coupled, asynchronous fashion, use *Messaging* (53) to enable frequent exchanges of small amounts of data, ones that are perhaps used to invoke remote functionality.

Messaging

An enterprise has multiple applications that are being built independently, with different languages and platforms. The enterprise needs to share data and processes in a responsive way.

> How can I integrate multiple applications so that they work together and can exchange information?

File Transfer (43) and *Shared Database* (47) enable applications to share their data but not their functionality. *Remote Procedure Invocation* (50) enables applications to share functionality, but it tightly couples them as well. Often the challenge of integration is about making collaboration between separate systems as timely as possible, without coupling systems together in such a way that they become unreliable either in terms of application execution or application development.

File Transfer (43) allows you to keep the applications well decoupled but at the cost of timeliness. Systems just can't keep up with each other. Collaborative behavior is way too slow. *Shared Database* (47) keeps data together in a responsive way but at the cost of coupling everything to the database. It also fails to handle collaborative behavior.

Faced with these problems, *Remote Procedure Invocation* (50) seems an appealing choice. But extending a single application model to application integration dredges up plenty of other weaknesses. These weaknesses start with the essential problems of distributed development. Despite that RPCs look like local calls, they don't behave the same way. Remote calls are slower, and they are much more likely to fail. With multiple applications communicating across an enterprise, you don't want one application's failure to bring down all of the other applications. Also, you don't want to design a system assuming that calls are fast, and you don't want each application knowing the details about other applications, even if it's only details about their interfaces.

What we need is something like *File Transfer* (43) in which lots of little data packets can be produced quickly and transferred easily, and the receiver application is automatically notified when a new packet is available for consumption.

The transfer needs a retry mechanism to make sure it succeeds. The details of any disk structure or database for storing the data needs to be hidden from the applications so that, unlike *Shared Database* (47), the storage schema and details can be easily changed to reflect the changing needs of the enterprise. One application should be able to send a packet of data to another application to invoke behavior in the other application, like *Remote Procedure Invocation* (50), but without being prone to failure. The data transfer should be asynchronous so that the sender does not need to wait on the receiver, especially when retry is necessary.

Use *Messaging* to transfer packets of data frequently, immediately, reliably, and asynchronously, using customizable formats.

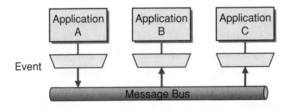

Asynchronous messaging is fundamentally a pragmatic reaction to the problems of distributed systems. Sending a message does not require both systems to be up and ready at the same time. Furthermore, thinking about the communication in an asynchronous manner forces developers to recognize that working with a remote application is slower, which encourages design of components with high cohesion (lots of work locally) and low adhesion (selective work remotely).

Messaging systems also allow much of the decoupling you get when using *File Transfer* (43). Messages can be transformed in transit without either the sender or receiver knowing about the transformation. The decoupling allows integrators to choose between broadcasting messages to multiple receivers, routing a message to one of many receivers, or other topologies. This separates integration decisions from the development of the applications. Since human issues tend to separate application development from application integration, this approach works with human nature rather than against it.

The transformation means that separate applications can have quite different conceptual models. Of course, this means that semantic dissonance will occur.

However, the messaging viewpoint is that the measures used by *Shared Database* (47) to avoid semantic dissonance are too complicated to work in practice. Also, semantic dissonance is going to occur with third-party applications and with applications added as part of a corporate merger, so the messaging approach is to address the issue rather than design applications to avoid it.

By sending small messages frequently, you also allow applications to collaborate behaviorally as well as share data. If a process needs to be launched once an insurance claim is received, it can be done immediately by sending a message when a single claim comes in. Information can be requested and a reply made rapidly. While such collaboration isn't going to be as fast as *Remote Procedure Invocation* (50), the caller needn't stop while the message is being processed and the response returned. And messaging isn't as slow as many people think—many messaging solutions originated in the financial services industry where thousands of stock quotes or trades have to pass through a messaging system every second.

This book is about *Messaging*, so you can safely assume that we consider *Messaging* to be generally the best approach to enterprise application integration. You should not assume, however, that it is free of problems. The high frequency of messages in *Messaging* reduces many of the inconsistency problems that bedevil *File Transfer* (43), but it doesn't remove them entirely. There are still going to be some lag problems with systems not being updated quite simultaneously. Asynchronous design is not the way most software people are taught, and as a result there are many different rules and techniques in place. The messaging context makes this a bit easier than programming in an asynchronous application environment like X Windows, but asynchrony still has a learning curve. Testing and debugging are also harder in this environment.

The ability to transform messages has the nice benefit of allowing applications to be much more decoupled from each other than in *Remote Procedure Invocation* (50). But this independence does mean that integrators are often left with writing a lot of messy glue code to fit everything together.

Once you decide that you want to use *Messaging* for system integration, there are a number of new issues to consider and practices you can employ.

How do you transfer packets of data?

A sender sends data to a receiver by sending a *Message* (66) via a *Message Channel* (60) that connects the sender and receiver.

How do you know where to send the data?

If the sender does not know where to address the data, it can send the data to a *Message Router* (78), which will direct the data to the proper receiver.

How do you know what data format to use?

If the sender and receiver do not agree on the data format, the sender can direct the data to a *Message Translator* (85) that will convert the data to the receiver's format and then forward the data to the receiver.

If you're an application developer, how do you connect your application to the messaging system?

An application that wishes to use messaging will implement *Message Endpoints* (95) to perform the actual sending and receiving.

Chapter 3

Messaging Systems

Introduction

In Chapter 2, "Integration Styles," we discussed the various options for connecting applications with one another, including *Messaging* (53). Messaging makes applications loosely coupled by communicating asynchronously, which also makes the communication more reliable because the two applications do not have to be running at the same time. Messaging makes the messaging system responsible for transferring data from one application to another, so the applications can focus on what data they need to share as opposed to how to share it.

Basic Messaging Concepts

Like most technologies, *Messaging* (53) involves certain basic concepts. Once you understand these concepts, you can make sense of the technology even before you understand all of the details about how to use it. The following are the basic messaging concepts.

Channels—Messaging applications transmit data through a *Message Channel* (60), a virtual pipe that connects a sender to a receiver. A newly installed messaging system typically doesn't contain any channels; you must determine how your applications need to communicate and then create the channels to facilitate it.

Messages—A *Message* (66) is an atomic packet of data that can be transmitted on a channel. Thus, to transmit data, an application must break the data into one or more packets, wrap each packet as a message, and then send the message on a channel. Likewise, a receiver application receives a message and must extract the data from the message to process it. The message system will

57

try repeatedly to deliver the message (e.g., transmit it from the sender to the receiver) until it succeeds.

Pipes and Filters—In the simplest case, the messaging system delivers a message directly from the sender's computer to the receiver's computer. However, certain actions often need to be performed on the message after it is sent by its original sender but before it is received by its final receiver. For example, the message may have to be validated or transformed because the receiver expects a message format different from the sender's. The *Pipes and Filters* (70) architecture describes how multiple processing steps can be chained together using channels.

Routing—In a large enterprise with numerous applications and channels to connect them, a message may have to go through several channels to reach its final destination. The route a message must follow may be so complex that the original sender does not know what channel will get the message to the final receiver. Instead, the original sender sends the message to a *Message Router* (78), an application component that takes the place of a filter in the *Pipes and Filters* (70) architecture. The router then determines how to navigate the channel topology and directs the message to the final receiver, or at least to the next router.

Transformation—Various applications may not agree on the format for the same conceptual data; the sender formats the message one way, but the receiver expects it to be formatted another way. To reconcile this, the message must go through an intermediate filter, a *Message Translator* (85), which converts the message from one format to another.

Endpoints—Most applications do not have any built-in capability to interface with a messaging system. Rather, they must contain a layer of code that knows both how the application works and how the messaging system works, bridging the two so that they work together. This bridge code is a set of coordinated *Message Endpoints* (95) that enable the application to send and receive messages.

Book Organization

The patterns in this chapter provide you with the basic vocabulary and understanding of how to achieve enterprise integration using *Messaging* (53). Each subsequent chapter builds on one of the base patterns in this chapter and covers that particular topic in more depth.

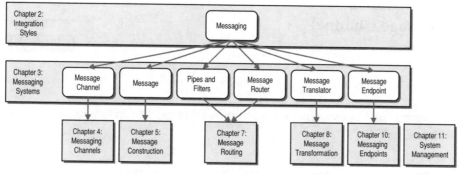

Relationship of Root Patterns and Chapters

You can read this chapter straight through for an overview of the main topics in *Messaging* (53). For more details about any one of these topics, skip ahead to the chapter associated with that particular pattern.

Message Channel

An enterprise has two separate applications that need to communicate by using *Messaging* (53).

How does one application communicate with another using messaging?

Once a group of applications has a messaging system available, it's tempting to think that any application can communicate with any other application anytime you want it to. Yet, the messaging system does not magically connect all of the applications.

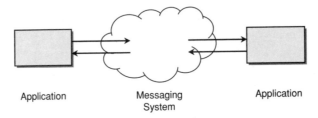

Application   Messaging   Application
                      System

Applications Magically Connected

Likewise, it's not as though an application just randomly throws out information into the messaging system while other applications just randomly grab whatever information they run across. (Even if this worked, it wouldn't be very efficient.) Rather, the application sending out the information knows what sort of information it is, and the applications that would like to receive information aren't looking for just any information but for particular types of information they can use. So the messaging system isn't a big bucket that applications throw information into and pull information out of. It's a set of connections that enables applications to communicate by transmitting information in predetermined, predictable ways.

Connect the applications using a *Message Channel*, where one application writes information to the channel and the other one reads that information from the channel.

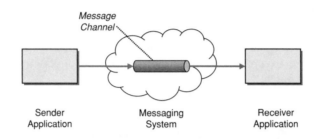

Message Channel

When an application has information to communicate, it doesn't just fling the information into the messaging system but adds the information to a particular *Message Channel*. An application receiving information doesn't just pick it up at random from the messaging system; it retrieves the information from a particular *Message Channel*.

The application sending information doesn't necessarily know what particular application will end up retrieving it, but it can be assured that the application that retrieves the information is interested in the information. This is because the messaging system has different *Message Channel*s for different types of information the applications want to communicate. When an application sends information, it doesn't randomly add the information to any channel available; it adds it to a channel whose specific purpose is to communicate that sort of information. Likewise, an application that wants to receive particular information doesn't pull info off some random channel; it selects what channel to get information from based on what type of information it wants.

Channels are logical addresses in the messaging system. How they're actually implemented depends on the messaging system product and its implementation. Perhaps every *Message Endpoint* (95) has a direct connection to every other endpoint, or perhaps they're all connected through a central hub. Perhaps several separate logical channels are configured as one physical channel that nevertheless keeps straight which messages are intended for which destination. The set of defined logical channels hides these configuration details from the applications.

A messaging system doesn't automatically come preconfigured with all of the message channels the applications need to communicate. Rather, the developers designing the applications and the communication between them have to decide what channels they need for the communication. Then the system administrator who installs the messaging system software must also configure it to set up the channels that the applications expect. Although some messaging system implementations support creating new channels while the applications are running, this isn't very useful because other applications besides the one that creates the channel must know about the new channel so they can start using it too. Thus, the number and purpose of channels available tend to be fixed at deployment time. (There are exceptions to this rule; see the introduction to Chapter 4, "Messaging Channels.")

Message Channel

A Little Bit of Messaging Vocabulary

So what do we call the applications that communicate via a *Message Channel*? There are a number of terms out there that are largely equivalent. The most generic terms are probably *sender* and *receiver*; an application sends a message to a *Message Channel* to be received by another application. Other popular terms are *producer* and *consumer*. You will also see *publisher* and *subscriber*, but they are geared more toward *Publish-Subscribe Channels* (106) and are often used in generic form. Sometimes we say that an application *listens* on a channel to which another application *talks*. In the world of Web services, we generally talk about a *requester* and a *provider*. These terms usually imply that the requester sends a message to the provider and receives a response back. In the olden days we called these *client* and *server* (the terms are equivalent, but saying "client" and "server" is not cool).

Now it gets confusing. When dealing with Web services, the application that sends a message to the service provider is often referred to as the *consumer* of the service even though it sends the request message. We can think of it in such a way that the consumer sends a message to the provider and then consumes the response. Luckily, use of the term with this meaning is limited to *Remote Procedure Invocation* (50) scenarios. An application that sends or receives messages may be called a *client* of the messaging system; a more specific term is *endpoint* or *message endpoint*.

Something that often fools developers when they first get started with using a messaging system is what exactly needs to be done to create a channel. A developer can write Java code that calls the method createQueue defined in the JMS

API or .NET code that includes the statement new MessageQueue, but neither code actually allocates a new queue resource in the messaging system. Rather, these pieces of code simply instantiate a runtime object that provides access to a resource that was already created in the messaging system using its administration tools.

There is another issue you should keep in mind when designing the channels for a messaging system: Channels are cheap, but they're not free. Applications need multiple channels for transmitting different types of information and transmitting the same information to lots of other applications. Each channel requires memory to represent the messages; persistent channels require disk space as well. Even if an enterprise system had unlimited memory and disk space, any messaging system implementation usually imposes some hard or practical limit to how many channels it can service consistently. So plan on creating new channels as your application needs them, but if it needs thousands of channels or needs to scale in ways that may require thousands of channels, you'll need to choose a highly scalable messaging system implementation and test that scalability to make sure it meets your needs.

Channel Names

If channels are logical addresses, what do these addresses look like? As in so many cases, the detailed answer depends on the implementation of the messaging system. Nevertheless, in most cases channels are referenced by an alphanumeric name, such as MyChannel. Many messaging systems support a hierarchical channel-naming scheme, which enables you to organize channels in a way that is similar to a file system with folders and subfolders. For example, MyCorp/Prod/OrderProcessing/NewOrders would indicate a channel that is used in a production application at MyCorp and contains new orders.

There are two different kinds of message channels: *Point-to-Point Channel*s (103) and *Publish-Subscribe Channel*s (106). Mixing different data types on the same channel can cause a lot of confusion; to avoid this, use separate *Datatype Channel*s (111). *Selective Consumer* (515) makes one physical channel act logically like multiple channels. Applications that use messaging often benefit from a special channel for invalid messages, an *Invalid Message Channel*. Applications that wish to use *Messaging* (53) but do not have access to a messaging client can still connect to the messaging system using *Channel Adapter*s (127). A well-designed set of channels forms a *Message Bus* (137) that acts like a messaging API for a whole group of applications.

Example: *Stock Trading*

When a stock trading application makes a trade, it puts the request on a *Message Channel* for trade requests. Another application that processes trade requests will look for those it can process on that same message channel. If the requesting application needs to request a stock quote, it will probably use a different *Message Channel*, one designed for stock quotes, so that the quote requests stay separate from the trade requests.

Example: *J2EE JMS Reference Implementation*

Let's look at how to create a *Message Channel* in JMS. The J2EE SDK ships with a reference implementation of the J2EE services, including JMS. The reference server can be started with the j2ee command. Message channels have to be configured using the j2eeadmin tool. This tool can configure both queues and topics.

```
j2eeadmin -addJmsDestination jms/mytopic topic
j2eeadmin -addJmsDestination jms/myqueue queue
```

Once the channels have been administered (created), they can be accessed by JMS client code.

```
Context jndiContext = new InitialContext();
Queue myQueue = (Queue) jndiContext.lookup("jms/myqueue");
Topic myTopic = (Topic) jndiContext.lookup("jms/mytopic");
```

The JNDI lookup doesn't create the queue (or topic); it was already created by the j2eeadmin command. The JNDI lookup simply creates a Queue instance in Java that models and provides access to the queue structure in the messaging system.

Example: *IBM WebSphere MQ*

If your messaging system implementation is IBM's WebSphere MQ for Java, which implements JMS, you'll use the WebSphere MQ JMS administration tool to create destinations. This will create a queue named myQueue.

```
DEFINE Q(myQueue)
```

Once that queue exists in WebSphere MQ, an application can access the queue.

WebSphere MQ, without the full WebSphere Application Server, does not include a JNDI implementation, so we cannot use JNDI to look up the queue as we did in the J2EE example. Rather, we must access the queue via a JMS session, like this.

```
Session session = // create the session
Queue queue = session.createQueue("myQueue");
```

Message Channel

Example: *Microsoft MSMQ*

MSMQ provides a number of different ways to create a message channel, called a queue. You can create a queue using the Microsoft Message Queue Explorer or the Computer Management console (see figure). From here you can set queue properties or delete queues.

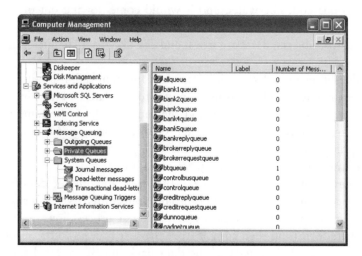

Alternatively, you can create the queue using code.

```
using System.Messaging;
...
MessageQueue.Create("MyQueue");
```

Once the queue is created, an application can access it by creating a Message-Queue instance, passing the name of the queue.

```
MessageQueue mq = new MessageQueue("MyQueue");
```

Message

An enterprise has two separate applications that are communicating via *Messaging* (53), using a *Message Channel* (60) that connects them.

> How can two applications connected by a Message Channel exchange a piece of information?

A *Message Channel* (60) can often be thought of as a pipe, a conduit from one application to another. It might stand to reason then that data could be poured into one end, like water, and it would come flowing out of the other end. But most application data isn't one continuous stream; it consists of units, such as records, objects, database rows, and the like. So a channel must transmit units of data.

What does it mean to "transmit" data? In a function call, the caller can pass a parameter by reference by passing a pointer to the data's address in memory; this works because both the caller and the function share the same memory heap. Similarly, two threads in the same process can pass a record or object by passing a pointer, since they both share the same memory space.

Two separate processes passing a piece of data have more work to do. Since they each have their own memory space, they have to copy the data from one memory space to the other. The data is usually transmitted as a byte stream, the most basic form of data. This means that the first process must *marshal* the data into byte form, and then copy it from the first process to the second one; the second process will *unmarshal* the data back into its original form, such that the second process then has a copy of the original data in the first process. Marshaling is how a Remote Procedure Call (RPC) sends arguments to the remote process and how the process returns the result.

So messaging transmits discrete units of data, and it does so by marshaling the data from the sender and unmarshaling it in the receiver so that the receiver has its own local copy. What would be helpful would be a simple way to wrap a unit of data such that it is appropriate to transmit the data on a messaging channel.

Package the information into a *Message*, a data record that the messaging system can transmit through a Message Channel.

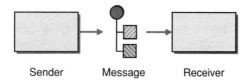

Sender   Message   Receiver

Thus, any data that is to be transmitted via a messaging system must be converted into one or more messages that can be sent through messaging channels. A message consists of two basic parts.

1. **Header**—Information used by the messaging system that describes the data being transmitted, its origin, its destination, and so on.

2. **Body**—The data being transmitted, which is generally ignored by the messaging system and simply transmitted as is.

This concept is not unique to messaging. Both postal service mail and e-mail send data as discrete mail messages. An Ethernet network transmits data as packets, as does the IP part of TCP/IP such as the Internet. Streaming media on the Internet is actually a series of packets.

To the messaging system, all messages are the same: some body of data to be transmitted as described by the header. However, to the applications programmer, there are different types of messages—that is, different application styles of use. Use a *Command Message* (145) to invoke a procedure in another application. Use a *Document Message* (147) to pass a set of data to another application. Use an *Event Message* (151) to notify another application of a change in this application. If the other application should send back a reply, use *Request-Reply* (154).

If an application wishes to send more information than one message can hold, break the data into smaller parts and send the parts as a *Message Sequence* (170). If the data is only useful for a limited amount of time, specify this use-by time as a *Message Expiration* (176). Since all the various senders and receivers of messages must agree on the format of the data in the messages, specify the format as a *Canonical Data Model* (355).

Example: *JMS Message*

In JMS, a message is represented by the type Message, which has several subtypes. In each subtype, the header structure is the same; it's the body format that varies by type.

Message

1. TextMessage—The most common type of message. The body is a string, such as literal text or an XML document. textMessage.getText() returns the message body as a String.

2. BytesMessage—The simplest, most universal type of message. The body is a byte array. bytesMessage.readBytes(byteArray) copies the contents into the specified byte array.

3. ObjectMessage—The body is a single Java object, specifically one that implements java.io.Serializable, which enables the object to be marshaled and unmarshaled. objectMessage.getObject() returns the Serializable.

4. StreamMessage—The body is a stream of Java primitives. The receiver uses methods like readBoolean(), readChar(), and readDouble() to read the data from the message.

5. MapMessage—The body acts like a java.util.Map, where the keys are Strings. The receiver uses methods like getBoolean("isEnabled") and getInt("numberOfItems") to read the data from the message.

Example: *.NET Message*

In .NET, the Message class implements the message type. It has a property, Body, which contains the contents of the message as an Object; BodyStream stores the contents as a Stream. Another property, BodyType, specifies the type of data the body contains, such as a string, a date, a currency, a number, or any other object.

Example: *SOAP Message*

In the SOAP protocol [SOAP 1.1], a SOAP message is an example of *Message*. A SOAP message is an XML document that is an envelope (a root SOAP-ENV:Envelope element) that contains an optional header (a SOAP-ENV:Header element) and required body (a SOAP-ENV:Body element). This XML document is an atomic data record that can be transmitted (typically the transmission protocol is HTTP) so it is a message.

Here is an example of a SOAP message from the SOAP spec that shows an envelope containing a header and a body.

```
<SOAP-ENV:Envelope
  xmlns:SOAP-ENV="http://schemas.xmlsoap.org/soap/envelope/"
  SOAP-ENV:encodingStyle="http://schemas.xmlsoap.org/soap/encoding/"/>
  <SOAP-ENV:Header>
     <t:Transaction
         xmlns:t="some-URI"
         SOAP-ENV:mustUnderstand="1">
             5
     </t:Transaction>
  </SOAP-ENV:Header>
  <SOAP-ENV:Body>
     <m:GetLastTradePrice xmlns:m="Some-URI">
         <symbol>DEF</symbol>
     </m:GetLastTradePrice>
  </SOAP-ENV:Body>
</SOAP-ENV:Envelope>
```

Message

SOAP also demonstrates the recursive nature of messages, because a SOAP message can be transmitted via a messaging system, which means that a messaging system message object (e.g., an object of type javax.jms.Message in JMS or System.Messaging.Message in .NET) contains the SOAP message (the XML SOAP-ENV:Envelope document). In this scenario, the transport protocol isn't HTTP but the messaging system's internal protocol (which in turn may be using HTTP or some other network protocol to transmit the data, but the messaging system makes the transmission reliable). For more information on transporting a message across a different messaging system, see *Envelope Wrapper* (330).

Pipes and Filters

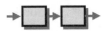

In many enterprise integration scenarios, a single event triggers a sequence of processing steps, each performing a specific function. For example, let's assume a new order arrives in our enterprise in the form of a message. One requirement may be that the message is encrypted to prevent eavesdroppers from spying on a customer's order. A second requirement is that the messages contain authentication information in the form of a digital certificate to ensure that orders are placed only by trusted customers. In addition, duplicate messages could be sent from external parties (remember all the warnings on the popular shopping sites to click the Order Now button only once?). To avoid duplicate shipments and unhappy customers, we need to eliminate duplicate messages before subsequent order processing steps are initiated. To meet these requirements, we need to transform a series of possibly duplicated, encrypted messages containing extra authentication data into a series of unique, simple plain-text order messages without the extraneous data fields.

> ▼
>
> How can we perform complex processing on a message while maintaining independence and flexibility?
>
> ▲

One possible solution would be to write a comprehensive "incoming message massaging module" that performs all the necessary functions. However, such an approach would be inflexible and difficult to test. What if we need to add a step or remove one? For example, what if orders can be placed by large customers who are on a private network and do not require encryption?

Implementing all functions inside a single component also reduces opportunities for reuse. Creating smaller, well-defined components allows us to reuse them in other processes. For example, order status messages may be encrypted but do not need to be de-duped because duplicate status requests are generally not harmful. Separating the decryption function into a separate module allows us to reuse this function for other messages.

Integration solutions typically connect a collection of heterogeneous systems. As a result, different processing steps may need to execute on different physical machines, such as when individual processing steps can only execute on specific systems. For example, it is possible that the private key required to decrypt incoming messages is only available on a designated machine and cannot be accessed from any other machine for security reasons. This means that the decryption component has to execute on this designated machine, whereas the other steps may execute on other machines. Likewise, different processing steps may be implemented using different programming languages or technologies that prevent them from running inside the same process or even on the same computer.

Implementing each function in a separate component can still introduce dependencies between components. For example, if the decryption component calls the authentication component with the results of the decryption, we cannot use the decryption function without the authentication function. We could resolve these dependencies if we could "compose" existing components into a sequence of processing steps in such a way that each component is independent from the other components in the system. This would imply that components expose generic external interfaces so that they are interchangeable.

If we use asynchronous messaging, we should take advantage of the asynchronous aspects of sending messages from one component to another. For example, a component can send a message to another component for further processing without waiting for the results. Using this technique, we could process multiple messages in parallel, one inside each component.

▼

Use the *Pipes and Filters* architectural style to divide a larger processing task into a sequence of smaller, independent processing steps (filters) that are connected by channels (pipes).

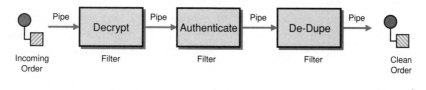

Each filter exposes a very simple interface: It receives messages on the inbound pipe, processes the message, and publishes the results to the outbound pipe. The pipe connects one filter to the next, sending output messages from one filter to the next. Because all components use the same external interface, they can be *composed* into different solutions by connecting the components to different pipes. We can add new filters, omit existing ones, or rearrange them into a new sequence—all without having to change the filters themselves. The connection between filter and pipe is sometimes called a *port*. In the basic form, each filter component has one input port and one output port.

When applied to our example problem, the *Pipes and Filters* architecture results in three filters connected by two pipes (see figure). We need one additional pipe to send messages to the decryption component and one to send the clear-text order messages from the de-duper to the order management system. This makes a total of four pipes.

Pipes and Filters

Pipes and Filters describes a fundamental architectural style for messaging systems: Individual processing steps (filters) are chained together through the messaging channels (pipes). Many patterns in this and the following sections, such as routing and transformation patterns, are based on this *Pipes and Filters* architectural style. This lets you easily combine individual patterns into larger solutions.

The *Pipes and Filters* style uses abstract pipes to decouple components from each other. The pipe allows one component to send a message into the pipe so that it can be consumed later by another process that is unknown to the component. The obvious implementation for such a pipe is a *Message Channel* (60). Typically, a *Message Channel* (60) provides language, platform, and location independence between the filters. This affords us the flexibility to move a processing step to a different machine for dependency, maintenance, or performance reasons. However, a *Message Channel* (60) provided by a messaging infrastructure can be quite heavyweight if all components can in fact reside on the same machine. Using a simple in-memory queue to implement the pipes would be much more efficient. Therefore, it is useful to design the components so that they communicate with an abstract pipe interface. The implementation of that interface can then be swapped out to use a *Message Channel* (60) or an alternative implementation such as an in-memory queue. The *Messaging Gateway* (468) describes how to design components for this flexibility.

One of the potential downsides of a *Pipes and Filters* architecture is the larger number of required channels. First, channels may not be an unlimited resource, since channels provide buffering and other functions that consume memory and CPU cycles. Also, publishing a message to a channel involves a certain amount of overhead because the data has to be translated from the application-internal format into the messaging infrastructure's own format. At the receiving end, this process has to be reversed. If we are using a long chain of filters, we are paying for the gain in flexibility with potentially lower performance due to repeated message data conversion.

The pure form of *Pipes and Filters* allows each filter to have only a single input port and a single output port. When dealing with *Messaging* (53), we can relax this property somewhat. A component may consume messages off more than one channel and also output messages to more than one channel (for example, a *Message Router* [78]). Likewise, multiple filter components can consume messages off a single *Message Channel* (60). A *Point-to-Point Channel* (103) ensures that only one filter component consumes each message.

Using *Pipes and Filters* also improves testability, an often overlooked benefit. We can test each individual processing step by passing a *Test Message* (66) to the component and comparing the result message to the expected outcome. It is more efficient to test and debug each core function in isolation because we can tailor the test mechanism to the specific function. For example, to test the encryption/decryption function we can pass in a large number of messages containing random data. After we encrypt and decrypt each message we compare it with the original. On the other hand, to test authentication, we need to supply messages with specific authentication codes that match known users in the system.

Pipes and Filters

Pipeline Processing

Connecting components with asynchronous *Message Channel*s (60) allows each unit in the chain to operate in its own thread or its own process. When a unit has completed processing one message, it can send the message to the output channel and immediately start processing another message. It does not have to wait for the subsequent components to read and process the message. This allows multiple messages to be processed concurrently as they pass through the individual stages. For example, after the first message has been decrypted, it can be passed on to the authentication component. At the same time, the next message can already be decrypted (see figure). We call such a configuration a *processing pipeline* because messages flow through the filters like liquid flows through a pipe. When compared to strictly sequential processing, a processing pipeline can significantly increase system throughput.

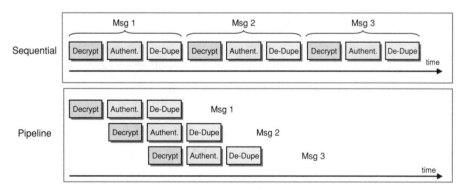

Pipeline Processing with Pipes and Filters

Parallel Processing

However, the overall system throughput is limited by the slowest process in the chain. We can deploy multiple parallel instances of that process to improve throughput. In this scenario, a *Point-to-Point Channel* (103) with *Competing Consumers* (502) is needed to guarantee that each message on the channel is consumed by exactly one of N available processors. This allows us to speed up the most time-intensive process and improve overall throughput. We need to be aware, though, that this configuration can cause messages to be processed out of order. If the sequence of messages is critical, we can run only one instance of each component or we must use a *Resequencer* (283).

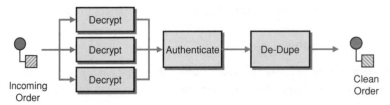

Increasing Throughput with Parallel Processing

For example, if we assume that decrypting a message is much slower than authenticating it, we can use the configuration shown in the figure, running three parallel instances of the decryption component. Parallelizing filters works best if each filter is stateless—that is, it returns to the previous state after a message has been processed. This means that we cannot easily run multiple parallel de-dupe components because the component maintains a history of all messages that it already received and is therefore not stateless.

History of Pipes and Filters

Pipes and Filters architectures are by no means a new concept. The simple elegance of this architecture combined with the flexibility and high throughput makes it easy to understand the popularity of *Pipes and Filters* architectures. The simple semantics also allow formal methods to be used to describe the architecture.

[Kahn] described Kahn Process Networks in 1974 as a set of parallel processes that are connected by unbounded FIFO (First-In, First-Out) channels. [Garlan] contains a good chapter on different architectural styles, including *Pipes and Filters*. [Monroe] gives a detailed treatment of the relationships between architectural styles and design patterns. [PLoPD1] contains Regine

Meunier's "The Pipes and Filters Architecture," which formed the basis for the *Pipes and Filters* pattern included in [POSA]. Almost all integration-related implementations of *Pipes and Filters* follow the "Scenario IV" presented in [POSA], using active filters that pull, process, and push independently from and to queuing pipes. The pattern described by [POSA] assumes that each element undergoes the same processing steps as it is passed from filter to filter. This is generally not the case in an integration scenario. In many instances, messages are routed dynamically based on message content or external control. In fact, routing is such a common occurrence in enterprise integration that it warrants its own patterns, the *Message Router* (78).

Vocabulary

When discussing *Pipes and Filters* architectures, we need to be cautious with the term *filter*. We later define two additional patterns, the *Message Filter* (237) and the *Content Filter* (342). While both of these are special cases of a generic filter, so are many other patterns in this pattern language. In other words, a pattern does not have to involve a filtering function (e.g., eliminating fields or messages) in order to be a filter in the sense of *Pipes and Filters*. We could have avoided this confusion by renaming the *Pipes and Filters* architectural style. However, we felt that *Pipes and Filters* is such an important and widely discussed concept that it would be even more confusing if we gave it a new name. We are trying to use the word *filter* cautiously throughout these patterns and trying to be clear about whether we are talking about a generic filter as in *Pipes and Filters* or a *Message Filter* (237)/*Content Filter* (342) that filters messages. If we thought there might still be confusion, we called the generic filter a *component*, which is a generic enough (and often abused enough) term that it should not get us into any trouble.

Pipes and Filters share some similarities with the concept of Communicating Sequential Processes (CSPs). Introduced by Hoare in 1978 [CSP], CSPs provide a simple model to describe synchronization problems that occur in parallel processing systems. The basic mechanism underlying CSPs is the synchronization of two processes via input-output (I/O). I/O occurs when process A indicates that it is ready to output to process B, and process B states that it is ready to input from process A. If one of these happens without the other being true, the process is put on a wait queue until the other process is ready. CSPs are different from integration solutions in that they are not as loosely coupled, nor do the "pipes" provide any queuing mechanisms. Nevertheless, we can benefit from the extensive treatment of CSPs in the academic world.

Example: *Simple Filter in C# and MSMQ*

Pipes and Filters

The following code snippet shows a generic base class for a filter with one input port and one output port. The base implementation simply prints the body of the received message and sends it to the output port. A more interesting filter would subclass the Processor class and override the ProcessMessage method to perform additional actions on the message—that is, transform the message content or route it to different output channels.

You notice that the Processor receives references to an input and output channel during instantiation. Thus, the class is tied to neither specific channels nor any other filter. This allows us to instantiate multiple filters and to chain them together in arbitrary configurations.

```
using System;
using System.Messaging;

namespace PipesAndFilters
{
    public class Processor
    {
        protected MessageQueue inputQueue;
        protected MessageQueue outputQueue;

        public Processor (MessageQueue inputQueue, MessageQueue outputQueue)
        {
            this.inputQueue = inputQueue;
            this.outputQueue = outputQueue;
        }

        public void Process()
        {
            inputQueue.ReceiveCompleted += new ReceiveCompletedEventHandler(OnReceiveCompleted);
            inputQueue.BeginReceive();
        }

        private void OnReceiveCompleted(Object source, ReceiveCompletedEventArgs asyncResult)
        {
            MessageQueue mq = (MessageQueue)source;

            Message inputMessage = mq.EndReceive(asyncResult.AsyncResult);
            inputMessage.Formatter =  new XmlMessageFormatter
                                    (new String[] {"System.String,mscorlib"});
```

```
        Message outputMessage = ProcessMessage(inputMessage);

        outputQueue.Send(outputMessage);

        mq.BeginReceive();
    }

    protected virtual Message ProcessMessage(Message m)
    {
        Console.WriteLine("Received Message: " + m.Body);
        return (m);
    }
  }
}
```

This implementation is an *Event-Driven Consumer* (498). The Process method registers for incoming messages and instructs the messaging system to invoke the method OnReceiveCompleted every time a message arrives. This method extracts the message data from the incoming event object and calls the virtual method ProcessMessage.

This simple filter example is not transactional. If an error occurs while processing the message (before it is sent to the output channel), the message is lost. This is generally not desirable in a production environment. See *Transactional Client* (484) for a solution to this problem.

Message Router

Message
Router

Multiple processing steps in a *Pipes and Filters* (70) chain are connected by *Message Channels* (60).

> How can you decouple individual processing steps so that messages can be passed to different filters depending on a set of conditions?

The *Pipes and Filters* (70) architectural style connects filters directly to each other with fixed pipes. This makes sense because many applications of the *Pipes and Filters* (70) pattern (e.g., [POSA]) are based on a large set of data items, each of which undergoes the same sequential processing steps. For example, a compiler will always execute the lexical analysis first, the syntactic analysis second, and the semantic analysis last. Message-based integration solutions, on the other hand, deal with individual messages that are not necessarily associated with a single, larger data set. As a result, individual messages are more likely to require a different series of processing steps.

A *Message Channel* (60) decouples the sender and the receiver of a *Message* (66). This also means that multiple applications can publish *Messages* (66) to a *Message Channel* (60). As a result, a *Message Channel* (60) can contain messages from different sources that may have to be treated differently based on the type of the message or other criteria. You could create a separate *Message Channel* (60) for each message type (a concept explained in more detail later as a *Datatype Channel* [111]) and connect each channel to the required processing steps for that message type. However, this would require the message originators to be aware of the selection criteria for different processing steps in order to publish the message to the correct channel. It could also lead to an explosion of the number of *Message Channels* (60). Furthermore, the decision on which steps the message undergoes may not just depend on the origin of the message. For example, we could imagine a situation where the destination of a message varies depending on the number of messages that have passed through the channel so far. No single originator would know this number and would therefore be unable to send the message to the correct channel.

*Message Channel*s (60) provide a very basic form of routing capabilities. An application publishes a *Message* (66) to a *Message Channel* (60) and has no further knowledge of that *Message*'s (66) destination. Therefore, the path of the *Message* (66) can change depending on which component subscribes to the *Message Channel* (60). However, this type of "routing" does not take into account the properties of individual messages. Once a component subscribes to a *Message Channel* (60), it will by default consume all messages from that channel regardless of the individual message's specific properties. This behavior is similar to the use of the pipe symbol in UNIX to process text files. It allows you to compose processes into a *Pipes and Filters* (70) chain, but for the lifetime of the chain, all lines of text undergo the same steps.

Message Router

We could make the receiving component itself responsible for determining whether it should process a message that arrives on a common *Message Channel* (60). This is problematic, though, because once the message is consumed and the component determines that it does not want the message, it can't just put the message back on the channel for another component to check out. Some messaging systems allow receivers to inspect message properties without removing the message from the channel so that it can decide whether to consume the message. However, this is not a general solution and also ties the consuming component to a specific type of message because the logic for message selection is now built right into the component. This would reduce the potential for reuse of that component and eliminate the composability that is the key strength of the *Pipes and Filters* (70) model.

Many of these alternatives assume that we can modify the participating components to meet our needs. In most integration solutions, however, the building blocks (components) are large applications that in most cases cannot be modified at all—for example, because they are packaged applications or legacy applications. This makes it uneconomical or even impossible to adjust the message-producing or -consuming applications to the needs of the messaging system or other applications.

One advantage of *Pipes and Filters* (70) is the composability of the individual components. This property enables us to insert additional steps into the filter chain without having to change existing components. This opens up the option of decoupling two filters by inserting between them another filter that determines what step to execute next.

Message Router

Insert a special filter, a *Message Router*, which consumes a Message from one Message Channel and republishes it to a different Message Channel, depending on a set of conditions.

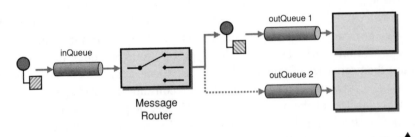

The *Message Router* differs from the basic notion of *Pipes and Filters* (70) in that it connects to multiple output channels (i.e., it has more than one output port). However, thanks to the *Pipes and Filters* (70) architecture, the components surrounding the *Message Router* are completely unaware of the existence of a *Message Router*. They simply consume messages off one channel and publish them to another. A defining property of the *Message Router* is that it does not modify the message contents; it concerns itself only with the destination of the message.

The key benefit of using a *Message Router* is that the decision criteria for the destination of a message are maintained in a single location. If new message types are defined, new processing components are added, or routing rules change, we need to change only the *Message Router* logic, while all other components remain unaffected. Also, since all messages pass through a single *Message Router*, incoming messages are guaranteed to be processed one by one in the correct order.

While the intent of a *Message Router* is to decouple filters from each other, using a *Message Router* can actually cause the opposite effect. The *Message Router* component must have knowledge of all possible destination channels in order to send the message to the correct channel. If the list of possible destinations changes frequently, the *Message Router* can turn into a maintenance bottleneck. In those cases, it would be better to let the individual recipients decide which messages they are interested in. You can accomplish this by using a *Publish-Subscribe Channel* (106) and an array of *Message Filters* (237). We contrast these two alternatives by calling them *predictive routing* and *reactive filtering* (for a more detailed comparison, see the *Message Filter* (237) in Chapter 7, "Message Routing").

Because a *Message Router* requires the insertion of an additional processing step, it can degrade performance. Many message-based systems have to decode the message from one channel before it can be placed on another channel, which causes computational overhead if the message itself does not really change. This overhead can turn a *Message Router* into a performance bottleneck. By using multiple routers in parallel or adding additional hardware, this effect can be minimized. As a result, the message throughput (number of messages processed per time unit) may not be impacted, but the latency (time for one message to travel through the system) will almost certainly increase.

Message Router

Like most good tools, *Message Router*s can also be abused. Deliberate use of *Message Router*s can turn the advantage of loose coupling into a disadvantage. Loosely coupled systems can make it difficult to understand the "big picture" of the solution—the overall flow of messages through the system. This is a common problem with messaging solutions, and the use of routers can exacerbate the problem. If everything is loosely coupled to everything else, it becomes impossible to understand in which direction messages actually flow. This can complicate testing, debugging, and maintenance. A number of tools can help alleviate this problem. First, we can use the *Message History* (551) to inspect messages at runtime and see which components they traversed. Alternatively, we can compile a list of all channels to which each component in the system subscribes or publishes. With this knowledge we can draw a graph of all possible message flows across components. Many EAI packages maintain channel subscription information in a central repository, making this type of static analysis easier.

Message Router Variants

A *Message Router* can use any number of criteria to determine the output channel for an incoming message. The most trivial case is a fixed router. In this case, only a single input channel and a single output channel are defined. The fixed router consumes one message off the input channel and publishes it to the output channel. Why would we ever use such a brainless router? A fixed router may be useful to intentionally decouple subsystems so that we can insert a more intelligent router later. Or, we may be relaying messages between multiple integration solutions. In most cases, a fixed router will be combined with a *Message Translator* (85) or a *Channel Adapter* (127) to transform the message content or send the message over a different channel type.

Many *Message Router*s decide the message destination only on properties of the message itself—for example, the message type or the values of specific message fields. We call such a router a *Content-Based Router* (230). This type of router is so common that the *Content-Based Router* (230) pattern describes it in more detail.

Other *Message Router*s decide the message's destination based on environment conditions. We call these routers *context-based routers*. Such routers are commonly used to perform load-balancing, test, or failover functionality. For example, if a processing component fails, the context-based router can reroute messages to another processing component and thus provide failover capability. Other routers split the flow of messages evenly across multiple channels to achieve parallel processing similar to a load balancer. Some *Message Channel*s (60) already provide basic load-balancing capabilities without the use of a *Message Router* because multiple *Competing Consumers* (502) can each consume messages off the same channel as fast as they can. However, a *Message Router* can have additional built-in intelligence to route the messages as opposed to a simple round-robin implemented by the channel.

Many *Message Router*s are *stateless*—in other words, they look at only one message at a time to make the routing decision. Other routers take the content of previous messages into account when making a routing decision. For example, the *Pipes and Filters* (70) example used a router that eliminates duplicate messages by keeping a list of all messages it already received. These routers are *stateful*.

Most *Message Router*s contain hard-coded logic for the routing decision. However, some variants connect to a *Control Bus* (540) so that the middleware solution can change the decision criteria without having to make any code changes or interrupting the flow of messages. For example, the *Control Bus* (540) can propagate the value of a global variable to all *Message Router*s in the system. This can be very useful for testing to allow the messaging system to switch from test to production mode. The *Dynamic Router* (243) configures itself dynamically based on control messages from each potential recipient.

Chapter 7, "Message Routing," introduces more variants of the *Message Router*.

Example: *Commercial EAI Tools*

The notion of a *Message Router* is central to the concept of a *Message Broker* (322), implemented in virtually all commercial EAI tools. These tools accept incoming messages, validate them, transform them, and route them to the correct destination. This architecture alleviates the participating applications from having to be aware of other applications altogether because the *Message Broker* (322) brokers between the applications. This is a key function in enterprise integration because most applications to be connected are packaged or legacy

---

Message Router

applications and the integration has to happen nonintrusively—that is, without changing the application code. Therefore, the middleware has to incorporate all routing logic so the applications do not have to. The *Message Broker* (322) is the integration equivalent of a *Mediator* presented in [GoF].

Example: *Simple Router with C# and MSMQ*

This code example demonstrates a very simple router that routes an incoming message to one of two possible output channels based on a simple condition.

```
class SimpleRouter
{
    protected MessageQueue inQueue;
    protected MessageQueue outQueue1;
    protected MessageQueue outQueue2;

    public SimpleRouter(MessageQueue inQueue, MessageQueue outQueue1, MessageQueue outQueue2)
    {
        this.inQueue = inQueue;
        this.outQueue1 = outQueue1;
        this.outQueue2 = outQueue2;

        inQueue.ReceiveCompleted += new ReceiveCompletedEventHandler(OnMessage);
        inQueue.BeginReceive();
    }

    private void OnMessage(Object source, ReceiveCompletedEventArgs asyncResult)
    {
        MessageQueue mq = (MessageQueue)source;
        Message message = mq.EndReceive(asyncResult.AsyncResult);

        if (IsConditionFulfilled())
            outQueue1.Send(message);
        else
            outQueue2.Send(message);

        mq.BeginReceive();
    }

    protected bool toggle = false;

    protected bool IsConditionFulfilled ()
    {
        toggle = !toggle;
        return toggle;
    }

}
```

The code is relatively straightforward. Like the simple filter presented in *Pipes and Filters* (70), the SimpleRouter class implements an *Event-Driven Consumer* (498) of messages using C# delegates. The constructor registers the method OnMessage as the handler for messages arriving on the inQueue. This causes the .NET framework to invoke the method OnMessage for every message that arrives on the inQueue. OnMessage figures out where to route the message by calling the method IsConditionFulfilled. In this trivial example, IsConditionFulfilled simply toggles between the two channels, dividing the sequence of messages evenly between outQueue1 and outQueue2. In order to keep the code to a minimum, this simple router is not transactional—that is, if the router crashes after it consumes a message from the input channel and before it publishes it to the output channel, the message would be lost. *Transactional Client* (484) explains how to make endpoints transactional.

Message Router

Message Translator

The previous patterns show how to construct messages and how to route them to the correct destination. In many cases, enterprise integration solutions route messages between existing applications such as legacy systems, packaged applications, homegrown custom applications, or applications operated by external partners. Each of these applications is usually built around a proprietary data model. Each application may have a slightly different notion of the Customer entity, the attributes that define a Customer, and other entities to which a Customer is related. For example, the accounting system may be more interested in the customer's taxpayer ID numbers, whereas the customer-relationship management (CRM) system stores phone numbers and addresses. The application's underlying data model usually drives the design of the physical database schema, an interface file format, or an application programming interface (API)—those entities with which an integration solution must interface. As a result, each application typically expects to receive messages that mimic the application's internal data format.

In addition to the proprietary data models and data formats incorporated in the various applications, integration solutions often interact with external business partners via standardized data formats that are independent from specific applications. A number of consortia and standards bodies define these protocols; for example, RosettaNet, ebXML, OAGIS, and many other industry-specific consortia. In many cases, the integration solution needs to be able to communicate with external parties using the "official" data formats, even though the internal systems are based on proprietary formats.

> How can systems using different data formats communicate with each other using messaging?

We could avoid having to transform messages if we could modify all applications to use a common data format. This turns out to be difficult for a number of reasons (see *Shared Database* [47]). First, changing an application's data format is risky, difficult, and requires a lot of changes to inherent business functionality. For most legacy applications, data format changes are simply not economically feasible. We may all remember the effort related to the Y2K retrofits, where the scope of the change was limited to the size of a single field!

Also, while we may get multiple applications to use the same data field names and maybe even the same data types, the physical representation may still be quite different. One application may use XML documents, whereas the other application uses COBOL copybooks.

Furthermore, if we adjust the data format of one application to match that of another application, we are tying the two applications more tightly to each other. One of the key architectural principles in enterprise integration is loose coupling between applications (see *Canonical Data Model* [355]). Modifying one application to match another application's data format would violate this principle because it makes two applications directly dependent on each other's internal representation. This eliminates the possibility of replacing or changing one application without affecting the other application, a scenario that is fairly common in enterprise integration.

We could incorporate the data format translation directly into the *Message Endpoint* (95). This way, all applications would publish and consume messages in a common format as opposed to in the application's internal data format. However, this approach requires access to the endpoint code, which is usually not the case for packaged applications. In addition, hard-coding the format translation to the endpoint would reduce the opportunities for code reuse.

Use a special filter, a *Message Translator*, between other filters or applications to translate one data format into another.

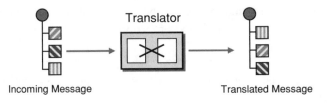

Incoming Message   Translated Message

The *Message Translator* is the messaging equivalent of the *Adapter* pattern described in [GoF]. An adapter converts the interface of a component into another interface so it can be used in a different context.

Levels of Transformation

Message translation may need to occur at a number of different levels. For example, data elements may share the same name and data types but may be used in different representations (e.g., XML file vs. comma-separated values vs. fixed-length fields). Or, all data elements may be represented in XML format but use different tag names. To summarize the different kinds of translation, we can divide it into multiple layers (loosely borrowing from the OSI Reference Model).

Layer	Deals With	Transformation Needs (Example)	Tools/ Techniques
Data Structures (Application Layer)	Entities, associations, cardinality	Condense many-to-many relationship into aggregation.	Structural mapping patterns, custom code
Data Types	Field names, data types, value domains, constraints, code values	Convert ZIP code from numeric to string. Concatenate First Name and Last Name fields to single Name field. Replace U.S. state name with two-character code.	EAI visual transformation editors, XSL, database lookups, custom code
Data Representation	Data formats (XML, name-value pairs, fixed-length data fields, EAI vendor formats, etc.)	Parse data representation and render in a different format.	XML parsers, EAI parser/ renderer tools, custom APIs
	Character sets (ASCII, UniCode, EBCDIC)	Decrypt/encrypt as necessary.	
	Encryption/compression		
Transport	Communications protocols: TCP/IP sockets, HTTP, SOAP, JMS, TIBCO RendezVous	Move data across protocols without affecting message content.	*Channel Adapter* (127), EAI adapters

The *Transport* layer at the bottom of the "stack" provides data transfer between the different systems. It is responsible for complete and reliable data transfer across different network segments and deals with lost data packets and other network errors. Some EAI vendors provide their own transport protocols (e.g., TIBCO RendezVous), whereas other integration technologies leverage

TCP/IP protocols (e.g., SOAP). Translation between different transport layers can be provided by the *Channel Adapter* (127) pattern.

The *Data Representation* layer is also referred to as the *syntax layer*. This layer defines the representation of data that is transported. This translation is necessary because the transport layer typically transports only character or byte streams. This means that complex data structures have to be converted into a character string. Common formats for this conversion include XML, fixed-length fields (e.g., EDI records), and proprietary formats. In many cases, data is also compressed or encrypted and carries check digits or digital certificates. In order to interface systems with different data representations, data may have to be decrypted, uncompressed, and parsed, and then the new data format must be rendered and possibly compressed and encrypted as well.

The *Data Types* layer defines the application data types on which the application (domain) model is based. Here we deal with such decisions as whether date fields are represented as strings or as native date structures, whether dates carry a time-of-day component, which time zone they are based on, and so on. We may also consider whether the field *Postal Code* denotes only a U.S. ZIP code or can contain Canadian postal codes. In the case of a U.S. zip code, do we include a ZIP+4? Is it mandatory? Is it stored in one field, or two? Many of these questions are usually addressed in so-called *Data Dictionaries*. The issues related to data types go beyond whether a field is of type *string* or *integer*. Consider sales data that is organized by region. The application used by one department may divide the country into four regions: West, Central, South, and East, identified by the letters W, C, S, and E. Another department may differentiate the Pacific region from the mountain region and distinguish the Northeast from the Southeast. Each region is identified by a two-digit number. What number does the letter E correspond to?

The *Data Structures* layer describes the data at the level of the application domain model. It is therefore also referred to as the *application layer*. This layer defines the logical entities that the application deals with, such as *customer, address,* or *account*. It also defines the relationships between these entities: Can one customer have multiple accounts? Can a customer have multiple addresses? Can customers share an address? Can multiple customers share an account? Is the address part of the account or the customer? This is the domain of entity-relationship diagrams and class diagrams.

Levels of Decoupling

Many of the design trade-offs in integration are driven by the need to decouple components or applications. Decoupling is an essential tool to enable the management of change. Integration typically connects existing applications and has to accommodate changes to these applications. *Message Channels* (60) decouple applications from having to know each other's location. A *Message Router* (78) can even decouple applications from having to agree on a common *Message Channel* (60). However, this form of decoupling achieves only limited independence between applications if they still depend on each other's data formats. A *Message Translator* (85) can remove this additional level of dependency.

Chaining Transformations

Many business scenarios require transformations at more than one layer. For example, let's assume an EDI 850 Purchase Order record represented as a fixed-format file has to be translated to an XML document sent over HTTP to the order management system, which uses a different definition of the Order object. The required transformation spans all four levels: The transport changes from file transfer to HTTP, the data format changes from a fixed-field format to XML, and both data types and data formats have to be converted to comply with the Order object defined by the order management system. The beauty of a layered model is that you can treat one layer without worrying about the lower layers and therefore can focus on one level of abstraction at a time (see the following figure).

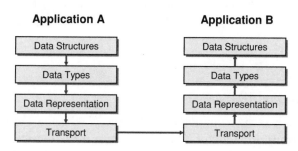

Mapping Across Multiple Layers

Chaining multiple *Message Translator* units using *Pipes and Filters* (70) results in the following architecture (see figure on the next page). Creating one *Message Translator* for each layer allows us to reuse these components in other scenarios. For example, the *Channel Adapter* (127) and the EDI-to-XML *Message Translator* can be implemented in a generic fashion so that they can be reused for any incoming EDI document.

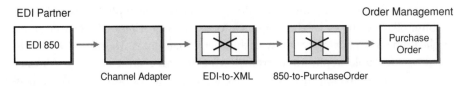

EDI Partner

EDI 850   Channel Adapter   EDI-to-XML   850-to-PurchaseOrder

Order Management

Purchase Order

Chaining Multiple Message Translators *(85)*

Message Translator

Chaining multiple *Message Translator*s also allows you to change the transformations used at an individual layer without affecting any of the other layers. You could use the same structural transformation mechanisms, but instead of converting the data representation into a fixed format, you could convert it into a comma-separated file by swapping out the data representation transformation.

There are many specializations and variations of the *Message Translator* pattern. An *Envelope Wrapper* (330) wraps the message data inside an envelope so that it can be transported across a messaging system. A *Content Enricher* (336) augments the information inside a message, whereas the *Content Filter* (342) removes information. The *Claim Check* (346) removes information but stores it for later retrieval. The *Normalizer* (352) can convert a number of different message formats into a consistent format. Last, the *Canonical Data Model* (355) shows how to leverage multiple *Message Translator*s to achieve data format decoupling. Inside each of those patterns, complex structural transformations can occur (e.g., mapping a many-to-many relationship into a one-to-one relationship).

Example: *Structural Transformation with XSL*

Transformation is such a common need that the W3C defined a standard language for the transformation of XML documents: the Extensible Stylesheet Language (XSL). Part of XSL is the XSL Transformation (XSLT) language, a rules-based language that translates one XML document into a different format. Since this is a book on integration and not on XSLT, we just present a simple example (for all the gory details, see the spec [XSLT 1.0], or to learn by reviewing code examples, see [Tennison]). In order to keep things simple, we explain the required transformation by showing example XML documents as opposed to XML schemas.

For example, let's assume we have an incoming XML document and need to pass it to the accounting system. If both systems use XML, the Data Representation layer is identical, and we need to cover any differences in field names, data types, and structure. Let's assume the incoming document looks like this.

```
<data>
    <customer>
        <firstname>Joe</firstname>
        <lastname>Doe</lastname>
        <address type="primary">
            <ref id="55355"/>
        </address>
        <address type="secondary">
            <ref id="77889"/>
        </address>
    </customer>
    <address id="55355">
        <street>123 Main</street>
        <city>San Francisco</city>
        <state>CA</state>
        <postalcode>94123</postalcode>
        <country>USA</country>
        <phone type="cell">
            <area>415</area>
            <prefix>555</prefix>
            <number>1234</number>
        </phone>
        <phone type="home">
            <area>415</area>
            <prefix>555</prefix>
            <number>5678</number>
        </phone>
    </address>
    <address id="77889">
        <company>ThoughtWorks</company>
        <street>410 Townsend</street>
        <city>San Francisco</city>
        <state>CA</state>
        <postalcode>94107</postalcode>
        <country>USA</country>
    </address>
</data>
```

This XML document contains customer data. Each customer can be associated with multiple addresses, each of which can contain multiple phone numbers. The XML represents addresses as independent entities so that multiple customers could share an address.

Let's assume the accounting system needs the following representation. (If you think that the German tag names are bit farfetched, keep in mind that one of the most popular pieces of enterprise software is famous for its German field names!)

Message
Translator

```
<Kunde>
    <Name>Joe Doe</Name>
    <Adresse>
        <Strasse>123 Main</Strasse>
        <Ort>San Francisco</Ort>
        <Telefon>415-555-1234</Telefon>
    </Adresse>
</Kunde>
```

**Message
Translator**

The resulting document has a much simpler structure. Tag names are different, and some fields are merged into a single field. Since there is room for only one address and phone number, we need to pick one from the original document based on business rules. The following XSLT program transforms the original document into the desired format. It does so by matching elements of the incoming document and translating them into the desired document format.

```
<xsl:stylesheet version="1.0" xmlns:xsl="http://www.w3.org/1999/XSL/Transform">
    <xsl:output method="xml" indent="yes"/>
    <xsl:key name="addrlookup" match="/data/address" use="@id"/>
    <xsl:template match="data">
        <xsl:apply-templates select="customer"/>
    </xsl:template>
    <xsl:template match="customer">
        <Kunde>
            <Name>
                <xsl:value-of select="concat(firstname, ' ', lastname)"/>
            </Name>
            <Adresse>
                <xsl:variable name="id" select="./address[@type='primary']/ref/@id"/>
                <xsl:call-template name="getaddr">
                    <xsl:with-param name="addr" select="key('addrlookup', $id)"/>
                </xsl:call-template>
            </Adresse>
        </Kunde>
    </xsl:template>
    <xsl:template name="getaddr">
        <xsl:param name="addr"/>
        <Strasse>
            <xsl:value-of select="$addr/street"/>
        </Strasse>
        <Ort>
            <xsl:value-of select="$addr/city"/>
        </Ort>
        <Telefon>
            <xsl:choose>
                <xsl:when test="$addr/phone[@type='cell']">
                    <xsl:apply-templates select="$addr/phone[@type='cell']" mode="getphone"/>
                </xsl:when>
```

```
            <xsl:otherwise>
                <xsl:apply-templates select="$addr/phone[@type='home']" mode="getphone"/>
            </xsl:otherwise>
        </xsl:choose>
    </Telefon>
</xsl:template>
<xsl:template match="phone" mode="getphone">
    <xsl:value-of select="concat(area, '-', prefix, '-', number)"/>
</xsl:template>
<xsl:template match="*"/>
</xsl:stylesheet>
```

XSL is based on pattern matching and can be a bit hairy to read if you are used to procedural programming like most of us. In a nutshell, the instructions inside an `<xsl:template>` element are called whenever an element in the incoming XML document matches the expression specified in the `match` attribute. For example, the line

```
<xsl:template match="customer">
```

causes the subsequent lines to be executed for each `<customer>` element in the source document. The next statements concatenate first and last name and output it inside the `<Name>` element. Getting the address is a little trickier. The XSL code looks up the correct instance of the `<address>` element and calls the subroutine `getaddr`. `getaddr` extracts the address and phone number from the original `<address>` element. It uses the cell phone number if one is present, or the home phone number otherwise.

Example: *Visual Transformation Tools*

If you find XSL programming a bit cryptic, you are in good company. Therefore, most integration vendors provide a visual transformation editor that displays the structure of the two document formats on the left-hand side and the right-hand side of the screen respectively. The users can then associate elements between the formats by drawing connecting lines between them. This can be a lot simpler than coding XSL. Some vendors, such as Contivo, specialize entirely in transformation tools.

The following figure shows the Microsoft BizTalk Mapper editor that is integrated into Visual Studio. The diagram shows the mapping between individual elements more clearly than the XSL script. On the other hand, some of the details (e.g., how the address is chosen) are hidden underneath the so-called functoid icons.

Message
Translator

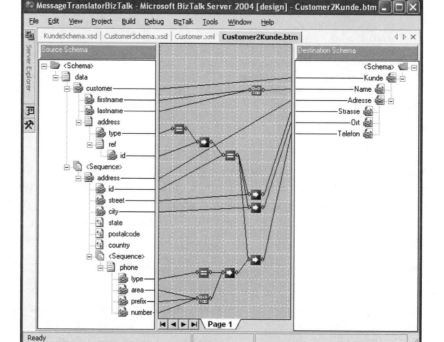

Creating Transformations: The Drag-Drop Style

Being able to drag and drop transformations shortens the learning curve for developing a *Message Translator* dramatically. As so often though, visual tools can also become a liability when it comes to debugging or when you need to create complex solutions. Therefore, many tools let you switch back and forth between XSL and the visual representation.

Message Endpoint

Applications are communicating by sending *Messages* (66) to each other via *Message Channel*s (60).

How does an application connect to a messaging channel to send and receive Messages?

The application and the messaging system are two separate sets of software. The application provides functionally for some type of user, whereas the messaging system manages messaging channels for transmitting messages for communication. Even if the messaging system is incorporated as a fundamental part of the application, it is still a separate, specialized provider of functionality, much like a database management system or a Web server. Because the application and the messaging system are separate, they must have a way to connect and work together.

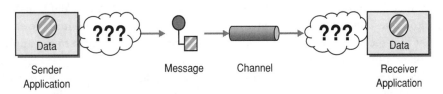

Applications Disconnected from a Message Channel

A messaging system is a type of server, capable of taking requests and responding to them. Like a database accepting and retrieving data, a messaging server accepts and delivers messages. A messaging system is a messaging server.

A server needs clients, and an application that uses messaging is a client of the messaging server. But applications do not necessarily know how to be messaging clients any more than they know how to be database clients. The messaging server, like a database server, has a client API that the application can use to interact with the server. The API is not application-specific but is domain-specific, where the domain is messaging. The application must contain a set of code that connects and unites the messaging domain with the application to allow the application to perform messaging.

Message Endpoint

Connect an application to a messaging channel using a *Message Endpoint*, a client of the messaging system that the application can then use to send or receive Messages.

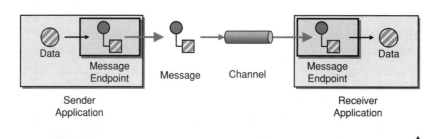

Message Endpoint code is custom to both the application and the messaging system's client API. The rest of the application knows little about message formats, messaging channels, or any of the other details of communicating with other applications via messaging. It just knows that it has a request or piece of data to send to another application, or is expecting those from another application. It is the messaging endpoint code that takes that command or data, makes it into a message, and sends it on a particular messaging channel. It is the endpoint that receives a message, extracts the contents, and gives them to the application in a meaningful way.

The *Message Endpoint* encapsulates the messaging system from the rest of the application and customizes a general messaging API for a specific application and task. If an application using a particular messaging API were to switch to another, developers would have to rewrite the message endpoint code, but the rest of the application should remain the same. If a new version of a messaging system changes the messaging API, this should only affect the message endpoint code. If the application decides to communicate with others via some means other than messaging, developers should ideally be able to rewrite the message endpoint code but leave the rest of the application unchanged.

A *Message Endpoint* can be used to send messages or receive them, but one instance does not do both. An endpoint is channel-specific, so a single application would use multiple endpoints to interface with multiple channels. An application may use multiple endpoint instances to interface to a single channel, usually to support multiple concurrent threads.

A *Message Endpoint* is a specialized *Channel Adapter* (127) one that has been custom developed for and integrated into its application.

A *Message Endpoint* should be designed as a *Messaging Gateway* (468) to encapsulate the messaging code and hide the message system from the rest of the application. It can employ a *Messaging Mapper* (477) to transfer data between domain objects and messages. It can be structured as a *Service Activator* (532) to provide asynchronous message access to a synchronous service or function call. An endpoint can explicitly control transactions with the messaging system as a *Transactional Client* (484).

Sending messages is pretty easy, so many endpoint patterns concern different approaches for receiving messages. A message receiver can be a *Polling Consumer* (494) or an *Event-Driven Consumer* (498). Multiple consumers can receive messages from the same channel either as *Competing Consumers* (502) or via a *Message Dispatcher* (508). A receiver can decide which messages to consume or ignore using a *Selective Consumer* (515). It can use a *Durable Subscriber* (522) to make sure a subscriber does not miss messages published while the endpoint is disconnected. And the consumer can be an *Idempotent Receiver* (528) that correctly detects and handles duplicate messages.

Example: *JMS Producer and Consumer*

In JMS, the two main endpoint types are MessageProducer, for sending messages, and MessageConsumer, for receiving messages. A *Message Endpoint* uses an instance of one of these types to either send messages to or receive messages from a particular channel.

Example: *.NET MessageQueue*

In .NET, the main endpoint class is the same as the main *Message Channel* (60) class, MessageQueue. A *Message Endpoint* uses an instance of MessageQueue to send messages to or receive messages from a particular channel.

Message
Endpoint

Chapter 4

Messaging Channels

Introduction

In Chapter 3, "Messaging Systems," we discussed *Message Channels* (60). When two applications want to exchange data, they do so by sending the data through a channel that connects the two. The application sending the data may not know which application will receive the data. However, by selecting a particular channel on which to send the data, the sender knows that the receiver will be one that is looking for that sort of data by looking for it on that channel. In this way, the applications that produce shared data have a way to communicate with those that wish to consume it.

Message Channel Themes

Deciding to use a *Message Channel* (60) is the simple part; if an application has data to transmit or data it wishes to receive, it will have to use a channel. The challenge is knowing what channels your applications will need and what to use them for.

> **Fixed set of channels**—One topic discussed in this chapter is that the set of *Message Channels* (60) available to an application tends to be static. When designing an application, a developer must know where to put what types of data in order to share that data with other applications and likewise where to look for particular types of data coming from other applications. These paths of communication cannot be dynamically created and discovered at runtime; they need to be agreed upon at design time so that the application knows where its data is coming from and where the data is going to. (While it is true that most channels must be statically defined,

99

there are exceptions, cases where dynamic channels are practical and useful. One exception is the reply channel in *Request-Reply* (154). The requestor can create or obtain a new channel that the replier knows nothing about and specify it as the *Return Address* (159) of a request message. The replier can then use it. Another exception is messaging system implementations that support hierarchical channels. A receiver can subscribe to a parent in the hierarchy, and then a sender can publish to a new child channel that the receiver knows nothing about. The subscriber will still receive the message. These relatively unusual cases notwithstanding, channels are usually defined before deployment, and applications are designed around a known set of channels.)

Introduction

Determining the set of channels—A related issue is, Who decides what *Message Channels* (60) are available—the messaging system or the applications? In other words, does the messaging system define certain channels and require the applications to make do with those? Or do the applications determine what channels they need and require the messaging system to provide them? There is no simple answer; designing the needed set of channels is iterative. First, the applications determine which channels the messaging system needs to provide. Subsequent applications will try to design their communication around the channels that are available, but when this is not practical, they will require that additional channels be added. When a set of applications already uses a certain set of channels, and new applications want to join in, they too will use the existing set of channels. When existing applications add new functionality, they may require new channels.

Unidirectional channels—Another common source of confusion is whether a *Message Channel* (60) is unidirectional or bidirectional. Technically, it's neither; a channel is more like a bucket that some applications add data to and other applications take data from (albeit a bucket that is distributed across multiple computers in some coordinated fashion). But because the data is in messages that travel from one application to another, that gives the channel direction, making it unidirectional. If a channel were bidirectional, that would mean that an application would both send messages to and receive messages from the same channel, which—while technically possible—makes little sense because the application would tend to keep consuming its own messages: the messages it's supposed to be sending to other applications. So, for all practical purposes, channels are unidirectional. As a consequence, for two applications to have a two-way conversation, they need two channels, one in each direction (see *Request-Reply* [154] in the next chapter).

Message Channel Decisions

Now that we understand what *Message Channels* (60) are, let's consider the decisions involved in using them.

One-to-one or one-to-many—When your application shares a piece of data, do you want to share it with just one other application or with any other application that is interested? To send the data to a single application, use a *Point-to-Point Channel* (103). This does not guarantee that every piece of data sent on that channel will necessarily go to the same receiver, because the channel might have multiple receivers. It does, however, ensure that any one piece of data will be received by only one of the applications. If you want all of the receiver applications to be able to receive the data, use a *Publish-Subscribe Channel* (106). When you send a piece of data this way, the channel effectively copies the data for each of the receivers.

What type of data—Any data in any computer memory has to conform to some sort of *type*: a known format or expected structure with an agreed-upon meaning. Otherwise, all data would just be a bunch of bytes, and there would be no way to make any sense out of it. Messaging systems work much the same way; the message contents must conform to some type so that the receiver understands the data's structure. *Datatype Channel* (111) is the idea that all of the data on a channel must be of the same type. This is the main reason that messaging systems need lots of channels. If the data could be of any type, the messaging system would only need one channel (in each direction) between any two applications.

Invalid and dead messages—The message system can ensure that a message is delivered properly, but it cannot guarantee that the receiver will know what to do with it. The receiver has expectations about the data's type and meaning. When it receives a message that doesn't meet these expectations, there's not much it can do. What it can do, though, is put the strange message on a specially designated *Invalid Message Channel* (60) in hopes that some utility monitoring the channel will pick up the message and figure out what to do with it. Many messaging systems have a similar built-in feature, a *Dead Letter Channel* (119), for messages that are successfully sent but ultimately cannot be successfully delivered. Again, a system management utility should monitor the *Dead Letter Channel* (119) and decide what to do with the messages that could not be delivered.

Crash proof—If the messaging system crashes or is shut down for maintenance, what happens to its messages? When it is back up and running, will its messages still be in its channels? By default, no; channels store their messages in memory. However, *Guaranteed Delivery* (122) makes channels persistent so that their messages are stored on disk. This hurts performance but makes messaging more reliable, even when the messaging system isn't.

Non-messaging clients—What if an application cannot connect to a messaging system but still wants to participate in messaging? Normally it would be out of luck, but if the messaging system can connect to the application somehow—through its user interface, its business services API, its database, or a network connection such as TCP/IP or HTTP—then a *Channel Adapter* (127) on the messaging system can be used. This allows you to connect a channel (or set of channels) to the application without having to modify the application and perhaps without requiring a messaging client running on the same machine as the application. Sometimes the "non-messaging client" really is a messaging client, but just for a different messaging system. In that case, an application that is a client on both messaging systems can build a *Messaging Bridge* (133) between the two, effectively connecting them into one composite messaging system.

Communications backbone—As more and more of an enterprise's applications connect to the messaging system and make their functionality available through messaging, the messaging system becomes a centralized point of one-stop shopping for shared functionality in the enterprise. A new application simply needs to know which channels to use to request functionality and which others to listen on for the results. The messaging system itself essentially becomes a *Message Bus* (137), a backbone providing access to all of the enterprise's various and ever-changing applications and functionality. You can achieve this integration nirvana more quickly and easily by specifically designing for it from the beginning.

As you can see, getting applications set up for *Messaging* (53) involves more than just connecting them to the messaging system so that they can send messages. The messages must have *Message Channels* (60) to transmit on. Simply slapping in some channels doesn't get the job done either. They have to be designed with a purpose, based on the datatype being shared, the sort of application making the data available, and the sort of application receiving the data. This chapter explains the decisions that go into designing these channels.

To help illustrate the patterns, each one has an example from a fictitious, simplified stock trading domain. While none of these examples should be used as the basis for implementing a real trading system, they do serve as brief and specific examples of how the patterns can be used.

Introduction

Point-to-Point Channel

An application is using *Messaging* (53) to make remote procedure calls (RPCs) or transfer documents.

How can the caller be sure that exactly one receiver will receive the document or perform the call?

One advantage of an RPC is that it's invoked on a single remote process, so either that receiver performs the procedure or it does not (and an exception occurs). And since the receiver was called only once, it performs the procedure only once. But with messaging, once a call is packaged as a *Message* (66) and placed on a *Message Channel* (60), potentially many receivers could see it on the channel and decide to perform the procedure.

The messaging system could prevent more than one receiver from monitoring a single channel, but this would unnecessarily limit callers that wish to transmit data to multiple receivers. All of the receivers on a channel could coordinate to ensure that only one of them actually performs the procedure, but that would be complex, create a lot of communications overhead, and generally increase the coupling between otherwise independent receivers. Multiple receivers on a single channel may be desirable so that multiple messages can be consumed concurrently, but any one receiver should consume any single message.

Send the message on a *Point-to-Point Channel*, which ensures that only one receiver will receive a particular message.

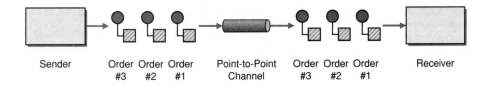

| Sender | Order #3 | Order #2 | Order #1 | Point-to-Point Channel | Order #3 | Order #2 | Order #1 | Receiver |

A *Point-to-Point Channel* ensures that only one receiver consumes any given message. The channel can have multiple receivers that can consume multiple messages concurrently, but only one of them can successfully consume a particular message. If multiple receivers try to consume a single message, the channel ensures that only one of them succeeds, so the receivers do not have to coordinate with each other.

When a *Point-to-Point Channel* has only one consumer, the fact that a message gets consumed only once is not surprising. When the channel has multiple consumers, then they become *Competing Consumers* (502), and the channel ensures that only one of the consumers receives each message. This design makes consuming and processing messages highly scalable because that work can be load-balanced across multiple consumers running in multiple applications on multiple computers.

Point-to-Point Channel

Whereas you use a *Point-to-Point Channel* to send a message to only one of the available receivers, to send a message to all available receivers, use a *Publish-Subscribe Channel* (106). To implement RPCs using messaging, use *Request-Reply* (154) with a pair of *Point-to-Point Channel*s. The call is a *Command Message* (145), and the reply is a *Document Message* (147).

Example: *Stock Trading*

In a stock trading system, the request to make a particular trade is a message that should be consumed and performed by exactly one receiver, so the message should be placed on a *Point-to-Point Channel*.

Example: *JMS Queue*

In JMS, a point-to-point channel implements the Queue interface. The sender uses a QueueSender to send messages; each receiver uses its own QueueReceiver to receive messages [JMS 1.1], [Hapner].

An application uses a QueueSender to send a message like this:

```
Queue queue = // obtain the queue via JNDI
QueueConnectionFactory factory = // obtain the connection factory via JNDI
QueueConnection connection = factory.createQueueConnection();
QueueSession session = connection.createQueueSession(true, Session.AUTO_ACKNOWLEDGE);
QueueSender sender = session.createSender(queue);

Message message = session.createTextMessage("The contents of the message.");

sender.send(message);
```

An application uses a `QueueReceiver` to receive a message like this:

```
Queue queue = // obtain the queue via JNDI
QueueConnectionFactory factory = // obtain the connection factory via JNDI
QueueConnection connection = factory.createQueueConnection();
QueueSession session = connection.createQueueSession(true, Session.AUTO_ACKNOWLEDGE);
QueueReceiver receiver = session.createReceiver(queue);

TextMessage message = (TextMessage) receiver.receive();
String contents = message.getText();
```

NOTE: JMS 1.1 unifies the client APIs for the point-to-point and publish-subscribe domains, so the code shown here can be simplified to use `Destination`, `ConnectionFactory`, `Connection`, `Session`, `MessageProducer`, and `MessageConsumer` rather than their `Queue`-specific counterparts.

Example: *.NET MessageQueue*

In .NET, the `MessageQueue` class implements a point-to-point channel [SysMsg]. MSMQ, which implements .NET messaging, supported only point-to-point messaging prior to version 3.0, so point-to-point is what .NET supports. Whereas JMS separates the responsibilities of the connection factory, connection, session, sender, and queue, a `MessageQueue` does it all.

Send a message on a `MessageQueue` like this:

```
MessageQueue queue = new MessageQueue("MyQueue");
queue.Send("The contents of the message.");
```

Receive a message on a `MessageQueue` like this:

```
MessageQueue queue = new MessageQueue("MyQueue");
Message message = queue.Receive();
String contents = (String) message.Body();
```

Publish-Subscribe Channel

An application is using *Messaging* (53) to announce events.

**Publish-
Subscribe
Channel**

How can the sender broadcast an event to all interested receivers?

Luckily, there are well-established patterns for implementing broadcasting. The *Observer* pattern [GoF] describes the need to decouple observers from their subject (that is, the originator of the event) so that the subject can easily provide event notification to all interested observers no matter how many observers there are (even none). The *Publisher-Subscriber* pattern [POSA] expands upon *Observer* by adding the notion of an event channel for communicating event notifications.

That's the theory, but how does it work with messaging? The event can be packaged as a *Message* (66) so that messaging will reliably communicate the event to the observers (subscribers). Then, the event channel is a *Message Channel* (60). But how will a messaging channel properly communicate the event to all of the subscribers?

Each subscriber needs to be notified of a particular event once but should not be notified repeatedly of the same event. The event cannot be considered consumed until all of the subscribers have been notified, but once they have, the event can be considered consumed and should disappear from the channel. Yet, having the subscribers coordinate to determine when a message is consumed violates the decoupling of the *Observer* pattern. Concurrent consumers should not compete but should be able to share the event message.

Send the event on a *Publish-Subscribe Channel*, which delivers a copy of a particular event to each receiver.

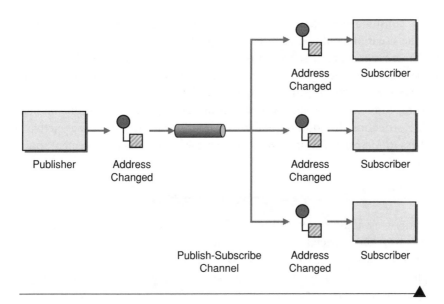

A *Publish-Subscribe Channel* works like this: It has one input channel that splits into multiple output channels, one for each subscriber. When an event is published into the channel, the *Publish-Subscribe Channel* delivers a copy of the message to each of the output channels. Each output end of the channel has only one subscriber, which is allowed to consume a message only once. In this way, each subscriber gets the message only once, and consumed copies disappear from their channels.

A *Publish-Subscribe Channel* can be a useful debugging tool. Even though a message is destined to only a single receiver, using a *Publish-Subscribe Channel* allows you to eavesdrop on a message channel without disturbing the existing message flow. Monitoring all traffic on a channel can be tremendously helpful when debugging messaging applications. It can also save you from inserting a ton of print statements into each application that participates in the messaging solution. Creating a program that listens for messages on all active channels and logs them to a file can provide many of the same benefits that a *Message Store* (555) brings.

However, the ability to eavesdrop on a *Publish-Subscribe Channel* can also turn into a disadvantage. If your messaging solution transmits payroll data between the payroll system and the accounting system, you may not want to allow anyone to write a simple program to listen to the message traffic. *Point-to-Point Channel*s alleviate the problem somewhat: Because the eavesdropper would consume messages off the channel and messages would suddenly be missing, the situation could be detected very quickly. However, many message queue implementations provide *peek* functions that let consumers look at messages inside a queue without consuming any of the messages. As a result, subscribing to a *Message Channel* (60) is an operation that should be restricted by security policies. Many (but not all) commercial messaging implementations implement such restrictions. In addition, creating a monitoring tool that logs active subscribers to *Message Channels* (60) can be a useful systems management tool.

Publish-
Subscribe
Channel

Wildcard Subscribers

Many messaging systems allow subscribers to *Publish-Subscribe Channels* to specify special wildcard characters. This is a powerful technique to allow subscribers to subscribe to multiple channels at once. For example, if an application publishes messages to the channels MyCorp/Prod/OrderProcessing/NewOrders and MyCorp/Prod/OrderProcessing/CancelledOrders, an application could subscribe to MyCorp/Prod/OrderProcessing/* and receive all messages related to order processing. Another application could subscribe to MyCorp/Dev/** to receive all messages sent by all applications in the development environment. Only subscribers are allowed to use wildcards; publishers are always required to publish a message to a specific channel. The specific capabilities and syntax for wildcard subscribers vary between the different messaging vendors.

An *Event Message* (151) is usually sent on a *Publish-Subscribe Channel* because multiple dependents are often interested in an event. A subscriber can be durable or nondurable—see *Durable Subscriber* (522) in the Chapter 10, "Messaging Endpoints." If notifications should be acknowledged by the subscribers, use *Request-Reply* (154), where the notification is the request and the acknowledgment is the reply. Storing each message on a *Publish-Subscribe Channel* until all subscribers consume the message can require a large amount of message storage. To help alleviate this issue, messages sent to a *Publish-Subscribe Channel* can use *Message Expiration* (176).

Example: *Stock Trading*

In a stock trading system, many systems may need to be notified of the completion of a trade, so make them all subscribers of a *Publish-Subscribe Channel* that publishes trade completions.

Likewise, many consumers are interested in displaying or processing current stock quote data. Therefore, stock quotes should be broadcast across a *Publish-Subscribe Channel*.

Example: *JMS Topic*

In JMS, a *Publish-Subscribe Channel* implements the Topic interface. The sender uses a TopicPublisher to send messages; each receiver uses its own Topic-Subscriber to receive messages [JMS 1.1], [Hapner].

An application uses a TopicPublisher to send a message like this:

```
Topic topic = // obtain the topic via JNDI
TopicConnectionFactory factory = // obtain the connection factory via JNDI
TopicConnection connection = factory.createTopicConnection();
TopicSession session = connection.createTopicSession(true, Session.AUTO_ACKNOWLEDGE);
TopicPublisher publisher = session.createPublisher(topic);

Message message = session.createTextMessage("The contents of the message.");

publisher.publish(message);
```

Publish-Subscribe Channel

An application uses a TopicSubscriber to receive a message like this:

```
Topic topic = // obtain the topic via JNDI
TopicConnectionFactory factory = // obtain the connection factory via JNDI
TopicConnection connection = factory.createTopicConnection();
TopicSession session = connection.createTopicSession(true, Session.AUTO_ACKNOWLEDGE);
TopicSubscriber subscriber = session.createSubscriber(topic);

TextMessage message = (TextMessage) subscriber.receive();
String contents = message.getText();
```

NOTE: JMS 1.1 unifies the client APIs for the point-to-point and publish-subscribe domains, so the code shown here can be simplified to use Destination, ConnectionFactory, Connection, Session, MessageProducer, and MessageConsumer rather than their Topic-specific counterparts.

Example: *MSMQ One-to-Many Messaging*

A new feature in MSMQ 3.0 [MSMQ] is a *one-to-many messaging model*, which has two different approaches.

1. **Real-Time Messaging Multicast**—This approach most closely matches publish-subscribe, but its implementation is entirely dependent on IP multicasting via the Pragmatic General Multicast (PGM) protocol, so this feature cannot be used with other protocols that are not based on IP.

2. **Distribution Lists and Multiple-Element Format Names**—A Distribution List enables the sender to explicitly send a message to a list of receivers (but this violates the spirit of the *Observer* pattern because the sender now has to be aware of the receivers). Therefore, this feature more closely resembles a *Recipient List* (249) than a *Publish-Subscribe Channel*. A Multiple-Element Format Name is a symbolic channel specifier that dynamically maps to multiple real channels, which is more the spirit of a *Publish-Subscribe Channel* but still forces the sender to choose between a real channel and a symbolic one.

The .NET Common Language Runtime (CLR) does not provide direct support for using the one-to-many messaging model. However, this functionality can be accessed through the COM interface [MDMSG], which can be embedded in .NET code.

Publish-Subscribe Channel

Example: *Simple Messaging*

The JMS Publish-Subscribe example in Chapter 6, "Interlude: Simple Messaging," shows an example of how to implement *Observer* across multiple processes using messaging.

Datatype Channel

An application is using *Messaging* (53) to transfer different types of data, such as different types of documents.

How can the application send a data item such that the receiver will know how to process it?

All messages are just instances of the same message type, as defined by the messaging system, and the contents of any message are ultimately just a byte array. While this simple structure—a bundle of bytes—is specific enough for a messaging system to be able to transmit a message, it is not specific enough for a receiver to be able to process a message's contents.

A receiver must know the message content's data structure and data format. The structure could be character array, byte array, serialized object, XML document, and so on. The format could be the record structure of the bytes or characters, the class of the serialized object, the schema definition of the XML document, and so on. All of this knowledge is loosely referred to as the message's type, referring to both the structure and format of the message's contents.

The receiver must know what type of messages it's receiving, or it won't know how to process them. For example, a sender may wish to send different objects such as purchase orders, price quotes, and queries. Yet, a receiver will probably take different steps to process each of those, so it has to know which is which. If the sender simply sends all of these to the receiver via a single message channel, the receiver will not know how to process each one.

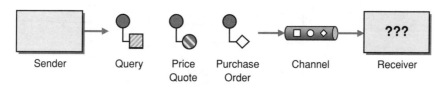

| Sender | Query | Price Quote | Purchase Order | Channel | Receiver |

Mixed Data Types

The sender knows what message type it's sending, so how can this be communicated to the receiver? The sender could put a flag in the message's header (see *Format Indicator* [180]), but then the receiver will need a case statement. The sender could wrap the data in a *Command Message* (145) with a different command for each type of data, but that presumes to tell the receiver what to do with the data when all that the message is trying to do is transmit the data to the receiver.

A similar problem—one separate from messaging—occurs when processing a collection of items. The collection must be homogeneous, meaning that all of the items are the same type, so that the processor knows what an item's type is and thus how to manipulate it. Many collection implementations do not force all of the items to be of a specific type, so programmers must design their code to ensure that all of the items in a collection are of the same type. Otherwise, items of different types can be added to a collection, but the code processing those items will not know how to manipulate each one because it won't know what type a particular item implements.

The same principle applies to messaging because the messages on a channel must likewise all be of the same type. The simplest solution is for all of the messages to be of the same format. If the formats must differ, they must all have a reliable *Format Indicator* (180). While the channel does not force all messages to be of the same type, the receiver needs them to be so that it knows how to process them.

Use a separate *Datatype Channel* for each datatype so that all data on a particular channel is of the same type.

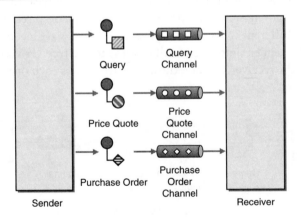

By using a separate *Datatype Channel* for each type of data, all of the messages on a given channel will contain the same type of data. The sender, knowing what type the data is, will need to select the appropriate channel to send it on. The receiver, knowing what channel the data was received on, will know what type it is.

As shown in the figures, since the sender wants to send three different types of data (purchase orders, price quotes, and queries), it should use three different channels. When sending an item, the sender must select the appropriate *Datatype Channel* for that item. When receiving an item, the receiver knows the item's type because of the datatype channel on which it received the item.

Datatype
Channel

Quality-of-Service Channel

A related strategy is a *Quality-of-Service Channel*. Sometimes, an enterprise wants to transmit one group of messages with a different level of service from another group of messages. For example, incoming New Order messages may be the primary source of revenue for a business and should be transported over a very reliable channel (e.g., using *Guaranteed Delivery* [122]) despite the potential performance overhead. On the other hand, losing a message that represents a request for order status is not the end of the world, so we may be inclined to use a faster but less reliable channel. This can sometimes be accomplished on a single channel, for example, by using message priorities. However, generally it is a better idea to define quality-of-service parameters when creating the channel rather than leaving the decision up to the application code that sends the messages. Therefore, it is best to transmit each group of messages on its own channel so that each channel's quality-of-service can be tuned for the needs of its group of messages.

As discussed under *Message Channel* (60), channels are cheap, but they are not free. An application may need to transmit many different datatypes, too many to create a separate *Datatype Channel* for each. In this case, multiple datatypes can share a single channel by using a different *Selective Consumer* (515) for each type. This makes a single physical channel act like multiple logical *Datatype Channel*s (a strategy called *multiplexing*). Whereas *Datatype Channel* explains why all messages on a channel must be of the same format, *Canonical Data Model* (355) explains how all messages on all channels in an enterprise should follow a unified data model.

If we would like to use *Datatype Channel*s but an existing message publisher simply sends all messages to a single channel, we can use a *Content-Based Router* (230) to *demultiplex* the messages. The router divides the message stream across multiple *Datatype Channel*s, each of which carries messages of only one type.

A *Message Dispatcher* (508), besides providing concurrent message consumption, can be used to process a generic set of messages in type-specific ways. Each message must specify its type (typically by a format indicator in the message's header); the dispatcher detects the message's type and dispatches it to a type-specific performer for processing. The messages on the channel are still all of the same type, but that type is the more general one that the dispatcher supports, not the more specific ones that the various performers require.

A *Format Indicator* (180) is used to distinguish different format versions of the same data, which in turn enables these different formats to be sent on the same *Datatype Channel*.

Datatype Channel

Example: *Stock Trading*

In a stock trading system, if the format of a quote request is different from that of a trade request, the system should use a separate *Datatype Channel* for communicating each kind of request. Likewise, a change-of-address announcement may have a different format from a change-of-portfolio-manager announcement, so each kind of announcement should have its own *Datatype Channel*.

Invalid Message Channel

An application is using *Messaging* (53) to receive *Messages* (66).

How can a messaging receiver gracefully handle receiving a message that makes no sense?

In theory, everything on a *Message Channel* (60) is just a message, and message receivers just process messages. However, to process a message, a receiver must be able to interpret its data and understand its meaning. This is not always possible: The message body may cause parsing errors, lexical errors, or validation errors. The message header may be missing needed properties, or the property values may not make sense. A sender might put a perfectly good message on the wrong channel, transmitting it to the wrong receiver. A malicious sender could purposely send an incorrect message just to mess up the receiver. A receiver may not be able to process all the messages it receives, so it must have some other way to handle messages it does not consider valid.

A *Message Channel* (60) should be a *Datatype Channel* (111), where each of the messages on the channel is supposed to be of the proper datatype for that channel. If a sender puts a message on the channel that is not the correct datatype, the messaging system will transmit the message successfully, but the receiver will not recognize the message and will not know how to process it.

One example of a message with an improper datatype or format is a byte message on a channel that is supposed to contain text messages. Another example is a message whose format is not correct, such as an XML document that is not well formed or that is not valid for the agreed-upon DTD or schema. There's nothing wrong with these messages as far as the messaging system is concerned, but the receiver will not be able to process them, so they are invalid.

Messages that do not contain the header field values that the receiver expects are also invalid. If a message is supposed to have header properties such as a *Correlation Identifier* (163), *Message Sequence* (170) identifiers, a *Return Address* (159), and so on, but the message is missing the properties, then the messaging system will deliver the message properly, but the receiver will not be able to process it successfully.

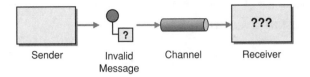

Invalid Message

When the receiver discovers that the message it's trying to process is not valid, what should it do with the message? It could put the message back on the channel, but then the message will just be reconsumed by the same receiver or another like it. Meanwhile, invalid messages that are being ignored will clutter the channel and hurt performance. The receiver could consume the invalid message and throw it away, but that would tend to hide messaging problems that need to be detected. What the system needs is a way to clean improper messages out of channels and put them in a place where they will be out of the way but can be detected to diagnose problems with the messaging system.

The receiver should move the improper message to an *Invalid Message Channel*, a special channel for messages that could not be processed by their receivers.

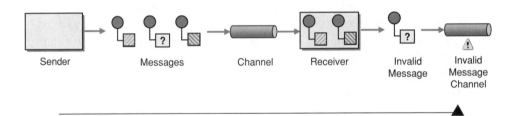

When designing a messaging system for applications to use, the administrator must define one or more *Invalid Message Channels* for the applications to use. The *Invalid Message Channel* will not be used for normal, successful communication, so if it is cluttered with improper messages, that will not be a problem. An error handler that wants to diagnose improper messages can use a receiver on the invalid channel to detect messages as they become available.

An *Invalid Message Channel* is like an error log for messaging. When something goes wrong in an application, it's a good idea to log the error. When something goes wrong processing a message, it's a good idea to put the message on the channel for invalid messages. If it won't be obvious to anyone browsing the channel why this message is invalid, the application should also log an error with more details.

Keep in mind that a message is neither inherently valid nor invalid, but it is the receiver's context and expectations that make this determination. A message that may be valid for one receiver may be invalid for another receiver; two such receivers should not share the same channel. A message that is valid for one receiver on a channel should be valid for all other receivers on that channel. Likewise, if one receiver considers a message invalid, all other receivers should as well. It is the sender's responsibility to make sure that a message it sends on a channel will be considered valid by the channel's receivers. Otherwise, the receivers will ignore the sender's messages by rerouting them to the *Invalid Message Channel*.

A similar but separate problem occurs when a message is structured properly, but its contents are semantically incorrect. For example, a *Command Message* (145) may instruct the receiver to delete a database record that does not exist. This is not a messaging error but an application error. As such, while it may be tempting to move the message to the *Invalid Message Channel*, there is nothing wrong with the message, so treating it as invalid is misleading. Rather, an error like this should be handled as an invalid application request, not an invalid message.

Invalid Message Channel

This difference between message-processing errors and application errors becomes simpler and clearer when the receiver is implemented as a *Service Activator* (532) or *Messaging Gateway* (468). These patterns separate message-processing code from the rest of the application. If an error occurs while processing the message, the message is invalid and should be moved to the *Invalid Message Channel*. If it occurs while the application processes the data from the message, that is an application error that has nothing to do with messaging.

An *Invalid Message Channel* whose contents are ignored is about as useful as an error log that is ignored. Messages on the *Invalid Message Channel* indicate application integration problems, so those messages should not be ignored; rather, they should be analyzed to determine what went wrong so that the problem can be fixed. Ideally, this would be an automated process that consumed invalid messages, determined their cause, and fixed the underlying problems. However, the cause is often a coding or configuration error that requires a developer or system analyst to evaluate and repair. At the very least, applications that use messaging and *Invalid Message Channel*s should have a process that monitors the *Invalid Message Channel* and alerts system administrators whenever the channel contains messages.

A similar concept implemented by many messaging systems is a *Dead Letter Channel* (119). Whereas an *Invalid Message Channel* is for messages that can be delivered and received but not processed, a *Dead Letter Channel* (119) is for messages that the messaging system cannot deliver properly.

Example: *Stock Trading*

In a stock trading system, an application for executing trade requests might receive a request for a current price quote, or a trade request that does not specify what security to buy or how many shares, or a trade request that does not specify to whom to send the trade confirmation. In any of these cases, the application has received an invalid message—one that does not meet the minimum requirements necessary for the application to be able to process the trade request. Once the application determines the message to be invalid, it should resend the message onto the *Invalid Message Channel*. The various applications that send trade requests may wish to monitor the *Invalid Message Channel* to determine if their requests are being discarded.

Example: *JMS Specification*

In JMS, the specification suggests that if a `MessageListener` gets a message it cannot process, a well-behaved listener should divert the message "to some form of application-specific 'unprocessable message' destination" [JMS 1.1]. This unprocessable message destination is an *Invalid Message Channel*.

Example: *Simple Messaging*

The JMS Request-Reply example and .NET Request-Reply example (both in Chapter 6, "Interlude: Simple Messaging") show an example of how to implement receivers that reroute messages they cannot process to an *Invalid Message Channel*.

Dead Letter Channel

An enterprise is using *Messaging* (53) to integrate applications.

> What will the messaging system do with a message it cannot deliver?

If a receiver receives a message it cannot process, it should move the invalid message to an *Invalid Message Channel* (60). But what if the messaging system cannot deliver the message to the receiver in the first place?

There are a number of reasons the messaging system may not be able to deliver a message. The messaging system may not have the message's channel configured properly. The message's channel may be deleted after the message is sent but before it can be delivered or while it is waiting to be received. The message may expire before it can be delivered (see *Message Expiration* [176]). A message without an explicit expiration may nevertheless time out if it cannot be delivered for a very long time. A message with a selection value that all *Selective Consumer*s (515) ignore will never be read and may eventually die. A message could have something wrong with its header that prevents it from being delivered successfully.

Once the messaging system determines that it cannot deliver a message, it has to do something with the message. It could just leave the message wherever it is, cluttering up the system. It could try to return the message to the sender, but the sender is not a receiver and cannot detect deliveries. It could just delete the message and hope no one misses it, but this may well cause a problem for the sender that has successfully sent the message and expects it to be delivered (and received and processed).

> When a messaging system determines that it cannot or should not deliver a message, it may elect to move the message to a *Dead Letter Channel*.

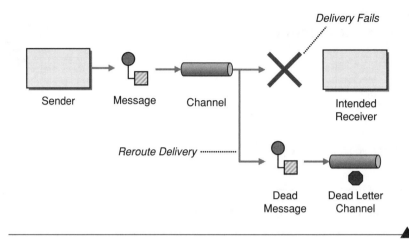

Dead Letter
Channel

The specific way a *Dead Letter Channel* works depends on the specific messaging system's implementation, if it provides one at all. The channel may be called a "dead message queue" [Monson-Haefel] or "dead letter queue" [MQSeries], [Dickman]. Typically, each machine the messaging system is installed on has its own local *Dead Letter Channel* so that whatever machine a message dies on, it can be moved from one local queue to another without any networking uncertainties. This also records what machine the message died on. When the messaging system moves the message, it may also record the original channel on which the message was supposed to be delivered.

The difference between a dead message and an invalid one is that the messaging system cannot successfully deliver what it then deems a dead message, whereas an invalid message is properly delivered but cannot be processed by the receiver. Determining if a message should be moved to the *Dead Letter Channel* is an evaluation of the message's header performed by the messaging system. On the other hand, the receiver moves a message to an *Invalid Message Channel* (60) because of the message's body or particular header fields the receiver is interested in. To the receiver, determination and handling of dead messages seem automatic, whereas the receiver must handle invalid messages itself. A developer using a messaging system is stuck with whatever dead message handling the messaging system provides, but she can design her own invalid message handling, including handling for seemingly dead messages that the messaging system doesn't handle.

Example: *Stock Trading*

In a stock trading system, an application that wishes to perform a trade can send a trade request. To make sure that the trade is received in a reasonable amount of time (less than five minutes, perhaps), the requestor sets the request's *Message Expiration* (176) to five minutes. If the messaging system cannot deliver the request in that amount of time, or if the trading application does not receive the message (e.g., read it off of the channel) in time, then the messaging system will take the message off of the trade request channel and put the message on the *Dead Letter Channel*. The trading system may wish to monitor the system's *Dead Letter Channels* to determine if it is missing trades.

**Dead Letter
Channel**

Guaranteed Delivery

An enterprise is using *Messaging* (53) to integrate applications.

How can the sender make sure that a message will be delivered even if the messaging system fails?

One of the main advantages of asynchronous messaging over RPC is that the sender, the receiver, and network connecting the two don't all have to be working at the same time. If the network is not available, the messaging system stores the message until the network becomes available. Likewise, if the receiver is unavailable, the messaging system stores the message and retries delivery until the receiver becomes available. This is the *store-and-forward* process that messaging is based on. So, where should the message be stored before it is forwarded?

By default, the messaging system stores the message in memory until it can successfully forward the message to the next storage point. This works as long as the messaging system is running reliably, but if the messaging system crashes (for example, because one of its computers loses power or the messaging process aborts unexpectedly), all of the messages stored in memory are lost.

Most applications have to deal with similar problems. All data that is stored in memory is lost if the application crashes. To prevent this, applications use files and databases to persist data to disk so that it survives system crashes. Messaging systems need a similar way to persist messages more permanently so that no message gets lost even if the system crashes.

Use *Guaranteed Delivery* to make messages persistent so that they are not lost even if the messaging system crashes.

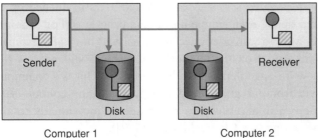

With *Guaranteed Delivery*, the messaging system uses a built-in datastore to persist messages. Each computer on which the messaging system is installed has its own datastore so that the messages can be stored locally. When the sender sends a message, the send operation does not complete successfully until the message is safely stored in the sender's datastore. Subsequently, the message is not deleted from one datastore until it is successfully forwarded to and stored in the next datastore. In this way, once the sender successfully sends the message, it is always stored on disk on at least one computer until it is successfully delivered to and acknowledged by the receiver.

Persistence increases reliability but at the expense of performance. Thus, if it's okay to lose messages when the messaging system crashes or is shut down, avoid using *Guaranteed Delivery* so messages will move through the messaging system faster.

Also consider that *Guaranteed Delivery* can consume a large amount of disk space in high-traffic scenarios. If a producer generates hundreds or thousands of messages per second, then a network outage that lasts multiple hours could use up a huge amount of disk space. Because the network is unavailable, the messages have to be stored on the producing computer's local disk drive, which may not be designed to hold this much data. For these reasons, some messaging systems allow you to configure a *retry timeout* parameter that specifies how long messages are buffered inside the messaging system. In some high-traffic applications (e.g., streaming stock quotes to terminals), this timeout may have to be set to a short time span, for example, a few minutes. Luckily, in many of these applications, messages are used as *Event Message*s (151) and can safely be discarded after a short amount of time elapses (see *Message Expiration* [176]).

It can also be useful to turn off *Guaranteed Delivery* during testing and debugging. This makes it easy to purge all message channels by stopping and restarting the messaging server. Messages that are still queued up can make it very tedious to debug even simple messaging programs. For example, you may have a sender and a receiver connected by a *Point-to-Point Channel* (103). If a message is still stored on the channel, the receiver will process that message before any new message that the sender produces. This is a common debugging pitfall in asynchronous, guaranteed messaging. Many commercial messaging implementations also allow you to purge queues individually to allow a fresh restart during testing (see *Channel Purger* [572]).

Guaranteed Delivery

How Guaranteed Is Guaranteed Messaging?

It is important to keep in mind that reliability in computer systems tends to be measured in the "number of 9s"—in other words, 99.9 percent. This tells us that something is rarely 100 percent reliable, with the cost already increasing exponentially to move from 99.9 to 99.99 percent. The same caveats apply to *Guaranteed Delivery*. There will always be a scenario where a message can get lost. For example, if the disk that stores the persisted messages fails, messages may get lost. You can make your disk storage more reliable by using redundant disk storage to reduce the likelihood of failure. This will possibly add another "9" to the reliability rating but likely not make it a true 100 percent. Also, if the network is unavailable for a long time, the messages that have to be stored may fill up the computer's disk, resulting in lost messages. In summary, *Guaranteed Delivery* is designed to protect the message delivery from expected outages, such as machine failures or network failures, but it is usually not 100 percent bulletproof.

With .NET's MSMQ implementation, for a channel to be persistent, it must be declared transactional, which means senders usually have to be *Transactional Client*s (484). In JMS, with *Publish-Subscribe Channel* (106), *Guaranteed Delivery* only ensures that the messages will be delivered to the active subscribers. To ensure that a subscriber receives messages even when it's inactive, the subscriber will need to be a *Durable Subscriber* (522).

Example: *Stock Trading*

In a stock trading system, trade requests and trade confirmations should probably be sent with *Guaranteed Delivery* to help ensure that none are lost. Change-of-address announcements should be sent with *Guaranteed Delivery*, but it is probably not necessary with price updates because losing some of them is not significant, and their frequency makes the overhead of *Guaranteed Delivery* prohibitive.

In *Durable Subscriber* (522), the stock trading example says that some price-change subscribers may wish to be durable. If so, then perhaps the price-change channel should guarantee delivery as well. Yet other subscribers may not need to be durable or want to suffer the overhead of *Guaranteed Delivery*. How can these different needs be met? The system may wish to implement two price-change channels, one with *Guaranteed Delivery* and another without. Only subscribers that require all updates should subscribe to the persistent channel, and their subscriptions should be durable. The publisher may wish to publish updates less frequently on the persistent channel because of its increased overhead. (See the *Quality-of-Service Channel* strategy discussed under *Datatype Channel* [111].)

Guaranteed Delivery

Example: *JMS Persistent Messages*

In JMS, message persistence can be set on a per-message basis. In other words, some messages on a particular channel may be persistent, whereas others might not be [JMS 1.1], [Hapner].

When a JMS sender wants to make a message persistent, it uses its `Message-Producer` to set the message's `JMSDeliveryMode` to `PERSISTENT`. The sender can set persistence on a per-message basis like this:

```
Session session = // obtain the session
Destination destination = // obtain the destination
Message message = // create the message
MessageProducer producer = session.createProducer(destination);
producer.send(
    message,
    javax.jms.DeliveryMode.PERSISTENT,
    javax.jms.Message.DEFAULT_PRIORITY,
    javax.jms.Message.DEFAULT_TIME_TO_LIVE);
```

If the application wants to make all of the messages persistent, it can set that as the default for the message producer.

```
producer.setDeliveryMode(javax.jms.DeliveryMode.PERSISTENT);
```

(And, in fact, the default delivery mode for a message producer is persistent.) Now, messages sent by this producer are automatically persistent, so they can simply be sent.

```
producer.send(message);
```

Meanwhile, messages sent by other message producers on the same channel may be persistent, depending on how those producers configure their messages.

Example: *IBM WebSphere MQ*

In WebSphere MQ, *Guaranteed Delivery* can be set on a per-channel basis or a per-message basis. If the channel is not persistent, the messages cannot be persistent. If the channel is persistent, the channel can be configured such that all messages sent on that channel are automatically persistent or that an individual message can be sent persistently or nonpersistently.

A channel is configured to be persistent (or not) when it is created in the messaging system. For example, the channel can be configured so that all of its messages will be persistent.

```
DEFINE Q(myQueue) PER(PERS)
```

Or the channel can be configured so that the message sender can specify with each message whether the message is persistent or transient.

```
DEFINE Q(myQueue) PER(APP)
```

If the channel is set to allow the sender to specify persistency, then a JMS `MessageProducer` can set that delivery-mode property as described earlier. If the channel is set to make all messages persistent, then the delivery-mode settings specified by the `MessageProducer` are ignored [WSMQ].

Example: *.NET Persistent Messages*

With .NET, persistent messages are created by making a `MessageQueue` transactional.

```
MessageQueue.Create("MyQueue", true);
```

All messages sent on this queue will automatically be persistent [Dickman].

Guaranteed
Delivery

Channel Adapter

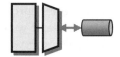

Many enterprises use *Messaging* (53) to integrate multiple, disparate applications.

How can you connect an application to the messaging system so that it can send and receive messages?

Channel
Adapter

Most applications were not designed to work with a messaging infrastructure. There are a variety of reasons for this limitation. Many applications were developed as self-contained, standalone solutions even though they contain data or functionality that can be leveraged by other systems. For example, many mainframe applications were designed as a one-in-all application that would never have to interface with other applications. Alas, legacy integration is nowadays one of the most common integration points for enterprise integration solutions. Another reason results from the fact that many message-oriented middleware systems expose proprietary APIs so that an application developer would have to code multiple interfaces to the messaging system, one for each potential middleware vendor.

If applications need to exchange data with other applications, they often are designed to use more generic interface mechanisms such as file exchange or database tables. Reading and writing files is a basic operating system function and does not depend on vendor-specific APIs. Likewise, most business applications already persist data into a database, so little extra effort is required to store data destined for other systems in a database table. Or an application can expose internal functions in a generic API that can be used by any other integration strategy, including messaging.

Other applications may be capable of communicating via a simple protocol like HTTP or TCP/IP. However, these protocols do not provide the same reliability as a *Message Channel* (60), and the data format used by the application is usually specific to the application and not compatible with a common messaging solution.

In the case of custom applications, we could add code to the application to allow it to send and receive messages. However, this can introduce additional complexity into the application and we need to be careful not to introduce any undesired side effects when making these changes. Also, this approach requires developers to be skilled with both the application logic and the messaging API. Both those approaches also assume that we have access to the application source code. If we deal with a packaged application that we purchased from a third-party software vendor, we may not even have the option of changing the application code.

Use a *Channel Adapter* that can access the application's API or data to publish messages on a channel based on this data and that likewise can receive messages and invoke functionality inside the application.

Channel Adapter

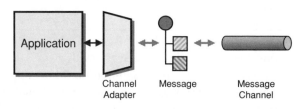

The adapter acts as a messaging client to the messaging system and invokes application functions via an application-supplied interface. Likewise, the *Channel Adapter* can listen to application-internal events and invoke the messaging system in response to these events. This way, any application can connect to the messaging system and be integrated with other applications as long as it has a proper *Channel Adapter*.

The *Channel Adapter* can connect to different layers of the application's architecture, depending on that architecture and the type of data the messaging system needs to access.

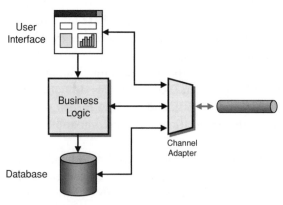

A Channel Adapter Connecting to Different Layers of an Application

1. **User Interface Adapter.** Sometimes disparagingly called "screen scraping," these types of adapters can be very effective in many situations. For example, an application may be implemented on a platform that is not supported by the messaging system. Or the owner of the application may have little interest in supporting the integration. This eliminates the option of running the *Channel Adapter* on the application platform. However, the user interface is usually available from other machines and platforms (e.g., 3270 terminals). Also, the surge of Web-based thin-client architectures has caused a certain revival of user interface integration. HTML-based user interfaces make it very easy to make an HTTP request and parse out the results. Another advantage of user interface integration is that no direct access to the application internals is needed. In some cases, it may not be desirable or possible to expose internal functions of a system to the integration solution. Using a user interface adapter, other applications have the exact same access to the application as a regular user. The downside of user interface adapters is the potential brittleness and low speed of the solution. The application has to parse "user" input and render a screen in response just so that the *Channel Adapter* can parse the screen back into raw data. This process involves many unnecessary steps, and it can be slow. Also, user interfaces tend to change more frequently than the core application logic. Every time the user interface changes, the *Channel Adapter* is likely to have to be changed as well.

2. **Business Logic Adapter.** Most business applications expose their core functions as an API. This interface may be a set of components (e.g., EJBs, COM objects, CORBA components) or a direct programming API (e.g., a C++, C#, or Java library). Since the software vendor (or developer) exposes these APIs expressly for access by other applications, they tend to be more stable than the user interface. In most cases, accessing the API is also more efficient. In general, if the application exposes a well-defined API, this type of *Channel Adapter* is likely to be the best approach.

3. **Database Adapter.** Most business applications persist their data inside a relational database. Since the information is already in the database, the *Channel Adapter* can extract information directly from the database without the application ever noticing, which is a very nonintrusive way to integrate the application. The *Channel Adapter* can even add a trigger to the relevant tables and send messages every time the data in these tables changes. This type of *Channel Adapter* can be very efficient and is quite universal, aided by the fact that only two or three database vendors dominate the market for relational databases. This allows us to connect to many different applications with a relatively generic adapter. The downside of a

database adapter is that we are poking around deep in the internals of an application. This may not be as risky if we simply read data, but making updates directly to the database can be very dangerous. Also, many application vendors consider the database schema "unpublished," meaning that they reserve the right to change it at will, which can make a database adapter solution brittle.

Channel Adapter

An important limitation of *Channel Adapter*s is that they can convert messages into application functions, but they require message formatting that closely resembles the implementation of the components being adapted. For example, a database adapter typically requires the message field names of incoming messages to be the same as the names of tables and fields in the application database. This kind of message format is driven entirely by the internal structure of the application and is not a good message format to use when integrating with other applications. Therefore, most *Channel Adapter*s must be combined with a *Message Translator* (85) to convert the application-specific message into a message format that complies with the *Canonical Data Model* (355).

*Channel Adapter*s can often run on a different computer than the application or the database itself. The *Channel Adapter* can connect to the application logic or the database via protocols such as HTTP or ODBC. While this setup allows us to avoid installing additional software on the application or database server, these protocols typically do not provide the same quality of service that a messaging channel provides, such as guaranteed delivery. Therefore, we must be aware that the remote connection to the database can represent a potential point of failure.

Some *Channel Adapter*s are unidirectional. For example, if a *Channel Adapter* connects to an application via HTTP, it may only be able to consume messages and invoke functions on the application, but it may not be able to detect changes in the application data except through repeated polling, which can be very inefficient.

An interesting variation of the *Channel Adapter* is the *Metadata Adapter*, sometimes called *Design-Time Adapter*. This type of adapter does not invoke application functions but extracts metadata, data that describes the internal data formats of the application. This metadata can then be used to configure *Message Translator*s (85) or to detect changes in the application data formats (see the introduction in Chapter 8, "Message Transformation"). Many application interfaces support this type of metadata extraction. For example, most commercial databases provide a set of system tables that contain metadata in the form of descriptions of the application tables. Likewise, most component frameworks (e.g., J2EE, .NET) provide special "reflection" functions that allow a component to enumerate methods provided by another component.

A special form of the *Channel Adapter* is the *Messaging Bridge* (133). The *Messaging Bridge* (133) connects the messaging system to another messaging system as opposed to a specific application. Typically, a *Channel Adapter* is implemented as a *Transactional Client* (484) to ensure that each piece of work the adapter does succeeds in both the messaging system and the other system being adapted.

Channel Adapter

Example: *Stock Trading*

A stock trading system may wish to keep a log of all of a stocks' prices in a database table. The messaging system may include a relational database adapter that logs each message from a channel to a specified table and schema. This channel-to-RDBMS adapter is a *Channel Adapter.* The system may also be able to receive external quote requests from the Internet (TCP/IP or HTTP) and send them on its internal quote-request channel with the internal quote requests. This Internet-to-channel adapter is a *Channel Adapter.*

Example: *Commercial EAI Tools*

Commercial EAI vendors provide a collection of *Channel Adapter*s as part of their offerings. Having adapters to all major application packages available greatly simplifies development of an integration solution. Most vendors also provide more generic database adapters as well as software development kits (SDKs) to develop custom adapters.

Example: *Legacy Platform Adapters*

A number of vendors provide adapters from common messaging system to legacy systems executing on platforms such as UNIX, MVS, OS/2, AS/400, Unisys, and VMS. Most of these adapters are specific to a certain messaging system. For example, Envoy Technologies' EnvoyMQ is a *Channel Adapter* that connects many legacy platforms with MSMQ. It consists of a client component that runs on the legacy computer and a server component that runs on a Windows computer with MSMQ.

Example: *Web Services Adapters*

Many messaging systems provide *Channel Adapter*s to move SOAP messages between an HTTP transport and the messaging system. This way, SOAP messages can be transmitted over an intranet using a reliable, asynchronous messaging system and over the global Internet (and through firewalls) using HTTP. One example of such an adapter is the Web Services Gateway for IBM's WebSphere Application Server.

Channel
Adapter

Messaging Bridge

An enterprise is using *Messaging* (53) to enable applications to communicate. However, the enterprise uses more than one messaging system, which confuses the issue of which messaging system an application should connect to.

Messaging
Bridge

> How can multiple messaging systems be connected so that messages available on one are also available on the others?

A common problem is an enterprise that uses more than one messaging system. This can occur because of a merger or acquisition between two different companies that have standardized around different messaging products. Sometimes a single enterprise that uses one messaging system to integrate its mainframe/legacy systems chooses another for its J2EE or .NET Web application servers and then needs to integrate the two messaging systems. Another common occurrence is an application that participates as part of multiple enterprises, such as a B2B client that wants to be a bidder in multiple auctioning systems. If the various auction clusters use different messaging systems, the bidder applications within an enterprise may wish to consolidate the messages from several external messaging systems onto a single internal messaging system. Another example is the extremely large enterprise with a huge number of *Message Channels* (60) and *Message Endpoints* (95) that may require more than one instance of the messaging system, which means those instances must be connected somehow.

If the messages on one system are of no interest to the applications using the other messaging system, then the systems can remain completely separate. But because the applications are part of the same enterprise, often some applications using one messaging system will be interested in messages being transmitted on another messaging system.

A common misconception is that a standardized messaging API such as JMS solves this problem; it does not. JMS makes two compliant messaging systems look the same to a client application, but it does nothing to make the two messaging systems work with each other. For the messaging systems to work together, they need to be interoperable, meaning that they use the same message format and transmit a message from one message store to the next in the same way. Messaging systems from two different vendors are rarely interoperable; a message store from one vendor can work only with other message stores from the same vendor.

Each application in the enterprise could choose to implement a client for each messaging system in the enterprise, but that would increase complexity and duplication in the messaging layer. This redundancy would become especially apparent if the enterprise added yet another messaging system and all of the applications had to be modified. On the other hand, each application could choose to interface with only one messaging system and ignore data on the other messaging systems. This would make the application simpler but could cause it to ignore a great deal of enterprise data. What is needed is a way for messages on one messaging system that are of interest to applications on another messaging system to be made available on the second messaging system as well.

Messaging Bridge

Use a *Messaging Bridge*, a connection between messaging systems that replicates messages between systems.

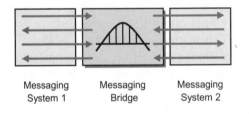

Messaging   Messaging   Messaging
System 1   Bridge   System 2

Typically, there is no practical way to connect two complete messaging systems, so instead we connect individual, corresponding channels between the messaging systems. The *Messaging Bridge* is a set of *Channel Adapter*s (127), where the non-messaging client is actually another messaging system and where each pair of adapters connects a pair of corresponding channels. The bridge acts as a map from one set of channels to the other and transforms the message format of one system to the other. The connected channels may be used to transmit messages between traditional clients of the messaging system or strictly for messages intended for other messaging systems.

You may need to implement the *Messaging Bridge* yourself for your enterprise. The bridge is a specialized *Message Endpoint* (95) application that is a client of both messaging systems. When a message is delivered on a channel of interest in one messaging system, the bridge consumes the message and sends another with the same contents on the corresponding channel in the other messaging system.

Many messaging system vendors have product extensions for bridging to messaging systems from other vendors. Thus, you may be able to buy a solution rather than build it yourself.

If the other "messaging system" is really a simpler protocol, such as HTTP, apply the *Channel Adapter* (127) pattern.

Messaging Bridge is necessary because different messaging system implementations have their own proprietary approaches for how to represent messages and how to forward them from one store to the next. Web services may be standardizing this, such that two messaging system installs, even from different vendors, may be able to act as one by transferring messaging using Web services standards. See the discussion of WS-Reliability and WS-ReliableMessaging in Chapter 14, "Concluding Remarks."

Messaging Bridge

Example: *Stock Trading*

A brokerage house may have one messaging system that the applications in its various offices use to communicate. A bank may have a different messaging system that the applications in its various branches use to communicate. If the brokerage and the bank decide to merge into a single company that offers bank accounts and investment services, which messaging system should the combined company use? Rather than redesigning half of the company's applications to use the new messaging system, the company can use a *Messaging Bridge* to connect the two messaging systems. This way, for example, a banking application and a brokerage application can coordinate to transfer money between a savings account and a securities trading account.

Example: *MSMQ Bridges*

MSMQ defines an architecture based on connector servers that enables connector applications to send and receive messages using other (non-MSMQ) messaging systems. An MSMQ application using a connector server can perform the same operations on channels from other messaging systems that it can perform on MSMQ channels [Dickman].

Microsoft's Host Integration Server product contains an MSMQ-MQSeries Bridge service that makes the two messaging systems work together. It lets

MSMQ applications send messages via MQSeries channels and vice versa, making the two messaging systems act as one.

Envoy Technologies, licenser of the MSMQ-MQSeries Bridge, also has a related product called Envoy Connect. It connects MSMQ and BizTalk servers with messaging servers running on non-Windows platforms, especially the J2EE platform, coordinating J2EE and .NET messaging within an enterprise.

Example: *SonicMQ Bridges*

Sonic Software's SonicMQ has SonicMQ Bridge products that support IBM MQSeries, TIBCO TIB/Rendezvous, and JMS. This enables messages on Sonic channels to be transmitted on other messaging systems' channels as well.

Messaging
Bridge

Message Bus

An enterprise contains several existing systems that must be able to share data and operate in a unified manner in response to a set of common business requests.

▼

What architecture enables separate applications to work together but in a decoupled fashion such that applications can be easily added or removed without affecting the others?

▲

Message Bus

An enterprise often contains a variety of applications that operate independently but must work together in a unified manner. Enterprise Application Integration (EAI) defines a solution to this problem but doesn't describe how to accomplish it.

For example, consider an insurance company that sells different kinds of insurance products (life, health, auto, home, etc.). As a result of corporate mergers and of the varying winds of change in IT development, the enterprise consists of a number of separate applications for managing the company's various products. An insurance agent trying to sell a customer several different types of policies must log onto a separate system for each policy, wasting effort and increasing the opportunity for mistakes.

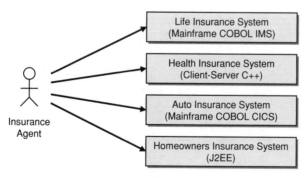

Insurance Company EAI Scenario

The agent needs a single, unified application for selling customers a portfolio of policies. Other types of insurance company employees, such as claims adjusters and customer service representatives, need their own applications for working with the insurance products, but they also want their applications to present a unified view. The individual product applications must be able to work together, perhaps to offer a discount when purchasing more than one policy and to process a claim that is covered by more than one policy.

The IT department could rewrite the product applications to all use the same technology and work together, but the amount of time and money to replace systems that already work (even though they don't work together) is prohibitive. IT could create a unified application for the agents, but this application needs to connect to the systems that actually manage the policies. Rather than unifying the systems, this new application creates one more system that doesn't integrate with the others.

The agent application could integrate with all of these other systems, but that would make it much more complex. The complexity would be duplicated in the applications for claims adjusters and customer service representatives. Furthermore, these unified user applications would not help the product applications integrate with each other.

Even if all of these applications could be made to work together, any change to the enterprise's configuration could make it all stop working. Not all applications will be available all of the time, yet the ones that are running must be able to continue with minimal impact from those that are not running. Over time, applications will need to be added to and removed from the enterprise, with minimal impact on the other applications. What is needed is an integration architecture that enables the product applications to coordinate in a loosely coupled way and for user applications to be able to integrate with them.

Structure the connecting middleware between these applications as a *Message Bus* that enables them to work together using messaging.

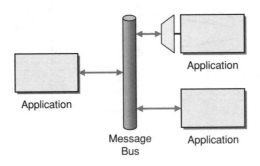

A *Message Bus* is a combination of a *Canonical Data Model* (355), a common command set, and a messaging infrastructure to allow different systems to communicate through a shared set of interfaces. This is analogous to a communications bus in a computer system, which serves as the focal point for communication between the CPU, main memory, and peripherals. Just as in the hardware analogy, there are a number of pieces that come together to form the message bus.

1. **Common communication infrastructure**—Just as the physical pins and wires of a PCI bus provide a common, well-known physical infrastructure for a PC, a common infrastructure must serve the same purpose in a message bus. Typically, a messaging system is chosen to serve as the physical communications infrastructure, providing a crossplatform, cross-language universal adapter between the applications. The infrastructure may include *Message Router* (78) capabilities to facilitate the correct routing of messages from system to system. Another common option is to use *Publish-Subscribe Channel*s (106) to facilitate sending messages to all receivers.

2. **Adapters**—The different systems must find a way to interface with the *Message Bus*. Some applications may be ready-built to connect to the bus, but most will need adapters to connect to the messaging system. These adapters are commonly commercial or custom *Channel Adapter*s (127) and *Service Activator*s (532). They may be specialized to handle tasks like invoking CICS transactions with the proper parameters or converting the bus's general data structures to the specific representation an application uses. This also requires a *Canonical Data Model* (355) that all systems can agree on.

3. **Common command structure**—Just as PC architectures have a common set of commands to represent the different operations possible on the physical bus (read bytes from an address, write bytes to an address), there must be common commands that all the participants in the *Message Bus* can understand. *Command Message* (145) illustrates how this feature works. Another common implementation for this is the *Datatype Channel* (111), where a *Message Router* (78) makes an explicit decision as to how to route particular messages (like purchase orders) to particular endpoints. It is at the end that the analogy breaks down, since the level of the messages carried on the bus are much more fine-grained than the "read/write" kinds of messages carried on a physical bus.

In our EAI example, a *Message Bus* could serve as a universal connector between the various insurance systems and as a universal interface for client applications that wish to connect to the insurance systems.

Message Bus

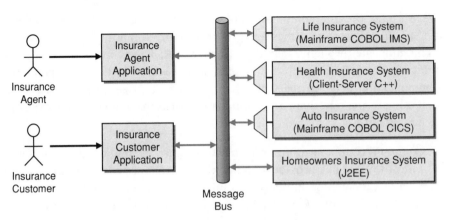

Insurance Company Message Bus

Here we have two GUIs that know only about the *Message Bus*; they are entirely unaware of the complexities of the underlying systems. The bus is responsible for routing *Command Messages* (145) to the proper underlying systems. In some cases, the best way to handle the command messages is to build an adapter to the system that interprets the command and then communicates with the system in a way it understands (invoking a CICS transaction, for instance, or calling a C++ API). In other cases, it may be possible to build the command-processing logic directly into the existing system as an additional way to invoke current logic.

Once the *Message Bus* has been developed for the agent GUI, it is easy to reuse for other GUIs, such as those for claims processors, customer service representatives, and customers who use a Web interface for to browse their own accounts. The features and security control of these GUI applications differ, but their need to work with the back-end applications is the same.

A *Message Bus* forms a simple, useful *service-oriented architecture* for an enterprise. Each service has at least one request channel that accepts requests of an agreed-upon format and probably a corresponding reply channel that supports a specified reply format. Any participant application can use these services by making requests and waiting for replies. The request channels, in effect, act as a directory of the services available.

A *Message Bus* requires that all of the applications using the bus use the same *Canonical Data Model* (355). Applications adding messages to the bus may need to depend on *Message Routers* (78) to route the messages to the appropriate final destinations. Applications not designed to interface with a messaging system may require *Channel Adapters* (127) and *Service Activators* (532).

Example: *Stock Trading*

A stock trading system may wish to offer a unified suite of services including stock trades, bond auctions, price quotes, portfolio management, and so on. This may require several separate back-end systems that have to coordinate with each other. To unify the services for a front-end customer GUI, the system could employ an intermediate application that offered all of these services and delegated their performance to the back-end systems. The back-end systems could even coordinate through this intermediary application. However, the intermediary application would tend to become a bottleneck and a single point of failure.

Rather than an intermediary application, a better approach might be a *Message Bus* with channels for requesting various services and getting responses. This bus could also enable back-end systems to coordinate with each other. A front-end system could simply connect to the bus and use it to invoke services. The bus could be distributed relatively easily across multiple computers to provide load distribution and fault tolerance.

Message Bus

Once the *Message Bus* is in place, connecting front-end GUIs would be easy; they each just need to send and receive messages from the proper channels. One GUI might enable a retail broker to manage his customers' portfolios. Another Web-based GUI could enable any customer with a Web browser to manage his own portfolio. Another non-GUI front end might support personal finance programs like Intuit's Quicken and Microsoft's Money, enabling customers using those programs to download trades and current prices. Once the *Message Bus* is in place, developing new user applications is much simpler.

Likewise, the trading system may want to take advantage of new back-end applications, such as by switching one trading application for another or spreading price quote requests across multiple applications. Implementing a change like this is as simple as adding and removing applications from the *Message Bus*. Once the new applications are in place, none of the other applications have to change; they just keep sending messages on the bus's channels as usual.

Chapter 5

Message Construction

Introduction

In Chapter 3, "Messaging Systems," we discussed *Message* (66). When two applications want to exchange a piece of data, they do so by wrapping it in a message. Whereas a *Message Channel* (60) cannot transmit raw data per se, it can transmit the data wrapped in a message. Creating and sending a *Message* (66) raises several other issues.

Message Construction

Message intent—Messages are ultimately just bundles of data, but the sender can have different intentions for what it expects the receiver to do with the message. It can send a *Command Message* (145), specifying a function or method on the receiver that the sender wishes to invoke. The sender is telling the receiver what code to run. It can send a *Document Message* (147), enabling the sender to transmit one of its data structures to the receiver. The sender is passing the data to the receiver but not specifying what the receiver should necessarily do with it. Or it can send an *Event Message* (151), notifying the receiver of a change in the sender. The sender is not telling the receiver how to react, just providing notification.

Returning a response—When an application sends a message, it often expects a response confirming that the message has been processed and providing the result. This is a *Request-Reply* (154) scenario. The request is usually a *Command Message* (145), and the reply is a *Document Message* (147) containing a result value or an exception. The requestor should specify a *Return Address* (159) in the request to tell the replier what channel to use to transmit the reply. The requestor may have multiple requests in process, so the reply should contain a *Correlation Identifier* (163) that specifies which request this reply corresponds to.

There are two common *Request-Reply* (154) scenarios worth noting; both involve a *Command Message* (145) request and a corresponding *Document Message* (147) reply. In the first scenario, Messaging RPC, the requestor not only wants to invoke a function on the replier, but also wants the return value from the function. This is how applications perform an RPC (Remote Procedure Call) using *Messaging* (53). In the other scenario, Messaging Query, the requestor performs a query; the replier executes the query and returns the results in the reply. This is how applications use messaging to perform a query remotely.

Huge amounts of data—Sometimes applications want to transfer a really large data structure, one that may not fit comfortably in a single message. In this case, break the data into more manageable chunks and send them as a *Message Sequence* (170). The chunks must be sent as a sequence, not just a bunch of messages, so the receiver can reconstruct the original data structure.

Introduction

Slow messages—A concern with messaging is that the sender often does not know how long it will take for the receiver to receive the message. Yet, the message contents may be time-sensitive, so if the message isn't received by a certain deadline, it should be ignored and discarded. In this situation, the sender can use *Message Expiration* (176) to specify an expiration date. If the messaging system cannot deliver a message by its expiration, it should discard the message or move it to a *Dead Letter Channel* (119). Likewise, if a receiver gets a message after its expiration, it should discard the message.

In summary, simply choosing to use a *Message* (66) is insufficient. When data must be transferred, it *must* be done through a *Message* (66). This chapter explains other decisions that are part of making messages work.

Command Message

An application needs to invoke functionality provided by other applications. It would typically use *Remote Procedure Invocation* (50), but it would like to take advantage of the benefits of using *Messaging* (53).

How can messaging be used to invoke a procedure in another application?

The advantage of *Remote Procedure Invocation* (50) is that it's synchronous, so the call is performed immediately while the caller's thread blocks. But that's also a disadvantage. If the call cannot be executed immediately—either because the network is down or because the remote process isn't running and listening—then the call doesn't work. If the call were asynchronous, it could keep trying until the procedure in the remote application is successfully invoked.

A local invocation is more reliable than a remote invocation. If the caller could transmit the procedure's invocation to the receiver as a *Message* (66), then the receiver could execute the invocation locally. So, the question is how to make a procedure's invocation into a message.

There's a well-established pattern for encapsulating a request as an object. The *Command* pattern [GoF] shows how to turn a request into an object that can be stored and passed around. If this object were a message, then it could be stored in and passed around through a *Message Channel* (60). Likewise, the command's state (such as method parameters) can be stored in the message's state.

**Command
Message**

Use a Command Message to reliably invoke a procedure in another application.

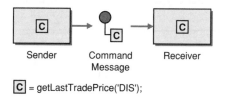

There is no specific message type for commands; a *Command Message* is simply a regular message that happens to contain a command. In JMS, the command message could be any type of message; examples include an ObjectMessage containing a Serializable command object, a TextMessage containing the command in XML form, and so on. In .NET, a command message is a *Message* (66) with a command stored in it. A Simple Object Access Protocol (SOAP) request is a command message.

*Command Message*s are usually sent over a *Point-to-Point Channel* (103) so that each command will be consumed and invoked only once.

Example: *SOAP and WSDL*

With the SOAP protocol [SOAP 1.1] and WSDL service description [WSDL 1.1], when using RPC-style SOAP messages, the request message is an example of this *Command Message* pattern. With this usage, the SOAP message body (an XML document) contains the name of the method to invoke in the receiver and the parameter values to pass into the method. This method name must be the same as one of the message names defined in the receiver's WSDL.

This example from the SOAP specification invokes the receiver's GetLastTradePrice method with a single parameter called symbol.

```
<SOAP-ENV:Envelope
  xmlns:SOAP-ENV="http://schemas.xmlsoap.org/soap/envelope/"
  SOAP-ENV:encodingStyle="http://schemas.xmlsoap.org/soap/encoding/">
  <SOAP-ENV:Body>
      <m:GetLastTradePrice xmlns:m="Some-URI">
          <symbol>DIS</symbol>
      </m:GetLastTradePrice>
  </SOAP-ENV:Body>
</SOAP-ENV:Envelope>
```

In a SOAP command, one might expect the method name to be the value of some standard <method> element; actually, the method name is the name of the method element, prefixed by the m namespace. Having a separate XML element type for each method makes validating the XML data much more precise, because the method element type can specify the parameters' names, types, and order.

Command Message

Document Message

An application would like to transfer data to another application. It could do so using *File Transfer* (43) or *Shared Database* (47), but those approaches have shortcomings. The transfer might work better using *Messaging* (53).

How can Messaging be used to transfer data between applications?

Document
Message

This is a classic problem in distributed processing: One process has data that another one needs. *File Transfer* (43) is easy to use, but it doesn't coordinate applications very well. A file written by one application may sit unused for quite a while before another application reads it. If several applications are supposed to read it, it'll be unclear who should take responsibility for deleting it.

Shared Database (47) requires adding new schema to the database to accommodate the data or force-fitting the data into the existing schema. Once the data is in the database, there's the risk that other applications that should not have access to the data now do. Triggering the receiver of the data to come and read it can be difficult, and coordinating multiple readers can create confusion about who should delete the data.

Remote Procedure Invocation (50) can be used to send the data, but then the caller is also telling the receiver—via the procedure being invoked—what to do with the data. Likewise, a *Command Message* (145) would transfer the data but would be overly specific about what the receiver should do with the data. Also, *Remote Procedure Invocation* (50) assumes two-way communication, which is unnecessary if we only want to pass data from one application to another.

Yet, we do want to use *Messaging* (53) to transfer the data. *Messaging* (53) is more reliable than an RPC. A *Point-to-Point Channel* (103) can be used to make sure that only one receiver gets the data (no duplication), or a *Publish-Subscribe Channel* (106) can be used to make sure that any receiver who wants the data gets a copy of it. So, the trick is to take advantage of *Messaging* (53) without making the *Message* (66) too much like an RPC.

Use a *Document Message* to reliably transfer a data structure between applications.

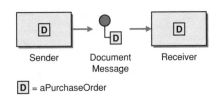

Whereas a *Command Message* (145) tells the receiver to invoke certain behavior, a *Document Message* just passes data and lets the receiver decide what, if anything, to do with the data. The data is a single unit of data, a single object or data structure that may decompose into smaller units.

Document Message

*Document Message*s can seem very much like *Event Message*s (151); the main difference is a matter of timing and content. The important part of a *Document Message* is its content: the document. Successfully transferring the document is important; the timing of when it is sent and received is less important. *Guaranteed Delivery* (122) may be a consideration; *Message Expiration* (176) probably is not. In contrast, an *Event Message*s (151) existence and timing are often more important than its content.

A *Document Message* can be any kind of message in the messaging system. In JMS, the document message may be an `ObjectMessage` containing a `Serializable` data object for the document, or it may be a `TextMessage` containing the data in XML form. In .NET, a document message is a *Message* (66) with the data stored in it. A Simple Object Access Protocol (SOAP) reply message is a document message.

*Document Message*s are usually sent using a *Point-to-Point Channel* (103) to move the document from one process to another without duplicating it. *Messaging* (53) can be used to implement simple workflow by passing a document to an application that modifies the document and then passes it to another application. In some cases, a document message can be broadcast via a *Publish-Subscribe Channel* (106), but this creates multiple copies of the document. The copies need to be read-only; otherwise, if the receivers change the copies, there will be multiple copies of the document in the system, each containing different data. In *Request-Reply* (154), the reply is usually a *Document Message*, where the result value is the document.

Example: *Java and XML*

The following example (drawn from the example XML schema in [Graham]) shows how a simple purchase order can be represented as XML and sent as a message using JMS.

```
Session session = // Obtain the session
Destination dest = // Obtain the destination
MessageProducer sender = session.createProducer(dest);
String purchaseOrder =
"    <po id=\"48881\" submitted=\"2002-04-23\">
        <shipTo>
            <company>Chocoholics</company>
            <street>2112 North Street</street>
            <city>Cary</city>
            <state>NC</state>
            <postalCode>27522</postalCode>
        </shipTo>
        <order>
            <item sku=\"22211\" quantity=\"40\">
                <description>Bunny, Dark Chocolate, Large</description>
            </item>
        </order>
    </po>";
TextMessage message = session.createTextMessage();
message.setText(purchaseOrder);
sender.send(message);
```

Document Message

Example: *SOAP and WSDL*

With the SOAP protocol [SOAP 1.1] and WSDL service description [WSDL 1.1], when using document-style SOAP messages, the SOAP message is an example of a *Document Message* . The SOAP message body is an XML document (or some kind of data structure that has been converted into an XML document), and the SOAP message transmits that document from the sender (e.g., the client) to the receiver (e.g., the server).

When using RPC-style SOAP messaging, the response message is an example of this pattern. With this usage, the SOAP message body (an XML document) contains the return value from the method that was invoked. This example

from the SOAP specification returns the answer from invoking the GetLastTrade-
Price method.

```
<SOAP-ENV:Envelope
  xmlns:SOAP-ENV="http://schemas.xmlsoap.org/soap/envelope/"
  SOAP-ENV:encodingStyle="http://schemas.xmlsoap.org/soap/encoding/"/>
  <SOAP-ENV:Body>
      <m:GetLastTradePriceResponse xmlns:m="Some-URI">
          <Price>34.5</Price>
      </m:GetLastTradePriceResponse>
  </SOAP-ENV:Body>
</SOAP-ENV:Envelope>
```

**Document
Message**

Event Message

Several applications would like to use event notification to coordinate their actions and would like to use *Messaging* (53) to communicate those events.

How can messaging be used to transmit events from one application to another?

    Sometimes, an event occurs in one object that another object needs to know about. The classic example is a Model-View-Controller architecture [POSA], where the model changes its state and must notify its views so that they can redraw themselves. Such change notification can also be useful in distributed systems. For example, in a B2B system, one business may need to notify others of price changes or a whole new product catalog.

    A process can use *Remote Procedure Invocation* (50) to notify other applications of change events, but that requires that the receiver accept the event immediately, even if it doesn't want events right now. RPC also requires that the announcing process know every listener process and invoke an RPC on each listener.

    The *Observer* pattern [GoF] describes how to design a subject that announces events and observers that consume events. A subject notifies an observer of an event by calling the observer's Update() method. Update() can be implemented as an RPC, but it would have all of RPC's shortcomings.

    It would be better to send the event notification asynchronously, as a *Message* (66). This way, the subject can send the notification when it's ready, and each observer can receive the notification if and when it's ready.

Use an *Event Message* for reliable, asynchronous event notification between applications.

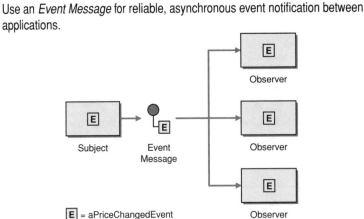

Subject   Event   Observer
             Message

Observer

Observer

E = aPriceChangedEvent

When a subject has an event to announce, it creates an event object, wraps it in a message, and sends it on a channel as an *Event Message*. The observer receives the *Event Message*, gets the event, and processes it. Messaging does not change the event that's being announced, but just makes sure that the notification gets to the observer.

An *Event Message* can be any kind of message in the messaging system. In Java, an event can be an object or data, such as an XML document. Thus, it can be transmitted through JMS as an ObjectMessage, TextMessage, and so on. In .NET, an event message is a Message with the event stored in it.

The difference between an *Event Message* and a *Document Message* (147) is a matter of timing and content. An event's contents are typically less important. Many events even have an empty message body; their mere occurrence tells the observer to react. An event's timing is very important; the subject should issue an event as soon as a change occurs, and the observer should process it quickly while it's still relevant. *Guaranteed Delivery* (122) is usually not very helpful with events, because they're frequent and need to be delivered quickly. *Message Expiration* (176) can be very helpful to make sure that an event is processed quickly or not at all.

The B2B system that must notify other businesses of price or product changes, for example, could use *Event Messages*, *Document Messages* (147), or a combination of the two. If a message says that the price for computer disk drives has changed, that's an event. If the message provides information about the disk drive, including its new price, that's a document being sent *as* an event.

Another message that announces the new catalog and its URL is an event, whereas a similar message that actually contains the new catalog is an event that contains a document.

Which is better? The *Observer* pattern describes this as a trade-off between a push model and a pull model. The *push model* sends information about the change as part of the update, whereas the *pull model* sends minimal information, and observers that want more information request it by sending GetState() to the subject. The two models relate to messaging like this.

Push model—The message is a combined document/event message; the message's delivery announces that the state has occurred and the message's contents are the new state. This is more efficient if all observers want these details, but otherwise it can be the worst of both worlds: a large message that is sent frequently and often ignored by many observers.

Pull model—There are three messages:

1. **Update** is an *Event Message* that notifies the observer of the event.

2. **State Request** is a *Command Message* (145) an interested observer uses to request details from the subject.

3. **State Reply** is a *Document Message* (147) the subject uses to send the details to the observer.

Event
Message

The advantages of the pull model are that the update messages are small, only interested observers request details, and potentially each interested observer can request the details it specifically is interested in. The disadvantage is the additional number of channels needed and the resulting traffic caused by more than one message.

For more details on how to implement *Observer* using messaging, see the section "JMS Publish/Subscribe Example" in Chapter 6, "Interlude: Simple Messaging."

There is usually no reason to limit an event message to a single receiver via a *Point-to-Point Channel* (103); the message is usually broadcast via a *Publish-Subscribe Channel* (106) so that all interested processes receive notification. Whereas a *Document Message* (147) needs to be consumed so that the document is not lost, a receiver of *Event Messages* can often ignore the messages when it's too busy to process them, so the subscribers can often be nondurable (not *Durable Subscribers* [522]). *Event Message* is a key part of implementing the *Observer* pattern using messaging.

Request-Reply

When two applications communicate via *Messaging* (53), the communication is one-way. The applications may want a two-way conversation.

Request-Reply

When an application sends a message, how can it get a response from the receiver?

Messaging (53) provides one-way communication between applications. *Messages* (66) travel on a *Message Channel* (60) in one direction; they travel from the sender to the receiver. This asynchronous transmission makes the delivery more reliable and decouples the sender from the receiver.

The problem is that communication between components often needs to be two-way. When a program calls a function, it receives a return value. When it executes a query, it receives query results. When one component notifies another of a change, it may want to receive an acknowledgment. How can messaging be two-way?

Perhaps a sender and receiver could share a message simultaneously. Then, each application could add information to the message for the other to consume. But that is not how messaging works. A message is first sent and then received, so the sender and receiver cannot both access the message at the same time.

Perhaps the sender could keep a reference to the message. Then, once the receiver placed its response into the message, the sender could pull the message back. This may work for notes clipped to a clothesline, but it is not how a *Message Channel* (60) works. A channel transmits messages in one direction. What is needed is a two-way message on a two-way channel.

Send a pair of *Request-Reply* messages, each on its own channel.

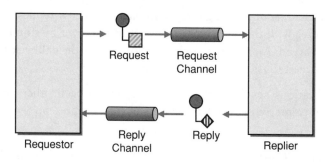

Request-Reply has two participants:

1. **Requestor** sends a request message and waits for a reply message.

2. **Replier** receives the request message and responds with a reply message.

The request channel can be a *Point-to-Point Channel* (103) or a *Publish-Subscribe Channel* (106). The difference is whether the request should be broadcasted to all interested parties or should be processed by only a single consumer. The reply channel, on the other hand, is almost always point-to-point, because it usually makes no sense to broadcast replies—they should be returned only to the requestor.

When a caller performs a *Remote Procedure Invocation* (50), the caller's thread must block while it waits for the response. With *Request-Reply*, the requestor has two approaches for receiving the reply.

1. **Synchronous Block**—A single thread in the caller sends the request message, blocks (as a *Polling Consumer* [494]) to wait for the reply message, and then processes the reply. This is simple to implement, but if the requestor crashes, it will have difficulty reestablishing the blocked thread. The request thread awaiting the response implies that there is only one outstanding request or that the reply channel for this request is private for this thread.

2. **Asynchronous Callback**—One thread in the caller sends the request message and sets up a callback for the reply. A separate thread listens for reply

messages. When a reply message arrives, the reply thread invokes the appropriate callback, which reestablishes the caller's context and processes the reply. This approach enables multiple outstanding requests to share a single reply channel and a single reply thread to process replies for multiple request threads. If the requestor crashes, it can recover by simply restarting the reply thread. An added complexity, however, is the callback mechanism that must reestablish the caller's context.

Two applications sending requests and replies to each other are not very helpful. What is interesting is what the two messages represent.

Request-
Reply

1. **Messaging RPC**—This is how to implement *Remote Procedure Invocation* (50) using messaging. The request is a *Command Message* (145) that describes the function the replier should invoke. The reply is a *Document Message* (147) that contains the function's return value or exception.

2. **Messaging Query**—This is how to perform a remote query using messaging. The request is a *Command Message* (145) containing the query, and the reply is the results of the query, perhaps a *Message Sequence* (170).

3. **Notify/Acknowledge**—This provides for event notification with acknowledgment, using messaging. The request is an *Event Message* (151) that provides notification, and the reply is a *Document Message* (147) acknowledging the notification. The acknowledgment may itself be another request, one seeking details about the event.

The request is like a method call. As such, the reply is one of three possibilities:

1. **Void**—Simply notifies the caller that the method has finished so that the caller can proceed.

2. **Result value**—A single object that is the method's return value.

3. **Exception**—A single exception object indicating that the method aborted before completing successfully, and indicating why.

The request should contain a *Return Address* (159) to tell the replier where to send the reply. The reply should contain a *Correlation Identifier* (163) that specifies which request this reply is for.

Example: *SOAP 1.1 Messages*

SOAP messages come in Request-Reply pairs. A SOAP request message indicates a service the sender wants to invoke on the receiver, whereas a SOAP response message contains the result of the service invocation. The response message contains either a result value or a fault—the SOAP equivalent of an exception [SOAP 1.1].

Example: *SOAP 1.2 Response Message Exchange Pattern*

Whereas SOAP 1.1 has loosely described response messages, SOAP 1.2 introduces an explicit *Request-Response Message Exchange* pattern [SOAP 1.2 Part 2]. This pattern describes a separate, potentially asynchronous response to a SOAP request.

Request-
Reply

Example: *JMS Requestor Objects*

JMS includes a couple of features that can be used to implement *Request-Reply*.

A TemporaryQueue is a Queue that can be created programmatically and that lasts only as long as the Connection used to create it. Only MessageConsumers created by the same connection can read from the queue, so it is effectively private to the connection [JMS 1.1].

How do MessageProducers know about this newly created, private queue? A requestor creates a temporary queue and specifies it in the reply-to property of a request message (see *Return Address* [159]). A well-behaved replier will send the reply back on the specified queue, one that the replier wouldn't even know about if it weren't a property of the request message. This is a simple approach the requestor can use to make sure that the replies always come back to it.

The downside with temporary queues is that when their Connection closes, the queue and any messages in it are deleted. Likewise, temporary queues cannot provide *Guaranteed Delivery* (122); if the messaging system crashes, then the connection is lost, so the queue and its messages are lost.

JMS also provides QueueRequestor, a simple class for sending requests and receiving replies. A requestor contains a QueueSender for sending requests and a QueueReceiver for receiving replies. Each requestor creates its own temporary queue for receiving replies and specifies that in the request's reply-to property

[JMS 1.1]. A requestor makes sending a request and receiving a reply very simple:

```
QueueConnection connection = // obtain the connection
Queue requestQueue = // obtain the queue
Message request = // create the request message
QueueSession session = connection.createQueueSession(false, Session.AUTO_ACKNOWLEDGE);
QueueRequestor requestor = new QueueRequestor(session, requestQueue );
Message reply = requestor.request(request);
```

One method—request—sends the request message and blocks until it receives the reply message.

TemporaryQueue, used by QueueRequestor, is a *Point-to-Point Channel* (103). Its *Publish-Subscribe Channel* (106) equivalents are TemporaryTopic and TopicRequestor.

Request-
Reply

Return Address

My application is using *Messaging* (53) to perform a *Request-Reply* (154).

▼————————————————————————————————

How does a replier know where to send the reply?

————————————————————————————————▲

Messages are often thought of as completely independent, such that any sender can send a message on any channel whenever it likes. However, messages are often associated. With *Request-Reply* (154) pairs, two messages appear independent, but the reply message has a one-to-one correspondence with the request message that caused it. Thus, the replier that processes the request message cannot simply send the reply message on any channel it wants; it must send it on the channel on which the requestor expects the reply.

Each receiver could automatically know which channel to send replies on, but hard-coding such assumptions makes the software less flexible and more difficult to maintain. Furthermore, a single replier could be processing calls from several different requestors, so the reply channel is not the same for every message; it depends on which requestor sent the request message.

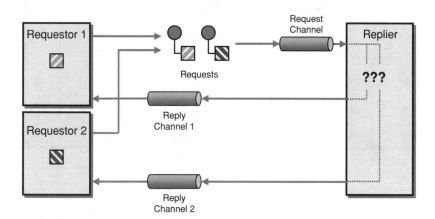

Uncertain Where to Send Replies

A requestor potentially may not want a reply sent back to itself. Rather, it may have an associated callback processor to process replies, and the callback processor may monitor a different channel than the requestor does (or the requestor may not monitor any channels at all). The requestor could have multiple callback processors, requiring replies for different requests from the same requestor to be sent to different processors.

The reply channel will not necessarily transmit replies back to the requestor; it will transmit them to whomever the requestor wants to process the replies, because it's listening to the channel the requestor specified. So, knowing what requestor sent a request or what channel it was sent on does not necessarily tell the replier what channel to send the reply on. Even if it did, the replier would still have to infer which reply channel to use for a particular requestor or request channel. It's easier for the request to explicitly specify which reply channel to use. What is needed is a way for the requestor to tell the replier where and how to send back a reply.

Return Address

The request message should contain a *Return Address* that indicates where to send the reply message.

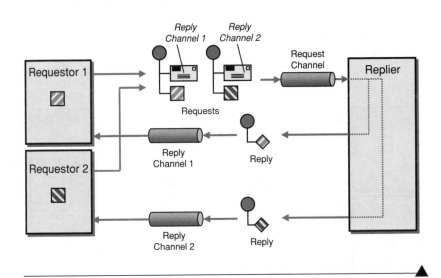

This way, the replier does not need to know where to send the reply; it can just obtain the reply channel address from the request message. If different messages to the same replier require replies to different places, the replier can determine from each request message where to send the reply for that request. This encapsulates the knowledge of what channels to use for requests and replies within the requestor so those decisions do not have to be hard-coded within the replier. A *Return Address* is put in the header of a message because it's not part of the application data being transmitted.

A message's *Return Address* is analogous to the reply-to field in an e-mail message. The reply-to e-mail address is usually the same as the from address, but the sender can set it to a different address to receive replies in an account other than the one used to send the original message.

When the reply is sent back over the channel indicated by the *Return Address*, it may also need a *Correlation Identifier* (163). The *Return Address* tells the receiver what channel to put the reply message on; the *Correlation Identifier* (163) tells the sender which request a reply is for.

Return Address

Example: *JMS Reply-To Property*

JMS messages have a predefined property for *Return Address*es, JMSReplyTo. Its type is a Destination (a Topic or Queue) rather than just a string for the destination name, which ensures that the destination (e.g., *Message Channel* [60]) really exists, at least when the request is sent [JMS 1.1], [Monson-Haefel].

A sender that wishes to specify a reply channel that is a Queue would do so like this:

```
Queue requestQueue = // Specify the request destination
Queue replyQueue = // Specify the reply destination
Message requestMessage = // Create the request message
requestMessage.setJMSReplyTo(replyQueue);
MessageProducer requestSender = session.createProducer(requestQueue);
requestSender.send(requestMessage);
```

Then, the receiver would send the reply message like this:

```
Queue requestQueue = // Specify the request destination
MessageConsumer requestReceiver = session.createConsumer(requestQueue);
Message requestMessage = requestReceiver.receive();
Message replyMessage = // Create the reply message
Destination replyQueue = requestMessage.getJMSReplyTo();
MessageProducer replySender = session.createProducer(replyQueue);
replySender.send(replyMessage);
```

Example: *.NET Response-Queue Property*

.NET messages also have a predefined property for *Return Addresses*, Response-Queue. Its type is a MessageQueue (e.g., *Message Channel* [60]), the queue that the application should send a response message to [SysMsg], [Dickman].

Example: *Web Services Request/Response*

SOAP 1.2 incorporates the *Request-Response Message Exchange* pattern [SOAP 1.2 Part 2], but the address to which to send the reply is unspecified and therefore implied. This SOAP pattern will need to support an optional *Return Address* to truly make SOAP messages asynchronous and to delink the responder from the requestor.

The emerging WS-Addressing standard helps address this issue by specifying how to identify a Web service endpoint and what XML elements to use. Such an address can be used in a SOAP message to specify a *Return Address*. See the discussion of WS-Addressing in Chapter 14, "Concluding Remarks."

Return Address

Correlation Identifier

My application is using *Messaging* (53) to perform a *Request-Reply* (154) and has received a reply message.

How does a requestor that has received a reply know which request this is the reply for?

When one process invokes another via *Remote Procedure Invocation* (50), the call is synchronous, so there is no confusion about which call produced a given result. But *Messaging* (53) is asynchronous, so from the caller's point of view, it makes the call, and then sometime later a result appears. The caller may not even remember making the request, or it may have made so many requests that it no longer knows which one this is the result for. Now, when the caller finally gets the result, it may not know what to do with it, which defeats the purpose of making the call in the first place.

Correlation
Identifier

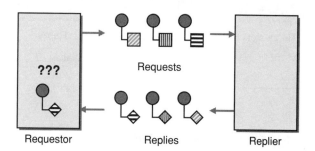

Cannot Match Reply to Request

There are a couple of approaches the caller can use to avoid this confusion. It can make just one call at a time and wait for a reply before sending another request, so there is at most one outstanding request at any given time. This, however, will greatly slow processing throughput. The caller could assume that it will receive replies in the same order it sent requests, but messaging does not guarantee what order messages are delivered in (see *Resequencer* [283]), and all requests may not take the same amount of time to process, so the caller's assumption would be faulty. The caller could design its requests so that they do not need replies, but this constraint would make messaging useless for many purposes.

What the caller needs is for the reply message to have a pointer or reference to the request message, but messages do not exist in a stable memory space where they can be referenced by variables. However, a message could have some sort of key, a unique identifier like the key for a row in a relational database table. Such a unique identifier could be used to identify the message from other messages, clients that use the message, and so on.

Correlation Identifier

Each reply message should contain a *Correlation Identifier*, a unique identifier that indicates which request message this reply is for.

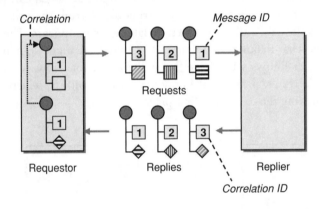

There are six parts to *Correlation Identifier*.

1. **Requestor**—An application that performs a business task by sending a request and waiting for a reply.

2. **Replier**—Another application that receives the request, fulfills it, and then sends the reply. It gets the request ID from the request and stores it as the correlation ID in the reply.

3. **Request**—A *Message* (66) sent from the requestor to the replier, containing a request ID.

4. **Reply**—A *Message* (66) sent from the replier to the requestor, containing a correlation ID.

5. **Request ID**—A token in the request that uniquely identifies the request.

6. **Correlation ID**—A token in the reply that has the same value as the request ID in the request.

This is how a *Correlation Identifier* works: When the requestor creates a request message, it assigns the request a request ID—an identifier that is different from those for all other currently outstanding requests, that is, requests that do not yet have replies. When the replier processes the request, it saves the request ID and adds that ID to the reply as a correlation ID. When the requestor processes the reply, it uses the correlation ID to know which request the reply is for. This is called a *Correlation Identifier* because of the way the caller uses the identifier to correlate (i.e., match; show the relationship) each reply to the request that caused it.

Correlation Identifier

As is often the case with messaging, the requestor and replier must agree on several details. They must agree on the name and type of the request ID property, and they must agree on the name and type of the correlation ID property. Likewise, the request and reply message formats must define those properties or allow them to be added as custom properties. For example, if the requestor stores the request ID in a first-level XML element named request_id and the value is an integer, the replier has to know this so that it can find the request ID value and process it properly. The request ID value and correlation ID value are usually of the same type; if not, the requestor has to know how the replier will convert the request ID to the reply ID.

This pattern is a simpler, messaging-specific version of the *Asynchronous Completion Token* pattern [POSA2]. The requestor is the Initiator, the replier is the Service, the consumer in the requestor that processes the reply is the Completion Handler, and the *Correlation Identifier* the consumer uses to match the reply to the request is the Asynchronous Completion Token.

A correlation ID (and also the request ID) is usually put in the header of a message rather than in the body. The ID is not part of the command or data the requestor is trying to communicate to the replier. In fact, the replier does not really use the ID at all; it just saves the ID from the request and adds it to the reply for the requestor's benefit. Since the message body is the content being transmitted between the two systems, and the ID is not part of that, the ID goes in the header.

The gist of the pattern is that the reply message contains a token (the correlation ID) that identifies the corresponding request (via its request ID). There are several different approaches for achieving this.

The simplest approach is for each request to contain a unique ID, such as a message ID, and for the response's correlation ID to be the request's unique ID. This relates the reply to its corresponding request. However, when the requestor is trying to process the reply, knowing the request message often isn't very helpful. What the requestor really wants is a reminder of what business task caused it to send the request in the first place so that the requestor can complete the business task using the data in the reply.

The business task, such as needing to execute a stock trade or to ship a purchase order, probably has its own unique business object identifier (such as an order ID), so that the business task's unique ID can be used as the request-reply correlation ID. Then, when the requestor gets the reply and its correlation ID, it can bypass the request message and go straight to the business object whose task caused the request in the first place. In this case, rather than use the messages' built-in request message ID and reply correlation ID properties, the requestor and replier should use a custom business object ID property in both the request and the reply that identifies the business object whose task this request-reply message pair is performing.

A compromise approach is for the requestor to keep a map of request IDs and business object IDs. This is especially useful when the requestor wants to keep the object IDs private or when the requestor has no control over the replier's implementation and can only depend on the replier copying the request's message ID into the reply's correlation ID. In this case, when the requestor gets the reply, it looks up the correlation ID in the map to get the business object ID and then uses that to resume performing the business task using the reply data.

Messages have separate message ID and correlation ID properties so that request-reply message pairs can be chained. This occurs when a request causes a reply, and the reply is in turn another request that causes another reply, and so on. A message's message ID uniquely identifies the request it represents; if the message also has a correlation ID, then the message is also a reply for another request message, as identified by the correlation ID.

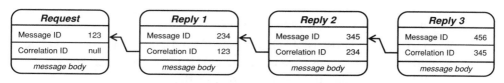

Request-Reply Chaining

Chaining is only useful if an application wants to retrace the path of messages from the latest reply back to the original request. Often, all the application wants to know is the original request, regardless of how many reply steps occurred in between. In this situation, once a message has a non-null correlation ID, it is a reply, and all subsequent replies that result from it should also use the same correlation ID.

While a *Correlation Identifier* is used to match a reply with its request, the request may also have a *Return Address* (159) that states what channel to put the reply on. Whereas a correlation identifier is used to matching a reply message with its request, a *Message Sequence*'s (170) identifiers are used to specify a message's position within a series of messages from the same sender.

Correlation
Identifier

Example: *JMS Correlation-ID Property*

JMS messages have a predefined property for correlation identifiers: JMSCorrelationID, which is typically used in conjunction with another predefined property, JMSMessageID [JMS 1.1], [Monson-Haefel]. A reply message's correlation ID is set from the request's message ID like this:

```
Message requestMessage = // Get the request message
Message replyMessage = // Create the reply message
String requestID = requestMessage.getJMSMessageID();
replyMessage.setJMSCorrelationID(requestID);
```

Example: *.NET CorrelationId Property*

Each Message in .NET has a CorrelationId property, a string in an acknowledgment message that is usually set to the ID of the original message. MessageQueue also has special peek and receive methods, PeekByCorrelationId(string) and ReceiveByCorrelationId(string), for peeking at and consuming the message on the queue (if any) with the specified correlation ID (see *Selective Consumer* [515]) [SysMsg], [Dickman].

Example: *Web Services Request-Response*

Web services standards, as of SOAP 1.1 [SOAP 1.1], do not provide very good support for asynchronous messaging, but SOAP 1.2 starts to plan for it. SOAP 1.2 incorporates the *Request-Response Message Exchange* pattern [SOAP 1.2 Part 2], a basic part of asynchronous SOAP messaging. However, the request-response pattern does not mandate support for "multiple ongoing requests," so it does not define a standard *Correlation Identifier* field, not even an optional one.

As a practical matter, service requestors often do require multiple outstanding requests. "Web Services Architecture Usage Scenarios" [WSAUS] discusses several different asynchronous Web services scenarios. Four of them—Request-Response, Remote Procedure Call (where the transport protocol does not support [synchronous] request-response directly), Multiple Asynchronous Responses, and Asynchronous Messaging—use message-id and response-to fields in the SOAP header to correlate a response to its request. This is the request-response example:

Correlation Identifier

SOAP Request Message Containing a Message Identifier

```
<?xml version="1.0" ?>
<env:Envelope xmlns:env="http://www.w3.org/2002/06/soap-envelope">
  <env:Header>
    <n:MsgHeader xmlns:n="http://example.org/requestresponse">
      <n:MessageId>uuid:09233523-345b-4351-b623-5dsf35sgs5d6</n:MessageId>
    </n:MsgHeader>
  </env:Header>
  <env:Body>
      ........
  </env:Body>
</env:Envelope>
```

SOAP Response Message Containing Correlation to Original Request

```
<?xml version="1.0" ?>
<env:Envelope xmlns:env="http://www.w3.org/2002/06/soap-envelope">
  <env:Header>
    <n:MsgHeader xmlns:n="http://example.org/requestresponse">
      <n:MessageId>uuid:09233523-567b-2891-b623-9dke28yod7m9</n:MessageId>
      <n:ResponseTo>uuid:09233523-345b-4351-b623-5dsf35sgs5d6</n:ResponseTo>
    </n:MsgHeader>
  </env:Header>
  <env:Body>
      ........
  </env:Body>
</env:Envelope>
```

Like the JMS and .NET examples, in this SOAP example, the request message contains a unique message identifier, and the response message contains a response (e.g., a correlation ID) field whose value is the message identifier of the request message.

Correlation
Identifier

Message Sequence

My application needs to send a huge amount of data to another process, more than may fit in a single message. Or, my application has made a request whose reply contains too much data for a single message.

How can messaging transmit an arbitrarily large amount of data?

Message Sequence

It's nice to think that messages can be arbitrarily large, but there are practical limits to how much data a single message can hold. Some messaging implementations place an absolute limit on how big a message can be. Other implementations allow messages to get quite big, but large messages nevertheless hurt performance. Even if the messaging implementation allows large messages, the message producer or consumer may place a limit on the amount of data it can process at once. For example, many COBOL-based and mainframe-based systems will consume or produce data only in 32 Kb chunks.

So, how do you get around this? One approach is to limit your application so it never needs to transfer more data than the messaging layer can store in a single message. This is an arbitrary limit, though, which can prevent your application from producing the desired functionality. If the large amount of data is the result of a request, the caller could issue multiple requests, one for each result chunk, but that increases network traffic and assumes the caller even knows how many result chunks will be needed. The receiver could listen for data chunks until there are no more (but how does it know there aren't any more?) and then try to figure out how to reassemble the chunks into the original, large piece of data, but that would be error-prone.

Inspiration comes from the way a mail order company sometimes ships an order in multiple boxes. If there are three boxes, the shipper marks them as "1 of 3," "2 of 3," and "3 of 3," so the receiver knows which ones he has received and whether he has received all of them. The trick is to apply the same technique to messaging.

Whenever a large set of data needs to be broken into message-size chunks, send the data as a *Message Sequence* and mark each message with sequence identification fields.

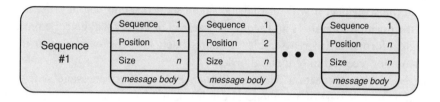

The three *Message Sequence* identification fields are as follows.

1. **Sequence identifier**—Distinguishes this cluster of messages from others.

2. **Position identifier**—Uniquely identifies and sequentially orders each message in a sequence.

3. **Size** or **End indicator**—Specifies the number of messages in the cluster or marks the last message in the cluster (whose position identifier then specifies the size of the cluster).

Message
Sequence

The sequences are typically designed so that each message in a sequence indicates the total size of the sequence—that is, the number of messages in that sequence. As an alternative, you can design the sequences so that each message indicates whether it is the final message in that sequence.

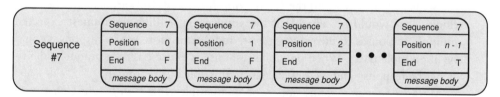

Message Sequence with End Indicator

Let's say a set of data needs to be sent as a cluster of three messages. The sequence identifier of the three-message cluster will be some unique ID. The position identifier for each message will be different: either 1, 2, or 3 (assuming that numbering starts from 1, not 0). If the sender knows the total number of messages from the start, the sequence size for each message is 3. If the sender does not know the total number of messages until it runs out of data to send (e.g., the sender is streaming the data), each message except the last will have a "sequence end" flag that is false. When the sender is ready to send the final message in the sequence, it will set that message's sequence end flag as true. Either way, the position identifiers and sequence size/end indicator will give the receiver enough information to reassemble the parts back into the whole, even if the parts are not received in sequential order.

If the receiver expects a *Message Sequence*, then every message sent to it should be sent as part of a sequence, even if it is only a sequence of one. Otherwise, when a single-part message is sent without the sequence identification fields, the receiver may become confused by the missing fields and may conclude that the message is invalid (see *Invalid Message Channel* [115]).

If a receiver gets some of the messages in a sequence but doesn't get all of them, it should reroute the ones it did receive to the *Invalid Message Channel* (60).

Message Sequence

An application may wish to use a *Transactional Client* (484) for sending and receiving sequences. The sender can send all of the messages in a sequence using a single transaction. This way, none of the messages will be delivered until all of them have been sent. Likewise, a receiver may wish to use a single transaction to receive the messages so that it does not truly consume any of the messages until it receives all of them. If any of the messages in the sequence are missing, the receiver can choose to roll back the transaction so that the messages can be consumed later. In many messaging system implementations, if a sequence of messages is sent in one transaction, the messages will be received in the order they are sent, which simplifies the receiver's job of putting the data back together.

When the *Message Sequence* is the reply message in a *Request-Reply* (154), the sequence identifier and the *Correlation Identifier* (163) are usually the same thing. They would be separate if the application sending the request expected multiple responses to the same request, and one or more of the responses could be in multiple parts. When only one response is expected, then uniquely identifying the response and its sequence is permissible but redundant.

Message Sequence tends not to be compatible with *Competing Consumers* (502) or *Message Dispatcher* (508). If different consumers/performers receive different messages in a sequence, none of the receivers will be able to reassemble the original data without exchanging message contents with each other. Thus, a message sequence should be transmitted via a *Message Channel* with a single consumer.

An alternative to *Message Sequence* is to use a *Claim Check* (346). Rather than transmitting a large document between two applications, if the applications both have access to a common database or file system, store the document and just transmit a key to the document in a single message.

Using *Message Sequence* is similar to using a *Splitter* (259) to break up a large message into a sequence of messages and using an *Aggregator* (268) to reassemble the message sequence back into a single message. *Splitter* (259) and *Aggregator* (268) enable the original and final messages to be very large, whereas *Message Sequence* enables the *Message Endpoint*s (95) to split the data before any messages are sent and to aggregate the data after the messages are received.

Message
Sequence

Example: *Large Document Transfer*

Imagine that a sender needs to send a receiver an extremely large document, so large that it will not fit within a single message or is impractical to send all at once. In this case, the document should be broken into parts, and each part can be sent as a message. Each message needs to indicate its position in the sequence and how many messages there are in all. For example, the maximum size of an MSMQ message is 4 MB. [Dickman] discusses how to send a multipart message sequence in MSMQ.

Example: *Multi-Item Query*

Consider a query that requests a list of all books by a certain author. Because this could be a very large list, the messaging design might choose to return each match as a separate message. Then, each message needs to indicate the query this reply is for, the message's position in the sequence, and how many messages to expect.

Example: *Distributed Query*

Consider a query that is performed in parts by multiple receivers. If the parts have some order to them, this will need to be indicated in the reply messages so that the complete reply can be assembled properly. Each receiver will need to know its position in the overall order and will need to indicate that position is the reply's message sequence.

Example: *JMS and .NET*

Neither JMS nor .NET has built-in properties for supporting message sequences. Therefore, messaging applications must implement their own sequence fields. In JMS, an application can define its own properties in the header, so that is an option. .NET does not provide application-defined properties in the header. The fields could also be defined in the message body. Keep in mind that if a receiver of the sequence needs to filter for messages based on their sequence, such filtering is much simpler to do if the field is stored in the header rather than in the body.

Example: *Web Services: Multiple Asynchronous Responses*

Web services standards currently do not provide very good support for asynchronous messaging, but the W3C has started to think about how it could. "Web Services Architecture Usage Scenarios" [WSAUS] discusses several different asynchronous Web services scenarios. One of them—Multiple Asynchronous Responses—uses `message-id` and `response-to` fields in the SOAP header to correlate a response to the request, and `sequence-number` and `total-in-sequence` fields in the body to sequentially identify the responses. This is the multiple responses example:

SOAP Request Message Containing a Message Identifier

```
<?xml version="1.0" ?>
<env:Envelope xmlns:env="http://www.w3.org/2002/06/soap-envelope">
  <env:Header>
    <n:MsgHeader xmlns:n="http://example.org/requestresponse">
      <n:MessageId>uuid:09233523-345b-4351-b623-5dsf35sgs5d6</n:MessageId>
    </n:MsgHeader>
  </env:Header>
  <env:Body>
    ........
  </env:Body>
</env:Envelope>
```

First SOAP Response Message Containing Sequencing and Correlation to Original Request

```
<?xml version="1.0" ?>
<env:Envelope xmlns:env="http://www.w3.org/2002/06/soap-envelope">
  <env:Header>
    <n:MsgHeader xmlns:n="http://example.org/requestresponse">
      <!-- MessageId will be unique for each response message -->
```

**Message
Sequence**

```
    <!-- ResponseTo will be constant for each response message in the sequence-->
    <n:MessageId>uuid:09233523-567b-2891-b623-9dke28yod7m9</n:MessageId>
    <n:ResponseTo>uuid:09233523-345b-4351-b623-5dsf35sgs5d6</n:ResponseTo>
  </n:MsgHeader>
  <s:Sequence xmlns:s="http://example.org/sequence">
    <s:SequenceNumber>1</s:SequenceNumber>
    <s:TotalInSequence>5</s:TotalInSequence>
  </s:Sequence>
 </env:Header>
 <env:Body>
    ........
 </env:Body>
</env:Envelope>
```

Final SOAP Response Message Containing Sequencing and Correlation to Original Request

```
<?xml version="1.0" ?>
<env:Envelope xmlns:env="http://www.w3.org/2002/06/soap-envelope">
  <env:Header>
    <n:MsgHeader xmlns:n="http://example.org/requestresponse">
      <!-- MessageId will be unique for each response message -->
      <!-- ResponseTo will be constant for each response message in the sequence-->
      <n:MessageId>uuid:40195729-sj20-pso3-1092-p20dj28rk104</n:MessageId>
      <n:ResponseTo>uuid:09233523-345b-4351-b623-5dsf35sgs5d6</n:ResponseTo>
    </n:MsgHeader>
    <s:Sequence xmlns:s="http://example.org/sequence">
      <s:SequenceNumber>5</s:SequenceNumber>
      <s:TotalInSequence>5</s:TotalInSequence>
    </s:Sequence>
  </env:Header>
  <env:Body>
    ........
  </env:Body>
</env:Envelope>
```

The message-id in the header is used as the sequence identifier in the responses. The sequence-number and total-in-sequence in each response are a position identifier and a size indicator respectively.

Message Sequence

Message Expiration

My application is using *Messaging* (53). If a *Messages* (66) data or request is not received by a certain time, it is useless and should be ignored.

Message Expiration

How can a sender indicate when a message should be considered stale and thus shouldn't be processed?

Messaging (53) practically guarantees that the *Message* (66) will eventually be delivered to the receiver. What it cannot guarantee is how long the delivery may take. For example, if the network connecting the sender and receiver is down for a week, then it could take a week to deliver a message. Messaging is highly reliable, even when the participants (sender, network, and receiver) are not, but messages can take a very long time to transmit in unreliable circumstances. (For more details, see *Guaranteed Delivery* [122].)

Often, a message's contents have a practical limit for how long they're useful. A caller issuing a stock quote request probably loses interest if it does not receive an answer within a minute or so. That means the request should not take more than a minute to transmit but also that the answer had better transmit back very quickly. A stock quote reply more than a minute or two old is probably too old and therefore irrelevant.

Once the sender sends a message and does not get a reply, it has no way to cancel or recall the message. Likewise, a receiver could check when a message was sent and reject the message if it's too old, but different senders under different circumstances may have different ideas about how long is too long, so how does the receiver know which messages to reject? What is needed is a way for the sender to specify the message's lifetime.

Set the *Message Expiration* to specify a time limit for how long the message is viable.

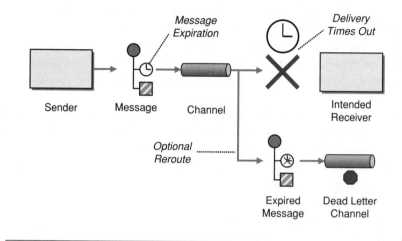

Once the time for which a message is viable passes, and the message still has not been consumed, then the message will expire. The messaging system's consumers will ignore an expired message; they treat the message as if it where never sent in the first place. Most messaging system implementations reroute expired messages to the *Dead Letter Channel* (119), whereas others simply discard expired messages; this may be configurable.

A *Message Expiration* is like the expiration date on a milk carton. After that date, you shouldn't drink the milk. Likewise, when a message expires, the messaging system should no longer deliver it. If a receiver still receives a message but cannot process it before the expiration, the receiver should throw away the message.

A *Message Expiration* is a timestamp (date and time) that specifies how long the message will live or when it will expire. The setting can be specified in relative or absolute terms. An absolute setting specifies a date and time when the message will expire. A relative setting specifies how long the message should live before it expires; the messaging system will use the time when the message is sent to convert the relative setting into an absolute one. The messaging system is responsible for adjusting the timestamp for receivers in different time zones from the sender, for adjustments in daylight savings times, and any other issues that can keep two different clocks from agreeing on what time it is.

The message expiration property has a related property, *sent time*, which specifies when the message was sent. A message's absolute expiration timestamp must be later than its sent timestamp (or else the message will expire immediately). To avoid this problem, senders usually specify expiration times relatively, in which case the messaging system calculates the expiration timestamp by adding the relative timeout to the sent timestamp (expiration time = sent time + time to live).

When a message expires, the messaging system may simply discard it or may move it to a *Dead Letter Channel* (119). A receiver that finds itself in possession of an expired message should move it to the *Invalid Message Channel* (60). With a *Publish-Subscribe Channel* (106), each subscriber gets its own copy of the message; some copies of a message may reach their subscribers successfully, whereas other copies of the same message expire before their subscribers consume them. When using *Request-Reply* (154), a reply message with an expiration setting may not work well—if the reply expires, the sender of the request will never know whether the request was ever received in the first place. If reply expirations are used, the request sender has to be designed to handle the case where expected replies are never received.

Example: *JMS Time-to-Live Parameter*

Message expiration is what the JMS specification calls "message time-to-live" [JMS 1.1], [Hapner]. JMS messages have a predefined property for message expiration, `JMSExpiration`, but a sender should not set it via `Message.setJMSExpiration(long)` because the JMS provider will override that setting when the message is sent. Rather, the sender should use its `MessageProducer` (`QueueSender` or `TopicPublisher`) to set the timeout for all messages it sends; the method for this setting is `MessageProducer.setTimeToLive(long)`. A sender can also set the time-to-live on an individual message using the `MessageProducer.send(Message message, int deliveryMode, int priority, long timeToLive)` method, where the fourth parameter is the time-to-live in milliseconds. Time-to-live is a relative setting specifying how long after the message is sent it should expire.

Message Expiration

Example: *.NET Time-to-Be-Received and Time-to-Reach-Queue Properties*

A .NET Message has two properties for specifying expiration: `TimeToBeReceived` and `TimeToReachQueue`. The reach-queue setting specifies how long the message has to reach its destination queue, after which the message might sit in the queue indefinitely. The be-received setting specifies how long the message has to be consumed by a receiver, which limits the total time for transmitting the message to its destination queue plus the amount of time the message can spend sitting on the destination queue. `TimeToBeReceived` is equivalent to JMS's `JMSExpiration` property. Both time settings have a value of type `System.TimeSpan`, a length of time [SysMsg], [Dickman].

Message
Expiration

Format Indicator

Several applications, communicating via *Messages* (66), follow an agreed-upon data format, perhaps an enterprise wide *Canonical Data Model* (355). However, that format may need to change over time.

How can a message's data format be designed to allow for possible future changes?

Format
Indicator

Even when you design a data format that works for all participating applications, future requirements may change. New applications may be added that have new format requirements, new data may need to be added to the messages, or developers may find better ways to structure the same data. Whatever the case, designing a single enterprise data model is difficult enough; designing one that will never need to change in the future is darn near impossible.

When an enterprise's data format changes, there would be no problem if all of the applications changed with it. If every application stopped using the old format and started using the new format, and all did so at exactly the same time, then conversion would be simple. The problem is that some applications will be converted before others, while some less-used applications may never be converted at all. Even if all applications could be converted at the same time, all messages would have to be consumed so that all channels are empty before the conversion could occur.

Realistically, applications will have to be able to support the old format and the new format simultaneously. To do this, applications must be able to tell which messages follow the old format and which follow the new.

One solution might be to use a separate set of channels for the messages with the new format. That, however, would lead to a huge number of channels, duplication of design, and configuration complexity as each application has to be configured for an ever-expanding assortment of channels.

A better solution is for the messages with the new format to use the same channels that the old format messages are using. This means that receivers need a way to distinguish messages of different formats that are using the same channel. Each message must specify what format it is using, and it needs a simple way to indicate its format.

Design a data format that includes a *Format Indicator* so that the message specifies what format it is using.

The *Format Indicator* enables the sender to tell the receiver the format of the message. This way, a receiver expecting several possible formats knows which one a message is using and therefore how to interpret the message's contents.

There are three main alternatives for implementing a *Format Indicator*:

1. **Version Number**—A number or string that uniquely identifies the format. Both the sender and receiver must agree on which format is designated by a particular indicator. The advantage of this approach is that the sender and receiver do not have to agree on a shared repository for format descriptors, but the drawback is that each must know what descriptor is indicated and where to access it.

Format Indicator

2. **Foreign Key**—A unique ID—such as a filename, a database row key, a home primary key, or an Internet URL—that specifies a format document. The sender and receiver must agree on the mapping of keys to documents and the format of the schema document. The advantage of this approach is that the foreign key is very compact and can point to a detailed data format description in a shared repository. The main drawback lies in the fact that each messaging participant has to retrieve the format document from a potentially remote resource.

3. **Format Document**—A schema that describes the data format. The schema document does not have to be retrieved via a foreign key or inferred from a version number; it is embedded in the message. The sender and the receiver must agree on the format of the schema. The advantage of this alternative is that messages are self-contained. However, message traffic increases because each message carries format information that rarely changes.

A version number or foreign key can be stored in a header field that the senders and receivers agree upon. Receivers that are not interested in the format version can ignore the field. A format document may be too long or complex to store in a header field, in which case the message body must have a format that contains two parts: the schema and the data.

Example: *XML*

XML documents have examples of all three approaches. One example is an XML declaration, like this:

```
<?xml version="1.0"?>
```

Here, 1.0 is a version number that indicates the document's conformance to that version of the XML specification. Another example is the document type declaration, which can take two forms. It can be an external ID containing a system identifier, like this:

```
<!DOCTYPE greeting SYSTEM "hello.dtd">
```

Format Indicator

The system identifier, hello.dtd, is a foreign key that indicates the file containing the DTD document that describes this XML document's format. The declaration can also be included locally, like this:

```
<!DOCTYPE greeting [
  <!ELEMENT greeting (#PCDATA)>
]>
```

The markup declaration, [<!ELEMENT greeting (#PCDATA)>], is a format document, an embedded schema document that describes the XML's format [XML 1.0].

Chapter 6

Interlude: Simple Messaging

Introduction

So far, we've introduced a lot of patterns. We've seen the basic messaging components, such as *Message Channel* (60), *Message* (66), and *Message Endpoint* (95). We've also seen detailed patterns for messaging channels and for message construction. So, how do all of these patterns fit together? How does a developer integrate applications using these patterns? What does the code look like, and how does it work?

This is the chapter where we really get to see the code. We have two examples:

Interlude:
Simple
Messaging

- **Request-Reply**—Demonstrates (in Java and .NET/C#) how to use messaging to send a request message and respond with a reply message.

- **Publish-Subscribe**—Explores how to use a JMS Topic to implement the *Observer* [GoF] pattern.

These two simple examples should get you started on adding messaging to your own applications.

Request-Reply Example

This is a simple but powerful example, transmitting a request and transmitting back a reply. It consists of two main classes:

- **Requestor**—The object that sends the request message and expects to receive the reply message.

- **Replier**—The object that receives the request message and sends a reply message in response.

183

These two simple classes sending simple messages illustrate a number of the patterns:

- *Message Channel* (60) and *Point-to-Point Channel* (103)—One channel for transmitting the requests, another for transmitting the replies.

- *Document Message* (147)—The default type of message, used as both the request and the reply.

- *Request-Reply* (154)—A pair of messages sent over a pair of channels, allowing the two applications to have a two-way conversation.

- *Return Address* (159)—The channel to send the response on.

- *Correlation Identifier* (163)—The ID of the request that caused this response.

- *Datatype Channel* (111)—All of the messages on each channel should be of the same type.

- *Invalid Message Channel* (115)—What happens to messages that aren't of the right type.

The example code also demonstrates a couple of patterns from Chapter 10, "Messaging Endpoints":

- *Polling Consumer* (494)—How the requestor consumes reply messages.

- *Event-Driven Consumer* (498)—How the replier consumes request messages.

While this book is technology-, product-, and language-neutral, code cannot be, so we've chosen two messaging programming platforms to implement this example:

- The JMS API in Java J2EE

- The MSMQ API in Microsoft .NET using C#

The same request-reply example is implemented in both platforms. Choose your favorite platform as an example of how messaging works. If you'd like to see how messaging works on the other platform but don't know how to write code for that platform, you can figure it out by comparing it to the code in the language you already know.

Introduction

Publish-Subscribe Example

This example explores how to implement the *Observer* pattern using a *Publish-Subscribe Channel* (106). It considers distribution and threading issues and discusses how messaging greatly simplifies these issues. The example shows how to implement both the push and pull models of notification and compares the consequences of each. It also explores how to design an adequate set of channels needed for a complex enterprise with numerous subjects notifying numerous observers.

The discussion and sample code illustrate several patterns:

- *Publish-Subscribe Channel* (106)—The channel that provides publish-subscribe notification.

- *Event Message* (151)—The message type used to send notifications.

- *Request-Reply* (154)—The technique used as part of the pull model for an observer to request the state from the subject.

- *Command Message* (145)—The message type used by an observer to request the state from the subject.

- *Document Message* (147)—The message type used by a subject to send its state to an observer.

- *Return Address* (159)—Tells the subject how to send the state to the observer.

- *Datatype Channel* (111)—The main guideline for whether two unrelated subjects can use the same channel to update the same group of observers.

The example code also demonstrates a couple of patterns from Chapter 10, "Messaging Endpoints":

- *Messaging Gateway* (468)—How the subject and observer encapsulate the messaging code so that they are not messaging-specific.

- *Event-Driven Consumer* (498)—How the observers consume notification messages.

- *Durable Subscriber* (522)—An observer that does not want to miss notifications, even if the observer is temporarily disconnected when the notification is sent.

This example is implemented in Java using JMS because JMS supports *Publish-Subscribe Channel* (106) as an explicit feature of the API through its Topic interface. .NET does not provide a similar level of support for using the publish-subscribe semantics in MSMQ. When it does, the techniques in the JMS example should be readily applicable to .NET programs as well.

Introduction

JMS Request-Reply Example

This is a simple example of how to use messaging, implemented in JMS [JMS]. It shows how to implement *Request-Reply* (154), where a requestor application sends a request, a replier application receives the request and returns a reply, and the requestor receives the reply. It also shows how an invalid message will be rerouted to a special channel.

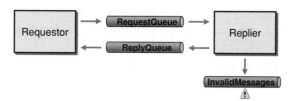

Components of the Request-Reply Example

This example was developed using JMS 1.1 and run using the J2EE 1.4 reference implementation.

Request-Reply Example

This example consists of two main classes:

1. **Requestor**—A *Message Endpoint* (95) that sends a request message and waits to receive a reply message as a response.

2. **Replier**—A *Message Endpoint* (95) that waits to receive the request message; when it does, it responds by sending the reply message.

The requestor and the replier each run in a separate Java Virtual Machine (JVM), which is what makes the communication distributed.

This example assumes that the messaging system has these three queues defined:

1. **jms/RequestQueue**—The queue the requestor uses to send the request message to the replier.

2. **jms/ReplyQueue**—The queue the replier uses to send the reply message to the requestor.

3. **jms/InvalidMessages**—The queue to which the requestor and replier move a message when they receive a message that they cannot interpret.

Here's how the example works. When the requestor is started in a command-line window, it starts and prints output like this:

```
Sent request
        Time:       1048261736520 ms
        Message ID: ID:_XYZ123_1048261766139_6.2.1.1
        Correl. ID: null
        Reply to:   com.sun.jms.Queue: jms/ReplyQueue
        Contents:   Hello world.
```

This shows that the requestor has sent a request message. Notice that this works even though the replier isn't even running and therefore cannot receive the request.

When the replier is started in another command-line window, it starts and prints output like this:

```
Received request
        Time:       1048261766790 ms
        Message ID: ID:_XYZ123_1048261766139_6.2.1.1
        Correl. ID: null
        Reply to:   com.sun.jms.Queue: jms/ReplyQueue
        Contents:   Hello world.
Sent reply
        Time:       1048261766850 ms
        Message ID: ID:_XYZ123_1048261758148_5.2.1.1
        Correl. ID: ID:_XYZ123_1048261766139_6.2.1.1
        Reply to:   null
        Contents:   Hello world.
```

**JMS
Request-
Reply
Example**

This shows that the replier received the request message and sent a reply message.

There are several interesting items in this output. First, notice the request sent and received timestamps; the request was received after it was sent (30270 ms later). Second, notice that the message ID is the same in both cases, because it's the same message. Third, notice that the contents, Hello world, are the same, which is very good because this is the data being transmitted, and it must be the same on both sides. (The request in this example is pretty lame. It is basically a *Document Message* (147); a real request would usually be a *Command Message* [145].) Fourth, the queue named jms/ReplyQueue has been specified in the request message as the destination for the reply message (an example of *Return Address* [159]).

Next, let's compare the output from receiving the request to that for sending the reply. First, notice the reply was not sent until after the request was received

(60 ms after). Second, the message ID for the reply is different from that for the request; this is because the request and reply messages are different, separate messages. Third, the contents of the request have been extracted and added to the reply (in this example, the replier acts as a simple "echo" service). Fourth, the reply-to destination is unspecified because no reply is expected (the reply does not use *Return Address* [159]). Fifth, the reply's correlation ID is the same as the request's message ID (the reply does use *Correlation Identifier* [163]).

Finally, back in the first window, the requestor received the following reply:

```
Received reply
     Time:       1048261797060 ms
     Message ID: ID:_XYZ123_1048261758148_5.2.1.1
     Correl. ID: ID:_XYZ123_1048261766139_6.2.1.1
     Reply to:   null
     Contents:   Hello world.
```

This output contains several items of interest. The reply was received after it was sent (30210 ms). The message ID of the reply was the same when it was received as when it was sent, which proves that it is indeed the same message. The message contents received are the same as those sent, and the correlation ID tells the requestor which request this reply is for (*Correlation Identifier* [163]).

Notice too that the requestor is designed to simply send a request, receive a reply, and exit. So, having received the reply, the requestor is no longer running. The replier, on the other hand, doesn't know when it might receive a request, so it never stops running. To stop it, we go to its command shell window and press the return key, which causes the replier program to exit.

So, that's the JMS request-reply example. A request was prepared and sent by the requestor. The replier received the request and sent a reply. Then, the requestor received the reply to its original request.

JMS Request-Reply Example

Request-Reply Code

First, let's take a look at how the requestor is implemented:

```
import javax.jms.Connection;
import javax.jms.Destination;
import javax.jms.JMSException;
import javax.jms.Message;
import javax.jms.MessageConsumer;
import javax.jms.MessageProducer;
import javax.jms.Session;
import javax.jms.TextMessage;
import javax.naming.NamingException;
```

```java
public class Requestor {

    private Session session;
    private Destination replyQueue;
    private MessageProducer requestProducer;
    private MessageConsumer replyConsumer;
    private MessageProducer invalidProducer;

    protected Requestor() {
        super();
    }

    public static Requestor newRequestor(Connection connection, String requestQueueName,
        String replyQueueName, String invalidQueueName)
        throws JMSException, NamingException {

        Requestor requestor = new Requestor();
        requestor.initialize(connection, requestQueueName, replyQueueName, invalidQueueName);
        return requestor;
    }

    protected void initialize(Connection connection, String requestQueueName,
        String replyQueueName, String invalidQueueName)
        throws NamingException, JMSException {

        session = connection.createSession(false, Session.AUTO_ACKNOWLEDGE);

        Destination requestQueue = JndiUtil.getDestination(requestQueueName);
        replyQueue = JndiUtil.getDestination(replyQueueName);
        Destination invalidQueue = JndiUtil.getDestination(invalidQueueName);

        requestProducer = session.createProducer(requestQueue);
        replyConsumer = session.createConsumer(replyQueue);
        invalidProducer = session.createProducer(invalidQueue);
    }

    public void send() throws JMSException {
        TextMessage requestMessage = session.createTextMessage();
        requestMessage.setText("Hello world.");
        requestMessage.setJMSReplyTo(replyQueue);
        requestProducer.send(requestMessage);
        System.out.println("Sent request");
        System.out.println("\tTime:        " + System.currentTimeMillis() + " ms");
        System.out.println("\tMessage ID:  " + requestMessage.getJMSMessageID());
        System.out.println("\tCorrel. ID:  " + requestMessage.getJMSCorrelationID());
        System.out.println("\tReply to:    " + requestMessage.getJMSReplyTo());
        System.out.println("\tContents:    " + requestMessage.getText());
    }

    public void receiveSync() throws JMSException {
        Message msg = replyConsumer.receive();
        if (msg instanceof TextMessage) {
            TextMessage replyMessage = (TextMessage) msg;
```

```
                System.out.println("Received reply ");
                System.out.println("\tTime:       " + System.currentTimeMillis() + " ms");
                System.out.println("\tMessage ID: " + replyMessage.getJMSMessageID());
                System.out.println("\tCorrel. ID: " + replyMessage.getJMSCorrelationID());
                System.out.println("\tReply to:   " + replyMessage.getJMSReplyTo());
                System.out.println("\tContents:   " + replyMessage.getText());
        } else {
                System.out.println("Invalid message detected");
                System.out.println("\tType:       " + msg.getClass().getName());
                System.out.println("\tTime:       " + System.currentTimeMillis() + " ms");
                System.out.println("\tMessage ID: " + msg.getJMSMessageID());
                System.out.println("\tCorrel. ID: " + msg.getJMSCorrelationID());
                System.out.println("\tReply to:   " + msg.getJMSReplyTo());

                msg.setJMSCorrelationID(msg.getJMSMessageID());
                invalidProducer.send(msg);

                System.out.println("Sent to invalid message queue");
                System.out.println("\tType:       " + msg.getClass().getName());
                System.out.println("\tTime:       " + System.currentTimeMillis() + " ms");
                System.out.println("\tMessage ID: " + msg.getJMSMessageID());
                System.out.println("\tCorrel. ID: " + msg.getJMSCorrelationID());
                System.out.println("\tReply to:   " + msg.getJMSReplyTo());
        }
    }
}
```

An application that wants to send requests and receive replies could use a requestor to do so. The application provides its requestor a connection to the messaging system. It also specifies the JNDI names of three queues: the request queue, the reply queue, and the invalid message queue. This is the information the requestor needs to initialize itself.

In the initialize method, the requestor uses the connection and queue names to connect to the messaging system.

- It uses the connection to create a session. An application needs only one connection to a messaging system, but each component in the application that wishes to send and receive messages independently needs its own session. Two threads cannot share a single session; they should each use a different session so that the sessions will work properly.

- It uses the queue names to look up the queues, which are Destinations. The names are JNDI identifiers; JndiUtil performs the JNDI lookups.

- It creates a MessageProducer for sending messages on the request queue, a MessageConsumer for receiving messages from the reply queue, and another producer for moving messages to the invalid message queue.

One thing that the requestor must be able to do is send request messages. For that, it implements the send() method.

- It creates a TextMessage and sets its contents to "Hello world."

- It sets the message's reply-to property to be the reply queue. This is a *Return Address* (159) that will tell the replier how to send back the reply.

- It uses the requestProducer to send the message. The producer is connected to the request queue, so that's the queue the message is sent on.

- It then prints out the details of the message it just sent. This is done after the message is sent because the message ID is set by the messaging system and is not set until the message is actually sent.

The other thing the requestor must be able to do is receive reply messages. It implements the receiveSync() method for this purpose.

JMS Request-Reply Example

- It uses its replyConsumer to receive the reply. The consumer is connected to the reply queue, so it will receive messages from there. It uses the receive() method to get the message, which synchronously blocks until a message is delivered to the queue and is read from the queue, so the requestor is a *Polling Consumer* (494). Because this receive is synchronous, the requestor's method is called receiveSync().

- The message should be a TextMessage. If so, the requestor gets the message's contents and prints out the message's details.

- If the message is not a TextMessage, then the message cannot be processed. Rather than just discarding the message, the requestor resends it to the invalid message queue. Resending the message will change its message ID, so before resending it, the requestor stores its original message ID in its correlation ID (see *Correlation Identifier* [163]).

In this way, a requestor does everything necessary to send a request, receive a reply, and route the reply to a special queue if the message does not make any sense. (Note: JMS provides a special class, QueueRequestor, whose purpose is to implement a requestor that receives replies just as we have here. We implemented the code ourselves rather than using a prebuilt JMS class so that we could show you how the code works.)

Next, let's take a look at how the replier is implemented.

```java
import javax.jms.Connection;
import javax.jms.Destination;
import javax.jms.JMSException;
import javax.jms.Message;
import javax.jms.MessageConsumer;
import javax.jms.MessageListener;
import javax.jms.MessageProducer;
import javax.jms.Session;
import javax.jms.TextMessage;
import javax.naming.NamingException;

public class Replier implements MessageListener {

    private Session session;
    private MessageProducer invalidProducer;

    protected Replier() {
        super();
    }

    public static Replier newReplier(Connection connection,
      String requestQueueName, String invalidQueueName)
        throws JMSException, NamingException {

        Replier replier = new Replier();
        replier.initialize(connection, requestQueueName, invalidQueueName);
        return replier;
    }

    protected void initialize(Connection connection, String requestQueueName,
    String invalidQueueName)
        throws NamingException, JMSException {

        session = connection.createSession(false, Session.AUTO_ACKNOWLEDGE);
        Destination requestQueue = JndiUtil.getDestination(requestQueueName);
        Destination invalidQueue = JndiUtil.getDestination(invalidQueueName);

        MessageConsumer requestConsumer = session.createConsumer(requestQueue);
        MessageListener listener = this;
        requestConsumer.setMessageListener(listener);

        invalidProducer = session.createProducer(invalidQueue);
    }

    public void onMessage(Message message) {
        try {
            if ((message instanceof TextMessage) && (message.getJMSReplyTo() != null)) {
                TextMessage requestMessage = (TextMessage) message;
```

```
            System.out.println("Received request");
            System.out.println("\tTime:       " + System.currentTimeMillis() + " ms");
            System.out.println("\tMessage ID: " + requestMessage.getJMSMessageID());
            System.out.println("\tCorrel. ID: " + requestMessage.getJMSCorrelationID());
            System.out.println("\tReply to:   " + requestMessage.getJMSReplyTo());
            System.out.println("\tContents:   " + requestMessage.getText());

            String contents = requestMessage.getText();
            Destination replyDestination = message.getJMSReplyTo();
            MessageProducer replyProducer = session.createProducer(replyDestination);

            TextMessage replyMessage = session.createTextMessage();
            replyMessage.setText(contents);
            replyMessage.setJMSCorrelationID(requestMessage.getJMSMessageID());
            replyProducer.send(replyMessage);

            System.out.println("Sent reply");
            System.out.println("\tTime:       " + System.currentTimeMillis() + " ms");
            System.out.println("\tMessage ID: " + replyMessage.getJMSMessageID());
            System.out.println("\tCorrel. ID: " + replyMessage.getJMSCorrelationID());
            System.out.println("\tReply to:   " + replyMessage.getJMSReplyTo());
            System.out.println("\tContents:   " + replyMessage.getText());
        } else {
            System.out.println("Invalid message detected");
            System.out.println("\tType:       " + message.getClass().getName());
            System.out.println("\tTime:       " + System.currentTimeMillis() + " ms");
            System.out.println("\tMessage ID: " + message.getJMSMessageID());
            System.out.println("\tCorrel. ID: " + message.getJMSCorrelationID());
            System.out.println("\tReply to:   " + message.getJMSReplyTo());

            message.setJMSCorrelationID(message.getJMSMessageID());
            invalidProducer.send(message);

            System.out.println("Sent to invalid message queue");
            System.out.println("\tType:       " + message.getClass().getName());
            System.out.println("\tTime:       " + System.currentTimeMillis() + " ms");
            System.out.println("\tMessage ID: " + message.getJMSMessageID());
            System.out.println("\tCorrel. ID: " + message.getJMSCorrelationID());
            System.out.println("\tReply to:   " + message.getJMSReplyTo());
        }
    } catch (JMSException e) {
        e.printStackTrace();
    }
  }
}
```

A replier is what an application might use to receive a request and send a reply. The application provides its requestor a connection to the messaging system, as well as the JNDI names of the request and invalid message queues. (It does not need to specify the name of the reply queue because, as we'll see, that will be provided by the message's *Return Address* [159].) This is the information the requestor needs to initialize itself.

The replier's `initialize` code is pretty similar to the requestor's, but there are a couple of differences.

- The replier does not look up the reply queue and create a producer for it. This is because the replier does not assume it will always send replies on that queue; rather, as we'll see later, it will let the request message tell it what queue to send the reply message on.

- The replier is an *Event-Driven Consumer* (498), so it implements `Message-Listener`. When a message is delivered to the request queue, the messaging system will automatically call the replier's `onMessage` method.

Once the replier has initialized itself to be a listener on the request queue, there's not much for it to do but wait for messages. Unlike the requestor, which has to explicitly check the reply queue for messages, the replier is event-driven and so does nothing until the messaging system calls its `onMessage` method with a new message. The message will be from the request queue because `initialize` created the consumer on the request queue. Once `onMessage` receives a new message, it processes the message like this.

- As with the requestor processing a reply message, the request message is supposed to be a `TextMessage`. It is also supposed to specify the queue on which to send the reply. If the message does not meet these requirements, the replier will move the message to the invalid message queue (same as the requestor).

- If the message meets the requirements, the replier implements its part of *Return Address* (159). Remember that the requestor set the request message's `reply-to` property to specify the reply queue. The replier now gets that property's value and uses it to create a `MessageProducer` on the proper queue. The important part here is that the replier is not hard-coded to use a particular reply queue; it uses whatever reply queue each particular request message specifies.

- The replier then creates the reply message. In doing so, it implements *Correlation Identifier* (163) by setting the reply message's `correlation-id` property to the same value as the request message's `message-id` property.

- The replier then sends out the reply message and displays its details.

Thus, a replier does everything necessary to receive a message (presumably a request) and send a reply.

Invalid Message Example

While we're at it, let's look at an example of *Invalid Message Channel* (115). Remember, one of the queues we need is the one named jms/InvalidMessages. This exists so that if a JMS client (a *Message Endpoint* [95]) receives a message it cannot process, it can move the strange message to a special channel.

To demonstrate invalid message handling, we have designed an InvalidMessenger class. This object is specifically designed to send a message on the request channel whose format is incorrect. The request channel is a *Datatype Channel* (111) in that the request receivers expect the requests to be in a certain format. The invalid messenger simply sends a message in a different format; when the replier receives the message, it does not recognize the message's format, so it moves the message to the invalid message queue.

We'll run the replier in one window and the invalid messenger in another window. When the invalid messenger sends its message, it displays output like this:

```
Sent invalid message
        Type:       com.sun.jms.ObjectMessageImpl
        Time:       1048288516959 ms
        Message ID: ID:_XYZ123_1048288516639_7.2.1.1
        Correl. ID: null
        Reply to:   com.sun.jms.Queue: jms/ReplyQueue
```

This shows that the message is an instance of ObjectMessage (whereas the replier is expecting a TextMessage). The replier receives the invalid message and resends it to the invalid message queue.

```
Invalid message detected
        Type:       com.sun.jms.ObjectMessageImpl
        Time:       1048288517049 ms
        Message ID: ID:_XYZ123_1048288516639_7.2.1.1
        Correl. ID: null
        Reply to:   com.sun.jms.Queue: jms/ReplyQueue
Sent to invalid message queue
        Type:       com.sun.jms.ObjectMessageImpl
        Time:       1048288517140 ms
        Message ID: ID:_XYZ123_1048287020267_6.2.1.2
        Correl. ID: ID:_XYZ123_1048288516639_7.2.1.1
        Reply to:   com.sun.jms.Queue: jms/ReplyQueue
```

One insight worth noting is that when the message is moved to the invalid message queue, it is actually being resent, so it gets a new message ID. Because of this, we apply *Correlation Identifier* (163); once the replier determines the message to be invalid, it copies the message's main ID to its correlation ID to preserve a record of the message's original ID. The code that handles this invalid-message processing is in the Replier class, shown earlier, in the onMessage method. Requestor.receiveSync() contains similar invalid-message processing code.

Conclusions

We've seen how to implement two classes, Requestor and Replier (*Message Endpoint*s [95]), that exchange request and reply *Messages* (66) using *Request-Reply* (154). The request message uses a *Return Address* (159) to specify what queue to send the reply on. The reply message uses a *Correlation Identifier* (163) to specify which request this is a reply for. The requestor implements a *Polling Consumer* (494) to receive replies, whereas the replier implements an *Event-Driven Consumer* (498) to receive requests. The request and reply queues are *Datatype Channels* (111); when a consumer receives a message that is not of the right type, it reroutes the message to the *Invalid Message Channel* (115).

JMS
Request-
Reply
Example

.NET Request-Reply Example

This is a simple example of how to use messaging, implemented in .NET [SysMsg] and C#. It shows how to implement *Request-Reply* (154), where a requestor application sends a request, a replier application receives the request and returns a reply, and the requestor receives the reply. It also shows how an invalid message will be rerouted to a special channel.

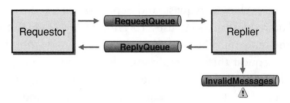

Components of the Request-Reply Example

This example was developed using the Microsoft .NET Framework SDK and run on a Windows XP computer with MSMQ [MSMQ] installed.

Request-Reply Example

This example consists of two main classes.

1. **Requestor**—A *Message Endpoint* (95) that sends a request message and waits to receive a reply message as a response.

2. **Replier**—A *Message Endpoint* (95) that waits to receive the request message; when it does, it responds by sending the reply message.

The requestor and the replier will each run as a separate .NET program, which is what makes the communication distributed.

This example assumes that the messaging system has these three queues defined:

1. **.\private$\RequestQueue**—The MessageQueue the requestor uses to send the request message to the replier.

2. **.\private$\ReplyQueue**—The MessageQueue the replier uses to send the reply message to the requestor.

3. **.\private$\InvalidQueue**—The MessageQueue to which the requestor and the replier move a message when they receive a message they cannot interpret.

Here's how the example works. When the requestor is started in a command-line window, it starts and prints output like this:

```
Sent request
      Time:        09:11:09.165342
      Message ID: 8b0fc389-f21f-423b-9eaa-c3a881a34808\149
      Correl. ID:
      Reply to:    .\private$\ReplyQueue
      Contents:    Hello world.
```

This shows that the requestor has sent a request message. Notice that this works even though the replier isn't even running and therefore cannot receive the request.

When the replier is started in another command-line window, it starts and prints output like this:

```
Received request
      Time:        09:11:09.375644
      Message ID: 8b0fc389-f21f-423b-9eaa-c3a881a34808\149
      Correl. ID: <n/a>
      Reply to:    FORMATNAME:DIRECT=OS:XYZ123\private$\ReplyQueue
      Contents:    Hello world.
Sent reply
      Time:        09:11:09.956480
      Message ID: 8b0fc389-f21f-423b-9eaa-c3a881a34808\150
      Correl. ID: 8b0fc389-f21f-423b-9eaa-c3a881a34808\149
      Reply to:    <n/a>
      Contents:    Hello world.
```

This shows that the replier received the request message and sent a reply message.

There are several interesting items in this output. First, notice the request sent and received timestamps; the request was received after it was sent (210302 microseconds later). Second, notice that the message ID is the same in both cases, because it's the same message. Third, notice that the contents, Hello world, are the same, which makes sense because that's the data that was sent, and it must be the same on both sides. Fourth, the request message specifies the queue that is the destination for the reply message (an example of *Return Address* [159]).

Next, let's compare the output from receiving the request to that for sending the reply. First, notice the reply was not sent until after the request was received (580836 microseconds after). Second, the message ID for the reply is different from that for the request; this is because the request and reply messages are different, separate messages. Third, the contents of the request have been extracted and added to the reply. Fourth, the reply-to destination is unspecified because no reply is expected (the reply does not use *Return Address* [159]).

Fifth, the reply's correlation ID is the same as the request's message ID (the reply does use *Correlation Identifier* [163]).

Finally, back in the first window, the requestor received the following reply:

```
Received reply
        Time:      09:11:10.156467
        Message ID: 8b0fc389-f21f-423b-9eaa-c3a881a34808\150
        Correl. ID: 8b0fc389-f21f-423b-9eaa-c3a881a34808\149
        Reply to:  <n/a>
        Contents:  Hello world.
```

This output contains several items of interest. The reply was received about two-tenths of a second after it was sent. The message ID of the reply was the same when it was received as when it was sent, which proves that it is indeed the same message. The message contents received are the same as those sent, and the correlation ID tells the requestor which request this reply is for (*Correlation Identifier* [163]).

The requestor doesn't run for very long; it sends a request, receives a reply, and exits. However, the replier runs continuously, waiting for requests and sending replies. To stop the replier, we go to its command shell window and press the return key, which causes the replier program to exit.

So, that's the .NET request-reply example. A request was prepared and sent by the requestor. The replier received the request and sent a reply. Then, the requestor received the reply to its original request.

Request-Reply Code

First, let's take a look at how the requestor is implemented.

```
using System;
using System.Messaging;

public class Requestor
{
    private MessageQueue requestQueue;
    private MessageQueue replyQueue;

    public Requestor(String requestQueueName, String replyQueueName)
    {
        requestQueue = new MessageQueue(requestQueueName);
        replyQueue = new MessageQueue(replyQueueName);

        replyQueue.MessageReadPropertyFilter.SetAll();
        ((XmlMessageFormatter)replyQueue.Formatter).TargetTypeNames =
          new string[]{"System.String,mscorlib"};
    }
```

```
public void Send()
{
    Message requestMessage = new Message();
    requestMessage.Body = "Hello world.";
    requestMessage.ResponseQueue = replyQueue;
    requestQueue.Send(requestMessage);


    Console.WriteLine("Sent request");
    Console.WriteLine("\tTime:      {0}", DateTime.Now.ToString("HH:mm:ss.ffffff"));
    Console.WriteLine("\tMessage ID: {0}", requestMessage.Id);
    Console.WriteLine("\tCorrel. ID: {0}", requestMessage.CorrelationId);
    Console.WriteLine("\tReply to:   {0}", requestMessage.ResponseQueue.Path);
    Console.WriteLine("\tContents:   {0}", requestMessage.Body.ToString());
}


public void ReceiveSync()
{
    Message replyMessage = replyQueue.Receive();


    Console.WriteLine("Received reply");
    Console.WriteLine("\tTime:      {0}", DateTime.Now.ToString("HH:mm:ss.ffffff"));
    Console.WriteLine("\tMessage ID: {0}", replyMessage.Id);
    Console.WriteLine("\tCorrel. ID: {0}", replyMessage.CorrelationId);
    Console.WriteLine("\tReply to:   {0}", "<n/a>");
    Console.WriteLine("\tContents:   {0}", replyMessage.Body.ToString());
}
}
```

An application that wants to send requests and receive replies could use a requestor to do so. The application specifies the pathnames of two queues: the request queue and the reply queue. This is the information the requestor needs to initialize itself.

In the requestor constructor, the requestor uses the queue names to connect to the messaging system.

- It uses the queue names to look up the queues, which are MessageQueues. The names are pathnames to MSMQ resources.

- It sets the reply queue's property filter so that when a message is read from the queue, all of the message's properties will be read as well. It also sets the formatter's TargetTypeNames so that the message contents will be interpreted as strings.

One thing that the requestor must be able to do is send request messages. For that, it implements the Send() method.

- It creates a message and sets its contents to "Hello world."

- It sets the message's ResponseQueue property to be the reply queue. This is a *Return Address* (159) that will tell the replier how to send back the reply.

- It then sends the message to the queue.

- It then prints out the details of the message it just sent. This is done after the message is sent because the message ID is set by the messaging system and is not set until the message is actually sent.

The other thing the requestor must be able to do is receive reply messages. It implements the ReceiveSync() method for this purpose.

- It runs the queue's Receive() method to get the message, which synchronously blocks until a message is delivered to the queue and is read from the queue, so the requestor is a *Polling Consumer* (494). Because this receive is synchronous, the requestor's method is called ReceiveSync().

- The requestor gets the message's contents and prints out the message's details.

In this way, a requestor does everything necessary to send a request and receive a reply.

Next, let's take a look at how the replier is implemented.

```
using System;
using System.Messaging;

class Replier {

    private MessageQueue invalidQueue;

    public Replier(String requestQueueName, String invalidQueueName)
    {
        MessageQueue requestQueue = new MessageQueue(requestQueueName);
        invalidQueue = new MessageQueue(invalidQueueName);

        requestQueue.MessageReadPropertyFilter.SetAll();
        ((XmlMessageFormatter)requestQueue.Formatter).TargetTypeNames =
          new string[]{"System.String,mscorlib"};

        requestQueue.ReceiveCompleted += new ReceiveCompletedEventHandler(OnReceiveCompleted);
        requestQueue.BeginReceive();
    }
```

```
public void OnReceiveCompleted(Object source, ReceiveCompletedEventArgs asyncResult)
{
    MessageQueue requestQueue = (MessageQueue)source;
    Message requestMessage = requestQueue.EndReceive(asyncResult.AsyncResult);

    try
    {
        Console.WriteLine("Received request");
        Console.WriteLine("\tTime:       {0}", DateTime.Now.ToString("HH:mm:ss.ffffff"));
        Console.WriteLine("\tMessage ID: {0}", requestMessage.Id);
        Console.WriteLine("\tCorrel. ID: {0}", "<n/a>");
        Console.WriteLine("\tReply to:   {0}", requestMessage.ResponseQueue.Path);
        Console.WriteLine("\tContents:   {0}", requestMessage.Body.ToString());

        string contents = requestMessage.Body.ToString();
        MessageQueue replyQueue = requestMessage.ResponseQueue;
        Message replyMessage = new Message();
        replyMessage.Body = contents;
        replyMessage.CorrelationId = requestMessage.Id;
        replyQueue.Send(replyMessage);

        Console.WriteLine("Sent reply");
        Console.WriteLine("\tTime:       {0}", DateTime.Now.ToString("HH:mm:ss.ffffff"));
        Console.WriteLine("\tMessage ID: {0}", replyMessage.Id);
        Console.WriteLine("\tCorrel. ID: {0}", replyMessage.CorrelationId);
        Console.WriteLine("\tReply to:   {0}", "<n/a>");
        Console.WriteLine("\tContents:   {0}", replyMessage.Body.ToString());
    }
    catch ( Exception ) {
        Console.WriteLine("Invalid message detected");
        Console.WriteLine("\tType:       {0}", requestMessage.BodyType);
        Console.WriteLine("\tTime:       {0}", DateTime.Now.ToString("HH:mm:ss.ffffff"));
        Console.WriteLine("\tMessage ID: {0}", requestMessage.Id);
        Console.WriteLine("\tCorrel. ID: {0}", "<n/a>");
        Console.WriteLine("\tReply to:   {0}", "<n/a>");

        requestMessage.CorrelationId = requestMessage.Id;

        invalidQueue.Send(requestMessage);

        Console.WriteLine("Sent to invalid message queue");
        Console.WriteLine("\tType:       {0}", requestMessage.BodyType);
        Console.WriteLine("\tTime:       {0}", DateTime.Now.ToString("HH:mm:ss.ffffff"));
        Console.WriteLine("\tMessage ID: {0}", requestMessage.Id);
        Console.WriteLine("\tCorrel. ID: {0}", requestMessage.CorrelationId);
        Console.WriteLine("\tReply to:   {0}", requestMessage.ResponseQueue.Path);
    }

    requestQueue.BeginReceive();
}
}
```

.NET
Request-
Reply
Example

When an application needs to receive a request and send a reply, it will implement something like this replier. The application specifies the pathnames of the request and invalid message queues. (It does not need to specify the name of the reply queue because, as we'll see later, that will be provided by the message's *Return Address* [159].) This is the information the requestor needs to initialize itself.

The replier constructor is pretty similar to the requestor's, but there are a couple of differences.

- One difference is that the replier does not look up the reply queue. This is because the replier does not assume it will always send replies on that queue; rather, as we'll see, it will let the request message tell it what queue to send the reply message on.

- Another difference is that the replier is an *Event-Driven Consumer* (498), so it sets up a ReceiveCompletedEventHandler. When a message is delivered to the request queue, the messaging system will automatically call the specified method, OnReceiveCompleted.

The replier initializes itself as a listener on the request queue, and then simply waits for messages to arrive. Unlike the requestor, which has to explicitly check the reply queue for messages, the replier is event-driven and so does nothing until the messaging system calls its OnReceiveCompleted method with a new message. The message will be from the request queue because the constructor created the event handler on the request queue. Once OnReceiveCompleted is called, this is what it does to get the new message and processes it:

- The source is a MessageQueue, the request queue.

- The message itself is obtained by running the queue's EndReceive method. The replier then prints out the details about the message.

- The replier implements its part of *Return Address* (159). Remember that the requestor set the request message's response-queue property to specify the reply queue. The replier now gets that property's value and uses it to reference the proper MessageQueue. The important part here is that the replier is not hard-coded to use a particular reply queue; it uses whatever reply queue each particular request message specifies.

- The replier then creates the reply message. In doing so, it implements *Correlation Identifier* (163) by setting the reply message's correlation-id property to the same value as the request message's message-id property.

- The replier then sends out the reply message and displays its details.

- If the message can be received but not successfully processed and an exception is thrown, the replier resends the message to the invalid message queue. In the process, it sets the new message's correlation ID to the original message's message ID.

- Once the replier has finished processing the message, it runs BeginReceive to start listening for the next message.

Thus, a replier does everything necessary to receive a message (presumably a request) and send a reply. If it cannot reply to a message, it routes the message to the invalid message queue.

Invalid Message Example

Let's now look at an example of *Invalid Message Channel* (115). Remember, one of the queues we need is the one named private$\InvalidMessages. This exists so that if an MSMQ client (a *Message Endpoint* [95]) receives a message it cannot process, it can move the strange message to a special channel.

.NET
Request-
Reply
Example

To demonstrate invalid message handling, we have designed an InvalidMessenger class. This object is specifically designed to send a message on the request channel whose format is incorrect. Like any channel, the request channel is a *Datatype Channel* (111) in that the request receivers expect the requests to be in a certain format. The invalid messenger simply sends a message in a different format; when the replier receives the message, it does not recognize the message's format, so it moves the message to the invalid message queue.

We'll run the replier in one window and the invalid messenger in another window. When the invalid messenger sends its message, it displays output like this:

```
Sent request
    Type:       768
    Time:       09:39:44.223729
    Message ID: 8b0fc389-f21f-423b-9eaa-c3a881a34808\168
    Correl. ID: 00000000-0000-0000-0000-000000000000\0
    Reply to:   .\private$\ReplyQueue
```

Type 768 means that the format of the message contents is binary (whereas the replier is expecting the contents to be text/XML). The replier receives the invalid message and resends it to the invalid message queue.

```
Invalid message detected
        Type:       768
        Time:       09:39:44.233744
        Message ID: 8b0fc389-f21f-423b-9eaa-c3a881a34808\168
        Correl. ID: <n/a>
        Reply to:   <n/a>
Sent to invalid message queue
        Type:       768
        Time:       09:39:44.233744
        Message ID: 8b0fc389-f21f-423b-9eaa-c3a881a34808\169
        Correl. ID: 8b0fc389-f21f-423b-9eaa-c3a881a34808\168
        Reply to:   FORMATNAME:DIRECT=OS:XYZ123\private$\ReplyQueue
```

One insight worth noting is that when the message is moved to the invalid message queue, it is actually being resent, so it gets a new message ID. Because of this, we apply *Correlation Identifier* (163); once the replier determines the message to be invalid, it copies the message's main ID to its correlation ID so as to preserve a record of the message's original ID. The code that handles this invalid-message processing is in the Replier class, shown earlier, in the OnReceive-Completed method.

.NET Request-Reply Example

Conclusions

We've seen how to implement two classes, Requestor and Replier (*Message Endpoints* [159]), that exchange a request and reply *Messages* (66) using *Request-Reply* (154). The request message uses a *Return Address* (159) to specify what queue to send the reply on. The reply message uses a *Correlation Identifier* (163) to specify which request this is a reply for. The requestor implements a *Polling Consumer* (494) to receive replies, whereas the replier implements an *Event-Driven Consumer* (498) to receive requests. The request and reply queues are *Datatype Channels* (111); when a consumer receives a message that is not of the right type, it reroutes the message to the *Invalid Message Channel* (115).

JMS Publish-Subscribe Example

This is a simple example that shows the power of publish-subscribe messaging and explores the alternative designs available. It shows how multiple subscriber applications can all be informed of a single event by publishing the event just once and considers alternative strategies for how to communicate details of that event to the subscribers.

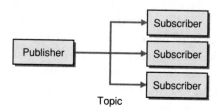

Publish-Subscribe Using a JMS Topic

To understand how helpful a simple *Publish-Subscribe Channel* (106) really is, we first need to consider what it is like to implement the *Observer* pattern in a distributed fashion among multiple applications. Before we get to that, let's review the basics of *Observer*.

The Observer Pattern

The *Observer* pattern [GoF] documents a design through which an object can notify its dependents of a change, while keeping that object decoupled from its dependents so that the object works just fine no matter how many dependents it has, even if it has none at all. Its participants are a Subject—the object announcing changes in its state—and Observers—objects interested in receiving notification of changes in the Subject. When a subject's state changes, it calls its Notify() method, whose implementation knows the list of observers and calls Update() on each of them. Some observers may not be interested in this state change, but those that are can find out what the new state is by calling GetState() on the subject. The subject must also implement Attach(Observer) and Detach(Observer) methods that the observers use to register interest.

Observer provides two ways to get the new state from the subject to the observer: the push model and the pull model. With the *push model*, the Update call to each observer contains the new state as a parameter. Thus, interested observers can avoid having to call GetState(), but effort is wasted passing data to uninterested observers. The opposite approach is the *pull model*, where the subject sends basic notification and each observer requests the new state from the subject. Thus, each observer can request the exact details it wants, even none at all, but the subject often has to serve multiple requests for the same data. The push model requires a single, one-way communication—the subject pushes the data to an observer as part of the update. The pull model requires three one-way communications—the subject notifies an observer, the observer requests the current state from the subject, and the subject sends the current state to the observer. As we'll see, the number of one-way communications affects both the design-time complexity and the runtime performance of the notification.

The easiest way to implement a subject's Notify() method is with a single thread, but that can have undesirable performance implications. A single thread will update each observer one at a time, in sequence, so those at the end of a long list of observers may need to wait a long time for updates. Also, a subject that spends a long time updating all of its observers isn't accomplishing anything else. Even worse, an observer may well use its update thread to react to the update by querying the subject for state and processing the new data; such observer work in the update thread makes the update process take even longer.

Thus, the more sophisticated way to implement a subject's Notify() method is to run each Update() call in its own thread. Then, all observers can be updated concurrently, and whatever work each may do in its update thread does not delay the other observers or the subject. The downside is that implementing multithreading and handling thread-management issues is more complex.

JMS Publish-Subscribe Example

Distributed Observer

The *Observer* pattern tends to assume that the subject and its observers all run in the same application. The pattern's design supports distribution, where the observers run in a separate memory space from the subject and perhaps from each other, but the distribution takes work. The Update() and GetState() methods, as well as the Attach and Detach methods, must be made remotely accessible (see *Remote Procedure Invocation* [50]). Because the subject must be able to call each observer, and vice versa, each object must be running in some type of object request broker (ORB) environment that allows the objects it contains to be invoked remotely. Because the update details and state data will be passed between memory spaces, the applications must be able to serialize, that is, marshal the objects they are passing.

Thus, implementing *Observer* in a distributed environment can get rather complex. Not only is a multithreaded *Observer* somewhat difficult to implement, but making methods remotely accessible—and invoking them remotely—adds more difficulty. It can be a lot of work just to notify some dependents of state changes.

Another problem is that a *Remote Procedure Invocation* (50) only works when the source of the call, the target, and the network connecting them are all working properly. If a subject announces a change and a remote observer is not ready to process the notification or is disconnected from the network, the observer loses the notification. While the observer may work fine without the notification in some cases, in other cases the lost notification may cause the observer to get out of sync with the subject—the very problem the *Observer* pattern is designed to prevent.

Distribution also favors the push model over the pull model. As discussed earlier, push requires a single, one-way communication, whereas pull requires three. When the distribution is implemented via RPCs (Remote Procedure Calls), push requires one call (`Update()`), whereas pull requires at least two calls (`Update()` and `GetState()`). RPCs have more overhead than nondistributed method invocations, so the extra calls required by the push approach can quickly hurt performance.

Publish-Subscribe

A *Publish-Subscribe Channel* (106) implements the *Observer* pattern, making the pattern much easier to use among distributed applications. The pattern is implemented in three steps.

1. The messaging system administrator creates a *Publish-Subscribe Channel* (106). (This will be represented in Java applications as a JMS `Topic`.)

2. The application acting as the subject creates a `TopicPublisher` (a type of `MessageProducer`) to send messages on the channel.

3. Each of the applications acting as an observer (e.g., a dependent) creates a `TopicSubscriber` (a type of `MessageConsumer`) to receive messages on the channel. (This is analogous to calling the `Attach(Observer)` method in the *Observer* pattern.)

This establishes a connection between the subject and the observers through the channel. Now, whenever the subject has a change to announce, it does so by sending a message. The channel will ensure that each of the observers receives a copy of this message.

Here is a simple example of the code needed to announce the change:

```java
import javax.jms.Connection;
import javax.jms.ConnectionFactory;
import javax.jms.Destination;
import javax.jms.JMSException;
import javax.jms.MessageProducer;
import javax.jms.Session;
import javax.jms.TextMessage;
import javax.naming.NamingException;

public class SubjectGateway {

    public static final String UPDATE_TOPIC_NAME = "jms/Update";
    private Connection connection;
    private Session session;
    private MessageProducer updateProducer;

    protected SubjectGateway() {
        super();
    }

    public static SubjectGateway newGateway() throws JMSException, NamingException {
        SubjectGateway gateway = new SubjectGateway();
        gateway.initialize();
        return gateway;
    }

    protected void initialize() throws JMSException, NamingException {
        ConnectionFactory connectionFactory = JndiUtil.getQueueConnectionFactory();
        connection = connectionFactory.createConnection();
        session = connection.createSession(false, Session.AUTO_ACKNOWLEDGE);
        Destination updateTopic = JndiUtil.getDestination(UPDATE_TOPIC_NAME);
        updateProducer = session.createProducer(updateTopic);

        connection.start();
    }

    public void notify(String state) throws JMSException {
        TextMessage message = session.createTextMessage(state);
        updateProducer.send(message);
    }

    public void release() throws JMSException {
        if (connection != null) {
            connection.stop();
            connection.close();
        }
    }
}
```

JMS
Publish-
Subscribe
Example

SubjectGateway is a *Messaging Gateway* (468) between the subject (not shown) and the messaging system. The subject creates the gateway and then uses it to broadcast notifications. Essentially, the subject's Notify() method is implemented to call SubjectGateway.notify(String). The gateway then announces the change by sending a message on the update channel.

Here is an example of the code needed to receive the change notification:

```
import javax.jms.Connection;
import javax.jms.ConnectionFactory;
import javax.jms.Destination;
import javax.jms.JMSException;
import javax.jms.Message;
import javax.jms.MessageConsumer;
import javax.jms.MessageListener;
import javax.jms.Session;
import javax.jms.TextMessage;
import javax.naming.NamingException;

public class ObserverGateway implements MessageListener {

    public static final String UPDATE_TOPIC_NAME = "jms/Update";
    private Observer observer;
    private Connection connection;
    private MessageConsumer updateConsumer;

    protected ObserverGateway() {
        super();
    }

    public static ObserverGateway newGateway(Observer observer)
        throws JMSException, NamingException {
        ObserverGateway gateway = new ObserverGateway();
        gateway.initialize(observer);
        return gateway;
    }

    protected void initialize(Observer observer) throws JMSException, NamingException {
        this.observer = observer;

        ConnectionFactory connectionFactory = JndiUtil.getQueueConnectionFactory();
        connection = connectionFactory.createConnection();
        Session session = connection.createSession(false, Session.AUTO_ACKNOWLEDGE);
        Destination updateTopic = JndiUtil.getDestination(UPDATE_TOPIC_NAME);
        updateConsumer = session.createConsumer(updateTopic);
        updateConsumer.setMessageListener(this);
    }
```

```java
public void onMessage(Message message) {
    try {
        TextMessage textMsg = (TextMessage) message; // assume cast always works
        String newState = textMsg.getText();
        update(newState);
    } catch (JMSException e) {
        e.printStackTrace();
    }
}

public void attach() throws JMSException {
    connection.start();
}

public void detach() throws JMSException {
    if (connection != null) {
        connection.stop();
        connection.close();
    }
}

private void update(String newState) throws JMSException {
    observer.update(newState);
}
}
```

JMS Publish-Subscribe Example

ObserverGateway is another *Messaging Gateway* (468), this time between the observer (not shown) and the messaging system. The observer creates the gateway, then uses attach() to start the connection (which is analogous to calling the Attach(Observer) method in the *Observer* pattern). The gateway is an *Event-Driven Consumer* (498), so it implements the MessageListener interface, which requires the onMessage method. In this way, when an update is received, the gateway processes the message to get the new state and calls its own update(String) method, which then calls the corresponding message in the observer.

These two classes implement the push model version of *Observer*. With the notification message sent by SubjectGateway.notify(String), the existence of the message tells the observer that a change has occurred, but it is the contents of the message that tell the observer what the subject's new state is. The new state is being pushed from the subject to the observer. As we'll see later, there's another way to implement this functionality using the pull model.

Comparisons

For distributed notification between applications, the publish-subscribe (e.g., messaging) approach has several advantages over the traditional, synchronous (e.g., RPC) approach of implementing *Observer*.

- **Simplifies notification.** The subject's implementation of Notify() becomes incredibly simple; the code just has to send a message on a channel. Likewise, Observer.Update() just has to receive a message.

- **Simplifies attach/detach.** Rather than attach to and detach from the subject, an observer needs to subscribe to and unsubscribe from the channel. The subject does not need to implement Attach(Observer) or Detach(Observer) (although the observer may implement these methods to encapsulate the subscribe and unsubscribe behavior).

- **Simplifies concurrent threading.** The subject needs only one thread to update all observers concurrently—the channel delivers the notification message to the observers concurrently—and each observer handles the update in its own thread. This simplifies the subject's implementation, and because each observer uses its own thread, what one does in its update thread does not affect the others.

- **Simplifies remote access.** Neither the subject nor the observers have to implement any remote methods, nor do they need to run in an ORB. They just need to access the messaging system, and it handles the distribution.

- **Increases reliability.** Because the channel uses messaging, notifications will be queued until the observer can process them, which also enables the observer to throttle the notifications. If an observer wants to receive notifications that are sent while that observer is disconnected, it should make itself a *Durable Subscriber* (522).

JMS
Publish-
Subscribe
Example

One issue that the publish-subscribe approach does not change is *serialization*. Whether *Observer* is implemented through RPC or messaging, state data is being distributed from the subject's memory space to each observer's memory space, so the data has to be serialized (i.e., marshaled). This behavior has to be implemented for either approach.

If the publish-subscribe approach has a downside, it's that the approach requires *messaging*, which means that the subject and observer applications must have access to a shared messaging system and must be implemented as clients of that messaging system. Still, making applications into messaging clients is no more difficult, and probably easier, than using the RPC approach.

Push and Pull Models

Another potential downside of the publish-subscribe approach is that the pull model is more complex than the push model. As discussed earlier, the pull model requires more back-and-forth discussion than the push model. When the discussion is among distributed applications, the extra communication can significantly hurt performance.

The communication is more complex with messaging than with RPC. In both cases, Update() is a one-way communication, either an RPC that returns void or a single *Event Message* (151) from the subject to the observer. The trickier part is when an observer needs to query the subject's state. GetState() is a two-way communication, either a single RPC that requests the state and returns it, or a *Request-Reply* (154)—a pair of messages where a *Command Message* (145) requests the state and a separate *Document Message* (147) returns it.

What makes *Request-Reply* (154) more difficult is not just that it requires a pair of messages, but that it requires a pair of channels to transmit those messages. One channel, the get-state-request channel, goes from an observer to the subject; an observer sends the state request on that channel. The other channel, the get-state-reply channel, goes from the subject back to the observer; the subject sends the state reply on that channel. All of the observers can share the same request channel, but they will probably each need their own reply channel. Each observer needs to receive not just any response but the particular response for its specific request, and the easiest way to ensure this is for each observer to have its own reply channel. (An alternative is to use a single reply channel and use *Correlation Identifier*s [163] to figure out which reply goes to which observer, but a separate channel per observer is a lot easier to implement.)

**JMS
Publish-
Subscribe
Example**

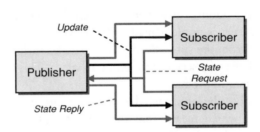

Publish-Subscribe Using the Pull Model

A reply channel for each observer can lead to an explosion of channels. Such a large number of channels may be manageable, but the messaging system administrator does not know how many static channels to create when the number of observers that must use these channels changes dynamically at runtime. Even if there are enough channels for all of the observers, how does each observer know which channel to use?

JMS has a feature, TemporaryQueue, specifically for this purpose [Hapner]. (Also see the discussion of *Request-Reply* [154].) An observer can create a temporary queue exclusively for its own use, specify that queue as the *Return Address* (159) in its request, and wait for the reply on that queue. Creating new queues frequently can be inefficient, depending on your messaging system's implementation, and temporary queues cannot be persistent (for use with *Guaranteed Delivery* [122]). However, if you don't want to use the push model, you can implement the pull model using temporary queues.

These two classes show how to implement the gateways using the pull model.

```
import javax.jms.Connection;
import javax.jms.ConnectionFactory;
import javax.jms.Destination;
import javax.jms.JMSException;
import javax.jms.Message;
import javax.jms.MessageConsumer;
import javax.jms.MessageListener;
import javax.jms.MessageProducer;
import javax.jms.Session;
import javax.jms.TextMessage;
import javax.naming.NamingException;

public class PullSubjectGateway {

    public static final String UPDATE_TOPIC_NAME = "jms/Update";
    private PullSubject subject;
    private Connection connection;
    private Session session;
    private MessageProducer updateProducer;

    protected PullSubjectGateway() {
        super();
    }

    public static PullSubjectGateway newGateway(PullSubject subject)
        throws JMSException, NamingException {
        PullSubjectGateway gateway = new PullSubjectGateway();
        gateway.initialize(subject);
        return gateway;
    }

    protected void initialize(PullSubject subject) throws JMSException, NamingException {
        this.subject = subject;

        ConnectionFactory connectionFactory = JndiUtil.getQueueConnectionFactory();
        connection = connectionFactory.createConnection();
```

```
        session = connection.createSession(false, Session.AUTO_ACKNOWLEDGE);
        Destination updateTopic = JndiUtil.getDestination(UPDATE_TOPIC_NAME);
        updateProducer = session.createProducer(updateTopic);

        new Thread(new GetStateReplier()).start();

        connection.start();
    }

    public void notifyNoState() throws JMSException {
        TextMessage message = session.createTextMessage();
        updateProducer.send(message);
    }

    public void release() throws JMSException {
        if (connection != null) {
            connection.stop();
            connection.close();
        }
    }
}

private class GetStateReplier implements Runnable, MessageListener {

    public static final String GET_STATE_QUEUE_NAME = "jms/GetState";
    private Session session;
    private MessageConsumer requestConsumer;

    public void run() {
        try {
            session = connection.createSession(false, Session.AUTO_ACKNOWLEDGE);
            Destination getStateQueue = JndiUtil.getDestination(GET_STATE_QUEUE_NAME);
            requestConsumer = session.createConsumer(getStateQueue);
            requestConsumer.setMessageListener(this);
        } catch (Exception e) {
            e.printStackTrace();
        }
    }

    public void onMessage(Message message) {
        try {
            Destination replyQueue = message.getJMSReplyTo();
            MessageProducer replyProducer = session.createProducer(replyQueue);

            Message replyMessage = session.createTextMessage(subject.getState());
            replyProducer.send(replyMessage);
        } catch (JMSException e) {
            e.printStackTrace();
        }
    }
}
}
```

`PullSubjectGateway` is very similar to `SubjectGateway`. The pull version now has a reference to its subject, so the gateway can query the subject for its state when requested by an observer. `notify(String)` has now become `notifyNoState()`, because the pull model simply sends out notification without including any state (and because Java already uses the method name `notify()`).

The big addition for the pull model is `GetStateReplier`, an inner class that implements `Runnable` so that it can run in its own thread. It is also a `Message-Listener`, which makes it an *Event-Driven Consumer* (498). Its `onMessage` method reads requests from the `GetState` queue and sends replies containing the subject's state to the queue specified by the request. In this way, when an observer makes a `GetState()` request, the gateway sends a reply (see *Request-Reply* [154]).

```java
import javax.jms.Destination;
import javax.jms.JMSException;
import javax.jms.Message;
import javax.jms.MessageConsumer;
import javax.jms.MessageListener;
import javax.jms.Queue;
import javax.jms.QueueConnection;
import javax.jms.QueueConnectionFactory;
import javax.jms.QueueRequestor;
import javax.jms.QueueSession;
import javax.jms.Session;
import javax.jms.TextMessage;
import javax.naming.NamingException;

public class PullObserverGateway implements MessageListener {

    public static final String UPDATE_TOPIC_NAME = "jms/Update";
    public static final String GET_STATE_QUEUE_NAME = "jms/GetState";
    private PullObserver observer;
    private QueueConnection connection;
    private QueueSession session;
    private MessageConsumer updateConsumer;
    private QueueRequestor getStateRequestor;

    protected PullObserverGateway() {
        super();
    }

    public static PullObserverGateway newGateway(PullObserver observer)
        throws JMSException, NamingException {
        PullObserverGateway gateway = new PullObserverGateway();
        gateway.initialize(observer);
        return gateway;
    }

    protected void initialize(PullObserver observer) throws JMSException, NamingException {
        this.observer = observer;
```

```
        QueueConnectionFactory connectionFactory = JndiUtil.getQueueConnectionFactory();
        connection = connectionFactory.createQueueConnection();
        session = connection.createQueueSession(false, Session.AUTO_ACKNOWLEDGE);
        Destination updateTopic = JndiUtil.getDestination(UPDATE_TOPIC_NAME);
        updateConsumer = session.createConsumer(updateTopic);
        updateConsumer.setMessageListener(this);

        Queue getStateQueue = (Queue) JndiUtil.getDestination(GET_STATE_QUEUE_NAME);
        getStateRequestor = new QueueRequestor(session, getStateQueue);
    }

    public void onMessage(Message message) {
        try {
            // message's contents are empty
            updateNoState();
        } catch (JMSException e) {
            e.printStackTrace();
        }
    }

    public void attach() throws JMSException {
        connection.start();
    }

    public void detach() throws JMSException {
        if (connection != null) {
            connection.stop();
            connection.close();
        }
    }

    private void updateNoState() throws JMSException {
        TextMessage getStateRequestMessage = session.createTextMessage();
        Message getStateReplyMessage = getStateRequestor.request(getStateRequestMessage);
        TextMessage textMsg = (TextMessage) getStateReplyMessage; // assume cast always works
        String newState = textMsg.getText();
        observer.update(newState);
    }
}
```

Again, PullObserverGateway is similar to ObserverGateway but with some more code to implement the pull model. In initialize, it sets up not only updateConsumer to listen for updates but also getStateRequestor to send GetState() requests. (getStateRequestor is a QueueRequestor; see *Request-Reply* [154].) In the pull version, the gateway's onMessage code ignores the message's contents because the message is empty. The message's existence tells the observer that the subject has changed, but it does not tell the observer what the subject's new state is. So, all there is to do is call updateNoState() (named similarly to notifyNoState()).

The difference for the observer between the push and pull models becomes apparent in the implementation of updateNoState() versus update(String). Whereas the push version gets the new state as a parameter and just has to update the observer, the pull version must go get the new state before it can update the observer. To get the new state, it uses the getStateRequestor to send a request and get the reply. The reply contains the subject's new state, which the gateway uses to update the observer. (Note that in this simple implementation, the gateway is single-threaded, so while it is sending the get-state request and waiting for the reply, it is not processing any more updates. Thus, if the request or reply messages take a really long time to transmit, the gateway will be stuck waiting, and any more updates that occur will simply queue up.)

As you can see, the pull model is more complex than the push model. It requires more channels (including a temporary one for every observer) and more messages (three messages per update per interested observer instead of one message for all observers), the subject and observer classes require more code to manage the additional messaging, and the objects at runtime require more threads to execute the additional messaging. If all of this is acceptable in your application, then the pull model is a viable approach. However, if in doubt, you should probably start with the push model because it is simpler.

Channel Design

So far, we've considered one subject with one piece of state notifying its observers. Using the push model, this requires one *Publish-Subscribe Channel* (106) for communicating changes in the subject's state to the observers.

Real enterprise applications are much more complex. An application can contain lots of subjects that need to announce changes. Each subject often contains several different pieces of state, called *aspects*, that can change independently. A single observer might be interested in several different aspects in several different subjects, where the subjects are not only multiple instances of the same class but may well be instances of different classes.

So, update semantics in sophisticated applications can quickly become complex. The *Observer* pattern addresses this as implementation issues like "Observing more than one subject" and "Specifying modifications of interest explicitly." Also, the *SASE* (Self-Addresses Stamped Envelope) pattern describes a combination of the *Observer* and *Command* patterns whereby an observer specifies the command a subject should send it when a certain change occurs [Alpert].

Without getting too deep into the issues of making sure observers receive only the updates they need, let's consider the implications for messaging, namely: How many channels will we need?

Let's first consider a simple case. An enterprise may have several different applications responsible for storing a customer's contact information, such as a mailing address. When a customer's address is updated in one of these applications, the application should notify other applications that may need this new information as well. Meanwhile, there may be several applications that need to know when an address changes, so they would like to register to receive notification.

This is a simple problem to solve. All that is needed is a single *Publish-Subscribe Channel* (106) for announcing address changes. Each application that can change an address then also has the responsibility to announce that change by publishing a message on the channel. Each application that wishes to receive notification subscribes to the channel. A particular change message might look like this.

```
<AddressChange customer_id="12345">
    <OldAddress>
        <Street>123 Wall Street</Street>
        <City>New York</City>
        <State>NY</State>
        <Zip>10005</Zip>
    </OldAddress>
    <NewAddress>
        <Street>321 Sunset Blvd</Street>
        <City>Los Angeles</City>
        <State>CA</State>
        <Zip>90012</Zip>
    </NewAddress>
</AddressChange>
```

JMS Publish-Subscribe Example

Now let's consider another problem. The enterprise may also have applications that need to announce when they are out of a product and others that need to receive these notifications so that can reorder the product. This is just a different example of the last problem, and it is solved the same way by using a *Publish-Subscribe Channel* (106) to make out-of-product announcements. One of these messages might look like this.

```
<OutOfProduct>
    <ProductID>12345</ProductID>
    <StoreID>67890</StoreID>
    <QuantityRequested>100</QuantityRequested>
</OutOfProduct>
```

But this leads us to wonder: Can we use the same channel for customer address changes and for out-of-product announcements? Probably not. First, *Datatype Channel* (111) tells us that all of the messages on a channel must be the same type, which in this case means that they must all conform to the same

XML schema. <AddressChange> is obviously a very different element type from <OutOfProduct>, so they should not be sent on the same channel. Perhaps the data formats could be reworked so that both message types fit the same schema, and then receivers could tell which messages were for addresses and which were for products. But then the problem is that the applications interested in address changes are probably not the same ones interested in product updates, so if the messages use the same channel, an application will frequently receive notifications it's not interested in. Thus, it makes sense to have two separate address change and product update channels.

Now, consider a third case where a customer's credit rating could change. The message might look like this:

```
<CreditRatingChange customer_id="12345">
    <OldRating>AAA</OldRating>
    <NewRating>BBB</NewRating>
</CreditRatingChange>
```

Like the case with product notifications, it might be tempting to solve the problem with a new credit-rating-changed channel (in addition to the address-changed and out-of-product channels). This would keep the credit rating changes separate from the address changes, and it would allow dependents to only register for the type of changes they're interested in.

The problem with this approach is that it can lead to a channel explosion. Consider all the pieces of data that may be known about a customer: name; contacts (address, phone number, e-mail) for mailing, shipping, and billing; credit rating; service level; standard discount; and so on. Each time any one of these aspects changes, other applications may need to know about it. Creating a channel for each can lead to lots of channels.

Large numbers of channels may tax the messaging system. Numerous channels with little traffic on each can waste resources and make load difficult to distribute. Numerous channels with lots of little messages can add to messaging overhead. Dependents can become confused as to which of a large number of channels to subscribe to. Multiple channels require multiple senders and receivers, perhaps leading to lots of threads checking lots of channels that are usually empty. So, creating yet more channels may not be such a good idea.

What may work better is to send both the address-changed and credit-rating-changed messages on the same channel, since they both concern changes to the customer and an application interested in one kind of change may be interested in the others as well. Yet, a separate out-of-product channel is still a good idea, since applications interested in customers may not be interested in products, and vice versa.

The address-changed and credit-rating-changed messages have different formats, yet *Datatype Channel* (111) tells us that to be on the same channel, the messages must have the same format. With XML, this means that all of the messages must have the same root element type but perhaps can have different optional nested elements. So, unified customer-changed messages might look like this:

```
<CustomerChange customer_id="12345">
    <AddressChange>
        <OldAddress>
            <Street>123 Wall Street</Street>
            <City>New York</City>
            <State>NY</State>
            <Zip>10005</Zip>
        </OldAddress>
        <NewAddress>
            <Street>321 Sunset Blvd</Street>
            <City>Los Angeles</City>
            <State>CA</State>
            <Zip>90012</Zip>
        </NewAddress>
    </AddressChange>
</CustomerChange>

<CustomerChange customer_id="12345">
    <CreditRatingChange>
        <OldRating>AAA</OldRating>
        <NewRating>BBB</NewRating>
    </CreditRatingChange>
</CustomerChange>
```

JMS Publish-Subscribe Example

There may still be the problem that shipping applications interested in address changes are not interested in credit rating changes, and billing applications are interested in the opposite. These applications can use *Selective Consumers* (515) to get only the messages of interest. If selective consumers prove to be complicated and a messaging system can easily support more channels, then perhaps separate channels would be better after all.

As with many issues in enterprise architecture and design, there are no simple answers and lots of trade-offs. With *Publish-Subscribe Channel* (106), as with any message channel, the goal is to help ensure that the observers receive only the notifications they need, without an explosion of separate channels and without taxing the typical observer with lots of threads running lots of consumers monitoring lots of channels.

Conclusions

This example shows that *Publish-Subscribe Channels* (106) are an implementation of the *Observer* pattern that makes the pattern much easier to use in distributed environments. When a channel is used, `Subject.Notify()` and `Observer.Update()` become much simpler because all they have to do is send and receive messages. The messaging system takes care of distribution and concurrency while making the remote notification more reliable. The push model is simpler and often more efficient than the pull model, especially for distributed notification and with messaging. Yet, the pull model can also be implemented using messaging. In complex applications where lots of data can change, it may be tempting to create a channel for every different thing that can change, but it's often more practical to use the same channel to transmit similar notifications going to the same observers. Even if your applications don't need messaging for anything else, if they need to notify each other of changes, it may well be worth using *Messaging* (53) just so you can take advantage of *Publish-Subscribe Channels* (106).

JMS
Publish-
Subscribe
Example

Chapter 7

Message Routing

Introduction

In Chapter 3, "Messaging Systems," we discussed how a *Message Router* (78) can be used to decouple a message source from the ultimate destination of the message. This chapter elaborates on specific types of *Message Routers* (78) to explain how to provide routing and brokering ability to an integration solution. Most patterns are refinements of the *Message Router* (78) pattern, while others combine multiple *Message Routers* (78) to solve more complex problems. Therefore, we can categorize the message routing patterns into the following groups:

- **Simple Routers** are variants of the *Message Router* (78) and route messages from one inbound channel to one or more outbound channels.

- **Composed Routers** combine multiple simple routers to create more complex message flows.

- **Architectural Patterns** describe architectural styles based on *Message Routers* (78).

Simple Routers

The *Content-Based Router* (230) inspects the content of a message and routes it to another channel based on the content of the message. Using such a router enables the message producer to send messages to a single channel and leave it to the *Content-Based Router* (230) to route them to the proper destination. This alleviates the sending application from this task and avoids coupling the message producer to specific destination channels.

225

A *Message Filter* (237) is a special form of a *Content-Based Router* (230). It examines the message content and passes the message to another channel only if the message content matches certain criteria. Otherwise, it discards the message. A *Message Filter* (237) performs a function that is very similar to that of a *Selective Consumer* (515) with the key difference that a *Message Filter* (237) is part of the messaging system, routing qualifying messages to another channel, whereas a *Selective Consumer* (515) is built into a *Message Endpoint* (95).

A *Content-Based Router* (230) and a *Message Filter* (237) can actually solve a similar problem. A *Content-Based Router* (230) routes a message to the correct destination based on the criteria encoded in the *Content-Based Router* (230). Equivalent behavior can be achieved by using a *Publish-Subscribe Channel* (106) and an array of *Message Filters* (237), one for each potential recipient. Each *Message Filter* (237) eliminates the messages that do not match the criteria for the specific destination. The *Content-Based Router* (230) routes predictively to a single channel and therefore has total control, but it is also dependent on the list of all possible destination channels. In contrast, the *Message Filter* (237) array filters reactively, spreading the routing logic across many *Message Filters* (237) but avoiding a single component that is dependent on all possible destinations. The trade-off between these solutions is described in more detail in the *Message Filter* (237) pattern.

A basic *Message Router* (78) uses fixed rules to determine the destination of an incoming message. Where we need more flexibility, a *Dynamic Router* (243) can be very useful. This router allows the routing logic to be modified by sending control messages to a designated control port. The dynamic nature of the *Dynamic Router* (243) can be combined with most forms of the *Message Router* (78).

Chapter 4, "Messaging Channels," introduced the concepts of *Point-to-Point Channel* (103) and *Publish-Subscribe Channel* (106). Sometimes, you need to send a message to more than one recipient but want to maintain control over the recipients. The *Recipient List* (249) allows you do just that. In essence, a *Recipient List* (249) is a *Content-Based Router* (230) that can route a single message to more than one destination channel.

Some messages contain lists of individual items. How do you process these items individually? Use a *Splitter* (259) to split the large message into individual messages. Each message can then be routed further and processed individually.

However, you may need to recombine the messages that the *Splitter* (259) created back into a single message. This is one of the functions an *Aggregator* (268) performs. An *Aggregator* (268) can receive a stream of messages, identify related

Introduction

messages, and combine them into a single message. Unlike the other routing patterns, the *Aggregator* (268) is a stateful *Message Router* (78) because it has to store messages internally until specific conditions are fulfilled. This means that an *Aggregator* (268) can consume multiple messages before it publishes a message.

Because we use messaging to connect applications or components running on multiple computers, multiple messages can be processed in parallel. For example, more than one process may consume messages off a single channel. One of these processes may execute faster than another, causing messages to be processed out of order. However, some components—for example, ledger-based systems—depend on the correct sequence of individual messages. The *Resequencer* (283) puts out-of-sequence messages back into sequence. The *Resequencer* (283) is also a stateful *Message Router* (78) because it may need to store a number of messages internally until the message that completes the sequence arrives. Unlike the *Aggregator* (268), though, the *Resequencer* (283) ultimately publishes the same number of messages it consumed.

The following table summarizes the properties of the *Message Router* (78) variants (we did not include the *Dynamic Router* [243] as a separate alternative because any router can be implemented as a dynamic variant):

Pattern	Number of Messages Consumed	Number of Messages Published	Stateful?	Comment
Content-Based Router	1	1	No (mostly)	
Filter	1	0 or 1	No (mostly)	
Recipient List	1	multiple (incl. 0)	No	
Splitter	1	multiple	No	
Aggregator	multiple	1	Yes	
Resequencer	multiple	multiple	Yes	Publishes same number it consumes

Composed Routers

A key advantage of the *Pipes and Filters* (70) architecture is that we can compose multiple filters into a larger solution. *Composed Message Processor* (294) and

Scatter-Gather (297) combine multiple *Message Router* (78) variants to create more comprehensive solutions. Both patterns allow us to retrieve information from multiple sources and recombine it into a single message. The *Composed Message Processor* (294) splits a single message into multiple parts, whereas the *Scatter-Gather* (297) sends a copy of the same message to multiple recipients.

Both the *Composed Message Processor* (294) and the *Scatter-Gather* (297) route a single message to a number of participants concurrently and reassemble the replies into a single message. We can say that these patterns manage the *parallel routing* of a message. Two additional patterns manage the *sequential routing* of a message, that is, routing a message through a sequence of individual steps. If we want to control the path of a message from a central point, we can use a *Routing Slip* (301) to specify the path the message should take. This pattern works just like the routing slip attached to office documents to pass them sequentially by a number of recipients. Alternatively, we can use a *Process Manager* (312), which gives us more flexibility but requires the message to return to a central component after each function.

Architectural Patterns

*Message Router*s (78) enable us to architect an integration solution using a central *Message Broker* (322). As opposed to the different message routing design patterns, this pattern describes a *hub-and-spoke* architectural style.

The Right Router for the Right Purpose

This chapter contains 12 patterns. How can we make it easy to find the right pattern for the right purpose? The following decision chart helps you find the right pattern for the right purpose through simple yes or no decisions. For example, if you are looking for a simple routing pattern that consumes one message at a time but publishes multiple messages in sequential order, you should use a *Splitter* (259). The diagram also helps illustrate how closely the individual patterns are related. For example, a *Routing Slip* (301) and a *Process Manager* (312) solve similar problems, while a *Message Filter* (237) does something rather different.

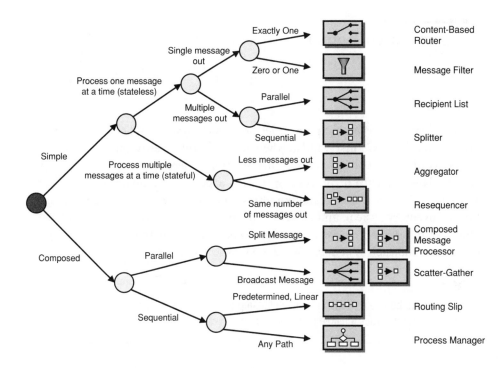

Introduction

Content-Based Router

Assume that we are building an order-processing system. When an incoming order is received, we first validate the order and then verify that the ordered item is available in the warehouse. This function is performed by the inventory system. This sequence of processing steps is a perfect candidate for the *Pipes and Filters* (70) style. We create two filters, one for the validation step and one for the inventory system, and route the incoming messages through both filters. However, in many enterprise integration scenarios more than one inventory system exists, and each system can handle only specific items.

> How do we handle a situation in which the implementation of a single logical function is spread across multiple physical systems?

Integration solutions connect existing applications so that they work together. Because many of these applications were developed without integration in mind, integration solutions rarely find an ideal scenario where a business function is well encapsulated inside a single system. For example, acquisitions or business partnerships often result in multiple systems performing the same business function. Also, many businesses that act as aggregators or resellers typically interface with multiple systems that perform the same functions (e.g., check inventory, place order). To make matters more complicated, these systems may be operated within the company or may be under the control of business partners or affiliates. For example, large e-tailers like Amazon allow you to order anything from books to chainsaws to clothing. Depending on the type of item, the order may be processed by a different "behind-the-scenes" merchant's order processing systems.

Let's assume that the company is selling widgets and gadgets and has two inventory systems: one for widgets and one for gadgets. Let's also assume that each item is identified by a unique item number. When the company receives an order, it needs to decide which inventory system should receive the order based on the type of item ordered. We could create separate channels for incoming orders based on the type of item ordered. However, this would require the customers to know our internal system architecture when in fact they may not even be aware that we distinguish between widgets and gadgets. Therefore, we should hide the fact that the implementation of the business function is spread across multiple systems from the remainder of the integration solution, including customers. Therefore, we must expect messages for different items to arrive on the same channel.

We could forward the order to all inventory systems (using a *Publish-Subscribe Channel* [106]), and let each system decide whether it can handle the order. This approach makes the addition of new inventory systems easy because we do not have to change any of the existing components when a new inventory system comes online. However, this approach assumes distributed coordination across multiple systems. What happens if the order cannot be processed by any system? Or if more than one system can process the order? Will the customer receive duplicate shipments? Also, in many cases an inventory system will treat an order for an item that it cannot handle as an error. If this is the case, each order would cause errors in all inventory systems but one. It would be hard to distinguish these errors from "real" errors, such as an invalid order.

An alternative approach would be to use the item number as a channel address. Each item would have its dedicated channel, and the customers could simply publish the order to the channel associated with the item's number without having to know about any internal distinctions between widgets and gadgets. The inventory systems could listen on all the channels for those items that it can process. This approach leverages the channel addressability to route messages to the correct inventory system. However, a large number of items could quickly lead to an explosion of the number of channels, burdening the system with runtime and management overhead. Creating new channels for each item that is offered would quickly result in chaos.

We should also try to minimize message traffic. For example, we could route the order message through one inventory system after the other. The first system that can accept the order consumes the message and processes the order. If it cannot process the order, it passes the order message to the next system. This approach eliminates the danger of orders being accepted by multiple systems simultaneously. Also, we know that the order was not processed by any system if the last system passes it back. The solution does require, however, that the systems know enough about each other to pass the message from one system to the next. This approach is similar to the *Chain of Responsibility* pattern [GoF]. However, in the world of message-based integration, passing messages through a chain of systems could mean significant overhead. Also, this approach would require collaboration of the individual systems, which may not be feasible if some systems are maintained by external business partners and are therefore not under our control.

Content-
Based
Router

In summary, we need a solution that encapsulates the fact that the business function is split across systems, is efficient in its use of message channels and message traffic, and ensures that the order is handled by exactly one inventory system.

Use a *Content-Based Router* to route each message to the correct recipient based on the message's content.

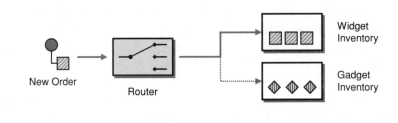

The *Content-Based Router* examines the message content and routes the message onto a different channel based on data contained in the message. The routing can be based on a number of criteria, such as existence of fields, specific field values, and so on. When implementing a *Content-Based Router*, special caution should be taken to make the routing function easy to maintain, as the router can become a point of frequent maintenance. In more sophisticated integration scenarios, the *Content-Based Router* can take on the form of a configurable rules engine that computes the destination channel based on a set of configurable rules.

Content- Based Router

Reducing Dependencies

Content-Based Router is a frequently used form of the more generic *Message Router* (78). It uses *predictive routing*—that is, it incorporates knowledge of the capabilities of all other systems. This makes for efficient routing because each outgoing message is sent directly to the correct system. The downside is that the *Content-Based Router* has to have knowledge of all possible recipients and their capabilities. As recipients are added, removed, or changed, the *Content-Based Router* has to be changed every time. This can become a maintenance nightmare.

We can avoid the dependency of the *Content-Based Router* on the individual recipients if the recipients assume more control over the routing process. These options can be summarized as *reactive filtering* because they allow each participant to filter relevant messages as they come by. The distribution of routing control eliminates the need for a *Content-Based Router,* but the solution is generally less efficient. These solutions and associated trade-offs are described in more detail in the *Message Filter* (237) and *Routing Slip* (301).

The *Dynamic Router* (243) describes a compromise between the *Content-Based Router* and the reactive filtering approach by having each recipient inform the *Content-Based Router* of its capabilities. The *Content-Based Router* maintains a list of each recipient's capabilities and routes incoming messages accordingly. The price we pay for this flexibility is the complexity of the solution and the difficulty of debugging such a system when compared to a simple *Content-Based Router.*

Example: *Content-Based Router with C# and MSMQ*

This code example demonstrates a very simple *Content-Based Router* that routes messages based on the first character in the message body. If the body text starts with W, the router routes the message to the widgetQueue; if it starts with G, it goes to the gadgetQueue. If it is neither, the router sends it to the dunno-Queue. This queue is actually an example of an *Invalid Message Channel* (115). This router is *stateless,* that is, it does not "remember" any previous messages when making the routing decision.

Content-
Based
Router

```
class ContentBasedRouter
{
    protected MessageQueue inQueue;
    protected MessageQueue widgetQueue;
    protected MessageQueue gadgetQueue;
    protected MessageQueue dunnoQueue;

    public ContentBasedRouter(MessageQueue inQueue, MessageQueue widgetQueue,
                            MessageQueue gadgetQueue, MessageQueue dunnoQueue)
    {
        this.inQueue = inQueue;
        this.widgetQueue = widgetQueue;
        this.gadgetQueue = gadgetQueue;
        this.dunnoQueue = dunnoQueue;

        inQueue.ReceiveCompleted += new ReceiveCompletedEventHandler(OnMessage);
        inQueue.BeginReceive();
    }

    private void OnMessage(Object source, ReceiveCompletedEventArgs asyncResult)
    {
```

```
        MessageQueue mq = (MessageQueue)source;
        mq.Formatter = new System.Messaging.XmlMessageFormatter
                            (new String[] {"System.String,mscorlib"});
        Message message = mq.EndReceive(asyncResult.AsyncResult);

        if (IsWidgetMessage(message))
            widgetQueue.Send(message);
        else if (IsGadgetMessage(message))
            gadgetQueue.Send(message);
        else
            dunnoQueue.Send(message);
        mq.BeginReceive();
    }

    protected bool IsWidgetMessage (Message message)
    {
        String text = (String)message.Body;
        return (text.StartsWith("W"));
    }

    protected bool IsGadgetMessage (Message message)
    {
        String text = (String)message.Body;
        return (text.StartsWith("G"));
    }
}
```

Content-
Based
Router

The example uses an event-driven message consumer by registering the method OnMessage as the handler for messages arriving on the inQueue. This causes the .NET framework to invoke the method OnMessage for every message that arrives on the inQueue. The message queue Formatter property tells the framework what type of message to expect; in our example, we only deal with simple string messages. OnMessage figures out where to route the message and tells .NET that it is ready for the next message by calling the BeginReceive method on the queue. In order to keep the code to a minimum, this simple router is not transactional: If the router crashes after it consumed a message from the input channel and before it published it to the output channel, we would lose a message. Later chapters explain how to make endpoints transactional (see *Transactional Client* [484]).

Example: *TIBCO MessageBroker*

Message routing is such a common need that most EAI tool suites provide built-in tools to simplify the construction of the routing logic. For example, in the C# example we had to code the logic to read a message off the incoming queue, deserialize it, analyze it, and republish it to the correct outgoing channel. In many EAI tools this type of logic can be implemented with simple drag-and-drop operations instead of by writing code. The only code to write is the actual decision logic for the *Content-Based Router*.

One such EAI tool that implements message routing is the TIBCO Active-Enterprise suite. The suite includes TIB/MessageBroker, which is designed to create simple message flows that include transformation and routing functions. The same widget router that routes incoming messages based on the first letter of the item number looks like this when implemented in TIB/MessageBroker:

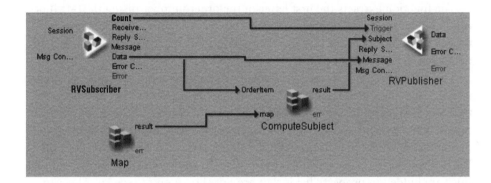

We can read the message flow from left to right. The component on the left (represented by a triangle pointing to the right) is the subscriber component that consumes messages off the channel router.in. The channel name is specified in a properties box not shown in this figure. The message content is directed to the message publisher (represented by the triangle on the right side of the screen). The direct line from the Data output of the subscriber to the Message input of the publisher represents the fact that a *Content-Based Router* does not modify the message body. In order to determine the correct output channel, the function ComputeSubject (in the middle) analyzes the message content. The function uses a so-called *dictionary* (labeled "Map" in the figure) as a translation table between message contents and the destination channel name. The dictionary is configured with the following values:

Item Code	Channel Name
G	gadget
W	widget

The ComputeSubject function uses the first letter of the incoming message's order item number to look up the destination channel from the dictionary. To form the complete name of the output channel, it appends the dictionary result to the string `router.out`, to form a channel name like `router.out.widget`. The result of this computation is passed to the publisher component on the right to be used as the name of the channel. As a result, any order item whose item number starts with a G is routed to the channel `router.out.gadget`, whereas any item whose item number starts with a W is routed to the channel `router.out.widget`.

The TIBCO implementation of the `ComputeSubject` function looks like this:

```
concat("router.out.",DGet(map,Upper(Left(OrderItem.ItemNumber,1))))
```

The function extracts the first letter of the order number (using the `Left` function) and converts it to uppercase (using the `Upper` function). The function uses the result as the key to the dictionary to retrieve the name of the outgoing channel (using the `DGet` function).

This example demonstrates the strengths of commercial EAI tools. Instead of a few dozen lines of code, we need to code only a single function to implement the same widget router functionality. Plus, we get features like transactionality, thread management, and systems management for free. But this example also highlights the difficulties of presenting a solution created with graphical tools. We had to relegate to screenshots to describe the solution. Many important settings are hidden in property fields that are not shown on the screen. This can make it difficult to document a solution built using graphical development tools.

Content-Based Router

Message Filter

Continuing with the order processing example, let's assume that company management decided to publish price changes and promotions to large customers. We would like to send a message to notify the customer whenever the price for an item changes. We do the same if we are running a special promotion, such as 10 percent off all widgets in the month of November. Some customers may be interested in receiving price updates or promotions related only to specific items. For example, if I purchase primarily gadgets, I may not be interested in knowing whether or not widgets are on sale.

How can a component avoid receiving uninteresting messages?

The most basic way for a component to receive only relevant messages is to subscribe only to those channels that carry relevant messages. This option leverages the inherent routing abilities of *Publish-Subscribe Channels* (106). A component receives only those messages that travel through channels to which the component subscribes. For example, we could create one channel for widget updates and another one for gadget updates. Customers would then be free to subscribe to one or the other channel or both. This has the advantage that new subscribers can join in without requiring any changes to the system. However, subscription to a *Publish-Subscribe Channel* (106) is generally limited to a simple binary condition: If a component subscribes to a channel, it receives all messages on that channel. The only way to achieve finer granularity is to create more channels. If we are dealing with a combination of multiple parameters, the number of channels can quickly explode. For example, if we want to allow consumers to receive all messages that announce all price cuts of widgets or gadgets by more than 5 percent, 10 percent, or 15 percent, we already need six (2 item types multiplied by 3 threshold values) channels. This approach would ultimately become difficult to manage and will consume significant resources due to the large number of allocated channels. So, we need to look for a solution that allows for more flexibility than channel subscription allows.

We also need a solution that can accommodate frequent change. For example, we could modify a *Content-Based Router* (230) to route the message to

Message
Filter

more than one destination (a concept described in the *Recipient List* [249]). This predictive router sends only relevant messages to each recipient so that the recipient does not have to take any extra steps. However, now we burden the message originator with maintaining the preferences for each and every subscriber. If the list of recipients or their preferences change quickly, this solution would prove to be a maintenance nightmare.

We could simply broadcast the changes to all components and expect each component to filter out the undesirable messages. However, this approach assumes that we have control over the actual component. In many integration scenarios this is not the case because we deal with packaged applications, legacy applications, or applications that are not under the control of our organization.

Use a special kind of Message Router, a *Message Filter*, to eliminate undesired messages from a channel based on a set of criteria.

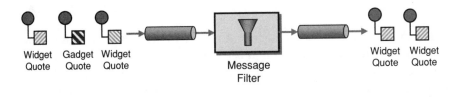

Widget Gadget Widget   Message   Widget Widget
Quote Quote Quote   Filter   Quote Quote

Message Filter

The *Message Filter* is a *Message Router* (78) with a single output channel. If the content of an incoming message matches the criteria specified by the *Message Filter*, the message is routed to the output channel. If the message content does not match the criteria, the message is discarded.

In our example we would define a single *Publish-Subscribe Channel* (106) that each customer is free to listen on. The customer can then use a *Message Filter* to eliminate messages based on criteria of his or her choosing, such as the type of item or the magnitude of the price change.

The *Message Filter* can be portrayed as a special case of a *Content-Based Router* (230) that routes the message either to the output channel or the *null channel*, a channel that discards any message published to it. The purpose of such a channel is similar to the /dev/null destination present in many operating systems or to a *Null Object* [PLoPD3].

Stateless versus Stateful Message Filters

The widget and gadget example describes a stateless *Message Filter*: The *Message Filter* inspects a single message and decides whether or not to pass it on based solely on information contained in that message. Therefore, the *Message Filter* does not need to maintain state across messages and is considered stateless. Stateless components have the advantage that they allow us to run multiple instances of the component in parallel to speed up processing. However, a *Message Filter* does not have to be stateless. For example, there are situations in which the *Message Filter* needs to keep track of the message history. A common scenario is the use of a *Message Filter* to eliminate duplicate messages. Assuming that each message has a unique message identifier, the *Message Filter* would store the identifiers of past messages so that it can recognize a duplicate message by comparing each message's identifier with the list of stored identifiers.

Filtering Functions Built into Messaging Systems

Some messaging systems incorporate aspects of a *Message Filter* inside the messaging infrastructure. For example, some publish-subscribe systems allow you to define a hierarchical structure for *Publish-Subscribe Channels* (106). Many publish-subscribe systems, including most JMS implementations, allow this. For example, one can publish promotions to the channel `wgco.update.promotion.widget`. A subscriber can then use wildcards to subscribe to a specific subset of messages; for example, if a subscriber listens to the topic `wgco.update.*.widget`, he would receive all updates (promotions and price changes) related to widgets. Another subscriber may listen to `wgco.update.promotion.*`, which would deliver all promotions related to widgets and gadgets, but no price changes. The channel hierarchy lets us refine the semantics of a channel by appending qualifying parameters, so that instead of a customer subscribing to all updates, customers can filter messages by specifying additional criteria as part of the channel name. However, the flexibility provided by the hierarchical channel naming is still limited when compared to a *Message Filter*. For example, a *Message Filter* could decide to pass on a price change message only if the price changed by more than 11.5 percent, something that would be hard to express by means of channel names.

Other messaging systems provide API support for *Selective Consumers* (515) inside the receiving application. Message selectors are expressions that evaluate header or property elements inside an incoming message before the application gets to see the message. If the condition does not evaluate to true, the message is

Message
Filter

ignored and not passed on to the application logic. A message selector acts as a *Message Filter* that is built into the application. While the use of a message selector still requires you to modify the application (something that is often not possible in EAI), the execution of the selection rules is built into the messaging infrastructure. One important difference between a *Message Filter* and a *Selective Consumer* (515) is that a consumer using a *Selective Consumer* (515) does not consume messages that do not match the specified criteria. On the other hand, a *Message Filter* removes all messages from the input channel, publishing to the output channel only those that match the specified criteria.

Because the *Selective Consumer* (515) registers the filter expression with the messaging infrastructure, the infrastructure is able to make smart internal routing decisions based on the filter criteria. Let's assume that the message receiver sits on a different network segment from the message originator (or even across the Internet). It would be rather wasteful to route the message all the way to the *Message Filter* just to find out that we want to discard the message. On the other hand, we want to use a *Message Filter* mechanism so that the recipients have control over the message routing instead of a central *Message Router* (78). If the *Message Filter* is part of the API that the messaging infrastructure provides to the message subscriber, the infrastructure is free to propagate the filter expression closer to the source. This will maintain the original intent of keeping control with the message subscriber, but allows the messaging infrastructure to avoid unnecessary network traffic. This behavior resembles that of a dynamic *Recipient List* (249).

Message Filter

Using Message Filters to Implement Routing Functionality

We can use a *Publish-Subscribe Channel* (106) connected to a set of *Message Filters* who eliminate unwanted messages to implement functionality equivalent to that of a *Content-Based Router* (230). The following diagrams illustrate the two options:

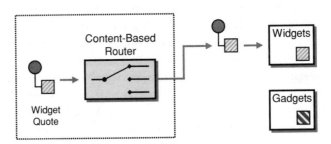

Option 1: Using a Content-Based Router

In this simple example, we have two receivers: receiver Gadgets is only interested in gadget messages, while receiver Widgets is only interested in widget messages. The *Content-Based Router* (230) evaluates each message's content and routes it predictively to the appropriate receiver.

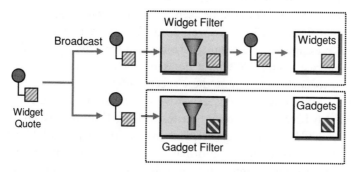

Option 2: Using a Broadcast Channel and a Set of Message Filters

The second option broadcasts the message to a *Publish-Subscribe Channel* (106). Each recipient is equipped with a *Message Filter* to eliminate unwanted messages. For example, the Widgets receiver employs a widget filter that lets only widget messages pass.

The following table characterizes some of the differences between the two solutions:

Content-Based Router	Publish-Subscribe Channel with Message Filters
Exactly one consumer receives each message.	More than one consumer can consume a message.
Central control and maintenance—predictive routing.	Distributed control and maintenance—reactive filtering.
Router needs to know about participants. Router may need to be updated if participants are added or removed.	No knowledge of participants required. Adding or removing participants is easy.
Often used for business transactions, e.g., orders.	Often used for event notifications or informational messages.
Generally more efficient with queue-based channels.	Generally more efficient with publish-subscribe channels.

How do we decide between the two options? In some cases, the decision is driven by the required functionality; for example, if we need the ability for multiple recipients to process the same message, we need to use a *Publish-Subscribe Channel* (106) with *Message Filters*. In most cases, though, we decide by which party has control over (and needs to maintain) the routing decision. Do we want to keep central control or farm it out to the recipients? If messages contain sensitive data that is only to be seen by certain recipients, we need to use a *Content-Based Router* (230)—we would not want to trust the other recipients to filter out messages. For example, let's assume we offer special discounts to our premium customers: We would not send those to our non-premium customers and expect them to ignore these special offers.

Network traffic considerations can drive the decision as well. If we have an efficient way to broadcast information (e.g., using IP multicast on an internal network), using filters can be very efficient and avoids the potential bottleneck of a single router. However, if this information is routed over the Internet, we are limited to point-to-point connections. In this case a single router is much more efficient, as it avoids sending individual messages to all participants regardless of their interests. If we want to pass control to the recipients but need to use a router for reasons of network efficiency, we can employ a dynamic *Recipient List* (249). This type of *Recipient List* (249) acts as a *Dynamic Router* (243), allowing recipients to express their preferences via control messages to the router. The *Recipient List* (249) stores the recipient preferences in a database or a rule base. When a message arrives, the *Recipient List* (249) forwards the message to all interested recipients whose criteria match the message.

Message Filter

Dynamic Router

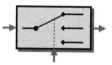

You are using a *Message Router* (78) to route messages between multiple destinations.

How can you avoid the dependency of the router on all possible destinations while maintaining its efficiency?

A *Message Router* (78) is very efficient because it can route a message directly to the correct destination. Other solutions to message routing, especially reactive filtering solutions, are less efficient because they use a trial-and-error approach: For example, a *Routing Slip* (301) routes each message to the first possible destination. If that destination is the correct one, it accepts the message; otherwise, the message is passed to the second possible destination and so on. Likewise, a *Message Filter* (237)–based approach sends the message to all possible recipients whether they are interested or not.

Distributed routing solutions also suffer the risk that there are multiple recipients of a message or none at all. Both situations can go undetected unless we use a central routing element.

In order to achieve this accuracy, we need to use a *Message Router* (78) that incorporates knowledge about each destination and the rules for routing messages to the destinations. However, this can turn the *Message Router* (78) into a maintenance burden if the list of possible destinations changes frequently.

Use a *Dynamic Router*, a router that can self-configure based on special configuration messages from participating destinations.

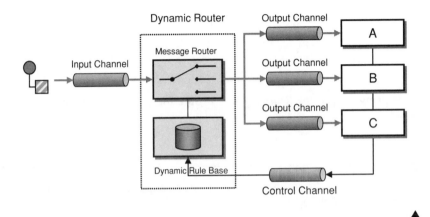

Besides the usual input and output channels, the *Dynamic Router* uses an additional *control channel*. During system startup, each potential recipient sends a special message to the *Dynamic Router* on this control channel, announcing its presence and listing the conditions under which it can handle a message. The *Dynamic Router* stores the preferences for each participant in a rule base. When a message arrives, the *Dynamic Router* evaluates all rules and routes the message to the recipient whose rules are fulfilled. This allows for efficient, predictive routing without the maintenance dependency of the *Dynamic Router* on each potential recipient.

In the most basic scenario, each participant announces its existence and routing preferences to the *Dynamic Router* at startup time. This requires each participant to be aware of the control queue used by the *Dynamic Router*. It also requires the *Dynamic Router* to store the rules in a persistent way. Otherwise, if the *Dynamic Router* fails and has to restart, it would not be able to recover the routing rules. Alternatively, the *Dynamic Router* could send a broadcast message to all possible participants to trigger them to reply with the control message. This configuration is more robust but requires the use of an additional *Publish-Subscribe Channel* (106).

It might make sense to enhance the control channel to allow participants to send both subscribe and unsubscribe messages to the *Dynamic Router*. This would allow recipients to add or remove themselves from the routing scheme during runtime.

Dynamic Router

Because the recipients are independent from each other, the *Dynamic Router* has to deal with rules conflicts, such as multiple recipients announcing interest in the same type of message. The *Dynamic Router* can employ a number of different strategies to resolve such conflicts:

1. Ignore control messages that conflict with existing messages. This option assures that the routing rules are free of conflict. However, the state of the routing table may depend on the sequence in which the potential recipients start up. If all recipients start up at the same time, this may lead to unpredictable behavior because all recipients would announce their preferences at the same time to the control queue.

2. Send the message to the first recipient whose criteria match. This option allows the routing table to contain conflicts but resolves them as messages come in.

3. Send the message to all recipients whose criteria match. This option is tolerant of conflicts but turns the *Dynamic Router* into a *Recipient List* (249). Generally, the behavior of a *Content-Based Router* (230) implies that it publishes one output message for each input message. This strategy violates that rule.

The main liabilities of the *Dynamic Router* are the complexity of the solution and the difficulty of debugging a dynamically configured system.

A *Dynamic Router* is another example where message-based middleware performs similar functions to lower level IP networking. A *Dynamic Router* works very similarly to the dynamic routing tables used in IP routing to route IP packets between networks. The protocol used by the recipients to configure the *Dynamic Router* is analogous to the IP Routing Information Protocol (RIP; for more information see [Stevens]).

A common use of the *Dynamic Router* is dynamic service discovery in service-oriented architectures. If a client application wants to access a service, it sends a message containing the name of the service to the *Dynamic Router*. The *Dynamic Router* maintains a service directory, a list of all services with their name and the channel they listen on. The router builds this directory based on control messages from each service provider. When a service request arrives, the *Dynamic Router* uses the service directory to look up the service by name, then routes the message to the correct channel. This setup allows the client application to send command messages to a single channel without having to worry about the nature or location of the specified service provider, even if the provider changes.

A related pattern, the *Client-Dispatcher-Server* pattern [POSA], allows a client to request a specific service without knowing the physical location of the service provider. The dispatcher uses a list of registered services to establish a connection between the client and the physical server implementing the requested service. The *Dynamic Router* performs a similar function but is different from the dispatcher in that it can use more intelligent routing than a simple table lookup.

Example: *Dynamic Router Using C# and MSMQ*

This example builds on the example presented in the *Content-Based Router* (230) and enhances it to act as a *Dynamic Router.* The new component listens on two channels: the inQueue and the controlQueue. The control queue can receive messages of the format X:QueueName, causing the *Dynamic Router* to route all messages whose body text begins with the letter X to the queue QueueName.

Dynamic Router

```csharp
class DynamicRouter
{
    protected MessageQueue inQueue;
    protected MessageQueue controlQueue;
    protected MessageQueue dunnoQueue;

    protected IDictionary routingTable = (IDictionary)(new Hashtable());


    public DynamicRouter(MessageQueue inQueue, MessageQueue controlQueue,
                         MessageQueue dunnoQueue)
    {
        this.inQueue = inQueue;
        this.controlQueue = controlQueue;
        this.dunnoQueue = dunnoQueue;

        inQueue.ReceiveCompleted += new ReceiveCompletedEventHandler(OnMessage);
        inQueue.BeginReceive();

        controlQueue.ReceiveCompleted +=
            new ReceiveCompletedEventHandler(OnControlMessage);
        controlQueue.BeginReceive();
    }

    protected void OnMessage(Object source, ReceiveCompletedEventArgs asyncResult)
    {
        MessageQueue mq = (MessageQueue)source;
        mq.Formatter = new System.Messaging.XmlMessageFormatter
                          (new String[] {"System.String,mscorlib"});
```

```
        Message message = mq.EndReceive(asyncResult.AsyncResult);

        String key = ((String)message.Body).Substring(0, 1);

        if (routingTable.Contains(key))
        {
            MessageQueue destination  = (MessageQueue)routingTable[key];
            destination.Send(message);
        }
        else
            dunnoQueue.Send(message);
        mq.BeginReceive();
    }

    // control message format is X:QueueName as a single string
    protected void OnControlMessage(Object source, ReceiveCompletedEventArgs asyncResult)
    {
        MessageQueue mq = (MessageQueue)source;
        mq.Formatter = new System.Messaging.XmlMessageFormatter
                        (new String[] {"System.String,mscorlib"});
        Message message = mq.EndReceive(asyncResult.AsyncResult);

        String text = ((String)message.Body);
        String [] split = (text.Split(new char[] {':'}, 2));
        if (split.Length == 2)
        {
            String key = split[0];
            String queueName = split[1];
            MessageQueue queue = FindQueue(queueName);
            routingTable.Add(key, queue);
        }
        else
        {
            dunnoQueue.Send(message);
        }
        mq.BeginReceive();
    }

    protected MessageQueue FindQueue(string queueName)
    {
        if (!MessageQueue.Exists(queueName))
        {
            return MessageQueue.Create(queueName);
        }
        else
            return new MessageQueue(queueName);
    }
}
```

This example uses a very simple conflict resolution mechanism—last one wins. If two recipients express interest in receiving messages that start with the letter X, only the second recipient will receive the message because the Hashtable stores only one queue for each key value. Also note that the dunnoQueue can now receive two types of messages: incoming messages that have no matching routing rules or control messages that do not match the required format.

Dynamic
Router

Recipient List

A *Content-Based Router* (230) allows us to route a message to the correct system based on message content. This process is transparent to the original sender in the sense that the originator simply sends the message to a channel, where the router picks it up and takes care of everything.

In some cases, though, we may want to specify one or more recipients for the message. A common analogy is the recipient lists implemented in most e-mail systems. For each e-mail message, the sender can specify a list of recipients. The mail system then ensures transport of the message content to each recipient. An example from the domain of enterprise integration would be a situation where a function can be performed by one or more providers. For example, we may have a contract with multiple credit agencies to assess the credit worthiness of our customers. When a small order comes in, we may simply route the credit request message to one credit agency. If a customer places a large order, we may want to route the credit request message to multiple agencies and compare the results before making a decision. In this case, the list of recipients depends on the dollar value of the order.

In another situation, we may want to route an order message to a select list of suppliers to obtain a quote for a requested item. Rather than sending the request to all vendors, we may want to control which vendors receive the request, possibly based on user preferences.

Recipient
List

▼───────────────────────────────────────

How do we route a message to a dynamic list of recipients?

───────────────────────────────────────▲

This problem is an extension to the issue that a *Content-Based Router* (230) solves, so some of the same forces and alternatives described in that pattern come into play here as well.

Most messaging systems provide *Publish-Subscribe Channels* (106), a type of channel that sends a copy of each published message to each recipient that subscribes to the channel. The set of recipients is based on subscription to the specific channel or subject. However, the list of active subscribers to a channel is somewhat static and cannot be controlled on a message-by-message basis. What we need is something like a *Publish-Subscribe Channel* (106) that can send each message to a different list of subscribers. This is difficult because subscribing to a

Publish-Subscribe Channel (106) is binary—you are either subscribed to all messages on the channel or none.

Each potential recipient could filter incoming messages based on message content, most likely using a *Message Filter* (237) or *Selective Consumer* (515). Unfortunately, this solution distributes the logic of who receives the message to the individual subscribers, which could become a maintenance burden. To retain a central point of control, the message could specify its intended recipients in a list attached to the message. Then, when the message is broadcast to all possible recipients, each recipient that is not in the message's recipient list would discard the message.

The problem with these approaches is their inefficiency: Each potential recipient must process every message, even though in many cases the recipient will decide to discard the message. The configuration also relies on a certain "honor system" on the part of the recipients, as a recipient could decide to process a message it is not supposed to process. This is definitely not desirable in situations where a message should be kept hidden from certain recipients, for example when forwarding a request for a quote to a select subset of suppliers and expecting the others to ignore the request when they receive it.

We could also require the message originator to publish the message individually to each desired recipient. In that case, though, we would place the burden of delivery to all recipients on the message originator. If the originator is a packaged application, this is generally not an option. Also, it would embed decision logic inside the application, which would couple the application more tightly to the integration infrastructure. In many cases, the applications that are being integrated are unaware that they even participate in an integration solution, so expecting the application to contain message routing logic is not realistic.

Recipient List

Define a channel for each recipient. Then use a *Recipient List* to inspect an incoming message, determine the list of desired recipients, and forward the message to all channels associated with the recipients in the list.

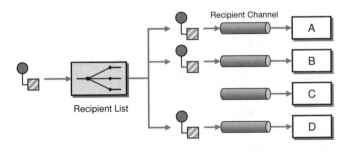

The logic embedded in a *Recipient List* can be pictured as two separate parts even though the implementation is often coupled together. The first part computes a list of recipients. The second part simply traverses the list and sends a copy of the received message to each recipient. Just like a *Content-Based Router* (230), the *Recipient List* usually does not modify the message contents.

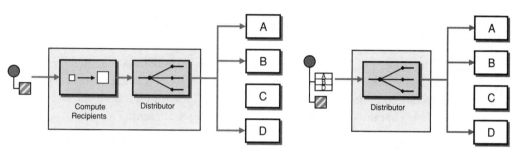

A Recipient List Can Compute the Recipients (left) or Have Another Component Provide a List (right)

The list of recipients can be derived from a number of sources. The creation of the list can be external to the *Recipient List* so that the message originator or another component attaches the list to the incoming message. In that case, the *Recipient List* only has to iterate through this ready-made list. The *Recipient List* usually removes the list from the message to reduce the size of the outgoing messages and prevent individual recipients from seeing who else is on the list. Alternatively, providing the list of recipients with the incoming message makes sense if the destinations of each message are driven by external factors, such as user selection.

In most cases, the *Recipient List* computes the list of recipients based on the content of the message and a set of rules embedded in the *Recipient List*. These rules may be hard-coded or configurable (see the following page).

The *Recipient List* is subject to the same considerations regarding coupling as discussed in *Message Router* (78). Routing messages predictively to individual recipients can lead to tighter coupling between components because a central component has to have knowledge of a series of other components.

In order for the *Recipient List* to control flow of information, we need to make sure that recipients cannot subscribe directly to the input channel into the *Recipient List*, bypassing any control the *Recipient List* exercises.

Recipient List

Robustness

The *Recipient List* component is responsible for sending the incoming message to each recipient specified in the recipient list. A robust implementation of the *Recipient List* must be able to process the incoming message but only "consume" it after all outbound messages have been successfully sent. As such, the *Recipient List* component has to ensure that the complete operation of receiving one message and sending multiple messages is atomic. If a *Recipient List* fails, it must be restartable, meaning it must be able to complete any operation that was in progress when the component failed. This can be accomplished in multiple ways:

1. *Single transaction:* The *Recipient List* can use transactional channels and place the message on the outbound channels as part of a single transaction. It does not commit the messages until all messages are placed on the channels. This guarantees that either all or no messages are sent.

2. *Persistent recipient list:* The *Recipient List* can "remember" which messages it already sent so that on failure and restart it can send messages to the remaining recipients. The recipient list could be stored on disk or a database so that it survives a crash of the *Recipient List* component.

3. *Idempotent receivers:* Alternatively, the *Recipient List* could simply resend all messages on restart. This option requires all potential recipients to be *idempotent* (see *Idempotent Receiver* [528]). Idempotent functions are those that do not change the state of the system if they are applied to themselves; that is, the state of the component is not affected if the same message is processed twice. Messages can be inherently idempotent (e.g., the messages "All Widgets on Sale until May 30" or "Get me a quote for XYZ widgets" are unlikely to do harm if they are received twice), or the receiving component can be made idempotent by inserting a special *Message Filter* (237) that eliminates duplicate messages. Idempotence is very handy because it allows us to simply resend messages when we are in doubt whether the recipient has received it. The TCP/IP protocol uses a similar mechanism to ensure reliable message delivery without unnecessary overhead (see [Stevens]).

Recipient List

Dynamic Recipient List

Even though the intent of the *Recipient List* is to maintain control, it can be useful to let the recipients themselves configure the rules stored in the *Recipient List*—for example, if recipients want to subscribe to specific messages based on rules that cannot easily be represented in the form of *Publish-Subscribe Chan-*

nel (106) topics. We mentioned these types of subscription rules under the *Message Filter* (237) pattern—for example "accept the message if the price is less than $48.31." To minimize network traffic, we would still want to send the messages only to interested parties as opposed to broadcasting it and letting each recipient decide whether or not to process the message. To implement this functionality, recipients can send their subscription preferences to the *Recipient List* via a special control channel. The *Recipient List* stores the preferences in a rules base and uses it to compile the recipient list for each message. This approach gives the subscribers control over the message filtering but leverages the efficiency of the *Recipient List* to distribute the messages. This solution combines the properties of a *Dynamic Router* (243) with a *Recipient List* to create a dynamic *Recipient List* (see figure).

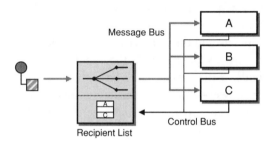

A Dynamic Recipient List Is Configured by the Recipients via a Control Channel

This approach would work well for the price update example discussed in the *Message Filter* (237) pattern. Since it assigns control to the individual recipients, it is not suitable for the price quote example mentioned at the beginning of this pattern, though, because we want to control the vendors that get to participate in the bid.

Network (In)Efficiencies

Whether it is more efficient to send one message to all possible recipients who then filter the message or to send individual messages to each recipient depends very much on the implementation of the messaging infrastructure. Generally, we can assume that the more recipients a message has, the more network traffic it causes. However, there are exceptions. Some publish-subscribe messaging systems are based on IP Multicast functionality and can route messages to multiple recipients with a single network transmission (requiring retransmission only for lost messages). IP Multicast takes advantage of Ethernet's bus architecture. When an IP packet is sent across the network, all network adapters (NIC) on the same Ethernet segment receive the packet. Normally, the NIC verifies the intended recipient of the packet and ignores it if the packet is not addressed to the IP address the NIC is associated with. Multicast routing allows all receivers that are part of a specified multicast group to read the packet off the bus. This results in a single packet being able to be received by multiple NICs who then pass the data to the respective application associated with the network connection. This approach can be very efficient on local networks due to the Ethernet bus architecture. It does not work across the Internet where point-to-point TCP/IP connections are required. In general, we can say that the further apart the recipients are, the more efficient it is to use a *Recipient List* instead of a *Publish-Subscribe Channel* (106).

Whether a broadcast approach is more efficient than a *Recipient List* depends not only on the network infrastructure, but also on the proportion between the total number of recipients and the number that are supposed to process the message. If on average most recipients are in the recipient list, it may be more efficient to simply broadcast the message and have the (few) nonparticipants filter the message out. If, however, on average only a small portion of all possible recipients are interested in a particular message, the *Recipient List* is almost guaranteed to be more efficient.

Recipient List

Recipient List versus Publish-Subscribe and Filters

A number of times we have contrasted implementing the same functionality using predictive routing with a *Recipient List* and using reactive filtering using a *Publish-Subscribe Channel* (106) and an array of *Message Filters* (237). Some of the decision criteria are the same as those of the comparison between the *Content-Based Router* (230) and the *Message Filter* (237) array. However, in case of a *Recipient List*, the message can travel to multiple recipients, making the filter option more attractive.

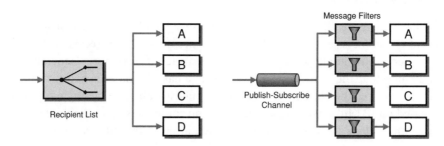

Recipient List versus Message Filter Array

The following table compares the two solutions:

Recipient List	Publish-Subscribe Channel with Message Filters
Central control and maintenance—predictive routing.	Distributed control and maintenance—reactive filtering.
Router needs to know about participants. Router may need to be updated if participants are added or removed (unless using dynamic router, but at expense of losing control).	No knowledge of participants required. Adding or removing participants is easy.
Often used for business transactions, e.g., request for quote.	Often used for event notifications or informational messages.
Generally more efficient if limited to queue-based channels.	Can be more efficient with publish-subscribe channels (depends on infrastructure).

If we send a message to multiple recipients, we may need to reconcile the results later. For example, if we send a request for a credit score to multiple credit agencies, we should wait until all results come back so that we can compare the results and accurately compute the median credit score. With other, less critical functions, we may just take the first available response to optimize message throughput. These types of strategies are typically implemented inside an *Aggregator* (268). *Scatter-Gather* (297) describes situations in which we start with a single message, send it to multiple recipients, and recombine the responses back into a single message.

A dynamic *Recipient List* can be used to implement a *Publish-Subscribe Channel* (106) if a messaging system provides only *Point-to-Point Channels* (103) but no *Publish-Subscribe Channels* (106). The *Recipient List* would keep a list of all *Point-to-Point Channels* (103) that are subscribed to the topic. Each topic can be represented by one specific *Recipient List* instance. This solution can also be useful if we need to apply special criteria to allow recipients to subscribe to a specific data source. While most *Publish-Subscribe Channels* (106) allow any component to subscribe to the channel, the *Recipient List* could easily implement logic to control access to the source data by limiting who gets to subscribe to the list. Of course, this assumes that the messaging system prevents the recipients from directly accessing the input channel into the *Recipient List*.

Recipient List

Example: *Loan Broker*

The composed messaging example in Chapter 9, "Interlude: Composed Messaging," uses a *Recipient List* to route a loan quote request only to qualified banks. The interlude shows implementations of the *Recipient List* in Java, C#, and TIBCO.

Example: *Dynamic Recipient List in C# and MSMQ*

This example builds on the *Dynamic Router* (243) example to turn it into a dynamic *Recipient List*. The code structure is very similar. The DynamicRecipientList listens on two input queues, one for incoming messages (inQueue) and a control queue (controlQueue) where recipients can hand in their subscription preferences. Messages on the control queue have to be formatted as a string consisting of two parts separated by a colon (:). The first part is a list of characters that indicate the subscription preference of the recipient. The recipient expresses that it wants to receive all messages starting with one of the specified letters. The second part of the control message specifies the name of the queue that the recipient listens on. For example, the control message W:WidgetQueue tells the DynamicRecipientList to route all incoming messages that begin with W to the queue WidgetQueue. Likewise, the message WG:WidgetGadgetQueue instructs the DynamicRecipientList to route messages that start with either W or G to the queue WidgetGadgetQueue.

```
class DynamicRecipientList
{
    protected MessageQueue inQueue;
    protected MessageQueue controlQueue;

    protected IDictionary routingTable = (IDictionary)(new Hashtable());

    public DynamicRecipientList(MessageQueue inQueue, MessageQueue controlQueue)
    {
        this.inQueue = inQueue;
        this.controlQueue = controlQueue;

        inQueue.ReceiveCompleted += new ReceiveCompletedEventHandler(OnMessage);
        inQueue.BeginReceive();

        controlQueue.ReceiveCompleted +=
            new ReceiveCompletedEventHandler(OnControlMessage);
        controlQueue.BeginReceive();
    }
```

Recipient List

```
protected void OnMessage(Object source, ReceiveCompletedEventArgs asyncResult)
{
    MessageQueue mq = (MessageQueue)source;
    mq.Formatter = new System.Messaging.XmlMessageFormatter
                        (new String[] {"System.String,mscorlib"});
    Message message = mq.EndReceive(asyncResult.AsyncResult);

    if (((String)message.Body).Length > 0)
    {
        char key = ((String)message.Body)[0];

        ArrayList destinations  = (ArrayList)routingTable[key];
        foreach (MessageQueue destination in destinations)
        {
            destination.Send(message);
            Console.WriteLine("sending message " + message.Body +
                            " to " + destination.Path);
        }
    }
    mq.BeginReceive();
}


// control message format is XYZ:QueueName as a single string
protected void OnControlMessage(Object source, ReceiveCompletedEventArgs asyncResult)
{
    MessageQueue mq = (MessageQueue)source;
    mq.Formatter = new System.Messaging.XmlMessageFormatter
                        (new String[] {"System.String,mscorlib"});
    Message message = mq.EndReceive(asyncResult.AsyncResult);

    String text = ((String)message.Body);
    String [] split = (text.Split(new char[] {':'}, 2));
    if (split.Length == 2)
    {
        char[] keys = split[0].ToCharArray();
        String queueName = split[1];
        MessageQueue queue = FindQueue(queueName);
        foreach (char c in keys)
        {
            if (!routingTable.Contains(c))
            {
                routingTable.Add(c, new ArrayList());
            }
            ((ArrayList)(routingTable[c])).Add(queue);
            Console.WriteLine("Subscribed queue " + queueName + " for message " + c);
        }
    }
    mq.BeginReceive();
}
```

```
protected MessageQueue FindQueue(string queueName)
{
    if (!MessageQueue.Exists(queueName))
    {
        return MessageQueue.Create(queueName);
    }
    else
        return new MessageQueue(queueName);
}
```

The DynamicRecipientList uses a bit more clever (read *complicated*) way to store the recipient's preferences. To optimize processing of incoming messages, the DynamicRecipientList maintains a Hashtable keyed by the first letter of incoming messages. Unlike in the *Dynamic Router* (243) example, the Hashtable contains not a single destination, but an ArrayList of all subscribed destinations. When the DynamicRecipientList receives a message, it locates the correct destination list from the Hashtable and then iterates over the list to send one message to each destination.

This example does not use a dunnoChannel (see *Content-Based Router* [230] or *Dynamic Router* [243]) for incoming messages that do not match any criteria. Typically, a *Recipient List* does not consider it an error if there are zero recipients for a message.

This implementation does not allow recipients to unsubscribe. It also does not detect duplicate subscriptions. For example, if a recipient subscribes twice for the same message type, it will receive duplicate messages. This is different from the typical publish-subscribe semantics where a specific recipient can subscribe to one channel only once. The DynamicRecipientList could easily be changed to disallow duplicate subscriptions if that is desired.

Recipient List

Splitter

Many messages passing through an integration solution consist of multiple elements. For example, an order placed by a customer typically consists of more than just a single line item. As outlined in the description of the *Content-Based Router* (230), each line item may need to be handled by a different inventory system. Thus, we need to find an approach to process a complete order but treat each order item contained in the order individually.

▼

How can we process a message if it contains multiple elements, each of which may have to be processed in a different way?

▲

The solution to this routing problem should be generic enough that it can deal with varying numbers and types of elements. For example, an order can contain any number of items, so we would not want to create a solution that assumes a fixed number of items. Nor would we want to make too many assumptions about what type of items the message contains. For example, if Widgets & Gadgets 'R Us starts selling books tomorrow, we want to minimize the impact on the overall solution.

Splitter

We also want to maintain control over the order items and avoid duplicated or lost processing. For example, we could send the complete order to each order management system using a *Publish-Subscribe Channel* (106) and let it pick out the items that it can handle. This approach has the same disadvantages described in the *Content-Based Router* (230); it would be very difficult to avoid losing or duplicating shipments of individual items.

The solution should also be efficient in its use of network resources. Sending the complete order message to each system that may process only a portion of the order can cause additional message traffic, especially as the number of destinations increases.

To avoid sending the complete message multiple times, we could split the original message into as many messages as there are inventory systems. Each message would then contain only the line items that can be handled by the specific system. This approach is similar to a *Content-Based Router* (230) except we are splitting the message and then routing the individual messages. This approach would be efficient but ties the solution to knowledge about the specific item types and associated destinations. What if we want to change the routing rules? We would now have to change this more complex "item router" component. We used the *Pipes and Filters* (70) architecture before to break out processing into well-defined, composable components as opposed to lumping multiple functions together, so we should be able to take advantage of this architecture here as well.

Use a *Splitter* to break out the composite message into a series of individual messages, each containing data related to one item.

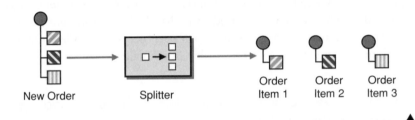

New Order   Splitter   Order   Order   Order
                                     Item 1   Item 2   Item 3

The *Splitter* publishes one message for each single element (or a subset of elements) in the incoming message. In many cases, we want to repeat some common elements in each resulting message. These extra elements may be required to make the resulting child message self-contained and enable stateless processing of each child message. It also allows reconciliation of associated child messages later on. For example, each order item message should contain a copy of the order number so we can properly associate the order item back to the order and all associated entities such as the customer placing the order (see figure).

Splitter

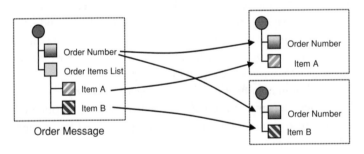

Copying a Common Data Element into Each Child Message

Iterating Splitters

As mentioned earlier, many enterprise integration systems store message data in a tree structure. The beauty of a tree structure is that it is recursive. Each child node underneath a node is the root of another subtree. This allows us to extract pieces of a message tree and process them further as a message tree on their own. If we use message trees, the *Splitter* can easily be configured to iterate through all children under a specified node and send one message for each child node. Such a *Splitter* implementation would be completely generic because it does not make any assumptions about the number and type of child elements. Many commercial EAI tools provide this type of functionality under the term *iterator* or *sequencer.* Since we are trying to avoid vendor vocabulary to reduce potential for confusion, we call this style of *Splitter* an *iterating Splitter.*

Static Splitters

Using a *Splitter* is not limited to repeating elements, though. A large message may be split into individual messages to simplify processing. For example, a number of B2B information-exchange standards specify very comprehensive message formats. These huge messages are often a result of design-by-committee, and large portions of the messages may rarely be used. In many instances it is helpful to split these mega-messages into individual messages, each centered on a specific portion of the large message. This makes subsequent transformations much easier to develop and can also save network bandwidth, since we can route smaller messages to those components that deal only with a portion of the mega-message. The resulting messages are often published to different channels rather than to the same channel because they represent messages of different subtypes. In this scenario, the number of resulting messages is generally fixed, whereas the more general *Splitter* assumes a variable number of items. To distinguish this style of *Splitter,* we call it *static Splitter.* A static *Splitter* is functionally equivalent to using a broadcast channel followed by a set of *Content Filters* (342).

Splitter

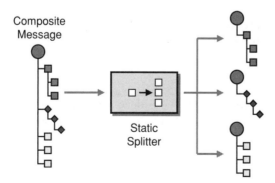

A Static Splitter Breaks Up a Large Message into a Fixed Number of Smaller Messages

Ordered or Unordered Child Messages

In some cases it is useful to equip child messages with sequence numbers to improve message traceability and simplify the task of an *Aggregator* (268). Also, it is a good idea to equip each message with a reference to the original (combined) message so that processing results from the individual messages can be correlated back to the original message. This reference acts as a *Correlation Identifier* (163).

If message envelopes are used (see *Envelope Wrapper* [330]), each new message should be supplied with its own message envelope to make it compliant with the messaging infrastructure. For example, if the infrastructure requires a message to carry a timestamp in the message header, we would propagate the timestamp of the original message to each message's header.

Example: *Splitting an XML Order Document in C#*

Many messaging systems use XML messages. For example, let's assume an incoming order looks as follows:

Splitter

```
<order>
    <date>7/18/2002</date>
    <ordernumber>3825968</ordernumber>
    <customer>
        <id>12345</id>
        <name>Joe Doe</name>
    </customer>
    <orderitems>
        <item>
            <quantity>3.0</quantity>
            <itemno>W1234</itemno>
            <description>A Widget</description>
        </item>
        <item>
            <quantity>2.0</quantity>
            <itemno>G2345</itemno>
            <description>A Gadget</description>
        </item>
    </orderitems>
</order>
```

We want the *Splitter* to split the order into individual order items. For the example document, the *Splitter* should generate the following two messages:

```
<orderitem>
    <date>7/18/2002</date>
    <ordernumber>3825968</ordernumber>
    <customerid>12345</customerid>
    <quantity>3.0</quantity>
```

```
    <itemno>W1234</itemno>
    <description>A Widget</description>
</orderitem>

<orderitem>
    <date>7/18/2002</date>
    <ordernumber>3825968</ordernumber>
    <customerid>12345</customerid>
    <quantity>2.0</quantity>
    <itemno>G2345</itemno>
    <description>A Gadget</description>
</orderitem>
```

Each orderitem message is being enriched with the order date, the order number, and the customer ID from the original order message. The inclusion of the customer ID and the order date makes the message self-contained and keeps the message consumer from having to store context across individual messages. This is important if the messages are to be processed by stateless servers. The addition of the ordernumber field is necessary for later reaggregation of the items (see *Aggregator* [268]). In this example we assume that the specific sequence of items inside an order is not relevant for completion of the order, so we did not have to include an item number.

Let's see what the *Splitter* code looks like in C#.

```
class XMLSplitter
{
    protected MessageQueue inQueue;
    protected MessageQueue outQueue;

    public XMLSplitter(MessageQueue inQueue, MessageQueue outQueue)
    {
        this.inQueue = inQueue;
        this.outQueue = outQueue;

        inQueue.ReceiveCompleted += new ReceiveCompletedEventHandler(OnMessage);
        inQueue.BeginReceive();

        outQueue.Formatter = new ActiveXMessageFormatter();
    }

    protected void OnMessage(Object source, ReceiveCompletedEventArgs asyncResult)
    {
        MessageQueue mq = (MessageQueue)source;
        mq.Formatter = new ActiveXMessageFormatter();
        Message message = mq.EndReceive(asyncResult.AsyncResult);

        XmlDocument doc = new XmlDocument();
        doc.LoadXml((String)message.Body);

        XmlNodeList nodeList;
        XmlElement root = doc.DocumentElement;
```

```
XmlNode date = root.SelectSingleNode("date");
XmlNode ordernumber = root.SelectSingleNode("ordernumber");
XmlNode id = root.SelectSingleNode("customer/id");
XmlElement customerid = doc.CreateElement("customerid");
customerid.InnerText = id.InnerXml;

nodeList = root.SelectNodes("/order/orderitems/item");

foreach (XmlNode item in nodeList)
{
    XmlDocument orderItemDoc = new XmlDocument();
    orderItemDoc.LoadXml("<orderitem/>");
    XmlElement orderItem = orderItemDoc.DocumentElement;

    orderItem.AppendChild(orderItemDoc.ImportNode(date, true));
    orderItem.AppendChild(orderItemDoc.ImportNode(ordernumber, true));
    orderItem.AppendChild(orderItemDoc.ImportNode(customerid, true));

    for (int i=0; i < item.ChildNodes.Count; i++)
    {
        orderItem.AppendChild(orderItemDoc.ImportNode(item.ChildNodes[i], true));
    }

    outQueue.Send(orderItem.OuterXml);
}

mq.BeginReceive();
}
```

Splitter

```
}
```

Most of the code centers on the XML processing. The XMLSplitter uses the same *Event-Driven Consumer* (498) structure as the other routing examples. Each incoming message invokes the method OnMessage, which converts the message body into an XML document for manipulation. First, we extract the relevant values from the order document. Then, we iterate over each <item> child element. We do this by specifying the XPath expression /order/orderitems/item. A simple XPath expression is very similar to a file path—it descends down the document tree, matching the element names specified in the path. For each <item> we assemble a new XML document, copying the fields carried over from the order and the item's child nodes.

Example: *Splitting an XML Order Document in C# and XSL*

Instead of manipulating XML nodes and elements manually, we can also create an XSL document to transform the incoming XML into the desired format and then create output messages from the transformed XML document. That is more maintainable when the document format is likely to change. All we have to do is change the XSL transformation without any changes to the C# code.

The new code uses the Transform method provided by the XslTransform class to convert the input document into an intermediate document format. The intermediate document format has one child element, orderitem, for each resulting message. The code simply traverses all child elements and publishes one message for each element.

```csharp
class XSLSplitter
{
    protected MessageQueue inQueue;
    protected MessageQueue outQueue;

    protected String styleSheet = "..\\..\\Order2OrderItem.xsl";
    protected XslTransform xslt;

    public XSLSplitter(MessageQueue inQueue, MessageQueue outQueue)
    {
        this.inQueue = inQueue;
        this.outQueue = outQueue;

        xslt = new XslTransform();
        xslt.Load(styleSheet, null);

        outQueue.Formatter = new ActiveXMessageFormatter();

        inQueue.ReceiveCompleted += new ReceiveCompletedEventHandler(OnMessage);
        inQueue.BeginReceive();
    }

    protected void OnMessage(Object source, ReceiveCompletedEventArgs asyncResult)
    {
        MessageQueue mq = (MessageQueue)source;
        mq.Formatter = new ActiveXMessageFormatter();
        Message message = mq.EndReceive(asyncResult.AsyncResult);

        try
        {
            XPathDocument doc = new XPathDocument
                                (new StringReader((String)message.Body));

            XmlReader reader = xslt.Transform(doc, null, new XmlUrlResolver());

            XmlDocument allItems = new XmlDocument();
            allItems.Load(reader);

            XmlNodeList nodeList = allItems.DocumentElement.
                                GetElementsByTagName("orderitem");
```

```
        foreach (XmlNode orderItem in nodeList)
        {
            outQueue.Send(orderItem.OuterXml);
        }
    }
    catch (Exception e) { Console.WriteLine(e.ToString()); }
    mq.BeginReceive();
}
}
```

We read the XSL document from a separate file to make it easier to edit and test. Also, it allows us to change the behavior of the *Splitter* without recompiling the code.

```xml
<xsl:stylesheet version="1.0" xmlns:xsl="http://www.w3.org/1999/XSL/Transform">
    <xsl:output method="xml" version="1.0" encoding="UTF-8" indent="yes"/>

    <xsl:template match="/order">
        <orderitems>
            <xsl:apply-templates select="orderitems/item"/>
        </orderitems>
    </xsl:template>

    <xsl:template match="item">
        <orderitem>
            <date>
                <xsl:value-of select="parent::node()/parent::node()/date"/>
            </date>
            <ordernumber>
                <xsl:value-of select="parent::node()/parent::node()/ordernumber"/>
            </ordernumber>
            <customerid>
                <xsl:value-of select="parent::node()/parent::node()/customer/id"/>
            </customerid>
            <xsl:apply-templates select="*"/>
        </orderitem>
    </xsl:template>

    <xsl:template match="*">
        <xsl:copy>
            <xsl:apply-templates select="@* | node()"/>
        </xsl:copy>
    </xsl:template>

</xsl:stylesheet>
```

Splitter

XSL is a declarative language, so it is not easy to make sense of unless you have written a fair bit of XSL yourself (or read a good XSL book like [Tennison]). This XSL transform looks for any occurrence of the order element (there is one in our document). Once it finds this element, it creates a new root element for the output document (all XML documents have to have a single root element) and goes on to process all item elements inside the orderitems element of the input document. The XSL specifies a new "template" for each item that is found. This template copies the date, ordernumber, and customerid elements from the order element (which is the item's parent's parent) and then appends any element from the item. The resulting document has one orderitem element for each item element in the input document. This makes it easy for the C# code to iterate over the elements and publish them as messages.

We were curious about how the two implementations would perform. We decided to run a real quick, nonscientific performance test. We simply piped 5,000 order messages into the input queue, started the *Splitter*, and measured the time it took for 10,000 item messages to arrive on the output queue. We executed this all inside a single program on one machine using local message queues. We measured 7 seconds for the XMLSplitter that uses the DOM to extract elements and 5.3 seconds for the XSL-based *Splitter*. To establish a baseline, a dummy processor that consumes one message of the input queue and publishes the same message twice on the output queue took just under 2 seconds for 5,000 messages. This time includes the dummy processor consuming 5,000 messages and publishing 10,000, and the test harness consuming the 10,000 messages the processor published. So, it looks like the XSL manipulation is a little more efficient than moving elements around "by hand" (if we subtract the baseline, the XSL is about 35 percent faster). We are sure that either program could be tuned for maximum performance, but it was interesting to see them execute side by side.

Splitter

Aggregator

A *Splitter* (259) is useful to break out a single message into a sequence of sub-messages that can be processed individually. Likewise, a *Recipient List* (249) or a *Publish-Subscribe Channel* (106) is useful to forward a request message to multiple recipients in parallel in order to get multiple responses to choose from. In most of these scenarios, the further processing depends on successful processing of the submessages. For example, we want to select the best bid from a number of vendor responses or we want to bill the client for an order after all items have been pulled from the warehouse.

How do we combine the results of individual but related messages so that they can be processed as a whole?

The asynchronous nature of a messaging system makes collecting information across multiple messages challenging. How many messages are there? If we broadcast a message to a broadcast channel, we may not know how many recipients listened to that channel and therefore cannot know how many responses to expect.

Even if we use a *Splitter* (259), the response messages may not arrive in the same sequence in which they were created. As individual messages can be routed through different network paths, the messaging infrastructure can usually guarantee the delivery of each message but may not be able to guarantee the order in which the individual messages are delivered. In addition, the individual messages may be processed by different parties with different processing speeds. As a result, response messages may be delivered out of order (see *Resequencer* [283] for a more detailed description of this problem).

In addition, most messaging infrastructures operate in a "guaranteed, ultimately" delivery mode, which means that messages are guaranteed to be delivered to the intended recipient, but there are no guarantees as to when the messages will be delivered. How long should we wait for a message? If we wait too long, we may delay subsequent processing. If we decide to move ahead without the missing message, we have to find a way to work with incomplete information. Even so, what should we do when the missing message (or messages) finally arrives? In some cases, we may be able to process the message separately, but in other cases, doing so may lead to duplicate processing. Also, if we ignore the latecomer messages, we permanently lose their information content.

All these issues can complicate the combined processing of multiple but related messages. It would be much easier to implement the business logic if a separate component could take care of these complexities and pass a single message to the subsequent processing business that depends on the presence of all individual submessages.

Use a stateful filter, an *Aggregator*, to collect and store individual messages until it receives a complete set of related messages. Then, the *Aggregator* publishes a single message distilled from the individual messages.

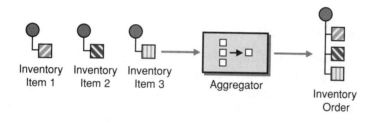

The *Aggregator* is a special filter (in a *Pipes and Filters* [70] architecture) that receives a stream of messages and identifies messages that are correlated. Once a complete set of messages has been received (more later on how to decide when a set is complete), the *Aggregator* collects information from each correlated message and publishes a single, aggregated message to the output channel for further processing.

Unlike most of the previous routing patterns, the *Aggregator* (268) is a *stateful* component. Simple routing patterns like the *Content-Based Router* (230) are often *stateless*, which means the component processes incoming messages one by one and does not have to keep any information between messages. After processing a message, such a component is in the same state as it was before the message arrived. Therefore, we call such a component stateless. The *Aggregator* cannot be stateless, since it needs to store each incoming message until all the messages that belong together have been received. Then, it must distill the information associated with each message into the aggregate message. The *Aggregator* does not necessarily have to store each incoming message in its entirety. For example, if we are processing incoming auction bids, we may need to keep only the highest bid and the associated bidder ID, not the history of all individual bid messages. Still, the *Aggregator* has to store some information across messages and is therefore stateful.

When designing an *Aggregator*, we need to specify the following properties:

1. **Correlation:** Which incoming messages belong together?

2. **Completeness Condition:** When are we ready to publish the result message?

3. **Aggregation Algorithm:** How do we combine the received messages into a single result message?

Correlation is typically achieved by either the type of the incoming messages or an explicit *Correlation Identifier* (163). Common choices for the completeness condition and aggregation algorithm are described on page 272.

Implementation Details

Due to the event-driven nature of a messaging system, the *Aggregator* may receive related messages at any time and in any order. To associate messages, the *Aggregator* maintains a list of active aggregates, that is, aggregates for which the *Aggregator* has received some messages already. When the *Aggregator* receives a new message, it needs to check whether the message is part of an already existing aggregate. If no aggregate related to this message exists, the *Aggregator* assumes that this is the first message of a set and creates a new aggregate. It then adds the message to the new aggregate. If an aggregate already exists, the *Aggregator* simply adds the message to the aggregate.

After adding the message, the *Aggregator* evaluates the completeness condition for the affected aggregate. If the condition evaluates to true, a new aggregate message is formed from the messages accumulated in the aggregate and published to the output channel. If the completeness condition evaluates to false, no message is published and the *Aggregator* keeps the aggregate active for additional messages to arrive.

The following diagram illustrates this strategy. In this simple scenario, incoming messages are related through a *Correlation Identifier* (163). When the first message with the *Correlation Identifier* (163) value of 100 arrives, the *Aggregator* initializes a new aggregate and stores the message inside that aggregate. In our example, the completeness condition specifies a minimum of three messages, so the aggregate is not yet complete. When the second message with the *Correlation Identifier* (163) value of 100 arrives, the *Aggregator* adds it to the already existing aggregate. Again, the aggregate is not yet complete. The third message specifies a different *Correlation Identifier* (163) value, 101. As a result, the *Aggregator* starts a new aggregate for that value. The fourth message relates to the first aggregate (identifier 100). After adding this message, the aggregate contains three messages, so the completeness condition is now fulfilled. As a result, the *Aggregator* computes the aggregate message, marks the aggregate as completed, and publishes the result message.

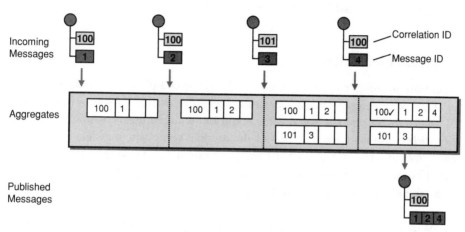

Aggregator Internals

This strategy creates a new aggregate whenever the *Aggregator* receives a message that cannot be associated with an existing aggregate. Therefore, the *Aggregator* does not need prior knowledge of the aggregates that it may produce. Accordingly, we call this variant a self-starting *Aggregator*.

Depending on the aggregation strategy, the *Aggregator* may have to deal with the situation that an incoming message belongs to an aggregate that has already been closed out—that is, the incoming message arrives after the aggregate message has been published. In order to avoid starting a new aggregate, the *Aggregator* must keep a list of aggregates that have been closed out. This list should be purged periodically so that it does not grow indefinitely. However, we need to be careful not to purge closed-out aggregates too soon because that would cause any messages that are delayed to start a new aggregate. Since we do not need to store the complete aggregate, but just the fact that it has been closed, we can store the list of closed aggregates quite efficiently and build a sufficient safety margin into the purge algorithm. We can also use *Message Expiration* (176) to ignore messages that have been delayed for an inordinate amount of time.

In order to increase the robustness of the overall solution, we can also allow the *Aggregator* to listen on a specific control channel that allows the manual purging of all active aggregates or a specific one. This feature can be useful if we want to recover from an error condition without having to restart the *Aggregator* component. Along the same lines, allowing the *Aggregator* to publish a list of active aggregates to a special channel upon request can be a very useful debugging feature. Both functions are excellent examples of the kind of features typically incorporated into a *Control Bus* (540).

Aggregation Strategies

There are a number of strategies for aggregator completeness conditions. The available strategies primarily depend on whether or not we know how many messages to expect. The *Aggregator* could know the number of submessages to expect because it received a copy of the original composite message or because each individual message contains the total count (as described in the *Splitter* [259] example). Depending on how much the *Aggregator* knows about the message stream, the most common strategies are as follows:

1. **Wait for All:** Wait until all responses are received. This scenario is most likely in the order example we discussed earlier. An incomplete order may not be meaningful. So, if all items are not received within a certain timeout period, an error condition should be raised by the *Aggregator*. This approach may give us the best basis for decision making, but may also be the slowest and most brittle (plus, we need to know how many messages to expect). A single missing or delayed message will prevent further processing of the whole aggregate. Resolving such error conditions can be a complicated matter in loosely coupled asynchronous systems because the asynchronous flow of messages makes it hard to reliably detect error conditions (how long should we wait before a message is "missing"?). One way to deal with missing messages is to re-request the message. However, this approach requires the *Aggregator* to know the source of the message, which may introduce additional dependencies between the *Aggregator* and other components.

2. **Timeout:** Wait for a specified length of time for responses and then make a decision by evaluating those responses received within that time limit. If no responses are received, the system may report an exception or retry. This heuristic is useful if incoming responses are scored and only the message (or a small number of messages) with the highest score is used. This approach is common in "bidding" scenarios.

Aggregator

3. **First Best:** Wait only until the first (fastest) response is received and ignore all other responses. This approach is the fastest but ignores a lot of information. It may be practical in a bidding or quoting scenario where response time is critical.

4. **Timeout with Override:** Wait for a specified amount of time or until a message with a preset minimum score has been received. In this scenario, we are willing to abort early if we find a very favorable response; otherwise, we keep going until time is up. If no clear winner was found at that point, rank ordering among all the messages received so far occurs.

5. **External Event:** Sometimes the aggregation is concluded by the arrival of an external business event. For example, in the financial industry, the end of the trading day may signal the end of an aggregation of incoming price quotes. Using a fixed timer for such an event reduces flexibility because it does not offer much variability. Also, a designated business event in the form of an *Event Message* (151) allows for central control of the system. The *Aggregator* can listen for the *Event Message* (151) on a special control channel or receive a specially formatted message that indicates the end of the aggregation.

Closely tied to the selection of a completeness condition is the selection of the aggregation algorithm. The following strategies are common to condense multiple messages into a single message:

Aggregator

1. **Select the "best" answer:** This approach assumes that there is a single best answer, such as the lowest bid for an identical item. This makes it possible for the *Aggregator* to make the decision and only pass the "best" message on. However, in real life, selection criteria are rarely this simple. For example, the best bid for an item may depend on time of delivery, the number of available items, whether the vendor is on the preferred vendor list, and so on.

2. **Condense data:** An *Aggregator* can be used to reduce message traffic from a high-traffic source. In these cases it may make sense to compute an average of individual messages or add numeric fields from each message into a single message. This works best if each message represents a numeric value, for example, the number of orders received.

3. **Collect data for later evaluation:** It is not always possible for an *Aggregator* to make the decision of how to select the best answer. In those cases it still makes sense to use an *Aggregator* to collect the individual messages and combine them into a single message. This message may simply be a compilation of the individual messages' data. The aggregation decision may be made later by a separate component or a human being.

In many instances, the aggregation strategy is driven by parameters. For example, a strategy that waits for a specified amount of time can be configured with the maximum wait time. Likewise, if the strategy is to wait until an offer exceeds a specific threshold, we will most likely let the *Aggregator* know in advance what the desired threshold is. If these parameters are configurable at runtime, an *Aggregator* may feature an additional input that can receive control messages, such as these parameter settings. The control messages may also contain information such as the number of correlated messages to expect, which can help the *Aggregator* implement more effective completion conditions. In such a scenario, the *Aggregator* does not simply start a new aggregate when the first message arrives, but rather receives up-front information related to an expected series of messages. This information can be a copy of the original request message (e.g., a *Scatter-Gather* [297] message) augmented by any necessary parameter information. The *Aggregator* then allocates a new aggregate and stores the parameter information with the aggregate (see figure). When the individual messages come in, they are associated with the corresponding aggregate. We call this variation an *initialized Aggregator* as opposed to the self-starting *Aggregator*. This configuration, obviously, is possible only if we have access to the originating message, which may not always be the case.

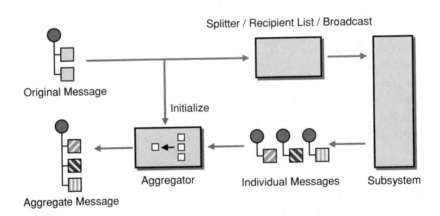

Aggregator

Original Message

Splitter / Recipient List / Broadcast

Initialize

Aggregate Message

Aggregator

Individual Messages

Subsystem

*Aggregator*s are useful in many applications. The *Aggregator* is often coupled with a *Splitter* (259) or a *Recipient List* (249) to form a composite pattern. See *Composed Message Processor* (294) and *Scatter-Gather* (297) for a more detailed description of these composite patterns.

Example: *Loan Broker*

The composed messaging example in Chapter 9, "Interlude: Composed Messaging," uses an *Aggregator* to select the best loan quote from the loan quote messages returned by the banks. The loan broker example uses an initialized *Aggregator*—the *Recipient List* (249) informs the *Aggregator* of the number of quote messages to expect. The interlude shows implementations of the *Aggregator* in Java, C# and TIBCO.

Example: *Aggregator as Missing Message Detector*

Joe Walnes showed us a creative use of an *Aggregator*. His system sends a message through a sequence of components, which are unfortunately quite unreliable. Even using *Guaranteed Delivery* (122) will not correct this problem because the systems themselves typically fail after consuming a message. Because the applications are not *Transactional Clients* (484), the message-in-progress is lost. To help remedy this situation, Joe routes an incoming message through two parallel paths: once through the required but unreliable components and once around the components using *Guaranteed Delivery* (122). An *Aggregator* recombines the messages from the two paths (see figure).

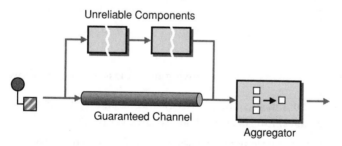

An Aggregator with Timeout Detects Missing Messages

The *Aggregator* uses a "Timeout with Override" completeness condition, which means that the *Aggregator* completes if either the timeout is reached or the two associated messages have been received. The aggregation algorithm depends on which condition is fulfilled first. If two messages are received, the processed message is passed on without modification. If the timeout event occurs, we know that one of the components failed and "ate" the message. As a result, we instruct the *Aggregator* to publish an error message that alerts the operators that one of the components has failed. Unfortunately, the components have to be restarted manually, but a more sophisticated configuration could likely restart the component and resend any lost messages.

Example: *Aggregator in JMS*

This example shows the implementation of an *Aggregator* using the Java Messaging Service (JMS) API. The *Aggregator* receives bid messages on one channel, aggregates all related bids, and publishes a message with the lowest bid to another channel. Bids are correlated through an Auction ID property that acts as a *Correlation Identifier* (163) for the messages. The aggregation strategy is to receive a minimum of three bids. The *Aggregator* is self-starting and does not require external initialization.

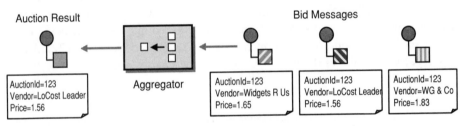

The Aggregator Example Selects the Lowest Bid

The solution consists of the following main classes (see the following figure):

1. Aggregator contains logic to receive messages, aggregate them, and send result messages. Interfaces with aggregates via the Aggregate interface.

2. AuctionAggregate implements the Aggregate interface. This class acts as an *Adapter* [GoF] between the Aggregate interface and the Auction class. This setup allows the Auction class to be free of references to the JMS API.

3. Auction is a collection of related bids that have been received. The Auction class implements the aggregation strategy, for example, finding the lowest bid and determining when the aggregate is complete.

4. Bid is a convenience class that holds the data items associated with a bid. We convert incoming message data into a Bid object so that we can access the bid data through a strongly typed interface, making the Auction logic completely independent from the JMS API.

Aggregator

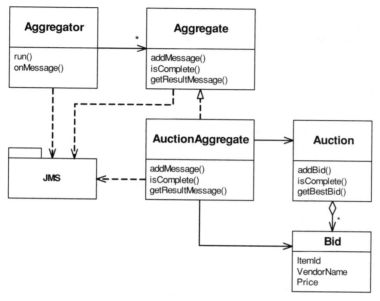

Auction Aggregator Class Diagram

The core of the solution is the `Aggregator` class. This class requires two JMS `Destinations`: one for input and another for output. `Destination` is the JMS abstraction for a `Queue` (*Point-to-Point Channel* [103]) or a `Topic` (*Publish-Subscribe Channel* [106]). The abstraction allows us to write JMS code independent from the type of channel. This feature can be very useful for testing and debugging. For example, during testing we may use publish-subscribe topics so that we can easily "listen in" on the message traffic. When we go to production, we may want to switch to queues.

Aggregator

```
public class Aggregator implements MessageListener
{
    static final String PROP_CORRID = "AuctionID";

    Map activeAggregates = new HashMap();

    Destination inputDest = null;
    Destination outputDest = null;
    Session session = null;

    MessageConsumer in = null;
    MessageProducer out = null;

    public Aggregator (Destination inputDest, Destination outputDest, Session session)
```

```
    {
        this.inputDest = inputDest;
        this.outputDest = outputDest;
        this.session = session;
    }

    public void run()
    {
        try {
            in = session.createConsumer(inputDest);
            out = session.createProducer(outputDest);
            in.setMessageListener(this);
        } catch (Exception e) {
            System.out.println("Exception occurred: " + e.toString());
        }
    }

    public void onMessage(Message msg)
    {
        try {
            String correlationID = msg.getStringProperty(PROP_CORRID);
            Aggregate aggregate = (Aggregate)activeAggregates.get(correlationID);
            if (aggregate == null) {
                aggregate = new AuctionAggregate(session);
                activeAggregates.put(correlationID, aggregate);
            }
            //--- ignore message if aggregate is already closed
            if (!aggregate.isComplete()) {
                aggregate.addMessage(msg);
                if (aggregate.isComplete()) {
                    MapMessage result = (MapMessage)aggregate.getResultMessage();
                    out.send(result);
                }
            }
        } catch (JMSException e) {
            System.out.println("Exception occurred: " + e.toString());
        }
    }
}
```

Aggregator

The Aggregator is an *Event-Driven Consumer* (498) and implements the
MessageListener interface, which requires it to implement the onMessage method.
Because the Aggregator is the message listener for the MessageConsumer, every time a
new message arrives on the consumer's destination, JMS invokes the method
onMesssage. For each incoming message, the Aggregator extracts the correlation ID
(stored as a message property) and checks whether an active aggregate exists
for this correlation ID. If no aggregate is found, the Aggregator instantiates a new
AuctionAggregate instance. The Aggregator then checks whether the aggregate is still
active (i.e., not complete). If the aggregate is no longer active, it discards the

incoming message. If the aggregate is active, it adds the message to the aggregate and tests whether the termination condition has been fulfilled. If so, it gets the best bid entry and publishes it.

The Aggregator code is very generic and depends on this specific example application only in two lines of code. First, it assumes that the correlation ID is stored in the message property AuctionID. Second, it creates an instance of the class AuctionAggregate. We could avoid this reference if we used a factory that returns an object of type Aggregate and internally creates an instance of type AuctionAggregate. Since this is a book on enterprise integration and not on object-oriented design, we kept things simple and let this dependency pass.

The AuctionAggregate class provides the implementation for the Aggregate interface. The interface is rather simple, specifying only three methods: one to add a new message (addMessage), one to determine whether the aggregate is complete (isComplete), and one to get the best result (getBestMessage).

```
public interface Aggregate {
    public void addMessage(Message message);
    public boolean isComplete();
    public Message getResultMessage();
}
```

Instead of implementing the aggregation strategy inside the AuctionAggregate class, we decided to create a separate class Auction that implements the aggregation strategy but is not dependent on the JMS API:

Aggregator

```
public class Auction
{
    ArrayList bids = new ArrayList();

    public void addBid(Bid bid)
    {
        bids.add(bid);
        System.out.println(bids.size() + " Bids in auction.");
    }

    public boolean isComplete()
    {
        return (bids.size() >= 3);
    }

    public Bid getBestBid()
    {
        Bid bestBid = null;

        Iterator iter = bids.iterator();
        if (iter.hasNext())
            bestBid = (Bid) iter.next();
```

```
        while (iter.hasNext()) {
            Bid b = (Bid) iter.next();
            if (b.getPrice() < bestBid.getPrice()) {
                bestBid = b;
            }
        }
        return bestBid;
    }
}
```

The Auction class is actually quite simple. It provides three methods similar to the Aggregate interface, but the method signatures differ in that they use the strongly typed Bid class instead of the JMS-specific Message class. For this example, the completeness condition is very simple, simply waiting until three bids have been received. However, separating the aggregation strategy from the Auction class and the JMS API makes it easy to enhance the Auction class to incorporate more sophisticated logic.

The AuctionAggregate class acts as an *Adapter* [GoF] between the Aggregate interface and the Auction class. An adapter is a class that converts the interface of a class into another interface.

```
public class AuctionAggregate implements Aggregate {
    static String PROP_AUCTIONID = "AuctionID";
    static String ITEMID = "ItemID";
    static String VENDOR = "Vendor";
    static String PRICE = "Price";

    private Session session;
    private Auction auction;

    public AuctionAggregate(Session session)
    {
        this.session = session;
        auction = new Auction();
    }

    public void addMessage(Message message) {
        Bid bid = null;
        if (message instanceof MapMessage) {
            try {
                MapMessage mapmsg = (MapMessage)message;
                String auctionID = mapmsg.getStringProperty(PROP_AUCTIONID);
                String itemID = mapmsg.getString(ITEMID);
                String vendor = mapmsg.getString(VENDOR);
                double price = mapmsg.getDouble(PRICE);
                bid = new Bid(auctionID, itemID, vendor, price);
                auction.addBid(bid);
            } catch (JMSException e) {
                System.out.println(e.getMessage());
```

```
            }
        }
    }

    public boolean isComplete()
    {
        return auction.isComplete();
    }

    public Message getResultMessage() {
        Bid bid = auction.getBestBid();
        try {
            MapMessage msg = session.createMapMessage();
            msg.setStringProperty(PROP_AUCTIONID, bid.getCorrelationID());
            msg.setString(ITEMID, bid.getItemID());
            msg.setString(VENDOR, bid.getVendorName());
            msg.setDouble(PRICE, bid.getPrice());
            return msg;
        } catch (JMSException e) {
            System.out.println("Could not create message: " + e.getMessage());
            return null;
        }
    }
}
```

The following sequence diagram summarizes the interaction between the
classes:

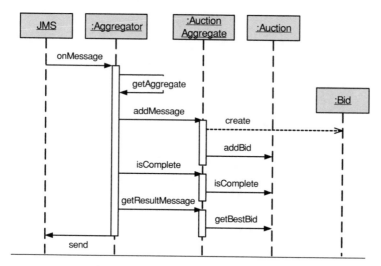

Auction Aggregator Sequence Diagram

This simple example assumes that Auction IDs are universally unique. This allows us to not worry about cleaning up the open auction list—we just let it grow. In a real-life application we would need to decide when to purge old auction records to avoid memory leaks.

Because this code references only JMS Destinations, we can run it with either Topics or Queues. In a production environment, this application may be more likely to employ a *Point-to-Point Channel* (103) (equivalent to a JMS Queue) because there should be only a single recipient for a bid, the *Aggregator*. As described in *Publish-Subscribe Channel* (106), topics can simplify testing and debugging. It is very easy to add an additional listener to a topic without affecting the flow of messages. When debugging a messaging application, it is often useful to run a separate listener window that tracks all messages that are exchanged between any participants. Many JMS implementations allow you to use wildcards in topic names so that a listener can simply subscribe to all topics by specifying a topic name of *. It is very handy to have a simple listener tool that displays all messages traveling on a topic and also logs the messages into a file for later analysis.

Aggregator

Resequencer

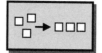

A *Message Router* (78) can route messages from one channel to different channels based on message content or other criteria. Because individual messages may follow different routes, some messages are likely to pass through the processing steps sooner than others, resulting in the messages getting out of order. However, some subsequent processing steps do require in-sequence processing of messages, for example, to maintain referential integrity.

How can we get a stream of related but out-of-sequence messages back into the correct order?

The obvious solution to the out-of-sequence problem is to keep messages in sequence in the first place. Keeping things in order is in fact easier than getting them back in order. That's why many university libraries like to prevent readers from putting books back into the (ordered) bookshelf. By controlling the insert process, correct order is (almost) guaranteed at any point in time. But keeping things in sequence when dealing with an asynchronous messaging solution can be about as difficult as convincing a teenager that keeping her room in order is actually the more efficient approach.

One common way things get out of sequence is when different messages take different processing paths. Let's look at a simple example. Let's assume we are dealing with a numbered sequence of messages. If all even-numbered messages have to undergo a special transformation, whereas all odd-numbered messages can be passed right through, then odd-numbered messages will appear on the resulting channel immediately while the even ones queue up at the transformation. If the transformation is quite slow, all odd messages may appear on the output channel before a single even message makes it, bringing the sequence completely out of order (see figure on the top of the following page).

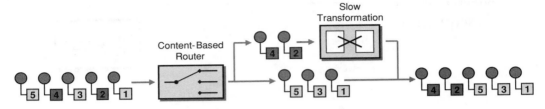

Messages Getting Out of Order

To avoid getting the messages out of order, we could introduce a loop-back (acknowledgment) mechanism that makes sure that only one message at a time passes through the system, meaning the next message will not be sent until the last one is done processing. This conservative approach will resolve the issue, but has two significant drawbacks. First, it can slow the system significantly. If we have a large number of parallel processing units, we would severely underutilize the processing power. In fact, in many instances the reason for parallel processing is that we need to increase performance, so throttling traffic to one message at a time would completely negate the purpose of the solution. The second issue is that this approach requires us to have control over messages being sent into the processing units. However, we often find ourselves at the receiving end of an out-of-sequence message stream without having control over the message origin.

An *Aggregator* (268) can receive a stream of messages, identify related messages, and aggregate them into a single message based on a number of strategies. During this process, the *Aggregator* (268) also must deal with the fact that individual messages can arrive at any time and in any order. The *Aggregator* (268) solves this problem by storing messages until all related messages arrive before it publishes a result message.

Resequencer

Use a stateful filter, a *Resequencer*, to collect and reorder messages so that they can be published to the output channel in a specified order.

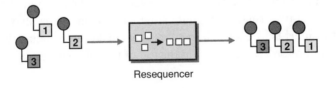

Resequencer

The *Resequencer* can receive a stream of messages that may not arrive in order. It stores out-of-sequence messages in an internal buffer until a complete sequence is obtained, and then publishes the messages to the output channel in the proper sequence. It is important that the output channel is order-preserving so messages are guaranteed to arrive in order at the next component. Like most other routers, a *Resequencer* usually does not modify the message contents.

Sequence Numbers

For the *Resequencer* to function, each message has to have a unique sequence number (see *Message Sequence* [170]). This sequence number is different from a message identifier or *Correlation Identifier* (163). A message identifier is a special attribute that uniquely identifies each message. However, in most cases, message identifiers are not comparable; they are basically random values and often not even numeric. Even if they happen to have numerical values, it is generally a bad idea to overload the sequence number semantics over an existing message identifier element. *Correlation Identifiers* (163) are designed to match incoming messages to original outbound requests (see *Request-Reply* [154]). The only requirement for *Correlation Identifiers* (163) is uniqueness; they do not to have to be numeric or in sequence. So, if we need to preserve the order of a series of messages, we should define a separate field to track the position of each message in the sequence. Typically, this field can be part of the message header.

Generating sequence numbers can be more time consuming than generating unique identifiers. Often, unique identifiers can be generated in a distributed fashion by combining unique location information (e.g., the MAC address of the NIC) and current time. Most GUID (globally unique identifier) algorithms work this way. To generate in-sequence numbers, we generally need a single counter that assigns numbers across the system. In most cases, it is not sufficient for the numbers to be simply in ascending order, but they need to be consecutive as well. Otherwise, it will be difficult to identify missing messages. If we are not careful, this sequence number generator could easily become a bottleneck for the message flow. If the individual messages are the result of using a *Splitter* (259), it is best to incorporate the numbering right into the *Splitter* (259). The *Identity Field* pattern in [EAA] contains a useful discussion on how to generate keys and sequence numbers.

Resequencer

Internal Operation

Sequence numbers ensure that the *Resequencer* can detect messages arriving out of sequence. But what should the *Resequencer* do when an out-of-sequence message arrives? An out-of-sequence message implies that a message with a higher sequence number arrives before a message with a lower sequence number. The *Resequencer* has to store the message with the higher sequence number until it receives all the "missing" messages with lower sequence numbers. Meanwhile, it may receive other out-of-sequence messages as well, which also have to be stored. Once the buffer contains a consecutive sequence of messages, the *Resequencer* sends this sequence to the output channel and then removes the sent messages from the buffer (see figure).

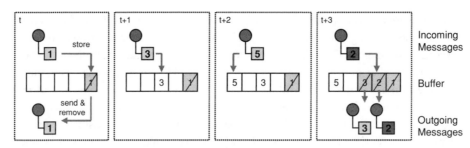

Internal Operation of the Resequencer

In this simple example, the *Resequencer* receives messages with the sequence numbers 1, 3, 5, and 2. We assume that the sequence starts with 1, so the first message can be sent right away and removed from the buffer. The next message has the sequence number 3, so we are missing message 2. Therefore, we store message 3 until we have a proper sequence of messages. We do the same with the next message, which has a sequence number of 5. Once message 2 comes in, the buffer contains a proper sequence of the messages 2 and 3. Therefore, the *Resequencer* publishes these messages and removes them from the buffer. Message 5 remains in the buffer until the remaining "gap" in the sequence is closed.

Avoiding Buffer Overrun

How big should the buffer be? If we are dealing with a long stream of messages, the buffer can get rather large. Worse yet, let's assume we have a configuration with multiple processing units, each of which deals with a specific message type. If one processing unit fails, we will get a long stream of out-of-sequence messages. A buffer overrun is almost certain. In some cases, we can use the message queue to absorb the pending messages. This works only if the messaging infrastructure allows us to read messages from the queue based on selection criteria as opposed to always reading the oldest message first. That way, we can poll the

Resequencer

queue and see whether the first missing message has come in yet without consuming all the messages in between. At some point, though, even the storage allocated to the message queue will fill up.

One robust way to avoid buffer overruns is to throttle the message producer by using active acknowledgment (see figure).

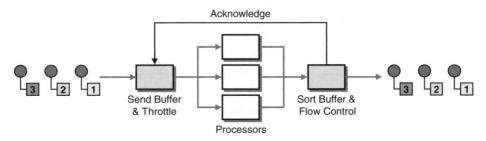

Active Acknowledgment Avoids Buffer Overflow

As we discussed earlier, sending only a single message at a time is very inefficient. We need to be a little smarter than that. A more efficient way is for the *Resequencer* to tell the producer how many slots it has available in its buffer. The message throttle can then fire off that many messages, since even if they get completely out of order, the *Resequencer* will be able to hold all of them in the buffer and re-sequence them. This approach presents a good compromise between efficiency and buffer requirements. However, it does require that we have access to the original in-sequence message stream in order to insert the send buffer and throttle.

This approach is very similar to the way the TCP/IP network protocol works. One of the key features of the TCP protocol is to ensure in-sequence delivery of packets over the network. In reality, each packet may be routed through a different network path, so out-of-sequence packets occur quite frequently. The receiver maintains a circular buffer that is used as a sliding window. Receiver and sender negotiate on the number of packets to send before each acknowledgment. Because the sender waits for an acknowledgment from the receiver, a fast sender cannot outpace the receiver or cause the buffer to overflow. Specific rules also prevent the so-called Silly Window Syndrome, where sender and receiver could fall into a very inefficient, one-packet-at-a-time mode [Stevens].

Another solution to the buffer overrun problem is to compute stand-in messages for the missing message. This works if the recipient is tolerant toward "good enough" message data and does not require precise data for each message or if speed is more important than accuracy. For example, in voice over IP transmissions, filling in a blank packet results in a better user experience than issuing a re-request for a lost packet, which would cause a noticeable delay in the voice stream.

Most of us application developers take reliable network communication for granted. When designing messaging solutions, it is actually helpful to look into some of the internals of TCP, because at its core, IP traffic is asynchronous and unreliable and has to deal with many of the same issues enterprise integration solutions do. For a thorough treatment of IP protocols see [Stevens] and [Wright].

Example: *Resequencer in Microsoft .NET with MSMQ*

To demonstrate the function of a *Resequencer* in a real-life scenario, we use the following setup:

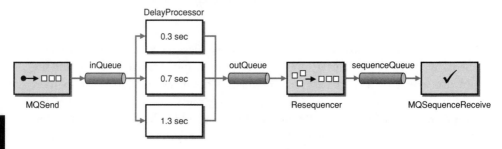

Resequencer Test Configuration

The test setup consists of four main components, each implemented as a C# class. The components communicate via MSMQ message queues provided by the Message Queuing service that is part of Windows 2000 and Windows XP.

1. MQSend acts as the *Test Message* (66) generator. The message body for each message contains a simple text string. MQSend also equips each message with a sequence number inside the AppSpecific property of each message. The sequence starts with 1, and the number of messages can be passed in from the command line. MQSend publishes the messages to the private queue inQueue.

2. DelayProcessor reads messages off inQueue. The only "processing" consists of a timed delay before the identical message is republished to outQueue. We use three DelayProcessors in parallel to simulate a load-balanced processing unit.

The processors act as *Competing Consumers* (502), so each message is consumed by exactly one processor. All processors publish messages to outQueue. Because of the different processing speeds, messages on outQueue are out of sequence.

3. The Resequencer buffers incoming out-of-sequence messages and republishes them in sequence to the sequenceQueue.

4. MQSequenceReceive reads messages off the sequenceQueue and verifies that the sequence numbers in the AppSpecific property are in ascending order.

If we fire up all components, we see debug output similar to the following figure. From the size of the processor output windows, we can see the different speeds at which the processors are working. As expected, the messages arriving at the *Resequencer* are not in sequence (in this run, the messages arrived as 3, 4, 1, 5, 7, 2, ...). We can see from the *Resequencer* output how the *Resequencer* buffers the incoming messages if a message is missing. As soon as the missing message arrives, the *Resequencer* publishes the now completed sequence in the correct order.

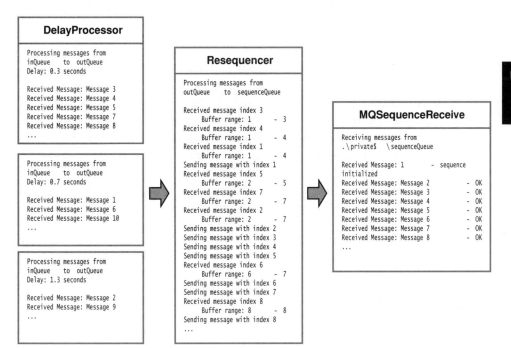

Output from the Test Components

Looking at the test setup, we realize that both the DelayProcessor and the *Resequencer* have a few things in common: They both read messages from an input queue and publish them to an output queue. The only difference is in what happens in between—the actual processing of the message. Therefore, we created a common base class that encapsulates the basic functionality of this generic filter (see *Pipes and Filters* [70]). It contains convenience and template methods for queue creation and asynchronous receiving, processing, and sending of messages. We call this base class Processor (see figure).

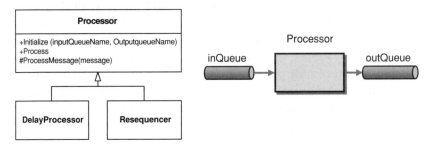

Both the DelayProcessor and the Resequencer Inherit from the Common Processor Class

The default implementation of the Processor simply copies messages from the input queue to the output queue. To implement the *Resequencer*, we have to override the default implementation of the ProcessMessage method. In the case of the *Resequencer*, the processMessage method adds the received message in the buffer, which is implemented as a Hashtable. The messages in the buffer are keyed by the message sequence number, which is stored in the AppSpecific property. Once the new message is added, the method SendConsecutiveMessages checks whether we have a consecutive sequence starting with the next outstanding messages. If so, the method sends all consecutive messages and removes them from the buffer.

Resequencer.cs

```
using System;
using System.Messaging;
using System.Collections;
using MsgProcessor;

namespace Resequencer
{
```

```
class Resequencer : Processor
{
    private int startIndex = 1;
    private IDictionary buffer = (IDictionary)(new Hashtable());
    private int endIndex = -1;

    public Resequencer(MessageQueue inputQueue, MessageQueue outputQueue)
                     : base (inputQueue, outputQueue) {}

    protected override void ProcessMessage(Message m)
    {
        AddToBuffer(m);
        SendConsecutiveMessages();
    }

    private void AddToBuffer(Message m)
    {
        Int32 msgIndex = m.AppSpecific;
        Console.WriteLine("Received message index {0}", msgIndex);
        if (msgIndex < startIndex)
        {
            Console.WriteLine("Out of range message index! Current start is: {0}",
                            startIndex);
        }
        else
        {
            buffer.Add(msgIndex, m);
            if (msgIndex > endIndex)
                endIndex = msgIndex;
        }
        Console.WriteLine("    Buffer range: {0} - {1}", startIndex, endIndex);
    }

    private void SendConsecutiveMessages()
    {
        while (buffer.Contains(startIndex))
        {
            Message m = (Message)(buffer[startIndex]);
            Console.WriteLine("Sending message with index {0}", startIndex);
            outputQueue.Send(m);
            buffer.Remove(startIndex);
            startIndex++;
        }
    }
}

}
```

Resequencer

As you can see, the *Resequencer* assumes that the message sequence starts with 1. This works well if the message producer also starts the sequence from 1 and the two components maintain the same sequence over the lifetime of the components. To make the *Resequencer* more flexible, the message producer should negotiate a sequence start number with the *Resequencer* before sending the first message of the sequence. This process is analogous to the SYN messages exchanged during the connect sequence of the TCP protocol (see [Stevens]).

The current implementation also has no provisions for a buffer overrun. Let's assume a DelayProcessor aborts or malfunctions and eats a message. The *Resequencer* will wait indefinitely for the missed message until the buffer overflows. In high-volume scenarios, the message and the *Resequencer* need to negotiate a window size describing the maximum number of messages the *Resequencer* can buffer. Once the buffer is full, an error handler has to determine how to deal with the missing message. For example, the producer could resend the message, or a "dummy" message could be injected.

The Processor base class is relatively simple. It uses asynchronous message processing by using the BeginReceive and EndReceive methods. Because it is easy to forget to call BeginReceive at the end of the message processing, we used a *template method* that incorporates this step. Subclasses can then override the ProcessMessage method without having to worry about the asynchronous processing.

Processor.cs

```
using System;
using System.Messaging;
using System.Threading;

namespace MsgProcessor
{
    public class Processor
    {
        protected MessageQueue inputQueue;
        protected MessageQueue outputQueue;

        public Processor (MessageQueue inputQueue, MessageQueue outputQueue)
        {
            this.inputQueue = inputQueue;
            this.outputQueue = outputQueue;
            inputQueue.Formatter = new System.Messaging.XmlMessageFormatter
                                (new String[] {"System.String,mscorlib"});
            inputQueue.MessageReadPropertyFilter.ClearAll();
            inputQueue.MessageReadPropertyFilter.AppSpecific = true;
            inputQueue.MessageReadPropertyFilter.Body = true;
            inputQueue.MessageReadPropertyFilter.CorrelationId = true;
            inputQueue.MessageReadPropertyFilter.Id = true;
            Console.WriteLine("Processing messages from " + inputQueue.Path +
                        " to " + outputQueue.Path);
        }
```

```
public void Process()
{
    inputQueue.ReceiveCompleted += new
        ReceiveCompletedEventHandler(OnReceiveCompleted);
    inputQueue.BeginReceive();
}

private void OnReceiveCompleted(Object source,
                             ReceiveCompletedEventArgs asyncResult)
{
    MessageQueue mq = (MessageQueue)source;

    Message m = mq.EndReceive(asyncResult.AsyncResult);
    m.Formatter =  new System.Messaging.XmlMessageFormatter
                     (new String[] {"System.String,mscorlib"});

    ProcessMessage(m);

    mq.BeginReceive();
}

protected virtual void ProcessMessage(Message m)
{
    string body = (string)m.Body;
    Console.WriteLine("Received Message: " + body);
    outputQueue.Send(m);
}
    }
}
```

Composed Message Processor

The order-processing example presented in the *Content-Based Router* (230) and *Splitter* (259) patterns processes an incoming order consisting of individual line items. Each line item requires an inventory check with the respective inventory system. After all items have been verified, we want to pass the validated order message to the next processing step.

> How can you maintain the overall message flow when processing a message consisting of multiple elements, each of which may require different processing?

This problem seems to contain elements of multiple patterns we have already defined. A *Splitter* (259) can split a single message into multiple parts. A *Content-Based Router* (230) could then route individual submessages through the correct processing steps based on message content or type. The *Pipes and Filters* (70) architectural style allows us to chain together these two patterns so that we can route each item in the composed message to the appropriate processing steps:

**Composed
Message
Processor**

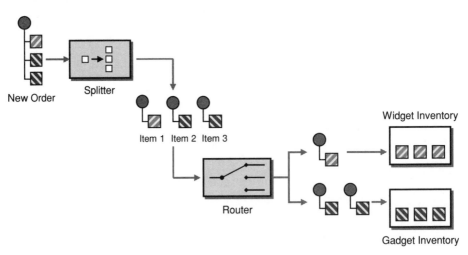

Combining a Splitter and a Router

In our example, this means that each order item is routed to the proper inventory system to be verified. The inventory systems are decoupled from each other, and each system receives only items that can be processed by it.

The shortcoming of the setup so far is that we cannot find out whether all items that have been ordered are actually in stock and can be shipped. We also need to retrieve the prices for all items (factoring volume discounts) and assemble them into a single invoice. This requires us to continue processing as if the order is still a single message even though we just chopped it up into many submessages.

One approach would be to just reassemble all those items that pass through a specific inventory system into a separate order. This order can be processed as a whole from this point on: The order can be fulfilled and shipped, and a bill can be sent. Each suborder is treated as an independent process. In some instances, lack of control over the downstream process may make this approach the only available solution. For example, Amazon follows this approach for a large portion of the goods it sells. Orders are routed to different fulfillment houses and managed from there.

However, this approach may not provide the best customer experience. The customer may receive more than one shipment and more than one invoice. Returns or disputes may be difficult to accommodate. This is not a big issue with consumers ordering books, but may prove difficult if individual order items depend on each other. Let's assume that the order consists of furniture items that make up a shelving system. The customer would not be pleased to receive a number of huge boxes containing furniture elements just to find out that the required mounting hardware is temporarily unavailable and will be shipped at a later time.

Composed Message Processor

The asynchronous nature of a messaging system makes distribution of tasks more complicated than synchronous method calls. We could dispatch each individual order item and wait for a response to come back before we check the next item. This would simplify the temporal dependencies but would make the system very inefficient. We would like to take advantage of the fact that each system can process multiple orders simultaneously.

Use a *Composed Message Processor* to process a composite message. The *Composed Message Processor* splits the message up, routes the submessages to the appropriate destinations, and reaggregates the responses back into a single message.

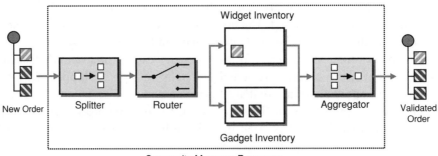

Composite Message Processor

The *Composed Message Processor* uses an *Aggregator* (268) to reconcile the requests that were dispatched to the multiple inventory systems. Each processing unit sends a response message to the *Aggregator* (268) stating the inventory on hand for the specified item. The *Aggregator* (268) collects the individual responses and processes them based on a predefined algorithm.

Because all submessages originate from a single message, we can pass additional information, such as the number of submessages, to the *Aggregator* (268) to define a more efficient aggregation strategy. Nevertheless, the *Composed Message Processor* still has to deal with issues around missing or delayed messages. If an inventory system is unavailable, do we want to delay processing of all orders that include items from that system? Or should we route them to an exception queue for a human to evaluate manually? If a single response is missing, should we resend the inventory request message? For a more detailed discussion of these trade-offs, see *Aggregator* (268).

This pattern demonstrates how several individual patterns can be composed into a single larger pattern. To the rest of the system, the *Composed Message Processor* appears like a simple filter with a single input channel and a single output channel. As such, it provides an effective abstraction of the more complex internal workings.

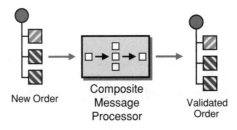

The Composite Message Processor as a Single Filter

Scatter-Gather

In the order-processing example introduced in the previous patterns, each order item that is not currently in stock could be supplied by one of multiple external suppliers. However, the suppliers may or may not have the respective item in stock, they may charge a different price, or they may be able to supply the part by a different date. To fill the order in the best way possible, we should request quotes from all suppliers and decide which one provides us with the best term for the requested item.

> How do you maintain the overall message flow when a message must be sent to multiple recipients, each of which may send a reply?

The solution should allow for flexibility in determining the recipients of the message. We can either determine the list of approved suppliers centrally or we can let any interested supplier participate in the bid. Since we have no (or little) control over the recipients, we must be prepared to receive responses from some, but not all, recipients. Such changes to the bidding rules should not impact the structural integrity of the solution.

The solution should hide the number and identity of the individual recipients from any subsequent processing. Encapsulating the distribution of the message locally keeps other components independent from the route of the individual messages.

We also need to coordinate the subsequent message flow. The easiest solution might be for each recipient to post the reply to a channel and let subsequent components deal with the resolution of the individual messages. However, this would require subsequent components to be aware of the message being sent to multiple recipients. It might also be harder for subsequent components to process the individual messages without having any knowledge of the routing logic that has been applied.

It makes sense to combine the routing logic, the recipients, and the postprocessing of the individual messages into one logical component.

Use a *Scatter-Gather* that broadcasts a message to multiple recipients and reaggregates the responses back into a single message.

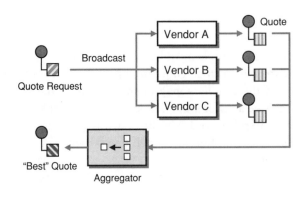

The *Scatter-Gather* routes a request message to a number of recipients. It then uses an *Aggregator* (268) to collect the responses and distill them into a single response message.

There are two variants of the *Scatter-Gather* that use different mechanisms to send the request messages to the intended recipients:

1. **Distribution** via a *Recipient List* (249) allows the *Scatter-Gather* to control the list of recipients but requires the *Scatter-Gather* to be aware of each recipient's message channel.

2. **Auction**-style *Scatter-Gather* uses a *Publish-Subscribe Channel* (106) to broadcast the request to any interested participant. This option allows the *Scatter-Gather* to use a single channel but also forces it to relinquish control.

The solution shares similarities with the *Composed Message Processor* (294). Instead of using a *Splitter* (259), we broadcast the complete message to all involved parties using a *Publish-Subscribe Channel* (106). We will most likely add a *Return Address* (159) so that all responses can be processed through a single channel. As with the *Composed Message Processor* (294), a *Scatter-Gather* aggregates responses based on defined business rules. In our example, the *Aggregator* (268) might take the best bids from suppliers that can fill the order. Aggregating the responses can be more difficult with a *Scatter-Gather* than with the *Composed Message Processor* (294), because we may not know how many recipients participate in the interaction.

Both the *Scatter-Gather* and the *Composed Message Processor* (294) route a single message to multiple recipients and combine the individual reply messages back into a single message by using an *Aggregator* (268). The *Composed Message Processor* (294) performs the task of synchronizing multiple parallel activities. If the individual activities take widely varying amounts of time, subsequent processing is held up even though many subtasks (or even all but one) have been completed. This consideration needs to be weighed against the simplicity and encapsulation the *Scatter-Gather* brings. A compromise between the two choices may be a cascading *Aggregator* (268). This design allows subsequent tasks to be initiated with only a subset of the results being available.

Example: *Loan Broker*

The Loan Broker example (Chapter 9, "Interlude: Composed Messaging") uses a *Scatter-Gather* to route requests for a loan quote to a number of banks and select the best offer from the incoming responses. The example implementations demonstrate both a solution based on a *Recipient List* (249)—see "Asynchronous Implementation with MSMQ" in Chapter 9—and a *Publish-Subscribe Channel* (106)—see "Asynchronous Implementation with TIBCO ActiveEnterprise" in Chapter 9.

Scatter-
Gather

Example: *Combining Patterns*

We can now use the *Scatter-Gather* to implement the widget and gadget order-processing example. We can combine the *Scatter-Gather* with the *Composed Message Processor* (294) to process each incoming order, sequence it into individual items, pass each item up for a bid, aggregate the bids for each item into a combined bid response, and then aggregate all bid responses into a complete quote. This is a very real example of how multiple integration patterns can be combined into a complete solution. The composition of individual patterns into larger patterns allows us to discuss the solution at a higher level of abstraction. It also allows us to modify details of the implementation without affecting other components.

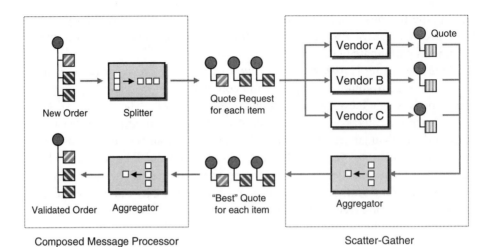

Combining a Scatter-Gather and a Composite Message Processor

This example also shows the versatility of the *Aggregator* (268). The solution uses two *Aggregators* (268) for quite different purposes. The first *Aggregator* (268)—part of the *Scatter-Gather*—chooses the best bid from a number of vendors. This *Aggregator* (268) may not require a response from all vendors (speed may be more important than a low price) but may require a complex algorithm to combine responses. For example, the order may contain 100 widgets, and the lowest price supplier has only 60 widgets in stock. The *Aggregator* (268) must be able to decide whether to accept this offer and fill the remaining 40 items from another supplier. The second *Aggregator* (268)—part of the *Composed Message Processor* (294)—might be simpler because it simply concatenates all responses received from the first *Aggregator* (268). However, this *Aggregator* (268) needs to make sure that all responses are in fact received and needs to deal with error conditions such as missing item responses.

Routing Slip

Most of the routing patterns presented so far route incoming messages to one or more destinations based on a set of rules. Sometimes, though, we need to route a message not just to a single component, but through a whole series of components. Let's assume, for example, that we use a *Pipes and Filters* (70) architecture to process incoming messages that have to undergo a sequence of processing steps and business rule validations. Since the nature of the validations varies widely and may depend on external systems (e.g., credit card validations), we implement each type of step as a separate filter. Each filter inspects the incoming message and applies the business rule(s) to the message. If the message does not fulfill the conditions specified by the rules, it is routed to an exception channel. The channels between the filters determine the sequence of validations that the message needs to undergo.

Now let's assume, though, that the set of validations to perform against each message depends on the message type (for example, purchase order requests do not need credit card validation, or customers who send orders over a VPN may not require decryption and authentication). To accommodate this requirement, we need to find a configuration that can route the message through a different sequence of filters depending on the type of the message.

Routing
Slip

▼

How do we route a message consecutively through a series of processing steps when the sequence of steps is not known at design time and may vary for each message?

▲

The *Pipes and Filters* (70) architectural style gives us an elegant approach to represent a sequence of processing steps as independent filters connected by pipes (channels). In its default configuration, the filters are connected by fixed pipes. If we want to allow messages to be routed to different filters dynamically, we can use special filters that act as *Message Routers* (78). The routers dynamically determine the next filter to route the message to.

The key requirements for a good solution to our problem can be summarized as follows:

- **Efficient message flow:** Messages should flow through only the required steps and avoid unnecessary components.

- **Efficient use of resources:** The solution should not use a huge amount of channels, routers, and other resources.

- **Flexible:** The route that individual messages take should be easy to change.

- **Simple to maintain:** If a new type of message needs to be supported, we would like to have a single point of maintenance to avoid introducing errors.

The following diagrams illustrate our alternative solutions to the problem. We assume that the system offers three separate processing steps, A, B, and C, and that the current message is required to pass only through steps A and C. The actual flow for this example message is marked with thick arrows.

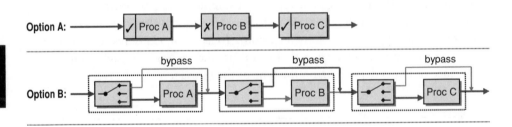

Routing Slip

We could form one long *Pipes and Filters* (70) chain of all possible validation steps and add code to each router to bypass the validation if the step is not required for the type of message being passed through (see Option A). This option essentially employs the reactive filtering approach described in the *Message Filter* (237). While the simplicity of this solution is appealing, the fact that the components blend both business logic (the validation) and routing logic (deciding whether to validate) will make them harder to reuse. Also, it is conceivable that two types of messages undergo similar processing steps but in different order. This hard-wired approach would not easily support this requirement.

In order to improve separation of concerns and increase the composability of the solution, we should replace the "gating" logic inside each component with

Content-Based Routers (230). We would then arrive at a chain of all possible validation steps, each prefixed by a *Content-Based Router* (230)—see Option B. When a message arrives at the router, it checks the type of the message and determines whether this type of message requires the validation step at hand. If the step is required, the router routes the message through the validation. If the step is not required, the router bypasses the validation and routes the message directly to the next router (in a way very similar to the *Detour* [545]). This configuration works quite well in cases where each step is independent from any other step and the routing decision can be made locally at each step. On the downside, this approach ends up routing the message though a long series of routers even though only a few validation steps may be executed. In fact, each message will be transmitted across a channel at a rate of two times the number of possible components. If we have a large component library, this will cause an enormous amount of message flow for a rather simple function. Also, the routing logic is distributed across many filters, making it hard to understand which validation steps a message of a specific type will actually undergo. Likewise, if we introduce a new message type, we may have to update each and every router. Finally, this option suffers from the same limitation as Option A in that messages are tied to executing steps in a predefined order.

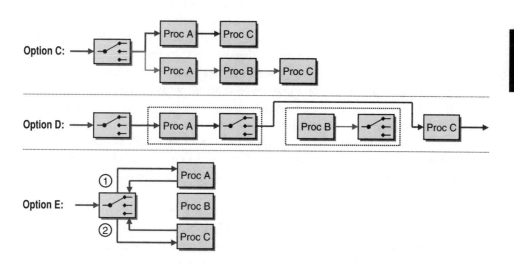

If we desire a central point of control, an up-front *Content-Based Router* (230) tended to be a good choice in our prior pattern discussions. We could envision a solution where we set up individual *Pipes and Filters* (70) chains for each message type. Each chain would contain the sequence of validations relevant to a specific type. We would then use a *Content-Based Router* (230) to route the incoming message to the correct validation chain based on message type (see Option C). This approach routes messages only through the relevant steps (plus the initial router). Thus, it is the most efficient approach so far because we add only a single routing step in order to implement the desired functionality. The solution also highlights the path that a message of a specific type will take quite nicely. However, it requires us to hard-wire any possible combination of validation rules. Also, the same component may be used in more than one path. This approach would require us to run multiple instances of such components, which leads to unnecessary duplication. For a large set of message types, this approach could result in a maintenance nightmare because of the large number of component instances and associated channels that we have to maintain. In summary, this solution is very efficient at the expense of maintainability.

If we want to avoid hard-wiring all possible combinations of validation steps, we need to insert a *Content-Based Router* (230) between each validation step (see Option D). In order not to run into the same issues associated with the reactive filtering approach (presented in Option B), we would insert the *Content-Based Router* (230) *after* each step instead of before (we need one additional router in front of the very first step to get started). The routers would be smart enough to relay the message directly to the next *required* validation step instead of routing it blindly to the next *available* step in the chain. In the abstract, this solution looks similar to the reactive filtering approach because the message traverses an alternating set of routers and filters. However, in this case the routers possess more intelligence than a simple yes or no decision, which allows us to eliminate unnecessary steps. For example, in our simple scenario, the message passes only through two routers as opposed to three with Option B. This option provides efficiency and flexibility but does not solve our goal of obtaining central control—we still have to maintain a potentially large number of routers because the routing logic is spread out across a series of independent routers.

To address this last shortcoming, we could combine all routers into a single "super-router" (see Option E). After each validation step, the message would be routed back to the super-router, which would determine the next validation step to be executed. This configuration routes the message only to those filters that are required for the specific type of message. Since all the routing decisions are now incorporated into a single router, we need to devise a mechanism to remember which steps we already finished processing. Therefore, the super-router would have to be stateful or each filter would have to attach a tag to the message telling the super-router the name of the last filter the message went through. Also, we are still dealing with the fact that each validation step requires the message to be passed through two channels: to the component and then back to the super-router. This results in about two times as much traffic as Option C.

Attach a *Routing Slip* to each message, specifying the sequence of processing steps. Wrap each component with a special message router that reads the *Routing Slip* and routes the message to the next component in the list.

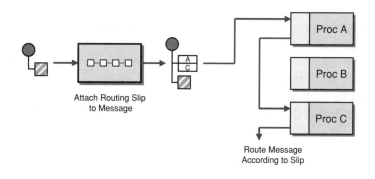

Attach Routing Slip
to Message

Route Message
According to Slip

We insert a special component into the beginning of the process that computes the list of required steps for each message. It then attaches the list as a *Routing Slip* to the message and starts the process by routing the message to the first processing step. After successful processing, each processing step looks at the *Routing Slip* and passes the message to the next processing step specified in the routing table.

This pattern works similarly to the routing slip attached to a magazine for circulation in a group or department. The only difference is that the *Routing Slip* has a defined sequence of components it traverses, whereas in most companies you can hand the magazine after reading it to any person on the list who has not read it (of course, the boss usually comes first).

The *Routing Slip* combines the central control of the super-router approach (Option E) with the efficiency of the hard-wired solution (Option C). We determine the complete routing scheme up front and attach it to the message, so we do not have to return to the central router for further decision making. Each component is augmented by simple routing logic. In the proposed solution, we assume that this routing logic is built into the processing component itself. If we look back at Option A, we remember that we dismissed this approach partly because we had to hard-code some logic into each component. How is the *Routing Slip* better? The key difference is that the router used in the *Routing Slip* is generic and does not have to change with changes in the routing logic. The routing logic incorporated into each component is similar to a *Return Address* (159), where the return address is selected from a list of addresses. Similarly to the *Return Address* (159), the components retain their reusability and composability even though a piece of routing logic is built into the component. Additionally, the computation of the routing table can now be done in a central place without ever touching the code inside any of the processing components.

As always, there is no free lunch, so we can expect the *Routing Slip* to have some limitations. First, the message size increases slightly. In most cases, this should be insignificant, but we need to realize that we are now carrying process state (which steps have been completed) inside the message. This can cause other side effects. For example, if we lose a message, we lose not only the message data but also the process data (i.e., where the message was going to go next). In many cases, it may be useful to maintain the state of all messages in a central place to perform reporting or error recovery.

Another limitation of the *Routing Slip* is that the path of a message cannot be changed once it is underway. This implies that the message path cannot depend on intermediate results generated by a processing step along the way. In many real-life business processes the message flow does change based on intermediate results, though. For example, depending on the availability of the ordered items (as reported by the inventory system), we may want to continue with a different path. This also means that a central entity has to be able to determine all steps a message should undergo in advance. This can lead to some brittleness in the design, similar to the concerns about using a *Content-Based Router* (230).

Implementing a Routing Slip with Legacy Applications

The *Routing Slip* assumes that we have the ability to augment the individual components with the router logic. If we are dealing with legacy applications or packaged applications, we may not be able to influence the functionality of the component itself. Rather, we need to use an external router that communicates with the component via messaging. This inevitably increases the number of channels and components in use. However, the *Routing Slip* still provides the best trade-off between our goals of efficiency, flexibility, and maintainability.

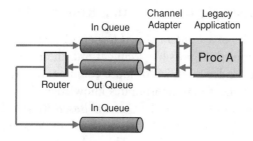

Implementing a Routing Slip with Legacy Applications

Common Usage

The *Routing Slip* is most useful in the following scenarios:

1. A sequence of binary validation steps. By not adding information to the message, the limitation that we cannot change the routing once the message is underway is no longer a factor. We still appreciate the flexibility to change the sequence of validation steps by reconfiguring the central *Routing Slip*. Each component has the choice between aborting the sequence due to error or passing the message on to the next step.

2. Each step is a stateless transformation. For example, let's assume that we receive orders from a variety of business partners. All orders arrive on a common channel but in different formats depending on the partner. As a result, each message may require different transformation steps. Messages from some partners may require decryption; others may not. Some may require transformation or enrichment; others may not. Keeping a *Routing Slip* for each partner gives us an easy way to reconfigure the steps for each partner in a central location.

3. Each step gathers data, but makes no decisions (see *Content Enricher* [336]). In some cases, we receive a message that contains reference identifiers to other data. For example, if we receive an order for a DSL line, the message may contain only the home phone number of the applicant. We need to go to external sources to determine the customer's name, the central office servicing the line, the distance from the central office, and so on. Once we have a complete message with all relevant data, we can decide what package to offer to the customer. In this scenario, the decision is postponed until the end, so we can use a *Routing Slip* to collect the necessary information. We need to assess, though, whether we really require the flexibility of the *Routing Slip*. Otherwise, a simple hard-wired chain of *Pipes and Filters* (70) may be sufficient.

Implementing a Simple Router with a Routing Slip

One of the downsides of a *Content-Based Router* (230) is that it has to incorporate knowledge about each possible recipient and the routing rules associated with that recipient. Under the spirit of loose coupling, it may be undesirable to have a central component that incorporates knowledge about many other components. An alternative solution to the *Content-Based Router* (230) is a *Publish-Subscribe Channel* (106) combined with an array of *Message Filters* (237) as described in the *Message Filter* (237). This solution allows each recipient to decide which messages to process but suffers from risk of duplicate message processing. Another option to enable individual recipients to decide whether to process a given message is to use a modified version of a *Routing Slip* acting as a *Chain of Responsibility* as described in [GoF]. The *Chain of Responsibility* allows each component to accept a message or route it to the next component in the list. The *Routing Slip* is a static list of all participants. This still implies that a central component has to have knowledge of all possible recipients. However, the component does not need to know which messages each component consumes.

Routing
Slip

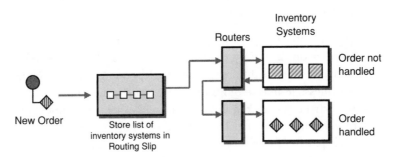

Using a *Routing Slip* avoids the risk of duplicate message processing. Likewise, it is easy to determine if a message was not processed by any component. The main trade-off is the slower processing and increased network traffic. While a *Content-Based Router* (230) publishes a single message regardless of the number of systems, the *Routing Slip* approach publishes an average number of messages equal to half the number of systems. We can reduce this number if we can arrange the systems in such a way that the first systems to receive the message have a higher chance of handling the message, but the number of messages will likely remain higher than with a predictive *Content-Based Router* (230).

There are cases where we need more control than a simple sequential list or we need to change the flow of a message based on intermediate results. The *Process Manager* (312) can fulfill these requirements because it supports branching conditions, forks, and joins. In essence, the *Routing Slip* is a special case of a dynamically configured business process. The trade-offs between using a *Routing Slip* and using a central *Process Manager* (312) should be carefully examined. A dynamic *Routing Slip* combines the benefits of a central point of maintenance with the efficiency of a hard-wired solution. However, as the complexity grows, analyzing and debugging the system may become increasingly difficult, since the routing state information is distributed across the messages. Also, as the semantics of the process definition begin to include constructs such as decisions, forks, and joins, the configuration file may become hard to understand and maintain. We could include conditional statements inside the routing table and augment the routing modules in each component to interpret the conditional commands to determine the next routing location. We need to be careful, though, to not overburden the simplicity of this solution with additional functionality. Once we require this type of complexity, it may be a good idea to give up the runtime efficiency of a *Routing Slip* and to start using a much more powerful *Process Manager* (312).

Example: *Routing Slip as a Composed Service*

When creating a service-oriented architecture, a single logical function is often composed of multiple independent steps. This situation occurs commonly for two primary reasons. First, packaged applications tend to expose fine-grained interfaces based on their internal APIs. When integrating these packages into an integration solution, we want to work at a higher level of abstraction. For example, the operation "New Account" may require multiple steps inside a billing system: Create a new customer, select a service plan, set address properties, verify credit data, and so on. Second, a single logical function may be spread across more than one system. We want to hide this fact from other systems so we have the flexibility to reassign responsibilities between systems without affecting the rest of the integration solution. We can easily use a *Routing Slip* to execute multiple internal steps in response to a single request message. The *Routing Slip* gives us the flexibility to execute different requests from the same channel. The *Routing Slip* executes the sequence of individual steps but appears to the outside like a single step (see figure on the following page).

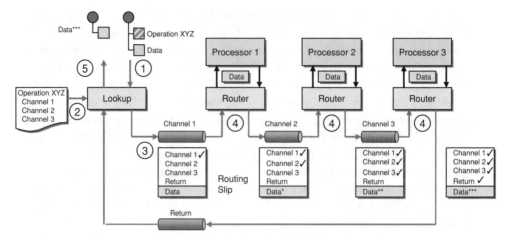

Using a Routing Slip as a Composed Service

1. The incoming request message, specifying the intended operation and any necessary data, is sent to the lookup component.

2. The lookup component retrieves the list of required processing steps associated with the intended operation from a service directory. It adds the list of channels (each channel equals one fine-grained operation) to the message header. The lookup component adds the return channel to the list so that completed messages are returned to the lookup component.

3. The lookup component publishes the message to the channel for the first activity.

4. Each router reads the request from the queue and passes it to the service provider. After the execution, the router marks the activity as completed and routes the message to the next channel specified in the routing table.

5. The lookup component consumes the message off the return channel and forwards it to the requestor. To the outside, this whole process appears to be a simple request-reply message exchange.

Example: *WS-Routing*

Frequently, a Web service request has to be routed through multiple intermediaries. For this purpose, Microsoft defined the Web Services Routing Protocol (WS-Routing) specification. WS-Routing is a SOAP-based protocol for routing messages from a sender through a series of intermediaries to a receiver. The semantics of WS-Routing are richer than those of the *Routing Slip*, but a *Routing Slip* can be easily implemented in WS-Routing. The following example shows the SOAP header for a message that is routed from node A to node D via the intermediaries B and C (denoted by the element <wsrp:via>).

```
<SOAP-ENV:Envelope
      xmlns:SOAP-ENV="http://www.w3.org/2001/06/soap-envelope">
   <SOAP-ENV:Header>
      <wsrp:path xmlns:wsrp="http://schemas.xmlsoap.org/rp/">
         <wsrp:action>http://www.im.org/chat</wsrp:action>
         <wsrp:to>soap://D.com/some/endpoint</wsrp:to>
         <wsrp:fwd>
            <wsrp:via>soap://B.com</wsrp:via>
            <wsrp:via>soap://C.com</wsrp:via>
         </wsrp:fwd>
         <wsrp:from>soap://A.com/some/endpoint</wsrp:from>
         <wsrp:id>uuid:84b9f5d0-33fb-4a81-b02b-5b760641c1d6</wsrp:id>
      </wsrp:path>
   </SOAP-ENV:Header>
   <SOAP-ENV:Body>
      ...
   </SOAP-ENV:Body>
</SOAP-ENV:Envelope>
```

Like most Web services specifications, WS-Routing is likely to evolve over time and/or be merged with other specifications. We included the example here as a snapshot of where the Web services community is going with respect to routing.

Routing
Slip

Process Manager

The *Routing Slip* (301) demonstrates how a message can be routed through a dynamic series of processing steps. The solution of the *Routing Slip* (301) is based on two key assumptions: The sequence of processing steps has to be determined up front, and the sequence is linear. In many cases, these assumptions may not be fulfilled. For example, routing decisions might have to be made based on intermediate results. Or, the processing steps may not be sequential, but multiple steps might be executed in parallel.

▼──

How do we route a message through multiple processing steps when the required steps may not be known at design time and may not be sequential?

──▲

One of the primary advantages of a *Pipes and Filters* (70) architectural style is the composability of individual processing units ("filters") into a sequence by connecting them with channels ("pipes"). Each message is then routed through the sequence of processing units (or components). If we need to be able to change the sequence for each message, we can use multiple *Content-Based Routers* (230). This solution provides the maximum flexibility but has the disadvantage that the routing logic is spread across many routing components. The *Routing Slip* (301) provides a central point of control by computing the message path up front, but does not provide the flexibility to reroute the message based on intermediate results or to execute multiple steps simultaneously.

We can gain flexibility and maintain a central point of control if, after each individual processing unit, we return control back to a central component. That component can then determine the next processing unit(s) to be executed. Following this approach, we end up with an alternating process flow: central component, processing unit, central component, processing unit, and so on. As a result, the central unit receives a message after each individual processing step. When the message arrives, the central component has to determine the next processing step(s) to be executed based on intermediate results and the current step in the sequence. This would require the individual processing units

Process Manager

to return sufficient information to the central unit to make this decision. However, this approach would make the processing units dependent on the existence of the central unit because they might have to pass through extraneous information that is not relevant to the processing unit, but only to the central component. If we want to decouple the individual processing steps and the associated message formats from the central unit, we need to provide the central unit with some form of "memory" that tells it what step in the sequence was executed last.

Use a central processing unit, a *Process Manager*, to maintain the state of the sequence and determine the next processing step based on intermediate results.

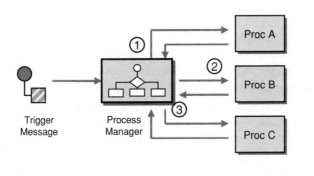

Trigger
Message

Process
Manager

Proc A

Proc B

Proc C

First of all, let's clarify that the design and configuration of a *Process Manager* is a pretty extensive topic. We could probably fill a whole book (Volume 2, maybe?) with patterns related to the design of workflow or business process management. Therefore, this pattern is intended primarily to "round off" the topic of routing patterns and to provide a pointer into the direction of workflow and process modeling. By no means is it a comprehensive treatment of business process design.

Using a *Process Manager* results in a so-called *hub-and-spoke* pattern of message flow (see diagram). An incoming message initializes the *Process Manager*. We call this message the *trigger message*. Based on the rules inside the *Process Manager*, it sends a message (1) to the first processing step, implemented by Processing Unit A. After unit A completes its task, it sends a reply message back to the *Process Manager*. The *Process Manager* determines the next step to be executed and sends a message (2) to the next processing unit. As a result, all message traffic runs through this central "hub," hence the term hub-and-spoke. The downside of this central control element is the danger of turning the *Process Manager* into a performance bottleneck.

The versatility of a *Process Manager* is at the same time its biggest strength and weakness. A *Process Manager* can execute any sequence of steps, sequential or in parallel. Therefore, almost any integration problem can be solved with a *Process Manager*. Likewise, most of the patterns introduced in this chapter could be implemented using a *Process Manager*. In fact, many EAI vendors make you believe that every integration problem is a process problem. We think that using a *Process Manager* for every situation may be overkill. It can distract from the core design issue and also cause significant performance overhead.

Managing State

One of the key functions of the *Process Manager* is to maintain state between messages. For example, when the second processing unit returns a message to the *Process Manager*, the *Process Manager* needs to remember that this is step 2 out of a sequence of many steps. We do not want to tie this knowledge to the processing unit because the same unit may appear multiple times inside the same process. For example, Processing Unit B may be both step 2 and step 4 of a single process. As a result, the same reply message sent by Processing Unit B may trigger the *Process Manager* to execute step 3 or step 5 based on the process context. To accomplish this without complicating the processing unit, the *Process Manager* needs to maintain the current position in the process execution.

It is useful for the *Process Manager* to be able to store additional information besides the current position in the process. The *Process Manager* can store intermediate results from previous processing if it is relevant to later steps. For example, if the results of step 1 are relevant to a later step, the *Process Manager* can store this information without burdening the subsequent processing units with passing this data back and forth. This allows the individual processing steps to be independent of each other because they do not have to worry about data produced or consumed by other units. Effectively, the *Process Manager* plays the role of a *Claim Check* (346) explained later.

Process Instances

Because the process execution can span many steps and can therefore take a long time, the *Process Manager* needs to be prepared to receive new trigger

Process Manager

messages while another process is still executing. In order to manage multiple parallel executions, the *Process Manager* creates a new *process instance* for each incoming trigger message. The process instance stores the state associated with the execution of the process initiated by the trigger message. The state includes the current execution step of the process and any associated data. Each process instance is identified by a unique process identifier.

It is important to separate the concepts of a *process definition* (also referred to as process template) and a process instance. The process definition is a design construct that defines the sequence of steps to be executed, comparable to a class in object-oriented languages. The process instance is an active execution of a specific template, comparable to an object instance in an OO language. The diagram below shows a simple example with one process definition and two process instances. The first instance (process identifier 1234) is currently executing step 1, while the second process instance (process identifier 5678) is executing steps 2 and 5 in parallel.

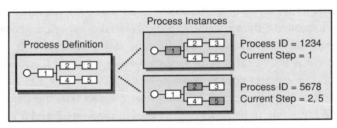

Multiple Process Instances Based on One Process Definition

**Process
Manager**

Correlation

Because multiple process instances may be executing simultaneously, the *Process Manager* needs to be able to associate an incoming message with the correct instance. For example, if the *Process Manager* in the previous example receives a message from a processing unit, which process instance is the message meant for? Multiple instances may be executing the same step, so the *Process Manager* cannot derive the instance from the channel name or the type of message. The requirement to associate an incoming message with a process instance reminds us of the *Correlation Identifier* (163). The *Correlation Identifier* (163) allows a component to associate an incoming reply message with the original request by storing a unique identifier in the reply message that correlates it to the request message. Using this identifier, the component can match the reply with the correct request even if the component has sent multiple requests and the replies arrive out of order. The *Process Manager* requires a similar mechanism. When the *Process Manager* receives a message from a processing unit, it must be able to associate the message with the process instance that sent the message to the processing unit. The *Process Manager* must include a *Correlation Identifier* (163) inside messages that it sends to processing units. The component needs to return this identifier in the reply message as a *Correlation Identifier* (163). If each process instance maintains a unique process identifier, it can use that identifier as a *Correlation Identifier* (163) for messages.

Keeping State in Messages

It is apparent that state management is an important feature of the *Process Manager*. How, then, did the previous patterns get away without managing state? In a traditional *Pipes and Filters* (70) architecture, the pipes (i.e., the *Message Channel*s [60]) manage the state. To continue the previous example, if we were to implement the process with hard-wired components connected by *Message Channel*s (60), it would look like the following figure. If we assume that this system is in the same state as the previous example (i.e., has two process instances), it equates to one message with the identifier 1234 sitting in a channel waiting to be processed by component 1 and two messages with the identifier 5678 waiting to be processed by the components 2 and 5 respectively. As soon as component 1 consumes the message and completes its processing tasks, it broadcasts a new message to components 2 and 4—exactly the same behavior as the *Process Manager* in the previous example.

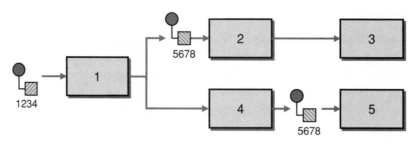

Keeping State in Channels

It is striking how much the message flow notation used for this example resembles a UML activity diagram that is often used to model the behavior of *Process Manager* components. Effectively, we can use an abstract notation to model the behavior of the system during design and then decide whether we want to implement the behavior as a distributed *Pipes and Filters* (70) architecture or as a hub-and-spoke architecture using a central *Process Manager*. Even though we don't have room in this book to dive too deeply into the design of process models, many of the patterns in this language do apply when designing a process model.

As with most architectural decisions, implementing a central *Process Manager* or a distributed *Pipes and Filters* (70) architecture is not a simple yes or no decision. In many cases, it makes most sense to use multiple *Process Manager* components, each of which houses a particular aspect of a larger process. The *Process Manager* components can then communicate with each other through a *Pipes and Filters* (70) architecture.

Managing state explicitly inside a *Process Manager* may require a more complex component, but it allows much more powerful process reporting. For example, most implementations of a *Process Manager* provide the ability to query process instance state. This makes it easy to see how many orders are currently waiting for approval or have been put on hold because of lacking inventory. We can also tell each customer the status of his or her order. If we used hard-wired channels, we would have to inspect all channels to obtain the same information. This property of the *Process Manager* is not only important for reporting, but also for debugging. Using a central *Process Manager* makes it easy to retrieve the current state of a process and the associated data. Debugging a fully distributed architecture can be a lot more challenging and is almost impossible without the assistance of such mechanisms as the *Message History* (551) or *Message Store* (555).

**Process
Manager**

Creating the Process Definition

Most commercial EAI implementations include a *Process Manager* component combined with visual tools to model the process definition. Most visual tools use a notation that resembles UML activity diagrams because the semantics of a *Process Manager* and those of an activity diagram are fairly similar. Also, activity diagrams are a good visual representation of multiple tasks executing in parallel. Until recently, most vendor tools converted the visual notation into an internal, vendor-proprietary process definition to be executed by the process engine. However, the push to standardize various aspects of distributed systems under the umbrella of Web services has not ignored the important role of process definitions. Three proposed "languages" have emerged as a result of these efforts. Microsoft defined XLANG, which is supported by its family of BizTalk orchestration modeling tools. IBM drafted the WSFL, the Web Services Flow Language [WSFL]. Recently, both companies have joined forces to create the specification for BPEL4WS, the Business Process Execution Language for Web Services (see [BPEL4WS]). The BPEL4WS is a powerful language that describes a process model as an XML document. The intent is to define a standardized intermediate language between the process modeling tools and the *Process Manager* engines. This way, we could model our processes with Vendor X's product and decide to execute the process on Vendor Y's process engine implementation. For more information on the impact of Web services standards on integration, see "Emerging Standards and Futures in Enterprise Integration" in Chapter 14.

The semantics of a process definition can be described in rather simple terms. The basic building block is an activity (sometimes called task or action). Usually, an activity can send a message to another component, wait for an incoming message, or execute a specific function internally (e.g., a *Message Translator* [85]). Activities can be connected in serial fashion, or multiple activities can be executed in parallel using a fork and join construct. A fork allows multiple activities to execute at the same time. It is semantically equivalent to a *Publish-Subscribe Channel* (106) in a hard-wired *Pipes and Filters* (70) architecture. A join synchronizes multiple parallel threads of execution back into a single thread. Execution after a join can continue only if all parallel threads have completed their respective activities. In the *Pipes and Filters* (70) style, an *Aggregator* (268) often serves this purpose. The process template also must be able to specify a *branch*, or decision point, so that the path of execution can change based on the content of a message field. This function is equivalent to a *Content-Based Router* (230). Many modeling tools include the ability to design a loop construct, but this is really a special case of the branch. The following figure highlights the semantic similarities between a process definition (depicted as a UML activity diagram) and a *Pipes and Filters* (70) implementation using the patterns defined in this pattern language, even though the physical implementations are very different.

Process Manager

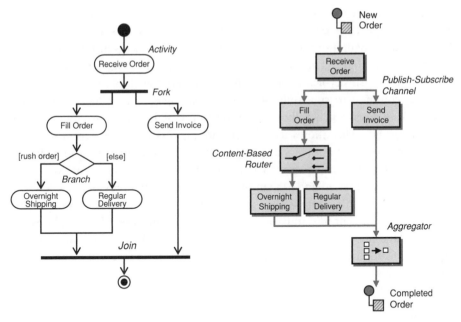

Example UML Activity Diagram and Corresponding Pipes-and-Filters Implementation

Comparing the Process Manager against Other Patterns

We have contrasted a basic *Pipes and Filters* (70) architecture, the *Routing Slip* (301), and the *Process Manager* several times. We compiled the key differences between these patterns into the following table to highlight the trade-offs involved in choosing the correct architecture.

Process Manager

Distributed Pipes and Filters	Routing Slip	Central Process Manager
Supports complex message flow	Supports only simple, linear flow	Supports complex message flow
Difficult to change flow	Easy to change flow	Easy to change flow
No central point of failure	Potential point of failure (compute routing table)	Potential point of failure
Efficient distributed runtime architecture	Mostly distributed	Hub-and-spoke architecture may lead to bottleneck
No central point of administration and reporting	Central point of administration, but not reporting	Central point of administration and reporting

A central point of control and state management can also mean a central point of failure or a performance bottleneck. For this reason, most *Process Manager* implementations allow persistent storage of process instance state in a file or in a database. The implementation can then leverage redundant data storage mechanisms typically implemented in enterprise-class database systems. It is also common to run multiple *Process Manager*s in parallel. Parallelizing *Process Manager*s is generally easy because process instances are independent from each other. This allows us to distribute process instances across multiple process engines. If the process engine persists all state information in a shared database, the system can become robust enough to survive the failure of a process engine—another engine can simply pick up where the previous one left off. The downside of this approach is that the state of each process instance has to be persisted in a central database after each processing step. This could easily turn the database into a new performance bottleneck. As so often happens, the architect has to find the correct balance between performance, robustness, cost, and maintainability.

Example: *Loan Broker*

The MSMQ implementation of the Loan Broker example (see "Asynchronous Implementation with MSMQ" in Chapter 9) implements a simple *Process Manager*. The example creates the *Process Manager* functionality from scratch by coding C# classes for both the process manager and process instances. The TIBCO implementation of the same example (see "Asynchronous Implementation with TIBCO ActiveEnterprise" in Chapter 9) uses a commercial process management tool.

Example: *Microsoft BizTalk Orchestration Manager*

Most commercial EAI tools include process design and execution capabilities. For example, Microsoft BizTalk lets users design process definitions via the Orchestration Designer tool that is integrated into the Visual Studio .NET programming environment.

Microsoft BizTalk 2004 Orchestration Designer

This simple example orchestration receives an order message and executes two parallel activities. One activity creates a request message to the inventory systems, and the other activity creates a request message to the credit system. Once both responses are received, the process continues. The visual notation makes it easy to follow the process definition.

Message Broker

Many patterns in this chapter present ways to route messages to the proper destination without the originating application being aware of the ultimate destination of the message. Most of the patterns focus on specific types of routing logic. However, in aggregate, these patterns solve a bigger problem.

▼

How can you decouple the destination of a message from the sender and maintain central control over the flow of messages?

▲

Using a simple *Message Channel* (60) already provides a level of indirection between sender and receiver—the sender knows only about the channel but not about the receiver. However, if each receiver has its own channel, this level of indirection becomes less meaningful. Instead of knowing the receiver's address, the sender has to know the correct channel name that is associated with the receiver.

Message Broker

All but the most trivial messaging solutions connect a number of different applications. If we created individual message channels to connect each application to each other application, the channels in the system would quickly explode into an unmanageable number, resulting in integration spaghetti (see figure).

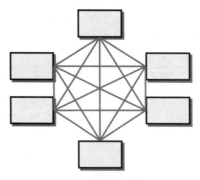

Integration Spaghetti as a Result of Point-to-Point Connections

This diagram illustrates that direct channels between individual applications can lead to an explosion of the number of channels and reduce many of the benefits of routing messages through channels in the first place. These types of integration architectures are often a result of a solution that grew over time. First, the customer care system had to talk to the accounting system. Then, the customer care system was also expected to retrieve information from the inventory system, and the shipping system was to update the accounting system with the shipping charges. It is easy to see how "adding one more piece" can quickly compromise the overall integrity of solution.

Requiring an application to explicitly communicate with all other applications can quickly hamper the maintainability of the system. For example, if the customer address changes in the customer care system, this system would have to send a message to all systems that maintain copies of the customer address. Every time a new system is added, the customer care system would have to know whether that system uses addresses and be changed accordingly.

*Publish-Subscribe Channel*s (106) provide some form of basic routing—the message is routed to each application that subscribed to the specific channel. This works in simple broadcast scenarios, but routing rules often are much more complicated. For example, an incoming order message may have to be routed to a different system based on the size or the nature of the order. To avoid making the applications responsible for determining a message's ultimate destination, the middleware should include a *Message Router* (78) that can route messages to the appropriate destination.

Message Broker

Individual message routing patterns have helped us decouple the sender from the receiver(s). For example, a *Recipient List* (249) can help pull the knowledge about all recipients out of the sender and into the middleware layer. Moving the logic into the middleware layer helps us in two ways. First, many of the commercial middleware and EAI suites provide tools and libraries that are specialized to perform these kinds of tasks. This simplifies the coding effort because we do not have to write the *Message Endpoint* (95)–related code, such as *Event-Driven Consumer*s (498) or thread management. Also, implementing the logic inside the middleware layer allows us to make the logic "smarter" than would be practical inside of the application. For example, using a dynamic *Recipient List* (249) can avoid coding changes when new systems are added to the integration solution.

However, having a large number of individual *Message Router* (78) components can be almost as hard to manage as the integration spaghetti we were trying to resolve.

Use a central *Message Broker* that can receive messages from multiple destinations, determine the correct destination, and route the message to the correct channel. Implement the internals of the *Message Broker* using other message routers.

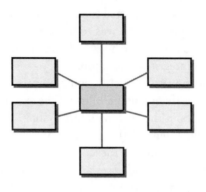

Using a central *Message Broker* is sometimes referred to as hub-and-spoke architectural style, which appears to be a descriptive name when looking at the figure above.

The *Message Broker* pattern has a slightly different scope than most of the other patterns presented in this chapter. It is an architecture pattern as opposed to individual design pattern. As such, it is comparable to the *Pipes and Filters* (70) architectural style, which gives us a fundamental way of chaining components together to form more complex message flows. Rather than just chaining individual components, the *Message Broker* concerns itself with larger solutions and helps us deal with the inevitable complexity of managing such a system.

The *Message Broker* is not a monolithic component. Internally, it uses many of the message routing patterns presented in this chapter. So, once you decide to use the *Message Broker* as an architectural pattern, you can choose the correct *Message Router* (78) design patterns to implement the *Message Broker*.

The advantage of central maintenance of a *Message Broker* can also turn into a disadvantage. Routing all messages through a single *Message Broker* can turn the *Message Broker* into a serious bottleneck. A number of techniques can help us alleviate this problem. For example, the *Message Broker* pattern only tells us to *develop* a single entity that performs routing. It does not prescribe how many instances of this entity we deploy in the system at deployment time. If the *Message Broker* design is stateless (i.e., if it is composed only of stateless components), we can easily deploy multiple instances of the broker to improve throughput. The

Message Broker

properties of a *Point-to-Point Channel* (103) ensure that only one instance of the *Message Broker* consumes any incoming message. Also, as in most real-life situations, the ultimate solution ends up being a combination of patterns. Likewise, in many complex integration solutions, it may make sense to design multiple *Message Broker* components, each specializing in a specific portion of the solution. This avoids creating the über-*Message Broker* that is so complex as to become unmaintainable. The apparent flip-side is that we no longer have a single point of maintenance and could create a new form of *Message Broker* spaghetti. One excellent architectural style that uses a combination of *Message Brokers* is a *Message Broker hierarchy* (see figure). This configuration resembles a network configuration composed out of individual subnets. If a message has to travel only between two applications inside a subnet, the local *Message Broker* can manage the routing of the message. If the message is destined for another subnet, the local *Message Broker* can pass the message to the central *Message Broker*, which then determines the ultimate destination. The central *Message Broker* performs the same functions as a local *Message Broker*, but instead of decoupling individual applications, it decouples whole subsystems consisting of multiple applications.

Message Broker

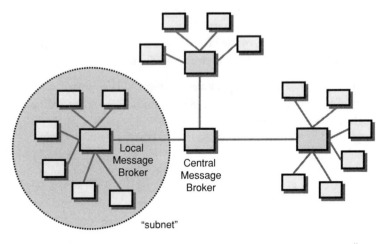

A Hierarchy of Message Brokers Provides Decoupling While Avoiding the Über-Broker

Because the purpose of the *Message Broker* is to reduce coupling between individual applications, it usually has to deal with translating message data formats between applications. Having a *Message Broker* abstract the routing of the message does not help the sending application if it has to format the message in the (supposedly hidden) destination's message format. The next chapter introduces a series of message transformation patterns to address these issues. In many cases, a *Message Broker* uses a *Canonical Data Model* (355) internally to avoid the *N*-square problem (the number of translators required to translate between each and every recipient in a system grows with the square of the number of participants).

Example: *Commercial EAI Tools*

Most commercial EAI suites provide tools to greatly simplify the creation of *Message Broker* components for integration solutions. These tool suites typically provide a number of features that support the development and deployment of *Message Broker*s:

1. **Built-in endpoint code:** Most EAI suites incorporate all code to send and receive messages to and from the message bus. The developer does not have to be concerned with writing any of the transport-related code.

2. **Visual design tools:** These tools allow the developer to compose the functionality of a *Message Broker* using visual components, such as routers, decision points, and transformers. These tools make the flow of messages visually intuitive and can reduce the coding effort for many of these components to single lines of code, such as an evaluation function or a rule.

3. **Runtime support:** Most EAI packages also provide sophisticated runtime support in both deploying the solution and monitoring the traffic flowing through the *Message Broker*.

Message Broker

Chapter 8

Message Transformation

Introduction

As described in the *Message Translator* (85), applications that need to be integrated by a messaging system rarely agree on a common data format. For example, an accounting system will have a different notion of a Customer object than will a customer relationship management system. On top of that, one system may persist data in a relational model, while another application uses flat files or XML documents. Integrating existing applications often means that we do not have the liberty of modifying the applications to work more easily with other systems. Rather, the integration solution has to accommodate and resolve the differences between the varying systems. The *Message Translator* (85) pattern offers a general solution to such differences in data formats. This chapter explores specific variants of the *Message Translator* (85).

Most messaging systems place specific requirements on the format and contents of a message header. We wrap message payload data into an *Envelope Wrapper* (330) that is compliant with the requirements of the messaging infrastructure. Multiple *Envelope Wrappers* (330) can be combined if a message is passed across different messaging infrastructures.

A *Content Enricher* (336) is needed if the target system requires data fields that the originating system cannot supply. It has the ability to look up missing information or compute it from the available data. The *Content Filter* (342) does the opposite—it removes unwanted data from a message. The *Claim Check* (346) also removes data from a message but stores it for later retrieval. The *Normalizer* (352) translates messages arriving in many different formats into a common format.

Eliminating Dependencies

Message transformation is a deep topic in integration. *Message Channels* (60) and *Message Routers* (78) can remove basic dependencies between applications by eliminating the need for one application to be aware of the other's location.

Message
Transformation

One application can send a message to a *Message Channel* (60) and not worry about what application will consume it. However, message formats impose another set of dependencies. If one application has to format messages in another application's data format, the decoupling in the form of the *Message Channel* (60) is somewhat of an illusion. Any change to the receiving application or the switch from one receiving application to another still requires a change to the sending application. *Message Translator*s (85) help remove this dependency.

Metadata Management

Transforming messages from one format into another requires us to deal with metadata—data that describes the format of actual data. While a message from one application to another may tell us that the customer with the ID 123 moved from San Francisco, California, to Raleigh, North Carolina, the associated metadata may tell us that this Address Change message uses a numeric customer ID field and stores the first and last names of the customer in two text fields of up to 40 characters each.

Metadata plays such an important role in integration that we can view most integration solutions as interplay between to two parallel systems. One deals with actual message data, the other with metadata. Many of the patterns used to design the flow of message data can also be used to manage the flow of metadata. For example, a *Channel Adapter* (127) not only can move messages in and out of a system, but can also extract metadata from external applications and load it into a central metadata repository. Using this repository, the integration developers can define transformations between the application metadata and the *Canonical Data Model* (355).

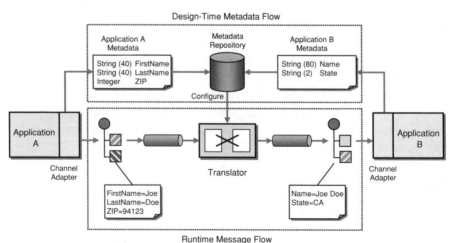

Metadata Integration

For example, the previous figure depicts the integration between two applications that need to exchange customer information. Each system has a slightly different definition of customer data. Application A stores first and last names in two separate fields, whereas Application B stores them in one field. Likewise, Application A stores the customer's ZIP code and not the state, while Application B stores only the state abbreviation. Messages flowing from Application A to Application B have to undergo a transformation so that Application B can receive data in the required format. Creating the transformation is much simplified if the *Channel Adapter*s (127) can also extract metadata (e.g., data describing the message format). This metadata can then be loaded into a repository, greatly simplifying the configuration and validation of the *Message Translator* (85). The metadata can be stored in a variety of formats. A common format used for XML messages is XSD—eXtensible Schema Definition. Other EAI tools implement proprietary metadata formats but allow administrators to import and export metadata into different formats.

Data Transformation Outside of Messaging

Many of the principles incorporated in these transformation patterns are applicable outside of message-based integration. For example, *File Transfer* (43) has to perform transformation functions between systems. Likewise, *Remote Procedure Invocation* (50) has to make requests in the data format specified by the service that is to be called even if the application's internal format is different. This typically requires the calling application to perform a transformation of data. Some of the most sophisticated transformation engines are incorporated into ETL (extract, transform, load) tools, such as Informatica or DataMirror. These tools typically transform a large set of data at once instead of transforming individual messages.

Introduction

This chapter focuses on variations of the basic *Message Translator* (85) pattern. It does not go into the details of structural transformations between entities (e.g., how to transform between two data models if one model supports many-to-many relationships between customer and address but the other model includes address fields on the customer record). One of the oldest and still most relevant books on the topic of presenting data and relationships is [Kent].

Envelope Wrapper

Most messaging systems divide the message data into a header and a body (see *Message* [66]). The header contains fields that are used by the messaging infrastructure to manage the flow of messages. However, most endpoint systems that participate in the integration solution generally are not aware of these extra data elements. In some cases, systems may even consider these fields as erroneous because they do not match the message format used by the application. On the other hand, the messaging components that route the messages between the applications may require the header fields and would consider a message invalid if it did not contain the proper header fields.

▼

How can existing systems participate in a messaging exchange that places specific requirements, such as message header fields or encryption, on the message format?

▲

For example, assume the messaging system is using a proprietary security scheme. A valid message would have to contain security credentials for the message to be accepted for processing by other messaging components. Such a scheme is useful to prevent unauthorized users from feeding messages into the system. Additionally, the message content may be encrypted to prevent eavesdropping by unauthorized listeners—a particularly important issue with publish-subscribe mechanisms. However, existing applications that are being integrated via the messaging systems are most likely not aware of the concepts of user identity or message encryption. As a result, "raw" messages need to be translated into messages that comply with the rules of the messaging system.

Some large enterprises use more than one messaging infrastructure. Thus, a message may have to be routed across messaging systems using a *Messaging Bridge* (133). Each messaging system is likely to have different requirements for the format of the message body as well as the header. This scenario is another case where we can learn by looking at existing TCP/IP-based network protocols. In many cases, connectivity to another system is restricted to a specific protocol, such as Telnet or Secure Shell (*ssh*). In order to enable communication using another protocol (for example, FTP), that protocol format has to be encapsulated into packets that conform to the supported protocol. At the other end, the packet payload can be extracted. This process is called *tunneling*.

Envelope
Wrapper

When one message format is encapsulated inside another, the system may lose access to the information inside the data payload. Most messaging systems allow components (for example, a *Message Router* [78]) to access only data fields that are part of the defined message header. If one message is packaged into a data field inside another message, the component may not be able to use the fields from the original message to perform routing or transformation functions. Therefore, some data fields may have to be elevated from the original message into the message header of the new message format.

Use an *Envelope Wrapper* to wrap application data inside an envelope that is compliant with the messaging infrastructure. Unwrap the message when it arrives at the destination.

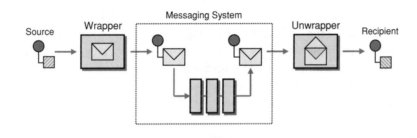

The process of wrapping and unwrapping a message consists of five steps:

1. The message source publishes a message in a raw format. This format is typically determined by the nature of the application and does not comply with the requirements of the messaging infrastructure.

2. The wrapper takes the raw message and transforms it into a message format that complies with the messaging system. This may include adding message header fields, encrypting the message, adding security credentials, and so on.

3. The messaging system transports the compliant messages.

4. A resulting message is delivered to the unwrapper. The unwrapper reverses any modifications the wrapper made. This may include removing header fields, decrypting the message, or verifying security credentials.

5. The message recipient receives a "clear text" message.

An envelope typically wraps both the message header and the message body, or payload. We can think of the header as being the information on the outside

Envelope Wrapper

of a postal envelope: It is used by the messaging system to route and track the message. The contents of the envelope is the payload or body—the messaging infrastructure does not care much about it (within certain limitations) until it arrives at the destination.

It is typical for wrappers to add information to the raw message. For example, before an internal message can be sent through the postal system, a ZIP code has to be looked up. In that sense, wrappers incorporate some aspects of a *Content Enricher* (336). However, wrappers do not enrich the actual information content, but add information that is necessary for the routing, tracking, and handling of messages. This information can be created on the fly (e.g., creating a unique message ID or adding a time stamp), it can be extracted from the infrastructure (e.g., retrieval of a security context), or the data may be contained in the original message body and then split by the wrapper into the message header (e.g., a key field contained in the raw message). This last option is sometimes referred to as *promotion* because a specific field is "promoted" from being hidden inside the body to being prominently visible in the header.

Frequently, multiple wrappers and unwrappers are chained (see the following postal system example), taking advantage of the layered protocol model. This results in a situation where the payload of a message contains a new envelope, which in turn wraps a header and a payload section (see figure).

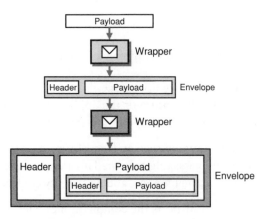

A Chain of Wrappers Creates a Hierarchical Envelope Structure

Envelope Wrapper

Example: *SOAP Message Format*

The basic SOAP message format [SOAP 1.1] is relatively simple. It specifies an envelope that contains a message header and a message body. The following example illustrates how the body can contain another envelope, which in turn contains another header and body. The combined message is sent to an intermediary that unwraps the outside message and forwards the inside message. This chaining of intermediaries is very common when crossing trust boundaries. We may encode all our messages and wrap them inside another message so that no intermediary can see the message content or header (e.g., the address of a message may be confidential). The recipient then unwraps the message, decodes the payload, and passes the unencoded message through the trusted environment.

```
<env:Envelope xmlns:env="http://www.w3.org/2001/06/soap-envelope">
    <env:Header env:actor="http://example.org/xmlsec/Bob">
        <n:forward xmlns:n="http://example.org/xmlsec/forwarding">
            <n:window>120</n:window>
        </n:forward>
    </env:Header>
    <env:Body>
        <env:Envelope xmlns:env="http://www.w3.org/2001/06/soap-envelope">
            <env:Header env:actor="http://example.org/xmlsec/Alice"/>
            <env:Body>
                <secret xmlns="http://example.org/xmlsec/message">
    The black squirrel rises at dawn</secret>
            </env:Body>
        </env:Envelope>
    </env:Body>
</env:Envelope>
```

Example: *TCP/IP*

While we commonly use *TCP/IP* as one term, it actually comprises two protocols. The IP protocol provides basic addressing and routing services, while TCP provides a reliable, connection-oriented protocol that is layered on top of IP. Following the OSI layer model, TCP is a *transport* protocol, while IP is a *network* protocol. Typically, TCP/IP data is transported over an Ethernet network, which implements the *link* layer.

As a result, application data is wrapped into a TCP envelope first, which is then wrapped into an IP envelope, which is then wrapped into an Ethernet envelope. Since networks are stream-oriented, an envelope can consist of both a header and a trailer, marking the beginning and the end of the data stream. The figure on the following page illustrates the structure of application data traveling over the Ethernet.

Envelope
Wrapper

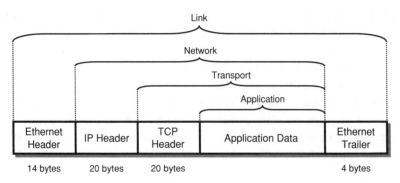

Application Data Is Wrapped Inside Multiple Envelopes to be Transported over the Network

You can see the successive wrapping of the application data into multiple envelopes: TCP (transport envelope), IP (network envelope), and Ethernet (link envelope). The TCP and the IP envelopes consist of only a header, while the Ethernet envelope adds both a header and a trailer. If you are interested in more details about TCP/IP, [Stevens] is guaranteed to quench your thirst for knowledge.

Example: *The Postal System*

Envelope Wrapper

The *Envelope Wrapper* pattern can be compared to the postal system (see figure on the next page). Let's assume an employee creates an internal memo to a fellow employee. Any sheet of paper will be an acceptable format for this message payload. In order for the memo to be delivered, it has to be "wrapped" into an intra-company envelope that contains the recipient's name and department code. If the recipient works in a separate facility, this intra-company message will be stuffed into a large envelope and mailed via the U.S. Postal Service. In order to make the new message comply with the USPS requirements, it needs to feature a new envelope with ZIP code and postage. The USPS may decide to transport this envelope via air. To do so, it stuffs all envelopes for a specific region into a mailbag, which is addressed with a bar code featuring the three-letter airport code for the destination airport. Once the mailbag arrives at the destination airport, the wrapping sequence is reversed until the original memo is received by the coworker. This example illustrates the term *tunneling*: Postal mail may be "tunneled" through air freight just as UDP mulitcast packets may be tunneled over a TCP/IP connection in order to reach a different WAN segment.

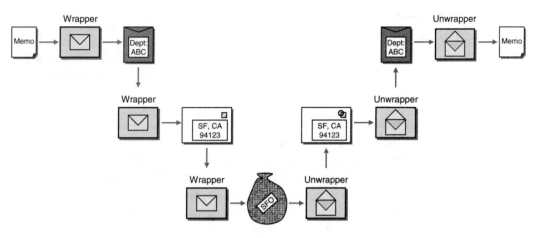

The postal system example also illustrates the common practice of chaining wrappers and unwrappers using the *Pipes and Filters* (70) architecture. Messages may be wrapped by more than one step and need to be unwrapped by a symmetric sequence of unwrapping steps. As laid out in *Pipes and Filters* (70), keeping the individual steps independent from each other gives the messaging infrastructure the flexibility to add or remove wrapping and unwrapping steps. For example, encryption may no longer be required because all traffic is routed across a VPN as opposed to the public Internet.

Envelope Wrapper

Content Enricher

When sending messages from one system to another, it is common for the target system to require more information than the source system can provide. For example, incoming Address messages may just contain the ZIP code because the designers felt that storing a redundant city and state information would be superfluous. Likely, another system will want to specify city and state as well as a ZIP code field. Yet another system may not actually use state abbreviations, but spell the state name out because it uses freeform addresses in order to support international addresses. Likewise, one system may provide us with a customer ID, but the receiving system actually requires the customer name and address. In yet another situation, an Order message sent by the order management system may just contain an order number, but we need to find the customer ID associated with that order so we can pass it to the customer management system. The scenarios are plentiful.

▼

How do we communicate with another system if the message originator does not have all the required data items available?

▲

This problem is a special case of the *Message Translator* (85), so some of the same considerations apply. However, this problem is slightly different from the basic examples described in the *Message Translator* (85). The description of the *Message Translator* (85) assumed that the data needed by the receiving application is already contained in the incoming message, albeit in the wrong format. In this new case, it is not a simple matter of rearranging fields; we actually need to inject additional information to the message.

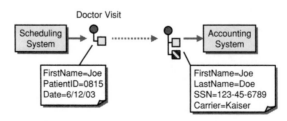

The Accounting System Requires More Information Than the Scheduling System Can Deliver

Let's consider the following example (see figure). A hospital scheduling system publishes a message announcing that the patient has completed a doctor's visit. The message contains the patient's first name, his or her patient ID, and the date of the visit. In order for the accounting system to log this visit and inform the insurance company, it requires the full patient name, the insurance carrier, and the patient's social security number. However, the scheduling system does not store this information; it is contained in the customer care system. What are our options?

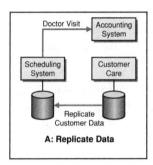
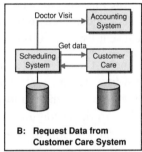
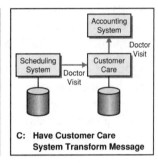

Possible Solutions for the Enricher Problem

Option A: We could modify the scheduling system so it can store the additional information. When the customer's information changes in the customer care system (e.g., because the patient switches insurance carriers), the changes need to be replicated to the scheduling system. The scheduling system can now send a message that includes all required information. Unfortunately, this approach has two significant drawbacks. First, it requires a modification to the scheduling system's internal structure. In most cases, the scheduling system is a packaged application and may not allow this type of modification. Second, even if the scheduling system is customizable, we need to consider that we are making a change to the system based on the specific needs of another system. For example, if we also want to send a letter to the patient confirming the visit, we would have to change the scheduling system again to accommodate the customer's mailing address. The integration solution would be much more maintainable if we decoupled the scheduling system from the specifics of the applications that consume the Doctor Visit message.

Option B: Instead of storing the customer's information inside the scheduling system, the scheduling system could request the SSN and carrier data from the customer care system just before it sends the Doctor Visit message. This solves the first problem—we no longer have to modify the storage of the scheduling system. However, the second problem remains: The scheduling system needs to know that the SSN and carrier information is required in order to notify the accounting system. Therefore, the semantics of the message are more similar to Notify Insurance than to Doctor Visit. In a loosely coupled system, we do not want one system to instruct the next one on what to do. We instead send an *Event Message* (151) and let the other systems decide what to do. In addition, this solution couples the scheduling system more tightly to the customer care system because the scheduling system now needs to know where to get the missing data. This ties the scheduling system to both the accounting system and the customer care system. This type of coupling is undesirable because it leads to brittle integration solutions.

Option C: We can avoid some of these dependencies if we send the message to the customer care system first instead of to the accounting system. The customer care system can then fetch all the required information and send a message with all required data to the accounting system. This decouples the scheduling system nicely from the subsequent flow of the message. However, now we implement the business rule that the insurance company receives a bill after the patient visits the doctor inside the customer care system. This requires us to modify the logic inside the customer care system. If the customer care system is a packaged application, this modification may be difficult or impossible. Even if we can make this modification, we now make the customer care system indirectly responsible for sending billing messages. This may not be a problem if all the data items required by the accounting system are available inside the customer care system. However, if some of the fields have to be retrieved from other systems, we are in a situation similar to where we started.

Option D (not shown): We could also modify the accounting system to require only the customer ID and to retrieve the SSN and carrier information from the customer care system. This approach has two disadvantages. First, we now couple the accounting system to the customer care system. Second, this option again assumes that we have control over the accounting system. In most cases, the accounting system is a packaged application with limited options for customization.

Content Enricher

Use a specialized transformer, a *Content Enricher*, to access an external data source in order to augment a message with missing information.

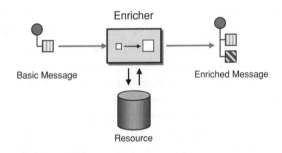

The *Content Enricher* uses information inside the incoming message (e.g., key fields) to retrieve data from an external source. After the *Content Enricher* retrieves the required data from the resource, it appends the data to the message. The original information from the incoming message may be carried over into the resulting message or may no longer be needed, depending on the specific needs of the receiving application.

The additional information injected by the *Content Enricher* has to be available somewhere in the system. Following are the most common sources for the new data:

1. **Computation:** The *Content Enricher* may be able to compute the missing information. In this case, the algorithm incorporates the additional information. For example, if the receiving system requires a city and state abbreviation, but the incoming message contains only a ZIP code, the algorithm can supply the city and state information. Or, a receiving system may require a data format that specifies the total size of the message. The *Content Enricher* can add the length of all message fields and thus compute the message size. This form of *Content Enricher* is very similar to the basic *Message Translator* (85) because it needs no external data source.

2. **Environment:** The *Content Enricher* may be able to retrieve the additional data from the operating environment. The most common example is a time stamp. For example, the receiving system may require each message to carry a time stamp. If the sending system does not include this field, the *Content Enricher* can get the current time from the operating system and add it to the message.

3. **Another System:** This option is the most common one. The *Content Enricher* has to retrieve the missing data from another system. This data resource can take on a number of forms, including a database, a file, an LDAP directory, an application, or a user who manually enters missing data.

Content
Enricher

In many cases, the external resource required by the *Content Enricher* may be situated on another system or even outside the enterprise. Accordingly, the communication between the *Content Enricher* and the resource can occur via *Messaging* (53) or via any other communication mechanism (see Chapter 2, "Integration Styles"). Since the interaction between the *Content Enricher* and the data source is by definition synchronous (the *Content Enricher* cannot send the enriched message until the data source returns the requested data), a synchronous protocol (e.g., HTTP or an ODBC connection to a database) may result in better performance than using asynchronous messaging. The *Content Enricher* and the data source are inherently tightly coupled, so achieving loose coupling through *Message Channel*s (60) is not as important.

Returning to our example, we can insert a *Content Enricher* to retrieve the additional data from the customer care system (see figure). This way, the scheduling system is nicely decoupled from having to deal with insurance information or the customer care system. All it has to do is publish the Doctor Visit message. The *Content Enricher* component takes care of retrieving the required data. The accounting system also remains independent from the customer care system.

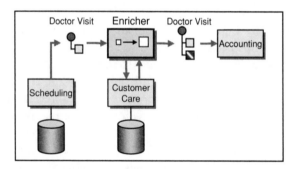

Applying the Enricher to the Patient Example

The *Content Enricher* is used on many occasions to resolve references contained in a message. In order to keep messages small and easy to manage, we often choose to pass simple references to objects rather than pass a complete object with all data elements. These references usually take the form of keys or unique IDs. When the message needs to be processed by a system, we need to retrieve the required data items based on the object references included in the original message. We use a *Content Enricher* to perform this task. There are some apparent trade-offs involved. Using references reduces the data volume in the original messages, but requires additional lookups in the resource. Whether the use of references improves performance depends on how many components can operate simply on references versus how many components need to use a *Content Enricher* to restore some of the original message content. For example, if a message passes through a long list of intermediaries before it reaches the final recipient, using an object reference can decrease message traffic significantly. We can insert a *Content Enricher* as the last step before the final recipient to load the missing information into the message. If the message already contains data that we might not want to carry along the way, we can use the *Claim Check* (346) to store the data and obtain a reference to it.

Example: *Communication with External Parties*

A *Content Enricher* is also commonly used when communicating with external parties that require messages to be compliant with a specific message standard (e.g., ebXML). Most of these standards require large messages with a long list of data. We can usually simplify our internal operations significantly if we keep internal messages as simple as possible and then use a *Content Enricher* to add the missing fields whenever we send a message outside of the organization. Likewise, we can use a *Content Filter* (342) to strip unnecessary information from incoming messages (see figure).

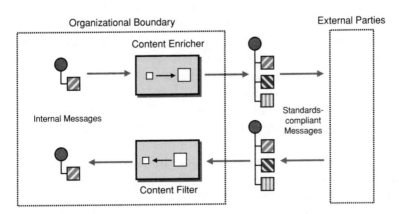

Using a Content Enricher/Content Filter Pair When Communicating with External Parties

Content Filter

The *Content Enricher* (336) helps us in situations where a message receiver requires more—or different—data elements than the message creator provides. There are surprisingly many situations where the opposite effect is desired: removing data elements from a message.

> ▼
>
> How do you simplify dealing with a large message when you are interested only in a few data items?

▲

Why would we want to remove valuable data elements from a message? One common reason is security. An application that requests data from a service may not be authorized to see all data elements that the reply message contains. The service provider may not have knowledge of a security scheme and may always return all data elements regardless of user identity. We need to add a step that removes sensitive data based on the requestor's proven identity. For example, the payroll system may expose only a simple interface that returns all data about an employee. This data may include payroll information, social security numbers, and other sensitive information. If you are trying to build a service that returns an employee's start date with the company, you may want to eliminate all sensitive information from the result message before passing it back to the requestor.

Another reason to remove data elements is to simplify message handling and to reduce network traffic. In many instances, processes are initiated by messages received from business partners. For obvious reasons, it is desirable to base communication with third parties on a standardized message format. A number of standards bodies and committees define standard XML data formats for certain industries and applications. Well-known examples are RosettaNet, ebXML, ACORD, and many more. While these XML formats are useful to conduct interaction with external parties based on an agreed-upon standard, the "design-by-committee" approach usually results in very large documents. Many of the documents have hundreds of fields, consisting of multiple nested levels. Such large documents are difficult to work with for internal message exchange. For example, most visual (drag-drop style) transformation tools become unusable if the documents to be mapped have hundreds of elements. Also, debugging becomes a major nightmare. Therefore, we want to simplify the incoming documents to include only the elements we actually require for our internal processing steps. In a sense, removing elements enriches the usefulness of such a message, because redundant and irrelevant fields are removed, leaving a more meaningful message and less room for developer mistakes.

Use a *Content Filter* to remove unimportant data items from a message, leaving only important items.

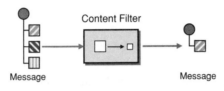

The *Content Filter* does not necessarily just remove data elements. A *Content Filter* is also useful to simplify the structure of the message. Often, messages are represented as tree structures. Many messages originating from external systems or packaged applications contain many levels of nested, repeating groups because they are modeled after generic, normalized database structures. Frequently, known constraints and assumptions make this level of nesting superfluous, and a *Content Filter* can be used to "flatten" the hierarchy into a simple list of elements that can be more easily understood and processed by other systems.

Content Filter

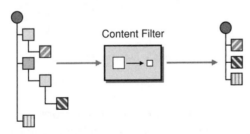

Flattening a Message Hierarchy with a Content Filter

Multiple *Content Filters* can be used as a *static Splitter* (see *Splitter* [259]) to break one complex message into individual messages that each deal with a certain aspect of the large message (see figure at the top of the next page).

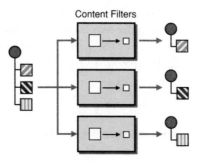

Using Multiple Content Filters as a Static Splitter

Example: *Database Adapter*

Many integration suites provide *Channel Adapter*s (127) to connect to existing systems. In many cases, these adapters publish messages whose format resembles the internal structure of the application. For example, let's assume we connect a database adapter to a database with the following schema:

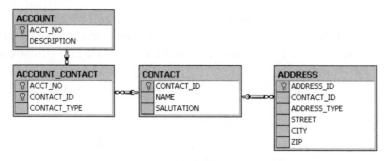

An Example Database Schema

It is desirable for a physical database schema to store related entities in separate tables that are linked by foreign keys and relation tables (e.g., ACCOUNT_CONTACT links the ACCOUNT and CONTACT tables). Many commercial database adapters translate these related tables into a hierarchical message structure that can contain additional fields such as primary and foreign keys that may not be relevant to the message receiver. In order to make processing a message easier, we can use a *Content Filter* to flatten the message structure and extract only relevant fields.

The example shows the implementation of a *Content Filter* using a visual transformation tool. We can see how we reduce the message from over a dozen fields spread across multiple levels into a simple message with five fields. It will be much easier (and more efficient) for other components to work with the simplified message.

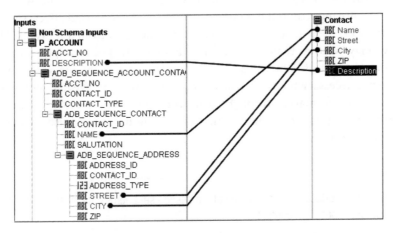

Simplifying a Message Published by a Database Adapter

A *Content Filter* is not the only solution to this particular problem. For example, we could configure a view in the database that resolves the table relationships and returns a simple result set. This may be a simple choice if we have the ability to add views to the database. In many situations, enterprise integration aims to be as little intrusive as possible and that guideline may include not adding views to a database.

Content
Filter

Claim Check

The *Content Enricher* (336) tells us how we can deal with situations where our message is missing required data items. To achieve the opposite effect, the *Content Filter* (342) lets us remove uninteresting data items from a message. However, we may want to remove fields only temporarily. For example, a message may contain a set of data items that are needed later in the message flow but that are not necessary for all intermediate processing steps. We may not want to carry all this information through each processing step, because it can cause performance degradation, and it makes debugging harder because we carry so much extra data.

▼

How can we reduce the data volume of a message sent across the system without sacrificing information content?

▲

Moving large amounts of data via messages may be inefficient. Some messaging systems even have hard limits as to the size of messages. Other messaging systems use an XML representation of data, which can increase the size of a message by an order of magnitude or more. So, while messaging provides the most reliable and responsive way to transmit information, it may not be the most efficient.

Claim
Check

Also, carrying less data in a message keeps intermediate systems from depending on information that was not intended for them. For example, if we send address information from one system to another via a series of intermediates, the intermediates could start making assumptions about the address data and therefore become dependent on the message data format. Making messages as small as possible reduces the possibility of introducing such hidden assumptions.

A simple *Content Filter* (342) helps us reduce data volume but does not guarantee that we can restore the message content later on. Therefore, we need to store the complete message information in a way that we can retrieve it later.

Because we need to store data for each message, we need a key to retrieve the correct data items associated with a message. We could use the message ID as the key, but that would not allow subsequent components to pass the key on, because the message ID changes with each message.

Store message data in a persistent store and pass a *Claim Check* to subsequent components. These components can use the *Claim Check* to retrieve the stored information.

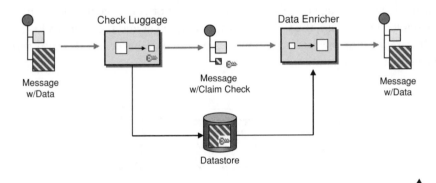

The *Claim Check* pattern consists of the following steps:

1. A message with data arrives.

2. The Check Luggage component generates a unique key for the information. This key will be used later as the *Claim Check*.

3. The Check Luggage component extracts the data from the message and stores it in a persistent store, such as a file or a database. It associates the stored data with the key.

4. It removes the persisted data from the message and adds the *Claim Check*.

5. Another component can use a *Content Enricher* (336) to retrieve the data based on the *Claim Check*.

This process is analogous to a luggage check at the airport. If you do not want to carry all of your luggage with you, you simply check it at the airline counter. In return, you receive a sticker on your ticket that has a reference number that uniquely identifies each piece of luggage you checked. Once you reach your final destination, you can retrieve your luggage.

As the figure illustrates, the data that was contained in the original message still needs to be "moved" to the ultimate destination. So, did we gain anything? Yes, because transporting data via messaging may be less efficient than storing it in a central datastore. For example, the message may undergo multiple routing steps that do not require the large amount of data. Using a messaging system, the message data would be marshaled and unmarshaled, possibly encrypted and decrypted, at every step. This type of operation can be very CPU-intensive and would be completely unnecessary for data that is not needed by any intermediate step but only by the final destination. The *Claim Check* also works well in a scenario where a message travels through a number of components and returns to the sender. In this case, the Check Luggage component and the *Content Enricher* (336) are local to the same component, and the data never has to travel across the network (see figure):

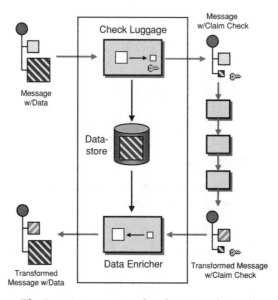

The Data May Be Stored and Retrieved Locally

Choosing a Key

How should we choose a key for the data? A number of options spring to mind:

1. A business key, such as a customer ID, may already be contained in the message body.

2. The message may contain a message ID that can be used to associate the data in the datastore with the message.

3. We can generate a unique ID.

Reusing an existing business key seems like the easiest choice. If we have to stow away some customer detail, we can reference it later by the customer ID. When we pass this key to other components, we need to decide whether we want these components to be aware that the key is a customer ID as opposed to just an abstract key. Representing the key as an abstract key has the advantage that we can process all keys in the same way and can create a generic mechanism to retrieve data from the datastore based on an abstract key.

Using the message ID as the key may seem convenient but is generally not a good idea. Using a message ID as a key for data retrieval results in dual semantics being attached to a single data element and can cause conflicts. For example, let's assume we need to pass the *Claim Check* reference on to another message. The new message is supposed to be assigned a new, unique ID, but then we can't use that new ID anymore to retrieve data from the datastore. The use of a message ID can be meaningful only in a circumstance where we want the data to be accessible only within the scope of the single message. Therefore, in general it is better to assign a new element to hold the key and avoid this bad form of "element reuse."

The data may be stored in the datastore only temporarily. How do we remove unused data? We can modify the semantics of the data retrieval from the datastore to delete the data when it is read. In this case, we can retrieve the data only once, which may actually be desirable in some cases for security reasons. However, it does not allow multiple components to access the same data. Alternatively, we can attach an expiration date to the data and define a garbage collection process that periodically removes all data over a certain age. As a third option, we may not want to remove any data. This may be the case because we use a business system as the datastore (e.g., an accounting system) and need to maintain all data in that system.

The implementation of a datastore can take on various forms. A database is an obvious choice, but a set of XML files or an in-memory message store can serve as a datastore just as well. Sometimes, we may use an application as the datastore. It is important that the datastore is reachable by components in other parts of the integration solution so that these parts can reconstruct the original message.

Using a Claim Check to Hide Information

While the original intent of the *Claim Check* is to avoid sending around large volumes of data, it can also serve other purposes. Often, we want to remove sensitive data before sending a message to an outside party (see figure). This means that outside parties receive data only on a need-to-know basis. For example, when we send employee data to an external party, we may prefer to reference employees by some magic unique ID and eliminate fields such as social security number. After the outside party has completed the required processing, we reconstruct the complete message by merging data from the datastore and the message returned from the outside party. We may even generate special unique keys for these messages so that we restrict the actions the outside party can take by the key it possesses. This will restrict the outside party from maliciously feeding messages into our system. Messages containing an invalid (or expired or already used) key will be blocked by the *Content Enricher* (336) when attempting to retrieve message data using the bad key.

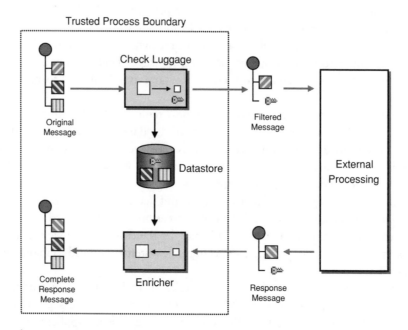

Eliminating Sensitive Message Data Outside of the Trusted Process Boundary

Using a Process Manager with a Claim Check

If we interact with more than one external party, a *Process Manager* (312) can provide the function of a *Claim Check*. A *Process Manager* (312) creates process instances (sometimes called tasks or jobs) when a message arrives. The *Process Manager* (312) allows additional data to be associated with each individual process instance. In effect, the process engine now serves as the datastore, storing our message data. This allows the *Process Manager* (312) to send messages to external parties that contain only the data relevant to that party. The messages do not have to carry all the information contained in the original message, since that information is kept with the process's datastore. When the *Process Manager* (312) receives a response message from an external party, it merges the new data with the data already stored by the process instance.

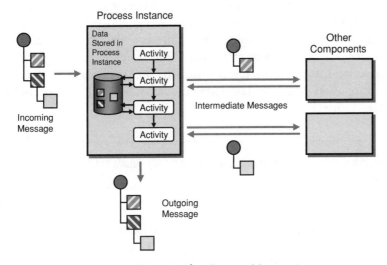

Storing Data Inside a Process Manager

Normalizer

In a business-to-business (B2B) integration scenario, it is quite common for an enterprise to receive messages from different business partners. These messages may have the same meaning but follow different formats, depending on the partners' internal systems and preferences. For example, at ThoughtWorks we built a solution for a pay-per-view provider that has to accept and process viewership information from over 1,700 affiliates, most of which did not conform to a standard format.

How do you process messages that are semantically equivalent but arrive in a different format?

The easiest solution from a technical perspective may seem to dictate a uniform format on all participants. This may work if the business is a large corporation and has control over the B2B exchange or the supply channel. For example, if General Motors would like to receive order status updates from its suppliers in a common message format, we can be pretty sure that Joe's Supplier business is likely to conform to GM's guidelines. In many other situations, however, a business is not going to have such a luxury. On the contrary, many business models position the message recipient as an "aggregator" of information, and part of the agreement with the individual participants is that a minimum of changes is required to their systems infrastructure. As a result, you find the aggregator willing to process information arriving in any data format ranging from EDI records or comma-separated files to XML documents or Excel spreadsheets arriving via e-mail.

One important consideration when dealing with a multitude of partners is the rate of change. Not only may each participant prefer a different data format to begin with, but the preferred format may also change over time. In addition, new participants may join while others drop off. Even if a specific partner makes changes to the data format only once every couple of years, dealing with a few dozen partners can quickly result in monthly or weekly changes. It is important to isolate these changes from the rest of the processing as much as possible to avoid a "ripple effect" of changes throughout the whole system.

To isolate the remainder of the system from the variety of incoming message formats, you need to transform the incoming messages into a common format. Because the incoming messages are of different types, you need a different *Message Translator* (85) for each message data format. The easiest way to accomplish this is to use a collection of *Datatype Channels* (111), one for each message type. Each *Datatype Channel* (111) is then connected to a different *Message Translator* (85). The drawback of this approach is that a large number of message formats translates into an equally large number of *Message Channels* (60).

▼

Use a *Normalizer* to route each message type through a custom Message Translator so that the resulting messages match a common format.

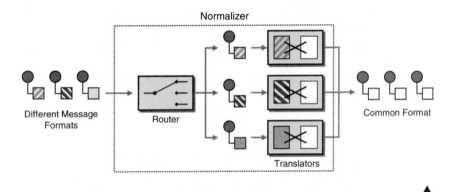

The *Normalizer* features one *Message Translator* (85) for each message format and routes the incoming message to the correct *Message Translator* (85) via a *Message Router* (78).

Detecting the Message Format

Routing the message to the correct *Message Translator* (85) assumes that the *Message Router* (78) can detect the type of the incoming message. Many messaging systems equip each message with a type specifier field in the message header to make this type of task simple. However, in many B2B scenarios, messages do not arrive as messages compliant with the enterprise's internal messaging system, but in diverse formats such as comma-separated files or XML documents without associated schema. While it is certainly best practice to equip any incoming data format with a type specifier, we know all too well that the world is far from perfect. As a result, we need to think of more general ways to identify the format of the incoming message. One common way for schema-less XML documents is to use the name of the root element to assume the correct type. If multiple data formats use the same root element, you can use XPath expressions to determine the presence of specific subnodes. Comma-separated files can require a little more creativity. Sometimes you can determine the type based on the number of fields and the type of the data (e.g., numeric vs. string). If the data arrives as files, the easiest way may be to use the file name or the file folder structure as a surrogate *Datatype Channel* (111). Each business partner can name the file with a unique naming convention. The *Message Router* (78) can then use the file name to route the message to the appropriate *Message Translator* (85).

The use of a *Message Router* (78) also allows the same transformation to be used for multiple business partners. That might be useful if multiple business partners use the same format or if a transformation is generic enough to accommodate multiple message formats. For example, XPath expressions are great at picking out elements from XML documents even if the documents vary in format.

Since a *Normalizer* is a common occurrence in messaging solutions, we created a shorthand icon for it:

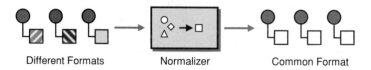

Different Formats   Normalizer   Common Format

The Normalizer in Action

Canonical Data Model

We are designing several applications to work together through *Messaging* (53). Each application has its own internal data format.

> How can you minimize dependencies when integrating applications that use different data formats?

Independently developed applications tend to use different data formats because each format was designed with just that application in mind. When an application is designed to send messages to or receive messages from some unknown application, the application will naturally use the message format that is most convenient for it. Likewise, commercial adapters used to integrate packaged applications typically publish and consume messages in a data format that resembles the application's internal data structure.

The *Message Translator* (85) resolves differences in message formats without changing the applications or having the applications know about each other's data formats. However, if a large number of applications communicate with each other, one *Message Translator* (85) may be needed between each pair of communicating applications (see figure).

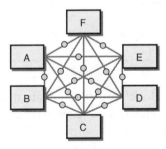

The Number of Connections Explodes with an Increasing Number of Systems

This approach requires a large number of *Message Translators* (85), especially when considering that each integrated application may publish or consume multiple message types. The number of required *Message Translator*s (85) increases exponentially with the number of integrated applications, which quickly becomes unmanageable.

While the *Message Translator* (85) provides an indirection between the message formats used by two communicating applications, it is still dependent on the message formats used by either application. As a result, if an application's data format changes, all *Message Translator*s (85) between the changing application and all other applications that it communicates with have to change. Likewise, if a new application is added to the solution, new *Message Translator*s (85) have to be created from each existing application to the new application in order to exchange messages. This situation creates a nightmare out of having to maintain all *Message Translator*s (85).

We also need to keep in mind that each additional transformation step injected into a message flow can increase latency and reduce message throughput.

Design a *Canonical Data Model* that is independent from any specific application. Require each application to produce and consume messages in this common format.

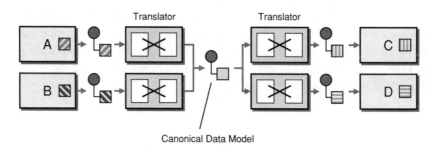

Canonical Data Model

The *Canonical Data Model* provides an additional level of indirection between applications' individual data formats. If a new application is added to the integration solution, only transformation between the *Canonical Data Model* has to be created, regardless of the number of applications that already participate.

The use of a *Canonical Data Model* may seem overly complicated if only a small number of applications participate in the integration solution. However, the solution quickly pays off as the number of applications increases. If we assume that each application sends and receives messages to and from each other application, a solution consisting of two applications would require only two *Message Translator*s (85) if we translate between the applications' data formats directly, whereas the *Canonical Data Model* requires four *Message Translator*s (85). A solution consisting of three applications requires six *Message Translator*s (85) with either approach. However, a solution consisting of six applications requires 30 (!) *Message Translator*s (85) without a *Canonical Data Model* and only 12 *Message Translator*s (85) when using a *Canonical Data Model*.

The *Canonical Data Model* can also be very useful if an existing application is likely to be replaced by another application in the future. For example, if a number of applications interface with a legacy system that is likely to be replaced by a new system in the future, the effort of switching from one application to the other is much reduced if the concept of a *Canonical Data Model* is built into the original solution.

Transformation Options

How do you make applications conform to the common format? You have three basic choices:

1. **Change the applications' internal data format.** This may be possible in theory, but it is unlikely in a complex, real-life scenario. If it was easy to just make each application to natively use the same data format, we would be better off using *Shared Database* (47) instead of *Messaging* (53).

2. **Implement a *Messaging Mapper* (477) inside the application.** Custom applications can use a mapper to generate the desired data format.

3. **Use an external *Message Translator* (85).** You can use an external *Message Translator* (85) to translate from the application-specific message format into the format specified by the *Canonical Data Model*. This may be your only option for transforming a packaged application's data.

Whether to use a *Messaging Mapper* (477) or an external *Message Translator* (85) depends on the complexity of the transformation and the maintainability of the application. Packaged applications usually eliminate the use of a *Messaging Mapper* (477) because the source code is not available. For custom applications the choice depends on the complexity of the transformation. Many

Canonical
Data Model

integration tool suites provide visual transformation editors that allow faster construction of mapping rules. However, these visual tools can get unwieldy if transformations are complex.

When using an external *Message Translator* (85), we need to distinguish between *public* (canonical) messages and *private* (application-specific) messages. The messages between an application and its associated *Message Translator* (85) are considered private because no other application should be using these messages. Once the *Message Translator* (85) transforms the message into a format compliant with the *Canonical Data Model*, the message is considered public and can be used by other systems.

Double Translation

The use of a *Canonical Data Model* does introduce a certain amount of overhead into the message flow. Each message now has to undergo two translation steps instead of one: one translation from the source application's format into the common format and one from the common format into the target application's format. For this reason, the use of a *Canonical Data Model* is sometimes referred to as *double translation* (transforming directly from one application's format to the other is called *direct translation*). Each translation step causes additional latency in the flow of messages. Therefore, for very high throughput systems, direct translation can be the only choice. This trade-off between maintainability and performance is common. The best advice is to use the more maintainable solution (i.e., the *Canonical Data Model*) unless performance requirements do not allow it. A mitigating factor may be that many translations are stateless and therefore lend themselves to load balancing with multiple *Message Translator*s (85) executing in parallel.

Canonical Data Model

Designing a Canonical Data Model

Designing a *Canonical Data Model* can be difficult; most enterprises have at least one failed "enterprise data model" effort under their belt. To achieve a balanced model, designers should strive to make the unified model work equally well for all applications being integrated. Unfortunately, in practice, this ideal is difficult to achieve. The chances of successfully designing a *Canonical Data Model* improve when considering that the *Canonical Data Model* does not have to model the complete set of data used inside all applications, but only the portion that participates in messaging (see figure). This can significantly reduce the complexity of creating the *Canonical Data Model*.

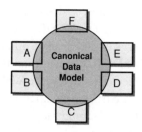

Modeling Only the Relevant Data

Using a *Canonical Data Model* can also have political advantages. Using a *Canonical Data Model* allows developers and business users to discuss the integration solution in terms of the company's business domain, not a specific package implementation. For example, packaged applications may represent the common concept of a customer in many different internal formats, such as "account," "payer," and "contact." Defining a *Canonical Data Model* is often the first step to resolving cases of semantic dissonance between applications (see [Kent]).

Data Format Dependencies

The figure at the beginning of this pattern showing the large number of transformers needed to translate between each and every application looks surprisingly similar to the figure shown in the *Message Broker* (322). This reminds us that dependencies between applications can exist at multiple levels. The use of *Message Channels* (60) provides a common transport layer between applications and removes dependencies between applications' individual transport protocols. *Message Routers* (78) can provide location-independence so that a sending application does not have to depend on the location of the receiving application. The use of a common data representation such as XML removes dependencies on any application-specific data types. Finally, the *Canonical Data Model* resolves dependencies on the data formats and semantics used by the applications.

As always, the only constant is change. Therefore, messages conforming to the *Canonical Data Model* should specify a *Format Indicator* (180).

Canonical
Data Model

Example: *WSDL*

When accessing an external service from your application, the service may already specify a *Canonical Data Model* to be used. In the world of XML Web services, the data format is specified by a WSDL (Web Services Definition Language; see [WSDL 1.1]) document. The WSDL specifies the structure of request and reply messages that the service can consume and produce. In most cases, the data format specified in the WSDL is different than the internal format of the application providing the service. Effectively, the WSDL specifies a *Canonical Data Model* to be used by both parties participating in the conversation. The double translation consists of a *Messaging Mapper* (477) or a *Messaging Gateway* (468) in the service consumer and a *Remote Facade* [EAA] in the service provider.

Example: *TIBCO ActiveEnterprise*

Many EAI tool suites provide a complete set of tools to define and describe the *Canonical Data Model*. For example, the TIBCO ActiveEnterprise suite provides the TIB/Designer that allows the user to inspect all common message definitions. Message definitions can be imported from or exported to XML schema definitions. When implementing a *Message Translator* (85) using a built-in visual tool set, the tool presents the designer with both the application-specific data format and the *Canonical Data Model* stored in the central data format repository. This simplifies the configuration of the *Message Translator* (85) between the two data formats.

Canonical Data Model

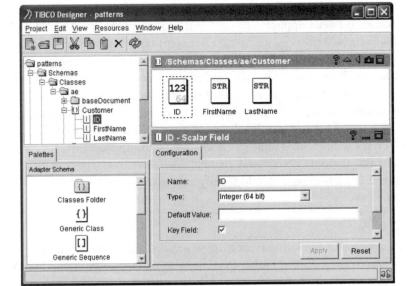

The TIBCO Designer: A GUI Tool to Maintain a Canonical Data Model

Chapter 9

Interlude: Composed Messaging

Loan Broker Example

This chapter demonstrates how to compose routing and transformation patterns into a larger solution. As an example scenario, we chose to model the process of a consumer obtaining quotes for a loan from multiple banks. We took the liberty to simplify the business process a little bit so we can focus on a discussion of integration patterns as opposed to holding a lecture in consumer financial services. Based on the patterns that we defined, we discuss and create three alternative implementations for this process, using different programming languages, technologies, and messaging models.

Obtaining a Loan Quote

When shopping for a loan, a customer usually calls several banks to find the deal with the best possible interest rate. Each bank asks the customer for his or her social security number, the amount of the loan, and the desired term (i.e., the number of months until the loan has to be paid off). Each bank then investigates the customer's credit background, usually by contacting a credit agency. Based on the requested terms and the customer's credit history, the bank responds with an interest rate quote to the consumer (or declines thankfully). Once the customer has received quotes from all banks, he or she can then select the best offer with the lowest interest rate.

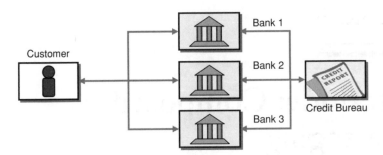

A Consumer Talking to Banks to Get a Loan Quote

Because contacting multiple banks with a loan quote request is a tedious task, loan brokers offer this service to consumers. A loan broker is typically not affiliated with any one bank but has access to many lending institutions. The broker gathers the customer data once and contacts the credit agency to obtain the customer's credit history. Based on the credit score and history, the broker presents the request to a number of banks that are best suited to meet the customer's criteria. The broker gathers the resulting quotes from the banks and selects the best offer to pass back to the consumer.

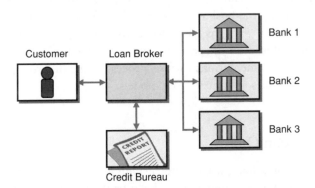

A Loan Broker Acting as Intermediary

Loan Broker Example

Designing the Message Flow

We want to design a loan broker system using integration patterns discussed in the previous chapters. To do this, let's first list the individual tasks that the loan broker needs to perform.

1. Receive the consumer's loan quote request.

2. Obtain credit score and history from credit agency.

3. Determine the most appropriate banks to contact.

4. Send a request to each selected bank.

5. Collect responses from each selected bank.

6. Determine the best response.

7. Pass the result back to the consumer.

Let's see which patterns could help us design and implement the loan broker. The first step describes how the broker receives the incoming request. We cover this topic in much more detail in Chapter 10, "Messaging Endpoints," so for now, let's skip over this step and assume the message is somehow received by the broker. Next, the broker has to retrieve some additional information: the customer's credit score. A *Content Enricher* (336) sounds like the ideal choice for this task. Once the broker has the complete information, the broker must determine the appropriate banks to route the request message to. We can accomplish this with another *Content Enricher* (336) that computes the list of recipients for the request. Sending a request message to multiple recipients and recombining the responses back into a single message is the specialty of the *Scatter-Gather* (297). The *Scatter-Gather* (297) can use a *Publish-Subscribe Channel* (106) or a *Recipient List* (249) to send the request to the banks. Once the banks reply with their rate quotes, the *Scatter-Gather* (297) aggregates the individual rate quotes into a single quote for the consumer using an *Aggregator* (268). If we model the message flow using these patterns, we arrive at the following design:

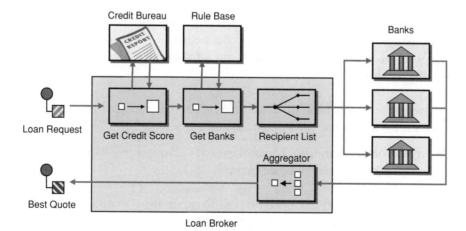

Simple Loan Broker Design

We have not yet accounted for the likely event that each bank may use a slightly different message format for the loan request and response. Because we want to separate the routing and aggregation logic from the banks' proprietary formats, we need to insert *Message Translators* (85) into the communication lines between the broker and the banks. We can use a *Normalizer* (352) to translate the individual responses into a common format:

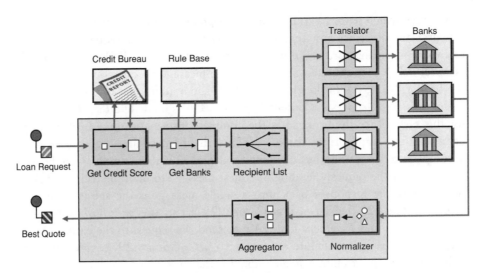

Complete Loan Broker Design

Sequencing: Synchronous versus Asynchronous

So far, we have described the flow of the messages and the routing and transformation patterns we can use to describe the design of the loan broker component. We have not yet discussed the timing of the broker operation. We have two primary choices:

- **Synchronous (Sequential):** The broker asks one bank for the quote and waits for a response before contacting the next bank.

- **Asynchronous (Parallel):** The broker sends all quote requests at once and waits for the answers to come back.

We can use UML sequence diagrams to illustrate the two options. The synchronous option implies a sequential processing of all loan requests (see the following figure). This solution has the advantage of being simpler to manage because we do not have to deal with any concurrency issues or threads. However, it is an inefficient solution because we do not take advantage of the fact that each bank possesses independent processing power and could be executing requests simultaneously. As a result, the consumer might have to wait a long time for an answer.

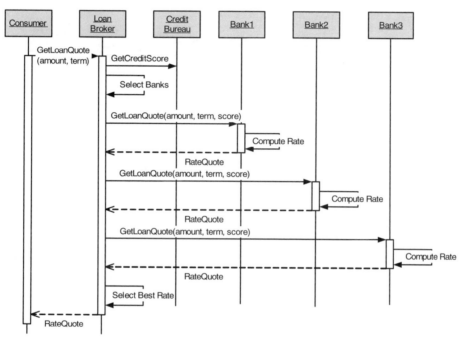

Synchronous, Sequential Processing of Loan Requests

The asynchronous solution issues all requests right away so that each bank can start processing. As the banks finish the computation, they return the results to the loan broker. This solution allows for a much quicker response. For example, if all banks take a similar amount of time to produce a loan quote, this solution is almost n times faster, where n is the number of banks we are dealing with. The loan broker now must be able to accept the loan quote reply messages in any order, because there is no guarantee that responses arrive in the same order that requests were made. The following sequence diagram

Loan
Broker
Example

illustrates this option. The open arrowhead on a loan quote request indicates an asynchronous invocation.

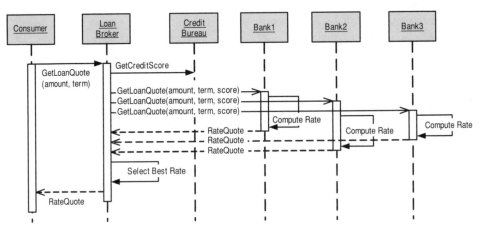

Asynchronous, Parallel Processing of Loan Requests

Another significant advantage of using asynchronous invocation via a message queue is the ability to create more than one instance of a service provider. For example, if it turns out that the credit bureau is a bottleneck, we could decide to run two instances of that component. Because the loan broker sends the request message to a queue instead of directly to the credit bureau component, it does not matter which component instance processes the message as long as the response is put back onto the response channel.

Addressing: Distribution versus Auction

Using a *Scatter-Gather* (297) to obtain the best quote allows us to choose from two addressing mechanisms, a *Recipient List* (249) or a *Publish-Subscribe Channel* (106). The decision primarily depends on how much control we want to exert over the banks who are allowed to participate in a specific loan request. Again, we have a number of choices:

- **Fixed:** The list of banks is hard-coded. Each loan request goes to the same set of banks.

- **Distribution:** The broker maintains criteria on which banks are a good match for a specific request. For example, it would not send a quote request for a customer with a poor credit history to a bank that specializes in premier customers.

- **Auction:** The broker broadcasts the request using a *Publish-Subscribe Channel* (106). Any bank that is interested is allowed to subscribe to the channel and "bid" on the request. Banks can subscribe or unsubscribe at will. Each bank can still apply its own criteria on whether to submit a bid.

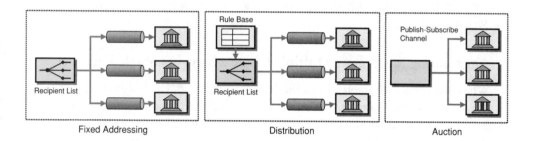

Fixed Addressing   Distribution   Auction

Which option is best for our scenario? As always, there is no simple "and the answer is...," but the choice is driven by both business and technical preferences and constraints. The first option is simple and gives the broker control over the list of banks. However, if new banks come and go frequently, the solution can result in an administrative burden. Also, the bank may not be happy to be receiving a bunch of irrelevant requests, because each request incurs a certain internal cost for the bank. Also, to maintain the simplicity of this approach, the aggregation strategy is more likely to require all banks to submit a response. Banks may want to reserve the right to withhold from the bid.

A distribution approach (using a *Recipient List* [249]) gives the broker more control over which bank to involve in each loan request. This allows the broker to be more efficient by reducing the number of requests. It also allows the broker to prefer certain banks based on the business relationship. On the downside, it requires additional business logic to be implemented and maintained inside the loan broker component. Both the distribution and the fixed approach require a separate *Message Channel* (60) for each participant in order to control the message flow.

Using a *Publish-Subscribe Channel* (106) broadcasts a loan request to all subscribing banks and lets each bank determine which requests to service. Each bank can use a *Message Filter* (237) or implement a *Selective Consumer* (515) to filter out undesirable loan requests. This approach renders the loan broker pretty much maintenance-free in cases of adding or removing banks, but it

Loan Broker Example

requires more work on the side of the banks. This solution requires only a single *Message Channel* (60), but it has to be implemented as a *Publish-Subscribe Channel* (106). Many efficient publish-subscribe schemes use IP Multicast that typically does not route across wide-area networks or the Internet. Other implementations emulate a *Publish-Subscribe Channel* (106) by using an array of *Point-to-Point Channels* (103) and a *Recipient List* (249). This approach preserves the simple semantics of a *Publish-Subscribe Channel* (106) but is less efficient in its use of channels and network bandwidth. For additional trade-offs between routing and publish-subscribe plus filtering, see the description of the *Message Filter* (237).

Aggregating Strategies: Multiple Channels versus Single Channel

When receiving loan quotes from the bank, we have similar design choices. We can have all banks submit their responses to a single response channel, or we can have a separate response channel for each bank. Using a single channel reduces the maintenance burden of setting up a separate channel for each participating bank but requires each bank's reply message to include a field identifying the bank who issued the quote. If we use a single response channel, the *Aggregator* (268) may not know how many response messages to expect unless the *Recipient List* (249) passes this information to the *Aggregator* (268) (we call this an initialized *Aggregator*). If we use an auction-style *Publish-Subscribe Channel* (106), the number of possible responses is unknown to the loan broker, so the *Aggregator* (268) has to employ a completeness condition that does not depend on the total number of participants. For example, the *Aggregator* (268) could simply wait until it has a minimum of three responses. But even that would be risky if temporarily only two banks participate. In that case, the *Aggregator* (268) could time out and report that it received an insufficient number of responses.

Managing Concurrency

Loan Broker Example

A service such as a loan broker should be able to deal with multiple clients wanting to use the service concurrently. For example, if we expose the loan broker function as a Web service or connect it to a public Web site, we do not really have any control over the number of clients and we may receive hundreds or thousands of concurrent requests. We can enable the loan broker to process multiple concurrent requests using two different strategies:

- Execute multiple instances.
- A single event-driven instance.

The first option maintains multiple parallel instances of the loan broker component. We can either start a new instance for each incoming request or maintain a "pool" of active loan broker processes and assign incoming requests to the next available process (using a *Message Dispatcher* [508]). If no process is available, we would queue up the requests until a process becomes available. A process pool has the advantage that we can allocate system resources in a predictable way. For example, we can decide to execute a maximum of 20 loan broker instances. In contrast, if we started a new process for each request, we could quickly choke the machine if a spike of concurrent requests arrives. Also, maintaining a pool of running processes allows us to reuse an existing process for multiple requests, saving time for process instantiation and initialization.

Because much of the processing required by the loan broker is to wait for replies from external parties (the credit bureau and the banks), running many parallel processes may not be a good use of system resources. Instead, we can run a single process instance that reacts to incoming message events as they arrive. Processing an individual message (e.g., a bank quote) is a relatively simple task, so that a single process may be able to service many concurrent requests. This approach uses system resources more efficiently and simplifies management of the solution, since we have to monitor only a single process instance. The potential downside is the limited scalability because we are tied to one process. Many high-volume applications use a combination of the two techniques, executing multiple parallel processes, each of which can handle multiple requests concurrently.

Executing multiple concurrent requests requires us to associate each message in the system to the correct process instance. For example, it may be most convenient for a bank to send all reply messages to a fixed channel. This means that the reply channel can contain messages related to different customers' concurrent quote requests. Therefore, we need to equip each message with a *Correlation Identifier* (163) to identify which customer request the bank is responding to.

Three Implementations

In order to implement the loan broker example, we have three main design decisions to make: We have to select a sequencing scheme for the requests, select an addressing scheme for the banks, and define an aggregation strategy. In addition, we have to select a programming language and a messaging infrastructure. In aggregate, these individual options result in a large number of potential implementation choices. We chose to implement three representative solutions to highlight the main trade-offs between the different implementation options. As with all examples in this book, the choice of specific technologies is

Loan Broker Example

somewhat arbitrary and does not indicate the superiority of a specific vendor's technology. The following table highlights the characteristics of each solution:

Implementation	Sequencing	Addressing	Aggregation	Channel Type	Product Technology
A	Synchronous	Distribution	Channel	Web Service/ SOAP	Java/ Apache Axis
B	Asynchronous	Distribution	Correlation ID	Message Queue	C#/ Microsoft MSMQ
C	Asynchronous	Auction	Correlation ID	Publish-Subscribe	TIBCO Active-Enterprise

The first implementation uses synchronous Web services implemented in Java and Apache Axis. The communication with each bank occurs over a separate HTTP channel, which serves as both a request and reply channel. Therefore, the aggregation strategy is based on individual reply channels and does not require correlation. The second implementation uses an asynchronous approach with message queues. We implement it using Microsoft's MSMQ, but an implementation using JMS or IBM WebSphere MQ could look very similar. The last implementation uses an Auction approach and leverages TIBCO's publish-subscribe infrastructure and the TIB/IntegrationManager tool that implements the *Process Manager* (312) pattern. In option B and C, all reply messages arrive on a single channel and the implementations use *Correlation Identifier*s (163) to associate reply messages to customer loan quote inquiries.

Synchronous Implementation Using Web Services

by Conrad F. D'Cruz

This section describes the implementation of the loan broker example using Java and XML Web services. We use the open source Apache Axis toolkit to take care of the Web services mechanics for us. We do not want this to be an exercise in Java development, so we chose this tool set to abstract the complexities of implementing a synchronous Web service interface. Instead, the discussion in this section focuses on the design decisions that we make in designing a synchronous messaging solution.

Solution Architecture

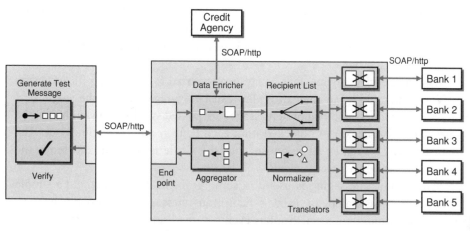

Web Services Solution Architecture

This figure shows the overall architecture of the synchronous predictive Web service implementation of the loan broker example. There are seven significant interfaces between the loan broker and the rest of the solution. As indicated, SOAP over HTTP is used to communicate between each pair of participants.

The first interface is the entry point into the loan broker that the client application uses to pass in the message containing the loan application information.

The client receives the results of the query back from the loan broker via the same interface. Although the Axis server is not shown in this diagram, it receives the Message from the client and implements the *Service Activator* (532).

The second interface is between the loan broker and the credit agency. The credit agency is an external bureau and provides a Web service interface for the loan broker to acquire additional customer data that is required by the banks. The loan broker enriches the incoming request with the data from the credit agency, implementing a *Content Enricher* (336).

The next five interfaces are between the loan broker and each of the five banks. Each interface is used to obtain the rate quote for a loan from that particular bank. Each bank interface provides the same functionality (obtain a quote) but may specify a different format for the associated SOAP messages. Therefore, the loan broker has to translate the quote request message to the format required by each particular bank before querying the bank.

The loan broker contacts each bank directly using predictive routing; that is, the set of banks that participate in the quote gathering is known right before they are called for a quote. In this stage the loan broker application sends the request to the selected banks using the *Recipient List* (249) pattern. Because each bank can use a different format for the request, the loan broker needs to use an array of *Message Translator*s (85) to convert the request into the format required by each bank.

Likewise, each reply message has to be converted to a common format using a *Normalizer* (352), so that all replies can be aggregated into the single best quote. The request and response messages are passed synchronously; that is, the client and loan broker are blocked until each bank responds or times out. The loan broker aggregates all responses into the single best quote and sends the best quote reply back to the client.

Synchronous messaging is useful in some problem domains where a simple solution is necessitated. By using synchronous messaging, we do not have to worry about handling asynchronous events, thread safety, or the infrastructure needed to support them. The client invokes the loan broker Web service and then waits for the response from the server. There are several components in this solution, and each component makes a synchronous call to the next component and waits for the response.

Synchronous Implementation Using Web Services

Web Services Design Considerations

XML Web services rely on the Simple Object Access Protocol (SOAP). The SOAP specification was submitted to the W3C and defines an XML-based protocol for the purpose of exchanging messages between decentralized and distributed systems. For more details on SOAP, please refer to the documents at the World Wide Web Consortium Web site *(www.w3.org/TR/SOAP)*.

Unfortunately, the *S* in SOAP is no longer valid. We have jokingly postulated that SOAP be renamed to Complex Remote Access Protocol—you figure out the acronym. Seriously, designing a robust Web services interface requires us to dive into a number of terminologies and associated design trade-offs. While this book is not an introduction to Web services, we feel it is important to briefly discuss the following design considerations:

- Transport protocol

- Asynchronous messaging versus synchronous messaging

- Encoding style (SOAP encoding vs. doc/literal)

- Binding style (RPC vs. document-style)

- Reliability and security

Transport Protocol The SOAP specification was created to allow applications to make synchronous RPC-style calls to a service across the network in a technology-neutral way. The SOAP specification actually defines a separate request and response message for each invocation to a Web service (as defined in the WSDL document describing the service). Even though SOAP was developed with messaging in mind, the vast majority of the Web service applications use HTTP as the transport protocol. HTTP is a natural choice because it is the most commonly used protocol on the Web and can sneak through firewalls. However, HTTP is the HyperText Transfer Protocol—it was designed to allow users with Web browsers to retrieve documents over the Internet, not for applications to communicate with each other. HTTP is inherently unreliable and designed for synchronous document retrieval—the client application uses the same connection for sending the request to the server and receiving the response. Therefore, Web services that use HTTP will invariably use synchronous request/response messaging because asynchronous messaging over an unreliable channel is about as useful as dropping a bottle into the ocean.

Asynchronous versus Synchronous In a synchronous implementation of a Web service, the client connection remains open from the time the request is submitted to the server. The client will wait until the server sends back the response message. The advantage of using the synchronous RPC communication is that the client application knows the status of the Web service operation

Synchronous
Implementation
Using Web
Services

in a very short time (either it receives a response or it times out). A serious limitation of using synchronous messaging is that the server may have to deal with a large number of concurrent connections because each concurrent client maintains an open connection while waiting for the results. This causes the server application to become increasingly complex. If one of the invocations to a synchronous service provider fails, the server application has to provide the mechanism to trap the failure and recover and reroute the processing or flag an error before continuing with the other synchronous invocations.

At the present time, most Web services toolkits support only synchronous messaging by default. However, using existing standards and tools such as asynchronous message queuing frameworks, some vendors have emulated asynchronous messaging for Web services. Several organizations, companies, and the Web services working groups have recognized the need for asynchronous messaging support and are moving toward defining standards (e.g., WS-Reliable-Messaging). For the latest on Web services standards, please refer to the World Wide Web Consortium Web site at *http://www.w3.org/* and see Chapter 14, "Concluding Remarks."

Encoding Style The notion of SOAP encoding has led to a fair amount of debate and confusion. The SOAP specification defines a mode called *encoding style* specified by the encodingStyle attribute. This mode can take on two values: *encoded* (by setting the attribute value to http://schemas.xmlsoap.org/soap/encoding/) and *literal* (by specifying a different [or no] attribute value). This mode determines how application objects and parameters are represented in the XML "on the wire." Encoded (also referred to as SOAP encoding) refers to Section 5 of the SOAP specification, which defines a primitive mechanism for mapping programming language types to XML. Literal (also called doc/literal) means don't do that. Instead, the type information is provided by an external mechanism, more likely than not a WSDL (Web Services Description Language) document that uses XML schema to define exactly what types are used in the SOAP message.

This came about   because the SOAP specification was written prior to the adoption of the W3C XML Schema Definition (XSD) specification. Thus, the original SOAP specification had to provide a way of encoding type information along with the parameters being sent for method calls because there was no accepted way of specifying it. Where this really comes into play is with complex data types such as Arrays. Section 5.4.2 of the SOAP specification defines a particular mechanism for representing programming language arrays in XML that uses a special SOAPEnc:Array schema type.

Synchronous Implementation Using Web Services

However, since the adoption of XML schema (see *http://www.w3.org/TR/xmlschema-0/*), most languages have rendered the need for SOAP encoding obsolete by specifying their own mappings (or serialization rules) from XML schema to the programming language types. For instance, the JAX-RPC specification uniquely specifies how Java types are mapped to XML schema elements, and vice versa. This obviates the need for extra encoding information in the XML. As a result, SOAP encoding is no longer favored and has been superceded by literal encoding with the mapping specified externally by an XML schema document, usually in the form of a WSDL document.

Binding Style The WSDL specification specifies two different *binding styles* in its SOAP binding. The values of the binding style attribute are RPC and Document. This means that if a WSDL document specifies an operation that has a binding style attribute set to RPC, then the receiver must interpret that message using the rules found in Section 7 of the SOAP specification. This means, for instance, that the XML element inside the SOAP body (called a *wrapper element*) must have a name identical to the name of the corresponding programming-language operation that is to be invoked, that each message part within that element must correspond exactly (in name and order) to a parameter of that programming-language operation, and that there must be only a single element returned (which must be named XXXResponse, where XXX is the name of the corresponding operation in the language) that contains inside it exactly one element, which is the return value of the operation.

The Document binding style is much looser. A message in the Document binding style must simply be made up of well-formed XML. It is up to the SOAP engine that receives it how it will be interpreted. Having said that, many tools (such as those from Microsoft) commonly use Document binding style and Literal encoding to represent RPC semantics. Even though a Document style is used, the message being sent represents a *Command Message* (145), with the operation to be invoked and the parameters to be passed encoded in the Document.

Synchronous
Implementation
Using Web
Services

Reliability and Security In Chapter 14, "Concluding Remarks," Sean Neville describes evolving standards that aim to address the issues of reliability and security for Web services.

Our solution uses the most basic and probably still most prevalent combination of these design choices. The loan broker implementation uses SOAP over HTTP with synchronous communication, encoding messages with the default

SOAP encoding style and RPC binding. This makes the Web service behave very much like a *Remote Procedure Invocation* (50). We went this route so that we do not get stuck debating Web services internals (well, not any more than we already did) but can focus on contrasting the synchronous Web services implementation with the other implementations.

Apache Axis

This section provides a brief description of the Axis architecture to help elucidate the significant points in our design. For additional details on Axis, please refer to the Apache Axis Web site at *http://ws.apache.org/axis*.

Chapter 3, "Messaging Systems," defines a *Message Endpoint* (95) as the mechanism an application uses to connect to a messaging channel in order to send and receive messages. In our loan broker application, the Axis framework itself represents the message channel, and its main function is to handle the processing of messages on behalf of the user application.

The Axis server implements the *Service Activator* (532) pattern. Chapter 10, "Messaging Endpoints," describes how a *Service Activator* (532) connects a *Message Channel* (60) to a synchronous service in an application so that when a message is received, the service is invoked.

The *Service Activator* (532) is implemented within the Axis server so that the developer does not need to bother with this functionality. Therefore, the application code contains only business logic for the application, and the Axis server takes care of all message-handling services.

The client-programming model of Axis provides the components for the client application to invoke an endpoint URL and then receive the response message from the server. The loan broker client in this application is a synchronous client that uses this client-programming model of Axis. Within the server there is a listener for each transport protocol supported by the server. When the client sends a message to the endpoint, a transport listener within the Axis framework creates a *message context* object and passes it through a request chain in a framework. The message context contains the actual message received from the client along with associated properties added by the transport client.

Synchronous Implementation Using Web Services

The Axis framework is made up of a series of Handlers, which are invoked in a particular order depending on the deployment configuration and whether the client or server is invoking the framework. Handlers are part of the Message Flow subsystem and are grouped together and called Chains. Request messages are processed by a sequence of request Handlers in a Chain. Any response messages are sent back on the corresponding response Chain through a sequence of response Handlers.

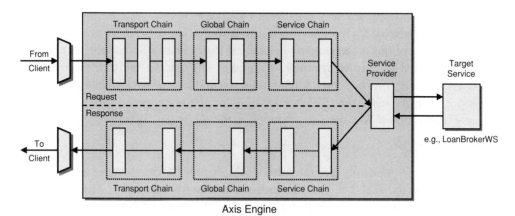

Axis Engine

The figure above shows a high-level representation of the internals of the Axis framework. A detailed discussion on the architecture of Axis can be found at *http://ws.apache.org/axis*.

Axis consists of several subsystems that work together to provide the functionality of a *Message Channel* (60). This framework is available for use by both the client and server applications.

The relevant Axis subsystems for our example are as follows:

- Message Model subsystem defines the XML syntax of the SOAP messages.

- Message Flow subsystem defines Handlers and Chains to pass the messages.

- Service subsystem defines the service handler (SOAP, XML-RPC).

- Transport subsystem provides alternatives for the transport of messages (e.g., HTTP, JMS, SMTP).

- Provider subsystem defines the providers for different types of classes (e.g., java:RPC, EJB, MDB).

As mentioned earlier, the developer only needs to focus on creating an application that implements the business logic, which can then be deployed in the Axis server. There are three techniques for deploying a Java class as a Web service and making it available as an endpoint service; we have named them as follows:

- Automatic deployment

- Using a Web Services Deployment Descriptor

- Generate proxies from an existing WSDL document

Synchronous
Implementation
Using Web
Services

The first and simplest way is to write the class containing the business logic as a Java Web Service (JWS) file (this is a Java source file with a *.jws extension). The methods of this class contain the business logic. The JWS file does not need to be compiled and can be instantly deployed by copying the source file into the webapps directory on the server. Each public method is now accessible as a Web service. The name of this JWS file forms part of the endpoint that the Axis server exposes as a Web service, as shown in the following URL:

```
http://hostname:portnumber/axis/LoanBroker.jws
```

Axis 1.1 automatically generates the WSDL document from services deployed within the server. WSDL is an XML format that describes the public interface of a Web service (i.e., the methods available through the interface) as well as the location of the service (i.e., the URL). The automatic generation of WSDL allows other applications to inspect the remote interface provided by the Web service class. It can also be used to automatically generate client stub classes that encapsulate the Web services call inside a regular Java class. The disadvantage of this method is that the developer cannot control the deployment parameters.

The second technique deploys a compiled class using a WSDD (Web Services Deployment Descriptor), which allows the developer to control the deployment parameters, such as the class scope. By default, a class gets deployed in the request scope; that is, a new instance of the class is instantiated for each request that is received. Once the processing is finished, the instance is destroyed. If the class has to persist for the entire session to service multiple requests from the same client over a period of time, we need to define the class in the session scope. For some applications, we need all clients to access a singleton class; that is, the class has to be instantiated and made available for the entire duration the application is active, and so the Web service is defined in the application scope.

The last technique is more complicated than the previous two techniques but allows the generation of proxies and skeletons from an existing WSDL document (using the wsdl2java tool). The proxies and skeletons encapsulate all SOAP-related code so that the developer does not have to write any SOAP-related (or Axis-related) code, but can instead insert the business logic right into the method bodies of the generated skeleton.

Synchronous Implementation Using Web Services

We chose to implement all our Web services using the Automatic Deployment technique, using JWS files, in order to keep the design and deployment requirements as simple as possible. On the client side, it is a lot easier to hand-code the call to the Web service. We could have used the wsdl2java tool to generate the stubs, which would then be called by the client code; however we tried to minimize the amount of code generation because it can make it difficult to walk through an example solution.

Service Discovery

Before we proceed with a discussion of the loan broker application, we need to describe a few general steps that we follow when implementing the solution to help create an application that is easy to deploy. In order to invoke a Web service that is deployed on a server, any client application needs to know the endpoint URL. In the Web services model, an application looks up the location of a Web service it would like to access from a common service registry.

UDDI (Universal Description, Discovery, and Integration) is a standard for such a repository. A discussion of UDDI is beyond the scope of this section; you can get additional information at *http://www.uddi.org*. In our example, we have hard-coded the endpoint URLs in the application itself. However, to make it easy to deploy the example code, we create properties files for both the server and client applications. The properties file has name-value pairs for the host-name and port number parameters, which match the parameters of your Axis server installation. This gives you some flexibility in deploying the loan broker application in your environment. We provide a utility method, readProps(), in some of the Java classes. This method is for reading files that contain the deployment parameters of the Axis server. The readProps() method is not used by any of the functional aspects of the loan broker application.

In any distributed computing framework, whether it is Java RMI, CORBA, or SOAP Web services, we need to define parameters of the method calls on remote objects as primitive data types or objects that can be serialized to and from the network. These parameters are the properties of the message objects that are sent from the client to the server. To keep the loan broker solution simple, we use a Java String object to return the response from the loan broker to the client. If the calling parameters are primitive data types (e.g., int, double, etc.), they have to be wrapped in the predefined object wrappers called the type wrappers (e.g., Integer, Double, etc.).

The Loan Broker Application

The figure on the following page shows the class diagram for the loan broker component. The core business logic for the loan broker is encapsulated inside the LoanBrokerWS class. This class inherits from a class provided by the Axis framework that implements a *Service Activator* (532) to invoke a method in the Loan-BrokerWS class when a SOAP request arrives. The LoanBrokerWS references a set of gateway classes that implement details of interfacing with external entities, such as the credit agency and the banks. This logic is encapsulated inside the classes CreditAgencyGateway, LenderGateway, and BankQuoteGateway.

Synchronous
Implementation
Using Web
Services

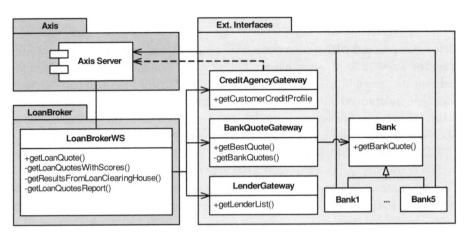

Loan Broker Class Diagram

The only service interface from the loan broker to the outside world is the message endpoint for the client to access the loan broker service. There is no need to define a *Messaging Gateway* (468), since the Axis framework acts as the gateway on behalf of the application.

The following sequence diagram illustrates the interaction between the components for the synchronous predictive Web service example. The loan broker first calls the credit agency gateway component, which enriches the minimum data provided with a credit score and the length of credit history for the customer. The loan broker uses the enriched data to call the lender gateway. This component implements the *Recipient List* (249) that uses all the data provided to choose the set of lenders that can service the loan request.

The loan broker then calls the bank quote gateway. This component performs the predictive routing operation by calling each bank in turn. The bank components model the interface to a real-world banking operation. For example, the Bank1 class is the interface to the Bank1WS.jws Web service that models the banking operation. When a loan request comes in, there is some amount of clerical work performed before generating the rate quote based on all the parameters. In this example, the rate quote is generated by a "dummy" banking Web service.

The bank quote gateway aggregates the responses from the banks and chooses the best quote from all the quotes received. The response is sent back to the loan broker, which formats the data from the best quote and returns the report to the client.

Synchronous Implementation Using Web Services

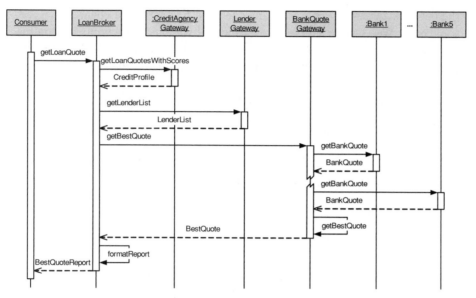

Loan Broker Sequence Diagram

We have shown only two of the five banks in the sequence diagram in the interest of keeping the figure manageable. Based on the *Recipient List* (249) generated for a particular request, the loan broker could contact exactly one bank or all five banks to service the client request.

The diagram highlights the sequential processing of the quote requests to each bank. The sequential processing has some advantages because we can run the application in a single thread, calling each bank in turn. The application does not need to spawn threads to request a quote from each bank, and so we don't have to worry about concurrency issues. However, the total time to get the response quote is high, since the loan broker has to wait for a response from each bank before submitting a request to the next bank in the lenders list. The net result is that the customer will have to wait a long time to get the result quote back after submitting the request.

Components of the Loan Broker Application

We now start designing the functional aspects of the loan broker application. As stated earlier, the Axis framework can support both the client and server application. This allows a remote client to access the published endpoint across

Synchronous Implementation Using Web Services

the network. A server application may also need to act like a client and access some other Web service endpoint, regardless of whether that endpoint is on the same server or a remote server. We demonstrate this by modeling the key components of our solution as Web services, albeit running on the same instance of our server.

The loan broker solution has to implement the following functions:

- Accept Client Requests
- Retrieve Credit Agency Data
- Implement the Credit Agency Service
- Obtain Quotes
- Implement the Banking Operations

Accepting Client Requests The loan broker is implemented in a JWS file named LoanBrokerWS.jws. It exposes a single public method as a Web service: GetLoanQuote. The loan broker needs three pieces of data from the client to start processing a loan request: the social security number (SSN) that acts as the customer identification number, the amount of the loan, and the duration of the loan in months:

LoanBrokerWS.jws

```
public String getLoanQuote(int ssn, double loanamount, int loanduration) {

    String results = "";

    results = results + "Client with ssn= " + ssn + " requests a loan of amount= " +
                        loanamount + " for " + loanduration + " months" + "\n\n";
    results = results + this.getLoanQuotesWithScores(ssn,loanamount,loanduration);

    return results;
}
```

The only step in this method is the call to the method getLoanQuotesWithScores. This method returns a string, which is sent back to the client along a response chain in the Axis framework. At the end of the chain, the transport listener that received the request accepts the response message from within the Axis framework and sends it back to the client on the network.

As described earlier, since we use the Automatic Deployment of the JWS file for the loan broker component, Axis generates the WSDL file for the LoanBrokerWS service. The WSDL file for the LoanBrokerWS.jws file is shown next.

```
<wsdl:definitions xmlns:wsdl="http://schemas.xmlsoap.org/wsdl/"
                  xmlns:wsdlsoap="http://schemas.xmlsoap.org/wsdl/soap/"
                  xmlns:xsd="http://www.w3.org/2001/XMLSchema">
    <wsdl:message name="getLoanQuoteRequest">
        <wsdl:part name="ssn" type="xsd:int"/>
        <wsdl:part name="loanamount" type="xsd:double"/>
        <wsdl:part name="loanduration" type="xsd:int"/>
    </wsdl:message>
    <wsdl:message name="getLoanQuoteResponse">
        <wsdl:part name="getLoanQuoteReturn" type="xsd:string"/>
    </wsdl:message>
    <wsdl:portType name="LoanBrokerWS">
        <wsdl:operation name="getLoanQuote" parameterOrder="ssn loanamount loanduration">
            <wsdl:input message="intf:getLoanQuoteRequest"
                        name="getLoanQuoteRequest"/>
            <wsdl:output message="intf:getLoanQuoteResponse"
                         name="getLoanQuoteResponse"/>
        </wsdl:operation>
    </wsdl:portType>
    <wsdl:binding name="LoanBrokerWSSoapBinding" type="intf:LoanBrokerWS">
        <wsdlsoap:binding style="rpc" transport="http://schemas.xmlsoap.org/soap/http"/>
        <wsdl:operation name="getLoanQuote">
            <wsdlsoap:operation soapAction=""/>
            <wsdl:input name="getLoanQuoteRequest">
                <wsdlsoap:body encodingStyle="http://schemas.xmlsoap.org/soap/encoding/"
                               namespace="..." use="encoded"/>
            </wsdl:input>
            <wsdl:output name="getLoanQuoteResponse">
                <wsdlsoap:body encodingStyle="http://schemas.xmlsoap.org/soap/encoding/"
                               namespace="..." use="encoded"/>
            </wsdl:output>
        </wsdl:operation>
    </wsdl:binding>
    <wsdl:service name="LoanBrokerWSService">
        <wsdl:port binding="intf:LoanBrokerWSSoapBinding" name="LoanBrokerWS">
            <wsdlsoap:address location="http://192.168.1.25:8080/axis/LoanBrokerWS.jws"/>
        </wsdl:port>
    </wsdl:service>
</wsdl:definitions>
```

Synchronous
Implementation
Using Web
Services

In the interest of space, we condensed the WSDL document to highlight the most significant elements. The <wsdl:service> element at the bottom of the document defines the service name (LoanBrokerWSService) and the endpoint location. The <wsdl:operation> element defines the method (operation) name along with the parameters required for the client to access the LoanBrokerWS Web service. The two messages defined in the <wsdl:message> tags define the request and the response messages for the getLoanQuote operation: getLoanQuoteRequest and getLoan-QuoteResponse with the appropriate parameters they pass in to or receive from the Web service. The <wsdlsoap:binding> element confirms that we are using the RPC binding style that we discussed at the beginning of this chapter, while the <wsdl-soap:body> reveals that we are using SOAP encoding (as opposed to doc/literal).

If you want to see the WSDL file from your server, you can type in the following URL in your browser window where hostname and portnumber are replaced with the appropriate values of your server installation:

```
http://hostname:portnumber/axis/LoanBrokerWS.jws?wsdl
```

Retrieving Credit Agency Data   Another requirement for the loan broker is to gather additional data on the customer to complete the loan request application. The next stage of the LoanBrokerWS implements the *Content Enricher* (336), as shown below.

LoanBrokerWS.jws

```
private String getLoanQuotesWithScores
            (int de_ssn, double de_loanamount, int de_duration) {
  String qws_results =
       "Additional data for customer: credit score and length of credit history\n";
  int ssn = de_ssn;
  double loanamount = de_loanamount;
  int loanduration = de_duration;
  int credit_score = 0;
  int credit_history_length = 0;

  CreditProfile creditprofile = CreditAgencyGateway.getCustomerCreditProfile(ssn);

  credit_score = creditprofile.getCreditScore();
  credit_history_length = creditprofile.getCreditHistoryLength();

  qws_results = qws_results + "Credit Score= " + credit_score +
                " Credit History Length= " + credit_history_length;
  qws_results = qws_results + "\n\n";
  qws_results = qws_results + "The details of the best quote from all banks that responded are
    shown below: \n\n";

  qws_results = qws_results + getResultsFromLoanClearingHouse
                (ssn,loanamount,loanduration,credit_history_length,credit_score);

  qws_results = qws_results + "\n\n";
  return qws_results;
}
```

Synchronous Implementation Using Web Services

We now design the credit agency operations, which is the next logical area of the loan broker application. In order to keep the SOAP code out of the loan broker application and minimize the dependencies between the loan broker and the credit agency, we use the *Gateway* pattern [EAA], which has two key advantages: First, it abstracts the technical details of the communication from the application. Second, if we choose to separate the gateway interface from the gateway implementation, we can replace the actual external service with a *Service Stub* [EAA] for testing.

Our CreditAgencyGateway abstracts the technical details of the communication between the CreditAgencyGateway and the credit agency Web service (CreditAgencyWS). We could replace the Web service with a test stub if needed. The gateway takes in the customer identification number (SSN) and acquires additional data from the credit agency. The two pieces of data returned by the credit agency are the credit score and the length of credit history for the customer, both of which are needed to complete the loan application. This gateway contains all the client-side code to access the CreditAgencyWS implemented in the CreditAgencyWS.jws file.

CreditAgencyGateway.java

```
public static CreditProfile getCustomerCreditProfile(int ssn){

  int credit_score = 0;
  int credit_history_length = 0;

  CreditProfile creditprofile = null;

  try{
    CreditAgencyGateway.readProps();

    creditprofile = new CreditProfile();

      String creditagency_ep = "http://" + hostname + ":" + portnum +
                          "/axis/CreditAgencyWS.jws";

      Integer i1 = new Integer(ssn);

      Service  service = new Service();
      Call     call    = (Call) service.createCall();
      call.setTargetEndpointAddress( new java.net.URL(creditagency_ep) );

      call.setOperationName("getCreditHistoryLength");
      call.addParameter( "op1", XMLType.XSD_INT, ParameterMode.IN );
      call.setReturnType( XMLType.XSD_INT );

      Integer ret1 = (Integer) call.invoke( new Object [] {i1});
      credit_history_length = ret1.intValue();

      call.setOperationName("getCreditScore");

      Integer ret2 = (Integer) call.invoke( new Object [] {i1});
      credit_score = ret2.intValue();

      creditprofile.setCreditScore(credit_score);
      creditprofile.setCreditHistoryLength(credit_history_length);
```

```
    Thread.sleep(credit_score);
  }catch(Exception ex){
    System.out.println("Error accessing the CreditAgency Webservice");
  }

  return creditprofile;
 }
}
```

The purpose of using this *Gateway* is to show how a server application uses the Axis client framework to access another Web service either on the same server or on a remote server.

Implementing the Credit Agency Service   The credit agency Web service is coded in CreditAgencyWS.jws, shown below. The two significant pieces of data needed to complete the loan application are the customer credit score and the length of the customer's credit history. The credit agency has this data for each customer with a credit history, and it can be accessed using the customer identification number.

CreditAgencyWS.jws

```
public int getCreditScore(int de_ssn) throws Exception
{
  int credit_score;

  credit_score = (int)(Math.random()*600+300);

  return credit_score;
}

public int getCreditHistoryLength(int de_ssn) throws Exception
{
  int credit_history_length;

  credit_history_length = (int)(Math.random()*19+1);

  return credit_history_length;
}
```

The following code shows the WSDL file for the CreditAgencyWS.jws file. This file was automatically generated by the Axis server.

```
<wsdl:definitions xmlns:wsdl="http://schemas.xmlsoap.org/wsdl/"
                xmlns:wsdlsoap="http://schemas.xmlsoap.org/wsdl/soap/">
    <wsdl:message name="getCreditScoreResponse">
        <wsdl:part name="getCreditScoreReturn" type="xsd:int"/>
    </wsdl:message>
    <wsdl:message name="getCreditHistoryLengthRequest">
        <wsdl:part name="de_ssn" type="xsd:int"/>
```

```
    </wsdl:message>
    <wsdl:message name="getCreditScoreRequest">
        <wsdl:part name="de_ssn" type="xsd:int"/>
    </wsdl:message>
    <wsdl:message name="getCreditHistoryLengthResponse">
        <wsdl:part name="getCreditHistoryLengthReturn" type="xsd:int"/>
    </wsdl:message>
    <wsdl:portType name="CreditAgencyWS">
        <wsdl:operation name="getCreditHistoryLength" parameterOrder="de_ssn">
            <wsdl:input message="intf:getCreditHistoryLengthRequest"
                        name="getCreditHistoryLengthRequest"/>
            <wsdl:output message="intf:getCreditHistoryLengthResponse"
                         name="getCreditHistoryLengthResponse"/>
        </wsdl:operation>
        <wsdl:operation name="getCreditScore" parameterOrder="de_ssn">
            <wsdl:input message="intf:getCreditScoreRequest"
                        name="getCreditScoreRequest"/>
            <wsdl:output message="intf:getCreditScoreResponse"
                         name="getCreditScoreResponse"/>
        </wsdl:operation>
    </wsdl:portType>
    <wsdl:binding name="CreditAgencyWSSoapBinding" type="intf:CreditAgencyWS">
        ...
    </wsdl:binding>
    <wsdl:service name="CreditAgencyWSService">
        <wsdl:port binding="intf:CreditAgencyWSSoapBinding" name="CreditAgencyWS">
            <wsdlsoap:address
             location="http://192.168.1.25:8080/axis/CreditAgencyWS.jws"/>
        </wsdl:port>
    </wsdl:service>
</wsdl:definitions>
```

The `<wsdl:service>` element defines the CreditAgencyWSService and exposes the endpoint that will be accessed by the client, in this case the loan broker. The `<wsdl:operation>` elements define the two public methods defined in the Credit-AgencyWS.jws file, getCreditScore, and getCreditHistoryLength. For each of these methods, a request-response message pair is defined, as can be seen in the `<wsdl:message>` elements. These are getCreditScoreRequest, getCreditScoreResponse, getCreditHistory-LengthRequest, and getCreditHistoryLengthResponse.

Once again, in the interest of space, we have collapsed most of the elements of the WSDL file to fit the format of the section. If you are interested in seeing the entire file, it can be accessed on your server using the following URL, where hostname and portnumber are the values for your server installation:

```
http://hostname:portnumber/axis/CreditAgencyWS.jws?wsdl
```

The credit agency Web service in our example does not provide real functionality. Rather, it stubs out the implementation and returns dummy data that can be used by other parts of the application.

Obtaining Quotes Having enriched the customer data, the loan broker now calls the loan clearinghouse function, which is part of the loan broker itself. As seen in the following call, the loan clearinghouse receives all the data for the loan application.

```
getResultsFromLoanClearingHouse(ssn, loanamount, loanduration,
                        credit_history_length, credit_score);
```

The loan clearinghouse function could be further demarcated into its own logical unit if the application gets more complex or if the loan broker requirements change to use an external loan clearinghouse. In our example, the loan clearinghouse functionality can be broken down into three steps:

- Get a list of lenders who can service the customer loan.

- Get the best quote out of all quotes from each bank in the lender list.

- Format the data from the best quote and return it to the loan broker.

The code shows these steps:

LoanBrokerWS.jws

```
private String getResultsFromLoanClearingHouse(int ssn, double loanamount,
                int loanduration, int credit_history_length, int credit_score) {
    String lch_results="Results from Loan Clearing House ";

    ArrayList lenderlist = LenderGateway.getLenderList
                        (loanamount, credit_history_length, credit_score);

    BankQuote bestquote = BankQuoteGateway.getBestQuote
            (lenderlist,ssn,loanamount,loanduration,credit_history_length,credit_score);

    lch_results = "Out of a total of " + lenderlist.size() +
                    " quote(s), the best quote is from" +
                    this.getLoanQuotesReport(bestquote);

    return lch_results;
}
```

The first requirement for the loan clearinghouse is to get a list of suitable lenders that can service the customer loan application. In order to abstract the functions of the lender selection process from the loan broker, we create a LenderGateway class. We could make the solution more interesting by encapsulating this function inside a Web service as well. However, Web services should be designed carefully, and the parameters and return types should be taken into consideration, since the types have to be serializable to and from the network. To keep things simple, we incorporate the lender selection logic in a simple Java class that is called by the loan broker.

It would be most convenient for the loan broker if the lender gateway returned a collection of service endpoints for the banks. The drawback of this approach is that the identification of the bank Web service would have to be hard-coded in the lender gateway. This becomes a maintenance nightmare in real life, especially since banks are bought, sold, or merged more often than IT architects change jobs. We discuss a robust solution for the bank and its Web service in the discussion of the BankQuoteGateway topic later in this section.

The getLenderList method, shown below, returns the set of lenders (i.e., banks) that can service the loan request.

LenderGateway.java

```java
public static ArrayList getLenderList(double loanamount,
                                      int credit_history_length,
                                      int credit_score){

  ArrayList lenders = new ArrayList();
  LenderGateway.readProps();

  if ((loanamount >= (double)75000) && (credit_score >= 600) &&
      (credit_history_length >= 8))
  {
    lenders.add(new Bank1(hostname, portnum));
    lenders.add(new Bank2(hostname, portnum));
  }

  if (((loanamount >= (double)10000) && (loanamount <= (double)74999)) &&
      (credit_score >= 400) && (credit_history_length >= 3))
  {
    lenders.add(new Bank3(hostname, portnum));
    lenders.add(new Bank4(hostname, portnum));
  }

  lenders.add(new Bank5(hostname, portnum));

  return lenders;
}
```

This method implements the *Recipient List* (249) pattern. In our example, the rule base consists of very simple if statements that choose one or more banks based on a set of predefined conditions. We have also set a default selection for every customer request so that every customer request will have at least one quote.

The loan broker now passes the list of lenders to the bank quote gateway to start gathering quotes and make a selection. We create another gateway, a class named BankQuoteGateway to abstract the internal functioning of the bank interface. All the loan broker needs to do is request the best quote from the BankQuoteGateway, as shown in the following method call:

```
BankQuote bestquote = BankQuoteGateway.getBestQuote(lenderlist, ssn, loanamount,
                          loanduration,credit_history_length,credit_score);
```

The BankQuoteGateway responds to the loan broker request by getting the quotes from all the banks and then selecting the best quote (i.e., the quote with the lowest rate). The getBestQuote method is shown here:

BankQuoteGateway.java

```
public static BankQuote getBestQuote(ArrayList lenders, int ssn, double loanamount,
                              int loanduration,
                              int credit_history_length,
                              int credit_score){

  BankQuote lowestquote = null;
  BankQuote currentquote = null;

  ArrayList bankquotes = BankQuoteGateway.getBankQuotes(lenders, ssn, loanamount,
                          loanduration, credit_history_length, credit_score);

  Iterator allquotes = bankquotes.iterator();

  while (allquotes.hasNext()){
    if (lowestquote == null){
      lowestquote = (BankQuote)allquotes.next();
    }
    else{
      currentquote = (BankQuote)allquotes.next();
      if (currentquote.getInterestRate() < lowestquote.getInterestRate()){
        lowestquote = currentquote;
      }
    }
  }
  return lowestquote;
}
```

Synchronous
Implementation
Using Web
Services

The most significant line in the preceeding code is the call to getBankQuotes. This method not only performs the controlled Auction but also implements the *Aggregator* (268) pattern. The following listing shows the getBankQuotes method:

```
public static ArrayList getBankQuotes(ArrayList lenders, int ssn, double loanamount,
                                int loanduration,
                                int credit_history_length,
                                int credit_score) {

  ArrayList bankquotes = new ArrayList();
```

```
    BankQuote bankquote = null;
    Bank bank = null;

    Iterator banklist = lenders.iterator();

    while (banklist.hasNext()){
      bank = (Bank)banklist.next();
      bankquote = bank.getBankQuote(ssn, loanamount, loanduration,
                              credit_history_length, credit_score);
      bankquotes.add(bankquote);
    }
  return bankquotes;
}
```

The functionality of a controlled auction is implemented by the while loop. It extracts each bank from the lender list, and then invokes the method to generate a bank quote, as highlighted in the code below. Pay special attention to the order of the parameter list in the call to the method, and we will explain the significance when we start designing the banks and the associated Web services.

```
bank.getBankQuote(ssn, loanamount, loanduration, credit_history_length, credit_score);
```

The response is aggregated using the bankquotes ArrayList. The getBestQuote method iterates over this collection of bank quotes and selects the lowest quote, which is sent back to the loan broker.

As mentioned earlier, we will design the bank and bank Web service to emulate a real-world bank operation and keep the functions of the bank separate, not tightly coupled with the functions of the loan broker. This will let our bank classes have the advantages of using the *Gateway* pattern described earlier in the CreditAgencyGateway class.

We define an abstract Bank class as follows:

Bank.java

```
public abstract class Bank {

  String bankname;
  String endpoint = "";
  double prime_rate;

  public Bank(String hostname, String portnum){
    this.bankname = "";
    this.prime_rate = 3.5;
  }

  public void setEndPoint(String endpt){this.endpoint = endpt;}
```

Synchronous
Implementation
Using Web
Services

```java
public String getBankName(){return this.bankname;}
public String getEndPoint(){return this.endpoint;}
public double getPrimeRate(){return this.prime_rate;}
public abstract BankQuote getBankQuote(int ssn, double loanamount, int loanduration,
                                       int credit_history_length, int credit_score);


public void arbitraryWait(){
  try{
    Thread.sleep((int)(Math.random()*10)*100);


  }catch(java.lang.InterruptedException intex){
    intex.printStackTrace();
  }
 }
}
```

In our example, the process for getting a quote from a bank is modeled roughly along the same lines a real-world bank operates. First, a small amount of clerical work is done, followed by an access to the computerized rate quote system, and then additional clerical work is done before the quote is returned to the BankQuoteGateway.

The Bank abstract class and the child bank classes (Bank1 to Bank5) model the operation of a regular bank. In our example, the bank receives the loan request, and the clerical staff conducts the due diligence research while verifying that the customer information is accurate. We chose to model the clerical work as an arbitrary wait method implemented in the Bank abstract class, as just shown, and invoked in the getBankQuote method. To make things interesting, we use Web services to model the bank's rate quote system for getting rate quotes. For a given bank (bank n), the rate quote system is modeled using a BanknWS and coded in a file named BanknWS.jws. There are five bank classes (Bank1 to Bank5) and five rate quote systems (Bank1WS to Bank5WS). Each of the rate quote systems uses a different format for the parameter list in the method call—just like, in real life, different banks are likely to use different data formats. This means the Bank class has to use a *Message Translator* (85) to translate the format of the message before calling the Web service. We will show this after discussing the Bank classes.

Note that the getBankQuote method in the abstract Bank class is an abstract method and has the parameters ordered in a particular format. We now look at one of the bank implementations and, for no particular reason, choose Bank1. The class structure of all the banks will be identical, and each will differ only in the values of its fields (the bank name and endpoint address), which are set when the bank object is constructed.

Bank1.java

```java
public class Bank1 extends Bank {

  public Bank1(String hostname, String portnum){
    super(hostname,portnum);
    bankname = "Exclusive Country Club Bankers\n";
    String ep1 = "http://" + hostname + ":" + portnum + "/axis/Bank1WS.jws";
    this.setEndPoint(ep1);
  }

  public void setEndPoint(String endpt){this.endpoint = endpt;}

  public String getBankName(){return this.bankname;}
  public String getEndPoint(){return this.endpoint;}

  public BankQuote getBankQuote(int ssn, double loanamount, int loanduration,
                                int credit_history_length, int credit_score) {

    BankQuote bankquote = new BankQuote();

    Integer i1 = new Integer(ssn);
    Double i2 = new Double(prime_rate);
    Double i3 = new Double(loanamount);
    Integer i4 = new Integer(loanduration);
    Integer i5 = new Integer(credit_history_length);
    Integer i6 = new Integer(credit_score);

    try{
      Service service = new Service();
      Call call = (Call) service.createCall();
      call.setTargetEndpointAddress( new java.net.URL(endpoint) );

      call.setOperationName("getQuote");

      call.addParameter( "op1", XMLType.XSD_INT, ParameterMode.IN );
      call.addParameter( "op2", XMLType.XSD_DOUBLE, ParameterMode.IN );
      call.addParameter( "op3", XMLType.XSD_DOUBLE, ParameterMode.IN );
      call.addParameter( "op4", XMLType.XSD_INT, ParameterMode.IN );
      call.addParameter( "op5", XMLType.XSD_INT, ParameterMode.IN );
      call.addParameter( "op6", XMLType.XSD_INT, ParameterMode.IN );

      call.setReturnType( XMLType.XSD_DOUBLE);

      Double interestrate = (Double) call.invoke( new Object [] {i1,i2,i3,i4,i5,i6});

      bankquote.setBankName(bankname);
      bankquote.setInterestRate(interestrate.doubleValue());
    }catch(Exception ex){
    System.err.println("Error accessing the axis webservice from " + bankname);

      BankQuote badbq = new BankQuote();
```

Synchronous
Implementation
Using Web
Services

```
    badbq.setBankName("ERROR in WS");
    return badbq;
  }

  arbitraryWait();

  return bankquote;
  }

}
```

As seen in the preceeding code, the getBankQuote method is implemented and has the parameters in a particular order.

```
public BankQuote getBankQuote(int ssn, double loanamount, int loanduration,
                            int credit_history_length, int credit_score)
```

Implementing the Banking Operations As described earlier, the format for the parameters of the rate quote system for each bank is different. This means the getBankQuote method of the Bank class implements the *Message Translator* (85) pattern and has to translate the order of the parameters before calling the respective bank Web service. The signature of the method getQuote for each bank Web service is shown below.

Bank1WS:

```
getQuote(int ssn, double prime_rate, double loanamount, int loanduration,
        int credit_history_length, int credit_score)
```

Bank2WS:

```
getQuote(double prime_rate, double loanamount, int loanduration,
        int credit_history_length, int credit_score, int ssn)
```

Bank3WS:

```
getQuote(double loanamount, int loanduration, int credit_history_length,
        int credit_score, int ssn, double prime_rate)
```

Bank4WS:

```
getQuote(int loanduration, int credit_history_length, int credit_score, int ssn,
        double prime_rate, double loanamount)
```

Bank5WS:

```
getQuote(int credit_history_length, int credit_score, int ssn, double prime_rate,
        double loanamount, int loanduration)
```

The actual implementation of the getQuote method is a placeholder and returns a rate quote using a simple algorithm, as shown below for Bank1WS.jws.

Bank1WS.jws

```
public class Bank1WS {

  public double getQuote(int ssn, double prime_rate, double loanamount,
                         int loanduration, int credit_history_length, int credit_score)
  {
    double ratepremium = 1.5;

    double int_rate = prime_rate + ratepremium + (double)(loanduration/12)/10 +
                      (double)(Math.random()*10)/10;

    return int_rate;
  }

}
```

In a real-world application, the formula is a lot more detailed and complicated. The return type of the getQuote method is a double precision number representing the rate the bank offers the customer, given the parameters in the loan application.

Once again, the Axis server automatically generates a WSDL file for each Bank JWS file (exposed at http://*hostname:portnum*/axis/Bank1WS.jws?wsdl). The WSDL files for the other banks will have a similar format but will differ in the definition of the parameters. The WSDL file for the Bank1WS.jws Web service is shown below.

```
<wsdl:definitions xmlns:wsdl="http://schemas.xmlsoap.org/wsdl/"
                  xmlns:wsdlsoap="http://schemas.xmlsoap.org/wsdl/soap/">
    <wsdl:message name="getQuoteRequest">
        <wsdl:part name="ssn" type="xsd:int"/>
        <wsdl:part name="prime_rate" type="xsd:double"/>
        <wsdl:part name="loanamount" type="xsd:double"/>
        <wsdl:part name="loanduration" type="xsd:int"/>
        <wsdl:part name="credit_history_length" type="xsd:int"/>
        <wsdl:part name="credit_score" type="xsd:int"/>
    </wsdl:message>
    <wsdl:message name="getQuoteResponse">
        <wsdl:part name="getQuoteReturn" type="xsd:double"/>
    </wsdl:message>
    <wsdl:portType name="Bank1WS">
        <wsdl:operation name="getQuote" parameterOrder="ssn prime_rate loanamount loanduration
          credit_history_length credit_score">
            <wsdl:input message="intf:getQuoteRequest" name="getQuoteRequest"/>
```

```
                <wsdl:output message="intf:getQuoteResponse" name="getQuoteResponse"/>
          </wsdl:operation>
      </wsdl:portType>
      <wsdl:binding name="Bank1WSSoapBinding" type="intf:Bank1WS">
          ...
      </wsdl:binding>
      <wsdl:service name="Bank1WSService">
          <wsdl:port binding="intf:Bank1WSSoapBinding" name="Bank1WS">
              <wsdlsoap:address location="http://192.168.1.25:8080/axis/Bank1WS.jws"/>
          </wsdl:port>
      </wsdl:service>
  </wsdl:definitions>
```

As we can see, the WSDL contains one operation, getQuote, defined in the <wsdl:operation> element, which Axis maps to the getQuote method in the Bank1WS.jws class. The <wsdl:service> element defines the Web service Bank1WS. There is a request-response message pair, each defined in a <wsdl:message> element: getQuote-Request and getQuoteResponse.

The rate quote for each bank is set in a bank quote bean (BankQuote), which is added to the collection sent back to the BankQuoteGateway. The bean does not require any formatting, and the beans returned by all the banks look essentially the same. This eliminates the need for a *Normalizer* (352) to convert the reply messages to a common format.

The BankQuoteGateway selects the lowest quote from the collection of bank quotes it gets back and sends one bank quote bean back to the loan broker. The loan broker accesses the data in the bean and formats a report to send back to the client application. The method that formats the report is shown below.

BankQuoteGateway.java

```
private static String getLoanQuotesReport(BankQuote bestquote){
    String bankname = bestquote.getBankName();
    double bestrate = ((double)((long)(bestquote.getInterestRate()*1000))/(double)1000);

    String results = "\nBank Name: " + bankname + "Interest Rate: " + bestrate;

    return results;
}
```

Client Application

The client application is the customer's interface to the loan broker application. The main requirement of the client is to gather information from the customer in a functional user interface environment with adequate error checking. Beneath the covers and far away from the eyes of the customer, the client application prepares the three pieces of data for delivery to the endpoint of the server application. For simplicity, we designed the client application to be a Java class with a main method that takes in the client information as command-line arguments. In reality, the user interface could be implemented as a window-based fat client or a browser-based thin client. The client could also be part of another business system that has the client-programming model deployed. The most significant part of the client application with respect to invoking the loan broker Web service is shown here:

```
Service service = new Service();
Call     call   = (Call) service.createCall();

call.setTargetEndpointAddress( new java.net.URL(endpoint) );
call.setOperationName( "getLoanQuote" );
call.addParameter( "op1", XMLType.XSD_INT, ParameterMode.IN );
call.addParameter( "op2", XMLType.XSD_DOUBLE, ParameterMode.IN );
call.addParameter( "op3", XMLType.XSD_INT, ParameterMode.IN );

call.setReturnType( XMLType.XSD_STRING );

String ret = (String) call.invoke( new Object [] {ssn, loanamount, loanduration});
```

The salient points in the code are the lines that define the method name (get-LoanQuote) and those that set the parameters and return types. The method get-LoanQuote takes in a customer ID, loan amount, and loan duration. The return value is a string.

Since we are not using UDDI, the Web services lookup service, we hard-code the endpoint URL for our Web service. Since we chose to deploy the loan broker application as a JWS file, the endpoint has the standard format, as defined by the Axis API for a JWS. The endpoint for our deployment is shown in the following URL, where hostname and portnumber are the values corresponding to your server installation,

```
http://hostname:portnumber/axis/LoanBroker.jws
```

The client application, which was blocked all along waiting for the response, will accept the formatted report and display it in the GUI area set up for it. Alternatively, it can be saved or sent to a printer.

Running the Solution

This section assumes that you have Axis and the loan broker application installed. The server now needs to be restarted or started if it was not running. Follow the documentation in the Tomcat help files for the proper steps to start

Synchronous
Implementation
Using Web
Services

or restart the server. You can then verify that Tomcat and Apache Axis are up and running by following these steps:

Open a shell or command window on the client machine and run the application as shown for either UNIX/Linux or Microsoft Windows:

```
java -classpath %CLASSPATH% LoanQueryClient [customerid] [loanamount] [loanduration in months]
```

or

```
java -classpath $CLASSPATH LoanQueryClient [customerid] [loanamount] [loanduration in months]
```

For example,

```
java -classpath %CLASSPATH% LoanQueryClient 199 100000.00 29
```

This invokes the loan broker Web service and returns the following results:

```
Calling the LoanBroker webservice at 1053292919270 ticks
LoanBroker service replied at 1053292925860 ticks

Total time to run the query = 6590 milliseconds

The following reply was received from the Loan Clearing House

Client with ssn= 199 requests a loan of amount= 100000.0 for 29 months

Additional data for customer: credit score and length of credit history
Credit Score= 756 Credit History Length= 12

The details of the best quote from all banks that responded are shown below:

Out of a total of 3 quote(s), the best quote is from
Bank Name: Exclusive Country Club Bankers
Interest Rate: 6.197
```

You can test the loan broker by entering different loan amounts when running the client. We will now analyze the output results with a single client running. Later, we launch multiple clients.

Synchronous
Implementation
Using Web
Services

Analyzing the Output The client application keeps track of the time when it invokes the loan broker Web service endpoint on the server. The client also notes the time when the server responds with the result. Both start and end times of the call to the Web service are reported in the client application together with the difference between the two.

```
Calling the LoanBroker webservice at 1053292919270 ticks
LoanBroker service replied at 1053292925860 ticks

Total time to run the query = 6590 milliseconds
```

The Loan Clearing House Web service reports all relevant details of the customer request sent across the network by the client application.

```
Client with ssn= 199 requests a loan of amount= 100000.0 for 29 months
```

The Loan Clearing House also reports additional credit data that was gathered to support the customer request.

```
Additional data for customer: credit score and length of credit history
Credit Score= 756 Credit History Length= 12
```

The LoanBroker analyzes the data and selects a set of banks that fit the customer loan request criteria. The LoanBroker submits the customer data in the format required for individual banks and waits for each bank to respond. Since this is a synchronous application, the loan broker blocks until the bank responds or the request times out or fails.

The LoanBroker collects all the responses, analyzes the return quotes, and chooses the best quote. This quote is formatted and sent back to the customer along with any relevant data. Here are the details of the best quote from all banks that responded:

```
Out of a total of 3 quote(s), the best quote is from
Bank Name: Exclusive Country Club Bankers
Interest Rate: 6.197
```

From the preceeding consule ouput, we see that the LoanBroker reports that three banks responded and that it selected the best quote and presented the quote to the user.

Performance Limitations

As explained when we discussed the sequence diagram earlier in this chapter, the total time to get the response quote is significant since the loan broker has to wait for a response from each bank before submitting the request to the next bank in the lenders list. As a result, the customer has to wait a long time after submitting the request to get the result quote back. We ran several baseline tests with a single client against the server and obtained an average of the total time to run the query (about 8 seconds). We then launched four instances of the client in separate windows on the same client machine and obtained the following average times:

```
Client 1: 12520 milliseconds
Client 2: 12580 milliseconds
Client 3: 15710 milliseconds
Client 4: 13760 milliseconds
```

While these tests could not be considered scientific by any stretch of imagination, the empirical evidence points to the fact that performance suffers tremendously when multiple clients try to simultaneously access our loan broker system.

Limitations of This Example

To make the discussion of the design of the loan broker example easier, we chose to implement all the Web services as JWS files. This gave us the advantage of deploying the service by simply copying it over to the server. The disadvantage, however, is that a new instance of the service class is instantiated for each request and is deallocated as soon as the request is complete. This means that some amount of the time lag we noticed is a result of the server creating instances of the class before invoking the service.

We could have chosen the more complicated route and designed a Java class file that would get deployed using a WSDD file. This would give us the flexibility of defining how long the instantiated class would persist: for the entire client session or for the duration of the application. The issue of how to deploy a Web service is a significant one when designing a real-world application. If we had chosen to include the deployment issue, the description of the example would have become very lengthy, and the design details would have become unnecessarily complicated for the purposes of this chapter.

Summary

In this section we stepped through the implementation of the loan broker application using synchronous SOAP/HTTP Web services. We used predictive routing to submit our loan request to a set of banks. We highlighted the strengths and drawbacks of using this approach. We made some design trade-offs to manage the discussion and avoid getting bogged down in describing deployment details. The overall intention was to provide a discussion on the merits and demerits of this approach. We also saw the use of many of the patterns described in this book, which will help in adapting the synchronous predictive approach to other business domains.

Synchronous
Implementation
Using Web
Services

Asynchronous Implementation with MSMQ

This section describes how to implement the loan broker example (see the introduction to this chapter) using Microsoft .NET, C#, and MSMQ. The Microsoft .NET framework includes the System.Messaging namespace that gives .NET programs access to the Microsoft Message Queuing Service included in the recent versions of the Windows operating system (Windows 2000, Windows XP, and Windows Server 2003). The example walks through many of the design decisions and shows the actual code required to make this solution work. As much as possible, we focus on the design aspects of the solution so that this example is of value even if you are not a hard-core C# developer. In fact, much of the application besides the actual interface into System.Messaging would look very similar if this implementation were done in Java and JMS.

Some of the functions demonstrated in this solution could likely be implemented with less coding effort by using an integration and orchestration tool such as Microsoft BizTalk Server. I intentionally avoided using such tools for two reasons. First, these tools are not free, and you would have to acquire a license just to run this simple example. Second, I wanted to demonstrate the explicit implementation of all necessary functions.

The solution is set up as multiple executables so that the different components can be distributed across multiple computers. For purpose of the example, local, private messages are used to keep the setup requirements simple and avoid having to install Active Directory. As a result, the solution "as is" must run on a single machine.

This implementation of the loan broker example uses asynchronous messaging over message queues. As described in the example overview, this allows us to process multiple quote requests concurrently but also requires us to correlate messages as they flow though the system and ultimately produce a response message to the loan quote request. Many of our design decisions over the course of this example are driven by the need for asynchronous processing.

Asynchronous Implementation with MSMQ

Loan Broker Ecosystem

It is a good idea to start understanding the loan broker design from the outside in. Let's start by examining all external interfaces that the loan broker has to support (see figure). Because message queues are unidirectional, we need a pair of queues to establish a request-response communication with another component (see section ".NET Request/Reply Example" in Chapter 6, "Interlude: Simple Messaging," for a simple case). As a result, the loan broker receives requests for loan quotes on the loanRequestQueue and replies to the test client on the loanReplyQueue. The interaction with the credit bureau happens over a similar pair of queues. Rather than create a pair of queues for each bank, we decided to have all banks reply to the same bankReplyQueue. The *Recipient List* (249) sends the request message to each individual bank queue, while the *Aggregator* (268) selects the best quote from the reply messages arriving on the loanReplyQueue. Together, the *Recipient List* (249) and the *Aggregator* (268) act as a distribution-style *Scatter-Gather* (297). For simplicity's sake, all banks in this example use the same message format so that a *Normalizer* (352) is not required. But because the common bank message format is different from the format expected by the consumer, we still need to use one *Message Translator* (85) to convert bank reply messages into a loan broker reply message. I decided to design the loan broker as a *Process Manager* (312). Rather than implementing the functions inside the loan broker as individual components separated by message queues, the loan broker is a single component that executes all functions internally. This approach eliminates the overhead that would be incurred by sending messages across queues between these functions, but it requires the loan broker to maintain multiple, concurrent process instances.

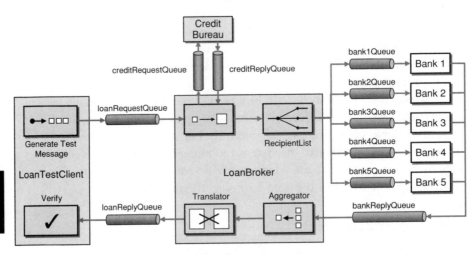

Loan Broker with Message Queue Interfaces

Laying the Groundwork: A Messaging Gateway

This section is not meant as an introduction into the System.Messaging namespace and MSMQ. Therefore, it makes sense to separate the MSMQ-specific functions into separate classes so that the application code will not be littered with MSMQ-specific commands. *Gateway* [EAA] is an excellent pattern to use for this purpose and provides two key advantages: First, it abstracts the technical details of the communication from the application. Second, if we choose to separate the gateway interface from the gateway implementation, we can replace the actual external service with a *Service Stub* [EAA] for testing.

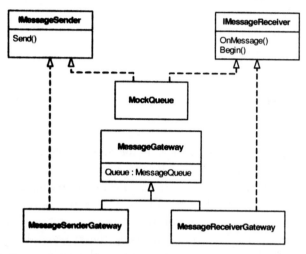

A Gateway Helps Keep MSMQ Details Out of the Application
and Improves Testability

In our case, we define two interfaces into the *Messaging Gateway* (468): IMessageSender and IMessageReceiver. We kept these interfaces almost trivially simplistic. All the IMessageSender can do is send a message, and all the IMessageReceiver can do is (surprise!) receive a message. Additionally, the receiver has a Begin method to tell it that it is okay to start receiving messages. Keeping the interfaces this simple makes it easy to define classes that implement the interface.

Asynchronous
Implementation
with MSMQ

IMessageSender.cs

```
namespace MessageGateway
{
    using System.Messaging;

    public interface IMessageSender
    {
        void Send(Message mess);
    }
}
```

IMessageReceiver.cs

```
namespace MessageGateway
{
    using System.Messaging;

    public interface IMessageReceiver
    {
        OnMsgEvent OnMessage
        {
            get;
            set;
        }

        void Begin();

        MessageQueue GetQueue();
    }
}
```

The actual implementations reside in the `MessageSenderGateway` and `Message-ReceiverGateway` classes. These classes take care of configuring the message queue properties, such as `MessageReadPropertyFilter` or `Formatter` settings. `MessageReceiver-Gateway` uses a *Template Method* [GoF] for the `ReceiveCompleted` event of the MSMQ message queue to take care of small but important details, such as calling the `mq.BeginReceive` method after processing the message. Instead of diving into the details of these features, we refer you to the online documentation on MSDN [MSMQ].

Because we defined very narrow interfaces, it is also possible to provide an implementation that does not even use a message queue. `MockQueue` implements both interfaces without even referencing a message queue! When an application sends a message, `MockQueue` immediately triggers the `OnMessage` event with that same message. This makes testing the application in a single address space much simpler without having to worry about the asynchronous aspects (more on testing follows).

The line `OnMsgEvent OnMessage` in `IMessageReceiver` may require a little bit of explanation for those who are new to C#. The .NET framework provides language features for the *Observer* pattern [GoF], called *delegates* and *events*. `OnMsgEvent` is a delegate defined in the `MessageReceiverGateway`:

```
public delegate void OnMsgEvent(Message msg);
```

A delegate allows objects to register with a certain type of event. When the event is invoked, .NET calls all registered methods. A delegate can be invoked in a number of ways, but the simplest form is the direct invocation by using the name of the delegate:

```
OnMsgEvent receiver;
Message message;
...
receiver(message);
```

If this leaves you more interested in delegates, have a look at a good .NET or C# book. If you want to know the dirty details on how the Common Language Runtime (CLR) implements them, have a look at [Box].

Base Classes for Common Functionality

When we look at the high-level design, we quickly realize that some of the components in the loan broker scenario have common functions. For example, both a bank and a credit bureau act as a service by receiving a request, processing the request, and publishing the result to another channel. Sounds easy enough. But since we live in the world of asynchronous messaging, we have to do a little extra work to implement even a simple request-reply scheme. First, we want the caller of the service to specify a *Return Address* (159) for the reply. This allows different callers to use the same service but use different reply queues. The service should also support a *Correlation Identifier* (163) so that the caller can reconcile incoming reply messages with request messages. Furthermore, if the service receives a message in an unrecognized format, it would be good manners to route the message to an *Invalid Message Channel* (115) instead of simply discarding it.

To eliminate code duplication (the deadly sin of object-oriented programming), I create the base class MQService. This class incorporates support for *Return Address* (159) and *Correlation Identifier* (163). Really, the server-side support for a *Correlation Identifier* (163) consists of nothing more than copying the message ID of the incoming message to the correlation ID of the reply message. In our example, we also copy the AppSpecific property because we will see later that sometimes we need to correlate by a property other than the message ID. The MQService also makes sure to send the response to the specified *Return Address* (159). Because the requestor supplies the *Return Address* (159), the only initialization parameter for the MQService is the name of the request queue—the queue where new request messages come in. If the requestor forgets to supply a *Return Address* (159), the RequestReplyService sends the reply to the *Invalid Message Channel* (115). We may also consider sending the request message to the *Invalid Message Channel* (115) because that's the message that caused the fault. For now, we will keep our lives simple and not get into the details of error handling.

Asynchronous Implementation with MSMQ

MQService.cs

```csharp
public abstract class MQService
{
    static protected readonly String InvalidMessageQueueName =
                                ".\\private$\\invalidMessageQueue";
    IMessageSender invalidQueue = new MessageSenderGateway(InvalidMessageQueueName);

    protected IMessageReceiver requestQueue;
    protected Type requestBodyType;

    public MQService(IMessageReceiver receiver)
    {
        requestQueue = receiver;
        Register(requestQueue);
    }

    public MQService(String requestQueueName)
    {
        MessageReceiverGateway q = new MessageReceiverGateway(requestQueueName,
                                                        GetFormatter());
        Register(q);
        this.requestQueue = q;
        Console.WriteLine("Processing messages from " + requestQueueName);
    }

    protected virtual IMessageFormatter GetFormatter()
    {
        return new XmlMessageFormatter(new Type[] { GetRequestBodyType() });
    }

    protected abstract Type GetRequestBodyType();

    protected Object GetTypedMessageBody(Message msg)
    {
        try
        {
            if (msg.Body.GetType().Equals(GetRequestBodyType()))
            {
                return msg.Body;
            }
            else
            {
                Console.WriteLine("Illegal message format.");
                return null;
            }
        }
        catch (Exception e)
        {
            Console.WriteLine("Illegal message format" + e.Message);
            return null;
        }
    }
```

```
    public void Register(IMessageReceiver rec)
    {
        OnMsgEvent ev = new OnMsgEvent(OnMessage);
        rec.OnMessage += ev;
    }

    public void Run()
    {
        requestQueue.Begin();
    }


    public void SendReply(Object outObj, Message inMsg)
    {
        Message outMsg = new Message(outObj);
        outMsg.CorrelationId = inMsg.Id;
        outMsg.AppSpecific = inMsg.AppSpecific;

        if (inMsg.ResponseQueue != null)
        {
            IMessageSender replyQueue = new MessageSenderGateway(inMsg.ResponseQueue);
            replyQueue.Send(outMsg);
        }
        else
        {
            invalidQueue.Send(outMsg);
        }
    }

    protected abstract void OnMessage(Message inMsg);
}
```

The class is abstract because it does not provide an implementation for the GetRequestedBodyType and OnMessage methods. Because we want our classes to deal as much as possible with strongly typed business objects as opposed to Message data types, we have the MQService verify the type of the message body and cast it to the correct type. The problem is that this abstract base class does not know which type to cast it to because the base class can be used by many different service implementations, each of which is likely to use a different message type. To perform as much work as possible in the base class, we created the method Get-TypedMessageBody and the abstract method GetRequestBodyType. Each subclass has to implement the method GetRequestBodyType to specify the type of the messages that it expects to receive. MQServer uses the type to initialize the XML formatter and to perform type checking. After these checks, the subclass can safely cast the incoming message body to the desired type without causing exceptions. The exception handling inside GetTypedMessageBody is admittedly primitive at this point—all it does is print a message to the console. If this weren't a simple demo app, we would definitely use a more sophisticated approach to logging or, better yet, a comprehensive *Control Bus* (540).

Asynchronous
Implementation
with MSMQ

The OnMessage method is left to be implemented by the subclasses of MQService. We provide two implementations, a synchronous one and an asynchronous one. The synchronous implementation (RequestReplyService) calls the virtual method ProcessMessage, which is expected to return a reply message, and calls SendReply right away. The asynchronous implementation (AsyncRequestReplyService), in contrast, defines the virtual ProcessMessage method without any return parameter. The inheriting subclasses are responsible for calling SendReply.

MQService.cs

```
public class RequestReplyService : MQService
{
    public RequestReplyService(IMessageReceiver receiver) : base(receiver) {}
    public RequestReplyService(String requestQueueName) : base (requestQueueName) {}

    protected override Type GetRequestBodyType()
    {
        return typeof(System.String);
    }

    protected virtual Object ProcessMessage(Object o)
    {
        String body = (String)o;
        Console.WriteLine("Received Message: " + body);
        return body;
    }

    protected override void OnMessage(Message inMsg)
    {
        inMsg.Formatter = GetFormatter();
        Object inBody = GetTypedMessageBody(inMsg);
        if (inBody != null)
        {
            Object outBody = ProcessMessage(inBody);

            if (outBody != null)
            {
                SendReply(outBody, inMsg);
            }
        }
    }
}

public class AsyncRequestReplyService : MQService
{
    public AsyncRequestReplyService(IMessageReceiver receiver) : base(receiver) {}
    public AsyncRequestReplyService(String requestQueueName) : base (requestQueueName) {}

    protected override Type GetRequestBodyType()
    {
```

Asynchronous Implementation with MSMQ

```
            return typeof(System.String);
    }

    protected virtual void ProcessMessage(Object o, Message msg)
    {
        String body = (String)o;
        Console.WriteLine("Received Message: " + body);
    }

    protected override void OnMessage(Message inMsg)
    {
        inMsg.Formatter =  GetFormatter();
        Object inBody = GetTypedMessageBody(inMsg);
        if (inBody != null)
        {
            ProcessMessage(inBody, inMsg);
        }

    }
}
```

Both classes provide a default implementation of the GetRequestBodyType and
ProcessMessage methods. GetRequestBodyType specifies that the message expects a simple string, and ProcessMessage prints that string to the console. Technically speaking, we could have omitted the default implementations of these methods from
the classes RequestReplyService and AsyncRequestReplyService so that they remain
abstract. This would allow the compiler to detect any subclass of one of these
classes that forgot to implement one of the abstract methods. However, it is nice
to have a default implementation of a service available for testing and debugging
purposes, so we let these classes be concrete so that they can be instantiated as is.

In summary, the class diagram for the base classes looks as follows (we discuss the bank, credit bureau, and loan broker classes shortly):

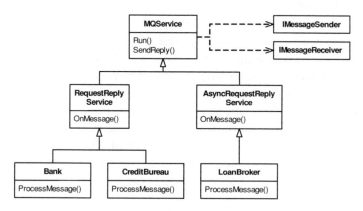

Base Classes for Message Services

Designing the Bank

Now that we have created a set of base classes and utility functions, it is time to start implementing the application logic. An easy way to start creating the solution is to build the application components by reverse order of dependency. This means, we first create components that do not depend on anything else. This allows us to run and test these components independently. The bank is certainly one of those components. The loan broker depends on the banks, but the banks themselves are self-contained. Conveniently enough, a bank is a prime example of a request-reply-service, so implementing a bank should be as simple as inheriting from `RequestReplyService` and filling in some business logic.

Before we start working on the internals of the bank, though, we should define the external interface. We need to define the message types for loan quote requests and replies. For our simple implementation, we define a common message format for all banks so we can use a common class for all five bank instances. C# supports structs, so we use those as message types:

Message Types for Bank

```csharp
public struct BankQuoteRequest
{
    public int SSN;
    public int CreditScore;
    public int HistoryLength;
    public int LoanAmount;
    public int LoanTerm;
}

public struct BankQuoteReply
{
    public double InterestRate;
    public String QuoteID;
    public int ErrorCode;
}
```

Because we want to use a single class for all bank instances, we need to parameterize the banks for different behavior. Our banks are very simple institutions, so the only parameters are `BankName`, `RatePremium`, and `MaxLoanTerm`. The `RatePremium` determines the number of interest rate points that the bank charges above the prime rate—basically, the bank's profit margin. The `MaxLoanTerm` specifies the longest loan term (in months) that the bank is willing to extend. If a loan request is for a longer duration than specified, the bank will thankfully decline. After plugging in the appropriate convenience constructors and accessors, we can build the `ProcessMessage` method of the bank:

Asynchronous Implementation with MSMQ

Bank.cs

```
internal class Bank : RequestReplyService
{
  ...

  protected override Type GetRequestBodyType()
  {
      return typeof(BankQuoteRequest);
  }


  protected  BankQuoteReply ComputeBankReply(BankQuoteRequest requestStruct)
  {
      BankQuoteReply replyStruct = new BankQuoteReply();

      if (requestStruct.LoanTerm <= MaxLoanTerm)
      {
        replyStruct.InterestRate = PrimeRate + RatePremium
                              + (double)(requestStruct.LoanTerm / 12)/10
                              + (double)random.Next(10) / 10;
          replyStruct.ErrorCode = 0;
      }
      else
      {
          replyStruct.InterestRate = 0.0;
          replyStruct.ErrorCode = 1;
      }
      replyStruct.QuoteID = String.Format("{0}-{1:00000}", BankName, quoteCounter);
      quoteCounter++;
      return replyStruct;
  }


  protected override Object ProcessMessage(Object o)
  {
      BankQuoteRequest requestStruct;
      BankQuoteReply replyStruct;

      requestStruct = (BankQuoteRequest)o;
      replyStruct = ComputeBankReply(requestStruct);

      Console.WriteLine("Received request for SSN {0} for {1:c} / {2} months",
                      requestStruct.SSN, requestStruct.LoanAmount,
                      requestStruct.LoanTerm);
      Thread.Sleep(random.Next(10) * 100);
      Console.WriteLine("  Quote: {0} {1} {2}",
                      replyStruct.ErrorCode, replyStruct.InterestRate,
                      replyStruct.QuoteID);

      return replyStruct;
  }
}
```

Asynchronous
Implementation
with MSMQ

We can see that the concrete service has to implement only the GetRequestBody-Type and ProcessMessage methods. The service can safely cast the object passed in by ProcessMessage because the base class has already verified the correct type. As we can see, the remaining implementation has rather little to do with messaging—all the details are taken care of in the base classes. The MQService and Request-ReplyService classes act as a *Service Activator* (532), keeping the application from having to dig into messaging system details.

The method ComputeBankReply contains the complete business logic for a bank. If life were only so simple! Well, this is not an introduction to macroeconomics, but an example of messaging, so we took some liberties to simplify things. The computed interest rate is the sum of the prime rate, the configured rate premium, the loan term, and a sprinkle of randomness. If the requested loan term is longer than the bank is comfortable with, it returns an error code. Each quote that the bank issues receives a unique quote ID so the customer may refer back to it later. In the current implementation, a simple incrementing counter creates these IDs.

The ProcessMessage method incorporates a small delay (between 1/10 and 1 second) to make the bank transaction a bit more realistic. The ProcessMessage also logs some activities to the console so we can see what is going on when we run it inside a simple console application.

To start a bank, first we instantiate it with the appropriate parameters, and then we call the Run method that it inherits from MQService. Since the processing happens through events, the Run method returns right away. Therefore, we must be careful not to terminate the program right after it starts. For our simple tests, I simply insert a Console.ReadLine() statement after the call to Run.

Designing the Credit Bureau

The credit bureau implementation is analogous to the bank. The only difference is in the message types and the business logic. The credit bureau can handle the following message types:

Message Types for Credit Bureau

```
public class CreditBureauRequest
{
    public int SSN;
}

public class CreditBureauReply
{
    public int SSN;
    public int CreditScore;
    public int HistoryLength;
}
```

The ProcessMessage method is nearly identical to the bank code, except it deals with different data structures and invokes different application logic. The credit bureau also has a built-in delay.

CreditBureau.cs

```
private int getCreditScore(int ssn)
{
    return (int)(random.Next(600) + 300);
}

private int getCreditHistoryLength(int ssn)
{
    return (int)(random.Next(19) + 1);
}
```

Designing the Loan Broker

Now that we have a functioning credit bureau and a bank class that lets us instantiate multiple incarnations of a bank, we are ready to work in the internal design of the loan broker. The routing and transformation patterns from this book help us segment the functions that the loan broker needs to provide. We can group the internal functions of the loan broker into three main portions (see figure): the request-reply interface that accepts requests from clients, the credit bureau interface, and the bank interface.

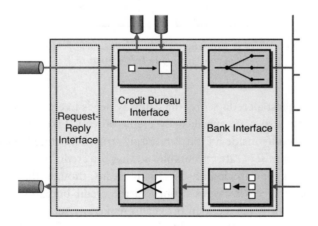

Internal Structure of the Loan Broker

Asynchronous
Implementation
with MSMQ

In a similar fashion to building the whole solution in reverse order of dependency, let's start building the pieces that depend only on what's already there. Because we just built a bank and a credit bureau service, it makes sense to create the interface from the loan broker to these external components. The credit bureau interface definitely seems simpler, so let's start there.

Credit Bureau Gateway   The loan broker needs to make requests to the credit bureau to obtain the customer's credit rating, which is required by the bank. This implies sending a message to the external loan broker component and receiving reply messages. Wrapping the details of sending a generic message inside a MessageGateway allowed us to hide many MSMQ details from the rest of the application. Following the same reasoning, we should encapsulate sending and receiving messages to the credit bureau inside a *credit bureau gateway*. This credit bureau gateway performs the important function of *semantic enrichment*, allowing the loan broker to call methods such as GetCreditScore as opposed to SendMessage. This makes the loan broker code more readable and provides a strong encapsulation of the communication between the loan broker and the credit bureau. The following diagram illustrates the levels of abstraction achieved by "chaining" the two gateways.

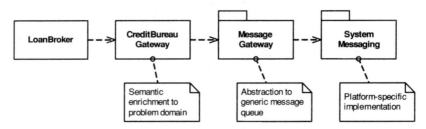

The Loan Broker Provides an Additional Level of Abstraction
from the Messaging Infrastructure

Asynchronous
Implementation
with MSMQ

In order to request a credit score, the gateway needs to create an instance of a CreditBureauRequest struct, as specified by credit bureau. Likewise, the interface will receive the results inside a CreditBureauReply struct. We stated earlier that the solution is built from separate executables so that the credit bureau can run on a different computer than the loan broker. This means, though, that the loan broker may not have access to types defined in the credit bureau's assembly, and really, we would not want the loan broker to make any references to the credit bureau internals, because that would eliminate the benefits of loose coupling over message queues. The loan broker is supposed to be completely unaware of what component services the credit score requests. The loan broker needs, however, access to the structs that define the message formats. Luckily, the Microsoft .NET Framework SDK contains a tool that lets us do just that, the XML Schema Definition Tool (xsd.exe). This tool can create XML schemas from an assembly and also create C# source code from XML schemas. The following figure describes the process:

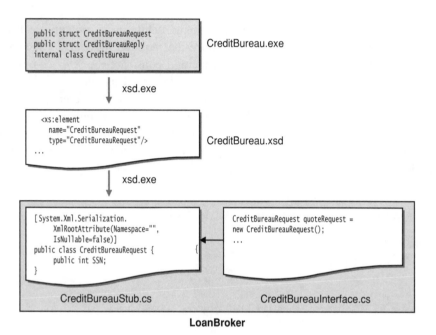

Creating Class Stubs from Another Assembly

xsd.exe extracts public type definitions and creates an XML schema file based on the type definition and optional attributes that control serialization. In our case, xsd.exe created the following schema:

Asynchronous Implementation with MSMQ

```xml
<?xml version="1.0" encoding="utf-8"?>
<xs:schema elementFormDefault="qualified" xmlns:xs="http://www.w3.org/2001/XMLSchema">
  <xs:element name="CreditBureauRequest" type="CreditBureauRequest" />
  <xs:complexType name="CreditBureauRequest">
    <xs:sequence>
      <xs:element minOccurs="1" maxOccurs="1" name="SSN" type="xs:int" />
    </xs:sequence>
  </xs:complexType>
  <xs:element name="CreditBureauReply" type="CreditBureauReply" />
  <xs:complexType name="CreditBureauReply">
```

```
    <xs:sequence>
      <xs:element minOccurs="1" maxOccurs="1" name="SSN" type="xs:int" />
      <xs:element minOccurs="1" maxOccurs="1" name="CreditScore" type="xs:int" />
      <xs:element minOccurs="1" maxOccurs="1" name="HistoryLength" type="xs:int" />
    </xs:sequence>
  </xs:complexType>
  <xs:element name="Run" nillable="true" type="Run" />
  <xs:complexType name="Run" />
</xs:schema>
```

Usually, a service would publish this schema definition to potential callers. This allows the caller the option to produce the required message format in a number of different ways. First, the caller could construct the XSD-compliant request message explicitly. Alternatively, the caller could use the .NET built-in serialization. In this case, the client would still have a choice of different programming languages since the .NET CLR is programming language–independent.

We decide to use .NET's built-in serialization. Therefore, we run xsd.exe again to create source files to be used by the service consumer, and we get a file that looks like this:

```
//
// This source code was auto-generated by xsd, Version=1.1.4322.573.
//
namespace CreditBureau {
    using System.Xml.Serialization;


    /// <remarks/>
    [System.Xml.Serialization.XmlRootAttribute(Namespace="", IsNullable=false)]
    public class CreditBureauRequest {

        /// <remarks/>
        public int SSN;
    }
    ...
}
```

It is worth noting that the .NET XML serialization and deserialization allows loose coupling. So, technically speaking, the request message that we send to the credit bureau does not have to be of the exact same CLR type that is used inside the credit bureau implementation as long as the XML representation contains the required elements. For example, this would allow a requestor to send a message whose XML representation contains additional elements without disturbing the communication. For our example, we assume that the loan broker is willing to conform to the credit bureau's specified format and use the same data types on both ends of the communication.

We are now ready to send messages in the correct format to the credit bureau. We need to keep in mind, though, that this communication is asynchronous with a separate, asynchronous request message and reply message. We could design the credit bureau gateway so that after sending a request, the gateway code waits until the response comes back. This approach has one significant drawback: The application will just sit and wait while the credit bureau is processing a message. This type of pseudo-synchronous processing can quickly result in a performance bottleneck. If we make each step of the process pseudo-synchronous, it means that the loan broker can process only one request process at a time. For example, it would not be able to request the credit score for a new request while it is still waiting for bank replies for the previous quote request. To visualize the difference, let's consider that the loan broker has to perform two main steps: Get the credit score and get the best quote from the banks. If we assume the loan broker runs only a single, sequential execution, the execution will look like the top half of the following figure:

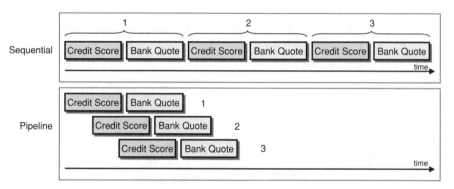

Pipeline Processing Can Provide Significantly Higher Throughput

Because the bulk of the actual work is executed by external components, the loan broker component basically sits around and waits for results—not an efficient use of computing resources. If we design the whole loan broker process as an *Event-Driven Consumer* (498), we can start processing multiple requests in parallel and process the results as they come in. We call this mode *pipeline* processing. The scalability of the system now depends only on the processing capacity of the external components and not on the loan broker. If we run only a single instance of the credit bureau process, the difference may not be as pronounced because the bureau request queue will queue up the requests anyway. However, if we decide to run multiple credit bureau instances in parallel, we will see immediate performance gains (more on performance to follow).

Asynchronous
Implementation
with MSMQ

There are two primary ways to make the loan broker process event-driven. We can create a sequential process but create a new thread for each incoming request message. Alternatively, we can let the messaging system notify the loan broker whenever an event is pending. This way, we let the messaging system control the threads of execution. Each approach has pros and cons. Coding a sequential process can make the code easier to understand; however, if our component is primarily a broker component that brokers messages between external entities, it would result in a potentially large number of threads that are doing nothing much but wait for incoming messages. These threads could consume a large amount of system resources and accomplish little. Therefore, we may be better off letting the messaging system drive the execution. Whenever a message is ready to be consumed, the system will invoke the broker execution. This lets us maintain a single thread of execution and not worry about thread management. However, we need to deal with the fact that the execution path is not a single sequential method, but multiple code segments that are executed as messages arrive.

You might have guessed that the way to make things event-driven in .NET is to use *delegates*. As expected, the credit bureau gateway defines a new delegate.

```
public delegate void OnCreditReplyEvent(CreditBureauReply creditReply, Object ACT);
```

This delegate allows other code segments to tell the credit bureau gateway which method to call when the result comes in. The credit bureau gateway passes a properly typed `CreditBureauReply` struct back to the caller. It also passes something we call ACT—an *Asynchronous Completion Token* [POSA2]. This token allows the caller to pass in data to the gateway and receive the data back when the corresponding reply message comes in (see *Messaging Gateway* [468]). Basically, the credit bureau gateway performs correlation for the request and reply messages so that the caller does not have to.

What's left are a method to request a credit score and a method that handles an incoming reply message, correlating the proper ACT and invoking the properly typed delegate.

Asynchronous Implementation with MSMQ

CreditBureauGateway.cs

```
internal struct CreditRequestProcess
{
    public int CorrelationID;
    public Object ACT;
    public OnCreditReplyEvent callback;
}
```

```
internal class CreditBureauGateway
{
    protected IMessageSender creditRequestQueue;
    protected IMessageReceiver creditReplyQueue;

    protected IDictionary activeProcesses = (IDictionary)(new Hashtable());

    protected Random random = new Random();

    public void Listen()
    {
        creditReplyQueue.Begin();
    }

    public void GetCreditScore(CreditBureauRequest quoteRequest,
                       OnCreditReplyEvent OnCreditResponse, Object ACT)
    {
        Message requestMessage = new Message(quoteRequest);
        requestMessage.ResponseQueue = creditReplyQueue.GetQueue();
        requestMessage.AppSpecific = random.Next();

        CreditRequestProcess processInstance = new CreditRequestProcess();
        processInstance.ACT = ACT;
        processInstance.callback = OnCreditResponse;
        processInstance.CorrelationID = requestMessage.AppSpecific;

        creditRequestQueue.Send(requestMessage);

        activeProcesses.Add(processInstance.CorrelationID, processInstance);
    }

    private void OnCreditResponse(Message msg)
    {
        msg.Formatter = GetFormatter();

        CreditBureauReply replyStruct;
        try
        {
            if (msg.Body is CreditBureauReply)
            {
                replyStruct = (CreditBureauReply)msg.Body;
                int CorrelationID = msg.AppSpecific;

                if (activeProcesses.Contains(CorrelationID))
                {
                    CreditRequestProcess processInstance =
                      (CreditRequestProcess)(activeProcesses[CorrelationID]);
                    processInstance.callback(replyStruct, processInstance.ACT);
                    activeProcesses.Remove(CorrelationID);
                }
                else { Console.WriteLine
                        ("Incoming credit response does not match any request"); }
```

```
        }
        else
        { Console.WriteLine("Illegal reply."); }
    }
    catch (Exception e)
    {
        Console.WriteLine("Exception: {0}", e.ToString());
    }
  }
}
```

When a caller requests a credit score via the GetCreditScore method, the credit bureau gateway allocates a new instance of the CreditRequestProcess structure. The collection activeProcesses contains one instance of CreditRequestProcess for each outstanding request, keyed by the *Correlation Identifier* (163) of the message. The structure also holds the delegate for the OnCreditReplyEvent event. Storing the delegate for each message allows each caller to specify a different callback location for each request. As we will see later, this allows the caller to use delegates to manage conversation state.

It is important to note that we do not use the message's built-in message ID field to correlate. Instead, we assign a random integer number to the AppSpecific field and correlate incoming messages by the value of that field (remember that we designed the RequestReplyService to copy both the ID field and the AppSpecific field to the reply message). Why would we want to correlate by something other than the message ID? The advantage of the message ID is that it is unique for each message in the system. But that also limits our flexibility. Requiring a reply message to correlate to the message ID of the request message does not allow us to insert intermediate steps (for example, a router) into the message flow. Because any intermediate step would consume the request message and publish a new message to the service, the reply message's CorrelationId would match the message the service received but not the message that the loan broker originally sent (see figure).

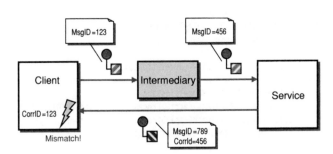

Intermediaries Hinder Correlation with System-Generated Message IDs

There are two solutions to this problem. First, any intermediate would be required to intercept both request and reply messages and to equip reply messages with the correct CorrelationId value (for an example of this approach, see the *Smart Proxy* [558]). Alternatively, we can use a separate field for correlation purposes so that all related messages that flow through the intermediary and the service carry the same *Correlation Identifier* (163). In this example, we chose the second approach to make it easier for an intermediary component to intercept request messages between the loan broker and the credit bureau (we will take advantage of this in Chapter 12, "Interlude: Systems Management Example"). How should we pick a value for the AppSpecific property? We could use sequential values, but then we have to be careful that two concurrent instances do not use the same starting value. We could also use a central ID generation module (e.g., a database) that guarantees systemwide uniqueness. This seemed a little too much trouble for this simple example, so we chose a random number. .NET generates random numbers as signed 32-bit integers so that the odds of a duplicate are 1 in 2 billion—a risk we are willing to take.

The credit bureau gateway now provides the clean abstraction from the Windows message queuing infrastructure that we were aiming for. The only public interface into the credit bureau gateway (besides constructors) is a delegate and two methods:

```
delegate void OnCreditReplyEvent(CreditBureauReply creditReply, Object ACT);
class CreditBureauGateway {
  void Listen() {...}
  void GetCreditScore(CreditBureauRequest quoteRequest,
              OnCreditReplyEvent OnCreditResponse,
              Object ACT) {...}
  ...
}
```

Neither construct makes any reference to a message or a message queue. This provides a number of benefits. First, we can easily implement a stubbed out version of the credit bureau gateway that does not rely on message queues at all (similar to the MockQueue). Second, we can replace the implementation of the credit bureau gateway if we decide to use a transport different from MSMQ. For example, if we were going to use a Web services interface using SOAP and HTTP instead of MSMQ, the methods exposed by the gateway would most likely not have to change at all.

Asynchronous Implementation with MSMQ

Bank Gateway The design of the bank gateway follows the same principles as the design of the credit bureau gateway. We use the same process as before to declare stubs for the request and reply message types specified by the bank.

The external portion of the bank gateway is very similar to the credit bureau gateway:

```
delegate void OnBestQuoteEvent(BankQuoteReply bestQuote, Object ACT);
class BankGateway {
    void Listen() {...}
    void GetBestQuote(BankQuoteRequest quoteRequest,
                      OnBestQuoteEvent onBestQuoteEvent,
                      Object ACT) {...}
    ...
}
```

The internal workings are slightly more complex because the *Scatter-Gather* (297) style of interaction routes a single BankQuoteRequest to multiple banks. Likewise, a single BankQuoteReply is usually the result of multiple bank quote reply messages. The former part is handled by a *Recipient List* (249), while the latter is handled by an *Aggregator* (268). Let's start with the *Recipient List* (249). It has to implement three main functions:

- Computation of appropriate recipients
- Sending the message to the recipients
- Initializing the *Aggregator* (268) to process incoming replies

As described in the introduction of this chapter, this implementation uses the *distribution* style of *Scatter-Gather* (297), actively determining which banks to route the request to. This approach makes business sense if the banks charge the broker for each quote or if the bank and the broker have an agreement that requires the broker to prequalify leads he or she generates. The loan broker makes the routing decision based on the customer's credit score, the amount of the loan and the length of the credit history. We encapsulate each connection to a bank inside a class that inherits from the abstract class BankConnection. This class contains a reference to the properly addressed message queue and a method CanHandleLoanRequest that determines whether the quote request should be forwarded to this bank. The BankConnectionManager simply iterates through the list of all bank connections and compiles a list of those that match the criteria of the loan quote. If the list of banks was longer, we could consider implementing a configurable rules engine. We prefer the current approach because it is simple and explicit.

Asynchronous Implementation with MSMQ

```
internal class BankConnectionManager
{
    static protected BankConnection[] banks =
                    {new Bank1(), new Bank2(), new Bank3(), new Bank4(), new Bank5() };

    public IMessageSender[] GetEligibleBankQueues
                    (int CreditScore, int HistoryLength, int LoanAmount)
```

```
    {
        ArrayList lenders = new ArrayList();

        for (int index = 0; index < banks.Length; index++)
        {
            if (banks[index].CanHandleLoanRequest(CreditScore, HistoryLength,
                                                  LoanAmount))
                lenders.Add(banks[index].Queue);
        }
        IMessageSender[] lenderArray = (IMessageSender [])Array.CreateInstance
                                  (typeof(IMessageSender), lenders.Count);
        lenders.CopyTo(lenderArray);
        return lenderArray;
    }
}



internal abstract class BankConnection
{
    protected MessageSenderGateway queue;
    protected String bankName = "";
    public MessageSenderGateway Queue
    {
        get { return queue; }
    }
    public String BankName
    {
        get { return bankName; }
    }
    public BankConnection (MessageQueue queue)
      { this.queue = new MessageSenderGateway(queue); }
    public BankConnection (String queueName)
      { this.queue = new MessageSenderGateway(queueName); }

    public abstract bool CanHandleLoanRequest(int CreditScore, int HistoryLength,
                                              int LoanAmount);
}

internal class Bank1 : BankConnection
{
    protected String bankname = "Exclusive Country Club Bankers";

    public Bank1 () : base (".\\private$\\bank1Queue") {}
    public override bool CanHandleLoanRequest(int CreditScore, int HistoryLength,
                                              int LoanAmount)
    {
        return LoanAmount >= 75000 && CreditScore >= 600 && HistoryLength >= 8;
    }
}
...
```

Once the list of relevant banks is compiled, sending the message is a simple matter of iterating over the list. In a production application, this iteration should occur inside a single transaction to avoid error conditions where a message may be sent to some banks but not to others. Once again, we chose to let simplicity prevail for this example.

```
internal class MessageRouter
{
    public static void SendToRecipientList (Message msg, IMessageSender[] recipientList)
    {
        IEnumerator e = recipientList.GetEnumerator();
        while (e.MoveNext())
        {
            ((IMessageSender)e.Current).Send(msg);
        }
    }
}
```

Now that request messages are on their way to the banks, we need to initialize the *Aggregator* (268) to expect incoming bank quotes. Due to the event-driven nature of the loan broker, the aggregator needs to be prepared to work on more than one aggregate concurrently—maintaining one active aggregate for each quote request that is pending. This means that incoming messages need to be uniquely correlated to a specific aggregate. Unfortunately, we cannot use the message ID as the correlation identifier because the *Recipient List* (249) needs to send individual messages to each of the banks. As a result, if three banks participate in a quote request, the *Recipient List* (249) needs to send three unique messages, one to each bank. Each of these messages will have a unique message ID, so if the banks were to correlate by message ID, the three responses will have different correlation IDs even though they belong to the same aggregate. This would make it impossible for the aggregator to identify related messages. We could have the aggregate store the message ID for each request message and thus correlate the incoming message's correlation ID back to the aggregate. However, this is more complicated than we need it to be. Instead, we just generate our own correlation IDs—one for each aggregate as opposed to one for each message. We store this (numeric) ID in the AppSpecific property of the outgoing request messages. The banks inherit from RequestReply-Service, which already transfers the incoming message's AppSpecific property to the reply messages. When a quote message comes in from a bank, the BankGateway can easily correlate the incoming message by the AppSpecific property of the message (see figure).

Asynchronous
Implementation
with MSMQ

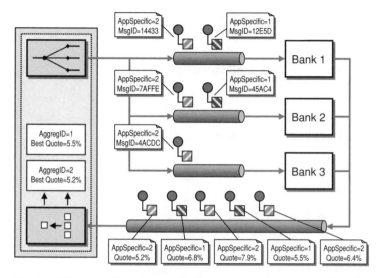

*The BankGateway Uses the AppSpecific Message Property to Correlate
Response Messages to Aggregates*

The bank gateway initializes an aggregate with the aggregate ID (generated
by a simple counter) and the number of expected messages. In addition, the
caller needs to supply a delegate and can optionally specify an object reference
to an ACT in the same way the credit bureau gateway functioned. The aggregation strategy is simple. The aggregate is considered complete when all selected
banks have responded with a reply message. The *Recipient List* (249) initializes
the aggregate with the number of expected messages. Remember that banks
have the option of declining to provide a quote. So that we can know when an
aggregate is complete, we require the banks to provide a reply message with the
error code set if they do not want to provide a quote. We could easily modify
the aggregation strategy, for example, to cut off the bidding after 1 second and
take the best response up to that point.

```
internal class BankQuoteAggregate
{
    protected int ID;
    protected int expectedMessages;
    protected Object ACT;
    protected OnBestQuoteEvent callback;

    protected double bestRate = 0.0;

    protected ArrayList receivedMessages = new ArrayList();
    protected BankQuoteReply bestReply = null;
```

```
public BankQuoteAggregate(int ID, int expectedMessages, OnBestQuoteEvent callback,
                          Object ACT)
{
    this.ID = ID;
    this.expectedMessages = expectedMessages;
    this.callback = callback;
    this.ACT = ACT;
}

public void AddMessage(BankQuoteReply reply)
{
    if (reply.ErrorCode == 0)
    {
        if (bestReply == null)
        {
            bestReply = reply;
        }
        else
        {
            if (reply.InterestRate < bestReply.InterestRate)
            {
                bestReply = reply;
            }
        }
    }
    receivedMessages.Add(reply);
}

public bool IsComplete()
{
    return receivedMessages.Count == expectedMessages;
}

public BankQuoteReply getBestResult()
{
    return bestReply;
}

public void NotifyBestResult()
{
    if (callback != null)
    {
        callback(bestReply, ACT);
    }
}
}
```

Asynchronous
Implementation
with MSMQ

Armed with the bank connection manager, the recipient list, and the aggregate, the implementation of the BankGateway's functions becomes relatively simple:

BankGateway.cs

```
internal class BankGateway
  {
      protected IMessageReceiver bankReplyQueue;
      protected BankConnectionManager connectionManager;

      protected IDictionary aggregateBuffer = (IDictionary)(new Hashtable());
      protected int aggregationCorrelationID;

      public void Listen()
      {
          bankReplyQueue.Begin();
      }

      public void GetBestQuote(BankQuoteRequest quoteRequest,
                              OnBestQuoteEvent onBestQuoteEvent, Object ACT)
      {

          Message requestMessage = new Message(quoteRequest);
          requestMessage.AppSpecific = aggregationCorrelationID;
          requestMessage.ResponseQueue = bankReplyQueue.GetQueue();
          IMessageSender[] eligibleBanks =
              connectionManager.GetEligibleBankQueues(quoteRequest.CreditScore,
                                            quoteRequest.HistoryLength,
                                            quoteRequest.LoanAmount);

          aggregateBuffer.Add(aggregationCorrelationID,
              new BankQuoteAggregate(aggregationCorrelationID, eligibleBanks.Length,
                            onBestQuoteEvent, ACT));
          aggregationCorrelationID++;

          MessageRouter.SendToRecipientList(requestMessage, eligibleBanks);
      }


      private void OnBankMessage(Message msg)
      {
          msg.Formatter = GetFormatter();

          BankQuoteReply replyStruct;
          try
          {
              if (msg.Body is BankQuoteReply)
              {
                  replyStruct = (BankQuoteReply)msg.Body;
                  int aggregationCorrelationID = msg.AppSpecific;
                  Console.WriteLine("Quote {0:0.00}% {1} {2}",
                                  replyStruct.InterestRate, replyStruct.QuoteID,
                                  replyStruct.ErrorCode);
```

Asynchronous
Implementation
with MSMQ

```
        if (aggregateBuffer.Contains(aggregationCorrelationID))
        {
            BankQuoteAggregate aggregate =
                (BankQuoteAggregate)(aggregateBuffer[aggregationCorrelationID]);
            aggregate.AddMessage(replyStruct);
            if (aggregate.IsComplete())
            {
                aggregate.NotifyBestResult();
                aggregateBuffer.Remove(aggregationCorrelationID);
            }
        }
        else
        { Console.WriteLine("Incoming bank response does not match any aggregate"); }
    }
    else
    { Console.WriteLine("Illegal request."); }
}
catch (Exception e)
{
    Console.WriteLine("Exception: {0}", e.ToString());
}
    }
}
```

When the bank gateway receives a quote reply from a bank, the OnBankMessage method executes. The method converts the incoming message to the correct type and goes on to locate the related aggregate via the AppSpecific property. It adds the new bid to the aggregate. Once the aggregate is complete (as defined in the Bank-QuoteAggregate class), the BankGateway invokes the delegate supplied by the caller.

Accepting Requests Now that we have a well-encapsulated credit bureau gateway and bank gateway, we are ready to have the loan broker accept requests. Earlier, we discussed the design of the MQService and AsyncRequestReply-Service base classes. The LoanBroker class inherits from AsyncRequestReplyService because it cannot send the results back to the reply queue right away, but only after several other asynchronous operations (obtaining the credit store and communicating with the banks) complete.

The first step in implementing the LoanBroker is to define the message types the loan broker handles:

```
public struct LoanQuoteRequest
{
    public int SSN;
    public double LoanAmount;
    public int LoanTerm;
}
```

Asynchronous
Implementation
with MSMQ

```
public struct LoanQuoteReply
{
    public int SSN;
    public double LoanAmount;
    public double InterestRate;
    public string QuoteID;
}
```

Next, we create a class that inherits from AsyncRequestReplyService and override the ProcessMessage method.

The Process The loan broker is different from the previous classes because the process that is triggered by an incoming message is not contained in any single method. Instead, the completion of the process depends on a sequence of external events. The loan broker can receive three types of events:

- A new loan request message arrives.
- A credit score reply message arrives (via the CreditBureauGateway).
- A bank quote message arrives (via the BankGateway).

Since the logic for the loan broker is spread across multiple event handlers, we need to keep the state of the broker across these functions. That's where the asynchronous completion tokens come in! Remember that the credit bureau gateway and the bank gateway allow the caller (the loan broker) to pass a reference to an object instance when sending a request. The gateway passes the object reference back when the reply message is received. To take advantage of this functionality, we declare an ACT in the loan broker as follows:

```
internal class ACT
{
    public LoanQuoteRequest loanRequest;
    public Message message;

    public ACT(LoanQuoteRequest loanRequest, Message message)
    {
        this.loanRequest = loanRequest;
        this.message = message;
    }
}
```

Asynchronous
Implementation
with MSMQ

The ACT contains a copy of the original request message (which contains the message ID and the reply address required to create the reply message) and the request data structure (needed to copy the SSN and the loan amount into the reply message). Technically speaking, the ACT stores a small amount of duplicate information because we could extract the content of the request structure from the request message. However, the convenience of accessing a strongly typed structure is worth the few extra bytes.

The remainder of the loan broker is implemented as follows:

LoanBroker.cs

```
internal class LoanBroker : AsyncRequestReplyService
{
    protected ICreditBureauGateway creditBureauInterface;
    protected BankGateway bankInterface;

    public LoanBroker(String requestQueueName,
                      String creditRequestQueueName, String creditReplyQueueName,
                      String bankReplyQueueName,
                      BankConnectionManager connectionManager): base(requestQueueName)
    {

        creditBureauInterface = (ICreditBureauGateway)
            (new CreditBureauGatewayImp(creditRequestQueueName, creditReplyQueueName));
        creditBureauInterface.Listen();

        bankInterface = new BankGateway(bankReplyQueueName, connectionManager);
        bankInterface.Listen();
    }

    protected override Type GetRequestBodyType()
    {
        return typeof(LoanQuoteRequest);
    }

    protected override void ProcessMessage(Object o, Message msg)
    {
        LoanQuoteRequest quoteRequest;
        quoteRequest = (LoanQuoteRequest)o;

        CreditBureauRequest creditRequest =
            LoanBrokerTranslator.GetCreditBureaurequest(quoteRequest);

        ACT act = new ACT(quoteRequest, msg);

        creditBureauInterface.GetCreditScore(creditRequest,
                                     new OnCreditReplyEvent(OnCreditReply), act);
    }

    private void OnCreditReply(CreditBureauReply creditReply, Object act)
    {
        ACT myAct = (ACT)act;

        Console.WriteLine("Received Credit Score -- SSN {0} Score {1} Length {2}",
                        creditReply.SSN, creditReply.CreditScore,
                        creditReply.HistoryLength);
```

```
        BankQuoteRequest bankRequest =
            LoanBrokerTranslator.GetBankQuoteRequest(myAct.loanRequest ,creditReply);
        bankInterface.GetBestQuote(bankRequest, new OnBestQuoteEvent(OnBestQuote), act);
    }

    private void OnBestQuote(BankQuoteReply bestQuote, Object act)
    {
        ACT myAct = (ACT)act;

        LoanQuoteReply quoteReply = LoanBrokerTranslator.GetLoanQuoteReply
                                    (myAct.loanRequest, bestQuote);
        Console.WriteLine("Best quote {0} {1}",
                        quoteReply.InterestRate, quoteReply.QuoteID);
        SendReply(quoteReply, myAct.message);
    }
}
```

LoanBroker inherits from AsyncRequestReplyService, which provides support for receiving requests and sending correlated replies. LoanBroker overrides the method ProcessMessage to deal with incoming request messages. ProcessMessage creates a new instance of the ACT and calls the credit bureau gateway to request a credit score. Interestingly, the method ends there. Processing continues when the credit bureau gateway invokes OnCreditReply, the delegate specified by the ProcessMessage method. This method uses the ACT and the credit bureau reply to create a bank quote request and calls the bank gateway to send the request messages. This time it specifies the method OnBestQuote as the callback delegate. Once the bank gateway receives all bank quote replies, it invokes this method via the delegate and passes back the instance of the ACT. OnBestQuote uses the bank quote and the ACT to create a reply to the customer and sends it off using the base class implementation of SendReply.

One class you probably noticed in the source code is the LoanBrokerTranslator. This class provides a handful of static methods that help convert between the different message formats.

The LoanBroker class demonstrates the trade-off we made in our design. The code is free of references to messaging or thread-related concepts (except for the inheritance from AsyncRequestReplyService), which makes the code very easy to read. However, the execution of the main function is spread across three methods that make no direct reference to each other besides the delegates. This can make the flow of execution hard to understand without considering the total solution, including all external components.

Asynchronous Implementation with MSMQ

Refactoring the Loan Broker

When we look at the way the loan broker functions, we realize that we are separating data and functionality. We have one instance of the LoanBroker class that emulates multiple instances by means of the ACT collection. While ACTs are very useful, they seem to go against the spirit of object-oriented programming by separating data and functionality—the two parts that make up an object. However, we can refactor the LoanBroker class to avoid the repeated lookup of the ACT if we use the delegates in a better way. Delegates are essentially type-safe function pointers. As such, they point to a specific object instance. So, rather than supplying the credit bureau and bank gateway with a reference to a method in the sole LoanBroker instance, we can use the delegates to point to a specific instance of a "process object" that maintains the current state, as an ACT does, but also contains the logic of the loan broker process. To do this, we turn the ACT into a new class called LoanBrokerProcess and move the message handler functions into this class:

```
internal class LoanBrokerProcess
{
    protected LoanBrokerPM broker;
    protected String processID;
    protected LoanQuoteRequest loanRequest;
    protected Message message;

    protected CreditBureauGateway creditBureauGateway;
    protected BankGateway bankInterface;

    public LoanBrokerProcess(LoanBrokerPM broker, String processID,
                            CreditBureauGateway creditBureauGateway,
                            BankGateway bankGateway,
                            LoanQuoteRequest loanRequest, Message msg)
    {
        this.broker = broker;
        this.creditBureauGateway = broker.CreditBureauGateway;
        this.bankInterface = broker.BankInterface;
        this.processID = processID;
        this.loanRequest = loanRequest;
        this.message = msg;

        CreditBureauRequest creditRequest =
            LoanBrokerTranslator.GetCreditBureaurequest(loanRequest);
        creditBureauGateway.GetCreditScore(creditRequest,
            new OnCreditReplyEvent(OnCreditReply), null);
    }

    private void OnCreditReply(CreditBureauReply creditReply, Object act)
    {
        Console.WriteLine("Received Credit Score -- SSN {0} Score {1} Length {2}",
            creditReply.SSN, creditReply.CreditScore, creditReply.HistoryLength);
        BankQuoteRequest bankRequest =
            LoanBrokerTranslator.GetBankQuoteRequest(loanRequest, creditReply);
        bankInterface.GetBestQuote(bankRequest, new OnBestQuoteEvent(OnBestQuote), null);
    }
```

```
    private void OnBestQuote(BankQuoteReply bestQuote, Object act)
    {
        LoanQuoteReply quoteReply = LoanBrokerTranslator.GetLoanQuoteReply
                                    (loanRequest, bestQuote);
        Console.WriteLine("Best quote {0} {1}",
                          quoteReply.InterestRate, quoteReply.QuoteID);
        broker.SendReply(quoteReply, message);
        broker.OnProcessComplete(processID);
    }
}
```

The methods no longer reference the ACT parameter provided by the credit bureau gateway and the bank gateway because all necessary information is stored in the instance of the LoanBrokerProcess. Once the process completes, it sends the reply message using the SendReply method that the LoanBrokerPM inherits from the AsyncRequestReplyService. Next, it notifies the LoanBrokerPM of the completion of the process. We could have implemented this notification using a delegate, but we decided to use a reference to the broker instead.

Using the LoanBrokerProcess class simplifies the main loan broker class:

```
internal class LoanBrokerPM : AsyncRequestReplyService
{
    protected CreditBureauGateway creditBureauGateway;
    protected BankGateway bankInterface;
    protected IDictionary activeProcesses = (IDictionary)(new Hashtable());

    public LoanBrokerPM(String requestQueueName,
                    String creditRequestQueueName, String creditReplyQueueName,
                    String bankReplyQueueName,
                    BankConnectionManager connectionManager): base(requestQueueName)
    {
        creditBureauGateway = new CreditBureauGateway(creditRequestQueueName,
                                            creditReplyQueueName);
        creditBureauGateway.Listen();

        bankInterface = new BankGateway(bankReplyQueueName, connectionManager);
        bankInterface.Listen();
    }

    protected override Type GetRequestBodyType()
    {
        return typeof(LoanQuoteRequest);
    }

    protected override void ProcessMessage(Object o, Message message)
    {
        LoanQuoteRequest quoteRequest;
        quoteRequest = (LoanQuoteRequest)o;
```

Asynchronous Implementation with MSMQ

```
    String processID = message.Id;
    LoanBrokerProcess newProcess =
        new LoanBrokerProcess(this, processID, creditBureauGateway,
                              bankInterface, quoteRequest, message);
    activeProcesses.Add(processID, newProcess);
}

public void OnProcessComplete(String processID)
{
    activeProcesses.Remove(processID);
}
}
```

This `LoanBrokerPM` is basically a generic implementation of a *Process Manager* (312). It creates a new process instance when a new message arrives. When a process completes, the process manager removes the process instance from the list of active processes. The process manager uses the message ID as the unique process ID assigned to each process instance. We can now change the behavior of the loan broker just by editing the `LoanBrokerProcess` class, which has no references to messaging besides passing the message object around. It looks like paying attention to proper encapsulation and refactoring paid off. The following class diagram summarizes the internal structure of the loan broker:

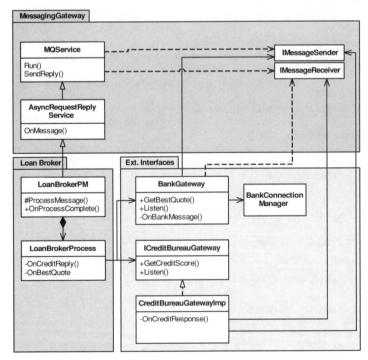

Loan Broker Class Diagram

Putting It All Together

The only remaining piece is the test client. The test client design is similar to that of the credit bureau gateway. The test client can make a specified number of repeated requests and correlate incoming responses to outstanding requests. Once we start all processes (banks, credit bureau, and the loan broker), we can execute the example. We use a number of simple main classes to start the respective components as console applications. We see a flurry of activity on the screen, indicating the flow of messages through the system (see figure).

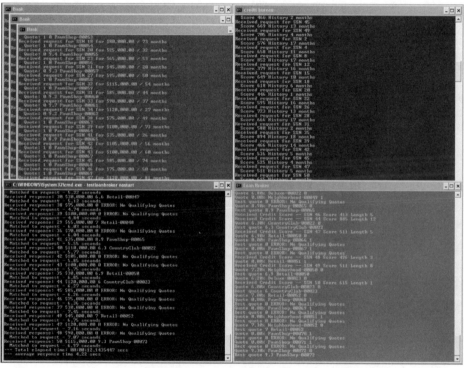

Running the MSMQ Example

Improving Performance

Now that we have the complete solution running, we can gather some performance metrics to compare the throughput of the asynchronous solution to the synchronous solution. Using the test data generator, we send 50 randomly generated requests to the loan broker. The test data generator, shown on the next page, reports that it took 33 seconds to receive the 50 reply messages.

```
Received response: 47 $65,000.00 7.3 Neighborhood-00015
  Matched to request - 26.80 seconds
Received response: 48 $110,000.00 5.6 CountryClub-00012
  Matched to request - 27.06 seconds
Received response: 49 $25,000.00 7.5 Retail-00016
  Matched to request - 27.55 seconds
Received response: 50 $110,000.00 0 ERROR: No Qualifying Quotes
  Matched to request - 27.78 seconds
=== Total elapsed time: 00:00:33.5627119 secs
=== average response time 15.31 secs
```

Sending 50 Quote Requests

It would be tempting to think that each request took 33/50 = 0.6 seconds. Wrong! The *throughput* of the loan broker is 50 requests in 33 seconds, but some of the requests took 27 seconds to complete. Why is the system so slow? Let's look at a snapshot of the message queue during the test run:

31 Messages Are Queued Up in the Credit Request Queue

Asynchronous Implementation with MSMQ

Thirty-one messages are queued up in the credit bureau request queue! Apparently, the credit bureau is our bottleneck, because all quote requests have to go through the credit bureau first. Now we can reap some of the rewards of loose coupling and start two additional instances of the credit bureau. We now have three parallel instances of the credit bureau service running. This should fix our bottleneck, right? Let's see:

```
Received response: 47 $70,000.00 0 ERROR: No Qualifying Quotes
  Matched to request - 15.61 seconds
Received response: 49 $115,000.00 0 ERROR: No Qualifying Quotes
  Matched to request - 15.61 seconds
Received response: 48 $90,000.00 9 PawnShop-00098
  Matched to request - 16.02 seconds
Received response: 50 $45,000.00 0 ERROR: No Qualifying Quotes
  Matched to request - 16.43 seconds
=== Total elapsed time: 00:00:21.5595550 secs
=== average response time 8.63 secs
```

Sending 50 Quote Requests, Using Three Credit Bureau Instances

The total time to process all 50 messages is reduced to 21 seconds, with the longest request waiting for a response for 16 seconds. On average, the client had to wait for a reply to the loan request for 8.63 seconds, half of the original version. It looks like we eliminated the bottleneck, but the message throughput did not increase as dramatically as we might have hoped. Remember, though, that for this simple example we are running all processes on a single CPU so that all processes compete for the same resources. Let's look at the new queue statistics to verify that the credit bureau bottleneck is in fact corrected:

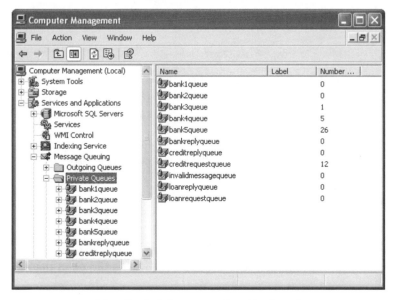

Asynchronous Implementation with MSMQ

Now Bank 5 Appears to Be a Bottleneck

It looks like we eliminated one bottleneck just to find a new one—Bank 5. Why Bank 5? Bank 5 is a pawn shop; it offers loans to everybody, so Bank 5 is part of almost every quote request. We could now go on to start multiple instances of Bank 5, but it's not realistic to expect the pawn shop to run multiple instances just to improve our throughput. Our other option is to change the routing logic for the bank requests. Since the pawn shop charges a substantial premium over the other banks, its quote tends to be the lowest quote only in those cases where no other bank provided a quote. Taking this observation into account, we can improve the efficiency of the system by not routing requests to the pawn shop if the quote can also be serviced by another bank. This change will not affect the overall behavior of the system.

We change the BankConnectionManager to include Bank 5 only for those quote requests that cannot be serviced by any other bank. The modified BankConnection-Manager looks like this:

```
internal class BankConnectionManager
{
    static protected BankConnection[] banks =
        {new Bank1(), new Bank2(), new Bank3(), new Bank4()
};
    static protected BankConnection catchAll = new Bank5();

    public IMessageSender[] GetEligibleBankQueues(int CreditScore, int HistoryLength,
                                                  int LoanAmount)
    {
        ArrayList lenders = new ArrayList();

        for (int index = 0; index < banks.Length; index++)
        {
            if (banks[index].CanHandleLoanRequest(CreditScore, HistoryLength,
                                                  LoanAmount))
                lenders.Add(banks[index].Queue);
        }
        if (lenders.Count == 0)
            lenders.Add(catchAll.Queue);
        IMessageSender[] lenderArray = (IMessageSender [])Array.CreateInstance
                                        (typeof(IMessageSender), lenders.Count);
        lenders.CopyTo(lenderArray);
        return lenderArray;
    }
}
```

Running with the modified code produces the results shown in the following figure.

Asynchronous Implementation with MSMQ

```
Received response: 43 $45,000.00 6.7 Retail-00023
  Matched to request - 6.01 seconds
Received response: 48 $50,000.00 0 ERROR: No Qualifying Quotes
  Matched to request - 5.70 seconds
Received response: 49 $30,000.00 7.4 Retail-00024
  Matched to request - 5.91 seconds
Received response: 50 $110,000.00 8.8 PawnShop-00034
  Matched to request - 6.29 seconds
=== Total elapsed time: 00:00:12.3232948 secs
=== average response time 3.68 secs
```

*Sending 50 Quote Requests Using Three Credit Bureau Instances
and a Modified BankConnectionManager*

The test results now show that all 50 requests were serviced in 12 seconds, half of the original time. More importantly, the average time to service a loan quote request is now under 4 seconds, a fourfold improvement over the initial version. This example demonstrates the advantage of predictive routing by using a *Recipient List* (249). Because the loan broker has control over the routing, we can decide how much "intelligence" we can build into the routing logic without requiring any changes to the external parties. The trade-off is that the loan broker becomes more and more dependent on knowledge about the internal parties. For example, while the original BankConnectionManager treated all banks as equal, the modified version relies on the fact that Bank 5 is a catch-all provider that should be contacted only if there are no other options. If Bank 5 starts to offer better rates, the clients may no longer get the best possible deal.

The screen clip also demonstrates that response messages do not necessarily arrive in the order in which the requests were made. We can see that the test client received the response to request number 48 right after the response to request 43. Because we are not missing any responses, this means that the test client received responses 44 through 47 before it received response 43. How did these requests pass number 43? It looks like request 43 was routed to the General Retail Bank (Bank 3). After the Pawn Shop, this bank has the next least restrictive selection criteria and is more likely than the other banks to be backed up with requests. If requests 44 through 47 did not match the General Retail Bank's criteria, the bank gateway would have received all responses for these requests, while the quote request for request 43 was still sitting in the bank3Queue. Because our loan broker is truly event-driven, it will reply to a loan request as soon as it receives all bank quotes. As a result, if the bank quotes for request 44 arrive before the bank quotes for number 43, the loan broker will send the reply message for request 44 first. This scenario also highlights the importance of the *Correlation Identifier* (163) in the messages so that the test client can match responses to requests even if they arrive out of order.

Tuning asynchronous, message-based systems can be a very complex task. Our example shows some of the most basic techniques of identifying and resolving bottlenecks. But even our simple example made it clear that correcting one problem (the credit bureau bottleneck) can cause another problem (the Bank 5 bottleneck) to surface. We can also clearly see the advantages of asynchronous messaging and event-driven consumers. We were able to process 50 quote requests in 12 seconds—a synchronous solution would have taken 8 or 10 times as long!

A Few Words on Testing

The loan broker example demonstrates how a simple application can become reasonably complex once it becomes distributed, asynchronous, and event-driven. We now have a dozen classes and use delegates throughout to deal with the event-driven nature of asynchronous message processing. The increased complexity also means increased risk of defects. The asynchronous nature makes these defects hard to reproduce or troubleshoot because they depend on specific temporal conditions. Because of these additional risks, messaging solutions require a very thorough approach to testing. We could write a whole book on testing messaging solutions, but for now I want to include some simple, actionable advice on testing, summarized in the following three rules:

- Isolate the application from the messaging implementation by using interfaces and implementation classes.

- Test the business logic with unit test cases before plugging it into the messaging environment.

- Provide a mock implementation of the messaging layer that allows you to test synchronously.

Asynchronous Implementation with MSMQ

Isolate the Application from the Messaging Implementation Testing a single application is much easier than testing multiple, distributed applications connected by messaging channels. A single application allows us to trace through the complete execution path, we do not need a complex startup procedure to fire up all components, and there is no need to purge channels between tests (see *Channel Purger* [572]). Sometimes it is useful to stub out some external functions while testing others. For example, while we are testing the bank gateway, we might as well stub out the credit bureau gateway instead of actually sending messages to an external credit bureau process.

How can we achieve some of the benefits of testing inside a single application with a minimal impact on the application code? We can separate the implementation of a *Messaging Gateway* (468) from the interface definition. That allows us to provide multiple implementations of the interface.

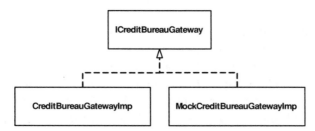

Separating Credit Bureau Interface from Implementation

Because we encapsulated all messaging-specific logic inside the credit bureau gateway, we can define a very simple interface:

```
public interface ICreditBureauGateway
{
    void GetCreditScore(CreditBureauRequest quoteRequest,
                    OnCreditReplyEvent OnCreditResponse, Object ACT);
    void Listen();
}
```

For example, we can create a mock credit bureau gateway implementation that does not actually connect to any message queue but rather invokes the specified delegate right inside the GetCreditScore method. This mock implementation contains the same logic as the actual credit bureau, so the remainder of the loan broker is completely unaware of this switcheroo.

```
public class MockCreditBureauGatewayImp : ICreditBureauGateway
{

    private Random random = new Random();

    public MockCreditBureauGatewayImp()
    { }

    public void GetCreditScore(CreditBureauRequest quoteRequest,
                        OnCreditReplyEvent OnCreditResponse, Object ACT)
    {
        CreditBureauReply  reply = new CreditBureauReply();
        reply.CreditScore =  (int)(random.Next(600) + 300);
        reply.HistoryLength = (int)(random.Next(19) + 1);
```

```
        reply.SSN = quoteRequest.SSN;
        OnCreditResponse(reply, ACT);
    }

    public void Listen()
    { }
}
```

Test the Business Logic with Unit Test Cases The implementation of the CreditBureau class demonstrated a clean separation of messaging-related functions (encapsulated in the base class) and the business logic (reduced to a randomizer in our simple example). In a real-life scenario, the business logic would (hopefully) be somewhat more complex. In that case, it pays off to move the getCreditScore and getCreditHistoryLength methods together into a separate class that does not have any dependency on the messaging layer (even though it is less visible, inheritance still carries dependencies from the subclass to the base class and related classes). We can then use a unit test tool such as nUnit (*http://www.nunit.org*) to write test cases without having to worry about messaging.

Provide a Mock Implementation of the Messaging Layer The mock implementation of the ICreditBureauGateway is simple and effective. But it also replaces all credit bureau gateway–related code so that the class CreditBureauGatewayImp has to be tested separately. If we want to eliminate the dependency (and the associated performance hit) on message queues but still execute the code inside the CreditBureauGatewayImp class, we can use a mock implementation of the IMessageReceiver and IMessageSender interfaces. A simple mock implementation could look like this:

Asynchronous Implementation with MSMQ

```
public class MockQueue: IMessageSender, IMessageReceiver
{
    private OnMsgEvent onMsg = new OnMsgEvent(DoNothing);

    public void Send(Message msg){
        onMsg(msg);
    }

    private static void DoNothing(Message msg){

    }

    public OnMsgEvent OnMessage
    {
        get { return onMsg; }
        set { onMsg = value; }
    }
}
```

```
public void Begin()
{

}

public MessageQueue GetQueue()
{
    return null;
}

}
```

We can see that the Send method triggers the onMsg delegate immediately without using any message queue. To use this mock queue for the credit bureau gateway, we would have to make sure to reply with a message of the correct type. We would not be able to simply pass the request message back to the reply message. This implementation is not shown here but can be simple if, for example, we use a canned reply message.

Limitations of This Example

This section reminded us that even a simple messaging system (the loan broker really has to execute only two steps: get the credit score and get the best bank quote) can get fairly complex due to the asynchronous nature and loose coupling between components. However, we still took a number of shortcuts to keep the example manageable. Specifically, the example does not address the following topics:

- Error handling

- Transactions

- Thread safety

The example has no managed mechanism to handle errors. At this point, components simply spit out messages into the various console windows—not a suitable solution for a production system. For a real implementation, error messages should be routed to a central console so they can notify an operator in a unified way. The systems management patterns in Chapter 11, "System Management" (e.g., the *Control Bus* [540]) address these requirements.

This example does not use transactional queues. For example, if the Message-Router crashes after sending two out of four quote request messages to the banks, some banks will process a quote request, while others will not. Likewise, if the loan broker crashes after it receives all bank quote replies but before it

Asynchronous Implementation with MSMQ

sends a reply to the client, the client will never receive a reply. In a real-life system, actions like these need to be encapsulated inside transactions so that incoming messages are not consumed until the corresponding outbound message had been sent.

The loan broker implementation executes only in a single thread and does not worry about thread safety. For example, the BeginReceive method on an inbound message queue (hidden away in MessageReceiverGateway) is not called until the processing of the previous message has been completed. This is just fine for an example application (and a lot faster than the synchronous implementation), but for a high-throughput environment, we would want to use a *Message Dispatcher* (508) that manages multiple performer threads.

Summary

This chapter walked us through the implementation of the loan broker application using asynchronous message queues and MSMQ. We intentionally did not shy away from showing implementation details in order to bring the real issues inherent in building asynchronous messaging applications to light. We focused on the design trade-offs more so than on the vendor-specific messaging API so that the example is also valuable for non-C# developers.

This example reminds us of the complexities of implementing even a simple messaging application. Many things that can be taken for granted in a monolithic application (e.g., invoking a method) can require a significant amount of coding effort when using asynchronous messaging. Luckily, the design patterns provide us with a language to describe some of the design trade-offs without having to descend too deeply into the vendor jargon.

Asynchronous
Implementation
with MSMQ

Asynchronous Implementation with TIBCO ActiveEnterprise

by Michael J. Rettig

The previous two implementations of the loan broker used integration frameworks that provided basic *Message Channel* (60) functionality. For example, both Axis and MSMQ provided APIs to send messages to or receive messages from a *Message Channel* (60), while the application had to take care of pretty much everything else. We chose this type of implementation intentionally to demonstrate how an integration solution can be built from the ground up, using commonly available Java or C# libraries.

Many commercial EAI product suites offer substantially more functionality to streamline the development of integration solutions. These product suites typically include visual development environments that allow for drag-drop configuration of *Message Translator*s (85) and *Process Manager*s (312). Many also provide sophisticated systems management and metadata management functions. We chose the TIBCO ActiveEnterprise integration suite for this example implementation. As with the previous implementations, we focus primarily on design decisions and trade-offs and introduce only as much product-specific language as is necessary to understand the solution. Therefore, this section should be useful even if you have not worked with TIBCO ActiveEnterprise before. If you are interested in detailed product or vendor information, please visit *http://www.tibco.com*.

This example implementation also differs in the solution design by using an Auction-style *Scatter-Gather* (297) approach. This approach uses a *Publish-Subscribe Channel* (106) instead of a *Recipient List* (249) so that the loan broker can send the quote request to any number of banks. This type of *Scatter-Gather* (297) pattern performs a dynamic *Request-Reply* (154) with an unknown number of listeners. Additionally, the implementation of the loan broker component uses the business process management functionality provided by TIBCO's *Process Manager* (312) tool.

Asynchronous
Implementation
with TIBCO
ActiveEnterprise

Solution Architecture

Our application is a simple bank quote request system. Customers submit quote requests to a loan broker interface. The loan broker fulfills the request by first obtaining a credit score, then requesting quotes from a number of banks. Once the loan broker obtains quotes from the banks, it selects the best quote and returns it to the customer (see figure).

Clients of the system expect a synchronous *Request-Reply* (154) interface to the loan broker—the client sends a quote request and waits for a reply message from the loan broker. The loan broker in turn uses a *Request-Reply* (154) interface to communicate with the credit bureau to obtain credit scores. Once the initial client request is received, the loan broker has the option to perform asynchronous operations behind the distributed, synchronous facade. This allows the loan broker to utilize an auction-style *Scatter-Gather* (297) with a *Publish-Subscribe Channel* (106) to acquire the bank quotes from multiple banks.

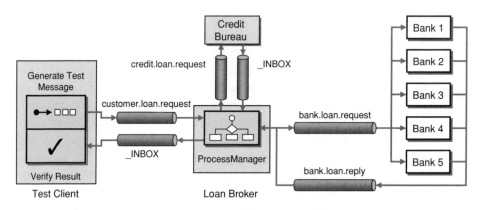

TIBCO Loan Broker Solution Architecture

The auction sequence begins by publishing the request for quotes message to the bank.loan.request *Publish-Subscribe Channel* (106) so that any interested bank can listen for the message and provide its own rates. The number of banks submitting replies is unknown and can vary for each quote request. The auction works by opening the auction to the banks, then waiting a predefined amount of time for response messages on the channel bank.loan.reply. Each time a bid is received, the timeout is reset, giving other banks time to submit another bid if possible. In this case, the bids of other banks are public, so another bank could actually listen for other bids and place a counter bid if desired.

The loan broker broadcasts the request for a quote to an unknown number of recipients. This is quite different from a *Recipient List* (249), which involves sending the request to a predefined list of banks. This is reflected in the *Aggregator*'s (268) completeness condition. Instead of waiting for a response from each bank as in the previous implementations, the *Aggregator* (268) relies solely on a timeout condition to terminate the auction. The *Aggregator* (268) simply ignores any responses received after the auction times out. If no bank replies within the specified interval, the *Aggregator* (268) sends a response message to the client indicating that no quotes were obtained.

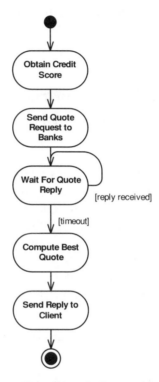

Activity Diagram Describing the Process Manager Behavior

In this implementation, the *Content Enricher* (336) and *Aggregator* (268) functions are implemented within the *Process Manager* (312) component. As a result, the solution architecture diagram does not describe the details of the interaction between the components, because they are embedded in a single component. Instead, we need to look at the activity diagram that represents the Process Template definition used by the *Process Manager* (312). An initial activity diagram cleanly defines the role of the loan broker and provides the basis for the Process Template. From the diagram, we can see that the loan broker has several responsibilities. This translates well into a process diagram, which graphically shows the exact order of events and decision paths.

The Implementation Toolset

In order to explain the design of our solution, we need to introduce some basic concepts about the TIBCO product suite. Implementing TIBCO solutions often requires evaluating different tools for a particular problem because at times, a problem can be solved with several different tools. The trick is picking the best one. We limit the discussion to only those TIBCO features that are required to construct the example implementation:

- TIB/RendezVous Transport

- TIB/IntegrationManager Process Manager tool

- TIBCO Repository for Metadata Management

TIB/RendezVous Transport   At the heart of TIBCO's messaging suite is the TIB/RendezVous transport layer. RendezVous provides the messaging mechanism for sending and receiving TIBCO messages on the *information bus*. TIBCO supports a wide range of transports, including (but not limited to) JMS, HTTP, FTP, and e-mail. RendezVous provides the underlying transport for the messages in our example. The transport supports both synchronous and asynchronous messages as well as *Point-to-Point Channels* (103) and *Publish-Subscribe Channels* (106). Each channel can be configured for different service levels:

- Reliable Messaging (RV)—provides high performance, but at the realistic risk of losing messages.

- Certified messages (RVCM)—at least once delivery.

- Transactional messaging (RVTX)—guaranteed once and only once delivery.

Asynchronous
Implementation
with TIBCO
ActiveEnterprise

Similar to the MSMQ examples in this book, TIBCO provides an open API for creating messaging solutions using Java or C++ and includes a range of tools for simplifying the development process.

TIB/IntegrationManager Process Manager Tool   TIB/IntegrationManager is a TIBCO development tool consisting of a rich user interface for designing workflow solutions and a Process Manager engine for executing them. The GUI provides an extensive array of configuration, workflow, and implementation options that are stored in the TIBCO Repository. TIBCO uses the repository as the central configuration artifact for the system. It holds all metadata, workflow, and custom code.

The workflow component of the solution is an aspect that sets it apart from code-level solution. For the loan broker example, TIB/IntegrationManager provides asynchronous and synchronous messaging as well as basic workflow, including *Server Session State* [EAA]. For our purposes, we can break TIB/ IntegrationManager into three parts: the channel, the job creator, and the process diagram.

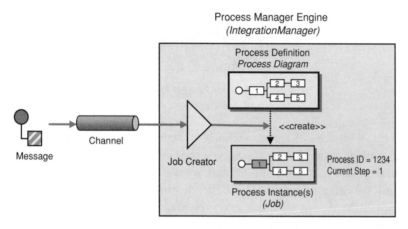

TIB/IntegrationManager Components

Every process in TIB/IntegrationManager creates a "job" (or *process instance*) that provides a central session object for maintaining state. This object includes a slotted environment with get and put operations for storing objects, as well as utility methods for interacting with the session. A simple GUI allows TIBCO developers to create *process definitions* (called Process Diagrams in TIBCO) that specify the sequence of tasks the job executes. Process definitions resemble UML-style activity diagrams consisting of tasks connected by transition lines (see figure on the next page). However, the diagrams provide only the skeleton; behind each activity (i.e., box on the diagram) is a good amount of configuration and code. For our example, we require some code for processing the loans. TIB/ IntegrationManager uses ECMAScript (commonly referred to as JavaScript) as the underlying scripting language.

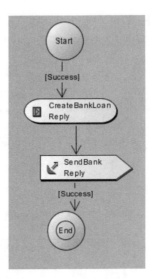

TIB/IntegrationManager Process Diagram Example

A typical process diagram includes a series of integration tasks. These include control tasks such as forks, sync bars or decision points, signal tasks to send and receive messages, and execution tasks such as data translation, routing, and system integration. The basic diagram pictured here includes two tasks: an ECMAScript task that executes some custom logic and a signal-out task that publishes a message to a channel. Task transitions can contain logic for selecting a particular route based upon message contents or other criteria.

TIBCO Repository for Metadata Management   Integration and messaging nearly always requires some form of self-describing data (see "Introduction" in Chapter 8, "Message Transformation"). TIBCO defines metadata classes as ActiveEnterprise (AE) objects stored in the TIBCO repository. Every AE object sent across a message channel includes a *Format Indicator* (180) to indicate the class definition that this message adheres to.

Managing message metadata is an important part of the development process. TIBCO developers can define the metadata directly within the development environment, can extract it from external systems such as relational databases (using a Metadata Adapter as described in *Channel Adapter* [xxx]), or import XML schemas. The metadata provides an explicit contract for objects and messages in the system. Once the classes are defined in the TIBCO repository, the objects are available for instantiation and manipulation within ECMA script:

```
//Instantiation of a TIBCO AE class
var bank = new aeclass.BankQuoteRequest();
bank.CorrelationID = job.generateGUID();
bank.SSN = job.request.SSN;
```

However, remember that this is a dynamic, scripted environment with limited compile-time type checking. Changing a metadata definition can easily break another part of your system. Without proper testing and development practices, message-based systems can easily become "add-only" systems, meaning metadata is only added to the system and never changed for fear of breaking something.

The Interfaces

The Solution Architecture diagram, on page 446, shows us that the solution requires the following services.

Loan Broker

- Receives the initial request

- Obtains a credit score

- Holds loan auction with banks

- Returns best loan offer to client

Credit Service

- Provides a credit score based upon SSN

Bank(s)

- Submit a quote based upon the credit rating and loan amount

Each service is accessible through an external interface. For each such interface, we have to make the following design decisions:

- Conversation Style: Synchronous vs. Asynchronous

- Quality of Service Level

The conversation styles for the interfaces have been predetermined by the solution architecture. The loan broker and credit service will both need synchronous interfaces, while the communication with the banks will be purely asynchronous.

Service levels for messaging solutions can become quite complicated, especially given failover scenarios. Fortunately, the loan example service level resolves to a simple solution. In event of failure (timeout, dropped messages, down systems), the original request can be resubmitted (the loan broker is an *Idempotent Receiver* [528]). Remember that we are only obtaining a quote at this point. It is not yet a legally binding agreement. Of course, this type of assumption needs to be documented in the system and understood by all parties involved. For example, the banks need to know that a quote request may be resubmitted a second time. If the banks track customer loan requests for fraud detection purposes, we may have to change the solution to avoid sending duplicate requests, for example by using *Guaranteed Delivery* (122).

Implementing the Synchronous Services

The loan broker system has two synchronous interfaces—between the customer and the loan broker and between the loan broker and the credit bureau. TIBCO implements RPC-style messaging with operations using *Request-Reply* (154) and *Command Message* (145). Essentially, this is a synchronous wrapper to the underlying TIBCO messaging engine. During the invocation of TIBCO operations, you can listen to the request and reply messages passing across the bus. The request message is published on the specified channel (for example, cus-tomer.loan.request). The message includes a *Return Address* (159) that specifies the address of a so-called INBOX channel for the reply. TIBCO hides the asynchronous details behind an RPC-style programming model. In TIB/Integration-Manager, the domain operations such as obtain credit score are defined as part of the AE classes and can be invoked from the process modeling tool. For example, to expose the loan broker as a synchronous interface, we must perform several implementation steps. The implementation of the credit bureau service follows closely to these same steps.

> **Asynchronous Implementation with TIBCO ActiveEnterprise**

Define the AE Class Definitions   AE classes define the data format for messages sent across TIB/RendezVous channels. Defining a class in TIB/Integration-Manager is quite different from creating a class in your favorite IDE. AE classes are defined through a series of dialog boxes (see figure) from the TIB/Integration-Manager IDE. The dialog boxes allow you to select a name for your class and then designate fields for the class. The fields can be typed as integers, floats, or doubles, or can be composed of other AE classes.

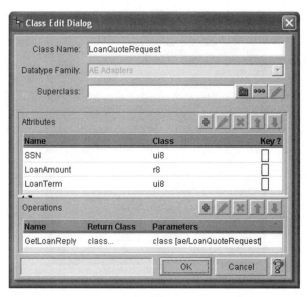

Defining an AE Class with Attributes and Operations

Define the AE Operation Definitions Similar to adding interface methods, operations can be added to an AE class. The parameters and the return types can be specified in the definition. True to an interface, no implementation is specified. The implementation is bound later when we use the job creator to bind a channel to a process instance.

Create a Process Diagram A process diagram provides the implementation for the operation. The operations implemented in this example require a return parameter. Unlike methods implemented in code, a process diagram doesn't have a "return" value. Instead, we specify the slot in the job where the return value will be placed. We designate this in the job creator, and we must remember to properly assign the value to the job slot in our process diagram. The actual implementation of the process diagram is discussed in detail in the following pages.

Asynchronous
Implementation
with TIBCO
ActiveEnterprise

Create a Client/Server Channel to Receive the Requests The channel allows us to define our transport, message definition, service, and subject. For our synchronous operations, we need a client/server channel. We can specify the AE classes that we created in step 1. From our initial interface definitions, we chose RendezVous with reliable messaging. Configuring these options is just a matter of clicking and selecting the proper options. (See figure.)

Defining Channel Properties

Configure a Job Creator to Instantiate the Process Diagram   The job creator retrieves values from the channel and passes them to the process diagram by creating a job and initializing its environment slots. Once the job is created, the process diagram is instantiated. Execution will follow the path defined by the activity diagram. Once the process finishes, the job creator returns the reply back to the channel. We can see in the job creator dialog the name of our operation.

Configuring the Job Creator

The Loan Broker Process

With our synchronous services in place, we can implement the loan broker to tie everything together. The included diagram represents the loan broker process. This process defines the behavior of the loan broker component. In our prior steps, we defined the AE operation, channel, and job creator to instantiate the process diagram when a client submits a message to the CreditRequest channel.

Design Considerations From a design perspective, we need to be very careful as to what is included in the process diagram. Large, complex diagrams quickly become unmanageable. It is critical to create an effective separation of concerns within the diagrams, avoiding an ugly mixture of business logic and process logic inside a single process definition. Defining what is process logic and what is business logic is hard. A good rule of thumb is to think of process logic as external system interaction: What system do I connect to next? What do I do if the system is not available? Business logic will typically involve more domain-specific language: How do I activate an order? How do I calculate a credit score? How do I create a quote for a bank loan? Given the complex nature of business code, a full-featured development language is often the best choice for implementation. Most process management tools, including TIB/IntegrationManager, allow you to integrate directly with Java or another language.

For those familiar with the MVC (Model, View, Controller) concept (for example, [POSA]), the implementation can be viewed in a similar context. By simply renaming view to workflow, our implementation falls into a concise definition.

1. Workflow—a visualized model of the workflow.

2. Controller—the process engine that receives events from the message bus, executing the proper component of the process workflow.

3. Model—the underlying business code (ECMAScript, JavaScript, Java, J2EE, etc.).

The Process Model Implementation   The following diagram contains a mix of script execution boxes and custom tasks that perform integration actions. One of the big advantages of modeling processes using a visual process modeling tool is that the running "code" looks very similar to the UML activity diagram that we used to design the solution. (See figure on page 447.)

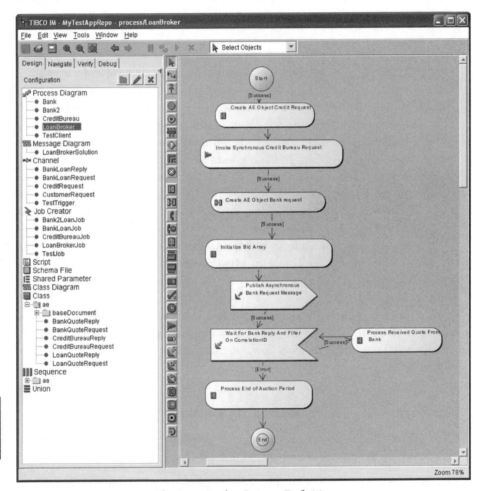

Asynchronous
Implementation
with TIBCO
ActiveEnterprise

The Loan Broker Process Definition

Since each task icon can contain actual code or important configuration parameters, we'll walk through each task and describe it in more detail.

The first box represents an ECMAScript that instantiates an AE object and assigns values to the fields.

```
var credit = new aeclass.CreditBureauRequest();
credit.SSN = job.request.SSN;
job.creditRequest = credit;
```

The credit request created is needed as a parameter in the next activity, which invokes the synchronous operations call to the credit bureau. The credit bureau is implemented as a separate process diagram consisting of a single ECMA task that receives the message and returns a credit score. The synchronous operation implies that the Loan Broker process will wait until a reply message from the credit bureau arrives.

Once the loan broker receives a reply from the credit bureau, we can see in the diagram that another AE object needs to be created to publish a quote request to any participating banks. To implement this function, we use the Mapper task that allows us to graphically map data items from multiple sources. The Mapper is a visual implementation of the *Message Translator* (85) pattern. The Mapper task demonstrates one of the advantages of managing metadata. Because TIB/IntegrationManager has access to the metadata defining the structure of each object, the Mapper displays the structure of the source and target objects and allows us to visually map the fields with a few mouse clicks. A new object is instantiated with the values from the input object. We use the job object's generateGUID method to generate a unique *Correlation Identifier* (163) and assign it to the Correlation ID field of the bankRequest object. As we will see later, the Correlation ID field is important to allow us to process more than one loan request at the same time.

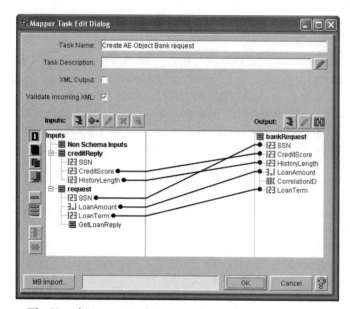

The Visual Mapper Task Creates the Bank Request Message

Instead of using the visual Mapper, we could have used an ECMAScript task to accomplish the same function. The equivalent code would look like the following. You can see how we create a new object of type BankQuoteRequest and assign each field from the source objects:

```
var bank = new aeclass.BankQuoteRequest();
//Create ID to uniquely identify this transaction.
// We will need this later to filter replies
bank.CorrelationID = job.generateGUID();
bank.SSN = job.request.SSN;
bank.CreditScore = job.creditReply.CreditScore;
bank.HistoryLength = job.creditReply.HistoryLength;
bank.LoanAmount = job.request.LoanAmount;
bank.LoanTerm = job.request.LoanTerm;

job.bankRequest = bank;
```

Whether to use the visual Mapper task or an ECMAScript task to implement a *Message Translator* (85) function depends on the type and complexity of a mapping. The Mapper task can give us a nice visual view of the connections between source and target objects but can become hard to read when the objects have many fields. On the other hand, the Mapper includes special functions that allow us to map repeating fields (i.e., Arrays) with a single line instead of having to code a loop.

Next, a very simple ECMAScript task instantiates a bid array that will hold the incoming bank responses. This script contains only a single line:

```
job.bids = new Array();
```

The next task is a Signal Out task that publishes the bankRequest object to the bank.loan.request channel. This is an asynchronous action, so the process immediately transitions to the next step without waiting for a reply.

The following tasks waits for incoming quote reply messages on the bank.loan. reply channel. If a message is received within the specified timeout interval, the script task adds the received message to the bids array:

```
job.bids[job.bids.length] = job.loanReply;
```

Once the auction period ends, the Signal In task times out and transitions the process to the final task. This ECMAScript task implements the aggregation algorithm of the *Aggregator* (268), selecting the best quote from all the bids. The code creates a new instance of the LoanQuoteReply, transfers the SSN and Loan-Amount fields from the request object to this reply object, and loops through the bids array to find the best quote.

Asynchronous Implementation with TIBCO ActiveEnterprise

```
var loanReply = new aeclass.LoanQuoteReply();
loanReply.SSN = job.request.SSN;
loanReply.LoanAmount = job.request.LoanAmount;

var bids = job.bids;
for(var i = 0; i < bids.length; i++){
    var item = bids[i];
    if(i == 0 || (item.InterestRate < loanReply.InterestRate)){
        loanReply.InterestRate = item.InterestRate;
        loanReply.QuoteID = item.QuoteID;
    }
}

job.loanReply = loanReply;
```

The last line of the ECMA script places the loan reply object to be returned to customer into a job slot. We configured the loan broker job creator to return the loanReply attribute of the job to the customer as the reply message (see figure). When the process finishes, the job creator pulls the message found in the loanReply attribute of the job, and returns the value to the client.

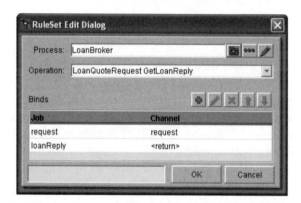

Configuring the Job Creator's Rule Set to Return the Best Quote

Asynchronous
Implementation
with TIBCO
ActiveEnterprise

Managing Concurrent Auctions

The implementation of the auction provided a few development hurdles. Concurrency adds a degree of complexity to the problem. For the auction to work, we need to publish an asynchronous message, then wait a specified amount of time for replies. However, if multiple auctions occur at once, we must ensure that each loan broker receives only the replies it is concerned about, not all the replies.

This functionality was implemented using a *Correlation Identifier* (163) and a *Selective Consumer* (515) to discard unrelated messages. Ideally, we would want this filtering to occur at the channel level and not at the process instance. However, that would require the dynamic creation of channel subjects at runtime, one for each pending auction. Presently, there are implementation constraints within TIB/IntegrationManager that prevent us from using this approach. When a process diagram is instantiated at runtime, it needs to register all subjects it is listening to. This allows the process engine to listen for any messages on those subjects and queue them as needed. Queuing prevents timing bugs due to process diagrams that publish on one subject and then transition to another state to listen for a reply. In an asynchronous world, if the transition takes too long, the reply could be received before the process diagram gets a chance to subscribe. Therefore, the process diagram conveniently queues inbound messages, but at the cost of disallowing dynamic subjects. Given the requirements of the present example, filtering at the process level works perfectly well. The *Correlation Identifier* (163) is a unique identifier assigned to each process that is then passed to each bank process and is included in each reply. A single line of ECMAScript provides the filtering in the Signal In task:

```
(event.msg.CorrelationID == job.bankRequest.CorrelationID)
```

Execution

With the example in place, we can now run the solution. Running the solution involves starting the TIB/IntegrationManager engine. To test the solution, a simple test client is included in the repository that submits loan requests every 5 seconds. Simple stubs are used for the implementations of the credit service and the banks. One of the advantages of *Publish-Subscribe Channel*s (106) is that we can easily listen to all messages on the message bus to inspect the message flow. We used a simple tool to log all messages to the console. For clarity, we truncated the message content to show only relevant fields and eliminated the format identification and tracking information included in each message. From the logs, we can see the times, subjects, and inboxes of messages. The inboxes are the return addresses for the synchronous services.

Asynchronous Implementation with TIBCO ActiveEnterprise

```
tibrvlisten: Listening to subject >

2003-07-12 16:42:30 (2003-07-12 21:42:30.032000000Z):
subject=customer.loan.request,
reply=_INBOX.C0A80164.1743F10809898B4B60.3,
SSN=1234567890 LoanAmount=100000.000000 LoanTerm=360

2003-07-12 16:42:30 (2003-07-12 21:42:30.052000000Z):
subject=credit.loan.request,
reply=_INBOX.C0A80164.1743F10809898B4B60.4,
SSN=1234567890
```

```
2003-07-12 16:42:30 (2003-07-12 21:42:30.092000000Z):
subject=bank.loan.request,
SSN=1234567890 CreditScore=345 HistoryLength=456 LoanAmount=100000.000000
CorrelationID="pUQI3GEWK5Q3d-QiuLzzwGM-zzw" LoanTerm=360

2003-07-12 16:42:30 (2003-07-12 21:42:30.112000000Z):
subject=bank.loan.reply,
InterestRate=5.017751 QuoteID="5E0x1K_dK5Q3i-QiuMzzwGM-zzw" ErrorCode=0 Correla-
tionID="pUQI3GEWK5Q3d-QiuLzzwGM-zzw"

2003-07-12 16:42:30 (2003-07-12 21:42:30.112000000Z):
subject=bank.loan.reply,
InterestRate=5.897514 QuoteID="S9iIAXqgK5Q3n-QiuNzzwGM-zzw" ErrorCode=0 Correla-
tionID="pUQI3GEWK5Q3d-QiuLzzwGM-zzw"
```

We see the request message from the test client on the channel cus-
tomer.loan.request. The message includes the social security number of the customer as well as the desired loan amount and term ($100,000 for 360 months).
The message specifies the test client's private reply channel, _INBOX.C0A80164.
1743F10809898B4B60.3, as the *Return Address* (159) so that the loan broker knows
where to send the reply message.

The next message represents the request from the loan broker to the credit
service, carrying the private inbox of the loan broker as the *Return Address*
(159). The credit service requires only the social security number. The reply
message is not captured by our logging tool because _INBOX channels are private
channels.

After the loan broker receives the credit score, it publishes a message to the
bank.loan.request channel. The two bank stubs in our example immediately reply
with one interest rate each. Each bank also assigns a unique QuoteID to the reply
so that the customer can refer back to it later. The auction period times out in a
few seconds. Because we cannot see the reply message from the loan broker
process to the test client, we can look in the debug log for the process manager
engine to verify that our test client received the lower interest rate. Within this
message we can see the CorrelationID and the *Format Indicator* (180) for the
class.

```
reply= class/LoanQuoteReply {
    SSN=1234567890
    InterestRate=5.017751017038945
    LoanAmount=100000.0
    QuoteID=5E0x1K_dK5Q3i-QiuMzzwGM-zzw
}
```

Asynchronous
Implementation
with TIBCO
ActiveEnterprise

Conclusions

The solution provides some interesting points for comparison. Visual workflows can be easy to view and understand, but just as in code, this relative simplicity can turn into a maze of confusion as implementations become more complex. The dynamic nature of the *Scatter-Gather* (297) allows for a clean decoupling of the publish-subscribe interface. The loan broker can publish bank loan requests without any knowledge of the subscribing banks. Similarly, the *Aggregator* (268) for the replies doesn't need to know the number of expected replies. The potential downside of this flexibility is that it can hide errors resulting from incorrect subject naming, developer error, or dropped messages.

The visual, GUI-driven implementation with TIBCO provides a corollary approach to the code-level implementations. While the sheer power and flexibility of code cannot be argued against, a more graphical environment can greatly simplify very complex tasks. Configuration is a very large part of integration, and graphical environments work well for this. At times, it may seem that developers have to choose between writing code and using a vendor development tool. However, they can often coexist effectively. For instance, you could choose to use TIB/IntegrationManager to model integration workflows and use J2EE session beans to implement domain logic.

For the sake of brevity, our example was relatively simple, leading to an easy-to-understand scenario. Real-world implementations are rarely this simple. Rapid development tools can facilitate faster initial development but can limit your development options. Process management tools can help hide the complexities of messaging, allowing developers to focus on integration tasks without worrying about what happens behind the scenes. However, ignorance of messaging infrastructure has led to the death of more than one project.

Asynchronous Implementation with TIBCO ActiveEnterprise

Chapter 10

Messaging Endpoints

Introduction

In Chapter 3, "Messaging Systems," we discussed *Message Endpoint* (95). This is how an application connects to a messaging system so that it can send and receive messages. As an application programmer, when you program to a messaging API such as JMS or the System.Messaging namespace, you're developing endpoint code. If you are using a commercial middleware package, most of this coding is already done for you through the libraries and tools provided by the vendor.

Send and Receive Patterns

Some endpoint patterns apply to both senders and receivers. They concern how the application relates to the messaging system in general.

Encapsulate the messaging code—In general, an application should not be aware that it is using *Messaging* (53) to integrate with other applications. Most of the application's code should be written without messaging in mind. At the points where the application integrates with others, there should be a thin layer of code that performs the application's part of the integration. When the integration is implemented with messaging, that thin layer of code that attaches the application to the messaging system is a *Messaging Gateway* (468).

Data translation—It's great when the sender and receiver applications use the same internal data representation and when the message format uses that same representation as well. However, this is often not the case. Either the sender and receiver disagree on data format, or the messages use a different format (usually to support other senders and receivers). In this situation, use

463

a *Messaging Mapper* (477) to convert data between the application's format and the message's format.

Externally controlled transactions—Messaging systems use transactions internally; externally, by default, each send or receive method call runs in its own transaction. However, message producers and consumers have the option of using a *Transactional Client* (484) to control these transactions externally, which is useful when you need to batch together multiple messages or to coordinate messaging with other transactional services.

Message Consumer Patterns

Other endpoint patterns apply only to message consumers. Sending messages is easy. There are issues involved in deciding when a message should be sent, what it should contain, and how to communicate its intent to the receiver—that's why we have the Message Construction patterns (see Chapter 5, "Message Construction")—but once the message is built, sending it is easy. Receiving messages, on the other hand—that's tricky. Therefore, many endpoint patterns are about receiving messages.

An overriding theme in message consumption is *throttling*: the ability of an application to control, or *throttle*, the rate at which it consumes messages. As discussed in the book's Introduction, a potential problem any server faces is that a high volume of client requests could overload the server. With *Remote Procedure Invocation* (50), the server is pretty much at the mercy of the rate that clients make calls. Likewise, with *Messaging* (53), the server cannot control the rate at which clients send requests—but the server can control the rate at which it processes those requests. The application does not have to receive and process the messages as rapidly as they're delivered by the messaging system; it can process them at a sustainable pace while the *Message Channel* (60) queues up the messages to be processed in a first come, first served basis. However, if the messages are piling up too much and the server has the resources to process more messages faster, the server can increase its message consumption throughput using concurrent message consumers. So use these message consumer patterns to let your application control the rate at which it consumes messages.

Many of the message consumer patterns come in pairs that represent alternatives, meaning that you can design an endpoint one way or the other. A single application may design some endpoints one way and some endpoints the other way, but a single endpoint can implement only one alternative. Alternatives from each pair can be combined, leading to a great number of choices for how to implement a particular endpoint.

Synchronous or asynchronous consumer—One alternative is whether to use a *Polling Consumer* (494) or an *Event-Driven Consumer* (498) [JMS 1.1], [Hapner], [Dickman]. Polling provides the best throttling because if the server is busy, it won't ask for more messages, so the messages will queue up. Consumers that are event-driven tend to process messages as fast as they arrive, which could overload the server; but each consumer can only process one message at a time, so limiting the number of consumers effectively throttles the consumption rate.

Message assignment versus message grab—Another alternative concerns how a handful of consumers process a handful of messages. If each consumer gets a message, they can process the messages concurrently. The simplest approach is *Competing Consumers* (502), where one *Point-to-Point Channel* (103) has multiple consumers. Each one could potentially grab any message; the messaging system's implementation decides which consumer gets a message. If you want to control this message-to-consumer matching process, use a *Message Dispatcher* (508). This is a single consumer that receives a message but delegates it to a performer for processing. An application can throttle message load by limiting the number of consumers/performers. Also, the dispatcher in a *Message Dispatcher* (508) can implement explicit throttling behavior.

Accept all messages or filter—By default, any message delivered on a *Message Channel* (60) becomes available to any *Message Endpoint* (95) listening on that channel for messages to consume. However, some consumers may not want to consume just any message on that channel, but wish to consume only messages of a certain type or description. Such a discriminating consumer can use a *Selective Consumer* (515) to describe what sort of message it's willing to receive. Then the messaging system will make only messages matching that description available to that receiver.

Subscribe while disconnected—An issue that comes up with *Publish-Subscribe Channel*s (106) is, What if a subscriber was interested in the data being published on a particular channel and will be again, but is currently disconnected from the network or shut down for maintenance? Will a disconnected application miss messages published while it is disconnected, even though it has subscribed? By default, yes, a subscription is only valid while the subscriber is connected. To keep the application from missing messages published between connections, make it a *Durable Subscriber* (522).

Idempotency—Sometimes the same message gets delivered more than once, either because the messaging system is not certain the message has been

Introduction

successfully delivered yet, or because the *Message Channel*'s (60) quality-of-service has been lowered to improve performance. Message receivers, on the other hand, tend to assume that each message will be delivered exactly once, and they tend to cause problems when they repeat processing because of repeat messages. A receiver designed as an *Idempotent Receiver* (528) handles duplicate messages gracefully and prevents them from causing problems in the receiver application.

Synchronous or asynchronous service—Another tough choice is whether an application should expose its services to be invoked synchronously (via *Remote Procedure Invocation* [50]) or asynchronously (via *Messaging* [53]). Different clients may prefer different approaches; different circumstances may require different approaches. Since it's often hard to choose just one approach or the other, let's have both. A *Service Activator* (532) connects a *Message Channel* (60) to a synchronous service in an application so that when a message is received, the service is invoked. Synchronous clients can simply invoke the service directly; asynchronous clients can invoke the service by sending a message.

Message Endpoint Themes

Another significant theme in this chapter is difficulty using *Transactional Client* (484) with other patterns. *Event-Driven Consumer* (498) usually cannot externally control transactions properly, *Message Dispatcher* (508) must be carefully designed to do so, and *Competing Consumers* (502) that externally manage transactions can run into significant problems. The safest bet for using *Transactional Client* (484) is with a single *Polling Consumer* (494), but that may not be a very satisfactory solution.

Special mention should be made of JMS-style message-driven beans (MDBs), one type of Enterprise JavaBeans (EJB) [EJB 2.0], [Hapner]. An MDB is a message consumer that is both an *Event-Driven Consumer* (498) and a *Transactional Client* (484) that supports J2EE distributed (e.g., XAResource) transactions, and it can be dynamically pooled as *Competing Consumers* (502), even for a *Publish-Subscribe Channel* (106). This is a difficult and tedious combination to

Introduction

implement in one's own application code, but this functionality is provided as a ready-built feature of compatible EJB containers (such as BEA's WebLogic and IBM's WebSphere). (How is the MDB framework implemented? Essentially, the container implements a *Message Dispatcher* [508] with a dynamically sized pool of reusable performers, where each performer consumes the message itself using its own session and transaction.)

Finally, keep in mind that a single *Message Endpoint* (95) may well combine several different patterns from this chapter. A group of *Competing Consumers* (502) may be implemented as *Polling Consumer*s (494) that are also *Selective Consumer*s (515) and act as a *Service Activator* (532) on a service in the application. A *Message Dispatcher* (508) may be an *Event-Driven Consumer* (498) and a *Durable Subscriber* (522) that uses a *Messaging Mapper* (477). Whatever other patterns an endpoint implements, it should also be a *Messaging Gateway* (468). So, don't think of what one pattern to use—think of the combinations. That's the beauty of solving the problems with patterns.

There are a lot of options for making an application into a *Message Endpoint* (95). This chapter explains what those options are and how to make the best use of them.

Messaging Gateway

An application accesses another system via *Messaging* (53).

▼

How do you encapsulate access to the messaging system from the rest of the application?

▲

Most custom applications access the messaging infrastructures through a vendor-supplied API. While there are many different flavors of such APIs, these libraries generally expose similar functions, such as "open channel," "create message," and "send message." While this type of API allows the application to send any kind of message data across any kind of channel, it is sometimes hard to tell what the intent of sending the message data is.

Messaging solutions are inherently asynchronous. This can complicate the code to access an external function over messaging. Instead of calling a method GetCreditScore that returns the numeric credit score, the application has to send the request message and expect the reply message to arrive at a later time (see *Request-Reply* [154]). The application developer may prefer the simple semantics of a synchronous function to dealing with incoming message events.

Loose coupling between applications provides architectural advantages, such as resilience to minor changes in message formats (i.e., adding fields). Usually, the loose coupling is achieved by using XML documents or other data structures that are not strongly typed like a Java or C# class. Coding against such structures is tedious and error-prone because there is no compile-type support to detect misspelled field names or mismatched datatypes. Therefore, we often gain the flexibility in data formats at the expense of application development effort.

Sometimes, a simple logical function to be executed via messaging requires more than one message to be sent. For example, a function to get customer information may in reality require multiple messages, one to get the address, another to get the order history, and yet another to get personal information. Each of these messages may be processed by a different system. We would not want to clutter the application code with all the logic required to send and receive three separate messages. We could take some of the burden off the application by using a *Scatter-Gather* (297) that receives a single message,

Messaging
Gateway

sends three separate messages, and aggregates them back into a single reply message. However, not always do we have the luxury of adding this function to the messaging middleware.

Use a *Messaging Gateway*, a class that wraps messaging-specific method calls and exposes domain-specific methods to the application.

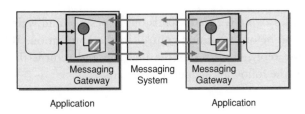

The Messaging Gateway encapsulates messaging-specific code (e.g., the code required to send or receive a message) and separates it from the rest of the application code. This way, only the Messaging Gateway code knows about the messaging system; the rest of the application code does not. The Messaging Gateway exposes a business function to the rest of the application so that instead of requiring the application to set properties like `Message.MessageRead-PropertyFilter.AppSpecific`, a *Messaging Gateway* exposes meaningful methods such as `GetCreditScore` that accept strongly typed parameters just like any other method. A *Messaging Gateway* is a messaging-specific version of the more general *Gateway* pattern [EAA].

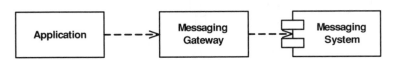

A Gateway Eliminates Direct Dependencies between the Application and the Messaging Systems

Messaging Gateway

A *Messaging Gateway* sits between the application and the messaging system and provides a domain-specific API to the application (see previous figure). Because the application doesn't even know that it's using a messaging system, we can swap out the gateway with a different implementation that uses another integration technology, such as remote procedure calls or Web services.

Many *Messaging Gateway*s send a message to another component and expect a reply message (see *Request-Reply* [154]). Such a *Messaging Gateway* can be implemented in two different ways:

1. Blocking (Synchronous) *Messaging Gateway*

2. Event-Driven (Asynchronous) *Messaging Gateway*

A blocking *Messaging Gateway* sends out a message and waits for the reply message to arrive before returning control to the application. When the gateway receives the reply, it processes the message and returns the result to the application (see the following sequence diagram).

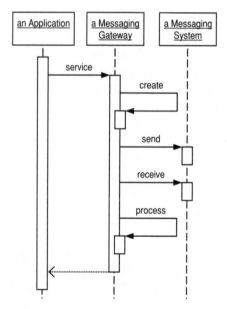

Blocking (Synchronous) Messaging Gateway

Messaging Gateway

A blocking *Messaging Gateway* encapsulates the asynchronous nature of the messaging interaction, exposing a regular synchronous method to the application logic. Thus, the application is unaware of any asynchronicity in the communication. For example, a blocking gateway may expose the following method:

```
int GetCreditScore(string SSN);
```

While this approach makes writing application code against the *Messaging Gateway* very simple, it can also lead to poor performance because the application ends up spending most of its time sitting around and waiting for reply messages while it could be performing other tasks.

An event-driven *Messaging Gateway* exposes the asynchronous nature of the messaging layer to the application. When the application makes the domain-specific request to the *Messaging Gateway*, it provides a domain-specific callback for the reply. Control returns immediately to the application. When the reply message arrives, the *Messaging Gateway* processes it and then invokes the callback (see the following sequence diagram).

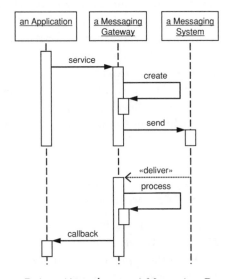

Event-Driven (Asynchronous) Messaging Gateway

For example, in C#, using delegates, the *Messaging Gateway* could expose the following public interface:

```
delegate void OnCreditReplyEvent(int CreditScore);
void RequestCreditScore(string SSN, OnCreditReplyEvent OnCreditResponse);
```

The method `RequestCreditScore` accepts an additional parameter that specifies the callback method to be invoked when the reply message arrives. The callback method has a parameter `CreditScore` so that the *Messaging Gateway* can pass the results to the application. Depending on the programming language or platform, the callback can be accomplished with function pointers, object references, or delegates (as shown here). Note that despite the event-driven nature of this interface, there is no dependency at all on a specific messaging technology.

Alternatively, the application can periodically poll to see whether the results arrived. This approach makes the higher-level interface simple without introducing blocking, essentially employing the *Half-Sync/Half-Async* pattern [POSA2]. This pattern describes the use of buffers that store incoming messages so that the application can poll at its convenience to see whether a message has arrived.

One of the challenges of using an event-driven *Messaging Gateway* is that the *Messaging Gateway* requires the application to maintain state between the request method and the callback event (the call stack takes care of this in the blocking case). When the *Messaging Gateway* invokes the callback event into the application logic, the application must be able to correlate the reply with the request it made earlier so that it can continue processing the correct thread of execution. The *Messaging Gateway* can make it easier for the application to maintain state if it allows the application to pass a reference to an arbitrary set of data to the request method. The *Messaging Gateway* will then pass this data back to the application with the callback. This way, the application has all necessary data available when the asynchronous callback is invoked. This type of interaction is commonly called ACT (Asynchronous Completion Token) [POSA2].

The public interface of an event-driven *Messaging Gateway* that supports an ACT may look like this:

```
delegate void OnCreditReplyEvent(int CreditScore, Object ACT);
void RequestCreditScore(string SSN, OnCreditReplyEvent OnCreditResponse, Object ACT);
```

The method `RequestCreditScore` features an additional parameter, a reference to a generic object. The *Messaging Gateway* stores this reference, waiting for the reply message to arrive. When the reply arrives, the gateway invokes the delegate of type `OnCreditReplyEvent`, passing in the result of the operation as well as the object reference. While supporting an ACT is a very convenient feature for the application, it does introduce the danger of a memory leak if the *Messaging Gateway* maintains a reference to an object but the expected reply message never arrives.

Messaging Gateway

Chaining Gateways

It can be beneficial to create more than one layer of *Messaging Gateway*s. The "lower-level" *Messaging Gateway* can simply abstract the syntax of the messaging system but maintain generic messaging semantics, for example, `Send-Message`. This *Messaging Gateway* can help shield the rest of the application when the enterprise changes messaging technologies, for example, from MSMQ to Web services. We wrap this basic *Messaging Gateway* with an additional *Messaging Gateway* that translates the generic messaging API into a narrow, domain-specific API, such as GetCreditScore. We use this configuration in the MSMQ implementation of the Loan Broker example (see the following figure; also see the section "Asynchronous Implementation with MSMQ" in Chapter 9, "Interlude: Composed Messaging").

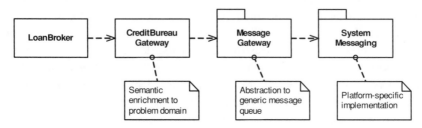

A Chain of Gateways Provides Different Levels of Abstraction

Dealing with Messaging Exceptions

Besides making coding the application simpler, the intent of the *Messaging Gateway* is also to eliminate dependencies of the application code on specific messaging technologies. This is easy to do by wrapping any messaging-specific method calls behind the *Messaging Gateway* interface. However, most messaging layers throw messaging-specific exceptions, such as the InvalidDestinationException raised by JMS. If we really want to make our application code independent from the messaging library, the *Messaging Gateway* has to catch any messaging-specific exception and throw an application-specific (or a generic) exception instead. This code can get a little tedious, but it is very helpful if we ever have to switch the underlying implementations, for instance, from JMS to Web services.

Generating Gateways

In many situations, we can generate the *Messaging Gateway* code from metadata exposed by the external resource. This is common in the world of Web services. Almost every vendor or open source platform provides a tool such as wsdl2java that connects to the Web Service Description Language (WSDL) exposed by an external Web service. The tool generates Java (or C#, or whatever language you need) classes that encapsulate all the nasty SOAP stuff and expose a simple function call. We created a similar tool that can read message schema definitions off the TIBCO repository and creates Java source code for a class that mimics the schema definition. This allows application developers to send correctly typed TIBCO ActiveEnterprise messages without having to learn the TIBCO API.

Using Gateways for Testing

*Messaging Gateway*s make great testing vehicles. Because we wrapped all the messaging code behind a narrow, domain-specific interface, we can easily create a dummy implementation of this interface. We simply separate interface and implementation and provide two implementations: one "real" implementation that accesses the messaging infrastructure and a "fake" implementation for testing purposes (see figure). The fake implementation acts as a *Service Stub* [EAA] and allows us to test the application without any dependency on messaging. A *Service Stub* can also be useful to debug an application that uses an event-driven *Messaging Gateway*. For example, a simple test stub for an event-driven *Messaging Gateway* can simply invoke the callback (or delegate) right from the request method, effectively executing both the request and the response processing in one thread. This can simplify step-by-step debugging enormously.

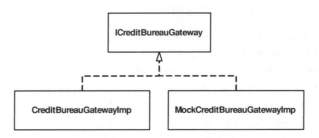

Gateways as a Testing Tool

Example: *Asynchronous Loan Broker Gateway in MSMQ*

This example shows a piece of the Loan Broker example introduced in Chapter 9, "Interlude: Composed Messaging" (see "Asynchronous Implementation with MSMQ").

```
public delegate void OnCreditReplyEvent(CreditBureauReply creditReply, Object ACT);

internal struct CreditRequestProcess
{
    public int CorrelationID;
    public Object ACT;
    public OnCreditReplyEvent callback;
}
```

```
internal class CreditBureauGateway
{
    protected IMessageSender creditRequestQueue;
    protected IMessageReceiver creditReplyQueue;

    protected IDictionary activeProcesses = (IDictionary)(new Hashtable());

    protected Random random = new Random();

    public void Listen()
    {
        creditReplyQueue.Begin();
    }

    public void GetCreditScore(CreditBureauRequest quoteRequest,
                               OnCreditReplyEvent OnCreditResponse,
                               Object ACT)
    {
        Message requestMessage = new Message(quoteRequest);
        requestMessage.ResponseQueue = creditReplyQueue.GetQueue();
        requestMessage.AppSpecific = random.Next();

        CreditRequestProcess processInstance = new CreditRequestProcess();
        processInstance.ACT = ACT;
        processInstance.callback = OnCreditResponse;
        processInstance.CorrelationID = requestMessage.AppSpecific;

        creditRequestQueue.Send(requestMessage);

        activeProcesses.Add(processInstance.CorrelationID, processInstance);
    }

    private void OnCreditResponse(Message msg)
    {
        msg.Formatter = GetFormatter();

        CreditBureauReply replyStruct;
        try
        {
            if (msg.Body is CreditBureauReply)
            {
                replyStruct = (CreditBureauReply)msg.Body;
                int CorrelationID = msg.AppSpecific;

                if (activeProcesses.Contains(CorrelationID))
                {
                    CreditRequestProcess processInstance =
                        (CreditRequestProcess)(activeProcesses[CorrelationID]);
                    processInstance.callback(replyStruct, processInstance.ACT);
                    activeProcesses.Remove(CorrelationID);
```

```
                }
                else
                {
                    Console.WriteLine("Incoming credit response does not match any request");
                }
            }
            else
            { Console.WriteLine("Illegal reply."); }
        }
        catch (Exception e)
        {
            Console.WriteLine("Exception: {0}", e.ToString());
        }
    }
}
```

You will notice that the public method GetCreditScore and the public delegate OnCreditReplyEvent make no references to messaging at all. This implementation allows the calling application to pass an arbitrary object reference as an ACT. The CreditBureauGateway stores this object reference in a dictionary indexed by the *Correlation Identifier* (163) of the request message. When the reply message arrives, the CreditBureauGateway can retrieve the data that was associated with the outbound request message. The calling application does not have to worry about how the messages are correlated.

Messaging
Gateway

Messaging Mapper

When applications use *Messaging* (53), the *Message*s' (66) data is often derived from the applications' domain objects. If we use a *Document Message* (147), the message itself may directly represent one or more domain objects. If we use a *Command Message* (145), some of the data fields associated with the command are likely to be extracted from domain objects as well. There are some distinct differences between messages and objects. For example, most objects rely on associations in the form of object references and inheritance relationships. Many messaging infrastructures do not support these concepts because they have to be able to communicate with a range of applications, some of which may not be object-oriented at all.

> How do you move data between domain objects and the messaging infrastructure while keeping the two independent of each other?

Why can't we make our messages look exactly like the domain objects and make the problem go away? In many cases, we are not in control of the message format because it is defined by a *Canonical Data Model* (355) or a common messaging standard (e.g., ebXML). We could still publish the message in a format that corresponds to the domain object and use a *Message Translator* (85) inside the messaging layer to make the necessary transformation to the common message format. This approach is commonly used by adapters to third-party systems that do not allow transformation inside the application (e.g., a database adapter).

Alternatively, the domain layer can create and publish a message in the required format without the need for a separate *Message Translator* (85). This option most likely results in better performance because we do not publish an intermediate message. Also, if our domain model contains many small objects, it may be beneficial to combine them into a single message first to simplify routing and improve efficiency inside the messaging layer. Even if we can afford the additional transformation step, we will run into limitations if we want to create messages that mimic domain objects. The shortcoming of this approach is that

Messaging Mapper

the domain becomes dependent on the message format, which makes domain maintenance difficult if the message format changes.

Most messaging infrastructures support the notion of a "Message" object as part of the API. This message object encapsulates the data to be sent over a channel. In most cases, this message object can contain only scalar datatypes such as strings, numbers, or dates, but does not support inheritance or object references. This is one of the key differences between RPC-style communications (i.e., RMI) and asynchronous messaging systems. Let's assume we send an asynchronous message containing an object reference to a component. In order to process the message, the component would have to resolve the object reference. It would do this by requesting the object from the message source. However, request-reply interaction would defeat some of the motivations of using asynchronous messaging in the first place (i.e., loose coupling between components). Worse yet, by the time the asynchronous message is received by the subscriber, the referenced object may no longer exist in the source system.

One attempt to resolve the issue of object references is to traverse the dependency tree of an object and include all dependent objects in the message. For example, if an Order object references five OrderItem objects, we would include the five objects in the message. This ensures that the receiver has access to all data references by the "root" object. However, if we use a fine-grained domain object model with many interrelated objects, messages can quickly explode in size. It would be desirable to have more control over what is included in a message and what is not.

Let's assume for a moment that our domain object is self-contained and does not have any references to other objects. We still cannot simply stick the whole domain object into a message, as most messaging infrastructures do not support objects because they have to be language-independent (the JMS interface ObjectMessage and the Message class in .NET's System.Messaging namespace are exceptions, since these messaging systems are either language-specific [Java] or platform-specific [.NET CLR]). We could think of serializing the object into a string and storing it in a string field called "data," which is supported by pretty much every messaging system. However, this approach has disadvantages as well. First, a *Message Router* (78) would not be able to use object properties for routing purposes because this string field would be "opaque" to the messaging layer. It would also make testing and debugging difficult, because we would have to decipher the contents of the data field. Also, constructing all messages so that they contain just a single string field would not allow us to route messages by message type because all messages look the same to the infrastructure. It would also be difficult to verify the correct format of the message because the messaging infrastructure would not verify anything inside the data field. Finally,

Messaging Mapper

we would not be able to use the serialization facilities provided by the language runtime libraries because these presentations are usually not compatible across languages. So, we would have to write our own serialization code.

Some messaging infrastructures now support XML fields inside messages so that we could serialize objects into XML. This can alleviate some of the disadvantages because the messages are easier to decipher now and some messaging layers can access elements inside an XML string directly. However, we now have to deal with quite verbose messages and limited datatype validation. Plus, we still have to create code that translates an object into XML and back. Depending on the programming language we use, this could be quite complex, especially if we use an older language that does not support reflection.

We are well advised to separate this mapping code from the domain object for a number of reasons. First of all, we may not want to blend code that concerns itself with low-level language features with application logic. In many cases, we will have a group of programmers dedicated to working with the messaging layer, while another group focuses on the domain logic. Sticking both pieces of code into one object will make it difficult for the teams to work in parallel.

Second, incorporating mapping code inside the domain object makes the domain object dependent on the messaging infrastructure because the mapping code will need to make calls into the messaging API (e.g., to instantiate the Message object). In most cases, this dependency is not desirable because it prevents the reuse of the domain objects in another context that does not use messaging or that uses another vendor's messaging infrastructure. As a result, we would seriously impede the reusability of the domain objects.

We often see people write "abstraction layers" that wrap the messaging infrastructure API, effectively making the code that deals with messaging independent from the messaging API. Such a layer provides a level of indirection because it separates the messaging interface from the messaging implementation. Therefore, we can reuse the messaging-related code even if we have to switch to another vendor's messaging layer. All we need to do is implement a new abstraction layer that translates the messaging interface to the new API. However, this approach does not resolve the dependency of the domain objects on the messaging layer. The domain objects would now contain references to the abstracted messaging interface as opposed to the vendor-specific messaging API. But we still cannot use the domain objects in a context that does not use messaging.

Messaging Mapper

Many messages are composed of more than one domain object. Since we cannot pass object references through the messaging infrastructure, it is likely that we need to include fields from other objects. In some cases, we may include the whole "dependency tree" of all dependent objects inside one message.

Which class should hold the mapping code? The same object may be part of multiple message types combined with different objects, so there is no easy answer to this question.

Create a separate *Messaging Mapper* that contains the mapping logic between the messaging infrastructure and the domain objects. Neither the objects nor the infrastructure have knowledge of the *Messaging Mapper*'s existence.

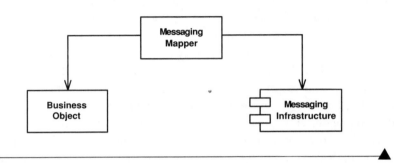

The *Messaging Mapper* accesses one or more domain objects and converts them into a message as required by the messaging channel. It also performs the opposite function, creating or updating domain objects based on incoming messages. Since the *Messaging Mapper* is implemented as a separate class that references both the domain object(s) and the messaging layer, neither layer is aware of the other. The layers don't even know about the *Messaging Mapper*.

The *Messaging Mapper* is a specialization of the *Mapper* pattern [EAA]. It shares some analogies with *Data Mapper* [EAA]. Anyone who has worked on O-R (Object-Relational) mapping strategies will understand the complexities of mapping data between layers that use different paradigms. The issues inherent in the *Messaging Mapper* are similarly complex, and a detailed discussion of all possible aspects is beyond the scope of this book. Many of the Data Source Architectural Patterns in [EAA] make a good read for anyone concerned with creating a *Messaging Mapper* layer.

A *Messaging Mapper* is different from the frequently used concept of an abstraction layer wrapped around the messaging API. In the case of an abstraction layer, the domain objects do not know about the messaging API, but they do know about the abstraction layer (the abstraction layer essentially performs the function of a *Messaging Gateway* [468]). In the case of a *Messaging Mapper*, the objects have no idea whatsoever that we are dealing with messaging.

The intent of a *Messaging Mapper* is similar to that of a *Mediator* [GoF], which is also used to separate elements. In the case of a *Mediator*, though, the elements are aware of the *Mediator*, whereas neither element is aware of the *Messaging Mapper*.

If neither the domain objects nor the messaging infrastructure know about the Messaging Mapper, how does it get invoked? In most cases, the Messaging Mapper is invoked through events triggered by either the messaging infrastructure or the application. Since neither one is dependent on the Messaging Mapper, the event notification can happen either through a separate piece of code or by making the *Messaging Mapper* an *Observer* pattern [GoF]. For example, if we use the JMS API to interface with the messaging infrastructure, we can implement the MessageListener interface to be notified of any incoming messages. Likewise, we can use an *Observer* to be notified of any relevant events inside the domain objects and to invoke the *Messaging Mapper*. If we have to invoke the *Messaging Mapper* directly from the application, we should define a *Messaging Mapper* interface so that the application does at least not depend on the *Messaging Mapper* implementation.

Reducing the Coding Burden

Some *Messaging Mapper* implementations may contain a lot of repetitive code: Get a field from the domain object and store it in a message object. Go on to the next field and repeat until all fields are done. This can be pretty tedious and also smells suspiciously like code duplication. We have a number of tools to help us avoid this tedium. First, we can write a generic *Messaging Mapper* that uses reflection to extract fields from a domain object in a generic way. For example, it could traverse the list of all fields inside the domain object and store it in a field of the same name in the message object. Obviously, this works only if the field names match. According to our previous discussions, we need to come up with some way to resolve object references, since we cannot store those in the message object. The alternative is to use a configurable code generator to generate the *Messaging Mapper* code. This allows us some more flexibility in the field naming (the message field name and the domain object field name do not have to match), and we can devise clever ways to deal with object references. The downside of code generators is that they can be difficult to test and debug, but if we make it generic enough, we have to write it only once.

Some frameworks, such as Microsoft .NET, feature built-in object serialization of objects into XML, and vice versa, and take away a lot of the grunt work involved in object serialization. Even if the framework does some of the legwork of converting an object into a message, this conversion is limited to the

Messaging Mapper

syntactic level of translation. It might be tempting to just let the framework do all the work, but it will just create messages that correspond to the domain objects one-to-one. As we explained earlier, this may not be desirable because the constraints and design criteria for messages are quite different from those for domain objects. It may make sense to define a set of "interface objects" that correspond to the desired messages structure and let the framework do the conversion between the messages and these objects. The *Messaging Mapper* layer will then manage the translation between the true domain objects and the interface objects. These interface objects bear some resemblance to *Data Transfer Objects* [EAA] even though the motivations are slightly different.

Mapper versus Translator

Even if we use a *Messaging Mapper,* it still makes sense to use a *Message Translator* (85) to translate the messages generated by the *Messaging Mapper* into messages compliant with the *Canonical Data Model* (355). This gives us an additional level of indirection. We can use the *Messaging Mapper* to resolve issues such as object references and datatype conversions, and leave structural mappings to a *Message Translator* inside the messaging layer. The price we pay for this additional decoupling is the creation of an additional component and a small performance penalty. Also, sometimes it is easier to perform complex transformations inside the application's programming language than to use the drag-and-drop "doodleware" supplied by the integration vendor.

If we use both a *Messaging Mapper* and a *Message Translator* (85), we gain an additional level of indirection between the canonical data format and the domain objects. It has been said that computer science is the area where every problem can be solved by adding just one more level of indirection, so does this rule hold true here? The additional indirection gives us the ability to compensate for changes in the canonical model inside the messaging layer without having to touch application code. It also allows us to simplify the mapping logic inside the application by leaving tedious field mappings and datatype changes (e.g., a numeric ZIP_Code field to an alphanumeric Postal_Code field) to the mapping tools of messaging layer that are optimized for this kind of work. The *Messaging Mapper* would then primarily deal with the resolution of object references and the elimination of unnecessary domain object detail. The apparent downside of the extra level of indirection is that a change in the domain object may now require changes to both the *Messaging Mapper* and the *Message Translator.* If we did manage to generate the *Messaging Mapper* code, this issue largely goes away.

**Messaging
Mapper**

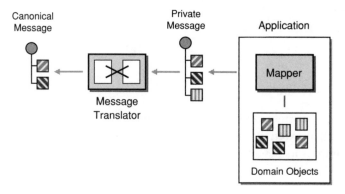

Combining Mapper and Message Translator

Example: *Messaging Mapper in JMS*

The AuctionAggregate class in the *Aggregator* (268) JMS example acts as a *Messaging Mapper* between the JMS messaging system and the Bid class. The methods addMessage and getResultMessage convert between JMS messages and Bid objects. Neither the messaging system nor the Bid class has any knowledge of this interaction.

Messaging
Mapper

Transactional Client

A messaging system, by necessity, uses transactional behavior internally. It may be useful for an external client to be able to control the scope of the transactions that impact its behavior.

▼
How can a client control its transactions with the messaging system?
▲

A messaging system must use transactions internally. A single *Message Channel* (60) can have multiple senders and multiple receivers, so the messaging system must coordinate the messages to make sure senders don't overwrite each other's *Messages* (66), multiple *Point-to-Point Channel* (103) receivers don't receive the same message, multiple *Publish-Subscribe Channel* (106) receivers each receive one copy of each message, and so on. To manage all of this, messaging systems internally use transactions to make sure a message gets added or doesn't get added to the channel, and gets read or doesn't get read from the channel. Messaging systems also have to employ transactions—preferably two-phase, distributed transactions—to copy a message from the sender's computer to the receiver's computer, such that at any given time, the message is "really" only on one computer or the other.

*Message Endpoint*s (95) sending and receiving messages are transactional, even if they don't realize it. The send method that adds a message to a channel does so within a transaction to isolate that message from any other messages simultaneously being added to or removed from that channel. Likewise, a receive method also uses a transaction, which prevents other point-to-point receivers from getting the same message and even assures that a publish-subscribe receiver won't read the same message twice.

Transactions are often described as being ACID: atomic, consistent, isolated, and durable. Only transactions for *Guaranteed Messaging* (53) are durable, and a message by definition is atomic. But all messaging transactions have to be consistent and isolated. A message can't be sort of in the channel—it either is or isn't. Also, an application's sending and receiving of messages has to be isolated from whatever other threads and applications might be sending and receiving messages via the same channel.

The messaging system's internal transactions are sufficient and convenient for a client that simply wants to send or receive a single message. However, an application may need a broader transaction to coordinate several messages or to coordinate messaging with other resources. Common scenarios like this include

- **Send-Receive Message Pairs**—Receive one message and send another, such as a *Request-Reply* (154) scenario or when implementing a message filter such as a *Message Router* (78) or *Message Translator* (85).

- **Message Groups**—Send or receive a group of related messages, such as a *Message Sequence* (170).

- **Message/Database Coordination**—Combine sending or receiving a message with updating a database, such as with a *Channel Adapter* (127). For example, when an application receives and processes a message for ordering a product, the application will also need to update the product inventory database. Likewise, the sender of a *Document Message* (147) may wish to delete a persisted document, but only when it is sent successfully; the receiver may want to persist the document before the message is truly considered to be consumed.

- **Message/Workflow Coordination**—Use a pair of *Request-Reply* (154) messages to perform a work item, and use transactions to ensure that the work item isn't acquired unless the request is also sent, and the work item isn't completed or aborted unless the reply is also received.

Scenarios like these require a larger atomic transaction that involve more than just a single message and may involve other transactional stores besides the messaging system. A transaction is required so that if part of the scenario works (receiving the message, for example) but another part does not (such as updating the database or sending another message), all parts can be rolled back as if they never happened, and then the application can try again.

Yet a messaging system's internal transaction model is insufficient to allow an application to coordinate handling a message with other messages or other resources. What is needed is a way for the application to externally control the messaging system's transactions and combine them with other transactions in the messaging system or elsewhere.

Transactional Client

Use a *Transactional Client*—make the client's session with the messaging system transactional so that the client can specify transaction boundaries.

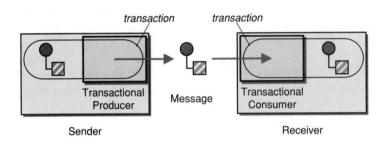

Both a sender and a receiver can be transactional. With a sender, the message isn't actually added to the channel until the sender commits the transaction. With a receiver, the message isn't actually removed from the channel until the receiver commits the transaction. A sender that uses explicit transactions can be used with a receiver that uses implicit transactions, and vice versa. A single channel might have a combination of implicitly and explicitly transactional senders; it could also have a combination of receivers.

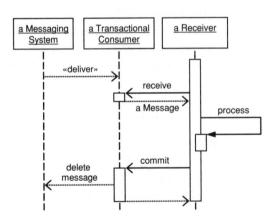

Transactional Receiver Sequence

With a transactional receiver, an application can receive a message without actually removing the message from the queue. At this point, if the application crashed, when it recovered, the message would still be on the queue; the mes-

Transactional Client

sage would not be lost. Having received the message, the application can then process it. Once the application is finished with the message and is certain it wants to consume it, the application commits the transaction, which (if successful) removes the message from the channel. At this point, if the application crashed, when it recovered, the message would no longer be on the channel, so the application had better truly be finished with the message.

How does controlling a messaging system's transactions externally help an application coordinate several tasks? Here's what the application would do in the scenarios described earlier:

Send-Receive Message Pairs

1. **What to do:** Start a transaction, receive and process the first message, create and send the second message, then commit. (This behavior is often implemented as part of *Request-Reply* [154], *Message Router* [78], and *Message Translator* [85].)

2. **What this does:** This keeps the first message from being removed from its channel until the second message is successfully added to its channel.

3. **Transaction type:** If the two messages are sent via channels in the same messaging system, the transaction encompassing the two channels is a simple one. However, if the two channels are managed by two separate messaging systems, such as with a *Messaging Bridge* (133), the transaction will be a distributed one coordinating the two messaging systems.

4. **Warning:** A single transaction only works for the receiver of a request sending a reply. The sender of a request cannot use a single transaction to send a request and wait for its reply. If it tries to do this, the request will never really be sent—because the send transaction isn't committed—so the reply will never be received.

Message Groups

1. **What to do:** Start a transaction, send or receive all of the messages in the group (such as a *Message Sequence* [170]), then commit.

2. **What this does:** When sending, none of the messages in the group will be added to the channel until they are all successfully sent. When receiving, none of the messages will be removed from the channel until all are received.

3. **Transaction type:** Since all of the messages are being sent to or received from a single channel, that channel will be managed by a single messaging

Transactional
Client

system, so the transaction will be a simple one. Also, in many messaging system implementations, sending a group of messages in a single transaction ensures that they will be received on the other end of the channel in the order they were sent.

Message/Database Coordination

1. **What to do:** Start a transaction, receive a message, update the database, and then commit. Or, update the database and send a message to report the update to others, and then commit. (This behavior is often implemented by a *Channel Adapter* [127].)

2. **What this does:** The message will not be removed unless the database is updated (or the database change will not stick if the message cannot be sent).

3. **Transaction type:** Since the messaging system and the database each has its own transaction manager, the transaction to coordinate them will be a distributed one.

Message/Workflow Coordination

1. **What to do:** Use a pair of *Request-Reply* (154) messages to perform a work item. Start a transaction, acquire the work item, send the request message, and then commit. Or, start another transaction, receive the reply message, complete or abort the work item, then commit.

2. **What this does:** The work item will not be committed unless the request is sent; the reply will not be removed unless the work item is updated.

3. **Transaction type:** Since the messaging system and the workflow engine each has its own transaction manager, the transaction to coordinate them will be a distributed one.

In this way, the application can assure that it will not lose the messages it receives or forget to send a message that it should. If something goes wrong in the middle, the application can roll back the transaction and try again.

Transactional clients using *Event-Driven Consumers* (498) may not work as expected. The consumer typically must commit the transaction for receiving the message before passing the message to the application. Then, if the application examines the message and decides it does not want to consume it, or if the application encounters an error and wants to roll back the consume action, it cannot because it does not have access to the transaction. So, an event-driven consumer tends to work the same whether or not its client is transactional.

Messaging systems are capable of participating in a distributed transaction, although some implementations may not support it. In JMS, a provider can act as an XA resource and participate in Java Transaction API [JTA] transactions. This behavior is defined by the XA classes in the javax.jms package, particularly javax.jms.XASession, and by the javax.transaction.xa package. The JMS specification recommends that JMS clients not try to handle distributed transactions directly, so an application should use the distributed transaction support provided by a J2EE application server. MSMQ can also participate in an XA transaction; this behavior is exposed in .NET by the MessageQueue.Transactional property and the MessageQueueTransaction class.

As discussed earlier, *Transactional Client*s can be useful as part of other patterns, such as *Request-Reply* (154), message filters in *Pipes and Filters* (70), *Message Sequence* (170), and *Channel Adapter* (127). Likewise, the receiver of an *Event Message* (151) may want to complete processing the event before removing its message from the channel completely. However, *Transactional Client*s do not work well with *Event-Driven Consumer*s (498) or *Message Dispatcher*s (508), can cause problems for *Competing Consumer*s (502), but work well with a single *Polling Consumer* (494).

Example: *JMS Transacted Session*

In JMS, a client makes itself transactional when it creates its session [JMS 1.1], [Hapner].

```
Connection connection = // Get the connection
Session session =
    connection.createSession(true, Session.AUTO_ACKNOWLEDGE);
```

This session is transactional because the first createSession parameter is set to true.

When a client is using a transactional session, it must explicitly commit sends and receives to make them real.

```
Queue queue = // Get the queue
MessageConsumer consumer = session.createConsumer(queue);
Message message = consumer.receive();
```

Transactional
Client

At this point, the message has only been consumed in the consumer's transactional view. But to other consumers with their own transactional views, the message is still available.

```
session.commit();
```

Now, assuming that the commit message does not throw any exceptions, the consumer's transactional view becomes the message system's, which now considers the message consumed.

Example: *.NET Transactional Queue*

In .NET, queues are not transactional by default, so to use a transactional client, the queue must be made transactional when it is created:

```
MessageQueue.Create("MyQueue", true);
```

Once a queue is transactional, each client action (send or receive) on the queue can be transactional or nontransactional. A transactional `Receive` looks like this:

```
MessageQueue queue = new MessageQueue("MyQueue");
MessageQueueTransaction transaction =
    new MessageQueueTransaction();
transaction.Begin();
Message message = queue.Receive(transaction);
transaction.Commit();
```

Although the client had received the message, the messaging system did not make the message unavailable on the queue until the client committed the transaction successfully [SysMsg].

Example: *Transactional Filter with MSMQ*

The following example enhances the basic filter component introduced in *Pipes and Filters* (70) to use transactions. This example implements the **Send-Receive Message Pair** scenario, receiving and sending a message inside the same transaction. We really have to add only a few lines of code to make the filter transactional. We use a variable of type `MessageQueueTransaction` to manage the transaction. We open a transaction before we consume the input `message` and commit after we publish the output message. If any exception occurs, we abort the transaction, which rolls back all message consumption and publication actions and returns the input message to the queue to be available to other queue consumers.

Transactional Client

```
public class TransactionalFilter
{
    protected MessageQueue inputQueue;
    protected MessageQueue outputQueue;
```

```
    protected Thread receiveThread;
    protected bool stopFlag = false;

    public TransactionalFilter (MessageQueue inputQueue, MessageQueue outputQueue)
    {
        this.inputQueue = inputQueue;
        this.inputQueue.Formatter = new System.Messaging.XmlMessageFormatter
                                (new String[] {"System.String,mscorlib"});
        this.outputQueue = outputQueue;
    }

    public void Process()
    {
        ThreadStart receiveDelegate = new ThreadStart(this.ReceiveMessages);
        receiveThread = new Thread(receiveDelegate);
        receiveThread.Start();
    }

    private void ReceiveMessages()
    {
        MessageQueueTransaction myTransaction = new MessageQueueTransaction();

        while (!stopFlag)
        {
            try
            {
                myTransaction.Begin();
                Message inputMessage = inputQueue.Receive(myTransaction);
                Message outputMessage = ProcessMessage(inputMessage);
                outputQueue.Send(outputMessage, myTransaction);
                myTransaction.Commit();
            }
            catch (Exception e)
            {
                Console.WriteLine(e.Message + " - Transaction aborted ");
                myTransaction.Abort();
            }
        }
    }


    protected virtual Message ProcessMessage(Message m)
    {
        Console.WriteLine("Received Message: " + m.Body);
        return m;
    }
}
```

How do we verify that our *Transactional Client* works as intended? We create a subclass of the basic TransactionalFilter class, the aptly named class RandomlyFailingFilter. For each consumed message, this filter draws a random

number between 0 and 10. If the number is less than 3, it throws an arbitrary
exception (ArgumentNullException seemed convenient enough for an example). If we
implemented this filter on top of our basic, nontransactional filter described in
Pipes and Filters (70), we would lose about one in three messages.

```
public class RandomlyFailingFilter : TransactionalFilter
{
    Random rand = new Random();

    public RandomlyFailingFilter(MessageQueue inputQueue, MessageQueue outputQueue)
      : base (inputQueue, outputQueue) { }

    protected override Message ProcessMessage(Message m)
    {
        string text = (string)m.Body;
        Console.WriteLine("Received Message: " + text);

        if (rand.Next(10) < 3)
        {
            Console.WriteLine("EXCEPTION");
            throw (new ArgumentNullException());
        }
        if (text == "end")
            stopFlag = true;
        return(m);
    }
}
```

To make sure that we do not lose any messages with the transactional version, we rigged up a simple test harness that publishes a sequence of messages
to the input queue and makes sure that it can receive all messages in the correct
order from the output queue. It is important to remember that the output messages remain in sequence only if we run a single instance of the transactional filter. If we run multiple filters in parallel, messages can (and will) get out of order
(see *Resequencer* [283]).

```
public void RunTests()
{
    MessageQueueTransaction myTransaction = new MessageQueueTransaction();

    for (int i=0; i < messages.Length; i++)
    {
        myTransaction.Begin();
        inQueue.Send(messages[i], myTransaction);
        myTransaction.Commit();
    }

    for (int i=0; i < messages.Length; i++)
```

Transactional Client

```
{
    myTransaction.Begin();
    Message message = outQueue.Receive(new TimeSpan(0,0,3), myTransaction);
    myTransaction.Commit();

    String text = (String)message.Body;
    Console.Write(text);
    if (text == messages[i])
        Console.WriteLine(" OK");
    else
        Console.WriteLine(" ERROR");
}

Console.WriteLine("Hit enter to exit");
Console.ReadLine();
}
```

Polling Consumer

An application needs to consume *Messages* (66), but it wants to control when it consumes each message.

▼

How can an application consume a message when the application is ready?

▲

Message consumers exist for one reason—to consume messages. The messages represent work that needs to be done, so the consumer needs to consume those messages and do the work.

But how does the consumer know when a new message is available? The easiest approach is for the consumer to repeatedly check the channel to see if a message is available. When a message is available, it consumes the message and then goes back to checking for the next one. This process is called *polling*.

The beauty of polling is that the consumer can request the next message when it is ready for another message. So, it consumes messages at the rate it wants to rather than at the rate they arrive in the channel.

▼

The application should use a *Polling Consumer*, one that explicitly makes a call when it wants to receive a message.

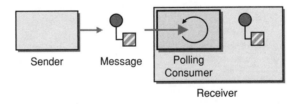

Sender   Message   Polling Consumer

Receiver

▲

This is also known as a synchronous receiver, because the receiver thread blocks until a message is received. We call it a Polling Consumer because the receiver polls for a message, processes it, then polls for another. As a convenience, messaging APIs usually provide a receive method that blocks until a message is delivered in addition to methods like receiveNoWait() and Receive(0) that return immediately if no message is available. This difference is only apparent when the receiver is polling faster than messages are arriving.

A *Polling Consumer* is an object that an application uses to receive messages by explicitly requesting them. When the application is ready for another message, it polls the consumer, which in turn gets a message from the messaging system and returns it. (How the consumer gets the message from the messaging system is implementation-specific and may or may not involve polling. All the application knows is that it doesn't get the message until it explicitly asks for one.)

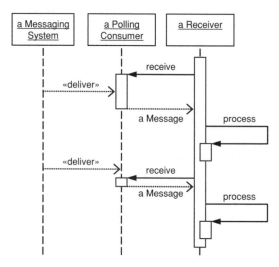

Polling Consumer Sequence

When the application polls for a message, the consumer blocks until it gets a message to return (or until some other condition is met, such as a time limit). Once the application receives the message, it can process it. Once it is through processing the message and wishes to receive another, the application can poll again.

By using *Polling Consumers*, an application can control how many messages are consumed concurrently by limiting the number of threads that are polling. This can help keep the receiving application from being overwhelmed by too many requests; extra messages queue up until the receiver can process them.

A receiver-application typically uses one thread (at least) per channel that it wishes to monitor, but it can also use a single thread to monitor multiple chan-

Polling Consumer

nels, which helps conserve threads when monitoring channels that are frequently empty. To poll a single channel, assuming that the thread has nothing to do until a message arrives, use a version of receive that blocks until a message arrives. To poll multiple channels with a single thread, or to perform other work while waiting for a message to arrive, use a version of receive with a timeout or receiveNoWait() so that if one channel is empty, the thread goes on to check another channel or perform other work.

A consumer that is polling too much or blocking threads for too long can be inefficient, in which case an *Event-Driven Consumer* (498) may be more efficient. Multiple *Polling Consumers* can be *Competing Consumers* (502). A *Message Dispatcher* (508) can be implemented as a *Polling Consumer*. A *Polling Consumer* can be a *Selective Consumer* (515); it can also be a *Durable Subscriber* (522). A *Polling Consumer* can also be a *Transactional Client* (484) so that the consumer can control when the message is actually removed from the channel.

Example: *JMS Receive*

In JMS, a message consumer uses MessageConsumer.receive to consume a message synchronously [JMS 1.1], [Hapner].

MessageConsumer has three different receive methods:

1. receive()—Blocks until a message is available and then returns it.

2. receiveNoWait()—Checks once for a message and returns it or null.

3. receive(long)—Blocks until a message is available and returns it, or until the timeout expires and returns null.

For example, the code to create a consumer and receive a message is very simple:

```
Destination dest = // Get the destination
Session session = // Create the session
MessageConsumer consumer = session.createConsumer(dest);
Message message = consumer.receive();
```

Polling Consumer

Example: *.NET Receive*

In .NET, a consumer uses MessageQueue.Receive to consume a message synchronously [SysMsg].

A MessageQueue client has several variations of receive. The two simplest are

1. Receive()—Blocks until a message is available, and then returns it.

2. Receive(TimeSpan)—Blocks until a message is available and returns it, or until the timeout expires and throws MessageQueueException.

The code to receive a message from an existing queue is quite simple:

```
MessageQueue queue = // Get the queue
Message message = queue.Receive();
```

Polling
Consumer

Event-Driven Consumer

An application needs to consume *Messages* (66) as soon as they're delivered.

> **How can an application automatically consume messages as they become available?**

The problem with *Polling Consumers* (494) is that when the channel is empty, the consumer blocks threads and/or consumes process time while polling for messages that are not there. Polling enables the client to control the rate of consumption but wastes resources when there's nothing to consume.

Rather than continuously asking the channel if it has messages to consume, it would be better if the channel could tell the client when a message is available. For that matter, instead of making the consumer poll for the message, just give the message to the consumer as soon as the message becomes available.

> **The application should use an *Event-Driven Consumer*, one that is automatically handed messages as they're delivered on the channel.**

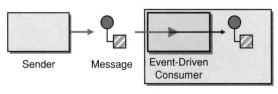

Receiver

Event-Driven Consumer

This is also known as an asynchronous receiver, because the receiver does not have a running thread until a callback thread delivers a message. We call it an *Event-Driven Consumer* because the receiver acts like the message delivery is an event that triggers the receiver into action.

An *Event-Driven Consumer* is an object that is invoked by the messaging system when a message arrives on the consumer's channel. The consumer passes the message to the application through a callback in the application's API. (How the messaging system gets the message is implementation-specific and may or may not be event-driven. All the consumer knows is that it can sit dormant with no active threads until it gets invoked by the messaging system passing it a message.)

An *Event-Driven Consumer* is invoked by the messaging system, yet it invokes an application-specific callback. To bridge this gap, the consumer has an application-specific implementation that conforms to a known API defined by the messaging system.

The code for an *Event-Driven Consumer* consists of two parts:

1. **Initialization**—The application creates an application-specific consumer and associates it with a particular *Message Channel* (60). After this code is run once, the consumer is ready to receive a series of messages.

2. **Consumption**—The consumer receives a message and passes it to the application for processing. This code is run once per message being consumed.

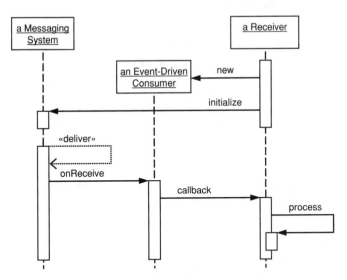

Event-Driven Consumer Sequence

Event-
Driven
Consumer

The application creates its custom consumer and associates it with the channel. Once the consumer is initialized, it (and the application) can then go dormant, with no running threads, waiting to be invoked when a message arrives.

When a message is delivered, the messaging system calls the consumer's message-received-event method and passes in the message as a parameter. The consumer passes the message to the application, using the application's callback API. The application now has the message and can process it. Once the application finishes processing the message, it and the consumer can then go dormant again until the next message arrives. Typically, a messaging system will not run multiple threads through a single consumer, so the consumer can process only one message at a time.

Event-Driven Consumers automatically consume messages as they become available. For more fine-grained control of the consumption rate, use a *Polling Consumer* (494). *Event-Driven Consumers* can be *Competing Consumers* (502). A *Message Dispatcher* (508) can be implemented as an *Event-Driven Consumer*. An *Event-Driven Consumer* can be a *Selective Consumer* (515); it can also be a *Durable Subscriber* (522). *Transactional Clients* (484) may not work as well with *Event-Driven Consumers* as they do with *Polling Consumers* (494); see the JMS example.

Example: *JMS MessageListener*

In JMS, an *Event-Driven Consumer* is a class that implements the MessageListener interface [Hapner]. This interface declares a single method, onMessage(Message). The consumer implements onMessage to process the message. Here is an example of a JMS performer:

```
public class MyEventDrivenConsumer implements MessageListener {
    public void onMessage(Message message) {
        // Process the message
    }
}
```

The initializer part of an *Event-Driven Consumer* creates the desired performer object (which is a MessageListener instance) and associates it with a message consumer for the desired channel:

```
Destination destination = // Get the destination
Session session = // Create the session
MessageConsumer consumer = session.createConsumer(destination);
MessageListener listener = new MyEventDrivenConsumer();
consumer.setMessageListener(listener);
```

Now, when a message is delivered to the destination, the JMS provider will call MyEventDrivenConsumer.onMessage with the message as a parameter.

Note that in JMS, an *Event-Driven Consumer* that is also a *Transactional Client* (484) will not work as expected. Normally, a transaction is rolled back

Event-Driven Consumer

when the code in the transaction throws an exception, but the `MessageLis-tener.onMessage` signature does not provide for an exception being thrown (such as `JMSException`), and a runtime exception is considered programmer error. If a runtime exception occurs, the JMS provider responds by delivering the next message, so the message that caused the exception is lost [JMS 1.1], [Hapner]. To successfully achieve transactional, event-driven behavior, use a message-driven EJB [EJB 2.0], [Hapner].

Example: *.NET ReceiveCompletedEventHandler*

With .NET, the performer part of an *Event-Driven Consumer* implements a method that is a `ReceiveCompletedEventHandler` delegate. This delegate method must accept two parameters: an object that is the `MessageQueue` and a `ReceiveCompletedEventArgs` that is the arguments from the `ReceiveCompleted` event [SysMsg]. The method uses the arguments to get the message from the queue and process it. Here is an example of a .NET performer:

```
public static void MyEventDrivenConsumer(Object source,
    ReceiveCompletedEventArgs asyncResult)
{
    MessageQueue mq = (MessageQueue) source;
    Message m = mq.EndReceive(asyncResult.AsyncResult);
    // Process the message
    mq.BeginReceive();
    return;
}
```

The initializer part of an event-driven client specifies that the queue should run the delegate method to handle a `ReceiveCompleted` event:

```
MessageQueue queue = // Get the queue
queue.ReceiveCompleted +=
    new ReceiveCompletedEventHandler(MyEventDrivenConsumer);
queue.BeginReceive();
```

Now, when a message is delivered to the queue, the queue will issue a `ReceiveCompleted` event, which will run the `MyEventDrivenConsumer` method.

Event-
Driven
Consumer

Competing Consumers

An application is using *Messaging* (53). However, it cannot process messages as fast as they're being added to the channel.

How can a messaging client process multiple messages concurrently?

Messages (66) arrive through a *Message Channel* (60) sequentially, so the natural inclination of a consumer is to process them sequentially. However, sequential consumption may be too slow, and messages may pile up on the channel, which makes the messaging system a bottleneck and hurts overall throughput of the application. This can happen either because of multiple senders on the channel, because a network outage causes a backlog of messages which are then delivered all at once, because a receiver outage causes a backlog, or because each message takes significantly more effort to consume and perform than it does to create and send.

The application could use multiple channels, but one channel might become a bottleneck while another sits empty, and a sender would not know which one of equivalent channels to use. Multiple channels would have the advantage, however, of enabling multiple consumers (one per channel), processing messages concurrently. Even if this worked, though, the number of channels the application defined would still limit the throughput.

What is needed is a way for a channel to have multiple consumers.

Competing Consumers

Create multiple *Competing Consumers* on a single channel so that the consumers can process multiple messages concurrently.

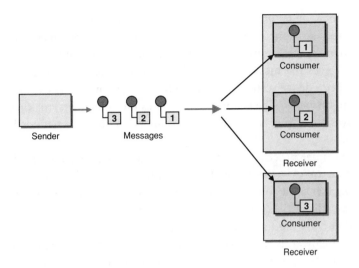

Competing Consumers are multiple consumers that are all created to receive messages from a single *Point-to-Point Channel* (103). When the channel delivers a message, any of the consumers could potentially receive it. The messaging system's implementation determines which consumer actually receives the message, but in effect the consumers compete with each other to be the receiver. Once a consumer receives a message, it can delegate to the rest of its application to help process the message. (This solution only works with *Point-to-Point Channels* (103); multiple consumers on a *Publish-Subscribe Channel* [106] just create more copies of each message.)

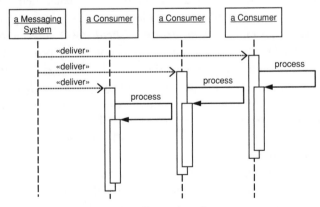

Competing Consumers Sequence

Each of the *Competing Consumers* runs in its own thread so that they all can consume messages concurrently. When the channel delivers a message, the messaging system's transactional controls ensure that only one of the consumers successfully receives the message. While that consumer is processing the message, the channel can deliver other messages, which other consumers can concurrently consume and process. The channel coordinates the consumers, making sure that each receives a different message; the consumers do not have to coordinate with each other.

Each consumer processes a different message concurrently, so the bottleneck becomes how quickly the channel can feed messages to the consumers instead of how long it takes a consumer to process a message. A limited number of consumers may still be a bottleneck, but increasing the number of consumers can alleviate that constraint as long as there are available computing resources.

To run concurrently, each consumer must run in its own thread. For *Polling Consumers* (494), this means that each consumer must have its own thread to perform the polling concurrently. For *Event-Driven Consumers* (498), the messaging system must use a thread per concurrent consumer; that thread will be used to hand the message to the consumer and will be used by the consumer to process the message.

A sophisticated messaging system will detect competing consumers on a channel and internally provide a *Message Dispatcher* (508) that ensures that each message is only delivered to a single consumer. This helps avoid conflicts that would arise if multiple consumers each thought they were the consumer of a single message. A less sophisticated messaging system will allow multiple consumers to attempt to consume the same message. When this happens, whichever consumer commits its transaction first wins; then the other consumers will not be able to commit successfully and will have to roll back their transactions.

A messaging system that allows multiple consumers to attempt consuming the same message can make a *Transactional Client* (484) very inefficient. The client thinks it has a message, consumes it, spends effort processing the message, then tries to commit and cannot (because the message has already been consumed by a competitor). Frequently performing work just to roll it back hurts throughput, whereas the point of this solution is to increase throughput. Thus, the performance of competing transactional consumers should be measured carefully; it could vary significantly on different messaging system implementations and configurations.

Not only can *Competing Consumers* be used to spread load across multiple consumer threads in a single application; they can also spread the consumption load across multiple applications (e.g., processes). This way, if one application

Competing
Consumers

cannot consume messages fast enough, multiple consumer applications—perhaps with each employing multiple consumer threads—can attack the problem. The ability to have multiple applications running on multiple computers using multiple threads to consume messages provides virtually unlimited message processing capacity, where the only limit is the messaging system's ability to deliver messages from the channel to the consumers.

The coordination of competing consumers depends on each messaging system's implementation. If the client wants to implement this coordination itself, it should use a *Message Dispatcher* (508). *Competing Consumers* can be *Polling Consumers* (494), *Event-Driven Consumers* (498), or a combination thereof. Competing *Transactional Clients* (484) can waste significant effort processing messages whose receive operations do not commit successfully and have to be rolled back.

Example: *Simple JMS Competing Consumers*

This is a simple example of how to implement a competing consumer in Java. An external driver/manager object (not shown) runs a couple of them. It runs each one in its own thread and calls stopRunning() to make it stop.

A JMS session must be single-threaded [JMS 1.1], [Hapner]. A single session serializes the order of message consumption [JMS 11], [Hapner]. So, for each competing consumer to work properly in its own thread, and for the consumers to be able to consume messages in parallel, each consumer must have its own Session (and therefore its own MessageConsumer). The JMS specification does not specify the semantics of how concurrent QueueReceivers (e.g., *Competing Consumers*) should work, or even require that this approach work at all. Thus, applications that use this technique are not assumed to be portable and may work differently with different JMS providers [JMS 1.1], [Hapner].

The consumer class implements Runnable so that it can run in its own thread; this allows the consumers to run concurrently. All of the consumers share the same Connection, but each creates its own Session, which is important, since each session can only support a single thread. Each consumer repeatedly receives a message from the queue and processes it.

Competing
Consumers

```
import javax.jms.Connection;
import javax.jms.Destination;
import javax.jms.JMSException;
import javax.jms.Message;
import javax.jms.MessageConsumer;
import javax.jms.Session;
import javax.naming.NamingException;
```

```
public class CompetingConsumer implements Runnable {

    private int performerID;
    private MessageConsumer consumer;
    private boolean isRunning;

    protected CompetingConsumer() {
        super();
    }

    public static CompetingConsumer newConsumer(int id, Connection connection,
                                                String queueName)
        throws JMSException, NamingException {
        CompetingConsumer consumer = new CompetingConsumer();
        consumer.initialize(id, connection, queueName);
        return consumer;
    }

    protected void initialize(int id, Connection connection, String queueName)
        throws JMSException, NamingException {
        performerID = id;
        Session session = connection.createSession(false, Session.AUTO_ACKNOWLEDGE);
        Destination dispatcherQueue = JndiUtil.getDestination(queueName);
        consumer = session.createConsumer(dispatcherQueue);
        isRunning = true;
    }

    public void run() {
        try {
            while (isRunning())
                receiveSync();
        } catch (Exception e) {
            e.printStackTrace();
        }
    }

    private synchronized boolean isRunning() {
        return isRunning;
    }

    public synchronized void stopRunning() {
        isRunning = false;
    }

    private void receiveSync() throws JMSException, InterruptedException {
        Message message = consumer.receive();
        if (message != null)
            processMessage(message);
    }

    private void processMessage(Message message)
      throws JMSException, InterruptedException {
        int id = message.getIntProperty("cust_id");
```

Competing
Consumers

```
        System.out.println(System.currentTimeMillis() + ": Performer #"
            + performerID + " starting; message ID " + id);
        Thread.sleep(500);
        System.out.println(System.currentTimeMillis() + ": Performer #"
            + performerID + " processing.");
        Thread.sleep(500);
        System.out.println(System.currentTimeMillis() + ": Performer #"
            + performerID + " finished.");
    }
}
```

So, implementing a simple *Competing Consumer* is easy. The main trick is to make the consumer a Runnable and run it in its own thread.

Competing
Consumers

Message Dispatcher

An application is using *Messaging* (53). The application needs multiple consumers on a single *Message Channel* (60) to work in a coordinated fashion.

> ▼
>
> How can multiple consumers on a single channel coordinate their message processing?
>
> ▲

Multiple consumers on a single *Point-to-Point Channel* (103) act as *Competing Consumers* (502). That's fine when the consumers are interchangeable, but it does not allow for specializing the consumers so that certain consumers are better able to consume certain messages.

Multiple consumers on a single *Publish-Subscribe Channel* (106) won't work as intended. Rather than distribute the message load, these consumers will duplicate the effort.

*Selective Consumer*s (515) can be used as specialized consumers. However, not all messaging systems support this feature. Even among those that do, they may not support selection based on values in the body of the message. Their selector value expressions may be too simple to adequately distinguish among the messages, or the performance of repeatedly evaluating those expressions may be slow. There may be numerous expressions that need to be carefully designed in a coordinated fashion so that they do not overlap but also do not leave any selector values unhandled. They may need to implement a default case for selector values that are not handled by other consumers or that are unexpected.

Datatype Channels (111) can be used to keep different types of messages separate and to enable consumers to specialize for those message types. But the type system may be too large and varied to justify creating a separate channel for each type. Or, the types may be based on dynamically changing criteria, which are difficult to handle with a static set of channels. The enterprise may already require a huge number of channels, taxing the messaging system, and multiplying many of those channels for distinct message types may simply require too many channels.

Each of these problems could be solved if consumers could work together. They could avoid duplicating work by being aware if another consumer had

Message Dispatcher

already processed that work. They could be specialized; if a consumer got the wrong kind of message for its specialty, it could hand off the message to another consumer with the right specialty. If an application had too many channels coming in, it could save channels by having all of its consumers share a single channel; they would coordinate to make sure that the right messages went to the right consumers.

Alas, consumers are very independent objects that are difficult to coordinate. Making specialized consumers general enough to handle any message and hand it off would add a lot of design and processing overhead to each consumer. They would all have to know about each other so they could hand off work, and they would all need to know which of the others were busy so as not to give a consumer a message to process while it's already processing another. Making consumers work together would radically change the typical consumer design.

The *Mediator* pattern [GoF] offers some help. A *Mediator* coordinates a group of objects so that they don't need to know how to coordinate with each other. What we need for messaging is a mediator that coordinates the consumers for a channel. Then, each consumer could focus on processing a particular kind of message, and the coordinator could make sure the right message gets to the right consumer.

Create a *Message Dispatcher* on a channel that will consume messages from a channel and distribute them to performers.

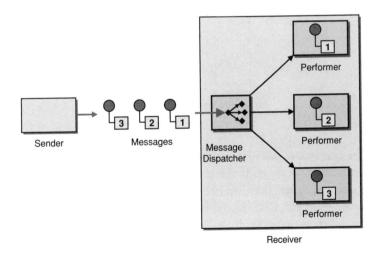

Message
Dispatcher

A *Message Dispatcher* consists of two parts:

1. **Dispatcher**—The object that consumes messages from a channel and distributes each message to a performer.

2. **Performer**—The object that is given the message by the dispatcher and processes it.

When a *Message Dispatcher* receives a message, it obtains a performer and dispatches the message to the performer to process it. A performer can delegate to the rest of its application to help process its message. The performer could be newly created by the dispatcher or could be selected from a pool of available performers. Each performer can run in its own thread to process messages concurrently. All performers may be appropriate for all messages, or the dispatcher may match a message to a specialized performer based on properties of the message.

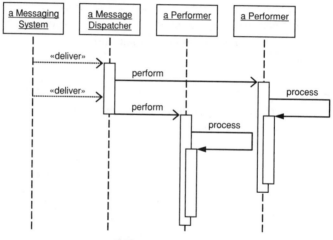

Message Dispatcher Sequence

Message Dispatcher

When the dispatcher receives a message, it delegates the message to an available performer to process it. If the performer processes the message using the dispatcher's thread, then the dispatcher blocks until the performer is finished processing the message. Conversely, if the performer processes the message in its own thread, then once the dispatcher starts that thread, it can immediately start receiving other messages and delegating them to other performers so that the messages are processed concurrently. This way, messages can be consumed as fast as the dispatcher can receive and delegate them, regardless of how long each message takes to process.

A dispatcher acts as a one-to-many connection between a single channel and a group of performers. The performers do most of the work; the dispatcher just acts as a matchmaker, matching each message with an available performer, and does not block as long as the performers run in their own threads. The dispatcher receives the message and then sends it to a performer to process it. Because the dispatcher does relatively little work and does not block, it potentially can dispatch messages as fast as the messaging system can feed them and thus avoids becoming a bottleneck.

This pattern is a simpler, messaging-specific version of the *Reactor* pattern [POSA2], where the message dispatcher is a Reactor and the message performers are Concrete Event Handlers. The *Message Channel* (60) acts as the Synchronous Event Demultiplexer, making the messages available to the dispatcher one at a time. The messages themselves are like Handles, but much simpler. A true handle tends to be a reference to a resource's data, whereas a message usually contains the data directly. (However, the message does not have to store the data directly. If a message's data is stored externally and the message is a *Claim Check* [346], then the message contains a reference to the data, which is more like a *Reactor* handle.) Different types of handles select different types of concrete event handlers, whereas a *Message Channel* (60) is a *Datatype Channel* (111), so all of the messages (handles) are of the same type, and there is typically only one type of concrete event handler.

Whereas *Datatype Channel* (111) designs a channel so that all messages are of the same type and all consumers process messages of that type, the *Reactor* pattern points out an opportunity to use *Message Dispatcher* to support multiple datatypes on the same channel and process them with type-specific performers. Each message must specify its type; the dispatcher detects the message's type and dispatches it to a type-specific performer for processing. In this way, a dispatcher with specialized performers can act as an alternative to *Datatype Channels* (111) and as a specialized implementation of *Selective Consumers* (515).

One difference between *Message Dispatcher* (508) and *Competing Consumers* (502) is the ability to distribute across multiple applications. Whereas a set of *Competing Consumers* (502) may be distributed among multiple processes (e.g., applications), a set of performers typically all run in the same process as the dispatcher (even if they run in different threads). If a performer were running in a different process from its dispatcher, the dispatcher would have to communicate with the performer in a distributed, *Remote Procedure Invocation* (50) manner, which is exactly what *Messaging* (53) intends to avoid in the first place.

Message
Dispatcher

Since a dispatcher is a single consumer, it works fine with both *Point-to-Point Channels* (103) and *Publish-Subscribe Channels* (106). With point-to-point messaging, a dispatcher can be a suitable alternative to *Competing Consumers* (502); this alternative may be preferable if the messaging system handles multiple consumers badly or if handling of multiple consumers across different messaging system implementations is inconsistent.

A dispatcher makes the performers work much like *Event-Driven Consumers* (498), even though the dispatcher itself could be event-driven or a *Polling Consumer* (494). As such, implementing a dispatcher as part of a *Transactional Client* (484) can be difficult. If the client is transactional, ideally the dispatcher should allow the performer to process a message before completing the transaction. Then, only if the performer is successful should the dispatcher commit the transaction. If the performer fails to process the message, the dispatcher should roll back the transaction. Since each performer may need to roll back its individual message, the dispatcher needs a session for each performer and must use that performer's session to receive the performer's message and complete its transaction. Since *Event-Driven Consumers* (498) often do not work well with *Transactional Clients*, the dispatcher should not be an *Event-Driven Consumer* (498), but rather should be a *Polling Consumer* (494).

It can be helpful to implement performers as *Event-Driven Consumers* (498). In JMS, this means implementing the performer as a `MessageListener`. A message listener has one method, `onMessage(Message)`; it accepts a message and performs whatever processing necessary. This forms a clean separation between the dispatcher and the performer. Likewise, in .NET, the performer should be a `ReceiveCompletedEventHandler` delegate, even though the dispatcher will not really issue `ReceiveCompleted` events. However, these event-driven approaches may not be compatible with the API necessary to run a performer in its own thread.

To avoid the effort of implementing your own *Message Dispatcher* (508), consider instead using *Competing Consumers* (502) on a *Datatype Channel* (111) or using *Selective Consumers* (515). A *Message Dispatcher* can be a *Polling Consumer* (494) or an *Event-Driven Consumer* (498). A *Message Dispatcher* does not make a very good *Transactional Client* (484).

Message Dispatcher

Example: *.NET Dispatcher*

Usually, a *Message Dispatcher* dispatches messages to the performers (see the Java example). .NET provides another option: The dispatcher can use Peek to detect a message and get its message ID, then dispatch the message ID (not the full message) to the performer. The performer then uses `ReceiveById` to consume the particular message it has been assigned. In this way, each performer can take responsibility not just for processing the message but for consuming it as well, which can help with concurrency issues, especially when the consumers are *Transactional Clients* (484).

Example: *Simple Java Dispatcher*

This is a simple example of how to implement a dispatcher and performer in Java. A more sophisticated dispatcher implementation might pool several performers, keep track of which ones are currently available to process messages, and make use of a thread pool. This simple example skips those details but does run each performer in its own thread so that they can run concurrently.

The driver/manager that controls the dispatcher (not shown) will run receiveSync() repeatedly. Each time, the dispatcher will receive() the next message, instantiate a new performer instance to process the message, and then start the performer in its own thread.

```java
import javax.jms.Connection;
import javax.jms.Destination;
import javax.jms.JMSException;
import javax.jms.Message;
import javax.jms.MessageConsumer;
import javax.jms.Session;
import javax.naming.NamingException;

public class MessageDispatcher {

    MessageConsumer consumer;
    int nextID = 1;

    protected MessageDispatcher() {
        super();
    }

    public static MessageDispatcher newDispatcher(Connection connection,
      String queueName)
        throws JMSException, NamingException {
        MessageDispatcher dispatcher = new MessageDispatcher();
        dispatcher.initialize(connection, queueName);
        return dispatcher;
    }

    protected void initialize(Connection connection, String queueName)
        throws JMSException, NamingException {
        Session session = connection.createSession(false, Session.AUTO_ACKNOWLEDGE);
        Destination dispatcherQueue = JndiUtil.getDestination(queueName);
        consumer = session.createConsumer(dispatcherQueue);
    }
```

```
    public void receiveSync() throws JMSException {
        Message message = consumer.receive();
        Performer performer = new Performer(nextID++, message);
        new Thread(performer).start();
    }
}
```

The performer must implement Runnable so that it can run in its own thread. The runnable's run() method simply calls processMessage(). When this is complete, the performer becomes eligible for garbage collection.

```
import javax.jms.JMSException;
import javax.jms.Message;

public class Performer implements Runnable {

    private int performerID;
    private Message message;

    public Performer(int id, Message message) {
        performerID = id;
        this.message = message;
    }

    public void run() {
        try {
            processMessage();
        } catch (Exception e) {
            e.printStackTrace();
        }
    }

    private void processMessage() throws JMSException, InterruptedException {
        int id = message.getIntProperty("cust_id");

        System.out.println(System.currentTimeMillis() + ": Performer #"
            + performerID + " starting; message ID " + id);
        Thread.sleep(500);
        System.out.println(System.currentTimeMillis() + ": Performer #"
            + performerID + " processing.");
        Thread.sleep(500);
        System.out.println(System.currentTimeMillis() + ": Performer #"
            + performerID + " finished.");
    }
}
```

Message Dispatcher

Implementing a simple dispatcher and performer is easy. The main trick is to make the performer a Runnable and run it in its own thread.

Selective Consumer

An application is using *Messaging* (53). It consumes *Messages* (66) from a *Message Channel* (60), but it does not necessarily want to consume all of the messages on that channel—just some of them.

How can a message consumer select which messages it wishes to receive?

By default, if a *Message Channel* (60) has only one consumer, all *Messages* (66) on that channel will be delivered to that consumer. Likewise, if there are multiple *Competing Consumers* (502) on the channel, any message can potentially go to any consumer, and every message will go to some consumer. A consumer normally does not get to choose which messages it consumes; it always gets whatever message is next.

This behavior is fine as long as the consumer wants to receive any and all messages on the channel, which is normally the case. This is a problem, however, when a consumer wants to consume only certain messages, because a consumer normally has no control over which messages on a channel it receives. Why would a consumer want to receive only certain messages? Consider an application processing loan request messages; it may want to process loans for up to $100,000 differently from those over $100,000. One approach would be for the application to have two different kinds of consumers, one for small loans and another for big loans. Yet, since any consumer can receive any message, how can the application make sure that the right messages go to the right consumer?

The simplest approach might be for each to consume whatever messages it gets. If it gets the wrong kind of message, it could somehow hand that message to the appropriate kind of consumer. That's going to be difficult, though; consumer instances usually don't know about each other, and finding one that isn't already busy processing another message can be difficult. Perhaps when the consumer realizes it doesn't want the message, it could put the message back on the channel. But then it's likely to just consume the message yet again. Perhaps every consumer could get a copy of every message and just discard the ones it

Selective Consumer

doesn't want. This will work but will cause a lot of message duplication and a lot of wasted processing on messages that are ultimately discarded.

Perhaps the messaging system could define separate channels for each type of message. Then, the sender could make sure to send each message on the proper channel, and the receivers could be sure that the messages they receive off of a particular channel are the kind desired. However, this solution is not very dynamic. The receivers may change their selection criteria while the system is running, which would require defining new channels and redistributing the messages already on the channels. It also means that the senders must know what the receivers' selection criteria are and when those criteria change. The criteria need to be a property of the receivers, not of the channels, and the messages on the channel need to specify what criteria they meet.

What is needed is a way for messages fitting a variety of criteria to all be sent on the same channel, for the consumers to be able to specify what criteria they're interested in, and for each consumer to receive only the messages that meet its criteria.

Make the consumer a *Selective Consumer*, one that filters the messages delivered by its channel so that it receives only the ones that match its criteria.

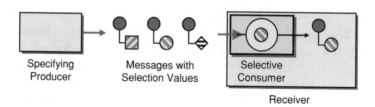

Specifying Producer — Messages with Selection Values — Selective Consumer — Receiver

---

There are three parts to this filtering process:

1. **Specifying Producer**—Specifies the message's selection value before sending it.

2. **Selection Value**—One or more values specified in the message that allow a consumer to decide whether to select the message.

3. **Selective Consumer**—Only receives messages that meet its selection criteria.

The message sender specifies each message's selection value before sending it. When a message arrives, a *Selective Consumer* tests the message's selection value to see if the value meets the consumer's selection criteria. If so, the consumer receives the message and passes it to the application for processing.

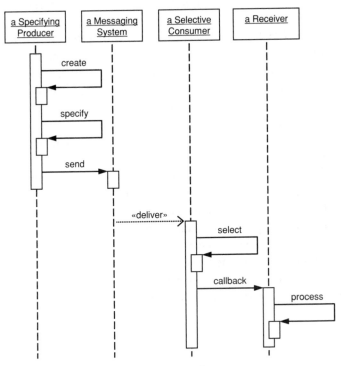

Selective Consumer Sequence

When the sender creates the message, it also sets the message's selection value; then it sends the message. When the messaging system delivers the message, the *Selective Consumer* tests the message's selection value to determine whether to select the message. If the message passes, the consumer receives the message and passes the message to the application, using a callback.

*Selective Consumer*s are often used in groups—one consumer filters for one set of criteria, while another filters for a different set, and so on. For the loan processing example, one consumer would select "amount < = $100,000" while another would select "amount > $100,000." Then, each consumer would only get the kinds of loans it is interested in.

When multiple *Selective Consumer*s are used with a *Point-to-Point Channel* (103), they effectively become *Competing Consumers* (502) that are also selective. If two consumers' criteria overlap, and a message's selection value meets both of their criteria, either consumer can consume the message. Consumers should be designed to ensure that at least one of them is eligible to consume every valid selection value. Otherwise, a message with an unmatched selection value will never be consumed and will clutter the channel forever (or at least until *Message Expiration* [176] occurs).

When multiple *Selective Consumers* are used with a *Publish-Subscribe Channel* (106), each message will be delivered to each subscriber, but a subscriber will simply ignore its copy of a message that does not fit its criteria. Once a consumer decides to ignore a message, the messaging system can discard the message, since it has been successfully delivered and will never be consumed. A messaging system can optimize this process by not even delivering a message it knows the consumer will ignore, thereby decreasing the number of copies of a message that must be produced and transmitted. This behavior of discarding ignored messages is independent of whatever *Guaranteed Delivery* (122), *Durable Subscriber* (522), and/or *Message Expiration* (176) settings are used.

Selective Consumers make a single channel act like multiple *Datatype Channels* (111). Different types of messages can have different selection values so that a consumer that is specialized for a particular type will only receive messages of that type. This can facilitate sending a large number of types using a small number of channels. This approach can also conserve channels in an enterprise that requires more channels than a messaging system can support.

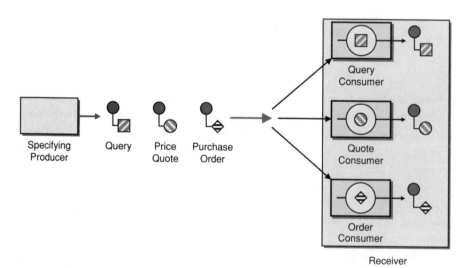

Competing, Selective Consumers

Using *Selective Consumer*s to emulate *Datatype Channels* (111) is not a good approach when trying to hide messages of a certain type from certain consumer applications. Whereas a messaging system can ensure only authorized applications successfully receive messages from a channel, they usually do not authorize a consumer's selection criteria, so a malicious consumer authorized to access the channel can gain access to unauthorized messages by changing its criteria. Separate datatype channels are needed to securely lock out applications.

An alternative to using *Selective Consumer*s is to use a *Message Dispatcher* (508). The selection criteria are built into the dispatcher, which then uses them to determine the performer for each message. If a message does not meet any of the performer's criteria, rather than leave it cluttering the channel or discarding it, the dispatcher can reroute the unmatched message to the *Invalid Message Channel* (60). As with the trade-off between *Message Dispatcher* (508) and *Competing Consumers* (502), the question is really whether you wish to let the messaging system do the dispatching or you want to implement it yourself. If a messaging system does not support *Selective Consumer* as a feature, you have no choice but to implement it yourself using a *Message Dispatcher* (508).

As mentioned earlier, if none of the *Selective Consumer*s on a channel match the message's selector value, the message will be ignored as if the channel has no receivers. A similar problem in procedural programming is a case statement where none of the cases match the value being tested. Thus, a case statement can have a default case that matches values that aren't matched by any other case. Applying this approach to messaging, it may seem tempting to create some sort of default consumer for messages that otherwise have no matching consumer. Yet, such a default consumer will not work as desired because it would require an expression that matches all selector values, so it would compete with all other consumers. Instead, to implement a default consumer, use a *Message Dispatcher* (508) that implements a case statement with a default option for unhandled cases that uses the default consumer.

Another alternative to *Selective Consumer*s is *Message Filters* (237). They accomplish much the same goal, but in different ways. With a *Selective Consumer*, all of the messages are delivered to the receivers, but each receiver ignores unwanted messages. A *Message Filter* (237) sits between a channel from the sender and a channel to the receiver and only transfers desired messages from the sender's channel to the receiver's. Thus, unwanted messages are never even delivered to the receiver's channel, so the receiver has nothing to ignore. *Message Filter* (237) is useful for getting rid of messages that no receiver wants. *Selective Consumer*s are useful when one receiver wants to ignore certain messages but other receivers want to receive those messages.

Selective Consumer

Another alternative to consider is *Content-Based Router* (230). This type of router, like a filter, makes sure that a channel gets only the messages that the receivers want, which can increase security and increase the performance of the consumers. *Selective Consumer* is more flexible, however, because each filtering option simply requires a new consumer (which is easy to create while the system is running), whereas each new option with a *Content-Based Router* (230) requires a new output channel (which is not so easy to create and use while the system is running) as well as a new consumer for the new channel. Consider a requirements change where you want to process medium-size loans ($50,000 to $150,000) differently from small and large loans. With *Content-Based Router* (230), you need to create a new channel for medium loans, as well as a consumer on that new channel, and adjust the way the router separates loans. You also need to worry about what happens when the change takes effect, because some messages that have already been routed onto the original channels may not have been consumed yet and may now be on the wrong channel. With *Selective Consumer*, you just replace the two types of consumers (less than $100,000 and greater than $100,000) with three types (less than $50,000, $50,000 to $150,000, and greater than $150,000). *Content-Based Router* (230) is a much more static approach, whereas *Selective Consumer* can be much more dynamic.

Ideally, a message's selection value should be specified in its header, not its body, so that a *Selective Consumer* can process the value without having to parse (and know how to parse) the message's body.

Selective Consumers make a single channel act like multiple *Datatype Channels* (111). They allow messages to be available for other receivers, whereas *Message Filter* (237) prevents unwanted messages from being delivered to any receiver, and they can be used more dynamically than a *Content-Based Router* (230). A *Selective Consumer* can be implemented as a *Polling Consumer* (494) or *Event-Driven Consumer* (498) and can be part of a *Transactional Client* (484). To implement the filtering behavior yourself, use a *Message Dispatcher* (508).

Example: *Separating Types*

Selective
Consumer

A stock trading system with a limited number of channels might need to use one channel for both quotes and trades. The receiver for performing a quote is very different from that for trading, so the right receiver needs to be sure to consume the right message. The sender would set the selector value on a quote message to QUOTE, and the *Selective Consumer* for quotes would consume only messages with that selector value. Trade messages would have their own TRADE selector value that their senders and receivers would use. In this way, two message types can successfully share a single channel.

Example: *JMS Message Selector*

In JMS, a MessageConsumer (QueueReceiver or TopicSubscriber) can be created with a message selector string that filters messages based on their property values [JMS 1.1], [Hapner]. First, a sender sets the value of a property in the message that the receiver could filter by:

```
Session session = // get the session
TextMessage message = session.createTextMessage();
message.setText("<quote>SUNW</quote>");
message.setStringProperty("req_type", "quote");
Destination destination = //get the destination
MessageProducer producer = session.createProducer(destination);
producer.send(message);
```

Second, a receiver sets its message selector to filter for that value:

```
Session session = // get the session
Destination destination = //get the destination
String selector = "req_type = 'quote'";
MessageConsumer consumer =
    session.createConsumer(destination, selector);
```

This receiver will ignore all messages whose request type property is not set to quote as if those messages were never delivered to the destination at all.

Example: *.NET Peek, ReceiveById, and ReceiveByCorrelationId*

In .NET, MessageQueue.Receive does not support JMS-style message selectors per se. Rather, what a receiver can do is use MessageQueue.Peek to look at a message. If it meets the desired criteria, then it can use MessageQueue.Receive to read it from the queue. This may not work very reliably, though, since the message returned by the Receive call may not necessarily be the same message that was peeked. Thus, use ReceiveById, whereby the consumer specifies the ID property value of the message it wishes to receive (instead of specifying Receive) to ensure getting the same message that was peeked.

Another option in .NET is the ReceiveByCorrelationId method with which the consumer specifies the CorrelationId property value of the message it wants to receive. A sender of a particular request message can use ReceiveByCorrelationId to receive the reply message specific to that request (see *Request-Reply* [154] and *Correlation Identifier* [163]).

Selective Consumer

Durable Subscriber

An application is receiving messages on a *Publish-Subscribe Channel* (106).

▼
How can a subscriber avoid missing messages while it's not listening for them?
▲

Why is this even an issue? Once a message is added to a channel, it stays there until it is either consumed, it expires (see *Message Expiration* [176]), or the system crashes (unless you're using *Guaranteed Delivery* [122]). This is true for a message on a *Point-to-Point Channel* (103), but a *Publish-Subscribe Channel* (106) works somewhat differently.

When a message is published on a *Publish-Subscribe Channel* (106), the messaging system must deliver the message to each subscriber. How it does this is implementation specific: It can keep the message until the list of subscribers that have not received it is empty, or it might duplicate and deliver the message to each subscriber. Whatever the case, which subscribers receive the message is completely dependent upon who is subscribed to the channel when the message is published. If a receiver is not subscribed when the message is published, even if the receiver subscribes an instant later, it will not receive that message. (There is also a timing issue of what happens when a subscriber subscribes and a message is published on the same channel at "about" the same time. Does the subscriber receive the message? How this issue is resolved depends on the messaging system's implementation. To be safe, subscribers should be sure to subscribe before messages of interest are published.)

As a practical matter, a subscriber unsubscribes from a channel by closing its connection to the channel. Thus, no explicit unsubscribe action is necessary; the subscriber just closes its connection.

Often, an application prefers to ignore messages published after it disconnects, because being disconnected means that the application is uninterested in whatever may be published. For example, a B2B/C application selling bricks may subscribe to a channel where buyers can request bricks. If the application stops selling bricks, or is temporarily out of bricks, it may decide to disconnect from the channel to avoid receiving requests it cannot fulfill anyway.

Yet this behavior can be disadvantageous, because the "you snooze, you loose" approach can cause an application to miss messages it needs. If an application crashes or must be stopped for maintenance, it may want to know what messages it missed while it wasn't running. The whole idea of messaging is to make communication reliable even if the sender and receiver applications and network aren't all working at the same time.

So, sometimes applications disconnect because they don't want messages from that channel anymore. But sometimes applications have to disconnect for a short time, and when they reconnect, they want to have access to all of the messages that were published during the connection lapse. A subscriber is normally either connected (subscribed) or disconnected (unsubscribed), but a third possible state is *inactive*, the state of a subscriber that is disconnected but still subscribed because it wants to receive messages published while it is disconnected.

If a subscriber was connected to a *Publish-Subscribe Channel* (106) but is disconnected when a message is published, how does the messaging system know whether or not to save the message for the subscriber so that it can deliver the message when the subscriber reconnects? That is, how does the messaging system know whether a disconnected subscriber is inactive or unsubscribed? There needs to be two kinds of subscriptions, those that end when the subscriber disconnects and those that survive even when the application disconnects and are broken only when the application explicitly unsubscribes.

By default, a subscription lasts only as long as its connection. So, what is needed is another type of subscription that survives disconnects by becoming inactive.

▼

Use a *Durable Subscriber* to make the messaging system save messages published while the subscriber is disconnected.

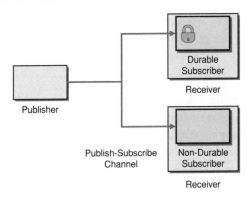

Durable Subscriber

A durable subscription saves messages for an inactive subscriber and delivers these saved messages when the subscriber reconnects. In this way, a subscriber does not lose any messages even though it disconnected. A durable subscription has no effect on the behavior of the subscriber or the messaging system while the subscriber is *active* (e.g., connected). A connected subscriber acts the same whether its subscription is durable or nondurable. The difference is in how the messaging system behaves when the subscriber is disconnected.

A *Durable Subscriber* is simply a subscriber on a *Publish-Subscribe Channel* (106). However, when the subscriber disconnects from the messaging system, it becomes inactive and the messaging system will save any messages published on its channel until it becomes active again. Meanwhile, other subscribers to the same channel may not be durable; they're nondurable subscribers.

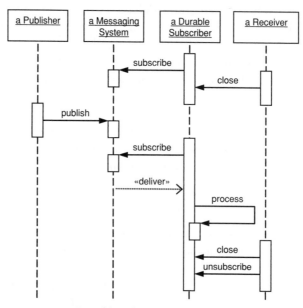

Durable Subscription Sequence

Durable Subscriber

To be a subscriber, the *Durable Subscriber* must establish its subscription to the channel. Once it has, when it closes its connection, it becomes inactive. While the subscriber is inactive, the publisher publishes a message. If the subscriber were nondurable, it would miss this message; but because it is durable, the messaging system saves this message for this subscriber. When the subscriber resubscribes, becoming active once more, the messaging system delivers the queued message (and any others saved for this subscriber). The subscriber receives the message and process it (perhaps delegating the message to the application). Once the subscriber is through processing messages, if it does not wish to receive any more messages, it closes its connection, becoming inactive again. Since it does not want the messaging system to save messages for it anymore, it also unsubscribes.

An interesting consideration is, What would happen if a durable subscriber never unsubscribed? The inactive durable subscription would continue to retain messages—that is, the messaging system would save all of the published messages until the subscriber reconnects. But if the subscriber does not reconnect for a long time, the number of saved messages can become excessive. *Message Expiration* (176) can help alleviate this problem. The messaging system may also wish to limit the number of messages that can be saved for an inactive subscription.

Example: *Stock Trading*

A stock trading system might use a *Publish-Subscribe Channel* (106) to broadcast changes in stocks prices; each time a stocks' price changes, a message is published. One subscriber might be a GUI that displays the current prices for certain stocks. Another subscriber might be a database that stores the day's trading range for certain stocks.

Both applications should be subscribers to the price-change channel so that they're notified when a stock's price changes. The GUI's subscription can be nondurable because it is displaying the current price. If the GUI crashes and loses its connection to the channel, there is no point in saving price changes the GUI cannot display. Conversely, the price range database should use a *Durable Subscriber*. While it is running, it can display the range thus far. If it loses its connection, when it reconnects, it can process the price changes that occurred and update the range as necessary.

Example: *JMS Durable Subscription*

JMS supports durable subscriptions for `TopicSubscribers` [JMS 1.1], [Hapner].

One challenge with durable subscriptions is differentiating between an old subscriber that is reconnecting and a completely new subscriber. In JMS, a durable subscription is identified by three criteria:

1. The topic being subscribed to

2. The connection's client ID

3. The subscriber's subscription name

**Durable
Subscriber**

The connection's client ID is a property of its connection factory, which is set when the connection factory is created using the messaging system's administration tool. The subscription name has to be unique for each subscriber (for a particular topic and client ID).

A *Durable Subscriber* is created using the Session.createDurableSubscriber method:

```
ConnectionFactory factory = // obtain the factory
// the factory has the client ID
Connection connection = factory.createConnection();
// the connection has the same client ID as the factory
Topic topic = // obtain the topic
String clientID = connection.getClientID(); // just in case you're curious
String subscriptionName = "subscriber1"; // some UID for the subscription

Session session =
    connection.createSession(false, Session.AUTO_ACKNOWLEDGE);
TopicSubscriber subscriber =
    session.createDurableSubscriber(topic, subscriptionName);
```

This subscriber is now active. It will receive messages as they are published to the topic (just like a nondurable subscriber). To make it inactive, close it, like this:

```
subscriber.close();
```

The subscriber is now disconnected and therefore inactive. Any messages published to its topic will be saved for this subscriber and delivered when it reconnects.

To make the subscription active again, you must create a new durable subscriber with the same topic, client ID, and subscription name. The code is the same as before, except that the connection factory, topic, and subscription name must be the same as before.

Because the code is the same to establish a durable subscription and to reconnect to it, only the messaging system knows whether this durable subscription had already been established or is a new one. One interesting consequence is that the application reconnecting to a subscription may not be the same application that disconnected earlier. As long as the new application uses the same topic, the same connection factory (and so the same client ID), and the same subscription name as the old application, the messaging system cannot distinguish between the two applications and will deliver all messages to the new application that weren't delivered to the old application before it disconnected.

Once an application has a durable subscription on a topic, it will have the opportunity to receive all messages published to that topic, even if the sub-

Durable Subscriber

scriber closes its connection (or if it crashes and the messaging system closes the subscriber's connection for it). To stop the messaging system from queuing messages for this inactive subscriber, the application must explicitly unsubscribe its durable subscription.

```
subscriber.close();
// subscriber is now inactive, messages will be saved
session.unsubscribe(subscriptionName);
// subscription is removed
```

Once the subscriber is unsubscribed, the subscription is removed from the topic, and messages will no longer be delivered to this subscriber.

Idempotent Receiver

Even when a sender application sends a message only once, the receiver application may receive the message more than once.

▼

How can a message receiver deal with duplicate messages?

▲

The channel patterns in Chapter 3, "Messaging Systems," discuss how to make messaging channels reliable by using *Guaranteed Delivery* (122). However, even some reliable messaging implementations can produce duplicate messages. In other scenarios, *Guaranteed Delivery* (122) may not be available because the communication relies on inherently unreliable protocols. This is the case in many B2B (business-to-business) integration scenarios where messages have to be sent over the Internet using HTTP. In these cases, message delivery can generally only be guaranteed by resending the message until an acknowledgment is returned from the recipient. However, if the acknowledgment is lost due to an unreliable connection, the sender may resend a message that the receiver had already received (see figure).

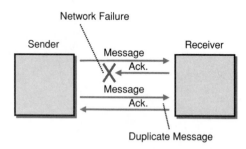

Message Duplication Because of Problem Sending Acknowledgment

Idempotent Receiver

Many messaging systems incorporate built-in mechanisms to eliminate duplicate messages so that the application does not have to worry about duplicates. However, eliminating duplicates inside the messaging infrastructure causes additional overhead. If the receiver is inherently resilient against duplicate messages—for example, a stateless receiver that processes query-style *Command Messages* (145)—messaging throughput can be increased if duplicates are allowed. For this reason, some messaging systems only provide at-least-once delivery and let the application deal with duplicate messages. Others allow the application to specify whether or not it deals with duplicates (for example, the JMS specification defines a DUPS_OK_ACKNOWLEDGE mode).

Another scenario that can produce duplicate messages is a failed distributed transaction. Many packaged applications that are connected to the messaging infrastructure through commercial adapters cannot properly participate in a distributed two-phase commit. When a message is sent to multiple applications and the message causes one or more of these applications to fail, it may be difficult to recover from this inconsistent state. If receivers are designed to ignore duplicate messages, the sender can simply resend the message to all recipients. Those recipients that had already received and processed the original message will simply ignore the resend. Those applications that were not able to properly consume the original message will apply the message that was resent.

▼

Design a receiver to be an *Idempotent Receiver,* one that can safely receive the same message multiple times.

▲

The term *idempotent* is used in mathematics to describe a function that produces the same result if it is applied to itself: $f(x) = f(f(x))$. In *Messaging* (53) this concepts translates into a message that has the same effect whether it is received once or multiple times. This means that a message can safely be resent without causing any problems even if the receiver receives duplicates of the same message.

Idempotency can be achieved through two primary means:

1. Explicit *de-duping*, which is the removal of duplicate messages.

2. Defining the message semantics to support idempotency.

The recipient can explicitly de-dupe messages (let's assume de-dupe is a proper English word) by keeping track of messages that it already received. A unique message identifier simplifies this task and helps detect those cases where two legitimate messages with the same message content arrive. By using a separate field, the message identifier, we do not tie the semantics of a duplicate message to the

Idempotent Receiver

message content. We then assign a unique message identifier to each message. Many messaging systems, such as JMS-compliant messaging tools, automatically assign unique message identifiers to each message without the applications having to worry about them.

In order to detect and eliminate duplicate messages based on the message identifier, the message recipient has to keep a list of already received message identifiers. One of the key design decisions is how long to keep this history of messages and whether to persist the history to permanent storage such as disk. This decision depends primarily on the contract between the sender and the receiver. In the simplest case, the sender sends one message at a time, awaiting the receiver's acknowledgment after every message. In this scenario, it is sufficient for the receiver to compare the message identifier of any incoming message to the identifier of the previous message. It will then ignore the new message if the identifiers are identical. Effectively, the receiver keeps a history of a single message. In practice, this style of communication can be very inefficient, especially if the latency (the time for the message to travel from the sender to the receiver) is significant relative to the desired message throughput. In these situations, the sender may want to send a whole set of messages without awaiting acknowledgment for each one. This implies, though, that the receiver has to keep a longer history of identifiers for already received messages. The size of the receiver's "memory" depends on the number of messages the sender can send without having gotten an acknowledgment from the receiver. This problem resembles the considerations presented in the *Resequencer* (283).

Eliminating duplicate messages is another example where we can learn quite a bit by having a closer look at the low-level TCP/IP protocol. When IP network packets are routed across the network, duplicate packets can be generated. The TCP/IP protocol ensures elimination of duplicate packets by attaching a unique identifier to each packet. Sender and receiver negotiate a "window size" that the recipient allocates in order to detect duplicates. For a thorough discussion of how TCP/IP implements this mechanism, see [Stevens].

In some cases, it may be tempting to use a business key as the message identifier and let the persistence layer handle the de-duping. For example, let's assume that an application persists incoming orders into a database. If each order contains a unique order number, and we configure the database to use a unique key on the order number field, the insert operation into the database would fail if a duplicate order message is received. This solution appears elegant because we delegated the checking of duplicates to the database systems, which is very efficient at detecting duplicate keys. But we have to be cautious because we associated dual semantics to a single field. Specifically, we tied infrastructure-related semantics (a duplicate message) to a business field (order number). Imagine that the business requirements change so that customers can amend existing orders by sending another message with the same order number (this is quite common). We would now have to make changes to our message structure, since we tied the unique message identifier to a business field. Therefore, it is best to avoid overloading a single field with dual semantics.

Using a database to force de-duping is sometimes done with database adapters provided by the messaging infrastructure vendors. In many cases, these adapters are not capable of eliminating duplicates, so this function has to be delegated to the database.

An alternative approach to achieve idempotency is to define the semantics of a message such that resending the message does not impact the system. For example, rather than defining a message as "Add $10 to account 12345," we could change the message to "Set the balance of account 12345 to $110." Both messages achieve the same result if the current account balance is $100. The second message is idempotent because receiving it twice will not have any effect. Admittedly, this example ignores concurrency situations—for example, the case where another message, "Set the balance of account 12345 to $150," arrives between the original and the duplicate message.

Example: *Microsoft IDL (MIDL)*

The Microsoft Interface Definition Language (MIDL) supports the concept of idempotency as part of the remote call semantics. A remote procedure can be declared as idempotent by using the [idempotent] attribute. The MIDL specification states that the "[idempotent] attribute specifies that an operation does not modify state information and returns the same results each time it is performed. Performing the routine more than once has the same effect as performing it once."

```
interface IFoo;
[
    uuid(5767B67C-3F02-40ba-8B85-D8516F20A83B),
    pointer_default(unique)
]

interface IFoo
{
    [idempotent]
    bool GetCustomerName
    (
        [in] int CustomerID,
        [out] char *Name
    );
}
```

Idempotent
Receiver

Service Activator

An application has a service that it would like to make available to other applications.

> How can an application design a service to be invoked both via various messaging technologies and via non-messaging techniques?

An application may not want to choose whether a service (an operation in a *Service Layer* [EAA]) can be invoked synchronously or asynchronously: It may want to support both approaches for the same service. Yet, technologies can seem to force the choice. For example, an application implemented using EJB may need to use a session bean to support synchronous clients but an MDB to support messaging clients.[1]

Developers designing an application to work with other applications, such as a B2B application, may not know what other applications they're communicating with and how the various communications will work. There are too many different messaging technologies and data formats to try to support every one just in case it's needed.[2]

Receiving and processing a message involves a number of steps; separating these steps can be difficult and unnecessarily complex. Yet, *Message Endpoint* (95) code that mixes together these tasks—receiving the message, extracting its contents, and acting on those contents to perform work—can be difficult to reuse.

When designing clients for multiple styles of communication, it may well seem necessary to reimplement the service for each style. This makes supporting each new style cumbersome and creates the risk that each style may not produce quite the same behavior. What is needed is a way for a single service to support multiple styles of communication.

Service Activator

---

1. Thanks to Mark Weitzel for this example.
2. Thanks to Luke Hohmann for this example.

Design a *Service Activator* that connects the messages on the channel to the service being accessed.

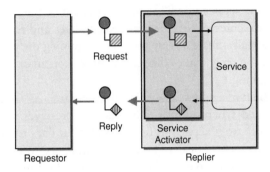

A *Service Activator* can be one-way (request only) or two-way (*Request-Reply* [154]). The service can be as simple as a method call—synchronous and non-remote—perhaps part of a *Service Layer* [EAA]. The activator can be hard-coded to always invoke the same service, or it can use reflection to invoke the service indicated by the message. The activator handles all of the messaging details and invokes the service like any other client, such that the service doesn't even know it's being invoked through messaging.

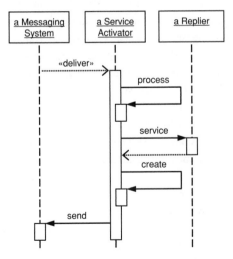

Service Activator Sequence for Request-Reply

The *Service Activator* handles receiving the request message (either as a *Polling Consumer* [494] or as an *Event-Driven Consumer* [498]). It knows the message's format and processes the message to extract the information necessary to know what service to invoke and what parameter values to pass in. The activator then invokes the service just like any other client of the service and blocks while the service executes. When the service completes and returns a value, the activator can optionally create a reply message containing the value and return it to the requestor. (The reply makes the service invocation an example of *Request-Reply* [154] messaging.)

A *Service Activator* enables a service to be written as though it's always going to be invoked synchronously. The activator receives the asynchronous message, determines what service to invoke and what data to pass it, and then invokes the service synchronously. The service is designed to work without messaging, yet the activator enables it to easily be invoked via messaging.

If the *Service Activator* cannot process the message successfully, the message is invalid and should be moved to an *Invalid Message Channel* (115). If the message can be processed and the service is invoked successfully, then any errors that occur as part of executing the service are semantic errors in the application and should be handled by the application.

Developers still may not be able to predict every way partners might wish to access their services, but they do at least know what services their application will provide and can implement those. Then, implementing new activators for different technologies and formats as needed is relatively easy.

This *Service Activator* pattern is also documented in [CoreJ2EE], which is where the pattern was originally named. That version of the pattern is somewhat different from this one—it assumes the activator is an *Event-Driven Consumer* (498) and that the service already exists so that the activator can be added to the service—but both versions propose the same solution to the same problem in a very similar fashion. *Service Activator* is related to the *Half-Sync/Half-Async* pattern [POSA2], which separates service processing into synchronous and asynchronous layers.

A *Service Activator* usually receives *Command Messages* (145), which describe what service to invoke. A *Service Activator* serves as a *Messaging Gateway* (468), separating the messaging details from the service. The activator can be a *Polling Consumer* (494) or an *Event-Driven Consumer* (498). If the service is transactional, the activator should be a *Transactional Client* (484) so that the message consumption can participate in the same transaction as the service invocation. Multiple activators can be *Competing Consumers* (502) or coordinated by a *Message Dispatcher* (508). If a *Service Activator* cannot process a message successfully, it should send the message to an *Invalid Message Channel* (115).

Example: *J2EE Enterprise JavaBeans*

Consider, for example, EJBs [EJB 2.0] in J2EE: Encapsulate the service as a session bean, and then implement MDBs for various messaging scenarios: one for a JMS destination using messages of one format; another for a different destination using another format; another for a Web service/SOAP message; and so on. Each MDB that processes the message by invoking the service is a *Service Activator*. Clients that wish to invoke the service synchronously can access the session bean directly.

Service
Activator

Chapter 11

System Management

Introduction

While developing a messaging solution is no easy task, operating such a solution in production is equally challenging: A message-based integration solution may produce, route, and transform thousands or even millions of messages in a day. We have to deal with exceptions, performance bottlenecks, and changes in the participating systems. To make things ever more challenging, components are distributed across many platforms and machines that can reside at multiple locations.

Besides the inherent complexities and scale of integrating distributed packaged and custom applications, the architectural benefits of loose coupling actually make testing and debugging a system harder. Martin Fowler refers to this as the "architect's dream, developer's nightmare" symptom: Architectural principles of loose coupling and indirection reduce the assumptions systems make about each other and therefore provide flexibility. However, testing a system where a message producer is not aware of who the consumers of a message are can be challenging. Add to that the asynchronous and temporal aspects of messaging and things get even more complicated. For example, the messaging solution may not even be designed for the message producer to receive a reply message from the recipient(s). Likewise, the messaging infrastructure typically guarantees the delivery of the message but not the delivery time. This makes it hard to develop test cases that rely on the results of the message delivery.

When monitoring a message solution, we can track the flow of messages at two different levels of abstraction. A typical *system management* solution monitors how many messages are being sent or how long it took a message to be processed. These monitoring solutions do not inspect the message data except maybe for some fields in the message header such as the message identifier or the *Message History* (551). In contrast, *business activity monitoring* (BAM) solutions focus on the payload data contained in the message, for example, the

537

dollar value of all orders placed in the last hour. Many of the patterns presented in this section are general enough that they can be used for either purpose. However, because BAM is a whole new field in itself and shares many complexities with data warehousing (something we have not touched on at all), we decided to discuss the patterns in the context of system management.

System management patterns are designed to address these requirements and provide the tools to keep a complex message-based system running. The patterns in this chapter fall into three categories: monitoring and controlling, observing and analyzing message traffic, and testing and debugging.

Monitoring and Controlling

A *Control Bus* (540) provides a single point of control to manage and monitor a distributed solution. It connects multiple components to a central management console that can display the status of each component and monitor message traffic through the components. The console can also be used to send control commands to components, for instance, to change the message flow.

We may want to route messages through additional steps, such as validation or logging. Because these steps can introduce performance overheads, we may want to be able to switch them on and off via the control bus. A *Detour* (545) gives us this ability.

Observing and Analyzing Message Traffic

Sometimes, we want to inspect the contents of a message without affecting the primary message flow. A *Wire Tap* (547) allows us to tap into message traffic.

When we debug a message-based system, it is a great aid to know where a specific message has been. The *Message History* (551) keeps a log of all components the message has visited without introducing dependencies between components.

While the *Message History* (551) is tied to an individual message, a central *Message Store* (555) can provide a complete account of every message that traveled through the system. Combined with the *Message History* (551), the *Message Store* (555) can analyze all possible paths messages can take through the system.

The *Wire Tap* (547), *Message History* (551), and *Message Store* (555) help us analyze the asynchronous flow of a message. In order to track messages sent to request-reply services, we need to insert a *Smart Proxy* (558) into the message stream.

Testing and Debugging

Testing a messaging system before deploying it into production is a very good idea. But testing should not stop there. You should be actively verifying that the running messaging system continues to function properly. You can do this by periodically injecting a *Test Message* (66) into the system and verifying the results.

When a component fails or misbehaves, it is easy to end up with unwanted messages on a channel. During testing it is very useful to remove all remaining messages from a channel so that the components under test do not receive "leftover" messages. A *Channel Purger* (572) does that for us.

Introduction

Control Bus

Naturally, enterprise integration systems are distributed. In fact, one of the defining qualities of an enterprise messaging system is to enable communication between disparate systems. Messaging systems allow information to be routed and transformed so that data can be exchanged between these systems. In most cases, these applications are spread across multiple networks, buildings, cities, or continents.

> How can we effectively administer a messaging system that is distributed across multiple platforms and a wide geographic area?

A distributed, loosely coupled architecture allows for flexibility and scalability. At the same time, it poses serious challenges for administration and control of such a system. For example, how can you tell whether all components are up and running? A simple process status won't suffice, because processes are distributed across many machines. Also, if you cannot obtain status from a remote machine, does it mean that the remote machine is not functioning, or might the communication with the remote machine be disturbed?

Besides just knowing whether a system or a component is up and running, you also need to monitor the dynamic behavior of the system. What is the message throughput? Are there any unusual delays? Are channels filling up? Some of this information requires tracking of message travel times between components or through components. This requires the collection and combination of information from more than one machine.

Also, just reading information from components may not be sufficient. Often, you need to make adjustments or change configuration settings while the system is running. For example, you may need to turn logging features on or off while the system is running. Many applications use property files and error logs to read configuration information and report error conditions. This approach tends to work well as long as the application consists of a single machine or possibly a small number of machines. In a large, distributed solution, property files would have to be copied to remote machines using some file transfer mechanism, which requires the file system on every machine to be accessible remotely. This can pose security risks and can be challenging if the machines are connected over the Internet or a wide-area network that may not support file mapping protocols. Also, the versions of the local property files would have to be managed carefully—a management nightmare waiting to happen.

It seems natural to try to leverage the messaging infrastructure to perform some of these tasks. For example, we could send a message to a component to change its configuration. This control message could be transported and routed just like a regular message. This would solve most of the communication problems but also poses new challenges. Configuration messages should be subject to stricter security policies than are regular application messages. For example, one wrongly formatted control message could easily bring a component down. Also, what if messages are queued up on a message channel because a component is malfunctioning? If we send a control message to reset the component, this control message would get queued up with all the other messages and not reach the component in distress. Some messaging systems support message priorities that can help move control messages to the front of the queue. However, not all systems provide this ability, and the priority may not help if a queue is filled to the limit and refuses to accept another message. Likewise, some control messages are of a lower priority than application messages. If we have components publish periodic status messages, delaying or losing an "I am alive" control message may be a lot less troublesome than delaying or losing the "Order for $1 million" message.

Use a *Control Bus* to manage an enterprise integration system. The *Control Bus* uses the same messaging mechanism used by the application data but uses separate channels to transmit data that is relevant to the management of components involved in the message flow.

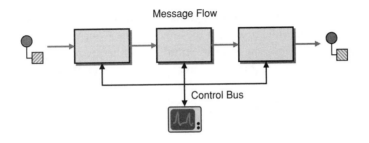

Control Bus

Each component in the system is now connected to two messaging subsystems:

1. The Application Message Flow
2. The *Control Bus*

The application message flow transports all application-related messages. The components subscribe and publish to these channels just as they would in an unmanaged scenario. In addition, each component also sends and receives messages from the channels that make up the *Control Bus*. These channels connect to a central management component.

The *Control Bus* is well suited to carry the following types of messages:

1. **Configuration**—Each component involved in the message flow should have configurable parameters that can be changed as required. These parameters include channel addresses, message data formats, timeouts, and so on. Components use the *Control Bus* rather than property files to retrieve this information from a central repository, allowing a central point of configuration and the reconfiguration of the integration solution at runtime. For example, the routing table inside a *Content-Based Router* (230) may need to be updated dynamically based on system conditions, such as overload or component failure.

2. **Heartbeat**—Each component may send a periodic *heartbeat* message on the *Control Bus* at specified intervals so that a central console application can verify that the component is functioning properly. This heartbeat may also include metrics about the component, such as number of messages processed and the amount of available memory on the machine.

3. **Test Messages**—Heartbeat messages tell the *Control Bus* that a component is still alive, but they may provide limited information on ability of the component to correctly process messages. In addition to having components publish periodic heartbeat messages to the *Control Bus,* we can inject test messages into the message stream that will be processed by the components. We extract the message later to see whether the component processed the message correctly. As this approach blurs the definition of the *Control Bus* and the application message flow, we defined a separate pattern for it (see *Test Message* [569]).

4. **Exceptions**—Each component can channel exception conditions to the *Control Bus* to be evaluated. Severe exceptions may cause an operator to be

**Control
Bus**

alerted. The rules to define exception handling should be specified in a central handler.

5. **Statistics**—Each component can collect statistics about the number of messages processed, average throughput, average time to process a message, and so on. Some of this data may be split out by message type, so we can determine whether messages of a certain type are flooding the system. Since this message tends to be lower priority than other messages, it is likely that the *Control Bus* uses nonguaranteed or lower-priority channels for this type of data.

6. **Live Console**—Most of the functions mentioned here can be aggregated for display in a central console. From here, operators can assess the health of the messaging system and take corrective action if needed.

Many of the functions that a *Control Bus* supports resemble traditional network management functions that are used to monitor and maintain any networked solution. A *Control Bus* allows us to implement equivalent management functions at the messaging system level—essentially elevating them from the low-level IP network level to the richer messaging level. Providing management functionality is as vital to the successful operation of a messaging infrastructure as it is for a network infrastructure. Unfortunately, the absence of management standards for messaging solutions makes it difficult to build enterprisewide, reusable management solutions for messaging systems.

When we design message processing components, we architect the core processor around three interfaces (see figure). The inbound data interface receives incoming messages from the message channel. The outbound data interface sends processed messages to the outbound channel. The control interface sends and receives control messages from and to the *Control Bus*.

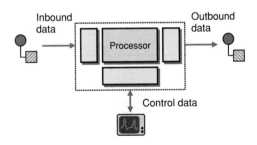

Key Interfaces of a Messaging Component

Example: *Instrumenting the Loan Broker Example*

In Chapter 12, "Interlude: Systems Management Example," we show how to use a *Control Bus* to instrument the loan broker example from Chapter 9, "Interlude: Composed Messaging." The instrumentation includes a simple management console that displays the status of components in real time (see "Loan Broker System Management" in Chapter 12).

Control
Bus

Detour

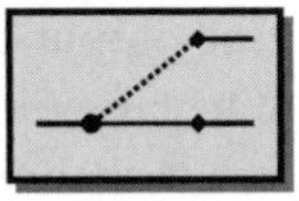

Sometimes we want to modify the route that messages take based on external factors.

How can you route a message through intermediate steps to perform validation, testing, or debugging functions?

Performing validations on messages that travel between components can be a very useful debugging tool. However, these extra steps may not always be required and would slow down the system if they are always executed.

Being able to include or skip these steps based on a central setting can be a very effective debugging or performance tuning tool. For example, while we test a system, we may want to pass messages through additional validation steps. Bypassing these steps during production may improve performance. We can compare these validations to assert statements in source code that are executed in the debug configuration but not in the release configuration of the executable.

Likewise, during troubleshooting, it may be useful to route messages through additional steps for logging or monitoring purposes. Being able to turn these logging steps on and off allows us to maximize message throughput under normal circumstances.

Construct a *Detour* with a Context-Based Router controlled via the Control Bus. In one state, the router routes incoming messages through additional steps, while in the other it routes messages directly to the destination channel.

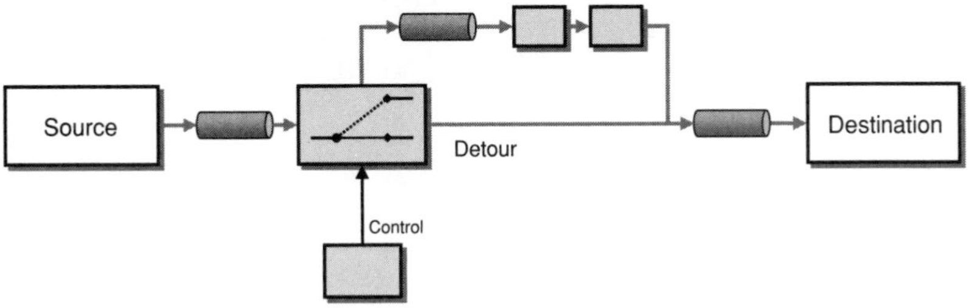

The *Detour* uses a simple context-based router with two output channels. One output channel passes the unmodified message to the original destination. When instructed by the *Control Bus* (540), the *Detour* routes messages to a different channel. This channel sends the message to additional components that can inspect and/or modify the message. Ultimately, these components route the message to the same destination.

If the detour route contains only a single component, it may be more efficient to combine the *Detour* switch and the component into a single filter. However, this solution assumes that the component in the detour path can be modified to include the bypass logic controlled via the *Control Bus* (540).

The strength of controlling the *Detour* over the *Control Bus* (540) is that multiple *Detour*s can be activated or deactivated simultaneously with a single command on the *Control Bus* (540) using a *Publish-Subscribe Channel* (106) from the control console to all *Detour*s.

Detour

Wire Tap

*Point-to-Point Channel*s (103) are often used for *Document Message*s (147) because they ensure that exactly one consumer will consume each message. However, for testing, monitoring, or troubleshooting, it may be useful to be able to inspect all messages that travel across the channel.

▼
How do you inspect messages that travel on a Point-to-Point Channel?
▲

It can be very useful to see which messages traverse a channel—for example, for simple debugging purposes or to store messages in a *Message Store* (555). You can't just add another listener to the *Point-to-Point Channel* (103), because it would consume messages off the channel and prevent the intended recipient from being able to consume the message.

Alternatively, you could make the sender or the receiver responsible to publish the message to a separate channel for inspection. However, this would force us to modify a potentially large set of components. Additionally, if we are dealing with packaged applications, we may not even be able to modify the application.

You could also consider changing the channel to a *Publish-Subscribe Channel* (106). This would allow additional listeners to inspect messages without disturbing the flow of messages. However, a *Publish-Subscribe Channel* (106) changes the semantics of the channel. For example, multiple *Competing Consumers* (502) may be consuming messages off the channel, relying on the fact that only one consumer can receive a specific message. Changing the channel to a *Publish-Subscribe Channel* (106) would cause each consumer to receive each message. This could be very undesirable, for example, if the incoming messages represent orders that now get processed multiple times. Even if only a single consumer listens on the channel, using a *Publish-Subscribe Channel* (106) may be less efficient or less reliable than using a *Point-to-Point Channel* (103).

Many messaging systems provide a peek method that allows a component to inspect messages inside a *Point-to-Point Channel* (103) without consuming the message. This approach has one important limitation though: Once the intended consumer consumes the message, the peek method can no longer see the message. Therefore, this approach does not allow us to analyze messages after they have been consumed.

You could insert a component into the channel (a form of "interceptor') that performs any necessary inspection. The component would consume a message off the incoming channel, inspect the message, and pass the unmodified message to the output channel. However, the type of inspection frequently depends on messages from more than one channel (e.g., to measure message runtime), so this function cannot be implemented by a single filter inside a single channel.

Insert a *Wire Tap* into the channel, a simple Recipient List that publishes each incoming message to the main channel as well as to a secondary channel.

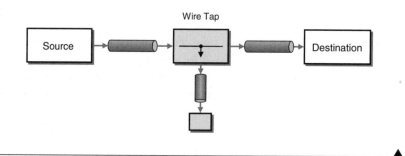

The *Wire Tap* (also known as *tee*) is a fixed *Recipient List* (249) with two output channels. It consumes messages off the input channel and publishes the unmodified message to both output channels. To insert the *Wire Tap* into a channel, you need to create an additional channel and change the destination receiver to consume the second channel. Because the analysis is performed by a separate component, we can insert a generic *Wire Tap* into any channel without any danger of unintentionally modifying the primary channel behavior. This improves reuse and reduces the risk of undesirable side effects when instrumenting an existing solution.

It might be useful to make the *Wire Tap* programmable over the *Control Bus* (540) so that the secondary channel (the "tap") can be turned on or off. This way, the *Wire Tap* can be instructed to publish messages to the secondary channel only during testing or debugging cycles.

The main disadvantage of the *Wire Tap* is the additional latency incurred by consuming and republishing a message. Many integration tool suites automatically decode a message even if it is published to another channel without modification. Also, the new message will receive a new message ID and new timestamps that are different from the original message. These operations can add up to additional overhead and cause existing mechanisms to break. For example, if the original message flow uses the message ID of the original message as a *Correlation Identifier* (163), the solution will break because the message ID of the republished message is different from the message ID of the original message. This is one of the reasons that it is generally not a good idea to use the message ID as a *Correlation Identifier* (163).

Because the *Wire Tap* publishes two separate messages, it is important not to correlate between these messages by their message ID. Even though the primary and the secondary channel receive identical messages, most messaging systems automatically assign a new message ID to each message in the system. This means that the original message and the "duplicate" message have different message IDs.

An existing *Message Broker* (322) can easily be augmented to act as a *Wire Tap* because all messages already pass through this central component.

An important limitation of the *Wire Tap* is that it cannot alter the messages flowing across the channel. If you need to be able to manipulate messages, use a *Detour* (545) instead.

Example: *Loan Broker*

In Chapter 12, "Interlude: Systems Management Example," we enhance the loan broker example to include a *Wire Tap* on the request channel to the credit bureau to keep a log of all requests made to this external service (see "Loan Broker System Management" in Chapter 12).

Example: *Using Multiple Wire Taps to Measure Message Runtime*

One of the strengths of the *Wire Tap* is that we can combine multiple *Wire Tap*s to send copies of messages to a central component for analysis. That component can be a *Message Store* (555) or another component that analyzes relationships between messages, such as the time interval between two related messages (see

Wire Tap

figure). When analyzing the message runtime, we should base the computation on the time when the secondary messages were sent so that the computation is not skewed by the travel time of the secondary messages.

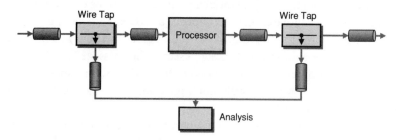

Using a Pair of Wire Taps to Analyze Message Runtime

Message History

One of key benefits of a message-based system is the loose coupling between participants; the message sender and recipient make no (or few) assumptions about each other's identity. If a message recipient retrieves a message from a message channel, it generally does not know nor care which application put the message on the channel. The message is by definition self-contained and is not associated with a specific sender. This is one of the architectural strengths of message-based systems.

However, the same property can make debugging and analyzing dependencies very difficult. If we are not sure where a message goes, how can we assess the impact of a change in the message format? Likewise, if we don't know which application published a particular message, it is difficult to correct a problem with the message.

How can we effectively analyze and debug the flow of messages in a loosely coupled system?

The *Control Bus* (540) monitors the state of each component that processes messages, but it does not concern itself with the route that an individual message takes. You could modify each component to publish the unique message identifier of each message that passes through it to the *Control Bus* (540). This information can then be collected in a common database, a *Message Store* (555). This approach requires a significant amount of infrastructure, including a separate datastore. Also, if a component needs to examine the history of a message, it would have to execute a query against a central database, running the risk of turning the database into a bottleneck.

Tracking the flow of a message through a system is not as simple as it appears. It would seem natural to use the unique message ID associated with each message. However, when a component (e.g., a *Message Router* [78]) processes a message and publishes it to the output channel, the resulting message will receive a new message identifier that is not associated with the message that the component consumed. Therefore, we would need to identify a new key that is copied from the incoming message to the outgoing message so that the two

Message
History

messages can be associated later. This can work reasonably well if the component publishes exactly one message for every message it consumes. However, this is not the case for many components, such as a *Recipient List* (249), an *Aggregator* (268), or a *Process Manager* (312), which typically publish multiple messages in response to a single input message.

Instead of identifying the path of each message by tagging the messages, the message itself could collect a list of components that it traversed. If each component in the messaging system carries a unique identifier, each component could add its identifier to each message it publishes.

Attach a *Message History* to the message. The *Message History* is a list of all applications or components that the message passed through since its origination.

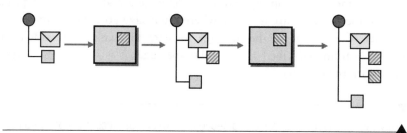

The *Message History* maintains a list of all components that the message passed through. Every component that processes the message (including the originator) adds one entry to the list. The *Message History* should be part of the message header because it contains system-specific control information. Keeping this information in the header separates it from the message body that contains application-specific data.

Not every message that a component publishes is the result of a single message. For example, an *Aggregator* (268) publishes a single message that carries information collected from multiple messages, each of which could have its own history. If we want to represent this scenario in the *Message History*, we have two choices. If we want to track the complete history, we can enhance the *Message History* to be stored as a hierarchical tree structure. Because of the recursive nature of a tree structure, we can store multiple message histories under a single node. Alternatively, we can keep a simple list and keep the history of only one incoming message. This approach can work well if one incoming message is more important to the result than other, auxiliary messages. For example, in an auction scenario we could choose to propagate only the history of the "winning" message.

Message History

The *Message History* is most useful if a series of messages flows through a number of different filters that together perform a specific business function or process. If it is important to manage the path that a message takes, a *Process Manager* (312) can be useful. The *Process Manager* (312) creates one process instance for each incoming trigger message. The flow of the message through various components is now managed centrally, alleviating the need to tag each message with its history.

Example: *Avoiding Infinite Loops*

Equipping a message with its history has another important benefit when using *Publish-Subscribe Channel*s (106) to propagate events. Assume we implement a system that propagates address changes to multiple systems via *Publish-Subscribe Channel*s (106). Each address change is broadcast to all interested systems so that they may update their records. This approach is very flexible toward the addition of new systems—the new system will automatically receive the broadcast message without requiring any changes to the existing messaging system. Assume the customer care system is one of the systems that stores addresses in the application database. Each change to the database fields causes a message to be triggered to notify all systems of the change. By nature of the publish-subscribe paradigm, all systems subscribing to the address-changed channel will receive the event. However, the customer care system itself has to subscribe to this channel as well in order to receive updates made in other systems, for example through a self-service Web site. This means that the customer care system will receive the message that it just published. This received message would result in a database update, which will in turn trigger another address-changed message. We could end up in an infinite loop of address-changed messages. To avoid such an infinite loop, the subscribing applications can inspect the *Message History* to determine whether the message originated from the very same system and ignore the incoming message if this is the case.

Example: *TIBCO ActiveEnterprise*

Many EAI integration suites include support for a *Message History*. For example, the message header of every TIBCO ActiveEnterprise message includes a tracking field that maintains a list of all components through which the message has passed. In this context it is important to note that a TIBCO ActiveEnterprise component assigns outgoing messages the same message ID as the consumed message. This makes tracking messages through multiple components easier, but

Message
History

it also means that the message ID is not a systemwide unique property, because multiple individual messages share the same ID. For example, when implementing a *Recipient List* (249), TIBCO ActiveEnterprise transfers the ID of the consumed message to each outbound message.

The following example shows the contents of a message that passed through multiple components, including two IntegrationManager processes, named OrderProcess and VerifyCustomerStub.

```
tw.training.customer.verify.response
{
  RVMSG_INT      2   ^pfmt^       10
  RVMSG_INT      2   ^ver^        30
  RVMSG_INT      2   ^type^       1
  RVMSG_RVMSG  108   ^data^
  {
    RVMSG_STRING  23   ^class^      "VerifyCustomerResponse"
    RVMSG_INT      4   ^idx^        1
    RVMSG_STRING   6   CUSTOMER_ID  "12345"
    RVMSG_STRING   6   ORDER_ID     "22222"
    RVMSG_INT      4   RESULT       0
  }
  RVMSG_RVMSG  150   ^tracking^
  {
    RVMSG_STRING  28   ^id^    "4OEaDEoiBIpcYk6qihzzwB5Uzzw"
    RVMSG_STRING  41   ^1^     "imed_debug_engine1-OrderProcess-Job-4300"
    RVMSG_STRING  47   ^2^     "imed_debug_engine1-VerifyCustomerStub-Job-4301"
  }
}
```

**Message
History**

Message Store

As the *Message History* (551) describes, the architectural principle of loose coupling allows for flexibility in the solution but can make it difficult to gain insight into the dynamic behavior of the integration solution.

How can we report against message information without disturbing the loosely coupled and transient nature of a messaging system?

The very properties that make messaging powerful can also make it difficult to manage. Asynchronous messaging guarantees delivery but does not guarantee when the message will be delivered. For many practical applications, though, the response time of a system may be critical. Also, while asynchronous messaging treats each message individually, information that spans multiple messages—for example, the number of messages passing through the system within a certain time interval—can be very useful.

The *Message History* (551) pattern illustrates the usefulness of being able to tell the "source" of a message. From this data, we can derive interesting message throughput and runtime statistics. The only downside is that the information is contained within each individual message. There is no easy way to report against this information, since it is spread across many messages. Also, the lifetime of a message can be very short. Once the message is consumed, the *Message History* (551) may no longer be available.

In order to perform meaningful reporting, we need to store message data persistently and in a central location.

Message Store

Use a *Message Store* to capture information about each message in a central location.

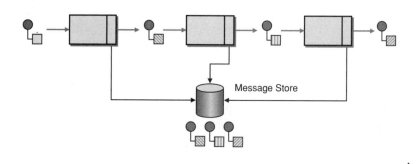

Message Store

When using a *Message Store*, we can take advantage of the asynchronous nature of a messaging infrastructure. When we send a message to a channel, we send a duplicate of the message to a special channel to be collected by the *Message Store*. This can be performed by the component itself, or we can insert a *Wire Tap* (547) into the channel. We can consider the secondary channel that carries a copy of the message as part of the *Control Bus* (540). Sending a second message in a "fire-and-forget" mode will not slow down the flow of the main application messages. It does, however, increase network traffic. That's why we may not store the complete message but just a few key fields that are required for later analysis, such as a message ID or the channel on which the message was sent combined with a timestamp.

How much detail to store is actually an important consideration. Obviously, the more data we have about each message, the better reporting abilities we have. The counterforces are network traffic and storage capacity of the *Message Store*. Even if we store all message data, our reporting abilities may still be limited. Messages typically share the same message header structure, but the message body is structured differently for each type of message and can be difficult to access by outside applications (for example, the message body might contain a serialized Java object). This can make it difficult to report against the data elements contained in the message body.

Since the data inside the message body can be formatted differently for each type of message, we need to consider different storage options. If we create a separate storage schema (e.g., tables) to match each message type's internal data structure, we can apply indexes and perform complex searches on the message content. However, this assumes that we have a separate storage structure for each message type. This could quickly turn into a maintenance burden. Instead, we could store the message data as unstructured data in XML format in a long character field. This allows us to use a generic storage schema. We could still query against header fields but would not be able to report against fields in the message body. However, once we identified a specific message, we could recreate the message content based on the XML document stored in the *Message Store*. Alternatively, we could use an XML repository to store the messages. These types of repositories index XML documents for later retrieval and analysis.

The *Message Store* may get very large, so most likely we will need to introduce a purging mechanism. This mechanism could move older message logs to a backup database or delete them altogether.

Example: *Commercial EAI Tools*

Some enterprise integration tools supply a *Message Store*. For example, MSMQ allows queues to automatically store sent or received messages in a *Journal Queue*. Microsoft BizTalk optionally stores all documents (messages) in a SQL Server database for later analysis.

Message
Store

Smart Proxy

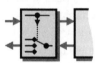

A pair of *Wire Tap*s (547) can be used to track messages that flow through a component, but this approach assumes that the component publishes messages to a fixed output channel. However, many service-style components publish reply messages to the channel specified by the *Return Address* (159) included in the request message.

How can you track messages on a service that publishes reply messages to the Return Address specified by the requestor?

In order to track messages flowing through a service, we need to capture both request and reply messages. Intercepting a request message using a *Wire Tap* (547) is easy enough. Intercepting reply messages is the tough part because the service publishes the reply message to different channels based on the requestor's preferred *Return Address* (159).

The support of a *Return Address* (159) is required for most *Request-Reply* (154) services so that a requestor can specify the channel that the reply message should be sent to. Changing the service to post reply messages to a fixed channel would make it hard for each requestor to extract the correct reply messages. Some messaging systems allow consumers to peek for specific messages inside a single reply queue, but that approach is implementation-specific and does not work in those instances where the reply message does not go back to the requestor but to a third party.

As discussed in the *Wire Tap* (547), modifying the component to inspect messages is not always feasible or practical. If we are dealing with a packaged application, we may not be able to modify the application code and may have to implement a solution that is external to the application. Likewise, we may not want to require each application to implement message inspection logic, especially because the nature of the logic may vary depending on whether we operate in test mode or production mode. Keeping the inspection functions in a separate, self-contained component improves flexibility, reuse, and testability.

Smart
Proxy

Use a *Smart Proxy* to store the Return Address supplied by the original requestor and replace it with the address of the *Smart Proxy.* When the service sends the reply message, route it to the original Return Address.

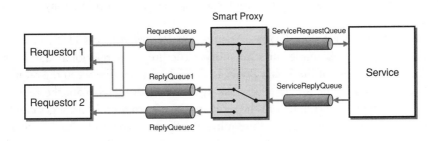

The *Smart Proxy* intercepts messages sent on the request channel to the *Request-Reply* (154) service. For each incoming message, the *Smart Proxy* stores the *Return Address* (159) specified by the original sender. It then replaces the *Return Address* (159) in the message with the reply channel that the *Smart Proxy* is listening on. When a reply message comes in on that channel, the *Smart Proxy* performs any desired analytical functions, retrieves the stored *Return Address* (159), and forwards the unmodified reply message to the original reply channel by using a *Message Router* (78).

The *Smart Proxy* is also useful in cases where an external service does not support a *Return Address* (159) but instead replies to a fixed reply channel. We can proxy such a service with a *Smart Proxy* to provide support for a *Return Address* (159). In this case, the *Smart Proxy* performs no analytical functions but simply forwards the reply message to the correct channel.

The *Smart Proxy* needs to store the *Return Address* (159) supplied by the original requestor in such a way that it can correlate incoming reply messages with the *Return Address* (159) and forward the reply message to the correct channel. The *Smart Proxy* can store this data in two places:

1. Inside the message

2. Inside the *Smart Proxy*

To store the *Return Address* (159) inside the message, the *Smart Proxy* can add a new message field together with the *Return Address* (159) to the message.

Smart
Proxy

The *Request-Reply* (154) service is required to copy this field to the reply message. All the *Smart Proxy* has to do is extract the special message field from the reply message, remove the field from the message, and forward the message to the channel specified by the field. This solution keeps the *Smart Proxy* simple, but it requires collaboration by the *Request-Reply* (154) service. If the *Request-Reply* (154) service is a nonmodifiable component, this option may not be available.

Alternatively, the *Smart Proxy* can store the *Return Address* (159) in dedicated storage, for example, in a memory structure or a relational database. Because the purpose of the *Smart Proxy* is to track messages between the request and reply message, the *Smart Proxy* usually has to store data from the request message anyway to correlate it to the reply message so that both messages can be analyzed in unison. This approach requires the *Smart Proxy* to be able to correlate the reply message back to the response message. Most *Request-Reply* (154) services support a *Correlation Identifier* (163) that the service copies from the request message to the reply message. If the *Smart Proxy* cannot modify the original message format, it can use (or abuse) this field to correlate request and reply messages.

However, it is better for the *Smart Proxy* to construct its own *Correlation Identifier* (163), because not all requestors will specify a *Correlation Identifier* (163) and also because the supplied *Correlation Identifier* (163) only needs to be unique only across requests made by a single requestor and may not be unique across multiple requestors. Because the single service reply queue from the service to the *Smart Proxy* now carries messages from multiple requestors, using the original *Correlation Identifier* (163) is not reliable. Therefore, the *Smart Proxy* stores the original *Correlation Identifier* (163) together with the original *Return Address* (159) and replaces the original *Correlation Identifier* (163) with its own *Correlation Identifier* (163) so that it can retrieve the original *Correlation Identifier* (163) and *Return Address* (159) when the reply message arrives.

Some services use the message ID of the request message as the *Correlation Identifier* (163) for the reply message. This introduces another problem. The service will now copy the message ID of the request message it received from the *Smart Proxy* to the reply message to the *Smart Proxy*. The *Smart Proxy* needs to replace this *Correlation Identifier* (163) in the reply message with the message ID of the original request message so that the requestor can properly correlate request and reply messages. The figure on the following page illustrates this process.

It is important to note that all four messages have unique message IDs even though they relate to the flow of a single "logical" message.

Smart
Proxy

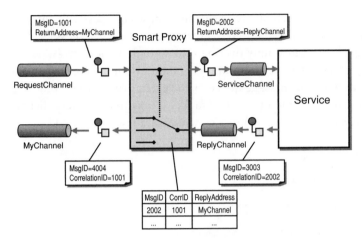

Storing and Replacing the Correlation Identifier and Return Address

Example: *Simple Smart Proxy in MSMQ and* C#

Implementing a *Smart Proxy* is not as complicated as it sounds. The following code implements a solution scenario consisting of two requestors, a *Smart Proxy* and a simple service. The *Smart Proxy* passes the message processing time to the control bus for display in the console. We want to allow the requestors to correlate by either the message ID or the numeric AppSpecific property provided by the Message object.

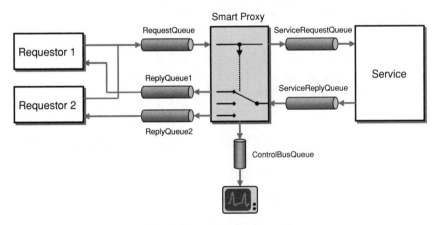

Simple Smart Proxy Example

For our coding convenience, we define a base class MessageConsumer that encapsulates the code that is required to create an event-driven message consumer. Inheriting classes can simply overload the virtual method ProcessMessage to perform any necessary message handling, and they do not have to worry about the configuration of the message queue or the event-driven processing. Separating this code into a common base class makes it easy to create test clients and a dummy *Request-Reply* (154) service with just a few lines of code.

MessageConsumer

```
public class MessageConsumer
{
    protected MessageQueue inputQueue;

    public MessageConsumer (MessageQueue inputQueue)
    {
        this.inputQueue = inputQueue;
        SetupQueue(this.inputQueue);
        Console.WriteLine(this.GetType().Name +  ": Processing messages from " +
                        inputQueue.Path);
    }

    protected void SetupQueue(MessageQueue queue)
    {
        queue.Formatter = new System.Messaging.XmlMessageFormatter
                        (new String[] {"System.String,mscorlib"});
        queue.MessageReadPropertyFilter.ClearAll();
        queue.MessageReadPropertyFilter.AppSpecific = true;
        queue.MessageReadPropertyFilter.Body = true;
        queue.MessageReadPropertyFilter.CorrelationId = true;
        queue.MessageReadPropertyFilter.Id = true;
        queue.MessageReadPropertyFilter.ResponseQueue = true;
    }

    public virtual void Process()
    {
        inputQueue.ReceiveCompleted +=
            new ReceiveCompletedEventHandler(OnReceiveCompleted);
        inputQueue.BeginReceive();
    }

    private void OnReceiveCompleted(Object source, ReceiveCompletedEventArgs asyncResult)
    {
        MessageQueue mq = (MessageQueue)source;

        Message m = mq.EndReceive(asyncResult.AsyncResult);
        m.Formatter =  new System.Messaging.XmlMessageFormatter
                        (new String[] {"System.String,mscorlib"});

        ProcessMessage(m);
```

Smart
Proxy

```
            mq.BeginReceive();
    }

    protected virtual void ProcessMessage(Message m)
    {
        String text = "";
        try
        {
            text = (String)m.Body;
        }
        catch (InvalidOperationException) {};
        Console.WriteLine(this.GetType().Name + ": Received Message " + text);
    }
}
```

With the MessageConsumer class as a starting point, we can create a *Smart Proxy*. A *Smart Proxy* contains two MessageConsumers, one for the request messages coming from the requestors (SmartProxyRequestConsumer) and one for the reply messages returned by the *Request-Reply* (154) service (SmartProxyReplyConsumer). The *Smart Proxy* also defines a Hashtable to store message data between request and reply messages.

SmartProxy

```
public class SmartProxyBase
{
    protected SmartProxyRequestConsumer requestConsumer;
    protected SmartProxyReplyConsumer replyConsumer;

    protected Hashtable messageData;

    public SmartProxyBase(MessageQueue inputQueue,
                          MessageQueue serviceRequestQueue,
                          MessageQueue serviceReplyQueue)
    {
        messageData = Hashtable.Synchronized(new Hashtable());
        requestConsumer = new SmartProxyRequestConsumer(inputQueue, serviceRequestQueue,
                                                        serviceReplyQueue, messageData);
        replyConsumer = new SmartProxyReplyConsumer(serviceReplyQueue, messageData);
    }

    public virtual void Process()
    {
        requestConsumer.Process();
        replyConsumer.Process();
    }
}
```

Smart
Proxy

The SmartProxyRequestConsumer is relatively simple. It stores relevant information from the request message (message ID, the *Return Address* [159], the AppSpecific property, and the current time) in the hashtable, indexed by the message ID of the new request message sent to the actual service. The request-reply service supports the *Correlation Identifier* (163) by copying this message ID to the CorrelationID field of the service reply message. This allows the *Smart Proxy* to retrieve the stored message data when the reply message arrives. The SmartProxyRequestConsumer also replaces the *Return Address* (159)—the ResponseQueue property—with the queue that the *Smart Proxy* listens on for reply messages. We included a virtual method AnalyzeMessage in this class so that subclasses can perform any desired analysis.

SmartProxyRequestConsumer

```
public class SmartProxyRequestConsumer : MessageConsumer
{
    protected Hashtable messageData;
    protected MessageQueue serviceRequestQueue;
    protected MessageQueue serviceReplyQueue;

    public SmartProxyRequestConsumer(MessageQueue requestQueue,
                                     MessageQueue serviceRequestQueue,
                                     MessageQueue serviceReplyQueue,
                                     Hashtable messageData) : base(requestQueue)
    {
        this.messageData = messageData;
        this.serviceRequestQueue = serviceRequestQueue;
        this.serviceReplyQueue = serviceReplyQueue;
    }

    protected override void ProcessMessage(Message requestMsg)
    {
        base.ProcessMessage(requestMsg);

        MessageData data = new MessageData(requestMsg.Id, requestMsg.ResponseQueue,
                                           requestMsg.AppSpecific);
        requestMsg.ResponseQueue = serviceReplyQueue;
        serviceRequestQueue.Send(requestMsg);
        messageData.Add(requestMsg.Id, data);
        AnalyzeMessage(requestMsg);
    }

    protected virtual void AnalyzeMessage(Message requestMsg)
    {
    }
}
```

Smart Proxy

The SmartProxyReplyConsumer listens on the service reply channel. The ProcessMessage method of this class retrieves the message data for the associated request message stored by the SmartProxyRequestConsumer and calls the AnalyzeMessage template method. It then copies the CorrelationID and the AppSpecific properties to the new reply message and routes it to the *Return Address* (159) specified in the original request message.

SmartProxyReplyConsumer

```
public class SmartProxyReplyConsumer : MessageConsumer
{
    protected Hashtable messageData;

    public SmartProxyReplyConsumer(MessageQueue replyQueue,
                                Hashtable messageData) : base(replyQueue)
    {
        this.messageData = messageData;
    }

    protected override void ProcessMessage(Message replyMsg)
    {
        base.ProcessMessage(replyMsg);

        String corr = replyMsg.CorrelationId;
        if (messageData.Contains(corr))
        {
            MessageData data = (MessageData)(messageData[corr]);

            AnalyzeMessage(data, replyMsg);

            replyMsg.CorrelationId = data.CorrelationID;
            replyMsg.AppSpecific = data.AppSpecific;

            MessageQueue outputQueue = data.ReturnAddress;
            outputQueue.Send(replyMsg);
            messageData.Remove(corr);
        }
        else
        {
            Console.WriteLine(this.GetType().Name + "Unrecognized Reply Message");
            //send message to invalid message queue
        }
    }

    protected virtual void AnalyzeMessage(MessageData data, Message replyMessage)
    {
    }
}
```

In order to collect metrics and send them to the control bus, we subclass both the generic SmartProxy and SmartProxyReplyConsumer classes. The new Metrics-SmartProxy instantiates the SmartProxyReplyConsumerMetrics as the class consuming

Smart
Proxy

reply messages. This class includes a simple implementation of the AnalyzeMessage method that computes the message runtime between request and response and sends this data together with the number of outstanding messages to the *Control Bus* (540) queue. We could easily enhance this method to perform more complex computations. The *Control Bus* (540) queue is connected to a simple file writer that writes each incoming message to a file.

MetricsSmartProxy

```
public class MetricsSmartProxy : SmartProxyBase
{
    public MetricsSmartProxy(MessageQueue inputQueue,
                             MessageQueue serviceRequestQueue,
                             MessageQueue serviceReplyQueue,
                             MessageQueue controlBus) :
                    base (inputQueue, serviceRequestQueue, serviceReplyQueue)
    {
        replyConsumer = new SmartProxyReplyConsumerMetrics
                            (serviceReplyQueue, messageData, controlBus);
    }
}
```

SmartProxyReplyConsumerMetrics

```
public class SmartProxyReplyConsumerMetrics : SmartProxyReplyConsumer
{
    MessageQueue controlBus;

    public SmartProxyReplyConsumerMetrics(MessageQueue replyQueue,
                                          Hashtable messageData,
                                          MessageQueue controlBus) :
                                base(replyQueue, messageData)
    {
        this.controlBus = controlBus;
    }

    protected override void AnalyzeMessage(MessageData data, Message replyMessage)
    {
        TimeSpan duration = DateTime.Now - data.SentTime;
        Console.WriteLine(" processing time: {0:f}", duration.TotalSeconds);
        if (controlBus != null)
        {
            controlBus.Send(duration.TotalSeconds.ToString() + "," + messageData.Count);
        }
    }
}
```

Smart Proxy

The following class diagram shows the relationship between the individual classes:

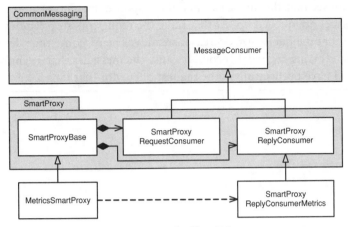

Smart Proxy Example Class Diagram

To test the proxy, we created a dummy request-reply service that does nothing but wait for a random interval between 0 and 200 ms. We feed the *Smart Proxy* from two requestors, each of which publishes 30 messages in 100 ms intervals. We capture the messages on the *Control Bus* (540) queue into a log file. For demonstration purposes, we loaded the resulting control bus file into a Microsoft Excel spreadsheet and created a nice looking chart.

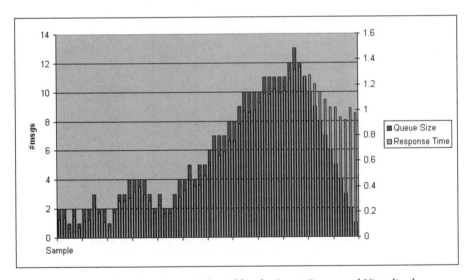

Response Time Statistics Collected by the Smart Proxy and Visualized by the Control Bus Console

We can see that the queue size and the response time increase steadily until 13 messages are queued up. At that time, the requestors stop sending new messages so that the queue size decreases steadily. The response time decreases as well, but remains around 1 second because the messages that are now being processed have been sitting in the request queue for that long.

Smart
Proxy

Test Message

The *Control Bus* (540) describes a number of approaches to monitor the health of the message processing system. Each component in the system can publish periodic heartbeat messages to the *Control Bus* (540) in order to keep the monitoring mechanism informed that the component is still active. The heartbeat messages can contain vital statistics of the component as well, such as the number of messages processed, the average time required to process a message, or the percentage of CPU utilization on the machine.

▼

What happens if a component is actively processing messages but garbles outgoing messages due to an internal fault?

▲

A simple heartbeat mechanism will not detect this error condition because it operates only at a component level and is not aware of application message formats.

▼

Inject a *Test Message* into the message stream to confirm the health of message processing components.

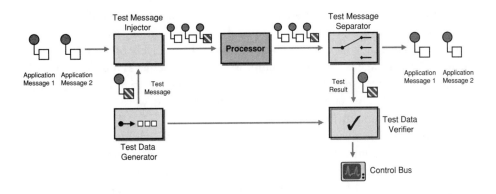

▲

The *Test Message* pattern relies on the following components:

1. The **Test Data Generator** creates messages to be sent to the component for testing. Test data may be constant, driven by a test data file, or generated randomly.

2. The **Test Message Injector** inserts test data into the regular stream of data messages sent to the component. The main role of the injector is to tag messages in order to differentiate real application messages from test messages. This can be accomplished by inserting a special header field. If we have no control over the message structure, we can try to use special values to indicate test messages (e.g., OrderID = 999999). This changes the semantics of application data by using the same field to represent application data (the actual order number) and control information (this is a test message). Therefore, this approach should be used only as a last resort.

3. The **Test Message Separator** extracts the results of test messages from the output stream. This can usually be accomplished by using a *Content-Based Router* (230).

4. The **Test Data Verifier** compares actual results with expected results and flags an exception if a discrepancy is discovered. Depending on the nature of the test data, the verifier may need access to the original test data.

An explicit Test Message Separator may not be needed if the component under test supports a *Return Address* (159). In this case, the test Data Generator can include a special test channel as the *Return Address* (159) so that test messages are not passed through the remainder of the system. Effectively, the *Return Address* (159) acts as the tag that distinguishes test messages from application messages.

Test Message is considered an *active monitoring* mechanism. Unlike passive mechanisms, active mechanisms do not rely on information generated by the components (e.g., log files or heartbeat messages) but actively probe the component. The advantage is that active monitoring usually achieves a deeper level of testing, since data is routed through the same processing steps as the application messages. It also works well with components that were not designed to support passive monitoring.

One possible disadvantage of active monitoring is the additional load placed on the processing unit. We need to find a balance between frequency of test and minimizing the performance impact. Active monitoring may also incur cost if we are being charged for the use of a component on a pay-per-use basis. This is

Test
Message

the case for many external components—for example, if we request credit reports for our customers from an external credit scoring agency.

Active monitoring does not work with all components. Stateful components may not be able to distinguish test data from real data and may create database entries for test data. We may not want to have test orders included in our annual revenue report!

Example: *Loan Broker: Testing the Credit Bureau*

In Chapter 12, "Interlude: Systems Management Example," we use a *Test Message* to actively monitor the external credit bureau.

Test
Message

Channel Purger

When we worked on the JMS request-reply example (see Chapter 6, "Interlude: Simple Messaging"), we ran into a simple but interesting problem. The example consists of a requestor that sends a message to a replier and waits for the response. The example uses two *Point-to-Point Channels* (103), RequestQueue and ReplyQueue (see figure).

We started the replier first, then the requestor. Then, a very odd thing happened. The requestor console window claimed to have gotten a response before the replier ever acknowledged receiving a request. A delay in the console output? Lacking any great ideas, we decided to shut the replier down, and we reran the requestor. Oddly enough, we still received a response to our request! Magic? No, just a side effect of persistent messaging. A superfluous message was present on the ReplyQueue, most likely caused by an earlier failure. Every time we started the requestor, it placed a new message on the RequestQueue and then immediately retrieved the extraneous reply message that was sitting on the ReplyQueue. We never noticed that this message was not the reply to the request the requestor had just made! Once the replier received the new request message, it placed a new reply message on the ReplyQueue so that the "magic" repeated during the next test. It can be amazing (or amazingly frustrating) how persistent, asynchronous messaging can play tricks on you in even the most simple scenarios!

▼

Channel Purger

How can you keep leftover messages on a channel from disturbing tests or running systems?

▲

*Message Channel*s (60) are designed to deliver messages reliably even if the receiving component is unavailable. In order to do so, the channel has to persist messages along the way. This useful feature can cause confusing situations during testing or if one of the components misbehaves (and does not use transactional message consumption and production). We can quickly end up with extraneous messages stuck on channels, as previously described. These messages make it impossible to pass test data into the system until the pending messages have been consumed. If the pending messages are orders worth a few million dollars, this is a good thing. If we are testing or debugging a system and have a channel full of query messages or reply messages, it can cause us a fair amount of headache.

In our simple example, some of our debugging pain could have been eased if we had used a *Correlation Identifier* (163). Using the identifier, the requestor would have recognized that the incoming message is actually not the response to the request it just sent. It could then discard the old reply message or route it to an *Invalid Message Channel* (115), which would effectively remove the "stuck" message. In other scenarios, it is not as easy to detect duplicate or unwanted messages. For example, if a specific message is malformed and causes the message recipient to fail, the recipient cannot restart until the bad message is removed, because it would just fail right away again. Of course, this example requires the defect in the recipient to be corrected (no malformed message should cause a component failure), but removing the message can get the system up and running quickly until the defect is corrected.

Another way to avoid leftover messages in channels is to use temporary channels (e.g., JMS provides the method `createTemporaryQueue` for this purpose). These channels are intended for request-reply applications and lose all messages once the application closes its connection to the messaging system. But again, this approach is limited to a simple request-reply example and does not protect against other messages being left over on other channels that need to be persistent.

It may be tempting to assume that transaction management can eliminate the extra message scenario because message consumption, message processing, and message publication are covered in a single transaction. So, if a component aborts in the middle of processing a message, the message would not be considered consumed. Likewise, a reply message would not be published until the component signals the final commit to send the message. We need to keep in mind, though, that transactions do not protect us against programming errors. In our simple request-reply example, a programmer error may have caused the requestor to not read a response from the `ReplyQueue` channel. As a result, despite

Channel Purger

potential transactionality, a message is stuck on that channel, causing the symptoms described earlier.

Use a *Channel Purger* to remove unwanted messages from a channel.

Message   Channel Purger

A basic *Channel Purger* simply removes all the messages from a channel. This may be sufficient for test scenarios where we want to reset the system into a consistent state. If we are debugging a production system, we may need to remove an individual message or a set of messages based on specific criteria, such as the message ID or the values of specific message fields.

In many cases, it is all right for the *Channel Purger* to simply delete the message from the channel and discard it. In other cases, we may need the *Channel Purger* to store the removed messages for later inspection or replay. This is useful if the messages on a channel cause a system to malfunction, so we need to remove them to continue operation. However, once the problems are corrected, we want to re-inject the message(s) so that the system does not lose the contents of the message. This may also include the requirement to edit message contents before re-injecting the message. This type of function combines some of the features of a *Message Store* (555) and a *Channel Purger*.

Example: *Channel Purger in JMS*

This example shows a simple *Channel Purger* implemented in Java. This example simply removes all messages on a channel. The ChannelPurger class references two external classes whose source code is not shown here:

1. JMSEndpoint—A base class to be used for any JMS participant. It provides pre-initialized instance variables for a Connection and Session instance.

2. JNDIUtil—Implements helper functions to encapsulate the lookup of JMS objects via JNDI.

```
import javax.jms.JMSException;
import javax.jms.MessageConsumer;
import javax.jms.Queue;

public class ChannelPurger extends JmsEndpoint
{

    public static void main(String[] args)
    {

        if (args.length != 1) {
            System.out.println("Usage: java ChannelPurger <queue_name>");
            System.exit(1);
        }
        String queueName = new String(args[0]);
        System.out.println("Purging queue " + queueName);

        ChannelPurger purger = new ChannelPurger();

        purger.purgeQueue(queueName);

    }

    private void purgeQueue(String queueName)
    {
        try {
            initialize();
            connection.start();
            Queue queue = (Queue) JndiUtil.getDestination(queueName);

            MessageConsumer consumer = session.createConsumer(queue);

            while (consumer.receiveNoWait() != null)
                System.out.print(".");
            connection.stop();
        } catch (Exception e) {
            System.out.println("Exception occurred: " + e.toString());
        } finally {
            if (connection != null) {
                try {
                    connection.close();
                } catch (JMSException e) {
                    // ignore
                }
            }
        }
    }
}
```

Channel
Purger

Chapter 12

Interlude: System Management Example

Loan Broker System Management

This chapter uses a more elaborate example to demonstrate how the system management patterns introduced in the previous chapter can be used to monitor and control a messaging solution. The example builds upon the C# and MSMQ implementation of the loan broker example from Chapter 9, "Interlude: Composed Messaging" (see "Asynchronous Implementation with MSMQ"). We augment rather than modify the original example solution, so it is not critical that you reviewed all the code of the original example. As with the original implementation, the intent of this example is not to explain the use of MSMQ-specific APIs but rather to illustrate the implementation of the patterns in this book using a queue-oriented messaging system. The structure of the solution would look very similar when implemented in Java using JMS queues or IBM WebSphere MQ. Because we focus mostly on the design decisions and trade-offs, this chapter should be valuable to you even if you are not a C# or MSMQ developer.

577

Instrumenting the Loan Broker

The loan broker implementation consists of the following four key components (see figure):

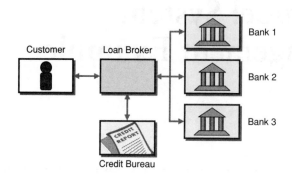

- The customer (or *test client*) makes requests for loan quotes.

- The *loan broker* acts as the central process manager and coordinates the communication between the credit bureau and the banks.

- The *credit bureau* provides a service to the loan broker, computing customers' credit scores.

- Each *bank* receives a quote request from the loan broker and submits an interest rate quote according to the loan parameters.

In most integration scenarios, we do not have access to the application internals but are limited to monitoring and managing components from the outside. To make this example as realistic as possible, we treat each of the existing components as a black box. Keeping this constraint in mind, we want the management solution to meet the following requirements:

- **Management Console:** We want a single front end that displays the health of all components and allows us to take compensating actions if something goes wrong.

- **Loan Broker Quality of Service:** In the original solution, we developed a test client that monitors the loan broker's response times between quote request and response. In a real production scenario, customers will not perform this function for us (they may, however, complain that the system is too slow). Therefore, we want the management solution to capture this information and relay it to the management console.

- **Verify the Credit Bureau Operation:** The credit bureau is an external service provided by a third party. We want to ensure the correct operation of this service by periodically sending test messages.

- **Credit Bureau Failover:** If the credit bureau malfunctions, we want to temporarily redirect the credit request messages to another service provider.

Management Console

To assess the health of the overall solution, we need to be able to collect metrics from multiple components to a single point, the management console. This console also has to be able to control message flow and component parameters so that we can address outages by rerouting messages or changing component behavior.

The management console communicates with the individual components via messaging. It uses a separate *Control Bus* (540) that only contains messages related to system management and not to application data.

Because this is a book on enterprise integration and not on user interface design, we keep the management console very, very simple. Many vendors offer real-time data displays, or you can even achieve visual miracles with Visual Basic and Microsoft Office components such as Excel. Also, many operating systems and programming platforms, offer their own instrumentation frameworks, such as Java/JMX (Java Management Extensions) or Microsoft's WMI (Windows Management Instrumentation). We hand-roll our solution to make it less dependent on a specific vendor's API and to demonstrate the inner workings of a monitoring solution. We will build up this console as we implement the specific management functions.

Loan Broker Quality of Service

The first requirement for the management solution is to measure the quality of service that the loan broker provides to its clients. For this type of monitoring, we are not interested in the business content of the individual messages—that is, the interest rate offered to the client—but only in the time elapsed between the request message and the reply message. The tricky part in tracking the time between these two messages is that the client can specify the channel for the reply message via a *Return Address* (159), so we cannot listen on a fixed channel for the reply. Luckily, the *Smart Proxy* (558) pattern solves this dilemma for us.

A *Smart Proxy* (558) intercepts a request message, stores the *Return Address* (159) supplied by the client, and replaces it with a fixed reply channel address. As a result, the service (the loan broker in our case) sends all reply messages to one channel. The *Smart Proxy* (558) listens to this channel and correlates incoming reply messages to stored request messages. It then forwards the reply message to the original *Return Address* (159) specified by the client (see figure).

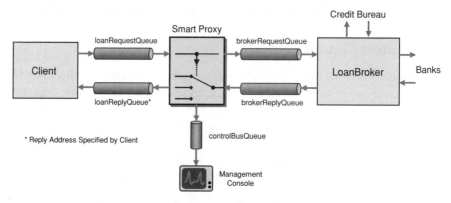

Instrumenting the Loan Broker with a Smart Proxy

In order to take advantage of the *Smart Proxy* (558) functionality, we "insert" the *Smart Proxy* (558) between the client and the loan broker (see figure above). This insertion is transparent to the client because the *Smart Proxy* (558) listens on the same channel that the loan broker originally listened on (loanRequestQueue). We now start the loan broker with new parameters so that it listens on the brokerRequestQueue instead of the loanRequestQueue channel. The *Smart Proxy* (558) instructs the loan broker to send all reply messages to the brokerReplyQueue channel from where it forwards the messages back to the correct *Return Address* (159) originally specified by the client.

We want to use the *Smart Proxy* (558) to measure both the response time for loan requests and the number of requests being processed by the loan broker at any one time. The *Smart Proxy* (558) can measure the time elapsed between request and reply messages by capturing the time that the request message was received. When it receives the associated reply message, the *Smart Proxy* (558) subtracts the request time from the current time to compute the time elapsed between request and reply. The *Smart Proxy* (558) can estimate how many active requests the loan broker is managing at one time by counting how many outstanding request messages there are (i.e., request messages that have not yet received reply messages). The *Smart Proxy* (558) cannot distinguish between messages queued up on the brokerRequestQueue and messages that the loan broker started processing, so this metric equals the sum of both. We can update the number of outstanding request messages whenever we receive a request message or a reply message.

The *Smart Proxy* (558) passes the metrics information to the management console for monitoring and analysis via the controlBusQueue channel. We could send the statistics for every single message, but that would clutter our network if we deal with high message volumes. Inserting a *Smart Proxy* (558) into the message flow already doubles the number of messages sent (two request and reply messages instead of one each), so we want to avoid sending another control message for each request message. Instead, we use a timer so that the *Smart Proxy* (558) sends a metrics message to the *Control Bus* (540) in predefined intervals, for example, every 5 seconds. The metrics message can contain either summary metrics (e.g., the maximum, minimum, and average response time) or the detailed information for all messages that passed through during the interval. In order to keep the metrics messages small and the management console simple, we decide to just pass the summary metrics to the console.

For the implementation of the loan broker *Smart Proxy* (558), we reuse the SmartProxy base classes introduced in the *Smart Proxy* (558) pattern. We subclass the SmartProxyBase, SmartProxyRequestConsumer, and SmartProxyReplyConsumer classes (see class diagram). Please refer to the *Smart Proxy* (558) pattern for the source code for these classes.

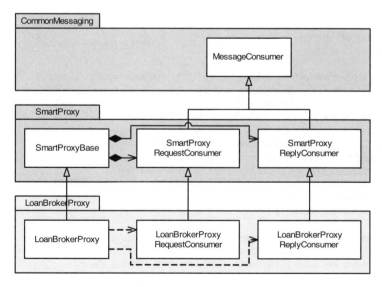

Loan Broker Smart Proxy Class Diagram

Just like the original SmartProxy, the new LoanBrokerProxy contains two separate message consumers, one for incoming request messages from the client (LoanBrokerProxyRequestConsumer) and one for incoming reply messages from the loan broker (LoanBrokerProxyReplyConsumer). Both consumer classes inherit from their respective base classes (SmartProxyRequestConsumer and SmartProxyReplyConsumer) and add a new implementation of the AnalyzeMessage method.

Let's have a look at the implementation of the LoanBrokerProxy class. The constructor takes the same parameters as the SmartProxyBase base class, plus a reference to a *Control Bus* (540) queue and the reporting interval in seconds.

The class maintains two ArrayLists with metrics, performanceStats, and queueStats. performanceStats collects data points of response-reply time intervals in seconds, while queueStats collects data points of the number of outstanding request messages (those either queued up in the brokerRequestQueue or in process by the loan broker). When the preprogrammed timer triggers, the method OnTimerEvent takes a snapshot of the data in both collections. We have to perform any further analysis of the data with this snapshot copy because the message consumers continue to add new data points as messages are received.

LoanBrokerProxy Class

```
public class LoanBrokerProxy : SmartProxyBase
{
    protected MessageQueue controlBus;

    protected ArrayList performanceStats;
    protected ArrayList queueStats;

    protected int interval;
    protected Timer timer;

    public LoanBrokerProxy(MessageQueue inputQueue, MessageQueue serviceRequestQueue,
                           MessageQueue serviceReplyQueue, MessageQueue controlBus,
                           int interval) :
        base (inputQueue, serviceRequestQueue, serviceReplyQueue)
    {
        messageData = Hashtable.Synchronized(new Hashtable());
        queueStats = ArrayList.Synchronized(new ArrayList());
        performanceStats = ArrayList.Synchronized(new ArrayList());

        this.controlBus = controlBus;
        this.interval = interval;

        requestConsumer = new LoanBrokerProxyRequestConsumer(inputQueue,
            serviceRequestQueue, serviceReplyQueue, messageData, queueStats);
        replyConsumer = new LoanBrokerProxyReplyConsumer(serviceReplyQueue,
            messageData, queueStats, performanceStats);
    }
```

```
public override void Process()
{
    base.Process();

    TimerCallback timerDelegate = new TimerCallback(OnTimerEvent);
    timer = new Timer(timerDelegate, null, interval*1000, interval*1000);
}

protected void OnTimerEvent(Object state)
{
    ArrayList currentQueueStats;
    ArrayList currentPerformanceStats;

    lock (queueStats)
    {
        currentQueueStats = (ArrayList)(queueStats.Clone());
        queueStats.Clear();
    }

    lock (performanceStats)
    {
        currentPerformanceStats = (ArrayList)(performanceStats.Clone());
        performanceStats.Clear();
    }

    SummaryStats summary = new SummaryStats(currentQueueStats,
                                            currentPerformanceStats);
    if (controlBus != null)
        controlBus.Send(summary);
    }
}
```

The LoanBrokerProxy uses the SummaryStats structure to condense the individual data points into maximum, minimum, and average values and then sends the summary data to the *Control Bus* (540). We could make the evaluation more efficient by updating the summary statistics with each incoming message so that we have to store only the summary data and not each data point. However, deferring the computation allows us to change the amount of detail we want to publish to the *Control Bus* (540).

The LoanBrokerProxyRequestConsumer class handles incoming request messages. The base class SmartProxyRequestConsumer takes care of storing relevant message data in the messageData hash table. Likewise, the base implementation of the Smart-ProxyReplyConsumer removes data from that hash table whenever it receives a reply message. As a result, we can derive the current number of outstanding request messages from the size of the messageData hash table. The LoanBrokerProxyRequest-Consumer maintains a reference to the queueStats collection stored inside the Loan-BrokerProxy so that it can add the new data point to this collection.

LoanBrokerProxyRequestConsumer Class

```
public class LoanBrokerProxyRequestConsumer : SmartProxyRequestConsumer
{
    ArrayList queueStats;

    public LoanBrokerProxyRequestConsumer(MessageQueue requestQueue,
                                          MessageQueue serviceRequestQueue,
                                          MessageQueue serviceReplyQueue,
                                          Hashtable messageData,
                                          ArrayList queueStats) :
        base(requestQueue, serviceRequestQueue, serviceReplyQueue, messageData)
    {
        this.queueStats = queueStats;
    }

    protected override void ProcessMessage(Message requestMsg)
    {
        base.ProcessMessage(requestMsg);
        queueStats.Add(messageData.Count);
    }
}
```

The LoanBrokerProxyReplyConsumer collects the two required metrics when a reply message arrives. First, it computes the time it took between sending the request message and receiving the reply message and adds that metric to the performanceStats collection. Second, it captures the remaining number of outstanding requests (again using the size of the messageData hash table) and adds that number to the queueStats collection.

LoanBrokerProxyReplyConsumer Class

```
public class LoanBrokerProxyReplyConsumer : SmartProxyReplyConsumer
{
    ArrayList queueStats;
    ArrayList performanceStats;

    public LoanBrokerProxyReplyConsumer(MessageQueue replyQueue,
                                        Hashtable messageData,
                                        ArrayList queueStats,
                                        ArrayList performanceStats) :
            base(replyQueue, messageData)
    {
        this.queueStats = queueStats;
        this.performanceStats = performanceStats;
    }
```

```
protected override void AnalyzeMessage(MessageData data, Message replyMessage)
{
    TimeSpan duration = DateTime.Now - data.SentTime;
    performanceStats.Add(duration.TotalSeconds);

    queueStats.Add(messageData.Count);
}
}
```

The SummaryStats structure computes maximum, minimum, and average values based on the captured data. It can derive the number of request messages processed by subtracting the number of performance data points (collected only for reply messages) from the number of queue size data points (collected for request and reply messages). The implementation of this structure is quite trivial, so we decided not to fill a whole page with the code.

Once we insert the new loan broker proxy into the message stream, we can start collecting performance metrics. To collect some example data, we configured two test clients to make 50 loan quote requests each. The proxy collected the following results (we used a simple XSL transform to render an HTML table off the metric data published in XML format to the controlBusQueue):

Time Stamp	Number of Requests	Number of Replies	Minimum Processing Time	Average Processing Time	Maximum Processing Time	Minimum Queue Size	Average Queue Size	Maximum Queue Size
14:11:02.96 44424	0	0	0.00	0.00	0.00	0	0	0
14:11:07.97 18424	89	7	0.78	2.54	3.93	1	42	82
14:11:12.97 92424	11	9	4.31	6.43	8.69	83	87	91
14:11:17.98 66424	0	8	9.39	10.83	12.82	77	80	84
14:11:22.99 40424	0	8	13.80	15.75	17.48	69	72	76
14:11:28.00 14424	0	7	18.37	20.19	22.18	62	65	68
14:11:33.00 88424	0	6	22.90	24.83	26.94	56	58	61
14:11:38.01 62424	0	10	27.74	29.53	31.62	46	50	55
14:11:43.02 36424	0	9	31.87	34.47	36.30	37	41	45

Table continued on next page

Time Stamp	Number of Requests	Number of Replies	Minimum Processing Time	Average Processing Time	Maximum Processing Time	Minimum Queue Size	Average Queue Size	Maximum Queue Size
14:11:48.03 10424	0	7	36.87	39.06	40.98	30	33	36
14:11:53.03 84424	0	9	41.75	43.82	45.14	21	25	29
14:11:58.04 58424	0	8	45.92	47.67	49.67	13	16	20
14:12:03.05 32424	0	8	50.86	52.58	54.59	5	8	12
14:12:08.06 06424	0	4	55.41	55.96	56.69	1	2	4
14:12:13.06 80424	0	0	0.00	0.00	0.00	0	0	0

Loaded into an Excel chart, the queue size data looks like this:

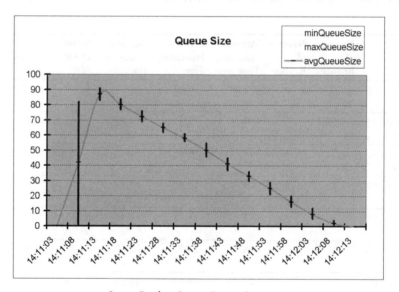

Loan Broker Smart Proxy Statistics

We can see that the two test clients pretty much flooded the loan broker, peaking at about 90 pending requests. The loan broker then processes the requests at a stable rate of about 2 request messages per second. Due to the large number of queued-up requests, the response times are pretty poor, peaking at almost 1 minute. The good news is that the loan broker handles a large number of sudden requests gracefully, while the bad news is that the response times are very long. In order to improve response times, we could execute multiple loan broker instances or multiple credit bureau instances (the credit bureau service turned out to be a bottleneck in the original implementation described in Chapter 9, "Interlude: Composed Messaging").

Verify the Credit Bureau Operation

The second requirement for the management solution is to monitor the correct operation of the external credit bureau service. The loan broker accesses this service to obtain credit scores for customers requesting a loan quote because the banks require this information to provide an accurate quote.

In order to verify the correct operation of the external credit bureau service, we decide to send periodic *Test Messages* (569) to the service. Because the credit bureau service supports a *Return Address* (159), it is easy to inject a *Test Message* (569) without disturbing the existing message flow. We simply provide a dedicated reply channel for test messages which avoids the need for a separate test message separator (see figure).

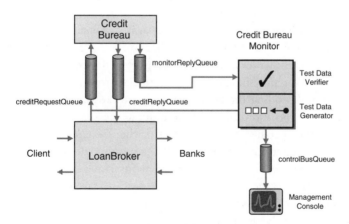

Monitoring the Credit Bureau Service

In order to verify the correct operation of the credit bureau service, we need a *test data generator* and a *test data verifier*. The test data generator creates test data to be sent to the service under test. A credit bureau test message is very simple; the only field that is required is a social security number (SSN). For our tests we use a special, fixed SSN that identifies a fictitious person. This allows us to verify the result data by comparing it to preestablished results. This way we can not only check whether we receive a reply message but also verify that the content of the message is correct. In our simple example introduced in Chapter 9, "Interlude: Composed Messaging," the credit bureau service is programmed to return random results regardless of the incoming SSN. As a result, our test data verifier does not check for specific result values but instead verifies whether the results are within the allowed range (e.g., 300 to 900 for a credit score). If the results fall outside the allowed range (for example, because a computational error set the score to zero), the test data verifier notifies the management console with a message.

The test data verifier also checks the response time of the external service. If we do not receive a reply message within a preset time interval, we also alert the management console. To minimize network bandwidth, the test data verifier notifies the console only if the response is delayed or malformed, not when the service is operating correctly. The only exception to this rule occurs when the monitor receives a correct reply message from the service subsequent to detecting an error. In that case, the monitor sends a "service OK" message to the management console to indicate that the credit bureau is working correctly again. Finally, during startup, the monitor sends a message to the console to announce its existence. This message allows the console to "discover" all active monitors so it can display the status for each.

The monitor implementation uses two separate timers: one to send *Test Messages* (569) in specified intervals and another to flag an exception if a response does not arrive within the specified timeout period (see diagram). The Send Timer determines the time interval between the last received message or the last timeout event and sending the next *Test Message* (569). The Timeout Timer is started whenever the monitor sends a request message. If a reply message arrives within the specified timeout interval, the Timeout Timer is reset and restarted with the next request message. If the monitor does not receive a reply message within the specified interval, the Timeout Timer triggers and the monitor sends an error message to the control bus. It then starts a new Send Timer to initiate a new request message after the send interval. A real-life scenario is likely to use a relatively short timeout (a few seconds) and a longer send interval (e.g., one minute).

The following figure illustrates the dependencies between the two timers. In this scenario, the monitor sends a *Test Message* (569) and starts the Timeout Timer. A response message arrives before the timer elapses, so the monitor cancels the Timeout Timer and starts the Interval Timer. When the Interval Timer elapses, the monitor sends a new *Test Message* (569) and starts a new Timeout Timer. This time, the Timeout Timer expires before the reply message arrives, causing the monitor to send a message to the *Control Bus* (540). At the same time, the monitor starts a new Interval Timer.

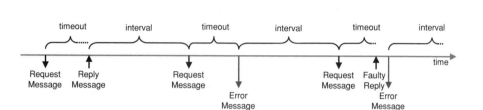

Monitoring the Credit Bureau Service

The implementation of the monitor requires only a single class. The `Monitor` class inherits from the `MessageConsumer` introduced in the *Smart Proxy* (558) pattern. This class configures an inbound channel and starts an *Event-Driven Consumer* (498) to receive messages. For each incoming message, it invokes the virtual `ProcessMessage` method. An inheriting class can simply override this method to add its own processing.

The `Process` method instructs a `MessageConsumer` to start consuming messages. The `Monitor` class augments the base implementation of this method by starting the Send Timer. When this timer triggers, it invokes the `OnSendTimerEvent` method. The `Process` method also sends a message of type `MonitorStatus` to the *Control Bus* (540) to announce its existence.

Monitor Class: Sending Messages

```
public override void Process()
{
    base.Process();
    sendTimer = new Timer(new TimerCallback
                     (OnSendTimerEvent), null, interval*1000, Timeout.Infinite);

    MonitorStatus status = new MonitorStatus(
             MonitorStatus.STATUS_ANNOUNCE, "Monitor On-Line", null, MonitorID);
    Console.WriteLine(status.Description);
    controlQueue.Send(status);
    lastStatus = status.Status;
}

protected void OnSendTimerEvent(Object state)
{
    CreditBureauRequest request = new CreditBureauRequest();
    request.SSN = SSN;
```

```
Message requestMessage = new Message(request);
requestMessage.Priority = MessagePriority.AboveNormal;
requestMessage.ResponseQueue = inputQueue;

Console.WriteLine(DateTime.Now.ToString() + " Sending request message");
requestQueue.Send(requestMessage);

correlationID = requestMessage.Id;

timeoutTimer = new Timer(new TimerCallback(OnTimeoutEvent), null,
                         timeout*1000, Timeout.Infinite);
}
```

The `OnSendTimerEvent` method creates a new request message. The only parameter in the request message is the customer's SSN. The method specifies a fixed SSN. The method also saves the message ID to verify the *Correlation Identifier* (163) of any incoming reply messages. Lastly, it starts the `timeoutTimer` so that the monitor is being notified after a set time interval if no reply message is received.

The method sets the test message's `Priority` property to `AboveNormal` to make sure that queued-up application messages do not let the service appear as if it is not available. Using a higher priority for *Test Messages* (569) causes the message queue to deliver these messages ahead of queued-up application messages. Setting a higher message priority is safe in this case because the test data generator injects a very small volume of *Test Messages* (569). If we injected a large volume of high-priority messages into the request channel, we could interrupt the flow of application messages. This would definitely violate the intention of a management solution to be as minimally intrusive as possible.

The `ProcessMessage` method is the heart of the `Monitor` class. It implements the test message verifier, evaluating incoming reply messages. After stopping the timeout timer, the method checks the incoming message for the correct *Correlation Identifier* (163), correct datatype of the message body, and reasonable values inside the message body. If any of these tests fail, the method sets up a `MonitorStatus` structure and sends it to the *Control Bus* (540) channel. The monitor also tracks the previous status that is stored in the `lastStatus` variable. If the status changes from "error" to "OK," the `ProcessMessage` method also sends a notification to the *Control Bus* (540).

Monitor Class: Receiving Messages

```
protected override void ProcessMessage(Message msg)
{
    Console.WriteLine(DateTime.Now.ToString() + " Received reply message");

    if (timeoutTimer != null)
        timeoutTimer.Dispose();
```

```
msg.Formatter = new XmlMessageFormatter(new Type[] {typeof(CreditBureauReply)});
CreditBureauReply replyStruct;
MonitorStatus status = new MonitorStatus();

status.Status = MonitorStatus.STATUS_OK;
status.Description = "No Error";
status.ID = MonitorID;

try
{
    if (msg.Body is CreditBureauReply)
    {
        replyStruct = (CreditBureauReply)msg.Body;
        if (msg.CorrelationId != correlationID)
        {
            status.Status = MonitorStatus.STATUS_FAILED_CORRELATION;
            status.Description =
                "Incoming message correlation ID does not match outgoing message ID";
        }
        else
        {
            if (replyStruct.CreditScore < 300 || replyStruct.CreditScore > 900 ||
                replyStruct.HistoryLength < 1 || replyStruct.HistoryLength > 24)
            {
                status.Status = MonitorStatus.STATUS_INVALID_DATA;
                status.Description = "Credit score values out of range";
            }
        }

    }
    else
    {
        status.Status = MonitorStatus.STATUS_INVALID_FORMAT;
        status.Description = "Invalid message format";        }
}
catch (Exception e)
{
    Console.WriteLine("Exception: {0}", e.ToString());
    status.Status = MonitorStatus.STATUS_INVALID_FORMAT;
    status.Description = "Could not deserialize message body";
}

StreamReader reader = new StreamReader (msg.BodyStream);
status.MessageBody =  reader.ReadToEnd();

Console.WriteLine(status.Description);

if (status.Status != MonitorStatus.STATUS_OK ||
    (status.Status == MonitorStatus.STATUS_OK &&
     lastStatus != MonitorStatus.STATUS_OK))
{
    controlQueue.Send(status);
}
```

```
    lastStatus = status.Status;
    sendTimer.Dispose();
    sendTimer = new Timer(new TimerCallback(OnSendTimerEvent), null,
                    interval*1000, Timeout.Infinite);
}
```

If no message arrives in the specified interval, the `timeoutTimer` will invoke the `OnTimeoutEvent` method. This method sends a `MonitorStatus` message to the *Control Bus* (540) and starts a new Send Timer so that a new request message is sent after the interval.

Monitor Class: Timeout

```
protected void OnTimeoutEvent(Object state)
{
    MonitorStatus status = new MonitorStatus(
                    MonitorStatus.STATUS_TIMEOUT, "Timeout", null, MonitorID);
    Console.WriteLine(status.Description);
    controlQueue.Send(status);
    lastStatus = status.Status;

    timeoutTimer.Dispose();
    sendTimer = new Timer(new TimerCallback(OnSendTimerEvent), null,
                    interval*1000, Timeout.Infinite);
}
```

Credit Bureau Failover

Now that we can monitor the status of the external credit bureau service, we want to use this data to implement a failover scheme so that the loan broker can continue operating even when the credit bureau service fails. It is worthwhile noting that *Point-to-Point Channel*s (103) already provide a basic form of failover. When we use multiple *Competing Consumers* (502) on a single *Point-to-Point Channel* (103), the failure of one consumer will not interrupt processing as long as the other consumer(s) still operate. When multiple consumers are active, they split the load, effectively implementing a simple load-balancing mechanism. Why then would we need to implement an explicit failover mechanism? When using external services, we may be limited to simple channels that do not support *Competing Consumers* (502), such as SOAP over HTTP. Also, we may not want multiple services to load balance. For example, we may have a volume agreement with the primary service provider that gives us substantial discounts if we meet certain usage quotas. Splitting the traffic across two providers will likely cost us more. Alternatively, we may be using a low-cost provider as our primary service provider and want to switch over to a premium provider only when the low-cost provider fails. (For an excellent discussion of architectural decisions driven by licensing considerations, see [Hohmann].)

In order to implement explicit failover, we insert a *Message Router* (78) into the credit bureau request channel (see figure). This router routes the request either to the primary credit bureau service (thick, black arrows) or to the secondary credit bureau service (thin, black arrows). Because the secondary service may use a different message format than the first service, we wrap the secondary service with a pair of *Message Translator*s (85). The *Message Router* (78) is a context-based *Message Router* (78) controlled by the management console over the *Control Bus* (540). The management console gets monitoring data from the credit bureau monitor we designed in the previous section. If the monitor indicates a failure, the management console instructs the *Message Router* (78) to reroute the traffic to the secondary service provider (see figure).

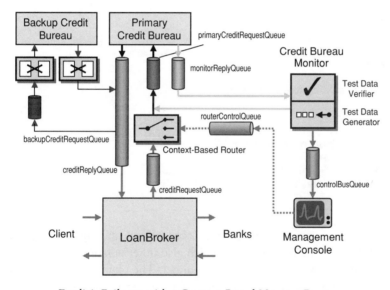

Explicit Failover with a Context-Based Message Router

While the request message traffic is rerouted to the secondary service provider, the monitor keeps on sending test messages to the primary provider. When the monitor confirms the correct operation of the service, the console instructs the *Message Router* (78) to return to routing request messages to the primary provider. The solution diagram does not show a monitor for the secondary service provider even though it would be very easy to use a second instance of the credit bureau monitor to monitor the health of the backup credit bureau service.

Let's look at the implementation of the context-based *Message Router* (78). The ContextBasedRouter class inherits from our trusty MessageConsumer base class to process incoming messages. The ProcessMessage method checks the value of the variable control and routes incoming messages to either the primary or secondary output channel based on the value of the variable.

ContextBasedRouter Class

```
delegate void ControlEvent(int control);

class ContextBasedRouter : MessageConsumer
{
...
    protected override void ProcessMessage(Message msg)
    {
        if (control == 0)
        {
            primaryOutputQueue.Send(msg);
        }
        else
        {
            secondaryOutputQueue.Send(msg);
        }
    }

    protected void OnControlEvent(int control)
    {
        this.control = control;
        Console.WriteLine("Control = " + control);
    }
}
```

The variable control is set by the OnControlEvent method. This method is invoked by the ControlReceiver class, which also inherits from MessageConsumer as it listens for messages from the control channel. The ContextBasedRouter class supplies the ControlReceiver with a delegate of type ControlEvent to invoke when it receives a control event with a numeric value. If you have not come across delegates, they are a really neat, type-safe way to implement callbacks without having to implement another interface or relegating to function pointers ([Box] goes into all the gory details).

ControlReceiver Class

```
class ControlReceiver : MessageConsumer
{
    protected ControlEvent controlEvent;
```

```
public ControlReceiver(MessageQueue inputQueue,
                       ControlEvent controlEvent) : base (inputQueue)
{
    this.controlEvent = controlEvent;
}

protected override void ProcessMessage(Message msg)
{
    String text = (string)msg.Body;
    Double resNum;

    if (Double.TryParse(text, NumberStyles.Integer,
                        NumberFormatInfo.InvariantInfo, out resNum))
    {
        int control = int.Parse(text);
        controlEvent(control);
    }
}
}
```

Enhancing the Management Console

The first version of the management console was so simple that we did not even bother showing the code. All it could do was receive a message and write the message content to a file for later analysis (such as rendering performance graphs from Excel). Now we want to inject some more intelligence into the management console. First, when the primary credit bureau monitor indicates a failure, the management console needs to instruct the context-based *Message Router* (78) to reroute messages to the secondary service provider. We opted to implement this functionality inside the management console so that we can decouple the monitor and the context-based *Message Router* (78)—effectively, the management console acts as a *Mediator* [GoF]. Also, implementing the failover logic in a central location gives us a single point of maintenance for the system management rules. Commercial management consoles typically include configurable rules engines to determine appropriate corrective actions based on events on the *Control Bus* (540).

Second, we want to build a simple user interface for the management console that displays the current state of the system. Obtaining a big-picture view of a messaging system can be quite difficult, especially if message paths change dynamically. Even a small number of components can make it difficult to reconcile where messages flow. Our user interface is simple but nevertheless quite useful. We use the iconic language defined in this book to represent the interaction between components. For now, the user interface displays only the credit bureau failover portion of the system, consisting of two services and one context-based *Message Router* (78); see figure on the following page.

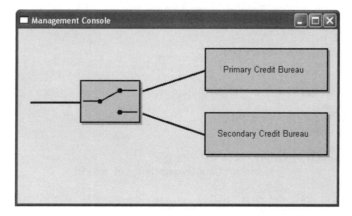

The Management Console Indicates That Both Credit Bureau Services Are Active

When the Monitor detects a failure and instructs the router to reroute the traffic, we want to update the user interface to reflect the new status (see figure). The router icon shows the new route for the request messages, and the primary credit bureau component changes colors to indicate the failure.

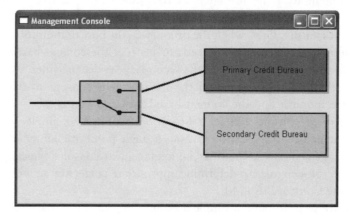

The Management Console Indicates That the Primary Credit Bureau Failed and Traffic Is Being Rerouted

Let's have a brief look at the code behind this console. We focus on the system management part of the code and do not dive into the details of the code that renders the pretty user interface pictures. First, the management console needs to be able to retrieve status messages from the monitor component. To make the console as robust as possible, we access the message content in a loosely coupled fashion, reading individual fields from the XML payload. This approach helps keep the management console operational even if the individual components decide to add new fields to the message format.

Not surprisingly, the console class also inherits from our good friend Message-Consumer, so we only show the implementation of the constructor and the Process-Message method. The method simply reads the message's BodyStream into a string variable and passes it to the different components for analysis.

ManagementConsole: ProcessMessage

```
public delegate void ControlMessageReceived(String body);

public class ManagementConsole : MessageConsumer
{
    protected Logger logger;
    public MonitorStatusHandler monitorStatusHandler;

    public ControlMessageReceived updateEvent;

    public ManagementConsole(MessageQueue inputQueue, string pathName) : base(inputQueue)
    {
        logger = new Logger(pathName);
        monitorStatusHandler = new MonitorStatusHandler();

        updateEvent += new ControlMessageReceived(logger.Log);
        updateEvent += new ControlMessageReceived(monitorStatusHandler.OnControlMessage);
    }

    protected override void ProcessMessage(Message m)
    {
        Stream stm = m.BodyStream;
        StreamReader reader = new StreamReader (stm);
        String body =  reader.ReadToEnd();

        updateEvent(body);
    }
    ...
}
```

The ManagementConsole class uses a delegate to notify the logger and the Monitor-StatusHandler. Using a delegate allows us to easily add other classes that also listen on incoming control messages without having to change the code inside the ProcessMessage method.

One of the components analyzing incoming control message data is the Monitor-StatusHandler class. First, this class checks whether the XML document contained in the body of the incoming message has the root element <MonitorStatus>.

If so, it loads the message body into an XML document to extract the relevant fields contained inside the ID and the Status elements. It then invokes the delegate updateEvent, which is of type MonitorStatusUpdate. Any interested class inside the management console application can add a callback method to this delegate and be notified any time a MonitorStatus message arrives. All the component has to do is provide an implementation of a method with a signature equal to MonitorStatusUpdate.

MonitorStatusHandler

```
public delegate void MonitorStatusUpdate(String ID, int Status);

public class MonitorStatusHandler
{
    public  MonitorStatusUpdate updateEvent;

    public void OnControlMessage(String body)
    {
        XmlDocument doc = new XmlDocument();
        doc.LoadXml(body);

        XmlElement root = doc.DocumentElement;
        if (root.Name == "MonitorStatus")
        {
            XmlNode statusNode = root.SelectSingleNode("Status");
            XmlNode idNode = root.SelectSingleNode("ID");

            if (idNode!= null && statusNode != null)
            {
                String msgID = idNode.InnerText;
                String msgStatus = statusNode.InnerText;
                Double resNum;
                int status = 99;

                if (Double.TryParse(msgStatus, NumberStyles.Integer,
                                NumberFormatInfo.InvariantInfo, out resNum))
                {
                    status = (int)resNum;
                }
                updateEvent(msgID, status);
            }
        }
    }
}
```

In our example, the first two components listening to the MonitorStatusUpdate event triggered by the MonitorStatusHandler are two user interface controls representing the primary and secondary credit bureau service in the user interface form. Each user interface control filters the events for the identifier that is unique to the respective component that is being monitored. When the status of the monitored component changes, the user interface control changes the color of the component. The following routine executes during the initialization of the display form and ties the two credit bureau display controls to the monitor-StatusHandler of the management console. This code causes the method OnMonitor-StatusUpdate of the controls to be invoked whenever the console receives a monitor status update message

Console Form Initialization

```
console = new ManagementConsole(controlBusQueue, logFileName);

primaryCreditBureauControl =
    new ComponentStatusControl("Primary Credit Bureau", "PrimaryCreditService");
primaryCreditBureauControl.Bounds =
    new Rectangle(300, 30, COMPONENT_WIDTH, COMPONENT_HEIGHT);

secondaryCreditBureauControl =
    new ComponentStatusControl("Secondary Credit Bureau", "SecondaryCreditService");
secondaryCreditBureauControl.Bounds =
    new Rectangle(300, 130, COMPONENT_WIDTH, COMPONENT_HEIGHT);

console.monitorStatusHandler.updateEvent += new
    MonitorStatusUpdate(primaryCreditBureauControl.OnMonitorStatusUpdate);
console.monitorStatusHandler.updateEvent += new
    MonitorStatusUpdate(secondaryCreditBureauControl.OnMonitorStatusUpdate);
```

Another component listening to the MonitorStatusUpdate events is the FailOver-Handler. This component is a nonvisual component that analyzes status messages to determine whether a failover switch should be set. If the status of the monitor has changed (we use a logical XOR denoted by the ∧ operator), the FailOver-Handler sends a command message to the designated command channel. In our case, this command channel is connected to the context-based *Message Router* (78) described earlier, which will start rerouting credit score request messages to a different credit bureau provider.

FailOverHandler Class

```
public delegate void FailOverStatusUpdate(String ID, string Command);

public class FailOverHandler
{
    ...
    public void OnMonitorStatusUpdate(String ID, int status)
    {
        if (componentID == ID)
        {
```

```
        if (IsOK(status) ∧ IsOK(currentStatus))
        {
            String command = IsOK(status) ? "0" : "1";
            commandQueue.Send(command);
            currentStatus = status;
            updateEvent(ID, command);
        }
    }
}

protected bool IsOK(int status)
{
    return (status == 0 || status >= 99);
}
}
```

The FailOverHandler also invokes the updateEvent, which is a delegate of type FailOverStatusUpdate. Similar to the MonitorStatusHandler, we can register any component that implements a method of this type to receive update notifications whenever the FailOverHandler changes status. In our example, we register the visual FailOverControl to receive these events so that it can redraw whenever the failover status changes. The console user interface initialization routine establishes the connection between these components:

Console Form Initialization

```
failOverControl = new FailOverControl("Credit Bureau Failover", "PrimaryCreditService");
failOverControl.Bounds = new Rectangle(100, 80, ROUTER_WIDTH, COMPONENT_HEIGHT);

FailOverHandler failOverHandler =
    new FailOverHandler(commandQueue, "PrimaryCreditService");
console.monitorStatusHandler.updateEvent +=
    new MonitorStatusUpdate(failOverHandler.OnMonitorStatusUpdate);

failOverHandler.updateEvent += new
    FailOverStatusUpdate(failOverControl.OnMonitorStatusUpdate);
```

Connecting the individual components inside the management console through delegates and events results in a loosely coupled architecture. This architecture allows us to reuse the individual components and recompose them into different constellations similar to the *Pipes and Filters* (70) architectural style introduced at the beginning of the book. Essentially, passing messages arriving on the *Control Bus* (540) by using delegates resembles creating an application-internal *Publish-Subscribe Channel* (106). Because the control bus events arrive on a *Point-to-Point Channel* (103), we have to use a single consumer, which then publishes the event to any interested subscriber inside the application.

The following collaboration diagram illustrates the propagation of events between the individual components inside the management console.

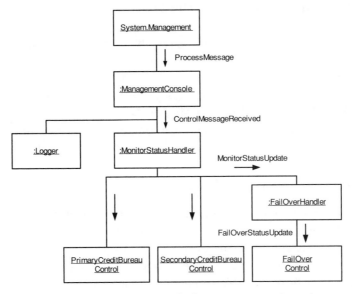

Propagation of Events Inside the Management Console

Using a user interface console to visualize the message flow between individual components is a powerful systems management tool. Some vendors include development suites that allow designers to visually arrange components and connect their input and outputs ports to create distributed message-flow application. For example, Fiorano's Tifosi product *(http://www.fiorano.com)* includes the *Distributed Applications Composer* that allows the design of a distributed solution from a single GUI even though each component may execute on a different machine or platform. This tool uses a *Control Bus* (540) to connect all distributed components to a central management and monitoring console.

Our simple example requires the management console to hard-code the visual connection between the individual components, for example, to draw a line between the failover router and the icons representing the credit bureau services. Many integration tools allow the user to design the solution from the beginning using a GUI. This approach makes it easy to use the same graphical design to display the status of the solution.

Alternatively, we can analyze the message flow in an existing messaging solution to create a graphical representation of the system. There are two fundamental approaches to perform this type of analysis: static and dynamic. A *static analysis* examines the channels that each component publishes and subscribes to. If one component publishes to the same channel another component subscribes to, the tool can draw a connecting line between the two components. Many EAI tool suites, for example, TIBCO ActiveEnterprise, store this type of information in a central repository, making this type of analysis much easier. The second approach uses *dynamic analysis* by inspecting individual messages flowing through the system and reverse-engineering connections between components based on the origin of messages arriving at a particular component. This task is greatly simplified if the messages in the system contain a *Message History* (551). Without the help of a *Message History* (551), we can still reconstruct the flow of messages if each message contains a field specifying the sender of the message (many systems include such a field for authentication purposes).

Limitations of This Example

In order to fit this example into the scope of a single chapter, we had to make some simplifying assumptions. For example, our failover mechanism does not deal with the messages that are already queued up when the primary credit bureau service fails—these messages remain queued up until the service is reinstated. The loan broker is able to continue functioning because it correlates incoming response messages to reply messages, but the loan quote requests associated with the "stuck" messages will not be processed until the primary credit bureau service comes back online. In order to improve response times in a failover scenario, we should implement a resend function that allows the loan broker to reissue request messages for those messages that are queued up indefinitely in front of a failed service. Alternatively, the failover router could store all request messages that have arrived since the correct function of the service was last confirmed. If a service failure is detected, the router could resend all these messages because some of them might not have been processed correctly. This approach can lead to duplicate request messages (and associated reply messages), but since both the credit bureau service and the loan broker are *Idempotent Receivers* (528) this does not cause any problems—duplicate reply messages are simply ignored.

This example demonstrated only a small subset of the system management functions that can be implemented with the patterns in the previous chapter. For example, we could monitor message traffic across all components, set performance thresholds, have each component send heartbeat messages, and more. In fact, adding robust systems management to a distributed messaging solution can require as much (or more) design and implementation effort as the original solution.

Chapter 13

Integration Patterns
in Practice

Case Study: Bond Pricing System

by Jonathan Simon

It is easy to distance yourself from a large collection of patterns or a pattern language. Patterns are the abstraction of an idea in a reusable form. Often, the very generic nature of patterns that makes them so useful also makes them hard to grasp. Sometimes, the best thing to help understand patterns is a real-world example—not a contrived scenario of what *could* happen, but what *actually* happens and what *will* happen.

This chapter applies patterns to solve problems using a discovery process. The system we discuss is a bond trading system that I worked with for two years from initial design through production. We explore scenarios and problems that were encountered and how to solve them with patterns. This involves the decision process of choosing a pattern as well as how to combine and adjust patterns to suit the needs of the system. This is all done taking into account the forces encountered in real systems, including business requirements, client decisions, architectural and technical requirements, and legacy system integration. The intent of this approach is to provide a clearer understanding of the patterns themselves through practical application.

Building a System

A major Wall Street investment bank sets out to build a bond pricing system in an effort to streamline the workflow of its bond trading desk. Currently, bond traders have to send prices for a large number of bonds to several different trading

603

venues, each with its own user interface. The goal for the system is to minimize the minutiae of pricing all of the bonds combined with advanced analytic functionality specific to the bond market in a single encapsulated user interface. This means integration and communication with several components over various communications protocols. The high-level flow of the system looks like this:

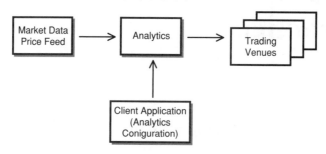

High-Level Flow

First, market data comes into the system. Market data is data regarding the price and other properties of the bond, representing what people are willing to buy and sell the bond for on the free market. The market data is immediately sent to the analytics engine that alters the data. Analytics refers to mathematical functions for financial applications that alter the prices and other attributes of bonds. These are generic functions that use input variables to tailor the results of the function to a particular bond. The client application that will run on each trader desktop will configure the analytics engine on a per-trader basis, controlling the specifics of the analytics for each bond the trader is pricing. Once the analytics are applied to the market data, the modified data is sent out to various trading venues where traders from other firms can buy or sell the bonds.

Architecture with Patterns

With this overview of the data flow in the system, we can approach some of the architectural problems we encounter during the design process. Let's take a look at what we know to date. Traders need a very responsive application on both Windows NT and Solaris workstations. Therefore, we decided to implement the client application as a Java thick client because of its platform-independence and its ability to quickly respond to user input and market data. On the server side, we are inheriting legacy C++ components that our system will utilize. The market data components communicate with the TIBCO Information Bus (TIB) messaging infrastructure.

We are inheriting the following components:

- **Market Data Price Feed Server:** Publishes incoming market data to the TIB.

- **Analytics Engine:** Performs analytics on incoming market data and broadcasts the modified market data to the TIB.

- **Contribution Server:** Performs all communication with trading venues. The trading venues are third-party components not controlled by the bank.

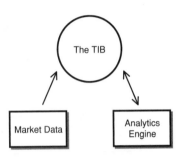

Legacy Market Data Subsystem

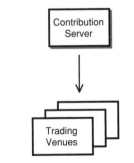

Legacy Contribution Subsystem

We need to decide how the separate subsystems (Java thick client, market data, and contribution) are going to communicate. We could have the thick client communicate directly with the legacy servers, but that would require too much business logic on the client. Instead, we'll build a pair of Java gateways to communicate with the legacy servers—the pricing gateway for market data and the contribution gateway for sending prices to trading venues. This will achieve nice encapsulation of the business logic related to these areas. The current components in the system are shown below. The connections marked as "???" indicate that we are still unsure how some of the components will communicate.

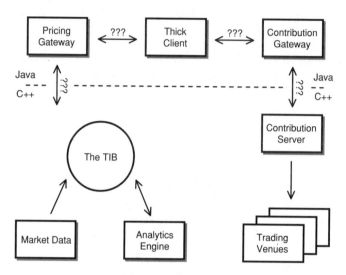

The System and Its Components

The first communication question is how to integrate the Java thick client and the two Java gateway components in order to exchange data. Let's look at the four integration styles suggested in this book: *File Transfer* (43), *Shared Database* (47), *Remote Procedure Invocation* (50), and *Messaging* (53). We can rule out *Shared Database* (47) immediately because we want to create a layer of abstraction between the client and the database, and we don't want to have database access code in the client. *File Transfer* (43), can similarly be ruled out, since minimal latency is required to ensure current prices are sent out to the trading venues. This leaves us with a choice between *Remote Procedure Invocation* (50) and *Messaging* (53).

The Java platform provides built-in support for both *Remote Procedure Invocation* (50) and *Messaging* (53). RPC-style integration can be achieved using Remote Method Invocation (RMI), CORBA, or Enterprise JavaBeans (EJB). The Java Messaging Service (JMS) is the common API for messaging-style integration. Both integration styles are easy to implement in Java.

So, which will work better for this project, *Remote Procedure Invocation* (50) or *Messaging* (53)? There's only one instance of the pricing gateway and one instance of the contribution gateway in the system, but usually many thick clients simultaneously connect to these services (one for each bond trader that happens to be logged in at a particular time). Furthermore, the bank would like this to be a generic pricing system that can be utilized in other applications. So, besides an unknown number of thick clients, there may be an unknown number of other applications using the pricing data coming out of the gateways.

Case Study: Bond Pricing System

A thick client (or other application using the pricing data) can fairly easily use RPC to make calls to the gateways to get pricing data and invoke processing. However, pricing data will constantly be published, and certain clients are only interested in certain data, so getting the relevant data to the proper clients in a timely manner could be difficult. The clients could poll the gateways, but that will create a lot of overhead. It would be better for the gateways to make the data available to the clients as soon as it is available. This, however, will require each gateway to keep track of which clients are currently active and which want what particular data; then, when a new piece of data becomes available (which will happen numerous times per second), the gateway will have to make an RPC to each interested client to pass the data to the client. Ideally, all clients should be notified simultaneously, so each RPC needs to be made in its own concurrent thread. This can work, but is getting very complicated very fast.

Messaging (53) greatly simplifies this problem. With *Messaging* (53), we can define separate channels for the different types of pricing data. Then, when a gateway gets a new piece of data, it will add a message containing that data to the *Publish-Subscribe Channel* (106) for that datatype. Meanwhile, all clients interested in a certain type of data will listen on the channel for that type. In this way, the gateways can easily send out new data to whomever is interested without needing to know how many listener applications there are or what they are.

The clients still need to be able to invoke behavior in the gateways as well. Since there are ever only two gateways, and the client can probably block while the method is invoked synchronously, these client-to-gateway invocations can fairly easily be implemented using RPC. However, since we are already using messaging for gateway-to-client communication, messages are probably just as good a way to implement client-to-gateway communication as well.

Therefore, all communication between the gateways and the clients will be accomplished through messaging. Because all of the components are written in Java, JMS presents an easy choice for the messaging system. This is effectively creating a *Message Bus* (137) or an architecture that will make it possible for future systems to integrate with the current system with little or no changes to the messaging infrastructure. This way, the business functionality of the application can be easily used by other applications the bank develops.

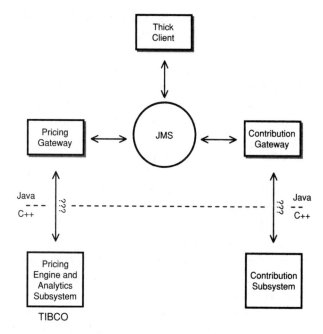

Java Components Communicating with JMS

JMS is simply a specification, and we need to decide on a JMS-compliant messaging system. We decided to use IBM MQSeries JMS because the bank is an "IBM shop," using WebSphere application servers and many other IBM products. As a result, we will use MQSeries, since we already have a support infrastructure in place and a site license of the product.

The next question is how to connect the MQSeries messaging system with the standalone C++ contribution server and the TIBCO-based market data and analytics engine servers. We need a way for the MQSeries consumers to have access to the TIB messages. But how? Perhaps we could use the *Message Translator* (85) pattern to translate TIB messages into MQSeries messages. Although the C++ client for MQSeries serves as a *Message Translator* (85), using it would sacrifice JMS server independence. And although TIBCO does have a Java API, the customer architect and manager have rejected it. As a result, the *Message Translator* (85) approach has to be abandoned.

The bridge from the TIB server to the MQSeries server requires communication between C++ and Java. We could use CORBA, but then what about the messaging? A closer look at the *Message Translator* (85) pattern shows it is related to the *Channel Adapter* (127) in its use of communication protocols. The heart of a *Channel Adapter* (127) is to connect non-messaging systems to messaging systems. A pair of channel adapters that connects two messaging systems is a *Messaging Bridge* (133).

The purpose of a *Messaging Bridge* (133) is to transfer messages from one messaging system to another. This is exactly what we are doing with the added complexity of the intralanguage Java to C++ communication. We can implement the cross-language *Messaging Bridge* (133) using a combination of *Channel Adapter*s (127) and CORBA. We will build two lightweight *Channel Adapter* (127) servers, one in C++ managing communication with the TIB and one in Java managing communication with JMS. These two *Channel Adapter*s (127), which are *Message Endpoint*s (95) themselves, will communicate with each other via CORBA. Like our choice for MQSeries, we will use CORBA rather than JNI, since it is a company standard. The messaging bridge implements the effectively simulated message translation between seemingly incompatible messaging systems and different languages.

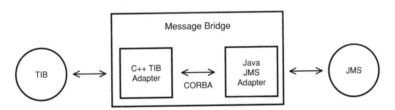

Messaging Bridge Using Channel Adapters

The next figure on the following page shows the current system design, including the gateways and other components. This is a good example of pattern application. We combined two *Channel Adapter*s (127) with a non-messaging protocol to implement the *Messaging Bridge* (133) pattern, effectively using one pattern to implement another pattern. Additionally, we changed the *Channel Adapter*s' (127) context to link two messaging systems with a non-messaging cross-language translation protocol rather than connecting a messaging system to a non-messaging system.

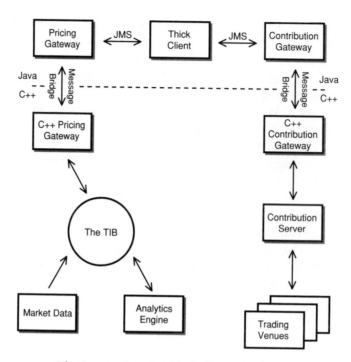

The Current System with the Channel Adapters

Structuring Channels

A key to working with patterns is knowing not only when to use which pattern, but also knowing how to most effectively use it. Each pattern implementation has to take into account specifics of the technology platform as well as other design criteria. This section applies the same discovery process to find the most efficient use of the *Publish-Subscribe Channel* (106) in the context of the market data server communicating with the analytics engine.

Real-time market data originates with market data feed, a C++ server that broadcasts market data on the TIB. The market data feed uses a separate *Publish-Subscribe Channel* (106) for each bond it is publishing prices for. This may seem a little extreme, since each new bond needs its own new channel. But this is not so severe, since you do not actually need to create channels in TIBCO. Rather, channels are referenced by a hierarchical set of topic names called *subjects*. The TIBCO server then filters a single message flow by subject, sending each unique subject to a single virtual channel. This results in a very lightweight message channel.

We could create a system that publishes on a few channels, and subscribers could listen only for prices they are interested in. This would require subscribers to use a *Message Filter* (237) or *Selective Consumer* (515) to filter the entire data flow for interesting bond prices, deciding whether each message should be processed as it is received. Given that the market data is published on bond-dedicated channels, subscribers can register for updates on a series of bonds. This effectively allows subscribers to "filter" by selectively subscribing to channels and only receiving updates of interest rather than deciding after the message is received. It is important to note that using multiple channels to avoid filtering is a nonstandard use of messaging channels. In context of the TIBCO technology, however, we are really deciding whether to implement our own filters or utilize the channel filtering built into TIBCO—rather than whether to use so many channels.

The next component we need to design is the analytics engine, another C++/TIB server that will modify the market data and rebroadcast it to the TIB. Although it is out of the scope of our Java/JMS development, we are working closely with the C++ team to design it, since we are the analytics engine's primary customer. The problem at hand is to find the channel structure that most efficiently rebroadcasts the newly modified market data.

Since we already have one dedicated *Message Channel* (60) per bond inherited from the market data price feed, it would be logical to modify the market data and rebroadcast the modified market data on the bond dedicated *Message Channel* (60). But this will not work since the analytics modifying the bonds prices are trader-specific. If we rebroadcast the modified data on the bond *Message Channel* (60), we will destroy the data integrity by replacing generic market data with trader-specific data. However, we could have a different message type for trader-specific market data that we publish on the same channel, allowing subscribers to decide which message they are interested in to avoid destroying the data integrity. But then clients will have to implement their own filters to separate out messages for other traders. Additionally, there will a substantial increase in messages received by subscribers, placing an unnecessary burden on them.

There are two options:

1. **One channel per trader:** Each trader has a designated channel for the modified market data. This way, the original market data remains intact, and each trader application can listen to its specific trader's *Message Channel* (60) for the modified price updates.

2. **One channel per trader per bond:** Create one *Message Channel* (60) per trader, per bond, solely for the modified market data of that bond. For

example, the market data for bond ABC would be published on channel "Bond ABC," while the modified market data for trader A would be published on channel "Trader A, Bond ABC," modified market data for trader B on channel "Trader B, Bond ABC," and so on.

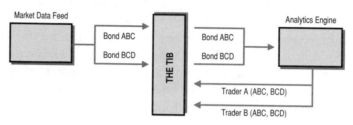

One Channel per Trader

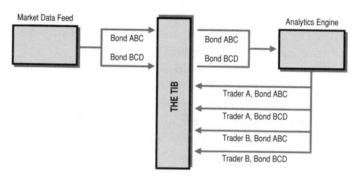

One Channel per Bond per Trader

There are advantages and disadvantages to each approach. The per-bond approach, for example, uses a lot more *Message Channels* (60). In the worst-case scenario, the number of *Message Channels* (60) will be the total number of bonds multiplied by the number of traders. We can put upper bounds on the number of channels that will be created, since we know that there are only around 20 traders and they never price more than a couple hundred bonds. This puts the upper limit below the 10,000 range, which is not so outlandish compared to the nearly 100,000 *Message Channels* (60) the market data price feed is using. Also, since we are using the TIB, and *Message Channels* (60) are quite inexpensive, the number of *Message Channels* (60) is not a severe issue. However, the sheer number of *Message Channels* (60) could be a problem from a management perspective. Every time a bond is added, a channel for each trader must be maintained. This could be severe in a very dynamic system. Our system, however, is essentially static. It also has an infrastructure for automatically managing *Message Channels* (60). This combined with the inherited architecture of a legacy component using a similar approach minimizes the downside. This is not to say we should make an unnecessarily excessive number of *Message Channels* (60). Rather, we can implement an architectural approach that uses a large number of *Message Channels* (60) when there is a reason.

And there *is* a reason in this case, which comes down to the location of logic. If we implement the per-trader approach, the Analytics Engine needs logic to group input and output channels. This is because the input channels from the Analytics Engine are per-bond, and the output *Message Channels* (60) would be per-trader, requiring the Analytics Engine to route all analytics input from multiple bonds for a particular trader to a trader-specific output *Message Channel* (60). This effectively turns the analytics engine into a *Content-Based Router* (230) to implement custom routing logic for our application.

Following the *Message Bus* (137) structure, the Analytics Engine is a generic server that could be used by several other systems in the system, so we don't want to cloud it with system-specific functionality. On the other hand, the per-bond approach works, since the idea of a trader owning the analytics output of bond prices is a company accepted practice. The per-bond approach keeps the *Message Channel* (60) separation of the market data feed intact while adding several more *Message Channels* (60). Before we reach the client, we want a *Content-Based Router* (230) to combine these several channels into a manageable number of channels. We don't want the client application running on the trader's desktop to be listening to thousands or tens of thousands of *Message Channels* (60). Now the question becomes where to put the *Content-Based Router* (230). We could simply have the C++/TIB *Channel Adapter* (127) forward all of the messages to the pricing gateway on a single *Message Channel* (60). This is bad for two reasons: We would be splitting up the business logic between C++ and Java, and we would lose the benefit of the separate *Message Channels* (60) on the TIB side that allows us to avoid filtering later in the data flow. Looking at our Java components, we could either place it in the pricing gateway or create an intermediary component between the pricing gateway and the client.

In theory, if we persisted the bond-based separation of *Message Channels* (60) all the way to the client, the pricing gateway would rebroadcast pricing information with the same channel structure as the pricing gateway and Analytics Engine. This means a duplication of all of the bond-dedicated TIB channels in JMS. Even if we create an intermediary component between the pricing gateway and the client, the pricing gateway will still have to duplicate all of the channels in JMS. However, implementing logic directly in the pricing gateway allows us to avoid duplicating the large number of channels in JMS—allowing us to create a much smaller number of channels in the order of one per trader. The pricing gateway registers itself through the C++/TIB *Channel Adapter* (127) as a consumer for each bond of every trader in the system. Then, the pricing gateway forwards each specific client only the messages related to that particular trader. This way, we use only a small number of *Message Channels* (60) on the JMS end while maximizing the benefit of the separation on the TIB end.

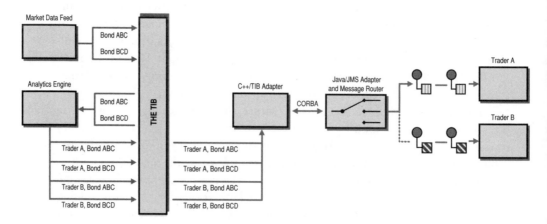

The Complete Market Data Flow to the Client

The *Message Channel* (60) layout discussion is a good example of how integrating patterns is important. The goal was to figure out how to effectively use the *Message Channels* (60). Saying you use a pattern isn't enough. You need to figure out how to best implement it and incorporate it into your system to solve the problems at hand. Additionally, this example shows business forces in action. If we could implement business logic in any of our components, we could have gone with the per-trader approach and implemented an overall more simple approach with many fewer channels.

Selecting a Message Channel

Now that we know the mechanics of the communication between the Java/JMS components and the C++/ TIBCO components, and we have seen some *Message*

Channel (60) structuring, we need to decide which type of JMS *Message Channels* (60) the Java components should use to communicate. Before we can choose between the different *Message Channels* (60) available in JMS, let's look at the high-level message flow of the system. We have two gateways (pricing and contribution) communicating with the client. Market data flows to the client from the pricing gateway, which sends it out to the contribution gateway. The client application sends messages to the pricing gateway to alter the analytics being applied to each bond. The contribution gateway also sends messages to the client application relaying the status of the price updates to the different trading venues.

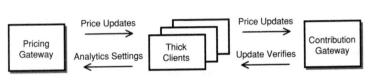

The System Message Flow

The JMS specification describes two *Message Channel* (60) types: Queue (a *Point-to-Point Channel* [103]) and Topic (a *Publish-Subscribe Channel* [106]). Recall that the case for using publish-subscribe is to enable all interested consumers to receive a message, while the case for using point-to-point is to ensure that only one eligible consumer receives a particular message.

Many systems would simply broadcast messages to all client applications, leaving each individual client application to decide for itself whether or not to process a particular message. This will not work for our application, since a large number of market data messages are being sent to each client application. If we broadcast market data updates to uninterested traders, we will be unnecessarily wasting client processor cycles deciding whether or not to process a market data update.

Point-to-Point Channels (103) initially sounds like a good choice, since the clients are sending messages to unique servers, and vice versa. But it was a business requirement that traders may be logged in to multiple machines at the same time. If we have a trader logged in at two workstations simultaneously and a point-to-point price update is sent, only one of the two client applications will get the message. This is because only one consumer on a *Point-to-Point Channel* (103) can receive a particular message (see figure on the next page). Notice that only the first of each group of a trader's client applications receives the message.

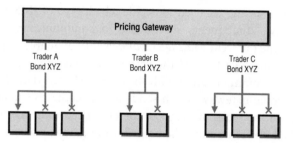

Point-to-Point Messaging for Price Updates

We could solve this using *Recipient List* (249), which publishes messages to a list of intended recipients, guaranteeing that only clients in the recipient list will receive messages. Using this pattern, the system could create recipient lists with all client application instances related to each trader. Sending a message related to a particular trader would in turn send the message to each application in the recipient list. This guarantees all client application instances related to a particular trader would receive the message. The downside of this approach is that it requires quite a bit of implementation logic to manage the recipients and dispatch messages.

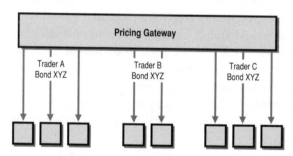

Recipient List for Price Updates

Even though point-to-point could be made to work, let's see if there is a better way. Using *Publish-Subscribe Channels* (106), the system could broadcast messages on trader-specific channels rather than client application–specific channels. This way, all client applications processing messages for a single trader would receive and process the message (see the following figure).

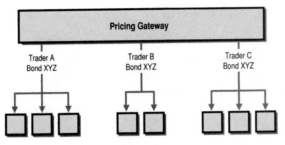

Publish-Subscribe Messaging for Price Updates

The downside of using *Publish-Subscribe Channel*s (106) is that unique message processing is not guaranteed with the server components. It would be possible for multiple instances of a server component to be instantiated and for each instance to process the same message, possibly sending out invalid prices.

Recalling the system message flow, only a single communication direction is satisfactory with each *Message Channel* (60). Server-to-client communication with publish-subscribe is satisfactory, while client-to-server communication is not, and client-to-server communication with point-to-point is satisfactory, while server-to-client is not. Since there is no need to use the same *Message Channel* (60) in both directions, we can use each *Message Channel* (60) in only one direction. Client-to-server communication will be implemented with point-to-point, while server-to-client communication will be implemented with publish-subscribe. Using this combination of *Message Channel*s (60), the system benefits from direct communication with the server components using point-to-point messaging and the multicast nature of publish-subscribe without either of the drawbacks.

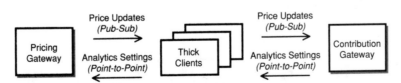

Message Flow with Channel Types

Problem Solving with Patterns

Patterns are tools, and collections of patterns are toolboxes. They help solve problems. Some think that patterns are only useful during design. Following the toolbox analogy, this is like saying that tools are only useful when you build a house, not when you fix it. The fact is that patterns are a useful tool throughout a project when applied well. In the following sections we use the same pattern exploration process we used in the previous section to solve problems in our now working system.

Flashing Market Data Updates

Traders want table cells to flash when new market data is received for a bond, clearly indicating changes. The Java client receives messages with new data, which triggers a client data cache update and eventually flashing in the table. The problem is that updates come quite frequently. The GUI thread stack is becoming overloaded and eventually freezing the client, since it can't respond to user interaction. We will assume that the flashing is optimized and concentrate on the data flow of messages through the updating process. An examination of performance data shows the client application is receiving several updates a second; two updates can occur less than a millisecond apart. Two patterns that seem like they could help slow down the message flow are *Aggregator* (268) and *Message Filter* (237).

A first thought is to implement a *Message Filter* (237) to control the speed of the message flow by throwing out updates received a short time after the reference message. As an example, let's say that we are going to ignore messages within 5 milliseconds of each other. The *Message Filter* (237) could cache the time of the last acceptable message and throw out anything received within the next 5 milliseconds. While other applications may not be able to withstand data loss to such an extent, this is perfectly acceptable in our system due to the frequency of price updates.

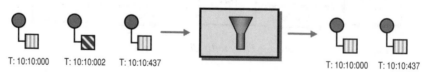

Time-Based Message Filter

The problem with this approach is that not all data fields are updated at the same time. Each bond has approximately 50 data fields displayed to the user, including price. We realize that not every field is updated in every message. If the system ignores consecutive messages, it may very well be throwing out important data.

The other pattern of interest is the *Aggregator* (268). The *Aggregator* (268) is used to manage the reconciliation of multiple, related messages into a single message, potentially reducing the message flow. The *Aggregator* (268) could keep a copy of the bond data from the first aggregated message, then update only new or changed fields from successive messages. Eventually, the aggregated bond data will be passed in a message to the client. For now, let's assume that the *Aggregator* (268) will send a message every 5 milliseconds like the *Message Filter* (237). Later, we'll explore another alternative.

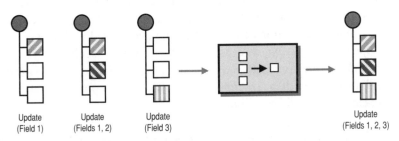

Aggregator with Partial Successive Updates

The *Aggregator* (268), like any other pattern, is not a silver bullet; it has its pluses and minuses that need to be explored. One potential minus is that implementing an *Aggregator* (268) would reduce the message traffic by a great amount in our case only if many messages are coming in within a relatively short time regarding the same bond. However, we would accomplish nothing if the Java client receives updates for only one field across all of the traders' bonds. For example, if we receive 1,000 messages in a specified timeframe with four bonds of interest, we would reduce the message flow from 1,000 to four messages over that timeframe. Alternatively, if we receive 1,000 messages in the same timeframe with 750 bonds of interest, we will have reduced the message flow from 1,000 to 750 messages: relatively little gain for the amount of effort. A quick analysis of the message updates proves that the Java client receives many messages updating fields of the same bond—and therefore related messages. So, *Aggregator* (268) is in fact a good decision.

What's left is to determine how the *Aggregator* (268) will know when to send a message it has been aggregating. The pattern describes a few algorithms for the *Aggregator* (268) to know when to send the message. These include algorithms to cause the *Aggregator* (268) to send out its contents after a certain amount of time has elapsed, after all required fields in a data set have been completed, and others. The problem with all of these approaches is that the *Aggregator* (268), not the client, is controlling the message flow—and the client, not the message flow, is the major bottleneck in this case.

This is because the *Aggregator* (268) is assuming the consumers of its purged messages (the client application in this case) are *Event-Driven Consumers* (498), or consumers that rely on events from an external source. We need to turn the client into a *Polling Consumer* (494), or a consumer that continuously checks for messages, so the client application can control the message flow. We can do this by creating a background thread that continuously cycles through the set of bonds and updates and flashes any changes that have occurred since the last iteration. This way, the client controls when messages are received, and as a result, guarantees that it will never become overloaded with messages during high update periods. We can easily implement this by sending a *Command Message* (145) to the *Aggregator* (268), initiating an update. The *Aggregator* (268) will respond with a *Document Message* (147) containing the set of updated fields that the client will process.

The choice of *Aggregator* (268) over *Message Filter* (237) is clearly a decision based solely on the business requirements of our system. Each could help us solve our performance problems, but using the *Message Filter* (237) would solve the problem at cost of the system data integrity.

Major Production Crash

With the performance of the flashing fixed, we are now in production. One day, the entire system goes down. MQSeries crashes, bringing several components down with it. We struggle with the problem for a while and finally trace it back to the MQSeries dead letter queue (an implementation of the *Dead Letter Channel* [119]). The queue grows so large that it brings down the entire server. After exploring the messages in the dead letter queue, we find they are all expired market data messages. This is caused by "slow consumers," or consumers that do not process messages fast enough. While messages are waiting to be processed, they time out (see the *Message Expiration* [176] pattern) and are sent to the *Dead Letter Channel* (119). The excessive number of expired market data messages in the dead letter queue is a clear indication that the message flow is too great—messages expire before the target application can consume them. We need to fix the message flow, and we turn to patterns for help in slowing down the message flow.

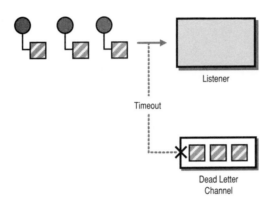

The Bottleneck

A reasonable first step is to explore solving this problem with the *Aggregator* (268), as we recently used this pattern to solve the similar flashing market data–control rate problem. The system design relies on the client application to immediately forward market data update messages to the trading venues. This means the system cannot wait to collect messages and aggregate them, so the *Aggregator* (268) must be abandoned.

There are two other patterns that deal with the problem of consuming messages concurrently: *Competing Consumers* (502) and *Message Dispatcher* (508). Starting with *Competing Consumers* (502), the benefit of this pattern is the parallel processing of incoming messages. This is accomplished using several consumers on the same channel. Only one consumer processes each incoming message, leaving the others to process successive messages. *Competing Consumers* (502), however, will not work for us, since we are using *Publish-Subscribe Channels* (106) in server-to-client communication. *Competing Consumers* (502) on a *Publish-Subscribe Channel* (106) means that all consumers process the same incoming message. This results in more work without any gain and completely misses the goal of the pattern. This approach also has to be abandoned.

The *Message Dispatcher* (508) describes an approach whereby you add several performers to a pool. Each performer can run its own execution thread. One main consumer listens to the *Message Channel* (60) and delegates the message on to an unoccupied performer in the pool, then immediately returns to listening on the channel. This achieves the parallel processing benefit of *Competing Consumers* (502) but works on *Publish-Subscribe Channel*s (106).

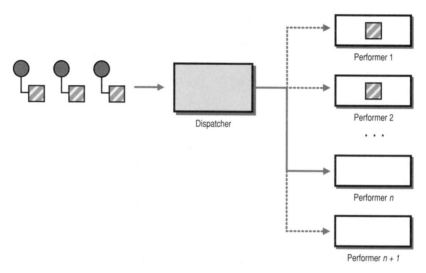

The Message Dispatcher in Context

Implementing this in our system is simple. We create a single `MessageListener` called the `Dispatcher`, which contains a collection of other `MessageListeners` called `Performers`. When the `onMessage` method of the `Dispatcher` is called, it in turn picks a `Performer` out of the collection to actually process the message. The result is a message listener (the `Dispatcher`) that always returns immediately. This guarantees a steady flow of message processing regardless of the message flow rate. This works equally as well on a *Publish-Subscribe Channel* (106) as it does on a *Point-to-Point Channel* (103). With this infrastructure, messages can be received by the client application at almost any rate. If the client application is still slow to process messages after receiving them, the client application can deal with the delayed processing and potentially outdated market data rather than the messages expiring in the JMS *Message Channel* (60).

The crash discussed in this section and the fix using the *Message Dispatcher* (508) are an excellent example of the limits of applying patterns. We encountered a performance problem based on a design flaw that prevented the client from processing messages in parallel. Applying patterns greatly reduced the problem but did not completely fix it, because the real problem was the client becoming a bottleneck. This couldn't be fixed with a thousand patterns. We later addressed this problem by refactoring the message flow architecture to route messages directly from the pricing gateway to the contribution gateway. So, patterns can help design and maintain a system, but they don't necessarily make up for poor upfront design.

Case Study: Bond Pricing System

Summary

Throughout this chapter, we have applied patterns to several different aspects of a bond trading system, including solving initial upfront design problems and fixing a nearly job-threatening production crash with patterns. We also saw these patterns as they already exist in third-party products, legacy components, and our JMS and TIBCO messaging systems. Most importantly, these are real problems with the same types of architectural, technical, and business problems we experience as we design and maintain our own systems. Hopefully, reading about applying patterns to this system has given you a better understanding of the patterns and how to apply them to your own systems.

Chapter 14

Concluding Remarks

Emerging Standards and Futures in Enterprise Integration

by Sean Neville

As data flows across system and domain boundaries through messaging conduits, and as developers and architects become more proficient in the patterns that govern messaging systems, new standards and products will emerge to extend the tactical reach of those patterns. Over time, patterns tend to strengthen but otherwise change little, if at all; but their implementation strategies often evolve rapidly to allow developers to apply them to much broader scales of sophistication. The fundamental *Message* (66) pattern, for example, finds its reach and applicability extended as implementation artifacts grow from Electronic Data Interchange (EDI) to proprietary Message-Oriented Middleware (MOM) to open XML and SOAP-based Web services to global Business Process Execution Language (BPEL) and beyond.

This chapter takes a look at the future of message-based enterprise integration in terms of the emerging standards that application developers will encounter in the mid-2000s. Many of these standards are not currently in common use but are coalescing with broad industry support and are likely to serve as the foundation of integration pattern implementations, particularly in service-oriented architectures. Most of them extend nascent Web services technologies to support the types of patterns presented in this book. We look at why these standards are important in relation to design patterns, which organizations are creating them and how they're going about it, and offer a brief summary of the technical solutions for business process integration that a few of the most promising Web services and Java standards aim to provide.

625

The Relationship between Standards and Design Patterns

Two mental artifacts provide the highest levels of abstraction in software architecture today: programming orientations, which include object-oriented programming, service-oriented programming, generative programming, and the like; and pattern languages, such as those documented in this book. If a particular orientation or design pattern proves useful, and if its context proves to recur frequently, the tactics and strategies used to implement the pattern often become very similar. Pattern solutions on multiple platforms, products, and applications end up owning very few differences—but those few differences are often frustrating growth inhibitors, typically semantic in nature, and produce interoperability that hinders sophistication of scale. To extend the reach of applications and the patterns on which they're based, such differences tend to be eliminated from products and platforms through formally agreed-upon standards.

When a pattern's tactic or implementation strategy is standardized, the pattern does not wane in usefulness, replaced by that standard; instead, quite the opposite occurs. Like rings within a tree trunk, a strong pattern grows upon itself to ever-broader levels of applicability, creating and then applying itself in broader instances of context. This growth in scale occurs because separate instances of a pattern's implementation become interoperable with one another. Taking a typical message-oriented J2EE application as an example, a pattern such as *Pipes and Filters* (70) exists at many levels—within the application as designed by the developer and also within the server product used to host the application, within the containers and services within that server, within the filters and components that compose the messaging subsystems, and so forth in recursive fashion.

Emerging messaging and Web service standards will serve to strengthen the patterns in this book by extending the reach of the developers who employ them. Standards such as BPEL and Web Services Reliability (WS-Reliability) propagate the scope of these patterns beyond bits, beyond languages, beyond products, and outward into increasingly useful compositions in the human- and system-centric circles of use cases and requirements. Application developers can stop using patterns such as *Correlation Identifier* (163) to match raw message replies to their senders and can start using that same pattern to correlate process components that consist of multiple asynchronous message senders and receivers. Without the benefit of messaging standards, a Java developer may implement *Message Router* (78) at the code level to inspect the contents of individual XML messages in order to programmatically forward the message to a particular service or filter. Emerging workflow and choreography standards will allow that same developer to apply his or her knowledge of the *Message Router* (78) pattern at a higher level of abstraction to route workflow among process compositions, where the tactical artifacts are business process components rather than raw sections of XML documents. In other words, application developers can stop spending precious time linking protocols and set about the business of linking business processes and services across domain boundaries.

The usefulness of design patterns and programming orientation for developing sophisticated systems is proportional to the application developer's ability to depend upon common, interoperable implementation strategies and tactics. Today, strategies for working with a messaging pattern in J2EE may mean use of JMS, JCA, or JAX-RPC; tomorrow, the strategies used by application developers may involve use of model-driven technology, schema-based scripts, aspects, or intentions—and any such shifts in implementation tactics only increase the significance of the patterns if the pattern's contextual definition and relevant standards are appropriately embraced. Standards provide the best way we currently know to enforce these commonalities to extend the software architect's mastery of design patterns.

Emerging
Standards
and Futures

Survey of Standards Processes and Organizations

Contrary to popular cynicism, standards are not intended to be developed in a vendor vacuum isolated from practical application development. They are intended to unify and improve the implementation approaches discovered and developed by application developers. By exercising the design patterns in this book, you may be contributing to the development of a standard even if you don't directly contribute to a specification working group. The organizations and consortiums that oversee specification working groups don't always do a great job of recognizing and assimilating implementation approaches, but that's the intention.

Standards are officially born when an inventor or group of inventors makes a formal proposal to a standards body. Usually, this requires membership in the standards body. Each standards body enforces its own process for shaping proposals into a standard, and all members are legally bound to those rules. The processes generally involve the forming of a working group or committee to further develop the specification under the oversight and eventual approval of the organization's management. Intellectual property rights and licensing policies are often hot topics in these organizations and can vary between standards bodies and even between working groups within the standards bodies.

Here's a look at the major standards organizations involved in creating the emerging messaging and Web service standards:

W3C: The World Wide Web Consortium *(http://www.w3c.org)* develops many of the basic Web technologies that are in turn used as building blocks by other standards organizations. It is managed by an international team of researchers and engineers, and consists of a large group of member vendors, content providers, governments, research laboratories, and other entities. The W3C makes use of an open, collaborative review process in working groups and subsequently in public that results in lengthy but generally high-quality iterations. Technologies created through the W3C are usually unencumbered by member claims to intellectual property rights. W3C technologies include SOAP and WSDL as well as all of the core XML specifications. The W3C Choreography Working Group will likely resolve conflicting business process specifications and provide the definitive basis for integration using Web services.

OASIS: One of several organizations that builds on W3C technologies is the Organization for the Advancement of Structured Information Standards, or OASIS *(http://www.oasis-open.org)*. Chartered to foster guidelines for SGML development, this nonprofit consortium of vendors now focuses on driving the adoption of global e-business standards. OASIS technical committees are producing many emerging Web service standards, such as ebXML and WS-Reliability. OASIS also hosts the xml.org portal.

WS-I: The Web Services Interoperability Organization (WS-I) *(http://www.ws-i.org)* aims to ensure that Web service technologies and standards are suitable for enabling business collaborations in a generic, interoperable manner. The organization promotes Web service protocols and practices that can apply across multiple systems, platforms, and languages. A key tactic in achieving these goals is the WS-I Basic Profile, which specifies the collection of Web service standards along with their version numbers—in the first profile these are XML Schema 1.0, SOAP 1.1, WSDL 1.1, and UDDI 1.0—as well as conventions governing how they should be used together. Thus, the WS-I intends to play a unifying role in ensuring that various vendors involved in Web services development can work together in a way that benefits application developers. It was founded and is managed by the leading Web services vendor companies, including Microsoft, IBM, BEA Systems, Oracle, and others.

JCP: The Java Community Process (JCP) *(http://www.jcp.org)* produces Java language bindings and J2EE APIs for technologies such as the Web services and messaging standards developed by other organizations. Led by Sun Microsystems, the JCP has not historically been an open process; although it makes use of expert groups and a proposal process similar to that of other standards organizations, intellectual property rights are typically retained by Sun and licensed to the Java and J2EE platform vendors for a fee. Most of the JSR expert groups are also led by Sun engineers. While lacking the openness of other organizations, the JCP has benefited from the focus that Sun has provided, somewhat unhindered by external agendas.

Ad Hoc Vendor Consortiums: In the race to establish control over portions of the emerging Web services technologies, particularly for the purposes of enterprise integration, traditional competitors such as IBM and Microsoft have in some cases united to publish would-be standards without submitting those works to any standards body. Many of the WS-* specifications fall into this bucket. Often, standards developed through vendor consortiums end up as submissions to standards organizations; the promising BPEL, for example, spent its early life as a creation of Microsoft and IBM before being submitted to OASIS. Interest in retaining intellectual property rights seems to be the catalyst for working in ad hoc fashion. These specifications achieve interoperability without the licensing openness, which is often satisfactory for application developers integrating platforms as popular as those produced by Microsoft and IBM, though whether these works are truly "open standards" is understandably the subject of much debate.

Business Process Components and Intra-Web Service Messaging

Not content merely to influence object-oriented programming, structural decomposition, and domain modeling, Aristotle also mischievously posed one of the most influential rhetorical questions ever to trouble software architecture: Is the world predominantly a series of processes, or is it a series of objects?

Messaging standards reply with an answer worthy of a Zen disciple: yes. The world is a series of objects whose most important characteristics are usually the processes through which they engage with and relate to other objects. It is often an object's behaviors related to other objects rather than its own internal composition that turn out to be most significant. In the realm of Web services and enterprise integration, this object/process hybrid view is referred to as the business process component. The business process component unites a series of services into a logical unit that interacts with other such units via messaging to achieve highly scalable, resilient flows of logic and data. The coalescence of process, object, and interaction patterns into a business process component is the future of messaging as seen by many Web services vendors and standards bodies.

The process component is a macro view of a set of services that is particularly relevant to enterprise integration. Taking a nontechnical example, a human can

Emerging
Standards
and Futures

drive a car, and both the human and the car are separate, highly-complex systems; the process view of the human and car, however, sees them as a single component defined by their interactions with one another and does not focus on the composition of either the human or the car separate from the interaction between them. Further, the process component view describes the interactions of that single component with others on the road, again without interest in the internal composition of other automobiles or drivers. This is not the same as simply presenting an external interface, as it also includes the rules that govern behaviors between usages of the interfaces.

The business process component, as emerging in standards, is a single component that internally consists of a set of Web services and a definition for how messages flow into and out of them. Web services and other message destinations are building blocks used to compose larger compositions whose interactions follow messaging patterns—both the composition of the process component and the linking of multiple process components into an application follow messaging patterns. Business process standards address the correlation of messages between Web services in order to create flows of execution and include behaviors related to errors, transactions, and data exchange.

A more technical business example is illustrated in the following figure in which the processing of a purchase order is handled by a component that consists of a number of service operations.

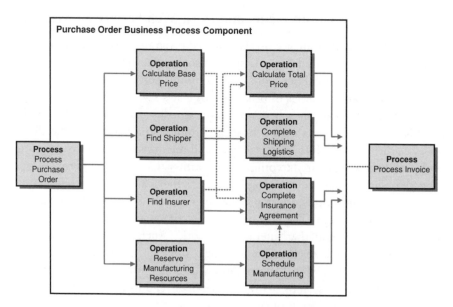

*The Business Process Component Exposing a Single Destination Endpoint
on Behalf of Multiple Internally Choreographed Web Services*

The example includes the following characteristics and activities:

- Each operation in the Process Purchase Order component is an operation available on the portType of a Web service, and the various Web services that expose the operations may reside on remote hosts in partner production facilities.

- When a purchase order is received, four operations are invoked concurrently, but some of the operations have dependencies that must be synchronously resolved (the dashed arrows in the illustration indicate dependencies).

- Two specific dependencies show that the shipping agreement and insurance costs are needed in order to calculate the final cost and that a binding insurance agreement must be received before the manufacturer will commit resources to a production schedule.

- Once all service operations have asynchronously completed, the purchase order has been processed. Rather than requiring the messaging client to interact with all of these services individually and manage the dependencies between them—that is, rather than requiring the client to create a *Process Manager* (312) implementation—the process component exposes a single network endpoint on behalf of all the services and manages all of the messaging and dependencies between services internally, simplifying the client's tasks.

- The Purchase Order process component is in turn linked to another business process component, the Process Invoice Component.

Four standards initiatives warrant a good look in the business process component and integration space: the ebXML initiative, two competing proposals called Business Process Execution Language and Web Services Choreography Interface, and a collection of individual specifications joined through the WS- prefix that address pieces of the same functionality in slightly narrower, more specific fashion.

ebXML and the Electronic Business Messaging Service (ebMS)

Even before the explosive popularity of SOAP and WSDL, many bright thinkers working on business collaboration and B2B integration projects saw a need to develop an open, secure, and interoperable infrastructure for exchanging business information using XML messaging. The several specifications and initiatives developed under the Electronic Business using eXtensible Markup

Language (ebXML) banner address that need, and as technologies such as SOAP have become popular, ebXML has grown to include and build upon them. The ebXML initiatives are jointly managed through OASIS and the United Nations UN/CEFACT organization. UN/CEFACT is the global group that brought the EDI standard into the world, and ebXML in many ways represents the next logical stage in the evolution of EDI.

Several specifications comprise ebXML, covering topics such as how enterprises advertise their business process and search for those of potential partners, how partners agree upon and initiate communication, the use of registries to facilitate the discovery and initialization of business conversations, and the behavior of the messaging infrastructure required to facilitate the conversations. This last element in particular has garnered a great deal of attention, and while it leverages the other ebXML specifications, it can also be considered separately, which is useful for the purposes of focusing on messaging patterns.

ebMS is not quite as "emerging" as some of the other standards mentioned here, as it has already achieved significant success as a means of integrating business processes, augmenting EDI systems, and extending SOAP to provide reliability and security for Web services. Developed by OASIS over a three-year period beginning in 1999, ebMS is also proving influential in the development of other business process standards.

The goal of ebMS is to ease the exchange of business messages within an XML framework, but that framework includes the use of message payloads that are not necessarily XML—the payload can take any form, including traditional EDI formats as well as binary formats. Thus ebMS can encapsulate existing messaging systems and serve as a flexible bridging technology, containing a set of *Message Translator* (85) implementations, which is particularly useful in scaling integration to extranets and to B2B communication between business partners. An important source of use cases for ebMS is the linkage of proprietary MOM systems across separate enterprises, and considerable testing between vendors and developers has occurred to verify this interoperability. Critical to ebMS is that it supports legacy EDI systems, allowing enterprises to leverage longstanding investments in EDI while compensating for EDI's shortcomings by incorporating features of the Web and XML.

While on the one hand ebMS is a compatible iteration of EDI, on the other hand it is also a sophisticated improvement of standard SOAP-based services. The XML transmissions used in an ebMS system consist of SOAP envelopes that include ebMS-specific SOAP Headers to record unique message identifiers, timestamps, digital signatures, and a manifest which provides metadata about the message's payload. Thus, ebMS uses the SOAP Header mechanism to implement the *message routing* patterns and many of the *messaging endpoints* patterns, such as *Idempotent Receiver* (528) and others related to guaranteed sequential delivery.

ebMS transports its payloads by using the SOAP with Attachments standard to attach the payload to the SOAP envelope in much the same way that attachments are added to email messages. These payloads, again, have no formatting restrictions placed upon them: A message's payload may be XML data, binary data, link-based references to external data, and so on. Further, each payload may have its own digital signature, and additional authentication and authorization may be provided by ebMS implementers.

Emerging Standards and Futures

An ebMS Message Is Composed as SOAP Messages with Attachments

Asynchronous message delivery is the default, but synchronous delivery is also possible through ebMS. The error-handling mechanism is also quite sophisticated, and depending on the implementation can provide SOAP Fault information along with payload-specific error messages.

To provide reliability, the critical element of an ebMS implementation—called ebXML Message Service Handlers—persist messages at the sending end of a conversation. Developers can provide semantic declarations such as "once-and-only-once" and "store-and-forward" for individual messages or for groups of messages. ebMS specifies services to manage sequential delivery and management as well; this last service is implemented through a Message Status Service that represents a *Control Bus* (540). It provides the ability to request the status of a message previously sent into the ebMS system, which underneath the covers operates through an implementation of *Message History* (551) and related patterns.

More information on ebXML can be found at *http://www.ebxml.org/*. The ebMS specification can be found at *http://www.ebxml.org/specs/ebMS2.pdf*.

Emerging Standards and Futures

Business Process Execution Language for Web Services (BEPL4WS)

A popular emerging standard for defining business process components and their interactions is Business Process Execution Language for Web Services (BPEL4WS). The name is often pronounced *bee-pel*—or even worse, *bee-pel for wuss*. This standard represents the merging of two competing proposals from IBM and from Microsoft. IBM's Web Services Flow Language (WSFL) specified a means of creating and linking service endpoints to choreograph Web service workflows, while Microsoft's XLANG provided a syntax and development model for creating workflow components as realized in the Microsoft BizTalk server product. BPEL4WS provides a bit of both: It includes a syntax for composing processes from existing services and for describing process interfaces for the purpose of linking them together in larger workflows. It was created by an ad hoc collaboration between BEA Systems, IBM, and Microsoft, and has been submitted to OASIS.

The design of BPEL calls for linkages of Web services, named *partners*, to put XML messages into and out of message stores, called *containers*, according to rules called *activities*. A logical set of service linkages, message containers, and activities comprise a single business process component. The BPEL specification essentially defines a *Process Manager* (312) that creates *Routing Slip* (301), *Durable Subscriber* (522), *Datatype Channel* (111), and others based on a declarative XML syntax. Developers declare behaviors in XML (perhaps with the aid of visual tools) in order to craft business process components (such as the one shown in the figure on page 630), and do not need to programmatically create the messaging between services.

WSDL documents are very important to BPEL, as the BPEL component will consist of and manage multiple Web services based on the services' WSDL documents. The business process instantiates and routes messages to the service endpoints declared within these services' WSDL documents using messages that are formatted according to the WSDL message declarations. The BPEL syntax links the portType and operations of a set of Web services by importing their WSDL files and declaring what sequences to use to receive the service messages, where to send them, when and how to reply, when to invoke other Web services, and so forth.

In order to establish the linkages between services, the application developer imports the WSDL of the Web services comprising the component and defines the partner relationships between them using the BPEL serviceLinkType element. This element refers to the portTypes of the Web services involved in a flow and the partner roles that they play in relation to the process; the developer is then able to refer to these linkages and partner roles when declaring how messages should flow into and out of them.

After declaring the relationships between services, the developer uses BPEL to create containers to hold the messages that the services use as input and output. Containers are very much like a *Datatype Channel* (111) for the message types defined in WSDL. Depending on the underlying container implementation, a container could also be considered from the perspective of the *Shared Database* (47) integration style, but with added encapsulation and built-in collaboration semantics; a container is a shared data repository used by separate services. In addition to connecting containers to services through the BPEL elements, a container's contents can be accessed directly via XPath extensions.

A BPEL component itself exposes its own input and output points as a single interface, and it does so in the same form that its internal Web services use: through WSDL. It should be evident, however, that the WSDL of a business process component is slightly different from a Web service WSDL document in that the business process WSDL's portTypes define entry points into and out of that single process, and not separate pieces of logic implemented as methods in a service interface.

The behavior of a BPEL component is declared as a set of actions. In any one specific action, a business processes can send messages to a service (in this case, the Web service is called an *invoked partner*), receive messages from a service (in this case, the service is called a *client partner*), reply to a message sent by a client partner, determine whether it should send or receive messages based on some logical rule, wait for a scheduled period of time, report an error, copy a message from one place to another, or do nothing at all.

The BPEL XML grammar reflects each of these basic actions. A developer uses the invoke element to send messages to an invoked partner and uses receive and reply to receive and reply to a client partner. Elements such as flow and pick fork logic into parallel and event-based channels of execution. The throw element facilitates error reporting, while the wait, empty, and terminate elements pause or halt execution. Elements to structure activities include while, sequence, and pick, and conditionals in BPEL are declared using XPath statements.

Emerging
Standards
and Futures

Once a developer has created the XML source file that defines the services that will compose a business process, declares the message containers that the services will use, and declares the sequence of operations involved in the message exchange, he or she is ready to deploy the business process component. This is where the runtime aspects of BPEL implementations come into play.

In addition to acting as declarations of service relationships and message flow, BPEL descriptions are also executable files that can be fed into a BPEL4WS engine. When this happens, the engine interprets the file and sets up a series of messaging constructs for the application developer that connects the Web services that are part of the business process. As a *Process Manager* (312) implementation, the BPEL4WS runtime is the governing entity that manages and correlates the flow of messages between services. The BPEL4WS engine accepts all of the necessary documents and dynamically generates and manages the messaging infrastructure.

The BPEL specification can be found at *http://www-106.ibm.com/developerworks/webservices/library/ws-bpel/*.

Web Service Choreography Interface (WSCI)

The Web Service Choreography Interface (WSCI; often pronounced *whiskey*) addresses the same problem domain tackled by BPEL. The two were competing specifications initially backed by competing vendor alliances (with the exception of BEA, which appears to be hedging bets by contributing to both specifications). WSCI was backed by Sun, Intalio, SAP, and BEA, and has been submitted to the W3C. However, several original supporters of WSCI are now lending support to BPEL.

WSCI is influenced by Business Process Modeling Language (BPML), which while not directly relevant to integration patterns, does bear mentioning for the sake of WSCI's historical context. BPML represents business processes in an XML-based metalanguage used in process modeling. BPML's workflow aspects are largely part of WSCI, but BPML also includes a companion graphical notation and query language.

Like BPEL, WSCI recognizes that enterprise integration involves lengthy conversations among composite services rather than the single operational invocations assumed by basic Web services protocols. WSCI provides a way to link service messages from multiple operations into these composite processes, ensuring along the way that messages are sent or received in the proper sequences, sent and received according to declarative business rules, sent in transactional fashion when needed, and portrayable and manageable as a single global process. Leveraging Web service advantages over traditional proprietary MOM solutions, WSCI also accommodates the dynamic discovery of services, heterogeneous protocols, and decentralized coordination of workflow.

Emerging
Standards
and Futures

Like BPEL, WSCI relies heavily upon WSDL's advertisement of service endpoints, portTypes, operations, and message types. WSCI actions directly map to operations exposed in the WSDL of the services within a choreography. Moreover, the WSCI syntax is embedded directly within a WSDL file; the declarations sit either in a WSDL document, which imports the WSDL documents of the choreographed services, or within the WSDL file of a single service whose operations are being choreographed. WSCI elements are contained within the WSDL definitions element.

The fundamental construct of WSCI is the action in which Web service messaging occurs. Actions are grouped within process elements so that they are declared to occur sequentially, in parallel, in loop, or conditionally. A set of processes is grouped with an interface declaration; this interface element is the interface to the process component, and it is directly embedded within the WSDL definitions of a Web service. Many of the activity elements are similar to those of BPEL, and like their BPEL counterparts, they include support for XPath expressions.

The WSCI specification can be found at *http://wwws.sun.com/software/xml/developers/wsci/wsci-spec-10.pdf*.

Java Business Process Component Standards

The JCP creates Java language APIs and bindings influenced by non-Java standards. In particular, standards developed by the Object Management Group (OMG) and the W3C have been shadowed by the JCP. Recently, the JCP has turned this approach toward Web services standards developed by groups such as the WS-I, and two new, much-ballyhooed JSRs are now underway to address Java bindings for business process components: Process Definition for Java (JSR-207), submitted by BEA Systems, and Java Business Integration (JSR-208), submitted by Sun Microsystems. While at first glance these two proposals may seem to overlap, they are actually fairly complementary. JSR-207 specifies a way for developers to craft messaging or process components quickly and easily using metadata attached to Java code; JSR-208 specifies how those components will interact with each other, with containers, and with the rest of the J2EE and Web services world. So, JSR-207 is more or less a micro-view, and JSR-208 is a macro-view of how the messaging between process components is to be standardized in Java.

Emerging
Standards
and Futures

Process Definition for Java (JSR-207)   Process Definition for Java (JSR-207), submitted by BEA Systems, aims to define metadata, interfaces, and a runtime model for creating business processes in the Java/J2EE environment. This very important JSR intends to specify the standard means of crafting business process components using the Java language and Javadoc-like metadata annotations. Proposed as an addition to J2EE, the mechanism could also be used to build Java implementations of business process initiatives such as BPEL4WS, WSCI, and those produced by the W3C Choreography Working Group.

This technology builds upon Java Language Metadata technology (JSR-175) in order to supply a simple syntax for describing business processes. Metadata can be applied directly to Java source code to dynamically generate and bind process behaviors, including support for asynchronous messaging, parallel execution, message correlation, message routing, error handling, and other common flow activities. The metadata semantics therefore need to be rich enough to support the parameters needed for a component's container to dynamically set up the messaging infrastructure and handle issues described in the introduction in Chapter 5, "Message Construction," upon the component's deployment.

It is worth noting that this JSR is not needed to enable developers to build business process components in J2EE. It is possible to build such processes today—but it is laborious work that requires developers to apply messaging patterns at a very low level and results in workflows that are costly to maintain. This specification intends to simplify the creation of process components so that developers can apply their skills at a higher level, creating more powerful applications more rapidly that are less expensive to evolve and administer over time.

More details on Process definition for Java can be found at *http://www. jcp.org/en/jsr/detail?id=207*.

Java Business Integration (JSR-208)   Sun proposed Java Business Integration (JBI) in JSR-208 with the intention of defining service provider interfaces (SPIs) for creating a business integration environment for specifications such as WSCI, BPEL4WS, and the work produced by the W3C Choreography Working Group. JBI proposes no new Java APIs or annotations, but does include a new deployment and packaging mechanism. Instead of adding APIs for developers, JBI focuses on integration infrastructure, and its SPIs will be visible primarily to product vendors who create messaging and process component models for performing integration work in a Java setting. The JBI expert group aims to follow the lead of the W3C Choreography Working Group and ensure that the work of that group will fit seamlessly into the J2EE platform.

JBI has a fairly lofty goal: Map various systems and protocol standards—that is, multiple syntaxes used to describe relationships between processes, including syntaxes that are proprietary and vendor-specific as well as those that become standard—to one another and to J2EE. It provides a Java binding for message choreography regardless of the underlying message and process specifics. It also includes a new packaging mechanism that extends J2EE packaging (such as WAR, JAR, RAR, and EAR) to support the deployment of a JBI component into a J2EE environment.

Emerging
Standards
and Futures

JBI sees three principal roles required for supporting process components: bindings, machines, and the environment. Bindings are about communication formats and include message formats and network transports along with their mappings as well as form an umbrella around workflow formats such as BPEL; machines are the service and process containers that host and manage business processes; the environment is the overarching process management system that links heterogeneous machines and bindings to one another. JBI focuses on the environment as the core of the integration system and specifies how machines and bindings interact with it. The JBI packaging and deployment mechanism is intended to provide a means of hooking processes up to the environment in a standard way, but the actual creation of those components is outside the scope of the specification.

JBI views the Process Definition for Java (JSR-207) described above as a way of composing process components, and the runtime that will host those components fits into the category of a JBI machine. That machine should implement the *Message Translator* (85), *Service Activator* (532), *Envelope Wrapper* (330) and other patterns necessary to expose their formats and protocol behaviors through JBI to ensure that it can integrate correctly with the integration environment.

More details on JBI can be found at *http://www.jcp.org/en/jsr/detail?id=208*.

WS-*

Less ambitious than the process integration specifications just described, a number of Web services specifications are emerging to extend SOAP- and WSDL-based Web services to include reliability, security, statefulness, and quality of service. Typically identifiable by the *WS-* prefix, these specifications build on the W3C technologies, and each addresses a fairly specific problem.

Unfortunately, the Web services standards landscape has become muddled with competing versions backed by competing vendor alliances, and perhaps as a result of this competition, many of these standards are rarely seen implemented in the wild today. A standards shake-out seems to be looming. Nevertheless, these specifications are worth noting, as their idioms and tactics might prove useful to application developers who are applying Web services technologies like SOAP and WSDL to messaging-based enterprise integration. These standards are also certain to find a home in the products of the vendors who propose them, including those of IBM, BEA, Microsoft, and Oracle.

A few of the more notable specifications in this category include those dealing with transactability, reliability, routing, conversational state, and security. These are described in the following pages.

WS-Coordination and WS-Transaction   Being stateless and unreliable, the most popular Web services protocols and transports do not provide the quality of service required by transactional processes. This shortcoming blossoms into a critically important problem. In practice, it means that if a developer wishes to use a Web services–based integration mechanism, that developer must grow his or her own transaction scheme within those integration mechanisms. A collection of service invocations that occur through asynchronous messaging must be capable of being batched atomically so that the messages function as a unit that can fail or roll back all at once or as a unit whose failure can trigger some form of compensation. This is common in proprietary MOM systems. The Web Services Coordination and Web Services Transaction specifications tackle this problem for Web services.

WS-Coordination, drafted by BEA, Microsoft, and IBM, specifies a way to create and propagate contextual information by all of the services participating in a flow, even asynchronously and over jagged time intervals. The specification describes an extensible framework for creating protocols that coordinate the actions of applications and services. These coordination protocols function by creating and registering XML-based contexts that are propagated with SOAP messages and used by coordinators located at all endpoints in an interaction.

Such contexts can be used to support a number of application behaviors, such as those that need to reach consistent agreement on the outcome of distributed transactions. Accordingly, the WS-Transaction specification uses WS-Coordination to implement distributed transactability across service invocations.

WS-Transaction defines a way to monitor and measure the success or failure of each action in a flow. Practically, this means that when a SOAP message arrives at an endpoint, the SOAP Header containing the coordination context must be filtered and pulled from the message (implementations may employ the *Content Filter* [342] and *Splitter* [259] patterns for this task) and then sent to the transaction coordinator for interpretation.

The SOAP envelope excerpt below provides a simple example of a coordination context used for making SOAP operations transactable through WS-Transaction. This context information in the SOAP header is used by coordinators to register applications to receive transaction events such as enlistments, the prepare stage of a two-phase commit process, rollbacks, and commits.

```
<SOAP-ENV:Envelope xmlns:SOAP-ENV="http://www.w3.org/2001/12/soap-envelope">

  <SOAP-ENV:Header>

    <wscoor:CoordinationContext
          xmlns:wscoor="http://schemas.xmlsoap.org/ws/2002/08/wscoor"
          xmlns:wsu="http://schemas.xmlsoap.org/ws/2002/07/utility"
          xmlns:myTransactableApp="http://foo.com/baz">

      <wsu:Identifier>http://foo.com/baz/bar</wsu:Identifier>
      <wsu:Expires>2004-12-31T18:00:00-08:00</wsu:Expires>

      <wscoor:CoordinationType>
        http://schemas.xmlsoap.org/ws/2002/08/wstx
      </wscoor:CoordinationType>

      <wscoor:RegistrationService>
        <wsu:Address>
          http://foo.com/coordinationservice/registration
        </wsu:Address>
      </wscoor:RegistrationService>

      <myTransactableApp:IsolationLevel>
        RepeatableRead
      </myTransactableApp:IsolationLevel>

    </wscoor:CoordinationContext>

  </SOAP-ENV:Header>

  <!-- SOAP BODY (snipped) -->

</SOAP-ENV:Envelope>
```

The WS-Transaction specification defines two coordination types for developers to use in their applications: atomic transaction (AT) and business activity (BA).

Atomic transactions map fairly well to traditional distributed transaction technology, such as XA. They are useful for relatively short-lived operations in which locking of resources—such as threads and portions of data sources—are acceptable and in which absolute rollbacks make sense. WS-Transaction provides a means of linking proprietary XA implementations, including support for two-phase commit, to Web services.

A business activity is typically a long-lived process that may consist of a number of atomic transactions. A global rollback is usually not desirable in the event of a single failure condition in a business activity; instead, a failure of one atomic transaction within a business activity should often trigger another set of service invocations and message exchanges. These exchanges might include compensation techniques to recover from the error in a way that preserves part of the history of the business activity. An example is a business activity that includes the booking of an airline flight, rental of a car, reservation of a hotel room, and reservation of theater tickets that a user makes over a two- or three-day period. Each activity in this flow may be an atomic transaction, and if one of the events should fail, the overarching business activity of making the travel arrangements should adjust via compensation rather than through coordinated rollback of all atomic transactions.

The WS-Coordination and WS-Transaction specifications are promising attempts to provide reliable, rich behaviors in the event of failures during service messaging. As they begin to wind their way into products, they should take the burden off of developers to craft their own transactability and contextual services around message-based service applications.

Information on WS-Transaction can be found at *http://dev2dev.bea.com/technologies/webservices/ws-transaction.jsp.*

WS-Reliability and WS-ReliableMessaging It is common for message-based interactions between Web services to require reliable, guaranteeable messaging even in the event of network, application, or component failures and to include persistence mechanisms and resend semantics. The most popular Web services technologies do not provide such reliability, however; SOAP without enhancements, for example, isn't comprehensively useful in many enterprise messaging scenarios because its most popular bindings don't reliably guarantee message delivery.

To remedy this, application developers are typically forced to implement reliability themselves using the extensibility of Web services mechanisms such as SOAP Headers. To eliminate the need for application developers to take on this task, new standards are emerging to tackle Web services reliability. Two such specifications are Web Services Reliability (WS-Reliability) and Web Services

Emerging
Standards
and Futures

Reliable Messaging (WS-ReliableMessaging). As is common in the nascent Web services standards space, these two standards are competing, backed by different groups of vendors aimed at the same problem domain.

WS-Reliability provides SOAP-based Web services with the ability to exchange messages asynchronously with guaranteed delivery, without duplicates, and with message ordering. It is a SOAP standard for managing message aggregation and sequencing, and provides a standard tactic for implementing the *Guaranteed Delivery* (122) and *Resequencer* (283) patterns, among others. WS-Reliability leverages the SOAP Header mechanism to add the header elements `MessageHeader`, `ReliableMessage`, `MessageOrder`, and `RMResponse` to SOAP messages. These elements denote message identifiers such as group IDs and sequence numbers, timestamps, time-to-live values, message type values, sender and receiver information, and acknowledgment callback information. WS-Reliability is produced by a number of vendors, including Sun, Oracle, and Sonic, and it has been submitted to OASIS. It is heavily influenced by the functionality of the ebMS.

To conform to WS-Reliability, the receiver of a SOAP message must respond with either a fault or an acknowledgment using the `<RMResponse>` element in a SOAP header. If such an acknowledgment is not received, then the sender resends the same message using the same message identifier. The sender is required to persist the message until its time-to-live value has expired or until acknowledgment or failure has occurred; the receiver is also required to persist the message until it can be reliably transmitted to the application layer.

To ensure that once-and-only-once message behaviors are enforced, WS-Reliability provides a sequence number mechanism that can be enabled based on application requirements. Separate messages that are grouped together may share the same group identifier but will advertise their own sequence numbers within the SOAP header, allowing receivers to resequence the messages before delivering them to the application.

The WS-Reliability specification can be found at *http://www.oasis-open.org/committees/documents.php?wg_abbrev=wsrm*.

The WS-ReliableMessaging specification describes a similar protocol that allows messages to be delivered reliably between distributed applications in the presence of failures. The protocol is described in an independent manner, allowing it to be implemented using a variety of network transport technologies and bindings. The specification does include one specific binding for SOAP. WS-ReliableMessaging is backed by BEA, IBM, and Microsoft, and has not yet been released to a standards body.

WS-ReliableMessaging operates on the same principles as WS-Reliability. It makes similar use of acknowledgments, callbacks, and identifiers; implies similar usage of persistent message caches; and offers detailed fault messages. It ensures that messages are delivered according to any of four basic delivery assurances: At most once, at least once, exactly once, and in order. An example of a message sequence delivered through WS-ReliableMessaging is illustrated below.

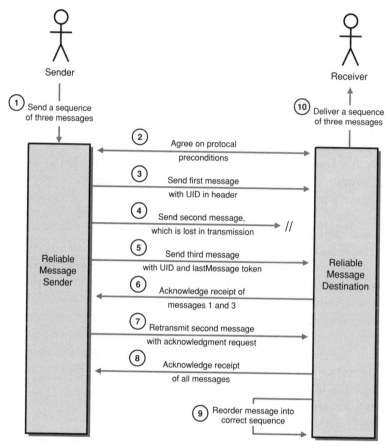

WS-ReliableMessaging Provides Guaranteed Sequential Delivery through a Series of Acknowledgment Callbacks That Rely on Unique IDs Inserted into the SOAP Header Element

A key difference between the two competing reliability specifications is that WS-ReliableMessaging includes usage of other critical Web services specifications, such as WS-Security and WS-Addressing. In practice, this means that WS-

ReliableMessaging uses specific idioms from other standards for supplying this information, whereas WS-Reliability supports the features but does not yet insist on the idiomatic forms specified in the other new standards.

More information on WS-ReliableMessaging can be found at *http://dev2dev. bea.com/technologies/webservices/ws-reliablemessaging.jsp*.

WS-Conversation   Web Services Conversation (WS-Conversation) specifies a protocol for managing stateful asynchronous message exchange between a sender and receiver, usually across two SOAP endpoints. In contrast to relying on an encapsulating business process component for managing stateful message exchange among multiple partners, this proposal provides a simple means of accomplishing the same thing between a single client and single service (where the client may also be a service).

The protocol leverages the SOAP Header mechanism to send identifiers, or token IDs, along with SOAP messages. When a stateful conversation is begun, the StartHeader element is used to supply a conversation identifier and callback URI. Subsequent messages that are part of the same conversation use the ContinueHeader and the CallbackHeader for further requests and replies, and these elements will include the same identifier established when the conversation was started.

The SOAP Header mechanism can be used to implement these patterns without use of these standard mechanisms, though there is benefit in establishing a common mechanism for clients and services across platforms. It is a formalization of the *Aggregator* (268) and *Composed Message Processor* (294) patterns using *Correlation Identifier* (163) for the purposes of mapping multiple messages to a single session.

The approach of externalizing state management through a process component or choreography seems more promising for larger scale integration projects where it is useful for simplicity's sake to consider the services and components as black boxes, but WS-Conversation is an example of what can be done when greater control over the services and clients is possible.

WS-Security   While standards such as WS-ReliableMessaging, WS-Coordination, and WS-Addressing provide various mechanisms that identify the sender of a message, none of those specifications guarantee that the sender actually owns the identity it claims. The elements of the WS-I Basic Profile—XML Schema, SOAP, WSDL, and UDDI—make no mention of how identity is verified and guaranteed or how message integrity is to be maintained. Early adopters of Web services either kept their services open and available to all or developed proprietary security protocols in order to fill this gap. The proprietary and private approaches created an undesirable coupling between message senders and receivers, something particularly galling in otherwise asynchronous and loosely coupled federations of message nodes.

WS-Security, also referred to as the Web Services Security Language, is the proposed standard means of addressing these issues. Of all the WS-* specifications, it enjoys perhaps the broadest level of consensus among the major Web services platform vendors. Created by a consortium consisting of Microsoft, IBM, and Verisign, it is now part of OASIS; it has received votes of confidence from the likes of Sun, BEA, Intel, SAP, IONA, RSA Security, and others.

**Emerging
Standards
and Futures**

WS-Security does not propose new security technologies, but rather it bridges SOAP and existing security technologies. It provides a generic, extensible means of associating security tokens with SOAP messages and propagating those tokens to SOAP endpoints. It also specifies the standard approach to encoding binary security tokens, such as digital certificates and Kerberos tickets, in SOAP messages. It does not describe specific fixed protocols but rather establishes a general set of mechanisms for implementing any number of security protocols and incorporating any number of trust domains, signature formats, and encryption technologies. In as much as it can include use of digital certificates, digests, and implementations of technologies such as PKI, Kerberos, SSL, and the like, WS-Security represents a way to apply familiar Internet security standbys to SOAP endpoints.

In addition to verification of sender identity, WS-Security may protect message integrity—that is, protect it from intermediary prying eyes during network transmission—by leveraging the W3C XML Signature and XML Encryption standards. In cases in which intermediary actors and third-party services are not involved, however, the use of HTTPS is a common alternative means of protecting SOAP messages in transit.

The security model specifies that a SOAP message sender makes a series of claims such as the sender's identity, group, privilege, and the like. These claims are collected in the form of a signed security token. The receiver of the message is charged with endorsing the claims. The tokens and signatures are carried in a SOAP Header block, specifically under the security header element in the WS-Security namespace. If an error occurs when the receiver endorses claims, that error will be one of two types: unsupported errors, which indicate that the endpoint does not support a particular token or encryption algorithm, and failure errors, which indicate most other errors, including all those related to invalid tokens and signatures. The specification does not mandate that failure errors always be reported, as they may be the result of an attack. When errors are reported, they take the form of SOAP Faults with fault codes defined in the specification.

The WS-Security specification can be found on the Web sites of each of its co-authoring vendors, including the following location at IBM: *http://www-106.ibm.com/developerworks/library/ws-secure/*.

WS-Addressing, WS-Policy, and Other WS-* Specifications

There are a number of other proposed WS-* specifications with varying degrees of support and acceptance. Some are quite narrow in scope, such as WS-Addressing, which defines XML elements to identify Web services endpoints in messages. This specification aims to support messaging through intermediaries such as endpoint managers, proxies, firewalls, and gateways in a transport-neutral manner. Essentially, WS-Addressing is a standard way to denote who a message is from ("From:") and who it is to ("To:"). It provides a means to plug SOAP-based Web services into *Recipient List* (249) solutions. As it provides a means of specifying where to direct a reply, it appears destined to be the standard Web services approach to resolving the issues raised in *Return Address* (159).

A means of supplying metadata about services, the Web Services Policy Framework (WS-Policy) offers a syntax for describing the policies of a Web service. Such policies include service requirements, preferences, capabilities, and quality of service metadata. The accompanying Web Services Policy Assertions Language (WS-PolicyAssertions) specifies a means of asserting that a message or service endpoint supports a particular policy. It involves investigating the WS-Policy declarations in search of a specific required policy. Finally, the Web Services Policy Attachment (WS-PolicyAttachment) describes how these policy standards fit into existing Web services technologies. It specifies how to associate policy expressions with WSDL type definitions and UDDI entities, and it defines how to associate implementation-specific policies with all or part of a WSDL portType.

New WS-* specifications are surfacing quickly as vendors race to formalize the implementation practices that application developers are following, staking a claim to valuable Web services intellectual property in the process. Wise application developers will keep an eye on interesting standards and cull idioms from them when useful, but will also bear in mind that the pattern and not the implementation idiom is most important to crafting a message-based application. The emerging WS-* standards are not yet required for implementing interoperable enterprise messaging systems, and where they become hindrances or distractions, they should boldly be ignored until mature.

Conclusions

At their best, standards extend the reach of design patterns by ensuring that different implementations of the same pattern are interoperable. Many efforts are underway to extend messaging patterns through Web services standards; many of these standards focus on the composition and behavior of workflow components called business process components. Standards such as BPEL, WSCI, and the WS-* specifications tackle many of the problems described in this book and implement several of the patterns in this pattern language.

Still, the emerging standards stories are occasionally conflicting and can be confusing. They're certainly not all ready for prime time. When applying a pattern, an application developer should avoid getting bogged down by standards and stay focused instead on the particular use cases at hand. Take a look at how certain standards are approaching a problem, and adopt those tactical, idiomatic implementations of a pattern if it makes sense or if it's helpful during implementation—regardless of whether the approach is standardized across vendor products. Developers can also provide feedback to standards organizations to challenge, criticize, and otherwise ensure that standards become practically useful and not academic or vendor exercises. As standards mature, architects are wise to consider how their use might extend enterprise integration solutions to broader, less risky, less costly, and more powerful levels of sophistication.

Emerging Standards and Futures

Bibliography

[Alexander]

A Pattern Language: Towns, Buildings, Construction, Christopher Alexander, Sara Ishikawa, & Murray Silverstein; Oxford University Press 1977, ISBN 0195019199

> Probably the most quoted book in any work related to patterns. I actually used a number of Alexander's patterns to design a beach house for an interior architecture class. It is interesting to note that Alexander's desire to dissect architecture and design into a set of composable constructs may stem from his study of mathematics. His thesis, published as "Notes on the synthesis of form," references a set of programs that he developed in IBM 7090 assembly code. So, the tremendous success of Alexander's patterns in the software community is not quite coincidental.

[Alpert]

The Design Patterns Smalltalk Companion, Sherman Alpert, Kyle Brown, & Bobby Woolf; Addison-Wesley 1998, ISBN 0201184621

> A second look at the *Design Patterns* material [GoF], this time for developers using a programming environment that has a common class library and runs on a virtual machine with garbage collection. At the time, that was Smalltalk, but many of the insights also apply to Java and .NET/C#.

[Box]

Essential .NET, Volume 1: The Common Language Runtime, Don Box; Addison-Wesley 2002, ISBN 0201734117

> More than you ever wanted to know about the inner workings of the CLR.

[BPEL4WS]

Business Process Execution Language for Web Services, Version 1.0, BEA, IBM, Microsoft; July 31, 2002, *http://www.ibm.com/developerworks/webservices/library/ws-bpel1/*

The BPEL4WS 1.0 specification.

[CoreJ2EE]

Core J2EE Patterns: Best Practices and Design Strategies (2nd edition), Deepak Alur, John Crupi, & Dan Malks; Prentice Hall PTR 2003, ISBN 0131422464

A very good book on enterprise application architecture patterns for Java.

[CSP]

"Communicating Sequential Processes," C. A. R. Hoare; *Communications of the ACM*, 1978

ACM online library access is required to see the full-text version of this article.

[Dickman]

Designing Applications with MSMQ, Alan Dickman; Addison-Wesley 1998, ISBN 0201325810

The book contains a great chapter on "Solutions to Messaging Problems" that deals with correlation, event-driven consumers and object serialization, and deserialization. Unfortunately, the age of the book means that all examples use Visual Basic with COM or C++.

[Douglass]

Real-Time Design Patterns, Bruce Powel Douglass; Addison-Wesley 2003, ISBN 0201699567

This book proves the transportability of patterns across domains. Some of Douglass's reliability patterns prove very useful in the context of enterprise messaging.

[EAA]

Patterns of Enterprise Application Architecture, Martin Fowler; Addison-Wesley 2003, ISBN 0321127420

The most comprehensive book yet on application architecture patterns. Even though it covers 51 patterns, it is an easy and interesting read while never sacrificing technical accuracy.

[EJB 2.0]

Enterprise JavaBeans Specification, Version 2.0, Sun Microsystems; August 14, 2001, *http://java.sun.com/products/ejb/docs.html*

The EJB 2.0 specification.

[Garlan]

Software Architecture: Perspectives on an Emerging Discipline, Mary Shaw & David Garlan; Prentice Hall 1996, ISBN 0131829572

The book contains a great chapter on architectural styles, including *Pipes and Filters*.

[GoF]

Design Patterns: Elements of Reusable Object-Oriented Software, Erich Gamma, Richard Helm, Ralph Johnson, & John Vlissides; Addison-Wesley 1995, ISBN 0201633612

Surely the second most quoted book in any work on patterns.

[Graham]

Building Web Services with Java: Making Sense of XML, SOAP and UDDI, Steve Graham, Simon Simeonov, Toufic Boubez, Glen Daniels, Doug Davis, Yuichi Nakamura, & Ryo Nyeama; SAMS Publishing 2002, ISBN 0672321815

A very good book on how Java and Web services come together.

[Hapner]

Java Messaging Service API Tutorial and Reference, Mark Hapner, Rich Burridge, Rahul Sharma, Joseph Fialli, & Kim Haase; Addison-Wesley 2002, ISBN 0201784726

How JMS works, from the authors who wrote the specification.

[Hohmann]

Beyond Software Architecture: Creating and Sustaining Winning Solutions, Luke Hohmann; Addison-Wesley 2003, ISBN 0201775948

Luke reminds us how many architectural decisions are not driven by technology alone but by business decisions, licensing schemes, and a host of other external factors.

[JMS]

Java Message Service (JMS), Sun Microsystems; 2001–2003, *http://java.sun.com/ products/jms/*

> The Java Message Service API, part of the Java 2, Enterprise Edition (J2EE) platform.

[JMS 1.1]

Java Message Service (the Sun Java Message Service 1.1 Specification), Sun Microsystems; April 12, 2002, *http://java.sun.com/products/jms/docs.html*

> The JMS 1.1 specification.

[JTA]

Java Transaction API (JTA), Sun Microsystems; 2001–2003, *http://java.sun.com/ products/jta/*

> The Java Transaction API, part of the Java 2, Enterprise Edition (J2EE) platform.

[Kahn]

"The Semantics of a Simple Language for Parallel Programming," G. Kahn, *Information Processing 74: Proc. IFIP Congress 74*, North-Holland Publishing Co., 1974

[Kaye]

Loosely Coupled: The Missing Pieces of Web Services, Doug Kaye; RDS Press 2003, ISBN 1881378241

> A refreshing look at Web services. Instead of wading through APIs, we get to read about the core principles at work in service-oriented architectures in a technology-neutral, jargon-free way. This book is likely too high-level for developers itching to make that SOAP call, but it is ideal for technical managers and architects who have to explain these concepts to non-techies.

[Kent]

Data and Reality, William Kent; 1stBooks 2000, ISBN 1585009709

> A classic book (the original edition is from 1978) that tells us why modeling reality inside a computer system is so hard.

[Lewis]

Advanced Messaging Applications with MSMQ and MQSeries, Rhys Lewis; Que 2000, ISBN 078972023X

[Leyman]

Production Workflow: Concepts and Techniques, Frank Leyman & Dieter Roller; Prentice-Hall PTR 1999, ISBN 0130217530

[MDMSG]

Multiple-Destination Messaging, Microsoft; February 2003, *http:// msdn.microsoft.com/library/en-us/msmq/msmq_about_messages_8aqv.asp*

Discusses the new feature in MSMQ 3.0 for sending messages to more than one destination.

[MicroWorkflow]

"Micro-Workflow: A Workflow Architecture Supporting Compositional Object-Oriented Software Development," Dragos Manolescu; University of Illinois 2000, *http://micro-workflow.com/PhDThesis/phdthesis.pdf*

[Monroe]

"Stylized Architecture, Design Patterns, and Objects," Robert T. Monroe, Drew Kompanek, Ralph Melton, & David Garlan; 1996, *http://www-2.cs.cmu.edu/ afs/cs/project/compose/ftp/pdf/ObjPatternsArch-ieee97.pdf*

[Monson-Haefel]

Java Message Service, Richard Monson-Haefel & David A. Chappell; O'Reilly 2001, ISBN 0596000685

Perhaps the best-known JMS book.

[MQSeries]

WebSphere MQ (formerly MQSeries), IBM; *http://www.software.ibm.com/ts/ mqseries*

One of the oldest and best known messaging and integration products.

[MSMQ]

Microsoft Message Queuing (MSMQ), Microsoft; *http://www.microsoft.com/windows2000/technologies/communications/msmq/*

> The messaging product built into Windows 2000, Windows XP, and Windows Server 2003.

[PatternForms]

Pattern Forms, *Wiki-Wiki-Web*, Cunningham & Cunningham; last edited on August 26, 2002, *http://c2.com/cgi/wiki?PatternForms*

> A list of commonly used pattern forms and their differences.

[PLoPD1]

Pattern Languages of Program Design, James Coplien & Douglas Schmidt (Editors); Addison-Wesley 1995, ISBN 0201607344

> The proceedings from the first PLoP conference. These proceedings contain a lot of papers that formed the basis for later books, such as [POSA]. This volume contains Frank Buschmann's and Regine Meunier's "A System of Patterns," Regine Meunier's "The Pipes and Filters Architecture," and Diane Mularz's "Pattern-Based Integration Architectures."

[PLoPD3]

Pattern Languages of Program Design 3, Robert Martin, Dirk Riehle, & Frank Buschmann (Editors); Addison-Wesley 1998, ISBN 0201310112.

> The third book from the PLoP conferences (PLoP, EuroPLoP, etc.; see *http://hillside.net/conferencesnavigation.htm*) contains patterns that became the basis for [POSA2]: Acceptor and Connector, Asynchronous Completion Token, and Double-Checked Locking. It also contains two patterns from the authors of this book: Null Object and Type Object.

[POSA]

Pattern-Oriented Software Architecture, Frank Buschmann, Regine Meunier, Hans Rohnert, Peter Sommerlad, & Michael Stal; Wiley 1996, ISBN 0471958697

> A great book on architecture and design patterns.

[POSA2]

Pattern-Oriented Software Architecture, Vol. 2, Douglas Schmidt, Michael Stal, Hans Rohnert, & Frank Buschmann; Wiley 2000, ISBN 0471606952

> More patterns focused on distributed systems and concurrency issues.

[Sharp]

Workflow Modeling: Tools for Process Improvement and Application Development, Alec Sharp & Patrick McDermott; Artech House 2001, ISBN 1580530214

> This book focuses on the modeling aspect of workflow—an interesting read for analysts and business architects alike.

[SOAP 1.1]

W3C Simple Object Access Protocol (SOAP) 1.1 Specification, World Wide Web Consortium; W3C Note, May 8, 2000, *http://www.w3.org/TR/SOAP/*

> The SOAP 1.1 specification.

[SOAP 1.2 Part 2]

SOAP Version 1.2, Part 2: Adjuncts, World Wide Web Consortium; W3C Recommendation, June 24, 2003, *http://www.w3.org/TR/soap12-part2/*

> The "extra parts" of the SOAP 1.2 specification.

[Stevens]

TCP/IP Illustrated, Volume 1: The Protocols, W. Richard Stevens; Addison-Wesley 1994, ISBN 0201633469

[SysMsg]

"System.Messaging namespace," .NET Framework, version 1.1, Microsoft; *http://msdn.microsoft.com/library/en-us/cpref/html/cpref_start.asp*

[Tennison]

XSLT and XPath on the Edge, Jeni Tennison; John Wiley & Sons 2001, ISBN 0764547763

[UML]

UML Distilled: A Brief Guide to the Standard Object Modeling Language (3rd edition), Martin Fowler; Addison-Wesley 2003, ISBN 0321193687

A excellent source for learning about UML diagrams—what they're supposed to look like and what they mean.

[UMLEAI]

"UML Profile for Enterprise Application Integration," Object Management Group; 2002, *http://www.omg.org/technology/documents/modeling_spec_catalog.htm*

[Wright]

TCP/IP Illustrated, Volume 2: The Implementation, Gary R. Wright & W. Richard Stevens; Addison-Wesley 1995, ISBN 020163354X

[WSAUS]

"Web Services Architecture Usage Scenarios," World Wide Web Consortium; W3C Working Draft, May 14, 2003, *http://www.w3.org/TR/ws-arch-scenarios/*

The W3C's latest thinking on how Web services will be used and what requirements the specifications need to fulfill.

[WSDL 1.1]

Web Services Description Language (WSDL) 1.1, World Wide Web Consortium; W3C Note March 15, 2001, *http://www.w3.org/TR/wsdl*

The WSDL 1.1 specification.

[WSFL]

Web Services Flow Language (WSFL) 1.0, IBM; May 2001, *http://www-3.ibm.com/ software/solutions/webservices/pdf/WSFL.pdf*

The WSFL 1.0 specification.

[WSMQ]

WebSphere MQ Using Java (2nd edition), IBM; October 2002, *http://publibfp.boulder.ibm.com/epubs/pdf/csqzaw11.pdf*

The developer's guide for Java programmers using IBM's WebSphere MQ messaging product [MQSeries].

[XML 1.0]

Extensible Markup Language (XML) 1.0 (2nd edition), World Wide Web Consortium; W3C Recommendation, October 6, 2000, *http://www.w3.org/TR/REC-xml*

The XML 1.0 specification.

[XSLT 1.0]

XSL Transformations (XSLT) Version 1.0, World Wide Web Consortium; W3C Recommendation, November 16, 1999, *http://www.w3.org/TR/xslt*

The XSLT 1.0 specification.

[Waldo]

"A Note on Distributed Computing" (Technical Report *SMLI TR-94-29*), Jim Waldo, Geoff Wyant, Ann Wollrath, & Sam Kendall; Sun Microsystems Laboratories, November 1994, *http://citeseer.nj.nec.com/waldo94note.html*

[Zahavi]

Enterprise Application Integration with CORBA, Ron Zahavi; John Wiley & Sons 1999, ISBN 0471327204

Index